STRAIGHT AND LEVEL

*For Captain David Holloway and
in memory of Squadron Leader Richard Holloway*

Straight and Level
Practical Airline Economics

Third Edition

STEPHEN HOLLOWAY

ASHGATE

Published by
Ashgate Publishing Limited
Gower House
Croft Road
Aldershot
Hampshire GU11 3HR
England

Ashgate Publishing Company
Suite 420
101 Cherry Street
Burlington, VT 05401-4405
USA

Ashgate website: http://www.ashgate.com

British Library Cataloguing in Publication Data
Holloway, Stephen, 1952–
    Straight and level : practical airline economics. – 3rd ed.
    1. Aeronautics, Commercial – Finance
    I. Title
    387.7'1

Library of Congress Cataloging-in-Publication
Holloway, Stephen, 1952–
    Straight and level : practical airline economics / by Stephen Holloway. -- 3rd ed.
        p. cm.
    Includes bibliographical references and index.
    ISBN 978-0-7546-7256-2 (hardback) -- ISBN 978-0-7546-7258-6 (pbk)
    1. Aeronautics, Commercial--Finance. I. Title.

HE9782.H65 2008
387.7'1--dc22

2008014374

ISBN: 978-0-7546-7256-2 (hardback)
ISBN: 978-0-7546-7258-6 (pbk)

Mixed Sources
Product group from well-managed forests and other controlled sources
www.fsc.org Cert no. SGS-COC-2482
© 1996 Forest Stewardship Council
FSC

Printed and bound in Great Britain by
TJ International Ltd, Padstow, Cornwall.

Contents

List of Figures

List of Tables

Acknowledgements

Once again, Maurice Flanagan has contributed a thoughtful and insightful foreword. It serves to underline that, notwithstanding most of what follows in this book being to one degree or another relatively technical, the human dimension is ultimately what makes the difference. His contribution is much appreciated.

Special thanks are also due to Bryson Monteleone (Tailwind Capital) and Rodger Robertson (Senior Visiting Fellow, UNSW Aviation), both of whom have again been exceptionally generous with their time. The following people kindly provided suggestions on how earlier editions might be improved upon: Natalie Lenoir (Ecole Nationale de l'Aviation Civile), Professor Douglas Marshall (University of North Dakota), Jim Oppermann (Ohio State University), Mal Sandford (Griffith University), Victor Ujimoto (University of Guelph), and Professor Roger Wootton (City University). None can be held responsible for errors of omission, commission or judgement – of which, in over 600 pages, there will doubtless be more than one or two. Thanks are also due to Professor Kenneth Button (George Mason University) and Simon Walker (Virtual Aviation College) for permission to use material.

Guy Loft at Ashgate Publishing deserves thanks for his professionalism and patience, and for being so straightforward to work with. Thanks also to Gillian Steadman, Rose James, Shirley Wood, and Carolyn Court for taking my presentational idiosyncrasies and turning them into a presentable product. Finally, special thanks are due to my wife Paula for tolerating with equanimity the absences and the ups and downs associated with a project such as this.

List of Abbreviations and Definitions

ABC	Activity-based costing.
ACARE	Advisory Council for Aeronautics Research in Europe.
ACARS	Aircraft communications addressing and reporting system.
ACMI	Aircraft, crew, maintenance and insurance (a form of wet-leasing).
ACP	Alternative content provider.
AD	Airworthiness directive.
ADS–B	Automatic dependent surveillance–broadcast.
AIRE	Atlantic Interoperability Initiative to Reduce Emissions.
ALF	Achieved (or actual) load factor.
ANSP	Air navigation services provider.
AOC	Air operator's certificate.
AOCC	Airline operations control centre.
AOG	Aircraft on the ground (i.e., unserviceable).
APEC	Asia-Pacific Economic Cooperation Forum.
APEX	Advance purchase excursion (fare).
APU	Auxiliary power unit.
APV	Acceptable perceived value.
ASA	Air services agreement.
ASEAN	Association of Southeast Asian Nations.
ASK	Available seat-kilometre: one seat flown one kilometre, whether occupied or not. A measure of output.
ASM	Available seat-mile: one seat flown one mile.
ATA	Air Transport Association of America.
ATC	Air Traffic Control.
ATK	Available tonne-kilometre: one tonne of payload capacity flown one kilometre, whether sold or not.
ATM	Available ton-mile: one ton of payload capacity flown one mile. (ATM is also a widely used abbreviation for 'air traffic management', but is not used as such in this book.)
ATPCO	Airline Tariff Publishing Company.
ATS	Air traffic services.
AVC	Average variable cost.
BALPA	British Air Line Pilots' Association.
BCBP	Barcoded boarding pass.

BELF	Break-even load factor.
BFE	Buyer-furnished equipment.
BIDT	Billing information data tape.
BV	Base value.
CAA	Civil Aviation Authority (UK).
CAB	Civil Aeronautics Board (US).
CASM	Cost per available seat-mile ('unit cost').
CCQ	Cross-crew qualification.
CDA	Continuous descent approach.
CEO	Chief executive officer.
CER	Certified Emissions Reduction.
CMV	Current market value.
CNS	Communication, navigation, and surveillance.
CPA	Capacity purchase agreement.
CRS	Computer reservation system.
CUSS	Common-use self-service (kiosks).
D^3	Demand-driven despatch.
DFM	Dynamic fleet management.
DOC	Direct operating cost.
DOJ	Department of Justice (US).
DOT	Department of Transportation (US).
EC	European Commission.
ECAA	European Common Aviation Area. (A single aviation market comprising members of the EEA.)
ECTM	Engine condition trend monitoring.
EDI	Electronic data interchange.
EEA	European Economic Area. (A free-trade area comprising members of the EU together with Iceland, Liechtenstein, Norway and Switzerland.)
EHM	Engine health monitoring.
ELFAA	European Low Fares Airline Association.
ERP	Enterprise resource planning.
ERU	Emission reduction unit (in the context of emissions trading).
ETOPS	Extended-range twin-engine operations.
ETS	Emissions trading scheme.
EU	European Union.
EUA	EU Emissions Allowance.
FAA	Federal Aviation Administration (US).
FAK	Freight-all-kinds (rate).
FFP	Frequent flyer programme.
FOD	Fuel over destination. (FOD is also a widely used abbreviation for 'foreign object damage', to airframes or engines, but is not used as such in this book.)
FTK	Freight tonne-kilometre.
FTM	Freight ton-mile.
GAAP	Generally accepted accounting principles.
GAO	General Accountability Office (US).
GATS	General Agreement on Trade in Services.

GDP	Gross domestic product.
GDS	Global distribution system.
GIT	Group inclusive tour.
GNE	GDS new entrant.
GNP	Gross national product.
GSA	General sales agent.
GSE	Ground support equipment.
HUD	Head-up display.
IATA	International Air Transport Association.
ICAO	International Civil Aviation Organization.
ICT	Information and communication technologies.
IFC	Inflight communications.
IFE	Inflight entertainment.
IO	Industrial organisation (economics).
IOC	Indirect operating cost.
IOSA	IATA Operational Safety Audit.
IP	Initial provisioning.
IPCC	Intergovernmental Panel on Climate Change.
IPO	Initial public offering.
IROPS	Irregular operations.
IRR	Internal rate of return.
ISAGO	IATA Safety Audit for Ground Operations.
IT	Information technology.
JIT	Just-in-time (inventory management).
JITI	Japan International Trade Institute.
JPDO	Joint Planning and Development Office.
LCC	Low-cost carrier.
LFA	Low-fare airline.
LRAC	Long-run average cost.
LRMC	Long-run marginal cost.
LROPS	Long-range operations.
LRU	Line-replaceable unit.
MAF	Minimum acceptable fare.
MALIAT	Multilateral Agreement on the Liberalisation of International Air Transportation.
MCT	Minimum connecting time.
MEL	Minimum equipment list.
MES	Minimum efficient scale.
MFF	Mixed fleet flying.
MIDT	Marketing information data tape.
MPA	Multilateral prorate agreement.
MPD	Maintenance planning document.
MPL	Multi-crew pilot licence.
MRO	Maintenance, repair, and overhaul.
MTOW	Maximum take-off weight.
NAS	National Airspace System (US).
NGATS	Next Generation (or NextGen) Air Transport System (US).
NPRM	Notice of proposed rule-making (US).

NPV	Net present value.
O&D	Origin and destination (markets).
OECD	Organisation for Economic Cooperation and Development.
OEM	Original equipment manufacturer.
PMA	Parts manufacturing approval.
PNR	Passenger name record.
PR	Public relations.
P-RNAV	Precision are navigation.
PV	Present value.
QC	Quick-change.
QSI	Quality of service index.
RASM	Revenue per available seat-mile (unit revenue).
RATM	Revenue per available ton-mile.
RBT	Resource-based theory of competitive advantage/strategy.
RFID	Radio frequency identification.
RJ	Regional jet.
RM	Revenue management.
RMS	Revenue management system.
RNAV	Area navigation.
RNP	Required navigation performance.
Rotables	High-value components that are either returned to service – not necessarily on the same aircraft – or held in inventory after repair or overhaul, rather than being consumed in use or discarded after use.
RPK	Revenue passenger-kilometre: one revenue passenger flown one kilometre. (A measure of sold output.)
RPM	Revenue passenger-mile: one revenue passenger flown one mile.
RTK	Revenue tonne-kilometre: one tonne of payload flown one kilometre.
RTM	Revenue ton-mile: one ton of payload flown one mile.
RV	Residual value.
RVSM	Reduced vertical separation minima.
SB	Service bulletin.
SCP	Structure–conduct–performance model of competitive strategy.
Seat pitch	The distance from the point where the back and pan of a seat join, to the same point on the seat in front.
SEC	Securities and Exchange Commission (United States).
SES	Single European Sky initiative.
SESAR	Single European Sky ATM Research.
SFE	Seller-furnished equipment.
SID	Standard instrument departure.
SPA	Special prorate agreement.
SRAC	Short-run average cost.
SRMC	Short-run marginal cost.
STB	Simplifying the business (an IATA programme).
TACO	Travel agency commission override.
TDC	Total distribution cost.
TFCs	Taxes, fees, and charges.
TMC	Travel management company.
TOC	Total operating cost.

TPF	Transaction processing facility. (An early operating system for high-volume transaction processing, developed by IBM for United Airlines.)
TTL	Ticketing time limit.
ULD	Unit load device.
UN	United Nations.
Unit cost	Operating cost per ASK, ASM, ATK or ATM.
Unit revenue	Operating revenue per ASK, ASM, ATK or ATM.
VDL	VHF datalink.
VFR	Visiting friends and relatives/relations.
VLJ	Very light jet.
XML	Extensible Markup Language.
Yield	Revenue per RPK/RPM or RTK/RTM.

ADDITIONAL COMMENTS ON DEFINITIONS AND USAGES ADOPTED IN THE BOOK

This book is consistent in its use of words or expressions that might be considered technical or terms of art. The following paragraphs clarify some of the usages adopted that might be considered open to debate.

Units of measurement   Miles and tons have generally been adopted rather than kilometres and tonnes, simply because the majority of sales of earlier editions were made in the United States. 'Dollars' and '$' refer to US dollars unless otherwise noted.

Capacity and output   Although the words 'capacity' and 'output' tend to be used interchangeably in the airline industry, they are not in fact synonymous. Assume an airline has one 300-mile route on which it operates a single 100-seat aircraft on one rotation (i.e., round-trip) each day. It is generating $(300 \times 2) \times 100 = 60,000$ ASMs per day. This is its *output* (although, as we will see in Chapter 4, output can also be measured using other metrics). If we further assume that the aircraft could feasibly be operated on as many as four rotations when fully utilised, it has the *capacity* to produce $60,000 \times 4 = 240,000$ ASMs each day. Its output is therefore currently well below capacity; in other words, its capacity is not being fully utilised.

It is of course very difficult – often impossible – for an airline to put a precise figure on the potential capacity of its fleet, and it is industry practice to refer to ASMs and ASKs actually produced as 'capacity' rather than 'output'. This book does not follow industry convention because it is analytically useful to retain a distinction between capacity (i.e., maximum potential output) and actual output.

Demand and traffic   Demand is a measure of potential customers willing and able to purchase air transport services in a market or group of markets given assumed price levels. Some of that demand will be unsatisfied because seats are not available and potential customers choose not to travel on alternative flights. Demand that is satisfied results in 'traffic' being carried.

Traffic as 'sold output'   As we will see in Chapter 2, traffic can be measured in terms of passenger enplanements or on a distance-weighted basis in terms of RPMs. Given that output is measured in ASMs, we can treat traffic expressed in RPMs as 'sold output'. The reason for adopting the expression 'sold output' will be made clear in Chapter 10; in the rest of the book, the word 'traffic' is used.

Unit cost, unit revenue, and yield   Unit cost is operating cost per ASM or ATM; unit revenue is operating revenue per ASM or ATM; and yield is operating revenue per RPM or RTM. Whilst unit cost and unit revenue are standard definitions, yield can be defined in other ways; none of the other definitions of yield is used in this book.

Revenue management versus yield management   The expression 'revenue management' has come to displace 'yield management' in recent years, although not universally. This book uses 'revenue management'.

GDS versus CRS   The abbreviation 'GDS' has come to displace 'CRS' – although, once again, not universally. This book actually uses the terms somewhat differently. 'CRS' here refers to an individual airline's internal reservation system – whether maintained inhouse, co-hosted in another airline's CRS or in a GDS, or maintained by a supplier such as IBM or EDS. 'GDS' here refers to industry-wide systems such as Amadeus and Sabre – systems which have until recently themselves been widely referred to as CRSs but whose expanding scope as travel service distributors for a range of companies and industries makes the expression 'GDS' more appropriate. The essence of this distinction is that a GDS is an industry-wide distribution system, whereas a CRS is a single-airline inventory management system.

Flight-legs, routes, markets, and segments   A flight-leg is a non-stop flight; it might be synonymous with a route and a market, or it might not. Orlando–Dallas non-stop is a flight-leg serving the Orlando–Dallas market; if it is part of an Orlando–Dallas–Salt Lake City (SLC) through-service, we can say that the Orlando–SLC route has two flight-legs (Orlando–Dallas and Dallas–SLC) and directly serves three origin and destination (O&D) markets (Orlando–Dallas, Orlando–SLC, and Dallas–SLC), together with a large number of connecting markets involving origins and destinations behind and/or beyond these three cities. If the Orlando–Dallas–SLC flight-legs are operated under one flight number, travel from Orlando to SLC represents one 'segment'. (Note that the word 'segment' is used in one of two contexts in this book: here we are talking about a flight-segment; elsewhere the word is used in reference to market segments. The context should make clear which usage applies.) Finally, a passenger's 'path' through an airline network describes the route(s) taken to get from their origin to their destination, whilst their 'itinerary' reflects actual flight-legs chosen.

Non-stop, through-plane, direct, and connecting service   Staying with the same example, Orlando–Dallas and Dallas–SLC are both non-stops, whilst Orlando–SLC is a through-plane service. According to different definitions encountered in the industry, the word 'direct' could be synonymous with either non-stop or through-plane service; this book adopts the latter approach, treating direct service as service on a one-stop or multi-stop route using the same aircraft (and generally the same flight number). Both non-stop and direct or through-plane services are distinct from connecting itineraries, which serve an O&D market with one or more change of planes (e.g., Dallas–Boise connecting at SLC).

Start-ups and new entrants   'Start-up' is used to refer to a newly launched carrier. 'New entrant' or 'entrant' refers to a carrier entering a market to challenge one or more incumbents; a new entrant might be a start-up, or it might be an established airline.

Cargo and freight   Some definitions treat these as synonymous, whereas others define freight as a subset of cargo (albeit by far the major subset in volume and revenue terms for the industry as a whole) alongside mail and unaccompanied baggage. This book takes the second approach.

Product 'Product' is an umbrella term which encompasses tangible goods (e.g., automobiles) and intangible services (e.g., life assurance). Airlines offer products that are primarily intangible services (i.e., the transportation of people and goods), but which nonetheless have significant tangible attributes (e.g., lounges, aircraft cabins, food, cargo documentation, etc.). This book generally refers to airline 'services', but the word 'product' is also used and can be treated in this case as synonymous with 'service'.

Fleets and subfleets A fleet is the aggregate of all aircraft operated by an airline, whereas a subfleet is comprised of one particular type (including variants). In the case of a single-type operator, the words are synonymous; a carrier operating more than one distinct type, on the other hand, has a number of subfleets.

Foreword

Steve has suggested that I might say something about leadership. Here goes.

In my early years in BOAC, I worked overseas in ten different countries in Africa, India, the Middle East, the Far East, and South America. What did I learn about leadership as a manager at increasingly senior levels? What are the common denominators of successful leadership in diverse cultural and ethnic environments?

What I found was that there really are natural leaders as well as appointed ones, and that there are natural followers, content to remain so. I also found that autocratic leadership (i.e., do this or else), which has to work in the armed forces, does not often work well elsewhere. Autocratic leaders tend to be absolutely, totally, 100 per cent convinced that what they are doing, and propose to do, is the one and only way. Such leaders are apt to be impatient with dissent, with the result that those reporting to them become afraid of exercising any initiative. I'm not saying that it never works, though.

In 1985 the airline Emirates was formed. I was made Managing Director and Sheikh Ahmed Bin Saeed Al Maktoum was appointed Chairman. Sheikh Ahmed was then only 25, both a born leader and born to lead – the two do not necessarily go together. His leadership reverberates throughout the organisation, and has been the driving force behind Emirates' success. The elements of his leadership are that he has great charisma, a powerful intellect, a memory like a steel trap, personal kindness, and exceptional management skills. There are very few such.

Some general comments. The very little I've read about leadership seems to assume that inborn qualities of leadership are necessarily benign. They are not, of course. Some of the world's most charismatic leaders – Hitler, Pol Pot, Ghengis Khan, and Lenin to name but a handful – have been guilty of monstrously evil acts on an epic scale.

One of my favourite leaders is the British Admiral Lord Nelson. Studies at Annapolis credit him with being the original leader by empowerment in the modern sense. He would clearly define his objective and strategy to his captains, and it was then up to them to get on with it, and deliver the objective within the strategy. The success of Nelson's method is illustrated by his two greatest victories, the Battle of the Nile in 1798 and the Battle of Trafalgar in 1805: at the first of these he was unconscious and at the second he was dead.

Leadership by stealth: I remember reading some years ago that the American General Vernon A. Walter said that you can get anything you want done in Washington, as long as you made sure somebody else got the credit. He had been educated at Stonyhurst College by the Jesuits there. It figures.

How in Emirates do we identify potential leaders? Just before we started the airline in 1985 I came across a paper by the British Institute of Manpower Studies on the correlation between different systems of selecting people for jobs, and subsequent success in the job. The usual method then was to define the job, select a shortlist from the applicants, interview, and make an appointment. The study concluded that you'd have been a bit better off tossing a coin. What did work was psychometric tests professionally interpreted, tailored specifically to the job profile. These tests analyse the characteristics that you want them to. They will measure followership, an essential quality in some jobs, as well as leadership.

Initially we used psychometric tests to identify leadership potential in some prospective managers and pilots, alongside others selected by interview, and compared the results. The superior effectiveness of psychometrics soon became clear. I mentioned pilots because we regard all of them as potential captains, and when captains are in command of our aircraft they are among the most important of our leaders.

Finally, and to tweak Shakespeare a bit, remember this: Some are born leaders, some achieve leadership, and some have leadership thrust upon them. Which of these are you, or would you rather not bother?

Maurice Flanagan
Executive Vice Chairman,
Emirates Airline and Group

Preface

The book is divided into four parts. Part 1 provides a strategic context within which to consider the industry's economics. Part 2 is structured around a relationship that lies at the heart of the business:

$$\text{TRAFFIC} \times \text{YIELD} > < \text{OUTPUT} \times \text{UNIT COST}$$
$$= \text{OPERATING PERFORMANCE (i.e., PROFIT or LOSS)}$$

Capacity management is clearly central to airline economics, and Part 3 looks at topics critical to capacity management: network design and scheduling, fleet management, and revenue management. Part 4 closes the book with a review of several macro-level metrics of operating performance.

The structure of the book is therefore unchanged from the last edition. There are two reasons for this: first, because several aviation masters degree programmes have been either partially or entirely designed around this structure there is a market requirement for consistency; second, and far more important, the operating performance model lying at the core of the book is both fundamental and constant – irrespective of what is happening in the industry. The preface to the last edition put the argument as follows: 'This book says little about the past evolution of the air transport industry, and neither does it forecast the future. Its sole objective is to describe in a practical way the fundamental economic forces that underlie the business. Unlike the industry itself, these fundamental forces change only slowly.' Given the transformation of the industry over the last several years, some might take issue with the last sentence. But if we look at the highly visible example of low-fare airlines – perhaps the most obvious heralds of change – it is the case that these carriers have *not* reinvented the economics of the industry. What the most successful of them have done is combine:

- market insight (e.g., recognising opportunity in unserved, underserved, and/or overpriced markets or market segments);
- technological developments (e.g., using the Internet to bypass traditional distribution channels);
- emerging approaches to enterprise management (e.g., creating simple organisational architectures and internal processes);
- commercial opportunity (e.g., seizing opportunities arising from the liberalisation or deregulation of a growing number of air transport markets).

The industry's strategies, business models, and institutional structure all change over time as do the environments (political, economic, social, and technological) within which it operates, but its fundamental, underlying economics are more enduring. What each edition of *Straight and Level* sets out to do is use those fundamental economic facts of life as a framework within which to outline current strategies, models, and challenges.

There is a caveat, however. This preface is being written against a background of surging jet fuel prices, increasingly rapacious taxation of airlines, deteriorating standards of service affecting a growing number of passengers both on the ground and in the air, shortfalls in infrastructural capacity, and a mounting anti-aviation bias in some parts of the world amongst the public, politicians, and the media. Time will tell whether or not the price of oil will fall back, but the other trends look enduring. None will change the industry's fundamental economics, but together they have the potential to profoundly affect its rate of growth and the viability of some current business models and strategies.

Several aspects of the book have been changed for this third edition, but within the same overarching structure shared with earlier editions. Chapter 1 has been largely rewritten, and both the content and organisation of Chapters 2 to 5 and Chapter 9 have been amended to varying degrees – in some cases substantially. The rapid evolution of the industry during its recovery from the post-9/11 downturn is reflected throughout the text, and examples have been brought up to date.

Finally, there are the perennial questions: what is the book intended to be, and who is it for? Let me approach this first by saying what it is not and who it is not for. It is not a descriptive text for readers with just a passing interest in the airline industry and it is not an introductory text for undergraduate students with little commercial background. These segments of the market are already well catered for. Neither is it a book for economic theoreticians; the word 'practical' in the title is entirely deliberate. *Straight and Level* has been written primarily for masters-level students on aviation management courses who want a comprehensive book to which they can refer for an understanding of the immutable forces which shape the industry and an interpretation of the impact these forces are having on its contemporary evolution. The book should also be useful to final year undergraduates wanting to prepare for more advanced study. Amongst practitioners, it will appeal in particular to established managers moving from functional posts into general management. More broadly, anyone with knowledge of the airline industry who wants to gain a deeper understanding of its economics at a practical level and an insight into the reasons for its financial volatility should find the book of interest.

Steve Holloway
Oxford, England

PART 1

Strategic Context

When your strategy is deep and far-reaching, then what you gain from your calculations is much. When your strategic thinking is shallow and near-sighted, then what you gain from your calculations is little and you lose before you do battle. Therefore victorious warriors win first and then go to war, while defeated warriors go to war first and then seek to win.

Sun Tzu

One point of view is that industry economics are our master, determining what can and cannot be done. Less deterministically, we can take the view that an understanding of industry economics is a tool which allows managers to work towards the vision they have for their airline's future and to meet the more explicit objectives established by stakeholders such as customers, employees, shareholders, alliance partners and members of the wider community. This book takes the latter approach. The single chapter in the opening part of the book outlines a customer-oriented strategic framework within which the understanding of industry economics developed in subsequent chapters can be applied.

1

Strategic Context

Never be afraid to try something new. Remember, amateurs built the ark; professionals built the Titanic.

Anonymous

CHAPTER OVERVIEW

Most airlines have a competitive strategy embodying the type of value they intend delivering. Its choice of competitive strategy is reflected in each carrier's operating strategy. The performance associated with an operating strategy depends on revenues earned from delivering expected benefits to targeted customers and on costs incurred delivering those benefits.

Part 2 of the book will look at airline revenues (traffic × yield) and costs (output × unit cost).

Part 3 will focus on key aspects of capacity management, which is in many respects the critical operations management challenge because it lies at the interface between cost and revenue streams.

Part 4 looks at several key macro-level metrics of operating performance.

What this opening chapter does is outline the strategic context within which costs and revenues are generated. It begins by identifying the scale of the challenge. It goes on to look at the theoretical underpinnings of the important but sometimes ill-defined concepts of 'strategy' and 'business model'. It then examines the changes currently taking place in airline business models. It ends by describing in more detail the structure of the book.

I. The Scale of the Challenge

Airlines have annual revenues of approximately half a trillion dollars and employ over 2 million people. They directly support another 2.9 million jobs at airports and civil aerospace manufacturers, and may indirectly support in excess of 15 million jobs in tourism (Air Transport Action Group 2005). Low-fare airlines in Europe are alone estimated to contribute close to half a million direct, indirect, and induced jobs (York Aviation 2007). The air transport industry, at the heart of which lie airlines, directly contributes US$330 billion per annum to world GDP (ibid.) and underpins as much as US$3.5 trillion (i.e., around 8 per cent) if direct output is aggregated with output generated elsewhere in the industry's supply chain, with the multiplier effect of corporate and personal spending by industry participants, and with the catalytic impact airlines have on tourism, trade, and investment (IATA 2007d). Airlines carry well over 2 billion passengers and between 25 and 30 per cent by value of world trade each year, and are therefore among the primary facilitators of global economic growth. Commercial aviation in the United States is estimated to be directly or indirectly responsible for 5.8 per cent of the country's economic activity, 5.0 per cent of personal earnings, and 8.8 per cent of employment (The Campbell-Hill Aviation Group 2006). Yet airlines, taken together, have historically been unable to cover their cost of capital (Pearce 2006). Table 1.1 illustrates the scale of the problem.

Although many carriers outperform industry averages and a handful generate returns which do exceed their cost of capital (e.g., Ryanair and AirAsia), the industry as a whole has not been capable of sustaining profitability throughout an entire economic cycle. At the end of 2007, the top of the most recent up-cycle, the industry remained almost $200 billion in debt and earned a net margin of little more than 1 per cent. A normally competitive industry would be expected to earn its cost of capital, but the airline industry has yet to achieve this. The problem has been particularly acute in the United States. Reviewing the period from deregulation in 1978 until 2005, Heimlich (2007) observes that:

- the median US airline net margin was -0.4 per cent, compared with 5.2 per cent for all US corporations;
- in their best year the airlines achieved a net margin of only 4.7 per cent, compared with 9.1 per cent for all corporations;
- in their worst year the airlines' net margin was -10.3 per cent, against 3.1 per cent for corporations generally;
- there was accordingly a 15-point spread for the airlines, as opposed to 6 points for all corporations.

By the end of 2005 the US airline industry had, according to the Air Transport Association (2007), made a cumulative net loss of US$16.8 billion since 1947. Clearly, the airlines most responsible for this performance have had to endure considerable strain on their balance sheets; many entered Chapter 11 bankruptcy protection, some on more than one occasion, and several have been liquidated.

Whilst the failings of senior management and the obduracy of labour have undoubtedly contributed to the economic downfall of particular airlines, the fact that underperformance has been so widespread across the industry over such a long period of time implies that there are structural impediments at work. The purpose of this book is to explain the nature

Table 1.1   Summary of airline profits and margins 1997–2008

US$ billions[1]	1997	1998	1999	2000	2001	2002	2003	2004	2005	2006	2007[3]	2008[4]
Operating revenue	291	295	305	328	307	306	321	378	413	452	490	514
Operating expense	274	279	293	317	319	311	323	375	409	440	474	498
Operating profit	17	16	12	11	-12	-5	-2	3	4	12	16	16
Operating margin (%)	5.8	5.4	3.9	3.3	-3.9	-1.6	-0.6	0.8	1.0	2.6	3.3	3.1
Net profit[2]	8.5	8.2	8.5	3.7	-13.0	-11.3	-7.6	-5.6	-4.1	-0.5	5.6	5.0
Net margin (%)	2.9	2.8	2.8	1.1	-4.2	-3.7	-2.4	-1.5	-1.0	-0.1	1.1	1.0

Source: ICAO, IATA.

Notes: 1. Figures are subject to rounding errors.
2. Excluding US airline bankruptcy charges.
3. Estimates.
4. IATA forecasts (made in late 2007, before subsequent spike in fuel prices).

of the challenge accepted by anybody responsible for an airline's income statement, and in doing this highlight the structural changes currently taking place in the industry. Because 'strategy' and 'business model' are concepts which are prominent in the discourse of change, and because they establish the context within which the economics of the industry are explained in subsequent chapters, the next section will briefly define them.

II. Strategies and Business Models: Some Theory

STRATEGY

'Our strategy is to be *the* low-cost provider.' 'Our strategy is to provide unrivalled customer service.' 'Our strategy is to be number one or number two in all our markets.' What each of these statements has in common is that none of them describes a strategy. They describe elements of a strategy (Hambrick and Frederickson 2005). Strategy can never be about service, price, output or cost in isolation; it has to address all of them in a coherent manner. There are many different definitions of strategy, but one which is compelling in both its simplicity and its information value states that 'effective strategy is a *coherent set* of individual actions in support of a system of goals' (Eden and Ackermann 1998, p. 4) [emphasis added].

Goals and the actions taken to achieve them will often be specified in detailed plans, but some of what is planned will inevitably fall by the wayside whilst alternatives emerge unplanned from the dynamics of the marketplace to augment or replace original intent (Mintzberg 1994). What is constant in any effective strategy, however, is a *theme*. According to Grant (1998, p. 3), 'Strategy is not a detailed plan or program of instructions; it is a unifying theme that gives coherence and direction to the actions and decisions of an individual or organization.' Porter (1996, p. 71) argues that, 'In companies with a clear strategic position, a number of higher-order themes can be identified and implemented through clusters of tightly linked activities.'

Whether the above definition is applied at the corporate, divisional or functional level, there should be a coherent theme uniting strategic action. But what is 'strategic'? The word has been devalued, often being used as a synonym for 'important'. To be truly 'strategic' an action must reinforce or change one or more of the following:

- the scope of the corporation's portfolio of businesses;
- the market (or 'horizontal') scope of an individual business in the portfolio;
- the value offered to customers of an individual business;
- the competitive advantage sought by a business;
- the operating strategy used by a business to deliver value to its customers.

These dimensions of strategy will be considered briefly in the context of the airline industry.

Corporate Strategy: The Industrial Scope Decision

The industrial scope decision addresses which businesses a corporation should be investing in. It is the essence of 'corporate', as different from 'competitive', strategy. During the 1970s and early 1980s, portfolio planning matrices such as the Boston Box, the McKinsey

Directional Policy Matrix, and the Arthur D. Little Life-Cycle Matrix were widely used to help structure industrial scope decisions (Bowman and Faulkner 1997); their underlying logic was to search continuously for ways to rebalance the corporate portfolio by investing free cash flow from slow-growing mature businesses into faster-growing new businesses. Since the late 1980s, emphasis has shifted towards analysis of shared competencies and the search for a better understanding of how it is that aggregating different businesses within the same corporate group actually creates more shareholder value than would be created were each independent; this has contributed to a move away from conglomerate diversification.

In the context of the airline industry, the industrial scope decision is a matter of whether and, if so, how far to diversify away from the air transport business. The decision might result in one of three group structures for an airline or its holding company:

1. *Single business* This is the model adopted by carriers concentrating on air transportation as their core business and outsourcing all activities considered 'non-core' relative to the carriage of passengers and cargo. Air transportation services might be offered using a single brand across all markets served, or a suite comprised of a master-brand and separately sub-branded 'production platforms'. For example, the JAL Group comprises master-brand Japan Airlines and sub-brands JALways, JAL Express, J-Air, Japan Asia Airways, and Transocean Air.

2. *Portfolio of related businesses* This model includes in addition to air transport operations a number of divisions, subsidiaries, and/or joint ventures in fields related to air transport. How to define 'relatedness' is an open question, but generally we would expect related businesses to share inputs, technology, competencies, and/ or markets and to reap economic benefits from this sharing. Whilst some airlines (e.g., British Airways) have for many years been focusing primarily on air transport operations, others (e.g., Lufthansa and Singapore Airlines) have been developing activities related to air transport into significant independent revenue-generators. Lufthansa made a strategic decision in the 1990s to diversify in order to reduce reliance on volatile earnings from passenger air transportation: it created Lufthansa Technik, Lufthansa Cargo, Lufthansa Service, and Lufthansa Systems, which within a decade together accounted for approximately 40 per cent of group revenue. Separately, several European charter airlines and Canadian carrier Air Transat are themselves a part of vertically integrated portfolios of related businesses within the leisure travel value chain.

3. *Portfolio of unrelated businesses* Most airlines and airline holding companies are now less inclined than some have been in the past to involve themselves in activities only tenuously related to air transport; All Nippon has stepped back from the hotel business, for example, but Icelandair's holding company has not. A few carriers, particularly in Asia where there is still a penchant for conglomerate diversification, are themselves part of broad industrial portfolios (e.g., Asiana, Cathay Pacific, EVA Air, and Kingfisher).

The corporate strategies of different airlines or airline holding companies can be outlined by using comparative bar charts to map the percentages of total revenue attributable to different businesses within their portfolios. Our interest in this book is limited to the economics of air transport businesses.

Competitive Strategy: Horizontal Scope, Customer Value, Competitive Advantage, And Operating Strategy

Airline managers do not confront the economics of the industry in a vacuum, but within the context of a particular competitive strategy. Competitive strategy is behaviour intended to build and/or leverage a competitive advantage. Each business, whether it stands alone or is part of a broader portfolio, should have a competitive strategy. The essence of a competitive strategy can be found in the answer to four questions that will be considered in the next four subsections: In which product and geographical markets should we compete? What value will we offer to targeted customers (or, more crudely, who would care if we ceased to exist and why)? How will we create and sustain an advantage over our competitors in each of those markets? How should we profitably organize the production of output to deliver the desired value to customers in targeted markets and to exploit our competitive advantage?

Figure 1.1 illustrates, at a generalised level, how competitive strategy might be formulated and how it relates to the concept of a 'business model'. The elements identified are all discussed below and will be encountered again in subsequent chapters; the purpose of this framework is to provide a context that can be referred to as necessary when reading through those chapters.

Horizontal scope: in which markets should we compete?   Purchase of air transportation involves simultaneous participation in both a geographical market and a service market (Holloway 2002).

1. *Geographical scope* can be:
    *   *Wide-market* There are several large international airlines, but no truly global carriers. Again, different production platforms may be used to serve different geographical markets; alliances are intended in part to broaden geographical scope within the constraints of both industry economics and the prevailing international aeropolitical regime – a regime which, as we will see in Chapter 4, is still on the whole relatively restrictive in some parts of the world but is rapidly liberalising in most major markets. An airline's network is, in fact, now widely perceived as a core attribute of its service – hence the imperative felt by many network carriers to build alliances.
    *   *Niche* This involves offering either a wide or a narrow range of services into a small number of geographical markets. What constitutes a geographical niche and what represents a geographical wide-market strategy is obvious at the extremes (e.g., regional carriers on the one hand and the US 'Big Three' on the other), but unclear in the middle ground. A large number of the world's international airlines make wide-market service offers into a relatively limited range of geographical markets, and are in this sense 'geographical niche carriers' – although they might not think of themselves as such. Many have moved out of geographical niches by joining global alliances; those that choose not to make this move will need confidence that they have distinctive and sustainable cost and/or service advantages with which to defend their niches. At the other end of the spectrum Belgian carrier VLM, bought by Air France-KLM in 2008, successfully established a geographical niche linking London's business-oriented City Airport to near-continental destinations and UK provincial

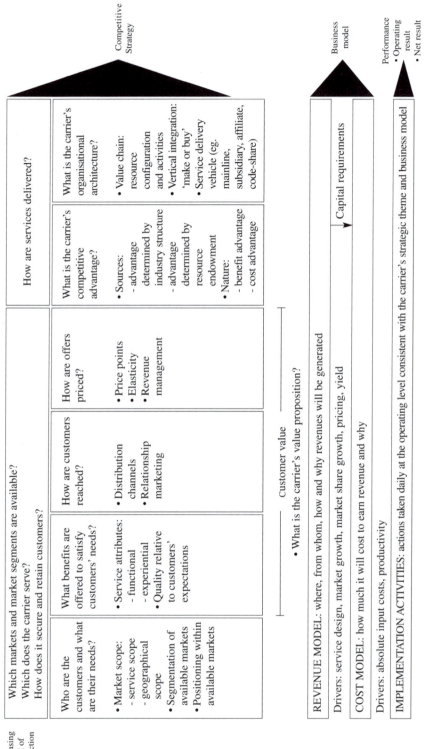

Figure 1.1   Relationships between competitive strategy, business model and performance

centres. Similarly, US carrier Allegiant Air was established to link relatively small communities to Las Vegas and Florida, tapping into thin vacation markets lacking intense competition. And at the time of writing, 23 of the 39 destinations served by Spirit are in the Caribbean and Latin American regions – a deliberate reorientation away from increasingly competitive domestic US markets.

Choice of geographical scope is clearly a fundamental underpinning of any airline's competitive strategy. In the mid-2000s, for example, bmi began to shift the emphasis of its mainline operations at London Heathrow away from short- and towards medium- and long-haul routes. Most US network carriers are growing their international operations in preference to expanding domestic output. In both cases this shift in geographical scope has been a response to intensifying competition from low-fare airlines, and further downward pressure on yields, in short-haul markets.

2. *Service scope* – the targeting of specific segments of demand within geographical markets, members of which want particular combinations of price and product – can be:

    - *Wide-market* A portfolio of passenger and cargo transport services is offered by a single carrier, either under its sole corporate brand or using a mixture of mainline, divisional, subsidiary, and/or franchised sub-brands to target distinct segments of demand.
    - *Niche* A single type of service, or a very narrow range, is offered. A typical example would be a low-fare carrier offering single-class service to one or a relatively narrow range of segments. Another would be a European charter carrier, offering single-class service to tour organizers and seat-only retail purchasers. The premium-only long-haul airlines which began operations in 2005 and 2006 provide examples at the other end of the service–price spectrum (e.g., Eos, Silverjet, L'Avion). Cargo carriers, including integrators such as UPS and DHL, are also niche operations insofar as their product range is narrower than that of combination carriers offering both passenger and cargo products. Clearly, niche does not necessarily mean small. It relates to degree of focus rather than size of revenues or scale of operations.

Geographical and service scope are distinct but closely linked choices. Indeed, in a network industry such as commercial air transportation these two scope decisions are fundamentally symbiotic: every departure is in itself a product offered to one or more geographical markets, and different levels of ground and onboard amenities provided to customers travelling in whatever separate classes are available on each departure can be characterised as product attributes offered to different segments of those markets. For example, European low-fare carriers are only able to serve many of the routes they have opened between secondary or tertiary centres by offering low fares to stimulate demand, and this in turn requires a type of service which costs less to produce than the traditional 'full-service' product that these markets have historically been unable to support.

Customer value: what is the carrier's value proposition? The concept of utility underlies neoclassical demand theory. Exchange takes place when two parties each give up something that provides them with less utility than what they receive in return (Fabrycky *et al.* 1998). The utility of a product may be intrinsic in the case of a 'status good', but in most cases is derived from the ability of the product to satisfy a particular consumer's needs and wants – hence the old marketing tenet that nobody needs a drill, what they need is a hole. Utility and customer value are closely related. Whereas utility (at least according to one definition) is the satisfaction a person derives from using a product, value is that person's appraisal of the worth of utility received net of any disutility – such as price paid, requirement to book in advance, having to change planes at a congested hub, or minimum and maximum stay restrictions. Customer value is neither the cost of a product nor its price, but a consumer's appraisal of what is to be gained from acquiring that product net of what has to be given up to acquire it (Lovelock and Wirtz 2004). Different consumers paying the same price may therefore not receive the same value (Ng 2006).

The question of who decides what amounts to value has been answered somewhat differently within different traditions of economics. The Austrian-subjectivist tradition places great store in the subjective opinions of individual actors. As Rothbard (1962, p. 19) puts it from this perspective, ' ... physically, there may be no discernible difference between one pound of butter and another. But if the actor chooses to evaluate them differently, they are no longer part of the supply of the same good.' Similarly, the services management literature holds that perception *is* reality as far as consumers are concerned (Carpenter *et al.* 1994; Holloway 2002). This view is adopted in the present book. Figure 1.2 proposes the following definitions:

1.   A customer's *perceived benefit* from using a service is equivalent to the gross benefits (or 'utility') offered by that particular service (e.g., safety, schedule convenience, ontime performance, inflight comfort, enhanced self-image through brand association, frequent flyer miles, etc.) less *non-monetary* costs (e.g., ticket conditionality, queues at various points in the service delivery system, elapsed journey time lengthened by having to connect at a hub, crowded airports and airplanes, etc.). This concept can be monetised by equating it to the maximum price the customer is prepared to pay.

It is important to stress again that we are talking about benefits as perceived by customers rather than by airline managers. Mid-1990s UK start-up Debonair tried to distinguish its low-fare product by adding a few minor cabin service benefits not offered by competitors such as Ryanair and easyJet. Unfortunately, most potential customers were either unaware of the incremental benefits or did not perceive them as meaningful

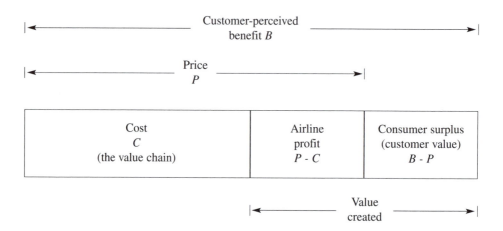

Figure 1.2   Cost, price, benefit and value

to the purchase decision. These benefits therefore generated costs uncompensated by incremental revenues, and were one factor (among several) contributing to Debonair's subsequent failure. In contrast, jetBlue's service offer was designed at launch to incorporate benefits that were both well-communicated to target customers and considered by those customers to be relevant to their purchase decisions.

2. *Value created* by a service is the customer-perceived benefit as just defined, less all the input costs that have been spent right along the value chain in order to create the service and deliver value to the customer.

3. *Consumer surplus* is perceived benefit less the monetary price paid by the customer. This is widely referred to as 'customer-perceived value' or simply 'customer value'; although the terms are not always used synonymously, they can be treated as such for our purposes here. In effect this is the part of 'value created' that the customer is capturing. Because each customer is likely to place a different value on any particular service, the amount of consumer surplus will vary between individuals; we will revisit this idea in Chapters 3 and 9, because it is the foundation of price discrimination and therefore of revenue management. Consumers are generally assumed, certainly by most economists, to make purchase decisions that maximise consumer surplus (Bowman and Ambrosini 1998). Sometimes there might be no consumer surplus: the price paid in this case equates exactly to the value placed by the consumer on perceived benefits. This is likely only where there is a monopoly supplier who knows each customer's valuation of the service and is able to price-discriminate accordingly (ibid.). (Note that in principle there can never be a negative consumer surplus insofar as nobody is likely to pay for a service from which they derive no value.)

4. *Seller's profit* is the monetary price paid by the customer less the cost of inputs. This is the portion of 'value created' that the airline – the final seller of the service fashioned out of all the inputs that went into creating and delivering it – is capturing. In terms of Porter's popular five-forces model (1980, 1985), we could characterise it as the proportion of whatever value has been created that the airline is able to appropriate for itself given the bargaining power of customers and suppliers (including suppliers of labour), the intensity of competitive rivalry, and inroads being made by substitutes and new entrants. The effect of a fare war, for example, would be to put downward pressure on P and result in reduced profit (lower, or perhaps even negative, $P-C$) and increased consumer surplus (higher $B-P$).

In practice, what has been happening in the post-deregulation era is that because widening choice has added to customers' benefits at the same time that increased competition and greater fare transparency have placed general downward pressure on prices, consumer surplus has been growing. According to Kahn (2004), the inability of airlines to equate the prices they charge to each customer's willingness to pay has been benefiting US consumers by more than $20 billion a year.

What airlines are, in principle, doing in the marketplace is trying to win business by manipulating service–price offers – that is, by managing gross benefits, non-monetary costs, and price. This is not an academic exercise. It is a response to the fundamental question that every manager with strategic responsibility needs to answer before anything else is tackled: Why should customers buy my product rather than a competitor's? Box 1.1 illustrates the point.

If we look at just the low-fare segment of the US industry, there are some very clear distinctions between value propositions that have been offered. The first generation of

Box 1.1: Southwest and Midwest – Different Types of Customer Value

When demand evaporated from low-fare carriers in the US domestic market during the summer of 1996 after a fatal accident involving one of their number, this was because the core benefit they were perceived to be delivering in respect of safety was being reassessed by customers. Despite the low prices they continued to offer, the value propositions put forward by these carriers (with the exception of long-established and highly regarded Southwest) had been unbalanced by changed consumer perceptions in respect of that key service attribute. Not even the most price-sensitive end of the US domestic market, it seems, is driven entirely by price; customer-perceived value is driven by both sides of the service–price offer, rather than by price alone. Customers may well buy into tight seat pitches and an absence of frills, but this does not mean that those service attributes that are in fact offered will necessarily be acceptable irrespective of quality; safety is perhaps the attribute which most strongly demonstrates this fact.

It is missing the point to assume that, say, Southwest sells on price alone. Southwest sells on value for money – on the right service–price offer. It has targeted customers who prefer not to pay as much as other carriers want them to pay, and it gives them good value. Many of the 'hard' service attributes offered by competing airlines until most pared-back their products after 9/11, such as meals and other amenities, have not traditionally been a feature of Southwest's value proposition; value has been embodied instead in emotional benefits derived from using the brand (e.g., the corporate ethos of 'fun') and from a culture supporting consistent standards of personal service, as well as in high frequencies, punctuality, and everyday low prices.

Whenever two competitors match each other's prices, consumers need to be given a reason to buy from one rather than the other. Observers who talk about the 'commoditisation' of the industry, because so many consumers are price-sensitive, and who dismiss branding as an irrelevant luxury miss this point. Southwest, on the other hand, proves it: low costs and strong branding are not incompatible, and together they help provide value that competitors cannot match as readily as they can match prices.

With the hallmark chocolate chip cookies and 2 × 2 leather seating of its original 'Signature Service', Midwest Airlines took a very different approach built around high standards of inflight service; nonetheless, it also sold on the basis of value for money. Different though their value propositions have been, these two carriers for many years shared one thing in common: clearly defined service concepts effectively translated into service packages designed to deliver the value expected by targeted customers. Neither the fact that Midwest has not been financially successful, has changed strategy by adding 'Saver' seats to its offer, and is no longer independent nor Southwest's 2007 introduction of a Business Select fare class with an augmented service offer weakens the point: there are many different ways to build value into a service. The key, of course, is to find sufficient customers who value the service enough to allow it to be sold at a meaningful profit.

post-deregulation low-fare entrants in the 1980s (e.g., People Express, Northeastern) offered rock-bottom prices and a 'sparse' customer experience, as did 1990s start-up ValuJet (since morphed into AirTran). The most recent wave includes not just carriers emphasising price above all else (e.g., Allegiant and, until its failure in 2008, Skybus), but others offering value propositions incorporating 'richer' service experiences (e.g., AirTran, jetBlue, Virgin America). The CEO of Southwest has had this to say in response to the increasing variety of service–price offers: 'The competitive landscape has changed.

We're going to need to compete less on price and more on something else' (Palmeri 2007). 'Something else' turned out to be a package of service upgrades for people willing to pay a fare premium. Similarly, when Aer Lingus reinvented itself to cope with low-fare competition from Ryanair, its objective was not to match the latter's unit costs, which was not feasible, but instead to narrow the cost difference between them and bridge it by offering an enhanced value proposition: that proposition was based on low (but not necessarily the lowest) fares, combined with service levels sufficiently in excess of what Ryanair was offering to justify a small price premium.

Price is critical, but products ultimately sell on value rather than price alone. Orbitz has noted that 30 per cent of its customers do not select the cheapest flight displayed (Dunleavy and Westerman 2005) – the implication being that notwithstanding the importance of price, a substantial body of customers is also to some degree product-sensitive. Similarly, in the final quarter of 2006 48 per cent of Air Canada's passengers purchased a fare higher than the lowest available to them; of those who did buy the lowest available fare, 25 per cent purchased an additional service from the airline (Gutschi 2007). However, customers must *perceive* value in what is offered if they are not to buy on price alone.

A brand offers good value relative to competitors when it provides:

- fewer benefits, sufficiently compensated by lower prices (e.g., Ryanair);
- similar benefits of similar quality at lower prices (e.g., all-premium carriers);
- unique benefits at the same price (e.g., Virgin Atlantic); or
- unique benefits which justify premium pricing (e.g., Singapore Airlines in respect of new business and first class cabins on the B777-300ER fleet first introduced in 2006, and the A380 Singapore Suites introduced in 2007).

The fundamental objective is to pitch a better bid for customers' business than competitors are pitching, by offering perceptibly more customer value to targeted segments. The ultimate purpose, of course, should be to do this and at the same time keep the price element of the service–price offer above input costs and ensure acceptable earnings. Figures 1.3 and 1.4 illustrate some of these ideas.

With reference to Figure 1.3:

- The acceptable perceived value (APV) curve is the theoretical indifference curve of a single consumer. In principle, a service–price offer positioned anywhere on this curve should be acceptable to the consumer. Bowman and Faulkner (1997) refer to this as a 'consumer surplus isoquant'. A service–price offer positioned off the curve has the potential to provide higher value (if to the left) or lower value (if to the right).
- There are two ways customer-perceived value could be improved relative to an existing value proposition on the indifference curve: by reducing price whilst maintaining or improving perceived benefits, or by improving benefits whilst maintaining or reducing price. Either would result in a new proposition located to the left of the indifference curve. Conversely, a reduction in benefits without downward adjustment in price, or an increase in price without an improvement in perceived benefits, would shift a proposition to the right of the curve.
- A segment of demand is comprised of customers whose similarly shaped APV curves imply broadly shared service expectations, attribute weightings, and

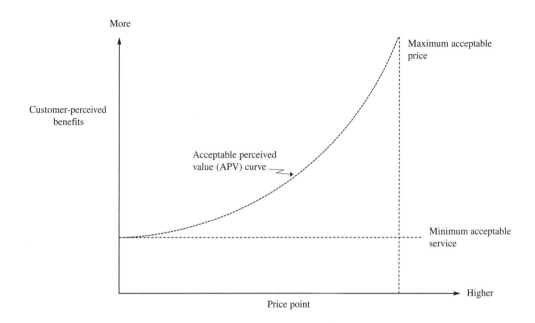

Figure 1.3   Customer-perceived value from a service–price offer

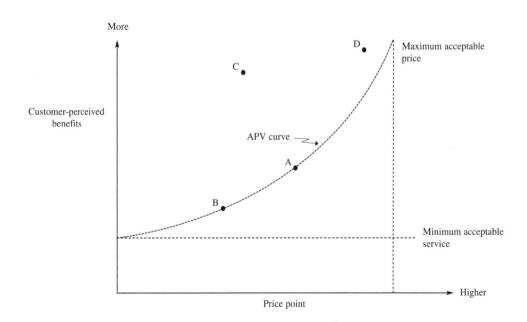

Figure 1.4   Positioning a value proposition

perceptions of value. The more congruent the expectations, weightings, and perceptions of value held by a group of customers, the tighter the segment; the less congruence there is, the stronger the case for further segmentation. This argument is consistent with the thinking behind benefits segmentation, which is discussed in Chapter 2.

Having identified one or more segments by hypothesising different APV curves, the next questions are which one(s) an airline should serve and where it should position itself in each targeted segment. The first question is answered by deciding upon a strategic position – as a wide-market or niche carrier focusing on product differentiation or cost leadership, for example. The second is answered by deciding upon a market position – something that in turn requires the carrier to distinguish itself from competitors in customers' perceptions. (Strategic positioning and market positioning are therefore closely related, but they are not identical concepts; whereas a carrier's *strategic* position refers to its choice of competitive scope – that is, whether in service and/or geographical dimensions it is to be a wide-market or niche differentiator or cost leader – its *market* position is a matter of how its brand is perceived in the minds of targeted customers relative to competing brands.)

Airlines can target a segment by designing a service–price offer that is believed to sit somewhere on that segment's APV curve – perhaps around its mid-point, as carrier A in Figure 1.4 has done. If all the firms in a market are located along the indifference curve, consumers will have little incentive to switch and market shares will be largely stable. One way of shifting market share is to locate away from the curve by offering a new price–benefit trade-off – that is, by making a new service–price offer. However, positions off the curve raise further questions. For example, staying with Figure 1.4 and using airline A as a benchmark:

- Airline B is offering fewer benefits at a lower price. The question is whether there is a subsegment of demand willing to forgo benefits in return for that lower price. If so, which benefits and how much lower price? An example in some US and European short-haul markets might be price-sensitive business travellers willing to forgo the ground and cabin amenities traditionally offered, provided there is a low-fare alternative offering high frequencies and reliable schedules.
- Airline C is offering more customer-perceived benefits than airline A and a lower price. Provided C can communicate its benefits effectively and further provided that the benefits it is perceived to be offering are sufficient to overcome the switching costs that A might have imposed by creating customer loyalty, whether emotional loyalty to the brand or functional loyalty to its frequent flyer programme, market share should shift from A to C. The question is whether C's cost structure will enable it to profitably sustain effective delivery of an enhanced benefits package and retain its increased share.
- Airline D is also offering more customer-perceived benefits than A, but unlike C it is charging a price premium. In other words, D is 'differentiating' its product. (Differentiation occurs when an airline is able to extract a price premium on the basis of unique or better-delivered benefits; in the absence of a price premium, those benefits might certainly enhance the brand distinctiveness of the airline delivering them, but they would not be a source of differentiation as defined by most economists.) The question in this case is whether there is a subsegment of demand prepared to pay for the augmented benefits being offered, or whether

the airline is 'over-delivering' in the context of the segment concerned. Long-haul carriers regularly introduce innovations into their business and first class cabins, and in some markets first-movers (e.g., Singapore Airlines) have been able to price above competitors serving broadly the same segments with products that are less benefit-rich. However, this strategy does impose an onerous and expensive requirement to be a consistent innovator.

Positions right of the APV curve are only sustainable in the long term if there are entry barriers preventing competition from carriers willing to position on or left of the curve, or if the segment is insufficiently profitable to attract such customer-driven competitors.

All this might sound vague and academic set against the cut-and-thrust of an airline's real-time product design and pricing environment in a highly competitive market. What the analysis does achieve is to underline why both strategic and market positioning need to be based on clearly understood sources of cost advantage and/or benefit advantage relative to identified competitors targeting the same customers in defined markets or market segments.

Competitive advantage: what do we do that others cannot do as well, as cheaply or at all? Anything that allows one firm to earn and sustain higher profitability than the average for its industry can be considered a source of competitive advantage. However, because the airline industry is a network business, each carrier can potentially face a wide range of different competitors depending upon which city-pair (or even which airport-pair) market is analysed; what gives an airline an advantage over competitors in one market might be insufficient to give it an advantage over perhaps different competitors in another market. Competitive advantage is therefore better characterised as a useful concept than a precise number. Its sources do nonetheless need to be understood and, where possible, proactively managed; it is the recognition and management of sources of competitive advantage that underpin a sound competitive strategy. 'Management' of competitive advantage requires understanding and acting upon the answers to three questions: What are the sources of competitive advantage? What is the nature of competitive advantage? How can competitive advantage be sustained?

1. *What are the sources of competitive advantage?* Competitive advantage is evident when a firm is able to provide better customer value for equivalent cost, or equivalent customer value at a lower cost than competitors (Porter 1985). To achieve either of these advantageous positions the firm chooses to perform particular activities, to perform those activities in a certain way, not to perform other activities, and to link those that it does perform in a particular manner (both internally and across organizational boundaries). From these choices flows an advantage over competitors targeting the same customers but making different choices (Porter 1991, 1996). What enables a firm to make the choices it does is its possession of resources and capabilities, relevant to the markets being served, with which it is able to distinguish itself from competitors in respect of what it can do and how it can do it. Resources might be structural (e.g., international route authorities), or they might be consciously created (e.g., brand image).

2. *What is the nature of competitive advantage?* This question is in effect asking what advantage a particular firm has that allows it to deliver at a profit the type of customer value it has chosen to offer. According to the resource-based theory of competitive strategy (RBT), some firms have resources that give them an advantage over others in producing certain types of output – that is, in offering certain types of customer

value. To be a source of competitive advantage, a resource must either contribute to something uniquely valuable that an airline can do for targeted customers, or to something that enables it to provide a given level of customer value at a lower cost than competitors (Barney 1986a).

- *Cost advantage* Referring back to Figure 1.2, an airline with a cost advantage has a lower C than its competitors. The critical question is the nature of the customer-perceived benefits B that it is offering and the price P it can charge for them. There are broadly two possibilities:
  - *Benefit parity* An airline offering the same benefits as competitors at the same price but off a lower cost base will earn higher profits. (This is what is meant by Porter's (1980) generic strategy of cost leadership; Porter's model describes above-average returns being earned by *the* lowest cost producer charging prices similar to others in the market. Contrary to a widespread misunderstanding, it is a model that hinges on *cost* leadership, not *price* leadership.)
  - *Benefit reduction* In this case, benefits offered are significantly fewer than most competitors are offering, and the price platform is lower in order to compensate. This is the essence of the original low-cost/low-fare model – a model which, as we will see later in the chapter, is now being blurred by an expanding range of offers. Profits depend upon whether a carrier's lower costs are sufficiently low to sustain its necessarily lower price platform.
- *Benefit advantage* An airline offering higher customer-perceived benefits (B) may have an advantage, depending on the costs it incurs and the price it is able to charge. Again, there are broadly two possibilities:
  - *Differentiation* If the supplementary benefits offered are sufficiently attractive to customers, the airline might be able to charge a premium price. This is what economists, and Porter's generic strategies model, refer to as 'differentiation'. Perhaps the most extreme example of differentiation was Concorde. The ability to differentiate can support higher production costs; lie-flat seats in long-haul business class cabins provide an obvious example insofar as they may allow an airline to charge a premium over less attractive 'standard' business class products to compensate for the lower seating densities they impose. If B increases more than C, incremental value will have been created; market forces, through their impact on P, will determine how this is shared between the airline (as profit) and the customer (as consumer surplus). Continuing with the same example, over time competitors will introduce their own upgraded cabins and any price premium is likely to be eroded – either by a general upward movement in competitors' prices, or by the innovator having to reduce its prices to compete with upgraded products introduced by carriers which decline to raise prices. (This example also illustrates that in highly competitive markets, investment in service innovations may be intended as much to protect the revenue stream as to enhance return on investment.)
  - *Distinctiveness* If an airline is unable to charge a premium for supplementary benefits, it is not technically 'differentiating' in an economic sense. These benefits may have merit insofar as they help distinguish the airline's offer and perhaps shift demand in its direction, but in the absence of an ability to differentiate (by increasing P) it is evident that any increase in costs (C) incurred in delivering them will reduce profits ($P-C$). Benefit advantage

in this case can therefore only arise from possession of resources and capabilities that contribute to distinctiveness *without* increasing costs. Box 1.2 explores this further.

The concepts of cost advantage and benefit advantage, set within a wider context established by strategic and market positioning, can be used to anchor the discussion of traffic, yield, output, and costs in Part 2 of the book.

3. *How can competitive advantage be sustained?* If a resource is to be a *sustainable* source of competitive advantage, it must be difficult for competitors to acquire, imitate or substitute (Bogner and Thomas 1994). In other words, resources need to be protected by 'isolating mechanisms' (Rumelt 1984). In practice, most tangible resources can in fact be acquired, imitated or substituted – albeit perhaps over time rather than immediately. Such resources, common to more than one competitor serving a particular market, are likely to be no more than 'enablers' rather than true sources of competitive advantage. The resources most likely to sustain competitive advantage over the long term are more often than not intangible. In a service business such as the airline industry, intangible

---

Box 1.2: Differentiation or Being Different?

In order to sell in a competitive market it is necessary to be different from competitors in some way that customers value. However, 'being different' is not necessarily the same as what is meant by economists when they talk of 'differentiation'. Economists say that two products A and B are 'differentiated' if there is some common price for the two at which consumers prefer, say, B over A; logically then, we can say that in order to get a consumer who prefers B to actually buy A, the price of A will have to be reduced sufficiently to compensate her for forgoing the benefits that drive her preference for B. If the price of A is indeed below the price of B but is not sufficiently low to convince all consumers to change allegiance, the producer of B is earning a price premium from those who do buy its product and so is reaping the benefit of differentiation.

The idea of differentiation, widely popularised by Porter (1980, 1985), in fact goes back to the 1930s when economists added the concept of 'monopolistic competition' to the microeconomic models of market structure which until then had recognised perfect competition, oligopoly, and monopoly (Hotelling 1929, Chamberlin 1933, Robinson 1934). The basic idea of monopolistic competition is that by differentiating their offers in some way that is valuable to customers, firms gain a degree of freedom to raise prices they would not otherwise have in a perfectly competitive market; in effect, what they do is create a 'mini-monopoly' for the differentiated product (Chamberlin op. cit.).

With this background in mind, it is worth taking a few paragraphs to explain what is meant by the expression 'service–price offer', which appears throughout this book.

Service An airline might offer a service that differs from competitors' offers in one or more ways which customers value. That difference could lie in functional attributes such as a better schedule or more comfortable cabins on long-haul services, or it might lie in less tangible but arguably more defensible emotional (i.e., psychosocial) attributes such as the style and tone of service delivery. (Note that 'attributes' are dimensions of a service offer that generate the benefits which customers buy to satisfy their needs and wants.)

*   If customers are willing to pay a premium for this augmented service, we have a case of 'differentiation' as defined by economists. The next questions would then be whether the price premium covers any incremental costs – a rough calculation at best, in most circumstances – and how sustainable the competitive advantage on which the differentiation has been built will prove to be over time. Some airlines have been able to

charge premia for non-stop services competing against connecting routes, for innovations such as lie-flat seats, for schedule strength at a dominated hub, and sometimes even for what they consider to be their 'high-quality' brand image; in India, for example, Kingfisher positioned itself as a premium carrier with first class fares 5–10 per cent above those charged by Jet. Sustaining premia on a long-term basis can prove challenging.

- If customers will not pay a premium in return for functional or psychosocial benefits, other than perhaps temporarily, these benefits are not technically a source of 'differentiation'. They are certainly 'points of difference', an expression widely used in the brand management literature, but in this case the airline is not earning 'economic rent' from the resources that make it different – much though it might like to; it is, nonetheless, giving customers a reason to buy in a competitive environment hallmarked by product sameness and widespread price-matching. For example, despite the cuts it was compelled to make in the 1990s, Alaska Airlines has retained a reputation for high standards of customer service; the fact that it competes with Southwest in many of its core west coast markets leaves little opportunity for Alaska to differentiate its fares, but even when fares are matched its reputation – distinct from Southwest's equally strong but different reputation – gives customers who prefer its value proposition a reason to buy.

In general, few airlines possess the unique, rare, or costly-to-imitate resources required to sustain either 'differentiation' or 'points of difference' based on purely functional service attributes. There are exceptions, most notably those built on possession of critical mass at a hub or in a particular market; either can lead to the building of a dominant position in customers' perceptions within a geographical area. On the whole, however, it is in respect of intangible attributes such as culture, service style, and brand image – providing predominantly psychosocial benefits – that sustainable points of difference can be found.

Price This is where we diverge further from the economists' idea of differentiation, because in this book price is treated as part of an overall service–price value proposition rather than as a reflection of whether or not an airline has been able to differentiate itself successfully in economists' terms. Take for example a low-fare carrier. It might be able to establish clear points of difference between itself and competitors based on corporate culture and a positive brand image, as Southwest has done; but it cannot earn a price premium – that is, 'differentiate'– because low price is a fundamental purchase criterion in the segment it is targeting. This does not mean that the points of difference built on corporate culture and brand image are irrelevant, because all other things being equal – including price and schedule, for example – these give customers a reason to choose, and remain loyal to, Southwest rather than another carrier. In other words, although Southwest might for the sake of argument score equally with the competition on price and on functional attributes such as frequency and departure timings, the points of difference it has established by nurturing psychosocial attributes driven by culture and image give its overall service–price offer a winning edge.

In summary, when we talk about price or service 'distinctiveness' in this book, we are in fact talking about what the brand management literature refers to as 'points of difference' rather than what economists mean by 'differentiation'. We are talking about design variables in a service–price offer which give customers a reason to purchase from the airline concerned rather than from competitors. When the word 'differentiation' is used, we mean that an airline is able to command a price premium over direct competitors.

resources – such as corporate culture and its impact on attitudes and the performance of routines – can be particularly important sources of competitive advantage because they have a profound effect on the efficiency and effectiveness of service delivery; evidence of the industry's continuing structural impediments, referred to at the beginning of the chapter, can be seen in the fact that slots and route authorities are also important to sustained competitive advantage in some markets.

However, it is not resources alone that matter, but how they are put to use in order to effectively and efficiently produce output for one or more segments of demand (Penrose 1959). Competitive strategy is a conscious attempt to build and capitalise on the firm's endowment of strategic resources (Zou and Cavusgil 1996). This takes us to the fourth element in this brief discussion of competitive strategy – the value chain and operating strategy.

Operating strategy: how should internal and external linkages be organized? Benefit and cost advantages are rooted in an airline's unique resources and capabilities, and reflected in its choice of strategic position; they are operationalised by the activities it chooses to undertake. Strategic management texts generally use the metaphor of a 'value chain' to characterise the way in which a firm's activities are organised to combine inputs and transform them into outputs valued by customers. A firm's value chain is itself part of a wider value system encompassing the value chains of suppliers, partners, distributors, and customers. Porter (1991, p. 104) has put the argument as follows:

> Competitive advantage results from a firm's ability to perform required activities at a collectively lower cost than rivals, or perform some activities in unique ways that create buyer value and hence allow the firm to command a premium price. The required mix and configuration of activities, in turn, is altered by competitive scope.

Returning once again to Figure 1.2, each activity in an airline's value chain has the potential to augment customer-perceived benefits (B), and each also has the potential to increase the cost (C) that the airline incurs assembling inputs and delivering service. The forces that influence benefits created and costs incurred – called 'activity drivers' – vary across different activities (Besanko *et al.* 2000). In principle, it is possible to generate value-added analyses which compare the incremental perceived benefit generated by a new activity, or a new way of performing an existing activity, with the cost incurred; in practice, it is often very difficult to isolate the impact that individual activities have on the overall value created by an airline.

At the macro-level, there are two decisions affecting the design of any value chain which together frame operating strategy: first, which activities are to be performed by external suppliers or partners rather than internally; second, how linkages between activities, whether performed internally or externally, are to be managed.

1. *Vertical boundaries of the firm* The strategic leaders of any business have to choose the extent to which they intend that business to be directly involved in the various activities that together contribute to the final service output delivered to their customers. This is a 'make or buy' decision, the outcome of which establishes the extent of vertical integration in the business. Vertical integration may be 'backward' if control over the supply of inputs is sought, or 'forward' if control over distribution channels is acquired. An example of backward integration is jetBlue's acquisition of inflight entertainment (IFE) supplier DIRECTV®. Another, highly unusual, example is Bangkok Airways' ownership of three airports in Thailand, including Koh Samui which is central to the carrier's niche strategy of providing high service quality into the country's smaller leisure destinations (Kuhlmann 2007c). More common, particularly in the United States, is airline ownership and leasing of terminals. With regard to forward integration,

the trend (in North America and Europe, but less so in Asia) has been to dispose of shareholdings in global distribution systems (GDSs) and close ticket offices, and to develop direct channels using the Internet. However, reflecting the fact that market differences can require very specific strategic responses, China's East Star Airlines and Spring Airlines rely heavily on distribution through their own chains of travel agencies, despite in other respects aspiring to a low-cost business model.

The difference between vertical integration and related diversification is open to debate, but can for practical purposes be described as follows: an airline which performs, for example, its own heavy maintenance and (at least at major stations) its own ground-handling and catering but does not generate significant revenue by selling these services to other carriers can be considered vertically integrated. Egyptair, for example, has a significant in-house maintenance, repair, and overhaul (MRO) capability, but it does little work for third parties. If, on the other hand, an airline's maintenance, catering, and other support operations are significant revenue generators in their own right because substantial third-party business is actively sought, the airline is pursuing a corporate strategy of related diversification; for example, two thirds of Lufthansa Technik's revenues are derived from outside the Lufthansa Group, clearly indicating a corporate (i.e., group-level) strategy of related diversification.

There are broadly five vertical scope options, with the word 'vertical' here being loosely defined to apply to any activity or process contributing ultimately to the delivery of customer value. They are outlined in Box 1.3.

Box 1.3: Vertical Scope Options

1. *In-house supply by an internal department/cost centre* This has been the traditional approach in large, highly integrated airlines.
2. *In-house supply by an internal profit centre* Some carriers that are prepared neither to spin internal service suppliers off into separate subsidiaries nor to outsource the services they supply have instead tried to instil a more entrepreneurial culture by enforcing greater cost transparency and expectations of profitability on what were previously accepted simply as necessary cost centres. How successful this approach will be might depend upon whether or not the core air transport operation remains a captive purchaser compelled to buy in-house (Doganis 2001).
3. *In-house supply by a subsidiary or joint venture* The objectives here are to cut costs by removing the 'monopoly supplier' mentality and to earn incremental revenues by competing more aggressively for third-party work; in the case of joint ventures (which might be with alliance partners or external suppliers), motives can extend to the realisation of cash from partial sale of existing assets or expertise, access to a captive source of external skills, or the sharing of future investment costs. Going a step further than a joint venture with one or more external parties, some airlines began in the 1990s to float their subsidiaries on public markets. As well as raising cash, an additional motive for a listing might be to realise shareholder value in that subsidiary not currently reflected in the parent's balance sheet or market rating.
4. *Tapered integration* This mixture of vertical integration and market exchange involves retaining in-house some of the work done in respect of a certain activity or process, and outsourcing the rest. One advantage is that tapered integration allows expansion of supply without having to invest in additional in-house capacity. Another is that retaining an in-house capability gives the airline concerned a first-hand knowledge of costs and achievable efficiency levels against which to benchmark outsourced work. This assumes that the in-house supplier represents an efficiency benchmark; one potential disadvantage of tapered integration is in fact that it might

deprive in-house suppliers of sufficient scale and scope to optimise their cost-effectiveness.

5. *External supply* Where the external supplier was previously an in-house unit we can refer to the arrangement as 'outsourcing', although in practice the word has come to encompass all forms of external supply. Cost savings and a preference for redirecting investment into core activities in which sources of real competitive advantage can be found are the most frequently cited motivations for outsourcing. Whatever the work being outsourced, however, somebody somewhere in the airline concerned has to be sufficiently qualified and knowledgeable to evaluate the quality of that work. The close monitoring of quality is particularly vital when safety or key operational and business processes are involved, and also when corporate reputation and brand integrity are at risk. (It is not only vertical transactions that can be outsourced; we will see in chapter six that airlines now commonly outsource capacity provision to franchisees and other code-share partners.)

Sometimes these five steps are followed sequentially in an evolutionary process. For example, Kuhlmann (2007a) traces the evolution of Swissair from the traditional model of in-house supply in the 1970s, to a group structure comprising Gate Gourmet, Swissport, SR Technics, and several other subsidiaries in the 1990s, and finally (in the guise of Swiss International) to being a subsidiary of Lufthansa focusing almost entirely on air transportation and purchasing most inputs from external suppliers (including some former Swissair subsidiaries which are now independently owned).

Readers with an interest in the topic can refer to Lajili *et al.* (2007) for an overview of empirical and theoretical research into vertical integration generally, concentrating on contributions from organizational economics.

Arguments in favour of vertical integration have generally included reliability of supply, better control over performance, and the economies of scale available to large in-house operations; other considerations might be the influence of trades unions wanting to retain work in-house or, particularly in developing countries, politicians wanting to build a local skills base. Arguments against vertical integration include the opportunity costs involved, the lack of competitive advantage that airlines sometimes face in respect of activities peripheral to their core air transport operations, the need to focus scarce management time on those core operations, and the fact that in-house suppliers bring with them fixed costs that can be difficult to shrink rapidly in response to a market downturn, whilst external suppliers largely represent a variable cost.

Because airlines in various parts of the world function in supplier markets having very different levels of sophistication, and also because each carrier has its own financial and emotional investment sunk into existing organizational architecture, there is little prescriptive that can be said about vertical integration in the industry. Airlines vary widely with regard to the choices they make. Large, long-established carriers frequently perform in-house many functions ancillary to the actual transportation of passengers and cargo that smaller, newer airlines prefer in most cases to outsource. However, airlines as a whole have been taking a closer look at which activities need to be in-house, and which could be outsourced – along with their overheads.

Whilst the outsourcing of activities is a trend that has been running for over a decade across the industry as a whole, managers in a handful of countries have recently been encouraged either by general market sentiment or the lobbying of activist investors to look deeper into their organizational structures for opportunities to 'unlock value' from their balance sheets. For example:

- Between 2005 and 2008, Air Canada's 75 per cent parent ACE Aviation Holdings sold the carrier's Aeroplan frequent flyer programme (FFP), raised three-quarters of a billion dollars selling 70 per cent of Air Canada Technical Services to private equity, and then earned a smaller sum selling down its interest in regional feeder Jazz to 9.9 per cent. (ACE's ultimate intention is to sell down its stake in Air Canada.)
- Following the failure of a bid for the entire company by private equity interests in early 2007, Qantas management launched a strategic review of its businesses which at the time of writing seems likely to result in the full or partial sale of – at the very least – the carrier's FFP.
- In late 2007 American announced that it was considering disposal of its AAdvantage FFP, American Eagle regional operation, and some of its MRO function.
- At the same time United was also considering sale of its Mileage Plus programme and MRO operation, whilst other US majors – with varying degrees of management enthusiasm – were similarly engaged in reviewing their options in respect of in-house MRO organizations, regionals, and/or FFPs (e.g., Delta's stated wish to sell wholly-owned subsidiary Comair). Whilst MRO organizations and FFPs are in many cases likely to have substantial intrinsic value to an external purchaser, whether the same is true for regional subsidiaries such as American Eagle and Comair remains to be seen.

Whether or not such spin-offs are sound strategic moves or simply short-term palliatives for lacklustre share prices is an open question. It is interesting that the Icelandic investors whose pressure brought spin-offs more firmly onto the agenda at American in 2007 appear to have had only a very short-term perspective, selling down their 9.1 per cent stake within a matter of weeks when a response from management was not immediately forthcoming.

The outcome of historical and commercial pressures has been a range of different decisions, reflecting divergent strategic perspectives with regard to what it is that constitutes a core activity for each carrier. Every management team must ultimately come to its own conclusion on whether retaining particular activities in-house builds or destroys shareholder value.

2. *Linkages between activities* The 'value' in a value chain can often be found in the way in which discrete activities are linked so that they make a coherent contribution to the business's strategic theme. For linkages to generate a competitive advantage, they must succeed in imbuing available resources with a greater 'value in use' to the airline concerned than the 'exchange value' these same resources have in factor markets. Hergert and Morris (1989, p. 17) explain the microeconomic roots of this idea:

> The firm is viewed as a collection of discrete but related production functions (activities), where some of them are not freely traded in external markets. These non-traded activities will generate rents for the firms able to perform them and also create entry barriers or cost disadvantages for other firms. Firms perform a variety of tasks in transforming raw materials and primary goods into final products. Although necessary, most of these activities do not distinguish a firm from its rivals. Competitive advantage must be based on those activities in which a firm has proprietary access to scarce resources (e.g., skills, patents, assets, distribution networks, etc.). The first step in strategy formulation is to identify which activities are the actual or potential source of such rents. This is the part of the firm which must be managed. [Anything else is a candidate for outsourcing.]

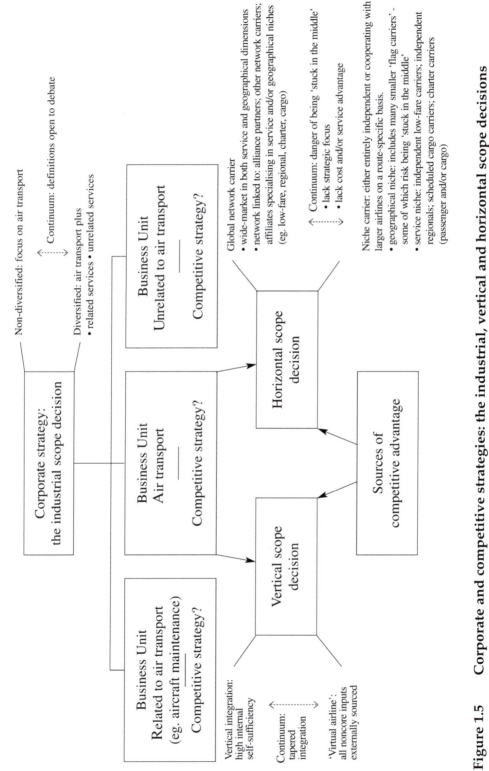

Figure 1.5   Corporate and competitive strategies: the industrial, vertical and horizontal scope decisions

The specialised linkages, such as organizational routines (Nelson and Winter 1982) and tacit knowledge (Nonaka 1994) which integrate a firm's resources, might be impossible to value or to imitate outside the context of that particular firm. The way in which linkages within an airline's corporate boundaries, and relationships with external suppliers and partners, are coordinated can therefore be important resources in their own right.

Summary

This section of the chapter has defined strategy as ' ... a coherent set of individual actions in support of a system of goals' (Eden and Ackermann 1998, p. 4) and noted that however a strategy is formulated, its implementation involves taking decisions which adhere to a consistent theme. To be truly 'strategic', a decision must reinforce or change: the scope of the corporation's portfolio of businesses; the market (or 'horizontal') scope of an individual business in the portfolio; the value offered to customers of an individual business; the competitive advantage sought by a business; or the operating strategy used by a business to deliver value to its customers. The first of these is 'corporate strategy', and the latter four taken together are the essence of 'competitive strategy'. Figure 1.5 summarises the range of possibilities.

The present book is not concerned with the industrial scope decision inherent in corporate strategy. Its concern is with the economics of just one business: the air transportation of passengers and cargo. Other businesses, such as MRO for example, are relevant only insofar as they affect the cost and delivery of airline services. Rather than *corporate* strategy, it is alternative *competitive* strategies in the air transport business which provide the background against which the discussion in subsequent chapters will be developed. Since the late 1990s, the product of competitive strategy has come to be widely referred to as a 'business model'. The next section defines this expression.

BUSINESS MODELS

If strategy is 'a coherent set of individual actions in support of a system of goals' (ibid.), then the business model is what lends it coherence – provided, of course, that the model is itself aligned with those goals. Like all models, a business model is a simplification of reality – the reality in this case being how the airline in question does business, which means how it buys, produces, and sells. Osterwalder (2004, p. 15) defines a business model as ' ... a description of the value a company offers to one or several segments of customers and the architecture of the firm and its network of partners for creating, marketing, and delivering this value'.

An airline's business model is therefore a description of the value the company delivers to targeted customers, and of how it configures resources internally and externally to achieve this. It has two elements:

1. A *revenue model* which describes how revenues will be earned, addressing matters such as product design and sources of ancillary revenue.
2. A *cost model* which describes the financial consequences of the revenue model, addressing business processes and enterprise architecture – specifically what is done, how it is done, and by whom it is done.

Over the last decade or so, airline business models have typically been categorised as:

- *legacy*, implying a full-service revenue model and an outdated cost model, or
- *low-cost*, implying a no-frills revenue model and an appropriately lean cost model.

The next section examines more carefully what has been happening in practice to airline business models and takes issue with the rhetoric used to describe them.

III. Airline Strategies and Business Models: What is Happening in Practice

The airline industry is clearly in a period of profound structural change which began with deregulation of the US passenger market in 1978, accelerated with European deregulation and the wider spread of both domestic liberalisation and less restrictive bilateral agreements in the 1990s, and gained further momentum from development of the Internet, the impact of 9/11, and significant increases in the cost of fuel. But two things remain unclear:

1. What form, as defined by number and identity of participants and variety of business models, the restructured industry will ultimately take.
2. Whether we should even be thinking in terms of a restructured industry in the sense of a new equilibrium eventually being reached, or whether instead we have entered an open-ended cycle which sees updated business models being introduced, competing on the basis of lower costs and prices, then becoming the norm and competing more on the basis of non-price attributes, and ultimately being replaced by further innovation (Treitel 2006). In this latter case the question is less about static structures than about the speed of the change cycle.

The present section of the chapter will start by identifying three developments that have driven the timing and speed of change in recent years. It will go on to highlight some of the more important new strategies and business models that are currently observable, take a critical look at the rhetorical labels used to describe these models, and finally draw some tentative conclusions.

WHY AIRLINE BUSINESS MODELS HAVE BEEN CHANGING SO RAPIDLY

Three factors have both enabled and mandated change: deregulation and liberalisation, the Internet, and advances in aircraft technologies.

Deregulation And Liberalisation

In a commercially regulated environment, output is controlled both as to nature (i.e., service attributes) and volume (i.e., size of aircraft and frequency of operation), whilst pricing tends to be cost-plus; there is little incentive to resist the accretion of complexity and cost, and little opportunity to enter and develop new markets or innovate in pursuit of new sources of revenue. In a deregulated environment, many (although not all) barriers to entry fall, with the result that output rises, prices are lowered as competition increases, service offers become more varied, and new airlines with lean process architectures, unerring focus on costs, and a capability for nimble decision-making (in respect of market entry and exit, for example) put pressure on the margins – even the economic survival – of established carriers. For example, even before the EU–US open skies accord came into effect in March 2008 liberalisation on the North Atlantic had already facilitated a number of different business models, including:

- wide-market offers from network carriers covering all market segments;
- all-premium niche offers (e.g., eos – first class equivalent, Silverjet – business class equivalent);
- low-fare niche offers (e.g., flyglobespan, Zoom).

To take another example, liberalisation of the Indian domestic market allowed entrants to challenge state-owned incumbent Indian Airlines with a wide range of value propositions, ranging from Air Deccan's basic low-cost carrier (LCC) model, through the hybrid models of IndiGo and Spice Jet, to the full-service offer of Jet and the premium positioning of Kingfisher.

There is an uneven but inexorable trend towards the liberalisation, and in a growing number of domestic and international markets the deregulation, of air transport services. We will return to this topic in Chapter 4.

The Internet

Growth in the capabilities and reduction in the cost of information and communication technologies (ICT) have together had four profound implications for airlines in the present context: first, by providing price transparency to consumers, they have put further downward pressure on real yields and this in turn has intensified the need for better control of costs; second, they have accelerated disintermediation in distribution channels and so contributed to lower distribution costs; third, they have significantly increased the available choice of feasible business configurations; fourth, they have reduced the cost of coordinating and transacting business within complex supply chains (Coase 1937, Williamson 1975). Cost models can now in principle be designed around the external supply of input goods and services without sacrificing quality or timeliness, whilst revenue models can be designed to offer a broader range of service attributes (e.g., Internet check-in), to incorporate ancillary revenue streams (e.g., charging for desk rather than kiosk or Internet check-in), and to exploit multi-channel distribution opportunities.

This development has had two consequences (Osterwalder 2004):

1. Instead of there being a small number of relatively homogeneous business models within the industry there are now several, and instead of the predominant organizational architecture being vertically integrated and functional there is now a trend towards the use of more complex networks of inter-firm relationships to deliver service to customers.

2. As industry 'clock-speed' (ibid, p. 13) has accelerated, sources of competitive advantage – particularly if based on resources that are easy to imitate or substitute – have become less stable, and this requires managers to adapt and innovate more or less continuously.

Advances In Aircraft Technologies

We will look at fleet planning in Chapter 8. For the purpose of the present discussion, two developments can be highlighted.

1. The increased reliability of aircraft generally, and in particular their powerplants and systems, has enabled the development of high-intensity, quick-turnaround short-haul operations. The capacity of young fleets to sustain high levels of utilisation reliably and with low cash maintenance costs has contributed to the ability of low-fare carriers to undercut the cost structures of established airlines in markets where they compete.
2. By offering increasingly capable new models and derivatives, aircraft manufacturers have over the last two decades broken the traditional link between aircraft payload and range capabilities which hitherto dictated that the longer a stage-length the larger the aircraft operating it had to be. This has opened up transcontinental non-stop markets to aircraft in the B737 and A320 category (and therefore to low-fare airlines), it has facilitated development of short- and medium-haul hub-bypass routes, it has contributed to accelerating fragmentation in long-haul markets, and it has brought much of the world within non-stop range of the rapidly growing hubs in the Middle East. We will return to this topic when network design is discussed in Chapter 6. A thought worth pondering is whether the next generation of replacements for the B737 and A320 series will have year-round full-payload westbound transatlantic range and, if so, what impact they might have on the future structure of traffic flows between Western Europe and the US eastern seaboard.

Conclusion

The last few paragraphs reviewed three factors that have driven and/or facilitated change in airline business models since the mid-1990s. Factors which may well be profound drivers of change going forward are the magnitude and speed of upward movements in the price of oil. The price per barrel breached $130 for the first time on the day these words were being written. Where it will go from here is anybody's guess. It may fall back once speculative excesses unwind – although how far and for how long are open questions. If on the other hand it remains at current levels for a sustained period (i.e., beyond the life of existing hedges) or rises inexorably towards the $150–200 range now anticipated by some observers, airfares and cargo rates will have to be very substantially increased. The implications of this would be a significant withdrawal of capacity in response to weaker demand and much slower than projected air traffic growth. The industry as currently structured is not built for $130 a barrel oil or worse. Many of the strategies and business models discussed in the next section would require further radical overhaul.

CHANGES IN STRATEGY AND BUSINESS MODEL

The following paragraphs identify the most significant global and regional trends to early 2008. However, they are generalisations from an increasingly complex reality and there is no shortage of exceptions.

Legacy Carriers: Reinventing The Business Model

The legacy business model as it existed in short-haul North American and European markets prior to 2000 relied for its profits almost entirely on the willingness of business travellers to pay high fares – a willingness sorely tested by the recession which began that year, and then by the impact of both 9/11 and the accelerating growth of cheaper, equally reliable alternatives. Whilst high fares still prevailed in some markets where legacy carriers remained unchallenged, as a system-wide approach to doing business the traditional high-cost/high-fare model was increasingly seen as obsolete in short- and medium-haul markets. The revenue environment had changed fundamentally, and the legacy carriers' business models – encompassing production processes, reward structures, network, fleet, pricing, and distribution – also had to change.

Changes to legacy carriers' revenue models   By 2003, LCCs were present in 2304 of the top 5000 US domestic city-pair markets and had access to 72.5 per cent of passengers (GAO 2006). Offered lower fares with fewer restrictions by reliable LCCs, business travel buyers in particular were no longer willing to accept the high walk-up fares that underpinned legacy revenue models. The legacy carriers were forced to respond with lower fares and fewer restrictions – at least in those markets where they faced serious competition. Whilst this has been equally true in Europe, US legacy carriers also responded to changes in the competitive environment by massively shrinking their output (a significant exception in this respect being Continental) and by shifting emphasis from domestic to international output growth. Between 2000 and 2006, US network carriers reduced their domestic output by 20.6 per cent; over the same period, LCCs and regionals increased output by 57.0 per cent and 141.3 per cent respectively (with the result that total domestic capacity increased by only 1.9 per cent over the period) (FAA 2007a). Whereas in 2000, 71 per cent of US domestic passenger enplanements were on network carriers, having been around 90 per cent in 1980, the percentage had fallen to 57 per cent by 2005; LCCs and regionals, on the other hand, increased their shares from 16 and 13 per cent respectively to 22 and 21 per cent. Two trends were therefore evident: first, a significant schedule shift from the network carriers to their regional partners – a shift which had begun to slow by mid-decade and by 2008 was coming under severe pressure due to the unprofitability of many 50-seat jet operations at prevailing fuel prices; and the inexorable growth of LCCs – primarily Southwest, but also AirTran, jetBlue and others.

In Chapter 3 we will take a closer look at pricing practices. For the purposes of the present chapter, it is worth highlighting that in short-haul North American and European markets the most fundamental change to legacy revenue models brought about by the spread of LCCs into progressively more markets was a new approach to pricing:

* old model: high unrestricted ('walk-up') fares, with increasingly deeper discounts available as restrictions on purchase, use, and/or refundability are added;

- new model: low basic fare, probably rising as departure date approaches, with – in the case of some but not all carriers – incremental charges for unbundled service attributes (e.g., priority boarding, seat assignment, refreshments, baggage checking).

Many network carriers, most notably the US majors, have also been changing their revenue models by increasing the proportion of output generated in medium- and long-haul international markets. There are three reasons:

1. Growth in these markets, particularly to/from Asia and Latin America and on the newly liberalised North Atlantic, is forecast to be higher than within North America and Western Europe; furthermore, unit revenues are expected to remain stronger in international markets, offering a better buffer against spikes in the price of fuel.
2. The majors already have in place much of the infrastructure which is essential to international network operations and which would be expensive for new competitors to duplicate.
3. The inherently lower unit costs associated with long-haul flying are expected to provide an additional buffer against the possibility of a low-cost onslaught on the scale experienced in short- and medium-haul markets; we will return to this claim in a moment.

Legacy carriers in various parts of the world have a track record of retreating to 'safe havens' in the face of LCC encroachment into what were previously thought to be 'their' markets. Under growing attack in shorter markets through the 1990s, US legacies believed as recently as the turn of the century that domestic transcontinental markets were safe; Southwest, jetBlue, and others proved this not to be true, with the result that average fares in these markets fell dramatically. Whether the same will happen over time in long-haul – particularly transatlantic – markets remains to be seen.

More generally, there has been a growing emphasis amongst legacy carriers on enhancing service to premium customers, most notably those flying medium- and long-haul in business class. Whilst sound enough in principle, the danger in this strategy is that a great deal of faith is being placed in just one segment of the market to generate a high percentage of revenue and profit. Particularly in the case of some of the higher cost European and (to a lesser extent) US legacy carriers, it will be interesting to see how this strategy copes with the next deep cyclical downturn.

Changes to legacy carriers' cost models In short- and medium-haul markets, legacy carriers have had to address costs in order to survive revenue environments that have been changed fundamentally by the rapid growth of LCCs, and in order to cope with a massive rise in the price of fuel. They have been redesigning their cost models by simplifying service delivery processes, depeaking hubs, increasing aircraft utilisation, renegotiating input costs (notably labour and leases, in several cases under Chapter 11 bankruptcy protection), exploiting low-cost distribution channels, shifting output into longer-haul markets, and (notably in the United States) removing service attributes from the onboard product. There was certainly work to be done: in 1996, Southwest's unit costs were 36 per cent below the average for US network carriers (adjusted to a 1400km stage-length), but by 2001 the gap had widened to 45 per cent (Pearce 2006). Notwithstanding the painful restructuring that most legacy carriers have undertaken, a fundamental problem remains: the gap between their short-haul unit costs and the unit costs of directly competing LCCs has in most cases been narrowed, but it has not been and cannot be eliminated. Legacy carriers therefore have to keep their costs firmly down yet at the same time avoid cutting service to the point where the revenue premia mandated by their higher costs can no longer be earned. Over the longer term, across entire economic cycles, it is difficult to see them being able to achieve this on a sustainable basis in short-haul point-to-point markets.

Separate low-cost divisions or subsidiaries have continued to be used to confront lower-cost competitors, but with mixed results. Although United's Ted lingered on primarily at Denver, no US major has successfully established a low-cost 'airline-within-an-airline'. Elsewhere, SAS quickly transformed its low-cost operation, Snowflake, into a branded fare class on mainline services, and Air Canada did the same with Tango. Gulf Air closed its all-economy Gulf Traveller unit. LOT has shifted the orientation of Centralwings from low-cost scheduled services to charters. On the other hand, whilst Qantas failed to separate Australian sufficiently from the mainline carrier's cost-base, it subsequently met with success by establishing Jetstar as a stand-alone entity (albeit on the ashes of failed independent start-up Impulse); indeed, much of Qantas group domestic and international growth is now coming through Jetstar, to the point where the latter is being positioned as the mass-market brand and Qantas itself is focused increasingly on smaller, higher-yield segments. In 2006 Iberia ventured into LCC territory with partly-owned start-up Clickair, and Air France/KLM extended its low-cost Transavia brand from the Netherlands to France. When Jet acquired Air Sahara in 2007 it rebranded the acquisition as Jet Lite and positioned it between Jet's premium master-brand and competing LCCs such as Air Deccan – which itself has since been rebranded and is now affiliated with full-service carrier Kingfisher. JAL is in the process of shifting almost 40 per cent of its international flights and 25 per cent of domestic operations to low-cost subsidiaries JALways, JAL Express, and J-Air. In 2008 Korean Air launched Jin Air to compete with domestic LCCs, including a recently announced joint venture between Tiger Airways and the municipal authorities at Korean's own Incheon hub; Asiana responded by purchasing a start-up. Several other carriers also have low-fare subsidiaries or affiliates in current operation, for example: Lufthansa (germanwings – possibly to be merged with TUIfly), Mexicana (Click Mexicana), Thai International (Nok Air), Turkish (Anatolia Jet), and Royal Air Maroc (Atlas Blue). An alternative approach adopted by British Airways and Malaysia Airlines has been to transfer substantial parts of their domestic operations directly to an independent LCC (Flybe and AirAsia respectively). Even where a low-cost offshoot is successful, this does not solve the parent airline's fundamental problem in its core operations: how to adapt the cost model to the revenue environment in the remaining markets it serves.

Conclusion

During late 2007 and on into 2008, US legacy carriers in particular came under intense pressure as a result of high fuel prices. Their response was to ground significant numbers of aircraft in pursuit of output reductions which, over time, would amount in scale to the elimination of a sizeable major. It is arguable that unprofitable capacity could have exited the system many years earlier had not Chapter 11 kept alive failed – or inadequately restructured – business models. In this context, a comment attributed to one of United's SVPs is enlightening:

'Low-cost carriers should do more. You still have significant low-cost carriers that have growth in their plans' (http://www.thestreet.com, 22 April 2008). With oil around $120 a barrel at the time, US network carriers such as United could not make money as structured whilst Southwest – the target of the quoted comment – could, just about. In a properly functioning free enterprise system, airlines suffering as a result of either a failing business model or inadequate execution would be allowed to go under, and those with models better suited to the harsh new environment would then be able to grow into whatever vacated market spaces they are able to serve profitably. That this has not been happening in significant parts of the industry is the source of one of its many economic challenges.

Network carriers, particularly in North America and Western Europe, have made significant and often painful efforts to narrow the gap between their unit costs and those of low-fare carriers. However, there are structural reasons why the gap can never be eliminated. These will be drawn out in the opening part of the next section.

Low-Cost Carriers: Blurring The Business Model

Low-cost carriers have been growing rapidly in North America, Europe, Asia, and Latin America. Their share of seats in 2007 stood at approximately 30 per cent intra-Europe, 25 per cent intra-North America, 20 per cent intra-Latin America, and 12 per cent intra-Asia (Airbus 2008). The next two paragraphs highlight critical elements in the archetypal LCC business model – a model based fundamentally on keeping processes as simple as possible and avoiding complexity; the challenge faced by legacy carriers in respect of each element is noted. After that we will look at how this archetypal model is evolving. All of the points made will be discussed in more detail later in the book.

1.   *The LCC revenue model*
     - Simple price structure based on one-way sectors, with few restrictions on ticket usage. (Any legacy carrier flight will generally carry not just point-to-point traffic, but also a complex mix of passengers flowing from and to other points on the network. The legacy carriers' pricing challenge is inevitably more complex than that of a point-to-point LCC.)
     - Basic ground product with fewer manned check-in desks, no lounges, and fewer passenger services staff. (Legacy carriers operating wide networks have to cater to the higher expectations of their business passengers, particularly those travelling long-haul in first, business, and perhaps also premium economy cabins.)
     - Basic inflight product with high seating densities in a single-class configuration, no free food or amenities, and cabin crew ratios at the legal minimum. (Legacy carriers have in many cases cut back on inflight service across their short-haul networks, but as long as they offer more than one cabin they will inevitably have lower seating densities and higher crew and catering costs.)
     - Maximum ancillary revenue, generated not only by cross-selling on the website but importantly by unbundling the air transportation product and making passengers pay for 'extras'. (Legacy carriers are also in many cases exploiting sources of ancillary revenue, but they face limits imposed by the willingness of their high-fare passengers to tolerate paying for extras and – perhaps more so outside North America – the sensitivity of their 'full-service' brand images to the appearance of 'gouging' customers.)

- Point-to-point route structures offering no interline or intraline (i.e., same-airline) connections for passengers and baggage, and therefore carrying no responsibility for missed connections. (Legacy airlines are for the most part operating extensive and integrated networks, and a major source of their product distinctiveness is the connectivity they offer. It is not, in the long term, feasible to sell connectivity without taking responsibility for connections.)
- Schedule reliability. (A legacy carrier's complex integrated network will inevitably have more potential fail-points than a point-to-point route structure, so maintaining a similar level of reliability requires slack to be built into the operating system – and slack costs money.)
- No help if things go wrong. (Legacy carriers are for structural reasons never going to be able to close the unit cost gap between themselves and the most efficient LCCs, and therefore need sources of distinctiveness to help them earn higher unit revenues. For some, the source is the strength of their networks. For most, it is willingness to help customers who are delayed or miss their connections. The fact that this service attribute is embedded in customers' expectations of legacy airlines is clear from the bad publicity accompanying any failure to deliver it – as seen too often in the United States in recent years. Nonetheless, in early 2008 Air Canada became the first network carrier to break the mould by selling a 'we'll look after you if things go wrong' insurance policy called 'On My Way'™.)

2. *The LCC cost model*
   - Lower distribution costs resulting from relying on direct sales rather than travel agencies and GDSs. (Legacy airlines have also been successful in moving a high proportion of bookings into direct channels (notably the Internet) and capping or eliminating agency commissions (particularly in respect of leisure travel in their home markets), but they still need access to business travellers who choose to book through agencies because of the travel management services many agencies now offer; these agencies in turn rely on GDSs.)
   - Use of secondary airports which charge low landing and passenger-handling fees, and in some cases offer financial incentives to airlines able to generate high traffic volumes. (Legacy carriers need access to major hubs to support network connectivity, and even when operating in point-to-point markets their business passengers would not accept some of the bucolic airports for which carriers such as Ryanair in particular have become noted.)
   - High seating densities, attributable to tight seat pitches and single-class cabins with limited galley and storage space, allowing an airline to generate more output from a given flight than a carrier operating the same type with fewer seats. (As noted above, to the extent that they use multi-cabin aircraft legacy carriers cannot reduce seating densities to LCC levels – notwithstanding that their seat pitches in the economy/coach cabin may be comparable to that of an LCC.)
   - High aircraft utilisation, which allows an airline to generate more flying time from its fleet each day. (This is based to a large extent on fast turnarounds, which are themselves based on using uncongested secondary airports and operating point-to-point networks. The benefit of the latter is that schedules can be designed to maximise aircraft utilisation rather than flight connections, and there is no pressure to hold outbound aircraft for late inbound connecting passengers. Legacy carriers have taken steps to improve aircraft utilisation, but as long as they operate hubs they cannot fully avoid the costs these impose.)

- Avoidance of passenger and baggage transfers, and therefore of the complex, labour-intensive, and expensive transfer systems required at hubs and the cost of compensating when things go wrong. (The largest legacy airlines are on the whole network carriers. A key part of the service they sell is therefore connectivity. The cost of providing an infrastructure to support connecting passengers inevitably gets allocated to all passengers – including those flying point-to-point who do not use it.)
- Heavy reliance on external suppliers of services such as aircraft- and passenger-handling, and aircraft maintenance. (Many legacy carriers have outsourced services traditionally delivered in-house, but dismantling an existing organizational architecture is never as straightforward as starting with a clean sheet of paper.)
- Single-type fleet. (Because they operate a greater variety of routes – that is, their product and geographical scope are generally wider – legacy carriers need more complex fleets than LCCs. Complexity costs money – higher maintenance and training costs and lower crew utilisation, for example.)
- Flexible, productive, and often heavily incentivised workforce. (Legacy carriers' work practices as well as job demarcations between different labour groups have evolved over decades. A great deal of progress has been made in bringing them up to date since 2000, but getting people to multi-task willingly so that fewer staff are needed to do the same job or so that a process can be completed more quickly takes time and reacculturation.)
- Simpler, cheaper processes generally, such as: not using premium airport facilities (e.g., using stairs to front and rear aircraft doors rather than an airbridge just to the front will be cheaper and will accelerate disembarkation and boarding); free rather than allocated seating should also speed boarding; returning aircraft and crews to their home bases each night avoids layover costs; and flat organizational structures cut corporate overhead.

Southwest is widely considered the original LCC template although it could be argued that Pacific Southwest, flying in the intra-California market, was ahead of them. The model subsequently spread to Europe when Ryanair re-invented itself as an LCC in 1991 but, again, the charter carriers had by then already been offering nonscheduled service with very lean cost models for several decades. More recently, Virgin Blue and AirAsia took the model into the Asia-Pacific region, Gol pioneered Latin America, and Air Arabia and Jazeera the Middle East.

Many LCCs (of which there are now more than 100) continue to apply the basic model, but others have blurred it in one or both of two ways: adding service attributes and complexity, and/or adding aircraft types. We look at these two developments next.

Adding service attributes   Some LCCs stick more or less rigidly to a low-cost model, in principle eschewing any activity which raises costs (e.g., Ryanair, Allegiant, Spirit, Gol, Tiger, and AirAsia). Others, in order to access higher yielding segments or in order to meet local market expectations, have been willing to add costs by offering additional service attributes such as:

- guaranteed early boarding (e.g., Southwest – free with higher-yielding Business Select fares);
- more generous seat-pitch (e.g., jetBlue, Virgin Blue, and Air Arabia);

- a first or business class cabin (e.g., AirTran);
- seating rows with extra leg-room (e.g., jetBlue and Spirit);
- through-check-in of passengers and baggage (e.g., jetBlue and Virgin Blue);
- interline connections (e.g., Jetstar with Qantas; Gol with Aerolineas Argentinas, Air France, Continental, Delta, KLM, and VRG; and Virgin Blue with United, Etihad, Malaysia, and Virgin Atlantic);
- code-sharing (e.g., Clickair with shareholder Iberia, and Gol with Copa);
- use of primary airports (e.g., easyJet and Clickair);
- FFPs (e.g., airberlin, Virgin America);
- complimentary assigned seating (e.g., airberlin and Virgin Blue);
- lounges (e.g., Virgin Blue – free with higher-yielding fares);
- inflight entertainment (e.g., AirTran and jetBlue);
- inflight communication (e.g., AirAsia);
- complimentary food and beverages (e.g., airberlin);
- network flow into and out of a hub (e.g., airberlin at Palma, AirTran at Atlanta, and – if current plans are implemented – Aer Lingus at Dublin);
- B2B travel management sites (e.g., easyJet); and
- distribution through channels other than the Internet and call centres (e.g., almost half of low-cost carriers use one or more of the GDSs at some level of functionality – for example airberlin, AirTran, easyJet, Southwest, and WestJet).

It is debateable whether a carrier such as jetBlue, with its relatively low seating densities, leather seats, free inflight entertainment, and attentiveness to a 'cool' brand image, has much in common with the traditional Southwest model or with AirAsia, Spirit, and Ryanair – beyond the fact that all pay far more attention to costs than legacy carriers used to. Jetblue offers a better short- and medium-haul product than most of its legacy competitors off a lower cost base – but a base which still leaves room for even lower cost producers to undercut it in the most price-sensitive segments of demand (something unlikely to happen to either Ryanair or AirAsia in the foreseeable future). Similarly, Virgin Blue started life in 2000 as a low-cost competitor to Qantas, but after adding service in pursuit of higher-yielding customers in mid-decade it preferred to call itself a 'New World Carrier'; in 2007 it even talked about launching its own low-cost subsidiary to combat the arrival in Australia of ultra-low-cost challenger Tiger, and the following year began exploring with AirAsia the possibility of a joint venture in this segment. With wholly-owned subsidiary Pacific Blue operating in New Zealand, joint venture Polynesian Blue in the South Pacific, and V Australia flying transpacific, Virgin Australia and its affiliates are developing a strategy which is a world away from the LCC template of just a few years ago. Considerably different is the case of airberlin which started as a charter carrier, then through both acquisition and organic growth moved first into low-cost scheduled operations and quickly thereafter into long-haul markets oriented both to the leisure segment (e.g., Florida) and the business segment (e.g., Beijing and Shanghai – since dropped). The challenges accompanying both integration of acquisitions and rapid implementation of a wide-market strategy will be considerable; it will be interesting to see whether the carrier remains independent in the long term. Finally, and perhaps uniquely, Brazilian LCC Gol rescued Varig and runs it as a full-service subsidiary (VRG).

Adding aircraft types Although something of an oversimplification, it can be argued that traditionally the legacy carriers have started with the networks they each wanted to serve and built their (often complex) fleet structures around the patterns of demand that this implied, whilst LCCs have started with the imperative of a single-type fleet (usually 150–180-seaters) and looked for suitably sized markets to attack or develop. Whilst there have been notable exceptions such as easyJet and AirTran, many LCCs retain single-type fleets; but others have begun pursuing revenue sources not otherwise available to them by adding smaller types (e.g., airberlin, Virgin Blue, and jetBlue). These incremental revenues might lie in a market segment which requires higher frequencies than can be sustained by a 150-seater; Virgin Blue, for example, has bought Embraers in part to allow it to penetrate the business segment by thickening its schedule in markets that could not support higher frequencies using the carrier's B737-700/800s. Or new revenues might be sought from markets too thin to support a larger aircraft type at all (i.e., the traditional domain of regionals).

Conclusion   In the most price-sensitive niche markets or market segments, the bare-bones LCC model – exploiting economies of scale, offering a completely commoditised experience, and charging for anything other than the air transport core – will be difficult to out-compete. However, in any market where there is demand for something more than the most basic service, either from business travellers or somewhat less price-sensitive discretionary purchasers, airlines which are not necessarily the lowest-cost producers may be able to prosper by drawing a revenue premium from people prepared to pay a small increment for some aspect of their service offer. As in the retail industry, niches are being identified and exploited by airlines keen to differentiate themselves – niches which the label 'LCC' no longer fully describes because the emphasis is on enhancing revenues rather than just underpinning rock-bottom fares. The key, inevitably, is only to add to costs if the increment adds more to revenue – something that is easy enough to write about, but very difficult to manage in such a complex business.

More generally, whilst LCCs are in many cases better placed to deal with high fuel prices than some legacy carriers, they are proportionately disadvantaged by the fact that the structure of their business model leads to fuel constituting a larger share of direct operating costs. The model also relies heavily on low fares to stimulate rapid volume growth, leading in turn to higher ancillary revenues and rising resource productivity; low fares are not easy to sustain in an environment of extreme fuel cost pressure. LCCs with wide brand recognition and critical mass are in most cases well positioned to survive high oil prices and sub-trend growth, but many of the 100 or so smaller airlines in this sector of the industry can be expected to disappear.

Regional Carriers: Blurring The Business Model

Regional carriers form a disparate sector of the industry, and in particular there are considerable distinctions between the structure of the business in Europe and North America. Nonetheless, some general comments can still be made:

1.   The average size of aircraft is getting larger, with growing emphasis on 70- to 120-seaters. This in part reflects the inevitable thickening over time of many existing regional routes, but it also brings thinner mainline routes more firmly into the geographical scope of regional carriers. In the United States, regionals became well-established on what were previously mainline routes as a result of the shift in output

from mainline between 2001 and 2006, and some relaxation of scope clauses permitted a growing proportion of these new services to be operated by 70- and 90-seat jets. Also contributing to the rising average size of regional aircraft is the adverse impact that high fuel prices have had on the operating economics of 50-seat (and smaller) jets.

2.   Just as the 'boundaries' between mainline and regional routes are blurring, so potentially are the boundaries between LCC and regional operations. There are two ways in which LCCs might impinge on regional networks:

   •   as just noted, some LCCs have been willing to add large regional jets to their fleets (e.g., jetBlue and Virgin Blue), and whilst the purpose of these aircraft is in part to boost off-peak frequencies on mainline routes where demand from business travellers in particular justifies it, these aircraft do open the opportunity to penetrate thinner markets over quite long ranges;

   •   LCCs with the lowest cost bases have shown themselves, particularly in Europe, to be able to use very low fares to stimulate discretionary travel in secondary point-to-point markets which the cost bases of many regional carriers preclude them from matching – with the result that the regionals are in many cases driven deeper into one or both of two niches: serving low-density, point-to-point business markets between secondary or tertiary centres and delivering feed to network hubs.

   Concerns such as this underlay Flybe's reinvention as a 'low-cost regional', and may encourage other independents which do not rely primarily on feeding network carriers' hubs to reconsider their cost and revenue models.

3.   In the United States, the trend over the last few years has been towards consolidation of previously independent regionals into a small number of larger groups, each diversifying code-share arrangements across several majors in preference to tying themselves to just one. Going forward, a significant problem is likely to be oversupply of 50-seat jets in US domestic service. In the face of a broad industry downturn leading to possible consolidation (and therefore hub closures) amongst the majors and announced reductions in their output, the ability to diversify contractual relationships appeared by mid-2008 to be insufficient to ensure the future of some regionals.

Long-Haul Markets: Segmentation By Aircraft Rather Than By Cabin

There have recently been several initiatives which target entire aircraft, rather than cabins, at particular segments of demand in long-haul markets.

Premium-only products   Some have been launched by established carriers. For example, KLM, Lufthansa, and Swiss have wet-leased A319s or Boeing Business Jets from PrivatAir for use in business-class-only configurations on medium- or long-haul routes with weak year-round economy/coach demand but sufficient premium traffic to justify their operation. In 2007 All Nippon launched business class B737-700ER service from Nagoya to Guangzhou and from Tokyo to Mumbai, whilst British Airways announced 32-seat all-business class A318 services between London City and New York. In 2008 Singapore Airlines reconfigured the A340-500s used on its non-stop New York and Los Angeles services from two classes with 181 seats to business class-only with 100 seats. Using a slightly different business model, Air France operates two-class A319s with low seating densities – 28 business and 54 economy – between Paris and points in Africa and the Middle East which generate thin but high-yield traffic. At the shorter end of the range spectrum, Lufthansa Private Jet flies several business jets and converted CRJ200s on services which primarily feed long-haul first class passengers in and out of the Group's Frankfurt, Munich, and Zurich hubs, but also offer intra-European hub-bypass opportunities. Austrian serves this sector of the market with a charter product provided by an independent partner, whilst Delta – through Delta AirElite, established in 1984 – offers fractional, charter, and fleet management programmes.

Other premium-only products have been offered not by incumbents but by start-ups that pitch price points well below those of existing business or first class products and aim to earn their margins by having significantly lower costs than established competitors. Examples have included eos (48-seat all first-class B757-200), L'Avion (90-seat all business class B757-200), MAXjet (102-seat all business-class B767-200), and Silverjet (102-seat all business-class B767-200ER). These services need to be offered in markets where premium traffic is sufficiently dense to support a daily or better frequency (at least on weekdays). London–New York, which generates around a million business and first class trips each year, for example, was used to launch eos, MAXjet, and Silverjet; both eos and Silverjet subsequently looked to diversify onto London–Dubai, a thinner market but one with substantial premium traffic. However, there are relatively few markets with sufficient traffic to support premium-only products at the frequency levels demanded by business travellers. Finally, low input costs and high productivity are essential given that costs have to be spread over far fewer seats in an all-premium operation than in a typical three-class widebody.

Historically, this is not a business model that has done well in short-haul markets (e.g., Regent Air, Legend, MGM Grand Air, and Fairlines). There must also be doubts about the survival of the premium-only model in long-haul markets outside the context of an established network carrier's corporate account relationships, FFP, and broad geographic scope. In early 2007 Eurofly terminated loss-making 48-seat all business-class A319LR flights between Milan Malpensa and New York JFK after only 9 months of operation, and MAXjet temporarily suspended services; the latter went bankrupt late in 2007, unable to raise additional finance – in part because of the threat that a softening economy would reduce demand for business travel, in part because of higher than budgeted fuel costs, and in significant measure because American entered the carrier's JFK–London Stansted market offering similar prices in business class but backed by its FFP and broad corporate relationships. American subsequently left the market. Silverjet and eos failed in spring 2008, and shortly afterwards L'Avion was targeted by British Airways for merger with its own OpenSkies venture.

Putting aside the profoundly damaging impact that economic slowdown and rapidly inflating fuel prices had on eos and the others, a particular challenge facing any independent start-up or legacy carrier selling premium seats out of another airline's hub is that it lacks feed/onward connections and, importantly, established access to local corporate accounts. Low frequencies relative to the dominant hub airline can be another impediment to penetration of the business segment. Certain aspects of British Airways' OpenSkies airline-within-an-airline designed to fly transatlantic from continental Europe are noteworthy in this context: after considering alternative city-pairs it launched between Paris and New York, which has a relatively dense flow of local traffic (with Amsterdam–New York following shortly afterwards); it offered three-class service (24 business, 28 premium economy, and 30 economy seats in a B757) rather than relying entirely on premium traffic – although the possibility of eliminating the 30 economy seats should premium traffic justify it was built into the business plan; and priority was placed on attracting small and medium-sized companies and entrepreneurs rather than large corporate accounts.

The premium-only business model has undoubted appeal in certain types of market, but is likely to remain a niche operation for some time to come. Existing carriers may have a better chance than start-ups unless the latter are very well capitalised and can quickly build critical mass. These products are expensive to deliver to the high standards required to compete in premium segments; critical mass can often be easier to build at the low-fare end of the market, where passenger service costs are less onerous.

Long-haul low-cost products   This is not a new business model: Icelandic carrier Loftleidir was connecting Europe and the United States over Keflavik in the 1960s, Laker Airways was briefly successful with its Skytrain venture in the 1970s, People Express also had a short period of success immediately after deregulation in 1978, and European charter airlines such as Britannia and LTU served a small number of dense long-haul inclusive tour markets from the 1980s onwards. What is different now is that liberalisation of international markets and the increasing availability of modern, medium-size long-haul twins offering attractive unit costs allow operators to build volume rapidly. As in short-haul markets, volume is a critical success factor to the extent that it provides scope for high asset productivity to help keep unit costs down; volume can also underpin revenue growth from higher ancillary sales as passenger numbers grow.

The traditional long-haul business model has been widely held to embody barriers to entry against long-haul LCCs on anything other than pure leisure routes with little premium traffic. Typical objections to migrating the short-haul low-cost model onto long-haul routes have included the following:

- Incumbents' utilisation of their long-haul aircraft is already high by virtue of the sector lengths involved. The scope to improve materially on their performance is limited by the fact that the interplay of departure and arrival airport curfews with time-zones imposes relatively narrow operating windows on many routes. It will also prove difficult to make substantial improvements to widebody turnaround times; the utilisation of long-haul aircraft is anyway less a function of turnaround times, as it is on short-haul routes, than of having a broad and coordinated network over which to deploy a fleet.
- Incumbents' long-haul economy class seat pitches are already, in many cases, quite tight and seat factors are high; the scope for using higher-density seating and better load factors to improve aircraft productivity and reduce the trip cost per passenger is therefore limited.
- Crewing costs tend to be higher for long-haul flights by virtue of the need to allow inflight rest-periods and to pay for accommodation and expenses on layovers. The scope for increasing utilisation of long-haul crews is also generally less than was the case in respect of short-haul crews at the time that LCCs began their period of rapid expansion in the mid-1990s.
- In all but the densest point-to-point markets it is generally true that the larger the aircraft operating a service the more reliant it is likely to be on traffic feed to maintain load factors – and most long-haul routes are operated by relatively large aircraft; the scope for introducing the low-cost model onto thin long-haul routes unsupported by network feed looks to be limited.

- Airport operators and ground-handling companies are commonly part of the same group in some parts of the world, and their willingness to cut a deal with low-fare carriers is more open to doubt than has been the case at secondary airports in North America and Europe. This is not a universal 'rule', however; Kuala Lumpur International Airport has been aggressive in its bid for Jetstar's business, whilst Singapore Changi has a budget terminal currently being expanded to a capacity of 7 million passengers a year.
- Incumbents already have an impressive supply of competitively priced, and effectively revenue-managed, output available in long-haul markets. It is broadly the case that most long-haul network carriers make a substantial proportion of their profits from a relatively small number of premium-cabin passengers, and that this rich vein of revenue together with the low unit costs associated with flying modern widebodies over long distances gives them the ability to offer competitively low economy/coach fares. Also, charter operators with very low cost bases already have a heavy presence in several of the densest long-haul leisure markets out of Europe (e.g., to Florida).
- Purchasers in some long-haul markets, notably outbound from Asia, still rely heavily on travel agencies, and to the extent that this remains true it will be difficult for LCCs to make savings in distribution costs (i.e., agency commissions and GDS fees) by moving to direct channels.
- The higher prices and longer times away from home associated with long-haul trips relative to short-haul, together with the relatively low fares already available, suggest that low-cost entry will have a somewhat weaker stimulatory effect on long-haul markets as a whole than has been the case in short-haul markets (CAA 2003). This implies that the model might be appropriate to relatively few markets.

Incumbents would therefore hope to be more insulated from attack by new-generation LCCs in these markets than in shorter markets out to, say, five hours. However, the launch of Jetstar, AirAsia X, Oasis, Viva Macau, and several other long-haul LCCs brought this orthodox view into question in mid-decade, as did Aer Lingus' efforts to establish a low-cost/low-fare transatlantic network hubbing over Ireland. Airberlin's acquisition of struggling leisure carrier LTU in 2007, together with a large order for B787s, is in the process of transforming Europe's third-largest LCC into a hybrid with an integrated short- and long-haul network (although there are doubts about the viability of this strategy).

It is too early to judge whether the low-fare long-haul business model represents a significant new trend, a narrow niche, or a brief flurry. Jetstar and AirAsia certainly deserve to be taken seriously given the identities of their owners, but Oasis has already failed and Viva Macau is a small operation that is hampered by the legal requirement to ask competitor Air Macau for permission to open new routes. Furthermore, these are not all pure single-class operations; indeed, some analyses suggest that having the additional revenues from a business class cabin – albeit one offering a relatively 'lean' product by network carrier standards – can make the difference between profit and loss for this business model. If claims that Jetstar's long-haul unit costs are as much as 45 per cent below those of its parent Qantas turn out to be true, however, the model may well have a future. Certainly, some of the entrepreneurs behind the early initiatives have a proven track record with successful short- and medium-haul LCCs, and this alone justifies taking the development seriously. The CEO of Ryanair has stated – albeit before the 2007/2008 run-up in oil prices – that he envisages launching a complementary long-haul airline alongside, but separate from, Ryanair itself; initial indications suggest a two-class operation connecting Ryanair's European bases with secondary airports in the United States. Separately, the trade-name easyAtlantic was registered several years ago – almost certainly to protect the 'easy' brand, but perhaps also with an eye to the future. Looking at the seat-mile costs of the B787 and A350 (or even, perhaps less feasibly given its capital cost, the A380) in high-density configuration, it is entirely possible that somebody with access to sufficient finance to build a plausible operation might eventually do serious damage to the economy class traffic of legacy carriers in the densest North Atlantic and Europe–Asia/Pacific markets.

In the meantime, there are seeds of a threat to network airlines' medium-haul operations. Asian and Australian low-cost carriers are in the process of stretching their narrowbody routes out beyond five hours, whilst in early 2008 low-cost carrier Norwegian announced the introduction of single-class B737-800 services from Oslo and Stockholm to Dubai. The latter may or may not prove themselves, but given the numbers of B737s and A320s Ryanair and easyJet have on order, the potential for increasing route overlap within Europe (or, some might argue, market saturation), and the capabilities of these aircraft, it will be interesting to see how the network strategies of the continent's two low-fare giants develop.

Industry Consolidation

'Concentration' rises when a growing share of output, assessed at either market or industry levels, is produced by a given number of producers. It can happen in two ways: as a result of the organic growth of a small number of competitors, with others growing more slowly or failing altogether; and as a result of consolidation. Consolidation, seen in a reduction in the number of competitors, can take one of several forms:

1. Acquisition followed by absorption (e.g., American acquiring and absorbing TWA). There have been many examples of this form, but most have been within individual countries (or within the EU single market).
2. Acquisition followed by continued separation of brand identities, either with the acquiree being a subsidiary of the acquirer or both becoming subsidiaries of a holding company majority-owned by owners of the acquirer (e.g., the Air France-KLM solution). ('Acquisition' here refers to purchase of a majority shareholding. There are several dozen examples of airlines taking minority stakes in other carriers, many involving cross-border investments, but history suggests that minority holdings can be relatively transitory, do not necessarily give rise to real strategic influence, and are at best only weak leading indicators of consolidation.)
3. Merger amongst true equals. There are relatively few precedents for this in any industry. The merger between BEA and BOAC initiated in 1974 might perhaps be an example, although the balance of power in the early years of British Airways tended, in respect of flight operations at least, to favour people from BOAC and a small regional subsidiary rather than BEA. Mergers between Japan Air Lines and Japan Air System and between Air India and Indian Airlines have also been presented as mergers of equals, but in each case it is arguable that the former could be more accurately cast as an acquirer than as a true equal. Again, mergers have generally been confined within national boundaries.

4.   Horizontal alliances (i.e., alliances between airlines, as opposed to vertical alliances between airlines and suppliers or distributors). These represent a weak form of consolidation, made notably attractive to airlines by their historic lack of freedom to enter into cross-border mergers. How weak depends upon the scope of the consolidation (e.g., route- or function-specific as opposed to global) and, if global, which of the three alliances is involved; oneworld is a looser, more marketing-oriented group than Star, which tends to operate with wider scope and more prescriptively, whilst SkyTeam takes a middle path with regard to governance. The longevity of alliances, particularly the global alliances, should barriers to cross-border airline acquisitions come down is a matter of debate.

The inevitability of consolidation and the increased concentration of output that would result are widely accepted in much of the industry; see, for example, the results of a survey reported by Iatrou and Oretti (2007, Chapter 8). Analysts, hedge funds long in airline stock, and senior airline managers anxious to trigger 'liquidity events' in their employment contracts are perennial enthusiasts for consolidation, most particularly in North America, and industry media are usually quite happy to fall into line. It is informative that there was scant mention of customers in the internal memos circulated by senior management at Delta and Northwest in early 2008 to boost their proposed merger.

The arguments cited in favour of consolidation are one or all of the following:

1.   *Bigger airlines will be more efficient* On this argument, presumably United should already be more efficient than Southwest. Consolidation will not make legacy carriers lean enough to compete profitably with LCCs in short-haul markets; diseconomies of scale mean that mating elephants rarely beget a racehorse.
2.   *Bigger airlines will be better able to compete* On 18 January 2008 Gordon Bethune, a highly respected former airline chief executive by then acting as a paid consultant to a hedge fund, told CNBC that another round of airline consolidation was 'inevitable' because 'no US airline can compete internationally'; Glenn Tilton, United's Chief Executive, made similar comments throughout 2007 and early 2008 (e.g., *Flight International*, 12–18 February 2008). Apparently, six of the world's largest airlines which collectively had protected access to international passengers connecting domestically to or from points in the United States were considered unable to compete with European and Asian carriers, most of which are considerably smaller by any measure of airline size, simply because they are not big enough. If US network majors are indeed unable to compete internationally, itself a highly questionable claim, the problem is more likely to be rooted in customer service than lack of scale; mergers do not have a history of improving service.
3.   *There is too much output, so capacity should be rationalised* How the load factors achieved between 2005 and 2007, particularly in the United States, can be equated to 'too much capacity' is a mystery, but leaving that aside the real question is what those in favour of consolidation expect to happen once capacity has been eliminated. Clearly, the expectation is that lower capacity will lead to higher yields, which will lead to higher profits. In fact, there has to this author's knowledge never been a rigorous study proving this chain of causality. On the contrary, in the course of a robust critique of myths surrounding consolidation, Pilarski (2007, pp. 116–117) presents evidence that there is no pattern of linkages between ASMs, yield, and profits across 103 data points taken from the US industry between 1981 and 2006. Anyway, the US majors'

reaction to surging fuel prices in 2008 – including a 12 per cent cull of domestic output announced by American in May – establishes clearly enough that consolidation is not a prerequisite for capacity reduction.

In the final analysis, the merger of any two US network carriers will undoubtedly lead to the running down of at least one hub per pairing (notwithstanding claims to the contrary made by senior managers at Delta and Northwest when boosting their proposed merger in 2008). Whilst barriers to entry at remaining hubs would be formidable, it seems highly unlikely that low-fare carriers would choose not to grow into vacated territory where they could profitably do so. The system as a whole might therefore not lose as much capacity as anticipated over the longer term, and network carriers will have handed some solid growth opportunities to their low-fare competitors.

If we move the arena from domestic to cross-border airline consolidation, it is necessary to bear in mind two institutional barriers to international mergers and acquisitions which will be considered in greater depth in Chapter 4:

1. Most countries have laws prohibiting majority foreign ownership of domestically incorporated airlines. Notable exceptions include Australia, New Zealand, Chile and one or two others, and for this purpose the European Union (EU) can be considered a single entity *within* which cross-border mergers and acquisitions are freely allowed.
2. Most of the bilateral air services agreements (ASAs) which govern international flights between signatory states specify that each country's designated carrier(s) must be majority owned and substantially controlled by nationals of that state.

With these considerations in mind, it is possible to make some generalisations about what is at the time of writing a fast-moving issue without any clear near-term outcome.

- *Consolidation within the United States*   Failure of the proposed US Airways takeover of Delta in early 2007 put back the timing of what many continued to see as an inevitable combination of the six largest US network carriers into three, but belief in that inevitability was largely undimmed. By the end of 2007, US hedge funds were busy hiring industry luminaries to tout the advantages of consolidation. By April 2008, Delta and Northwest had announced plans for a 'merger' (in reality a takeover of the latter by the former), whilst closer cooperation between United and Continental was anticipated. The outcome is uncertain at the time of writing.
- *Consolidation within the EU*   It has long been widely accepted that consolidation will leave Air France/KLM, British Airways, and Lufthansa as the only surviving legacy carriers, alongside residual niche players and a strong low-cost industry dominated by easyJet, Ryanair, and possibly a hybrid airberlin. Lufthansa's acquisition of Swiss and Air France's acquisition of KLM are held to have set precedents that will see Alitalia, Iberia, and probably SAS absorbed into one or other of the 'big three'. Time will tell. Airberlin has yet to fully and successfully digest its several acquisitions. There is nonetheless a good prospect of further consolidation in Europe, with mergers under consideration at the time of writing in both Spain and Germany, a number of former 'flag carriers' unlikely to survive as independent operations, and many of the smaller low-fare airlines struggling to reach long-term sustainability. The boards of British Airways and Iberia are believed to be discussing a merger (which would preserve the two

separate brands). The ownership of bmi, and its valuable holding of Heathrow slots, is also likely to change – with full absorption into the Lufthansa Group the most probable outcome but other possibilities (variously involving either Virgin Atlantic or British Airways) also being talked about.

- *Consolidation in other countries with significant domestic industries* There has already been substantial consolidation in China, Russia, India, and Brazil. In China, consolidation into a 'Big Three' was engineered by the government several years ago, and has continued with the fusion of several smaller carriers by Hainan Airlines into Grand China Air; separately, cross-shareholdings that bind together Air China and Cathay Pacific (including Dragonair) have the potential to create what might become within a decade one of the global industry's strongest groups – with a possible role also for China Eastern, although that carrier's future strategic direction is not clear at present. Acquisitions by Jet and by Kingfisher's parent UB Group, together with the merger of Indian Airlines and Air India in 2007, have signalled the onset of consolidation in India. Both China and India support highly entrepreneurial cultures, however, so further new entry cannot be ruled out. In Russia, where the AirUnion grouping already links several formerly independent airlines, Boeing (2007) estimates that the 120 commercial passenger and cargo carriers operating in 2007 will shrink to 15 major airlines by 2015.
- *Cross-border consolidation (outside the EU)* Domestic laws constraining foreign ownership of airlines impair the efficient allocation of capital, and commercial regulations imposed by tightly drawn bilateral ASAs impair the efficient production of output. The EU–US open skies agreement which came into effect in March 2008 has paved the way for further *intra*-continental consolidation by permitting any EU-owned carrier to fly to the United States from any EU country, but restrictions on ownership of US airlines by Europeans and of European airlines by Americans still limit the scope for *inter*-continental consolidation. Globally, further development of cross-border shareholdings seems a likelier first step towards international consolidation than an immediate rush to full mergers: countries unwilling to dispense fully with controls over which airlines other parties can designate under the terms of bilateral ASAs might nonetheless be prepared to forego the traditional requirement that airlines be under the ownership and effective control of nationals of their designating countries (Doganis 2006). This would allow airlines to be designated even if they are subsidiaries of carriers incorporated in a third country, provided their principal place of business is in the country designating them. ICAO endorsed the approach in 2003, and the willingness of countries to accept designation of Swiss by Switzerland and KLM by the Netherlands despite their foreign ownership shows that this is already beginning to happen.

Chapter 4 will look in greater depth at the impact of laws constraining the national ownership of airlines and at treaty terms limiting the nationality of airlines designated to operate international services under bilateral ASAs; both are coming under substantial pressure. There is a long way to go, but many observers predict their elimination over the next decade or so (see, for example, Doganis 2006). However, a number of other barriers still stand in the way of global consolidation. We will briefly look at these next.

Perceived national interest   Control over foreign ownership of airlines is widely assumed to be an anachronism, yet it persists. The reason is that there are powerful constituencies which see it as protecting their interests. Unionised US labour is one obvious example. Even more fundamental is the fact that in many countries we are some years away from political power-brokers and/or public opinion being prepared to see national airlines swallowed into global 'multinationals' controlled from overseas.

Political resistance in the United States to ceding national control of its airlines was made plain by the stance adopted towards Virgin America in 2006. Resistance is not universal: cross-border ownership and control are allowed in Australia and New Zealand and tolerated in parts of Latin America, whilst in Britain everything seems in principle to be for sale at the right price. However, it is difficult yet to envisage a near-term future in which governments in the United States, France, Germany, the Middle East or the larger Asia-Pacific countries (excluding Australia and New Zealand) will be willing to cede control of 'their' air transport industries to foreigners. Evidence of this could be seen in the fulminations surrounding Singapore Airlines' proposed minority stake in China Eastern, which appeared to have been agreed in 2007 but was subsequently opposed both by Air China and certain strands of central government opinion in Beijing.

In large countries, even local (rather than national) identities may slow domestic consolidation: US politicians are usually quite vocal in support of a threatened 'home-town' airline if independence remains a serious alternative – as most recently seen in Minneapolis when it became clear the city would not be the home for a merged Northwest and Delta. Local interests in Madrid were uncooperative when faced with the prospect of British Airways, together with private equity interests, taking control of Iberia – although the last has not yet been heard on the future ownership of this particular airline.

Economics   There is nothing in the history of airline mergers that can be taken to imply bigger always means better. United was one of the largest airlines in the world when it went into Chapter 11, so large airlines are just as capable of disappointing investors as small airlines; and the current successes – such as Air France-KLM and Lufthansa/Swiss – are arguably successful because the stronger partner has taken active steps to *avoid* outright absorption of the other. Too often mergers and acquisitions are accepted as part of some deterministic 'trend' rather than being assessed as what they are: individual transactions, each with its own commercial logic – or lack thereof. Even if potential diseconomies of scale are ignored in a victory of hope over experience, the question then remains, 'How big?' 'Big enough to eliminate effective competition', would doubtless be the answer in some quarters – which is why most developed legal systems have a body of competition law.

Competition law   In both Europe and the United States competition law may not stand in the way of consolidation as a principle, depending upon the specific circumstances of a proposed transaction, but its interpretation by those charged with enforcing it will certainly have a significant impact on timing and outcome – both domestically and across borders. Attorneys-general from 12 states joined the Department of Justice (DOJ) in opposing the proposed United/US Airways merger in 2001 on the grounds that it would lead to higher fares and reduced service for consumers. It is difficult to see anything that has happened in the interim (including the growth of LCCs) to warrant a change in this assessment – although shifting politics and/or the lobbying power of financial interests mean that history can be an imperfect guide to the future.

Practicalities Even when one is much smaller than the other, successfully merging airlines is a difficult challenge because of incompatible fleets, cultures, work practices, IT systems, and seniority lists. Examples of difficult mergers include: Northwest and Republic; American and AirCal, Reno Air, and TWA; and America West and US Airways. That is not to say that combinations cannot be successful: UTA and British Caledonian were digested by Air France and British Airways respectively in the 1980s with relatively little problem, as were Japan Air System by Japan Air Lines, Australian (i.e., the longstanding domestic airline, not its subsequent low-fare namesake) by Qantas, Canadian by Air Canada, and go and Buzz by easyJet and Ryanair many years later; the *gradual* fusing of Air France and KLM – the first large cross-border acquisition – appears to be proceeding smoothly; and Swiss, along with several smaller carriers, has been effectively integrated into the Lufthansa Group pursuant to a clear multi-brand strategy.

Nonetheless, the scope and magnitude of the challenges inherent in merging two large airlines with different cultures, perhaps national as well as corporate, and unique ways of producing and delivering service are often unjustifiably minimised by observers of the industry – particularly fee-earning advisers – who argue the inevitability of consolidation. It is a daunting task which demands a clearly articulated commercial rationale and a rarely available set of management and leadership skills. It also requires an understanding of possible diseconomies of scale – a consideration too frequently submerged under talk of synergies. To take just one example, it is easy to look at the networks of, say, Delta and Northwest then reach for the 'synergy' word; it is far less easy to integrate two such different fleets, operating systems, and corporate cultures.

Conclusion As regulation of the industry has gradually weakened over the last three decades, there has been a clear if uneven trend in the direction of consolidation; beginning in the United States in the 1980s, this trend has to date largely played out within individual countries and, more recently, within the EU. It is a trend that is likely to continue into the future, as the strong get stronger and at least some of the weak disappear. International cross-shareholdings might well accelerate. The three global alliances linking network carriers will probably continue to grow, albeit more slowly and subject to a number of membership changes, whilst linkages which allow cross-selling between low-fare carrier websites (such as those pioneered by Aer Lingus and jetBlue) may become more common.

However, the global 'mega-carriers' that have been discussed since the 1980s (see, for example, Gialloreto 1988) remain well in the future. Perhaps more likely is the prospect that a small number of financial holding companies and large airlines will assemble portfolios of carriers in different parts of the world, thereby going beyond today's relatively loose marketing alliances but holding short – at least for the time being – of difficult cross-border mergers, and all the brand dilution, labour issues, and political opposition they could engender. A great deal can be achieved by combining networks, scheduling, revenue management (where legally permissible), FFPs, sales teams, and cargo products and by uncovering synergies in MRO, ground-handling, purchasing, and IT – without rushing headlong into the merger of brand identities, cultures, passenger products, and seniority lists. The one certainty in this discussion is that truly *global* consolidation cannot and will not run its course until US restrictions on foreign ownership of airlines are removed. Odds on this happening soon appear to be long; second-stage US–EU open skies negotiations, with foreign ownership on the agenda, will show whether such pessimism is justified.

A CLOSER LOOK AT RHETORICAL LABELS

For convenience in what is an introductory and scene-setting chapter, widely recognised labels such as 'legacy carrier', 'full-service carrier', and 'low-cost carrier' have been used up to this point. The next few paragraphs will explain why they are in fact unhelpful, even as shorthand, and are as far as possible avoided in the rest of the book.

1. *Legacy carriers* Although there is no universally accepted definition, in the United States this expression is frequently used to refer to an airline which existed prior to the Airline Deregulation Act 1978 and is therefore burdened by 'legacy' fleets, labour contracts, organizational structures, and processes which disadvantage it relative to younger, leaner competitors. However, Southwest was incorporated in 1967 and began service in 1971, yet despite an organizational 'legacy' of 40 years is invariably characterised as a 'low-cost', rather than legacy, carrier. It would seem, therefore, that the expression has as much to do with an airline's cost base as its age. If this is so, at what unit cost threshold does a 'legacy carrier' which has successfully restructured its operations qualify as 'low-cost'? What of US Airways, a combination of airlines tracing their roots to both pre- and post-deregulation origins which has emerged from bankruptcy protection with a restructured cost base? What of Aer Lingus, which reinvented itself so thoroughly as a low-cost carrier that it no longer qualified for membership of oneworld? What of Emirates, an airline now more than two decades old which has a notably low cost base set against those of other airlines offering similar levels of service over international hub-and-spoke systems?
   Conversely, at what point might a long-established low-cost carrier be relegated to legacy status by newer, more flexible rivals? This is arguably happening to Southwest as its headlong growth in domestic markets slows and as its workforce and systems architecture continues to age. In response to what by its own high standards were lacklustre financial results in the winter of 2006–2007, Southwest acknowledged that it was looking at assigned seating, inflight entertainment, international flying, and increased cargo market penetration – strengthening the growing perception that as LCCs age they risk taking on 'legacy' characteristics which put upward pressure on their costs and leave openings in the market for well-financed, lower-cost start-ups. The term 'legacy carrier' is too imprecise and will not be used in the rest of the book.
2. *Full-service and no-frills airlines* The UK Civil Aviation Authority (CAA) still uses the term 'no-frills' to describe products that are less than full-service, but in doing this has explicitly declined to define the expression (CAA 2006a). Similarly, there is no commonly accepted definition of 'full-service'. There is in fact a broad palette of possible service attributes from which to choose when designing an airline's offer(s) to its customers (see Holloway 2002, Chapter 5), and no standard package which applies universally across any given business model – whether the label applied to such a model is 'legacy' or 'full-service', 'low-cost' or 'no-frills'. It has already been noted that boundaries are anyway being blurred by the augmenting of traditional no-frills models (e.g., by jetBlue and Virgin Blue) and the 'leaning' of traditional full-service products (e.g., the domestic products of several US majors, and the markedly higher short-haul seating densities introduced by Finnair in 2007). More generally, flying first class on Singapore Airlines is unquestionably a full-service experience whilst flying on Ryanair is not, but once the obvious extremes of the

full-service to no-frills continuum are left behind it becomes impossible to define precisely where to draw the line between the two concepts. The terms 'full-service' and 'no-frills' are too imprecise and will not be used in this book. It is more helpful to think in terms of the value being offered to customers by each airline's different service–price offer(s).

3. *Low-cost and low-fare carriers* 'Low-cost carrier' is an expression which is widely used both colloquially and in official sources (e.g., the US Bureau of Transportation Statistics). However, what qualifies as 'low-cost' is seldom defined either in general or, more importantly, in the context of any particular market. The European Travel Network has suggested that a low-cost carrier is one which sells at least 75 per cent of seats at its lowest published fares. Interestingly, that definition hinges on fares rather than costs. The rest of the present book avoids use of the expression 'low-cost' wherever possible, preferring instead 'low-fare'. This is open to criticism on the grounds that defining a low-fare carrier is as imprecise an exercise as defining a low-cost carrier: for example, it is not unusual to find KLM and British Airways pricing below easyJet on routes to and from Amsterdam; conversely, Southwest initiated US domestic industry fare increases on nine separate occasions in 2005–2006 and led industry price rises several times in 2007 as well. Where competition in a particular market is intense and pricing is dynamic, what qualifies as a low-fare carrier is as much a function of customer perception and brand identity as of actual pricing behaviour. Nonetheless, the expression 'low-fare' is preferred to 'low-cost' because:
   - passengers care about fares not costs;
   - it is possible to identify certain airlines which place consistently low fares at the centre of their brand identities, but impossible to find any airline manager who would admit to *not* focusing on costs;
   - when easyJet, Ryanair and others founded an association to lobby on their behalf in Brussels, they named it the European Low *Fares* Airline Association.

Descriptors Used In The Present Book

1. *Low-fare airline (LFA)* The reasons for preferring this expression over LCC have just been noted.
2. *Network carrier* This expression is used to distinguish airlines which primarily operate hub-and-spoke networks from others which primarily operate point-to-point services. A network carrier is willing and able to sell end-to-end journeys using connecting flight-legs or sectors, whereas a *purely* point-to-point operator (such as many of the LFAs) will generally sell just single sectors (CAA 2003) – something that makes pricing, revenue management, and route profitability analysis much easier. However, too much precision should not be read into this rhetorical label either:
   - we will see in Chapter 6 that whereas some hubs operate a pronounced wave structure with up to six or more complexes of synchronised arrival and departure banks each day, others facilitate transfers less by virtue of scheduled waves than by the high frequencies supported by a strong local origin and destination (O&D) market. Airlines operating the former are true network carriers in the sense used here (e.g., the US majors and Air France-KLM at Paris CDG), whereas airlines operating the latter are somewhat closer to being point-to-point operations;

- most network carriers also offer point-to-point services in addition to hub connections.

We can nonetheless say that whatever else they might be doing as well, the distinguishing characteristic of network carriers is the centrality of hub operation(s) to their strategic and brand positioning.

3. *Point-to-point carrier* This expression refers to airlines which do not have an integrated hub-and-spoke network at the core of their business model. The majority of their traffic does not flow across hubs on either interline or intraline connections. Most LFAs are point-to-point operators, as are some carriers with more service-oriented brands such as Virgin Atlantic and the all-premium airlines. Again, however, there are caveats:

   - some LFAs do have hubs, either in name (e.g., airberlin) or in effect (e.g., Southwest), and even carriers which are overwhelmingly point-to-point do nonetheless have some flow traffic (e.g., around 10 per cent of Virgin Atlantic's passengers);
   - most network carriers operate point-to-point hub-bypass services, and all operate point-to-point in and out of their hubs insofar as a variable but often high percentage of traffic originates from or is destined for each hub rather than connects across it.

4. *Regional* This term is used to describe airlines which specialise in operating aircraft smaller than 120 seats. These carriers might be owned or franchised by a network airline and strategically oriented towards feeding its hub(s), or they might be largely point-to-point operations operating under their own brand identities (e.g., Flybe).

What all this illustrates is that in an environment where business models are constantly evolving, labels – even those preferred for use in the present book – need to be treated cautiously.

Summary

A core theme runs throughout this book: the fundamental challenge confronting airline managers is to design services which provide the benefits that customers in targeted markets need and want, price them so that they are both competitive and capable of providing the type of customer value required, and deliver them for less than they cost to produce. This is a simple theme which the economics of the industry make exceedingly difficult to implement, and which terms such as 'legacy', 'full-service', 'no-frills', and 'low-cost' have a tendency to obscure. The expressions 'low-fare' and 'network carrier', both of which are used throughout the book, are also imprecise given the blurring of business models in the industry, but they do at least convey information about overall strategic positioning which the others arguably do not.

CONCLUSION

Until the 2000 recession and 9/11, network carriers were heavily focused on generating revenue by fine-tuning their networks and revenue management systems; in most cases they were less focused on managing costs, other than through quick fix programmes when crises hit. For LFAs the principal focus was on minimising costs; an important contributor to this was rapid volume growth. However, growth of LFAs into progressively more markets has compelled network carriers to manage their costs down towards more competitive levels, whilst the need to augment revenue has driven some LFAs to add product attributes; both are increasingly looking for sources of ancillary revenue by unbundling product attributes and selling them separately from the core transportation service. There has therefore been some convergence between the two types of carrier. There has also been convergence in Europe between LFAs and charter airlines, with the latter responding to the encroachment of the former into leisure markets by offering well over a third of their output on a seat-only scheduled basis. This convergence has given rise to a broad range of business models, with so many fine distinctions that the dichotomy between 'low-cost' and 'legacy' carriers is no longer informative; neither does the label 'new world carrier', applied to enhanced low-fare offers from carriers such as Virgin Blue, add very much descriptive power. The European Cockpit Association (2006, p. 3) has this to say on the subject: 'In the future a clear distinction between different *products* offered to passengers will be more useful in seeking to describe and analyse developments than a distinction between *types* of airlines.'

What we have is an expanding range of service–price offers, some emphasising price and others emphasising various tangible or intangible aspects of service for which it might be hoped that a price premium can be earned. But all, without exception, are selling on value. Ryanair certainly offers a different value proposition to easyJet or Aer Lingus, for example, but all three sell on the basis of the particular type of value that customers perceive them to be offering. Some customers will be drawn to the lowest fare; the lowest-cost producer will clearly have the best shot at serving this segment profitably on a *sustained* basis into the future. Others will be willing to pay for what they perceive as enhanced products; carriers selling to product-sensitive customers might find themselves competing in an overlapping space – to the extent that, say, somebody who would not choose Ryanair because of its sparse approach to customer service might instead see British Airways and easyJet as interchangeable depending upon price. This takes us back to the importance of brand distinctiveness, discussed earlier in the chapter.

The process of structural change which began with US deregulation in 1978 has still to run its course, both in the United States and elsewhere in the world. How it will unfold is clear in outline but far from certain in detail: some well-known brands will disappear through absorption or outright failure, others will prosper and expand, and new business models will emerge either from restructurings or new entrants. It is superficially appealing to accept that short- and medium-haul markets will become the preserve of low-fare airlines and a few niche carriers, whilst long-haul markets will be dominated by networks fashioned from combinations of long-established majors and former flag carriers. This is too simple.

1. First, a variety of different business models is emerging in both short- and long-haul markets.
2. Second, despite the undoubted preference that passengers have for avoiding hubs, there are still many markets both short- and long-haul which have traffic flows too small to support anything other than connecting service; established carriers with strong networks able to earn a premium from this aspect of their product will be able to survive in markets which relatively low traffic volumes make inaccessible to hub-bypass alternatives that might otherwise be offered by younger competitors with lower costs.

3. Third, where slowing market growth, increasing organizational size and complexity, and perhaps also product augmentation begin to put upward pressure on the costs of LFAs, the gap between their unit costs and those of established network carriers that have been successful in bringing their own costs under better control can be expected to shrink (as happened in the United States during the years after 9/11).
4. Fourth, it is likely that the industry is still some years away from spending as much energy on implementing global consolidation as is currently spent on touting its inevitability.
5. Fifth, the evolution of the price of jet fuel will have a profound effect on which business models are viable and which are not.
6. Sixth, the industry's future is more likely to be one of flux than one involving a linear transition from one static equilibrium to another.

It can nonetheless be argued that those most likely to prosper will fall into one of two loosely drawn camps:

1. Carriers with a *sustainably* low cost base relative to direct competitors, which enables them to do one of two things:
    *   consistently offer the lowest fares in their markets or market segments;
    *   match or exceed competitors' service and match their pricing, but off a lower cost base permitting higher margins.
2. Carriers which are not *the* cost leader in their markets but which nonetheless have a competitive advantage. The sources of this advantage could be one or more of:
    *   control over a substantial number of slots at a congested airport;
    *   the strength of a wide, high-frequency international network based around one or more well-located and efficient hubs – possibly in cooperation with alliance partners;
    *   a defensible position in niche geographical or product markets too small or too specialised to attract low-fare or network-carrier competition;
    *   a differentiated product able to support a price premium, albeit perhaps only a small premium, in markets sufficiently dense to contain a significant segment willing to buy on a basis other than price alone.

In either case, unremitting focus on what targeted customers need, want, and are prepared to pay for will have to be combined with an equally unremitting focus on keeping the cost of producing the designed products as low as it can be. Levine (2003) has clearly articulated the challenge:

> ... with any business model, you must have the lowest costs consistent with the strategy you have chosen and the product has to be attractive enough (along convenience, reliability, and comfort dimensions) to attract the revenue to cover them. Every survivor will be one form or another of LCC (even if an LCC created by reorganising a legacy airline), but they will not all use the same business model.

Because industry 'clock-speed' is now so fast, periodic cost reduction programmes in response to an economic downturn can no longer substitute for constant focus. Obvious though this undoubtedly is, it is not an imperative that has been universally recognised until relatively recently, and even when recognised it is seldom easy to act upon – especially for long-established carriers historically oriented more towards market share than profitability.

IV. The Rest Of The Book

This opening chapter has led us towards several questions, the answers to which help provide a strategic context for the rest of the book.

- What markets/segments are available and which should be served?
- What type of value – what combination of benefits and price – do customers in each of these markets/segments expect?
- What strategy-specific resources and capabilities do we have that enable us to deliver the value that targeted customers expect?
- What firm-specific resources and capabilities do we have that enable us to do this better than, and so outperform, competitors targeting the same customers?
- Can we do all this and also make money for our shareholders?

On an operating level, the answer to the last question will depend on how the elements in the following relationship are managed:

$$\text{TRAFFIC} \times \text{YIELD} > < \text{OUTPUT} \times \text{UNIT COST}$$
$$= \text{OPERATING PERFORMANCE (i.e., PROFIT or LOSS)}$$

Part 2 of the book is structured around this relationship, with separate chapters on traffic, yield, output, and cost. Given that capacity management is a critical driver of both revenues and costs, Part 3 contains chapters looking in turn at several of the most important topics in airline capacity management: network management (with separate chapters on design and scheduling); fleet management; and revenue management. Finally, Part 4 concludes the discussion with a review of some important macro-level performance metrics. Figure 1.6 maps the terrain to be covered.

Implicit in this are both demand-side and supply-side perspectives:

- *Demand side: service strategy and positioning* The fundamental issue here involves deciding which customers to target, understanding what targeted customers expect, and designing value propositions capable of delivering service that meets or exceeds expectations.
- *Supply side: operating strategy and resource advantage* Having designed one or more value propositions, it is then necessary to develop an operating strategy that is both consistent with the customer value to be delivered and able to exploit one or more sources of advantage over competitors.

If there is one core theme running through the book it is that the revenue and cost sides should always be considered together. In particular, costs must never be endowed with a life of their own, but should be looked at in the context of their contribution to customer value and to revenue.

V. Summary

We have seen in this chapter that the first strategic decision to address is the question of which businesses to invest in. This is the *corporate* strategy decision, and its outcome is reflected in a firm's 'industrial scope' or business portfolio. For a start-up with limited

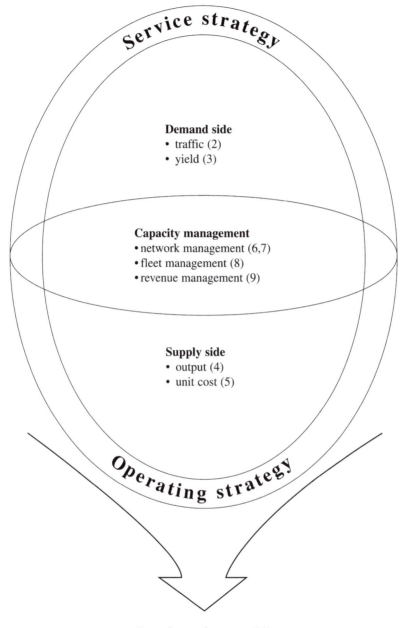

Operating performance (10)

Figure 1.6   The rest of the book

capital and narrow strategic intent focused entirely on air transport operations, the decision is likely to be straightforward; for a long-established carrier with an inherited portfolio the choices can be more difficult.

Each business, whether a stand-alone operation or part of a wider portfolio, requires its own *competitive* strategy founded on some sustainable competitive advantage.

Figure 1.1 suggested a three-level model, with each tier representing a particular level of abstraction:

- At the highest level of abstraction, a business needs to define its competitive strategy and the competitive advantage(s) on which that strategy is to be based (e.g., offering the lowest available fares to market segments which value price over a rich repertoire of amenities, supported by sustainably low input costs and high productivity).
- At a more focused level of abstraction, an airline's business model is a representation of the operational realities which flow from its choice of competitive strategy. There are two components: a revenue model which specifies how, from whom, and why it is able to earn revenue; and a cost model which specifies how it will organize itself to deliver service that satisfies targeted demand effectively at least cost.
- At the most focused level of abstraction are the processes, activity systems, and individual daily actions which, in an ideal world, should be mutually consistent and should reinforce the underlying theme mapped out in the competitive strategy and reflected in the business model.

Competitive strategy is built on one or both of cost advantage or benefit advantage. According to the resource-based theory of strategy, firms compete by deploying heterogeneous, imperfectly mobile resources. Resources that are rare, difficult for competitors to imitate, and causally ambiguous (i.e., not readily understood by outsiders) provide particularly strong foundations on which to build a competitive strategy (Nickerson *et al.* 2001). However, over time and in the absence of insurmountable barriers to entry it will be necessary to innovate within either or both the revenue model or the cost model in order to sustain superior financial performance. There is no silver bullet in any one strategy or business model: low-fare airlines can lose money as readily as network carriers (IATA 2006b).

PART 2

Operating Performance Drivers

The only prerequisite to economic success is to achieve a low cost base from which to build a desired service offering.

Unisys R2A (2003, p. 9)

Part 2 of the book has been structured around a model of performance at the operating level:

TRAFFIC × YIELD > < OUTPUT × UNIT COST
= OPERATING PERFORMANCE (i.e., PROFIT or LOSS)

Chapters 2 and 3 look at traffic and yield, which together drive operating revenue; ancillary operating revenues, derived from sources other than ticket sales, are considered at the end of Chapter 3. Chapters 4 and 5 look at output and unit cost, which together drive total operating cost.

The airline industry can claim many unique technological achievements. It also has a claim to uniqueness in the economic field: despite a history of expansion well above global gross domestic product (GDP) growth rates, despite impressive productivity gains, and despite the commercial and infrastructural barriers to entry that have arisen in some markets over recent years to dilute the benefits of deregulation and regulatory liberalisation, this is still an industry which in aggregate finds it difficult to cover its cost of capital across the duration of an economic cycle. Historically, and quite apart from the extraordinary impact of 9/11 or the 2007/2008 run-up in oil prices, the reasons for this have been clear enough: output growth has too often run ahead of traffic growth, and burgeoning costs have too frequently been put under pressure by declining yields. The next four chapters outline some of the complexities inherent in managing traffic, yield, output, and costs. They build on Chapter 1 by stressing the need for a focused, customer-oriented strategic framework within which to manage these critical variables.

2

Traffic

Markets don't buy services – customers do.

Tom Peters

Traffic is the first of four elements in the operating performance model around which Part 2 of the book has been structured:

TRAFFIC × YIELD > < OUTPUT × UNIT COST
= OPERATING PERFORMANCE (i.e., PROFIT or LOSS)

'Demand' is the quantity of a product that customers are willing and able to purchase over a defined period of time. 'Traffic' is that part of demand for air transport services that has been satisfied by carrying passengers and cargo; it is distinct from demand that has not been satisfied – demand that has been 'spilled', perhaps because space was not available when required and no alternative was acceptable. We will see in Part 3 of the book that 'spill' is a concept critical to network, fleet, and revenue management, and that 'spill models' are used in these functions. Nonetheless, the industry as a whole can only estimate rather than measure spill, and there is a tendency to treat 'demand' and 'traffic' as synonymous: in this book they are kept separate, with traffic treated as a subset of demand.

The first section of the chapter will provide a brief summary of economic concepts relevant to the discussion which follows; its purpose is to act as a refresher, not to duplicate material that is already covered in greater depth by business economics textbooks. Subsequent sections will introduce the most common metrics used to measure airline traffic and then consider: the identification and segmentation of available demand; the drivers (or determinants) of air transport demand; some unique characteristics of demand; and how air transport demand is modelled and forecasted. The chapter will end with a brief look at demand management as a precursor to the discussion of capacity management in Part 3 of the book.

I. The Modelling of Demand: A Brief Refresher

This section will review demand functions, demand schedules and curves, consumer choice, and elasticity of demand. All are relevant to the discussion of air transport demand and traffic in subsequent sections.

DEMAND FUNCTIONS

Market demand is an aggregate of demand for a product across all purchasers involved in the market concerned – whether this is a city-pair market (e.g., Los Angeles–Hong Kong), a regional market (e.g., US domestic), an interregional market (e.g., North Pacific), or the global air transport market as a whole. A statement, usually in tabular form, which relates determinants of demand (i.e., independent, or 'explanatory', variables) to a particular quantity of the service demanded (i.e., the dependent variable) is a 'demand function'. The relationships are commonly modelled in algebraic terms. For example:

$$D_a = f\ (P_a,\ P_1,\ P_2\ ...\ P_n,\ Y)$$

where demand (D_a) is a function of price (P_a), the prices of other products $(P_1,\ P_2\ ...P_n)$, and income (Y). In practice, more complex expressions incorporating coefficients for a far broader range of determinants than just price and income will be estimated; a comprehensive quantitative treatment of alternative models of demand can be found in Talluri and van Ryzin (2004, Chapter 7). It should be noted that 'price' in the above function would normally be taken to incorporate not just monetary expenditure, but non-monetary costs as well (e.g., the opportunity cost of time spent on the journey); however, reference to price in the present chapter refers to monetary expenditure alone unless otherwise stated.

The objective of estimating a demand function is to find out what impact on demand, and market share, will result from any assumed changes in the independent variables. Section IV of the chapter will take a closer look at those variables in the specific context of the demand for air transport services. At this point, it is worth noting that the construction of demand functions poses several practical challenges.

1. Establishing how each independent variable actually affects demand for passenger or freight services requires a great deal of historical data upon which to perform regression analysis. The availability of certain types of data can be an issue in some markets. Indeed, whereas supply-side data is relatively easy to come by, estimating a meaningful demand function using publicly available information is impossible in many countries.
2. The assumption that all demand-determining independent variables but the one under consideration can be held constant tends to assume away reality.
3. It also has to be assumed that historical relationships between independent and dependent variables, and indeed between independent variables themselves, are an accurate guide to future relationships. For example, just because a 1 per cent rise in personal disposable income has led to a 2 per cent rise in passenger traffic in the past does not mean that it will have the same impact on demand in the future; when air transport markets mature, as they are arguably doing in North America and to a lesser extent in Western Europe, a given level of economic growth tends to generate a weaker demand response than it does in less mature markets.
4. Perhaps the bravest assumption is that forecasts of independent variables will themselves prove accurate.

Airline managers can in principle create approximate demand functions for individual markets, for segments within each market, and even for specific flights. Different departures have different demand functions that ideally need to be understood, although relatively few airlines are equipped to deal with this level of analytical detail and in practice decisions are often based on imperfect and rapidly changing data.

DEMAND SCHEDULES AND DEMAND CURVES

A demand function is therefore a statement, in tabular or algebraic form, which relates determinants of demand at assumed states or levels to a particular quantity of the service demanded. Along with income, the independent variable that gets most attention is price. A table can be constructed which lists a range of alternative passenger fares and freight rates against the number of passengers or the volume of freight that would be carried at each price level in a particular market. This is a demand schedule. (If we were looking simultaneously at more than one market we would probably use yield as a proxy for price.) When price is graphed against the quantity demanded the result is a 'demand curve'. In other words, the demand curve is a graphical expression of the demand schedule. To summarise: whereas a demand function specifies the relationship between the quantity of a product demanded and *all* the independent variables affecting that demand, a demand curve is a graphical expression of the relationship between the quantity demanded and just one of the determinants in the demand function – price.

There are several generalisations worth noting with regard to demand curves:

- First, although referred to as 'curves' they are frequently modelled as straight lines.
- Second, there is an inverse relationship between price and the quantity demanded: other things being equal, when price goes up or down the quantity demanded will move in the opposite direction. (There are in fact exceptions to this 'law', but they are not relevant to the present discussion.)
- Third, other things are often not 'equal': when examining the effect on the quantity demanded of price movements along a single demand curve we are assuming that all other determinants of demand are held constant. Nonetheless, whilst this assumption is an oversimplification of reality, a demand curve does at least model one of the most critical parts of that reality – how price interacts with the quantity demanded.
- Fourth, the purpose of a demand curve and the schedule underlying it is to help managers manage: if the relationship between price and quantity demanded has been accurately modelled, that model can be used with reasonable confidence to forecast the impact of price changes.

The usefulness of demand curves to decision-makers actually stems from their simplicity, because they underline the existence of two different sources of demand variation – which may have very different short-run and strategic implications.

1. *Change in the quantity demanded* This graphs movement up or down a single unchanged demand curve; the significance of the word 'unchanged' is that because all the determinants of demand other than price are held constant, the curve itself does not shift position. The direction of movement along the demand curve reflects the inverse relationship referred to above: a rise in price leads to a fall in the quantity demanded, while a reduction in price will cause an increase in the quantity demanded. The

amount by which the quantity demanded reacts to a price change will depend upon the price-elasticity of the product. We will look at price-elasticity in a moment.

For example, in Figure 2.1 when the price falls from $400 to $300 along demand curve D, the quantity demanded rises from under 25 seats (point A) to more than 25 seats (point B).

2. *Change in demand* This does not involve a movement along a single unchanged demand curve, but the repositioning of the demand curve itself. Demand curves shift because of a change in one of the non-price variables in the demand function such as:
    -   macroeconomic conditions affecting personal and corporate incomes (or confidence in future incomes);
    -   consumer preferences for certain destinations;
    -   airline image or service (e.g., frequencies offered);
    -   size of available market (which might change for demographic reasons or because traffic feed is added or removed);
    -   activities of a major competitor, including service design, advertising and pricing initiatives.

    Such changes alter the demand schedule and, therefore, the position of the demand curve. Changes in demand favourable to the airline concerned will shift the curve rightwards, whilst unfavourable changes shift it to the left. For example, when an airline invests in a strong brand image and service enhancements it does so with the intention of influencing the preferences of potential passengers and shippers. The objective is to shift the demand curve of the targeted segment to the right so that either more people are willing to pay an unchanged fare or freight rate, or the fare or rate can be raised without a significant loss of volume; this would amount to an *increase in demand* (as opposed to an increase in the quantity demanded).

    Growth in income is a particularly common reason for changes in demand: when incomes grow, more of a product is likely to be demanded at a given price – until market saturation is reached. Sometimes demand continues to grow strongly notwithstanding significant fare increases; in 2006 and 2007 airlines heaped fare increases and fuel surcharges onto passengers, but demand kept growing strongly. One reason was the buoyant global macroeconomic environment at the time, supporting both corporate and personal spending despite the higher prices. In early 2008, however, fare increases necessitated by rapidly rising fuel prices came up against weakening US and European economies – the result in this case being a slowdown in traffic growth.

    Because a rise in income should, other things being equal, boost demand, a new demand curve will be established to the right of the previous curve. In Figure 2.1, the new curve is D_1. The effect of the illustrated shift is that at a price of $400 quantity A_1 is now demanded rather than quantity A, and at $300 quantity B_1 is demanded instead of quantity B.

Airline managers need to be able to distinguish between variations in demand resulting from a change in the quantity demanded (i.e., attributable, by definition, to an increase or decrease in price) and those attributable to a shift in demand (attributable to change in a non-price variable, such as an increase in income or a competitor's launch of a new product). If they are not able to do this, their response to market dynamics might be incorrect. In particular, it is always tempting to boost demand by reducing price along what is assumed to be an unchanged demand curve, whereas what the market could

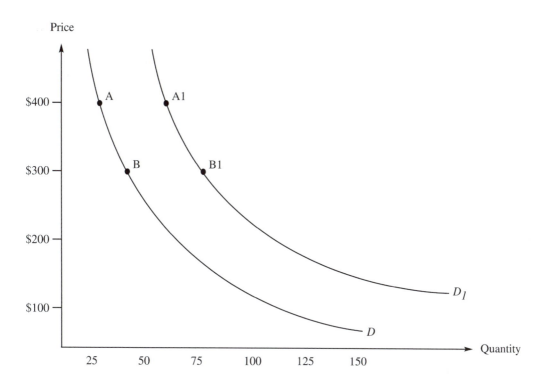

Figure 2.1   Change in the quantity demanded and shift in demand

really be signalling is that it wants a completely new service–price offer – which would be reflected in a repositioned demand curve.

To summarise: 'demand' refers to a schedule or curve constructed to relate the quantity of output demanded at different price points under a given set of non-price circumstances; a 'change in the quantity demanded' refers to movements up and down that demand curve; and a 'change in demand' refers to a shift in the position of the original demand curve, to the right or left, in response to a change in a non-price variable. Having briefly introduced the demand curve concept, the next two subsections will consider what it is that underlies the shape or steepness of a curve, and why shape matters.

CONSUMER CHOICE

Demand curves slope downwards from left to right simply because in most cases people will buy more of a product as its price falls. In other words, lowering the price of something will – other things being equal – increase the *quantity demanded*. This fact is fundamental to the volume-growth strategies implemented by LFAs: low costs underpin low fares, low fares stimulate demand, rapidly rising demand enables output to grow rapidly as well, and as output grows it is possible to raise the utilisation of aircraft, staff, airport facilities and other resources – which helps maintain downward pressure on unit costs.

The relationship between price and quantity demanded clearly depends upon the position and shape of the demand curve. The position and shape of the demand curve in turn depend upon non-price variables – notably incomes and consumer preferences.

Economics is at heart a science which tries to understand how individuals deal with scarcity – specifically, how they choose to allocate scarce resources such as time and money amongst a broad array of alternative options in such a way that their satisfaction is maximised. The concept used to help analyse preferences underlying consumers' choices is *utility*: everything done or bought yields utility, and the utility derived from one bundle of purchases can be compared with utility gained from alternative choices. Through this process *total utility* available given the particular resource constraint can be maximised.

If we think for the purposes of this limited discussion about just the amount of utility to be derived from a single product – say, leisure trips to Amsterdam from a home in London – it should be clear that were we to go every weekend it is unlikely that the amount of utility derived from each subsequent trip would be as high as that derived from the previous trip. In other words, *marginal utility* – the increase in total utility that a consumer achieves by consuming one extra unit of a product while the amounts of all other products purchased remain constant – would be diminishing. If marginal utility is diminishing whilst the price remains the same, the amount paid per unit of utility derived from each new trip would gradually rise; this is because less utility is being gained than before, but the price paid is unchanged. In order to induce continued purchase, the price would at some point have to fall. If it did not, funds available within the consumer's constrained budget would inevitably be redirected to purchase other products, now offering higher marginal utilities than another trip to Amsterdam; in this way total utility could be maintained at its existing level.

From this serious oversimplification of consumer choice theory we can conclude that the shape of a demand curve is derived, in part, from the diminishing marginal utility of the product concerned. Why the shape of the curve matters is the subject of the next subsection.

ELASTICITY OF DEMAND

Elasticity is a concept used to examine how sensitive demand is to changes in independent variables such as price, income, elapsed journey time or advertising expenditure. It is defined as the percentage change in demand arising from a 1 percentage point change in the value of an independent variable. In principle, an elasticity coefficient can be calculated for any independent variable in respect of which sufficient reliable data is held, and this coefficient can be inserted into an algebraic model of the demand function. Section iv will look at variables which are considered to be the principal drivers of air transport demand.

We have seen that whereas changes in non-price variables cause a demand curve to *shift*, changes in price cause movements up and down a *single demand curve*. How much movement is caused by a price change – that is, what impact a change in passenger fares or freight rates will have on the quantity demanded assuming all other variables remain unchanged – depends upon the slope of the demand curve; it is this which determines the price-elasticity of the product. Price might be defined as the yield, average fare, or (least likely) the full (i.e., unrestricted walk-up) fare in a market. However defined, the effect of a price change will depend upon the shape of the demand curve. In Figure 2.2, the effect of a price change from P_0 to P_1 will vary depending on whether we are facing demand curve D_A or D_B. In the former case, the price increase will lead to a relatively small demand decline from Q_0 to $Q1_A$, whereas in the latter case the decline to $Q1_B$ is substantially larger. Demand curve D_B is therefore more elastic than demand curve D_A; in other words, demand in the market or segment modelled by curve D_B is more sensitive to price changes.

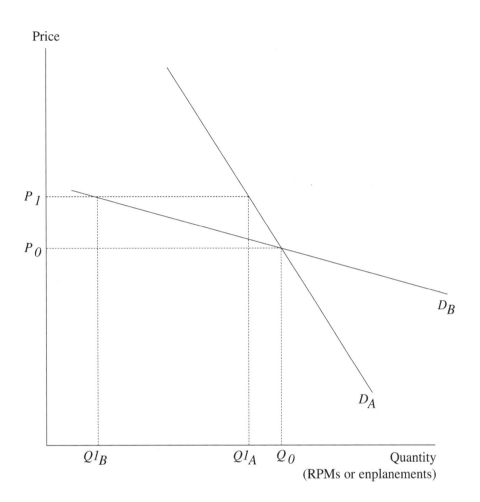

Figure 2.2   Price-elasticity and the shape of the demand curve

Since an infinitely elastic demand curve is horizontal and a perfectly inelastic curve (i.e., a curve with zero elasticity) is vertical, we can say that the steeper a demand curve becomes the less elastic it is and vice versa. This is critical to pricing and revenue management, as we will see in Chapters 3 and 9. The concern in this chapter lies not with the revenue impact of demand elasticities, however, but with their impact on airline traffic. The next section defines what is meant by 'traffic'.

II. Demand and Traffic

Demand is the quantity of a product that customers are willing and able to purchase over a defined period of time. In the case of air transport, demand is for transportation between different points which – depending on the purpose of analysis – can be geographically tiered:

- airport to airport (e.g., LAX to JFK)
- city to city (e.g., Los Angeles to New York)

- region to region – domestic (e.g., California to the north-east)
- country to country (e.g., USA to UK)
- region to region – international (e.g., North America to Europe – or 'North Atlantic')
- global.

Within each geographical market, demand can be further segmented into different product markets encompassing economy/coach, premium economy, business class and first class (although not all products are available in every geographical market).

'Traffic' is that subset of demand that has been satisfied by carrying passengers and cargo; it is distinct from demand that has not been satisfied – demand that has been spilled. Traffic is also analysed using the tiers listed above. However, there is a complication caused by the alternative network designs which airlines use to satisfy demand. Take for example a passenger travelling from Aberdeen (Scotland) to Colombo (Sri Lanka) on the following path:

Aberdeen (BA) → London (EK) → Dubai (EK) → Colombo

Demand arises in the Aberdeen–Colombo, UK–Sri Lanka, and Europe–Asia markets, but the traffic generated by serving this demand arises in the UK domestic, London–Dubai, UK–UAE, Dubai–Colombo, and UAE–Sri Lanka markets. In other words, the passenger creates traffic between Aberdeen and London, London and Dubai, and Dubai and Colombo despite not being part of the demand for service on those routes.

This example can be extended to underline one of the central challenges in airline management: network carriers in particular supply output and carry traffic by the flight-leg, but any one flight-leg might satisfy demand arising in multiple origin and destination (O&D) markets. Thus: the British Airways flight from Aberdeen will be carrying passengers connecting onwards to a variety of points other than Dubai; the Emirates flight from London will be carrying passengers from behind London and passengers connecting beyond Dubai to points other than Colombo; the Emirates flight to Colombo will be carrying passengers who connected from a variety of points behind Dubai other than London and may also be carrying onward transfers; and all the flights will be carrying local traffic. The points to bear in mind, particularly in respect of operations over a network carrier's hub, are that:

- any one flight-leg might be carrying traffic, and therefore satisfying demand, in multiple O&D markets (i.e., providing 'joint supply');
- any one passenger on a given flight-leg might have chosen one of several alternative paths from origin to destination (those alternatives, depending upon the geographical distance between origin and destination and how competing airlines have designed their networks, might involve non-stop, one-stop and/or connecting flights).

These ideas will resurface in Chapters 4 to 9.

TRAFFIC DEFINED

Airline traffic in any given period – in other words, the demand which has been met during that period – is measured by the following metrics:

1. For passengers:
    *   total enplanements (or 'boardings'), with one enplanement being the embarkation of a revenue passenger, whether originating, stopover, connecting or returning;
    *   revenue passenger-miles (RPMs) or -kilometres (RPKs), which are distance-weighted measures because they are generated by flying one revenue passenger one mile or kilometre.

        Thus, a regional airline might enplane the same number of passengers each year as Singapore Airlines, but the latter will generate considerably more RPMs because it carries each enplaned passenger much further. This will, in turn, be reflected in its longer average trip length per passenger, which can be calculated by dividing enplanements into RPMs or RPKs.
2. Distance-weighted traffic measurements are clearly a function of both enplanements and average journey length. For example, between 1978 and 2005 US airline revenue passenger enplanements rose 163.8 per cent (from 254 to 670 million) whilst RPMs grew 210.6 per cent (from 188 to 584 billion), reflecting longer average journey lengths (GAO 2006). Similar considerations apply in respect of other distance-weighted metrics. For example, the large size of the intra-North American air cargo market combined with its relatively short distances means that it accounts for a higher proportion of global air cargo tonnage than of global tonne-kilometres; air shipments across the North Pacific, on the other hand, account for less than 10 per cent of global tonnage but over 20 per cent of tonne-kilometres.
3. For cargo (i.e., freight, unaccompanied baggage, and mail): both tonnage and distance-weighted measures, such as cargo ton-miles (CTMs) or cargo tonne-kilometres (CTKs), are used. More commonly, freight is broken out and measured in terms of freight ton-miles (FTMs) or freight tonne-kilometres (FTKs); unaccompanied baggage is sometimes defined as freight and incorporated into these metrics.
4. For passengers and cargo combined: revenue ton-miles (RTMs) or revenue tonne-kilometres (RTKs), which are generated by flying one ton one mile or one tonne one kilometre. Use of an assumed weight per passenger and accompanying baggage, usually around 100kg, allows passenger traffic to be combined in a single measurement with cargo.

An airline's operating revenue is generated by selling individual services to customers, but it can usefully be analysed as the product of traffic (e.g., RPMs, RPKs, RTMs or RTKs) and yield (i.e., revenue per RPM, RPK, RTM or RTK) – which is the approach being taken in the present book; we will look at pricing and yield in the next chapter.

Table 2.1 clearly illustrates the strength of traffic during the early years of the upturn beginning in 2003. What the table does not show is that of the 2.1 billion passenger journeys in 2006, 10.5 per cent were in first or business class cabins. Global economic conditions contributed to strong demand for premium service, particularly in long-haul markets.

Looking ahead, Airbus (2008) forecasts 4.9 per cent global average annual growth in RPKs from 2007 to 2026, with the domestic US market returning amongst the lowest growth rates

Table 2.1   World airline scheduled traffic 1990–2006

	1990	1995	2000	2001	2002	2003	2004	2005	2006[1]
Revenue passengers (billions)	1.165	1.303	1.672	1.640	1.638	1.691	1.888	2.022	2.128
% change		11.8	28.3	-1.9	-0.1	3.2	11.6	7.1	5.2
RPKs (billions)	1894	2248	3037	2949	2964	3019	3445	3722	3940
% change		18.7	35.1	-2.9	0.5	1.8	14.1	8.0	5.8

[1] Preliminary figures.

Sources: ICAO and IATA

at 2.4 per cent per annum and the domestic Indian market returning the highest at 11.5 per cent. Because of their large existing traffic volumes, the relatively mature domestic US and intra-European markets are nonetheless expected to remain the two largest in 2026 – although domestic Chinese flows will have overtaken the North Atlantic for third position. If the frame of analysis is broadened to encompass all traffic flows from, to, and within individual regions, by 2026 Asian flows will account for 31 per cent of RPKs (2005: 26 per cent), European flows 27 per cent (2005: 29 per cent), and North American flows 25 per cent (2005: 31 per cent). The same source forecasts the annual average growth rate of FTKs through 2026 at 5.8 per cent, with the highest-growth market being domestic China at 10.5 per cent; both China–North America and China–Europe will not be far behind at 9.1 and 8.5 per cent respectively. The largest market in absolute terms is forecast to be China–North America.

Boeing's (2007) forecast is similar at the meta-level: average annual growth from 2007 to 2026 of 3.1 per cent in world GDP, 5.0 per cent in passenger traffic (RPKs), and 6.1 per cent in cargo traffic (i.e., freight and mail). Embraer's (2008) outlook for RPKs is 4.9 per cent average annual growth between 2007 and 2026, whilst Rolls Royce (2006) foresees 4.8 per cent and 6.8 per cent average annual growth in RPKs and FTKs respectively from 2006 to 2025. It will be interesting to see how subsequent editions of these forecasts respond to the behaviour of oil prices in 2007/2008.

III. Identification and Segmentation of Available Demand

The global air transport market is comprised of hundreds of thousands of city-pair markets – that is, points of origin and destination between which individual passengers and cargo shipments are transported. No airline has access to all of these markets. The availability of any particular market can be constrained by two sets of considerations (Holloway 2002):

1. *Barriers to entry* A barrier to entry might be externally imposed (e.g., government unwillingness to licence start-up airlines or grant additional route designations to existing carriers), it might grow over time through force of circumstance (e.g., slot constraints), or it might be deliberately created by an incumbent (e.g., network, brand, or distribution strengths, or a reputation for responding aggressively to new entrants). A barrier will either make entry impossible in a practical sense, or it will leave entrants with higher costs than incumbents. Higher costs suggest not only a weaker competitive position but a greater risk of commercial failure, and this perceived risk in itself is often sufficient to deter entry. Existing airlines, particularly

large carriers, generally find it considerably easier to overcome barriers to entry – except, perhaps, regulatory constraints and infrastructural congestion. Not only are they more likely to have the necessary marketing and operational resources, they are usually betting proportionately less than a start-up or other small carrier on the success of any one route.

2. *Vision* 'Vision', 'mission', and 'purpose' are variously defined in the strategy literature. Whatever the label used and whether articulated or not, strategic decision-makers at most airlines – start-up or incumbent – will have a sense of what their company is trying to achieve for its stakeholders, particularly its customers, and what it should aspire to in future. From this sense of purpose can be derived a 'strategic description' of the carrier, from which an idea of appropriate markets for targeting will emerge.

Having identified which markets are potentially available and formulated an outline strategy for surmounting any barriers to entry, the next step is to use the current strategic description of the airline as a first-cut filter through which to run market opportunities. One of two conclusions will emerge:

- the market concerned presents an opportunity consistent with the current strategic description of the carrier, or
- the opportunities presented are not consistent with that strategic description – in which case a decision will have to be taken as to whether or not a move away from the current description is justified.

Each potentially available market can be treated as a uniform source of demand. Alternatively, demand can be broken down into distinct segments.

SEGMENTING AVAILABLE MARKETS

I *need* food, I *want* a burger, I *prefer* a Big Mac®. I *need* liquid, I *want* a cola, I *prefer* a Coke. I *need* to be in Baltimore, I *want* to fly, I *prefer* Southwest. Looking at the first two of these statements, we can conclude the following: I *need* food and liquid because I am a biological organism that requires these inputs to survive – in other words, I have basic survival needs. I *want* a burger and a cola to satisfy these needs rather than anything else because I am part of a culture that shapes my desires – in other words, I want things that I have been acculturated into wanting. I *prefer* a Big Mac® and a Coke because I am an individual, and there is something about these products that appeals to me personally – in other words, I hold expectations that the attributes of these products (whether functional such as taste, or emotional such as brand association) will deliver benefits and overall value that at this moment I would prefer to the benefits and value offered by, say, Burger King or Pepsi. Similarly, perhaps I *need* to be in Baltimore because my job (and therefore maybe even the long-term survival of my lifestyle) requires me to be there, I *want* to fly because this will get me there faster than other modes of transport permit, and I *prefer* Southwest because the value being offered – the balance between benefits (both functional and emotional) and price – is at this time more appealing to me than what any other carrier is offering.

At a macro-level, we should understand markets – the actual and potential demand for burgers among the hungry, soda among the thirsty, and air travel among those who are somewhere else and need to be in Baltimore. But we also have to understand preferences – why certain people prefer Big Macs®, Coke, and Southwest, and how those who do not might be induced to change their preferences. Market segmentation can help. Box 2.1 provides some economic background, and the subsequent paragraphs look at various aspects of the technique. Any reader who believes air transport is a commodity sold only on the basis of price will probably take issue with what follows, because it is premised on the assumption articulated in Chapter 1 that airlines – all airlines – pitch value, in the form of different service–price offers, to customers who are not homogeneous in their preferences.

Box 2.1: Segmentation and Neoclassical Microeconomics

The benchmark model of market structure in the neoclassical tradition, perfect competition, assumes homogeneous intra-industry demand and homogeneous supply. Every industry is assumed to produce a single, commodity product and that is all that consumers demand; if this were not the case, there could be no single industry demand curve and therefore no market-clearing equilibrium price established at the point where such a curve would normally intersect with the industry supply curve. The problem is that when it speaks of 'commodities' the neoclassical tradition does not draw the line at primary products such as oil, wheat, or bauxite, but extends the idea to consumer goods and to services. To speak of a single demand curve for the automobile industry, for example, assumes that demand for Chevrolets and Porsches is homogeneous; it is not, and neither is demand for air transport services homogeneous. To speak of a single automobile industry supply curve implies that Chevrolets and Porsches are interchangeable; they are not, and neither are the different types of service that are offered into many air transport markets. Buyers have individual preferences, and most industries develop different products or product variants to satisfy different individuals; for convenience, these individuals are grouped into segments – each of which has its own demand curve.

It is the fact that there are many industries in respect of which it is meaningless to speak of a single industry demand curve that led Chamberlin (1933) to develop the idea of monopolistic competition as an alternative to perfect competition. This idea recognises that some industries do have multiple demand curves. Is air transport one of them? Those who treat the industry's output as a commodity, the purchase of which is by definition driven entirely by price, appear to think not; those who spend money on distinguishing their brand images and/ or designing differentiated service packages think it is. The view taken in this book is that the answer varies between markets, but on the whole this is not a commodity business. Certainly, many air travel purchase decisions are driven by price, and this is one of the hallmarks of a commodity business: concern for price above other considerations, and disregard for the identity of the producer. As emphasised in Chapter 1, however, when competitors are matched in terms of price consumers are left making a decision in response to other criteria – an understanding of which can provide the basis for market segmentation; furthermore, there are customers in some segments who are less sensitive to price than to particular service attributes, such as schedule and reliability.

If we look at LFAs, many have begun by offering basic products at low fares – the intention being to build traffic by stimulating demand from customers previously unable to afford air travel and from others who did travel but not as frequently as they would wish. Eventually, one or both of two things is likely to happen:

1.   Markets mature and growth slows: maintaining traffic and revenue growth may then require not just the price-stimulation of low fares, but also a shift of existing customers from competitors. At this point, efforts to develop consumer preference founded on something other than just price become necessary.

2.   High load factors are achieved and sustained: maintenance of revenue growth might require improvement to the traffic mix rather than continuing to rely on volume growth alone. At this point, an increase in traffic drawn from segments willing to pay slightly more than rock-bottom fares in return for slightly more than rock-bottom service becomes necessary.

Many LFAs have yet to face these circumstances and remain committed to the archetypal low-fare/no-frills service–price offer. Some, however, are refining their business models – particularly their revenue models – with the intention of building brands capable of driving preference and of generating demand and revenue from segments requiring more than the most basic product. This is in part what is behind the plethora of business models which are now bundled together under rather unhelpful labels such as 'new world', 'new generation', and 'new model' airlines. Whatever label is used, it is clear that segmentation is alive and well even amongst LFAs at the so-called commodity end of the business.

APPROACHES TO SEGMENTATION

The purpose of market segmentation is to identify groups of buyers who can be distinguished from other groups in order to help managers understand what is being bought or might in future be bought, by whom, where, when, and why. It can also be applied to identify specific competitors and how to outcompete them for segment dominance. The assumptions underlying market segmentation are that:

- customers are different;
- certain of the differences between them can be used to explain different behaviours, which in turn affect demand and so account for the existence of multiple demand curves within the same market;
- these differences can be used to isolate within the market as a whole separate groups of customers likely to respond in broadly the same manner to any given marketing initiative.

A market can be segmented in a variety of different ways depending on the purpose of the exercise:

1. If the purpose is to take an aggregated view across the global air transport industry as a whole, within a large region of the globe or across a network carrier's route structure, a top-down approach might be used to segment markets on the basis of:
    - Geography: contrasting short-, medium-, and long-haul flows or, alternatively, intra-regional and inter-regional flows.
    - Aeropolitics: contrasting domestic and international flows.
      This is the approach taken by trade associations, manufacturers, and analysts tracking the growth of the industry and forecasting its future; it is also likely to be used in the early stages of an airline's fleet planning process. Traffic data for both passengers and cargo is readily available from ICAO, IATA, and the various national and regional airline associations.
2. If the purpose is to design a tariff structure in a particular market, demand might be segmented according to willingness to pay different prices for each type of service offered, willingness to buy at different times ahead of departure, and willingness to tolerate restrictions on ticket purchase and usage. We will return to this in Chapters 3 and 9.

3. If the purpose is to take a more disaggregated view, perhaps as input into a marketing programme or in the more advanced stages of fleet planning, a bottom-up approach might be used to segment markets on the basis of different customer characteristics. For example, when acquiring and configuring aircraft, demand on the particular routes they will fly has to be segmented by cabin class whenever the carrier concerned is offering multi-class service; demand for space in each cabin is an aggregation of demand for the booking classes relevant to that cabin. Data for this type of exercise is not widely available to the public; much of it is proprietary, and in fact many airlines hold only sketchy data on customer characteristics. What we might mean by 'characteristics' will be discussed next.

Customer Characteristics: Descriptive And Behavioural Variables

Segments should ideally be comprised of customers who behave similarly in response to the same marketing stimuli – whether price, service design, promotions, or marketing communications. Whilst it is behavioural variables that ultimately matter, managers sometimes need to use descriptive variables instead to isolate segments – variables that do not themselves account for specific purchase behaviours, but which can nonetheless be used as a limited form of proxy. Descriptive characteristics used to profile consumer segments include geography (place of residence), demographics (gender, age, marital status, family structure, etc.), socio-economics (income, education, occupation, available leisure time, etc.), and psychographics (personality, attitudes, lifestyle, etc.); descriptive characteristics used to profile organizational segments include general company data (size, industry, geographic location, structure, etc.), and travel decision-making processes (unmanaged, in-house travel manager or use of a travel management company (TMC), etc.).

Encompassing both behavioural and descriptive approaches, four particularly powerful segmentation variables identified by Tapp (1998) are: required customer value, predicted response, lifetime value, and loyalty.

Required customer value   Segmentation is based on the benefits that different types of customer expect and what they are prepared to pay for them. At a strategic level, this is by far the most important demand segmentation variable (Piercy 1997). As we are in essence talking here about design of a service–price offer, there are two relevant variables:

1. *Price* Network carriers generally apply multiple booking (or 'fare') classes in every market they serve, each encompassing different tariffs targeted at segments of demand defined by reference to customers' different:
    *   price-elasticities (i.e., willingness to pay);
    *   time-preferences (i.e., willingness to book in advance and need to travel at specific times);
    *   flexibility (i.e., willingness to accept various purchase and usage conditions attached to their reservation).
    Most LFAs use fewer booking classes, but even so these still represent a form of price segmentation. We will return to this in Chapter 9.
2. *Service design* A service is a bundle of attributes, each designed to provide benefits relevant to targeted customers. Box 2.2 looks at benefits segmentation.

Box 2.2: Benefits Segmentation by Reference to Journey Purpose

Passenger markets   Journey purpose is still the most widely used proxy for determining customers' expected benefits, and for estimating willingness to pay for those benefits, on the passenger side of the industry. A fundamental distinction has long been drawn between 'business' and 'leisure' traffic.

1.   Business travel can be subsegmented into travel to intra-company meetings, external meetings, or for other purposes such as conferences, exhibitions, training or as part of an incentive package. A distinction is also now drawn between business travellers employed by large companies and those who run, or work for, smaller enterprises and so might be somewhat more price-sensitive. European LFAs, particularly those serving the main airports at major centres, are finding that over half the passengers on some of their flights are travelling for business purposes; often these people own or work for small or medium-sized companies (i.e., mid-market companies) rather than large corporations.

   Network carriers retain a strong position in the market for large corporate travel accounts for two reasons: first, their seat inventories are available on the GDSs that TMCs and corporate travel departments still largely rely on; second, most network carriers will negotiate significant price concessions in return for access to a substantial share of a large company's travel budget. Amongst LFAs, some – Southwest, jetBlue, Virgin Blue, and easyJet, for example – have been willing to change their sales and distribution strategies and/or service offers to increase access to revenue from corporate accounts; others, such as Ryanair, stick resolutely to the LFA template and simply rely on picking up business travellers who self-select their services.

   On the whole, the business segment is assumed to be less price-elastic than the leisure segment, but more sensitive to schedule and elapsed journey time – therefore requiring higher frequencies and direct routings. An IATA (2007a) survey of business travel between 1997 and 2006 reveals a more complex picture, however. The percentage of long-haul business travel moving in economy or premium economy has risen from just over 40 per cent to above 60 per cent, whilst in short-haul markets the percentage travelling economy/coach has risen from just over 60 per cent to above 80 per cent. On the other hand, in long-haul markets the lowest price is by no means the most significant criterion cited for carrier choice: FFPs, network, and reputation are the primary criteria – FFPs being the most frequently cited by customers in the Americas, network considerations in Europe, and reputation in Asia-Pacific.

   Business travel is believed to account for under 40 per cent of trips taken in the United States, down from over 70 per cent in the 1950s; the figures are probably not dissimilar in Europe. (The UK CAA [2006a] has found that 20 and 40 per cent respectively of passengers travelling on 'no-frills' and 'full-service' airlines in UK–EU and UK domestic markets were travelling on business. European regional airlines reporting annually to their trade association, however, tend to disclose a more balanced mix.)

2.   Leisure traffic is often subsegmented into:
   • vacation/holiday, which could be further subsegmented into:
      – independent traditional one- or two-week vacation (which can again be subsegmented by purpose or nature of destination – for example, activity or beach);
      – independent short-break (also open to subsegmentation by purpose and type of destination);
      – independent travel to a second property;
      – travel to cultural or sporting events;
      – travel to join a cruise;
      – inclusive tour.

- VFR (visiting friends and relatives), which could be further segmented into:
  - visits to friends and relatives who have moved abroad (e.g., UK to Australia);
  - visits by a person who has moved abroad, or whose parents emigrated, to friends and relatives in the country of origin (e.g., UK to Poland or India).

The leisure segment is generally more price-elastic than the business segment, and less sensitive to the lack of ground and inflight benefits. Globally, the segment is growing faster than business travel and is believed now to account for approximately 75 per cent of traffic; this implies that the demand for air travel as a whole is becoming more price-elastic. There are two particularly noteworthy trends likely to accelerate this process in coming decades (Amadeus 2007): first, active seniors with substantial disposable incomes will become a significant subsegment as baby-boomers retire in North America and elsewhere; second, globalisation and the acceleration of migration flows will expand an already large VFR subsegment. Demand from the former is likely to be less price-elastic than demand from the latter.

'Business' and 'leisure' segments are evidently far from homogeneous. Accordingly, several airlines have moved beyond basic business/leisure segmentation, looking in greater detail at some of the other variables discussed in the main text. Furthermore, depending on the market concerned additional distinctions might be drawn between domestic and international, inbound and outbound, short-haul and long-haul, or local and connecting flows; similarly, connecting flows can be subsegmented between short-haul to short-haul, short-haul to long-haul (and vice versa), or long-haul to long-haul – subject to the nature of the hub.

A third commonly recognised segment is 'personal travel' which, depending upon its precise purpose, might be closer to the business than to the leisure segment in respect of price-elasticity and benefits sought (e.g., late booking); travel to deal with a family crisis, for example, will have characteristics closer to business travel in time- and price-sensitivity than foreseeable journeys such as returning to an educational institution overseas. Whatever the purpose of travel, length of haul is clearly an important variable.

As well as benefits sought, journey purpose has been held to provide a good proxy for trip duration, booking pattern, frequency of travel, and both price- and income-elasticity of demand – all of which are important considerations when an airline comes to design a marketing programme. However, demand is more difficult to characterise than this suggests. Weekend breaks, single- or multiple-destination long vacations, a short-haul day-return business trip, a long-haul journey for an urgent meeting with just one client, and an extended marketing visit to the other side of the world planned some considerable time in advance can all be categorised as being either for business or leisure purposes; but in terms of service design, pricing, ticket conditionality, and marketing communications they are each in principle very different.

Cargo markets   Freight, which accounts for approximately 96 per cent of air cargo RTKs (the balance largely being mail), can be segmented into commodities which are never shipped by air (e.g., bulk commodities such as grain and ore) and others which are air-shippable. Those which are air-shippable can have an airfreight penetration factor in a particular market from zero to 100 (i.e., 100 per cent). What determines the penetration factor is:

1. Distance and surface infrastructure: a category of goods that is shipped by surface modes in some markets might, because of the length of haul or poor surface infrastructure, be air-shipped in other markets.
2. Size, weight, and value of the shipment: generally, the higher the value of a shipment (per unit of weight) the higher will be its air penetration factor – but this generalisation has to be moderated by consideration of volume and weight. Research suggests that commodities moved by air tend to exceed US$16 per kilogram in value (Boeing 2006b). The more valuable an item, the less impact air shipment cost will have on its final price to the purchaser – in other words, a shipment with a high value per kilogram is better able to support the high cost of air transportation than one with a low value. Also, valuable shipments tend to be more time-sensitive because of the capital tied up in them. This,

together with their weight and volume characteristics, is why well over half the electronic goods exported from China to Europe and North America are shipped by air.

3.   Time-sensitivity: commonly identified freight segments are 'emergency' and 'routine', with the former small in size but price-inelastic and the latter further subsegmented into 'non-perishable' and 'perishable'. The routine perishable subsegment, which covers goods that can be physically perishable such as flowers and fresh foodstuffs or economically perishable such as publications and fashion items, is likely to be less price-elastic than the routine non-perishable subsegment – at least in the short run.

Time has long been recognised as a key variable in emergency and routine perishable segments; as airfreight has come to play a greater role in international just-in-time (JIT) logistics systems, time has also become an important segmentation variable in respect of some routine non-perishable goods as well. The routine non-perishable subsegment – sometimes referred to as 'surface-divertible' – is therefore the area of the market most intensely fought over by airlines and surface carriers. Time is also a critical factor in respect of both mail and expedited small packages ('air express').

In recent years air cargo has been losing long-haul market share to the shipping industry. There are three broad reasons: first, fuel price increases hit shipping companies proportionately less than airlines, with the result that fuel surcharges are lower for sea transportation; second, a new generation of container ships has been introduced, bringing greater speed and efficiency to sea transportation; third, a small but growing trend has been the willingness of some forwarders to offer time-definite ocean transportation, backed by service guarantees.

High frequencies, ready space accessibility, late close-out times, a high 'flown-as-booked' rate, rapid transit, priority ground-handling, and in some cases door-to-door service are necessary product attributes in time-sensitive segments. Some carriers have developed niche markets such as the handling and transportation of foodstuffs, flowers, print media, fashion items, and live animals.

4.   Price: there has been an accelerating trend towards considering airfreight expenditures not as a separate line item cost but as just one element of total distribution costs, within the context of which high air shipment charges relative to surface modes need to be balanced against savings in respect of insurance premia and the cost (real or opportunity) of financing a shipment during a long ocean voyage. The 'total distribution cost' concept combines the inventory cost, security, and guaranteed time-to-market benefits of using airfreight in a shipper's logistics chain in order to emphasise that although the transportation element in that chain might be more expensive than competing surface modes, total cost can be lower when saved inventory financing and insurance charges are taken into account. Furthermore, the marketing benefits associated with speed and certainty can be the difference between success and failure in a shipper's marketplace. The trend towards consideration of total distribution cost within the broader context of an integrated logistics chain has been reinforced by use of JIT inventory management techniques and international sourcing.

As in passenger markets, what matters is not price alone but customer value – that is, the scope and quality of benefits being bought. Some shippers simply want airport-to-airport line-haul at the cheapest rate. On the other hand, since integrated carriers such as FedEx and UPS – specialising initially in the document and small package segments – began growing rapidly in the 1980s, committed door-to-door delivery times and automated shipment tracking have become increasingly sought-after benefits in freight markets generally. This is true in many cases irrespective of whether shipments are emergency, routine, high-value, small, or heavy.

Freight products are increasingly being segmented by reference to how time-definite (e.g., next day or second day delivery) and reach-definite (e.g., airport-to-airport or door-to-door) they are. However, the problem for airlines generally is that no matter how they design and package their cargo products, two immutable facts remain: first, the global market for express letters and parcels is totally dominated by integrators; second, around 90 per cent of international heavy freight moves through forwarders, and the forwarding industry is dominated by a dozen or so large firms.

In assessing value, customers weigh price against the type and quality of benefits they want. This leads to different types of behaviour:

1.   Some customer behaviour is driven largely or entirely by price. Customers in this segment are prepared to forgo many benefits offered by competing products in order to obtain the cheapest fare they can get at the time of booking. However, few are prepared to forgo safety; also, most expect reliability. Ryanair has designed its business model to serve this segment.
2.   Some customers who are price-sensitive and do not want a rich array of product benefits are nonetheless prepared to pay marginally more to be served by polite and friendly staff, to be flown to major rather than secondary airports, and to be looked after when things go wrong. EasyJet is commonly cited as being oriented towards this segment.
3.   Some customers want the opportunity to augment a basic product with purchased extras such as seat selection, lounges, or inflight food. Quite a few LFAs are now targeting this market segment, one example being Virgin Blue.
4.   Some customers want a broad range of benefits bundled into the price, but are prepared to compromise in return for paying a lower fare than competitors offering more upscale products would charge. Oasis, which operated long-haul low-fare services out of Hong Kong between 2006 and 2008, incorporated a heavily discounted business class into its two-class offer for two reasons: first, it believed that an all-economy business model was not sustainable on its initial routes; and second, it identified an unserved segment of demand comprised of price-sensitive self-employed business-people who would otherwise use incumbents' economy/coach products. (That Oasis failed in its execution does not necessarily mean the initial analysis of the market was flawed.)
5.   Some customers want a broad range of high-quality benefits and are prepared to pay. These are generally business travellers flying on larger companies' expense accounts, together with wealthy entrepreneurs and independent leisure travellers. They form the subsegments at which most incumbent network carriers target their premium cabins, and from which a high proportion of these airlines' profits is drawn.

This brief analysis goes some way to explaining the plethora of different airline business models that has arisen in recent years. However, matters are not really as simple as this, because when a particular customer travels reasonably frequently they might fit into one segment on one trip and another on a different trip – depending on variables such as length of haul or who is paying. Consider intra-European short-haul markets. Business and discretionary travellers from relatively high socio-economic groups are, at least on some routes, now very likely to be found using LFAs. People whose lifestyles might take them to expensive hotels in expensive rental cars when they reach their destination – people who might use premium cabins on long-haul journeys – can be just as satisfied with the value offered by LFAs as the highly price-sensitive customers that early stereotypes suggested were the only segment they serve. (The UK CAA [2006a] has found that in UK–EU and UK domestic markets there is little correlation between either the socio-economic group or the income level of leisure travellers on the one hand and their choice of 'no-frills' or 'full-service' airline on the other; amongst business travellers, only those in the highest income group show a distinct preference for 'full-service' airlines.)

Predicted response   We have seen that demand for air transport services is a function of certain independent variables – notably price and the income, time-sensitivity and product preferences of purchasers. We have also seen that independent variables each have an elasticity associated with them which determines how changes affect demand. In order to help develop and refine their marketing programmes (i.e., the design, pricing, promotion, and distribution of their services), managers benefit from knowing how customers would respond to changes in those programmes which affect demand-determining variables; this knowledge can provide a second basis on which to segment markets. One possible approach to gauging the reaction of different customers to variations in the marketing mix might be as follows:

1. Identify the behaviour of interest, which in most cases will be purchase in response to a particular type of marketing stimulus.
2. Measure that behaviour for a sample of customers.
3. Cluster members of the sample into segments. These segments would be comprised of people who can be expected to respond in broadly the same way to, say:
   • a price initiative;
   • advertising in particular electronic, broadcast or print media;
   • promotion in different distribution channels;
   • redesign of the product (e.g., revised schedule or new ground and inflight amenities).
   Segments identified for different purposes will certainly overlap, but they should nonetheless be distinct.
4. Isolate descriptors that characterise each segment, such as demographic or lifestyle variables or exposure to different types of media.
5. Target marketing initiatives at audiences defined by the relevant descriptors (Rao and Steckel 1998).

As already mentioned, however, identifying appropriate descriptors and then using them to predict behaviour with reasonable confidence is not easy. Neither is it cheap. Many airlines which either do not have the resources or consider themselves to be pitching a 'one size fits all' product at a largely homogeneous segment (e.g., extremely price-sensitive buyers) do not embark on this type of exercise.

More generally, people in many parts of the world are now being confronted with so much choice and are becoming so unpredictable in the ways they exercise consumer freedoms that it is increasingly difficult to isolate a single descriptive variable and assert that the individuals described will with some high degree of probability behave in a certain way. This can lead to a polarisation of marketing responses: either define segments increasingly sharply to help fine-tune product, communication, and distribution strategies (the approach of some network carriers), or simply pitch a single value proposition that speaks for itself (the approach of many LFAs). In between is the traditional 'mass marketing' approach of wide-market airlines that like to think they are segmenting their markets by offering separate cabins and a complex fare structure, but which in many cases have very little detailed customer insight.

Lifetime value   Segmentation can also be based on the worth of different customers in terms of future revenue and profit potential. Something approximating the 80/20 rule applies to long-haul operations insofar as a small percentage of customers (i.e., those travelling in premium cabins) account for the bulk of profitability. The lifetime value of customers such as this can usefully be cross-referenced to customer loyalty in order to help understand the potential profitability of different segments and to design relationship management/customer retention programmes (Payne and Frow 1999).

Most airlines have in fact yet to develop the sophisticated measurement capabilities required for such initiatives; some do not see any need to do so. A separate but related point is that value might lie less in the individual traveller, and therefore be less dependent upon class of travel, than in a relationship with the employer or travel management company that sets travel policy for many hundreds or thousands of ticket purchases.

Loyalty   Garvett and Avery (1998, p. 572) break traffic down into three customer types:

1. *Occasional flyers* These customers fly seldom and without regular patterns. Purchases are more likely to be stimulated by price than brand loyalty, and even FFP membership might not be relevant to choice of carrier. They nonetheless add density to traffic flows and may therefore lower unit production costs (something which will be discussed fully in Chapter 5).
2. *Infrequent flyers* These customers fly more often than occasionally and might have more regular travel patterns – perhaps to a particular company site or to visit friends or relations. Again, price may be more important than brand loyalty, although FFP membership can be influential up to a point.
3. *Frequent flyers* These are the relatively few customers whose high frequency of travel mark out as core drivers of revenue quality in the income statements of carriers to which they are loyal. In the United States, for example, the 8 per cent of 'frequent flyers' who take ten or more trips per year account for 40 per cent of total trips taken and, accordingly, for a disproportionately high share of revenue (Air Transport Association 2001). A similar dynamic applies in many long-haul international markets, where premium passengers may account for less than 15 per cent of traffic but a very much higher percentage of revenue.

Loyalty amongst frequent flyers is a particularly appealing basis for segmentation given its claimed linkage to profit (Reichheld 1996; Heskett *et al.* 1997). There are broadly three routes to achieving it:

- genuine brand preference;
- consumer loyalty programmes (notably FFPs);
- corporate loyalty programmes (corporate FFPs, negotiated deals in respect of prices and condition waivers, and/or end-of-period rebates).

An airline might try to 'ring-fence' and retain the most loyal and the most valuable of its customers, relying perhaps on more aggregated approaches to others in the market. The attraction of customer loyalty from an airline's perspective is that in its most extreme form it secures a segment of demand for the airline concerned and removes it from competitors' 'scopes'.

Loyalty, and its corollaries the customer retention and defection rates, can be important drivers of market share and revenue quality, but there are issues:

1. Because the effort required to understand customer loyalty (including retention and defection) and to effectively implement service recovery and complaint management

programmes is expensive, not only must significant resources be available but there has to be reasonable confidence that real payback is likely to flow from the effort in terms of revenue and yield improvement (Holloway 2002). In fact, the capability to predict customer defection, retention, and loyalty is still not well-developed in most of the industry. (See Ostrowski and O'Brien (1991) for an early study of the issues involved.)

2. With regard to FFPs:
   - They should be thought of and analysed as investments in the sense that resources are committed to customer retention, as a result of which future revenues will flow in over the life of the relationship. In practice this is relatively rare; loyalty programme costs are often buried in general marketing budgets, with neither costs nor benefits rigorously analysed on a market-by-market or segment-by-segment basis. Some programmes still track and reward usage (i.e., miles flown and trips taken) rather than the value (in terms of revenue and profit) that each member brings to the airline.
   - There are also other dynamics at work: first, several network carriers make considerable amounts of money from selling miles to other service providers such as credit card companies, hotel chains, and car rental firms – something which, because of different award policies, is not necessarily compatible with the objective of building customer loyalty to a particular airline (Watterson *et al.* 2006); second, high load factors and perceptions of a marked decline in the availability of award seats in the United States in particular have tended in recent years to reduce the value of airline loyalty programmes to customers; and third, many customers hold multiple FFP memberships.

3. An important challenge to loyalty segmentation is posed by the fact that the nature of the industry's product tends to generate only 'soft' brand loyalty (Crandall 1995), with price a prominent purchase driver in price-elastic segments and both schedule and punctuality dominant in business segments. Airlines have to work very hard to make other service attributes contribute substantially to brand loyalty. In the US domestic market, customers are often willing to switch away from their 'favourite' airline in response to minor differences in price or departure time – especially if they hold multiple FFP memberships (ibid.).

4. Whilst there is most probably a linkage between usage, loyalty, and profit it is ill-understood by the majority of carriers – and some loyal customers might well be unprofitable (Taneja 2002).

These issues notwithstanding, when core purchase criteria such as safety, price, schedule, and/or FFP membership are evenly matched it is essential for airlines to offer 'points of difference' that distinguish them from competitors and provide a basis for loyalty – even if only of the soft, 'all other things being equal' variety. This was emphasised in Chapter 1.

Summary The last few pages have looked at one possible approach to segmentation based on customer characteristics, focusing on four dimensions: required customer value, predicted response, lifetime value, and loyalty – but there are many other possibilities. For example, an alternative approach which projects macro trends forward to 2020, identifying four traveller 'tribes' (global executives, active seniors, cosmopolitan commuters, and global clans), has been suggested in a report by Amadeus (2007). Conversely, at a micro-level, time of booking is an important segmentation basis for some revenue management system applications (e.g., cancellation forecasting models).

Segmentation In Practice

Arguments in favour of segmentation are as follows:

- Markets are rarely homogeneous. The more sharply that any apparently homogeneous market is brought into focus, the greater the number of differences that can be identified amongst buyers. The more insightful an airline is in segmenting its markets, and the more precisely it can tailor its service design, pricing, marketing communications, and/or service delivery to what it has found out about customers but competitors do not yet know, the more likely it is that segment knowledge – in this context a key organizational resource – will lead to competitive advantage (Holloway 2002).
- Segments are not necessarily 'out there' objects waiting to be discovered; they can also be characterised as the constructions of individual managers' perceptions. Managers whose perceptions of 'reality' take them outside the established industry mindset might unearth segment insights that others have not developed. There are in fact as many possible ways of slicing a market as marketing executives have the imagination, time, data, and budget to come up with.

On the other hand, there are strong arguments against segmentation.

- Segmentation costs money, and some airline managers take the view that the rewards do not repay the costs; an undifferentiated approach to marketing is therefore justified. For example, from a product perspective many LFAs offer a single service concept targeted at a fairly broad market niche (e.g., cost-conscious travellers who want reliable service with minimal frills). To the extent that they segment their markets at all (e.g., into business and VFR or leisure segments) they use: schedule (e.g., higher frequencies to attract business travellers); revenue management (e.g., higher walk-up than advance-purchase fares – to make late-deciders, who are often business travellers, pay a premium for last-minute access to the seat inventory).
- Consumers are more unpredictable than they used to be, with the result that cultural, socio-economic and demographic characteristics no longer translate into a reasonably predictable set of behaviours. The inevitable result is that traditional demographic, psychographic, and geographic segmentation techniques are not as reliable in predicting purchase behaviours in response to marketing stimuli such as product design, price, and advertising as they have been in the past. This argues for a revenue model, increasingly seen in North American and European short-haul markets, which allows customers to self-select (Moorthy 1984) into segments by offering a range of different service–price offers on each flight – in other words, simultaneously offering the core transportation product at a base price (which will change as departure date approaches) alongside a menu of augmented service attributes (e.g., extra baggage, seat allocation, priority boarding, food, schedule flexibility) available at a fixed supplementary charge. If nothing else, this approach simplifies revenue management (Ng 2004).

Despite having separate cabins onboard (usually occupied by customers from a mix of different segments – albeit with one perhaps preponderant), and maybe also recognising an elite tier of FFP membership, many airlines still adopt a mass-marketing approach (Zakreski 1998). On the other hand, some network carriers are now identifying and targeting a broader range of more closely defined segments of demand. The wider an airline's geographic and product scope, and the more complex its customers' needs and purchase motivations, the more relevant segmentation is likely to be. Where segmentation is used, segments should be as homogeneous as possible, large enough to be meaningful, separately measurable, and accessible to marketing programmes. Whether a particular airline's approach to segmentation is rudimentary or sophisticated, it begs five questions once a segment has been identified: Is it structurally attractive? Is serving it consistent with the carrier's strategic description of itself? Does the carrier have a competitive advantage in serving it? Is that advantage sustainable? Can it be served profitably as well as effectively?

IV. The Drivers of Air Transport Demand

It was noted earlier in the chapter that demand is a function of a number of independent, or explanatory, variables. Two questions need to be answered:

1. What are these variables?
2. What is the elasticity of demand associated with each?

The most significant explanatory variables are price and income, and these will be the focus of this section of the chapter. Other variables will then be briefly highlighted. Some independent variables (e.g., income) influence aggregate market demand, some (e.g., price and schedule) can influence both market demand and market shares, whilst others (e.g., the ground and inflight product, and brand loyalty) are more likely to influence market share than aggregate market demand.

Other than in the immediate aftermath of a substantial exogenous shock such as 9/11 which undermines the willingness of some people to fly at all, price and income are always the most significant variables. The extent to which others influence demand will depend upon the scope and time-horizon of the analysis: the narrower the scope of a study and the shorter the time horizon, the more attention will need to be paid to other variables in addition to economic growth and price.

PRICE

Despite periodic increases in certain markets, airfares as a whole have on average and in most markets declined in real (i.e., inflation-adjusted) terms over the last several decades. By 2006, for example, US traffic had returned to pre-9/11 levels but the average fares necessary to generate this traffic were 15 per cent lower – despite a series of system-wide fare increases that year. Two years later average fares had still yet to return to their March 2000 peak, despite the imposition of surcharges and multiple fare increases in response to rapidly rising fuel costs; US network carriers therefore began cutting domestic output, and LFAs scaled back growth plans, in pursuit of greater pricing power.

Declining real airfares and cargo rates over the last several decades have been a product of the competition resulting from liberalisation and deregulation of air transport markets. They have forced airlines to manage costs more proactively. Productivity improvements attributable to increasingly efficient airframe and engine designs and to IT-enabled business process restructuring have made this possible; that certain carriers have been slower than others to respond to these possibilities has caused many of the industry's financial problems.

In some markets, the rapid expansion of LFAs with modern fleets and lean processes sufficient to support lower fares than previously available appears to have generated a significant price-stimulus. Box 2.3 considers the evidence.

When considering the price-elasticity of demand for air transport services, a distinction should be drawn between own-price elasticity and cross-price elasticity.

Box 2.3: Low-fare Airlines – Traffic Stimulation or Traffic Substitution?

Intuitively, it is difficult not to conclude that LFAs stimulate traffic. It is widely accepted that first in North America, then in Europe, and now in Asia and Latin America, LFAs have expanded by meeting a latent demand for affordable air travel. A corollary argument which often follows is that their (usually rapid) expansion of market share is attributable largely to new traffic that they have either stimulated or diverted from surface modes, and only to a much lesser extent to traffic captured from incumbent airlines (i.e., substitution). BAA, the UK airport operator, has expressed the view that on average around 50 per cent of traffic carried by 'no-frills carriers' is new rather than diverted from existing services (CAA 2003). Similarly, a study by the European Low Fares Airline Association (ELFAA 2004) claims, based on 2002 data, that LFAs sourced 59 per cent of their traffic from new demand and only 37 per cent from other carriers (no data being available for the remaining 4 per cent); of the new demand, 71 per cent would otherwise not have travelled whilst 21 per cent would have travelled instead by road or rail (no specific intentions being attributed to the remaining 8 per cent). Similar claims, based on both empirical and anecdotal sources, are plentiful. For example:

*   In a study of US markets before and after entry by an LFA, Perry (1995) found year-on-year average fare decreases ranging from 16 per cent (Reno–Portland) to 82 per cent (Cleveland–Baltimore), and passenger enplanements rising in the range of 58 per cent (Las Vegas–Oakland) to 745 per cent (Cleveland–Baltimore).
*   A study by Windle and Dresner (1999) has shown empirically that entry by LFAs into US domestic markets materially reduces fares.
*   Smith (2004) cites Southwest's entry into the Baltimore–Buffalo market as contributing to a reduction in fares exceeding 60 per cent and to a 300 per cent increase in traffic; jetBlue's entry into the New York–Burlington market drove down average fares by 50 per cent and helped stimulate a 140 per cent traffic increase.

On the other hand, a study of UK–EU and UK domestic markets by the CAA (2006a) came to markedly different conclusions:

*   Despite the high traffic growth figures achieved by LFAs since the mid-1990s and despite their growing share of total European scheduled traffic, no significant change was found in overall growth rates in the markets concerned during the decade to 2005. The trend rate, a 10-year moving average, remained in the same 5–6 per cent range in which it had been since the mid-1970s.
*   Although market growth might have been lower during the study period but for the expansion of LFAs, their traffic has largely been drawn from growth that would otherwise have been experienced by 'full-service scheduled carriers' and, even more so, charter airlines (ibid., p. 4).
*   The CAA accepted that on certain routes there has been 'considerable stimulation of new traffic' (ibid.), but went on to conclude that 'it is harder to discern a change in the rate of growth at the level of the market overall' (ibid.). The study cited routes such as London–Barcelona and Bristol–Amsterdam on which LFAs had a pronounced stimulatory effect, but identified others where this effect was short-lived (e.g., Edinburgh–Dublin) or where LFA traffic simply substituted for 'full-service' traffic (e.g., London–Milan) or charter traffic (e.g., Manchester–Malaga).

- The study found that 'full-service and charter traffic have generally been in decline since 2000 and, at present, they are broadly at the levels they were at some ten years ago [i.e., 1996]. The conclusion is that LFAs have taken up the aggregate market growth in this period, but that growth has not been substantially different from what would otherwise have been anticipated given established trends and elasticities.'

The CAA noted that one reason for the disparity between the ELFAA findings based on 2002 data and its own findings based on 10-year data could be that the stimulatory effect of low-fare entry is initially very strong on the routes affected, but over time this effect diminishes and the market taken as a whole returns to something closer to its long-term trend rate. The same might apply in respect of BAA's observations, noted above.

However, these comments cannot be taken to minimise the impact of LFAs. Whilst they might not have added a great deal to trend traffic growth in some markets during the period of the CAA's study, the authors of that study themselves make the point (Chapter 3, p. 6) that not only have LFAs caused a realignment of market share by absorbing nearly all of the traffic growth in those markets, they have also compelled established carriers to redesign their own business models. On a separate but related point, anecdotal evidence seems to suggest that the stimulatory impact of LFAs in South East Asia has been pronounced; also, whereas in more established air travel markets one of the stimulatory effects of LFAs is to encourage people in relatively high socio-economic groups to travel more often (CAA 2006a), in South East Asia LFAs are providing the opportunity to fly to people who previously did not have it.

By slightly modifying an analysis put forward by Binggeli and Pompeo (2005) and retaining their examples, we can identify the following broad outcomes of LFA entry:

1. Demand stimulation: new traffic is generated.
    - Previously unserved route (e.g., London–Treviso).
    - Route already served by network or charter carriers (e.g., London–Barcelona).
2. Shift in market share: little or no new traffic is stimulated by LFA entry, but the LFA takes market share from incumbents and compels them to reduce capacity (e.g., London–Genoa, London–Faro).
3. Demand stagnation.
    - The LFA stimulates new traffic, but growth quickly plateaus or reverses (e.g., London–Bologna, London–Aarhuis).
    - The LFA fails to stimulate traffic or attract market share from incumbents and exits the market (e.g., London–Marseille).

If we move the focus from diversion of growth away from incumbent carriers towards new entrant LFAs and look instead at diversion from established hubs to secondary airports, we can see again the market impact of those LFAs which show a strategic preference for using the latter. To avoid congestion at Boston Logan, Southwest chose to serve the Boston region by entering Providence in 1996 and Manchester in 1998. Subsequent passenger growth at both far exceeded their own historic performances as well as national averages; whereas in the first half of the 1990s Logan accounted for well over 80 per cent of the three airports' combined growth of 1.5 million passengers, in the second half of the decade it accounted for less than 40 per cent of growth recorded at 7.5 million passengers.

Own-Price Elasticity

We saw earlier in the chapter that a change in a fare or freight rate charged by a particular airline will, assuming all other determinant variables in the demand function are held constant, result in a change in the quantity demanded. In other words, there is movement along a demand curve which itself does not change. How much movement there is in response to a given price change will depend upon the curve's price-elasticity:

$$\text{Price-elasticity} = \frac{\% \text{ change in quantity demanded}}{\% \text{ change in price}}$$

Whilst price-elasticity varies between city-pair markets and also between market segments, demand for air travel as a whole tends to be price-elastic: the range in US domestic markets, for example, is -0.7 to -2.0. The fact that price elasticity is negative means that the short-run response of consumers to any price increase is to demand less of the service (i.e., traffic falls or grows more slowly than it otherwise would) whilst price decreases tend to stimulate demand. The key issue is the size of these effects. We can draw the following distinctions:

- *Price-elastic demand (below -1.0)* If the percentage change in quantity demanded exceeds the percentage change in price that caused it, demand is 'elastic'. Because vacationers are generally sensitive to fare movements, high price-elasticity is usual in the leisure (including VFR) segment.
- *Unitary price-elasticity (-1.0)* In this case, a given percentage change in price leads to the same percentage change in quantity demanded.
- *Price-inelastic demand (0 to -1.0)* If the percentage change in quantity demanded is less than the percentage change in price, the demand curve is considered 'inelastic'. Low price-elasticity is common in the business segment, although perhaps less so than before 2000 and amongst small and medium-sized companies (as opposed to large multinationals).

Demand from business travellers tends on the whole to exhibit lower price-elasticity than leisure demand, in part because their expenditure is drawn from corporate rather than personal budgets and in part because some level of business travel is always non-discretionary if an enterprise is to prosper. Also, whereas leisure travellers meet all their own expenditures, most business travellers receive a 'subsidy' equivalent to their company's marginal rate of tax as a result of the deductions they are able to claim.

However, since the late 1990s more companies have been taking a proactive stance towards the control of travel expenditures, resulting in the increasingly widespread implementation of travel management programmes and the stricter enforcement of travel policies. As a consequence, business travel demand in some markets is less price-inelastic than has historically been the case. (See Laney [2002] for an overview of US experience in this respect.) Corporations are now more prepared than in the past to search for low fares and/or negotiate private fares; some will buy fares off the Internet where these are cheaper than negotiated contract fares. Indeed, the 30 per cent decline in US business travel in 2001 even prior to 9/11 made it clear in retrospect that the network carriers had pushed their assumptions regarding the price-inelasticity of this segment too far by forcing through multiple fare increases in the face of deteriorating service. In Europe, the rapid growth of LFAs has changed consumer perceptions: there is no longer an acceptance that short-notice business travel inevitably has to be synonymous with extortionately high fares – although on routes without LFA competition it very often still is.

In the cargo market certain types of shipment are likely to be less price-sensitive than others. We saw earlier in the chapter that those which are physically perishable (e.g., flowers), economically perishable (e.g., newspapers or fashion items), high-value (e.g., currency or precious metals), or are needed urgently by the consignee will be less price-elastic than other goods. Conversely, price-elasticity is undoubtedly one of the reasons for the marked year-to-year volatility of air cargo traffic. For example, after growing 12 per cent in 2004 world air cargo traffic grew by only 2 per cent in 2005; in the northbound Latin America to North America market the swing was from 12.2 per cent growth to a 2.6 per cent decline. The imposition of fuel surcharges, which had relatively little impact on passenger traffic, was undoubtedly a significant contributor to this slowdown (Boeing 2006b).

Price-elasticity figures drawn from a number of studies are summarised in Appendix 2.1 at the end of this chapter. In a relatively recent survey which can be highly recommended as further reading on the subject of elasticity, Gillen *et al.* (2004) identify six market segments each with different median price-elasticities (as calculated from the findings of referenced empirical studies):

- long-haul international business: -0.265
- long-haul international leisure: -1.04
- long-haul domestic business: -1.15
- long-haul domestic leisure: -1.104
- short-haul business: -0.7
- short-haul leisure: -1.520.

Attention needs to be drawn to the caveats noted by the authors regarding the relatively small number of estimates and studies covering some of these segments, and the fact that they do not all analyse the same geographical markets in each of the identified segments. The figures are nonetheless interesting for illustrative purposes. For example, they suggest that in the long-haul international business markets covered by the studies reviewed, a 10 per cent increase in fares would lead to a 2.65 per cent drop in demand – implying a gain in total revenue; on the other hand, a 10 per cent increase in short-haul leisure fares would lead to a 15.2 per cent decline in demand – implying a decrease in total revenue. However, it cannot be stressed strongly enough that because we are dealing with a revenue-managed network industry in which demand varies by market, market segment, and individual flight departure and is served by a complex system of joint supply (i.e., any one flight might be satisfying demand in multiple markets), both the validity and practical application of figures such as these have to be considered with circumspection when pricing decisions are made in specific markets. For example, the CAA (2005) has found that UK outbound leisure demand has in fact exhibited quite *low* price elasticity in recent years (-0.8).

One final point: because elasticity measures proportionate change, price-elasticity is not necessarily the same at different points along a demand curve. Price-elasticity falls as we move down a demand curve. A change at one price point on a curve may therefore not generate the same demand response as a similar change at a different price point on the same curve.

Problems with price-elasticity estimations   There are two noteworthy points to bear in mind when estimating the effect of price adjustments in a particular market, both of which relate to possible changes in the shape of the demand curve that is being used as a basis for elasticity estimations.

1. Elasticities are calculated from historical traffic data which will have been influenced by variables other than price, yet today's non-price determinants of demand are likely

to be different. This can happen, for example, where income levels have changed or where there have been changes to non-price variables such as advertising, promotional activity or (in the longer term) service design. In other words, time-series data may be an unreliable guide to the future.

2. Competitors' pricing behaviour is also important. How the quantity demanded is affected by a change in price initiated by a particular airline in a given market will depend in part upon the manner in which that airline's competitors react. If all the competitors in a market were to raise or lower their fares simultaneously, for example, quantity demanded would most probably respond more or less as anticipated by the 'market price-elasticity'. On the other hand, were only one of several competitors in a market to vary its fares, price-relativities would change and demand curves would shift; we will look at cross-price elasticity next.

Cross-Price Elasticity Of Demand

Cross-price elasticity is used to measure how demand for an airline's services varies in response to changes in the prices of other products. Whereas own-price elasticity causes movement along a given demand curve, cross-price effects cause demand curves to shift; the effects of price-elasticity are then felt by changes in the quantity demanded as reflected by movement up or down the new demand curve. The cross-price elasticity of demand for products A and B is the percentage change in the quantity demanded of product A resulting from a 1 per cent change in the price of product B (and vice versa). The two types of product we are concerned with here are 'substitutes' and 'complements'. Whereas cross-price elasticity for substitutes is positive (i.e., direct) in the sense that an increase in the price of one stimulates demand for the other, cross-price elasticity for complements is negative (i.e., inverse) because a price increase in one causes demand for the other to decline. Products that are unrelated will have zero, or near-zero, cross-price elasticity.

Substitutes   There are potentially three sources of substitute products:

1. *Own industry*   The products of competing airlines are often viable substitutes. Customer-driven service design together with tools such as branding, FFPs, and travel agency commission overrides (TACOs) are intended to reduce cross-price elasticity to the extent that they induce loyalty, weaken the substitution value of competitors' products, and – except in the most price-elastic segments – soften the effect on demand of a competitor's price reduction. Clearly, the more information that consumers have regarding potential substitutes, the higher cross-price elasticity is likely to be; the Internet has had a profound impact in this regard. In practice, whether a new entrant's product is seen by an incumbent as a threat – that is, as a serious substitute which warrants pricing and perhaps output responses – might depend upon the market share the entrant can realistically target.
2. *Own products*   An airline with a large portfolio of products might need to look no further than the composition of that portfolio to find substitutes. Moving from the front to the rear of the aircraft, each class of service is a potential substitute for another: business for first, unrestricted (or premium) economy for business, discounted economy/coach for full-fare, travel on an in-house low-fare subsidiary for mainline coach (if network overlap is not carefully managed). An unmatched increase in,

say, an airline's business class fare may therefore lead not only to a loss of traffic to competitors, but also to an increase in demand for its own economy/coach product. Before fares are varied, the airline needs to understand these elasticities, and possibly to plan the use of non-price variables such as FFP bonus awards, other promotional activities, or different types of marketing communications to counter them.

Similarly, if demand for a peak departure is high enough to support firmer pricing, a customer with sufficient flexibility might switch to a cheaper departure. With regard to some leisure travel, different destinations might be substitutes for each other – as when people looking for weekend breaks are prepared to consider a range of alternatives on the basis of relative prices.

3. *Other industries* Videoconferencing, on-demand charters, fractional ownership or purchase of a personal or corporate aircraft might be viable substitutes for use of an airline in some business markets. Virtually any form of entertainment or any consumer durable could in principle be a substitute for leisure travel, particularly if such travel is not part of the main annual vacation that so many people in industrialised (and some middle-income developing) countries now take for granted. Surface modes might offer a viable substitute for short-haul passenger journeys and cargo shipments; concerns were raised in the aftermath of 9/11 that the introduction of lengthier security procedures would add an increment to total travel time sufficient in some short-haul US markets to make surface modes more attractive substitutes. (Conversely, low fares following market liberalisation in India and Mexico have made air travel a viable substitute for parts of those countries' rail and bus networks respectively.)

Cross-price elasticity can turn an apparent monopolist into an active competitor. For example, an airline holding a monopoly on short-haul domestic routes will not necessarily be able to price or to behave more generally as a pure monopolist would if it faces viable competition from potential substitutes such as surface transport modes. This is the case on some French domestic trunk routes, for example, where Air France faces state-subsidised competition from high-speed trains.

A rise in the price of a product can be expected to move demand towards available substitutes. The strength of the shift will depend upon whether we are dealing with 'close' or 'weak' substitutes – price movements in the former case having a more profound effect on demand. One purpose of product differentiation is to reduce cross-price elasticity by weakening the perception that competing products are real substitutes (Porter 1976). Knowledge of cross-price elasticities is clearly important for the management of pricing and other marketing strategies.

Complements These are products which are used together rather than as substitutes for each other. Bearing in mind that the demand for air transport is a derived demand for a product with no intrinsic value, complements are readily identifiable; what influence a particular complement has on demand will depend upon its share of total trip cost and the purpose of the trip. One example of a complementary relationship is passenger air transport and hotels. There is an inverse relationship between the demand for a product or service and the price of a complement, such that a major increase in the price of hotels at a particular destination will reduce (or slow the growth of) demand for travel to that destination. The air transport demand curve will shift leftwards. For example, increased hotel prices in a popular vacation spot, perhaps due to higher rates or an appreciating currency, might divert foreign vacationers to alternative destinations. Whereas carriers based in the outbound market (e.g., the UK or Germany) would be able to follow demand to newly preferred locations, carriers based in the re-priced destination (e.g., Cyprus) might not have the same network management flexibility. (This is a problem faced by any carrier with a network of limited scope based in a destination which for some reason loses its popularity (e.g., El Al or Middle East Airlines) – a problem not shared to the same extent by wide-market network carriers based in countries from which more diverse traffic flows originate.) Airlines in countries originating traffic can construct a portfolio of outbound routes which might be more resistant to the negative impact of cross-price elasticity than any portfolio of inbound routes. Conversely, of course, inbound route portfolios may be a useful hedge against a downturn in traffic from just one originating source.

Complements can also arise within an airline's network. Connecting flights are complements insofar as the price for one can impact upon demand for the other; this relationship might be transparent, as when a carrier offers combined single-segment fares – as Aer Lingus does over Dublin, for example, and Tiger does over Singapore – or it might be buried within the decision rules of a revenue management system.

The Strategic Implications Of Price-Elasticity

Knowledge of price-elasticities in different markets and segments is clearly helpful to pricing decisions – although, as already noted, airline managers commonly have to act on imperfect and rapidly changing data. These decisions also affect costs and interact with competitive strategy. Recalling the discussion of cost advantage and benefit advantage in Chapter 1, we can make the following generalisations.

Cost advantage   A price-elastic market is likely to offer greater opportunities to a low-fare carrier than to a differentiator, simply because it will not respond as favourably to the higher prices that differentiation implies. Low-fare carriers with a sustainable cost advantage should initially be focusing on price-elastic markets that have the potential to grow rapidly in response to the stimulus of low prices. In principle, this will allow them to benefit from improved operating economics as traffic density and their market share both increase. In practice, incumbents might choose to match low fares offered by a new entrant and – by virtue of their size and market presence – absorb much of any traffic growth, so leaving the challenger with little opportunity to expand output unless it is prepared to risk low load factors; the result could be a war of attrition between the low costs of the challenger and the deep pockets of the incumbent, which might be able to cross-subsidise from less competitive markets. The cards are initially stacked in favour of a large incumbent under these circumstances, but the success of Southwest in the United States and several LFAs in Europe and elsewhere shows that once a well-capitalised, well-managed low-fare carrier achieves critical mass it can be difficult to compete against.

It should always be borne in mind, however, that what pays the bills in practice is not traffic, but revenue. Low fares will under many circumstances stimulate incremental traffic, but because they will generally be matched by competitors the aggregate revenue generated may not actually increase by very much. We will return at the end of Chapter 3 to the importance of looking at traffic in conjunction with yield.

Benefit advantage   Differentiation on the strength of superior benefits is a strategy likely to be more successful in relatively price-inelastic markets. Were a new entrant or incumbent to price below competitors in a market heavily dominated by business travellers, for example, the relative price-inelasticity of the market and the importance of non-price determinants of demand (such as schedule, punctuality or brand loyalty) could justify a more muted price response than were the market dominated by highly price-elastic leisure travellers; this might particularly be the case if the lower fare were being offered either on a capacity-controlled basis or by a carrier producing a relatively small share of output in the market concerned. Most incumbents serving high-density North Atlantic routes did not initially react to the arrival of competitively priced all-premium airlines in 2006 and 2007, largely because the number of seats being offered by the new entrants was small relative to the several thousand business and first class passengers travelling in these markets each day; it was simply not worthwhile for the incumbents to dilute their own yields by matching prices or putting extra capacity onto the routes concerned – although American did eventually take on eos and MAXjet at Stansted. A similar threat to premium traffic on less dense routes should generate a more intense competitive reaction.

INCOME

As economic activity and trade increase, the demand for business air travel and for cargo space will grow. As people's incomes rise, they spend more on non-essential goods and services such as vacations. In both cases, as prosperity increases people tend to be less sensitive to price and more susceptible to manipulation of non-price variables in the marketing mix. Conversely, during a recession consumers still in the market are often more concerned about price than amenities and brand image.

Income-elasticity measures the responsiveness of demand to changes in customers' incomes, assuming all other demand-determining variables remain constant. Whilst in the real world all the independent variables used to model demand will be dynamic, for analytical purposes they have to be held constant. For example, a change in price can have an 'income effect' even without income itself changing: a fall in the price of something which is already in demand has an effect equivalent to a rise in income, and an increase in price has the opposite effect. Hence price must be held constant when considering income elasticity.

An income-elasticity figure above unity would be considered elastic, whilst anything below unity is inelastic. Unlike price elasticity, the relationship is positive rather than inverse, which means that increasing incomes lead to increasing demand.

$$\text{Income elasticity} = \frac{\%\ \text{change in demand}}{\%\ \text{change in income}}$$

When looking at income as one of the key determinants of air traffic growth, it can be useful to break the analysis down into two questions:

1. *Demographics* How many potential consumers are there in the market concerned?
2. *Income* What are their income levels?

The next subsection will touch briefly upon demographics. After that some of the metrics used as proxies for income in the business and leisure segments will be identified.

Demographics

Global demographic trends are likely to drive the continuing growth of air transport demand well into the future. Davies (2002) makes a compelling case for the inevitability of demand growth, and the threat of system congestion that this implies, based on widely accepted forecasts for the expansion of the world's population over the next several decades. The United Nations (2004) envisages this expansion being of the order of 1.5 billion between 2005 and 2025, by which time the global population will have reached 8 billion. In addition to its expansion, there are also foreseeable structural shifts within the world's population that will have a profound impact on demand in many air transport markets. Taneja (2002) explores the implications of current migration patterns as well as the growth in both population and purchasing power in developing countries.

Moving away from the global market, an individual city-pair market may be structurally attractive in the sense that pricing is high and competition is weak, but too small to justify entry by a carrier with a wide-market strategic position; it might, on the other hand, be attractive to a niche operator. Conversely, demographics can underpin network strategy. For example, because Emirates now operates some of the world's longest routes it is easy to overlook the fact that its network strategy owes a great deal to there being over 5 billion people living within 8 hours' flying time of its Dubai hub. Similarly, LFAs AirAsia and Tiger are based in countries which are within no more than 5 hours' flying time of well over 2 billion people.

Of course the presence of people is not in itself sufficient. They need a motivation to travel, and they need sufficient income to give them purchasing power. The next subsection looks at metrics of income.

Measuring Income

At a global level, world gross domestic product (GDP) is as good a metric of income as any. However, when measuring the income-elasticity of demand in a particular market the traffic mix is important because elasticities vary and because income in different segments is measured in a variety of different ways. Separately, it is worth bearing in mind that where a long-haul carrier relies heavily on sixth-freedom traffic flowing over its hub between city-pairs in different foreign countries (e.g., Singapore Airlines), income movements in its domestic economy will not necessarily have as significant an impact on demand as would be the case were it relying entirely on generating traffic to and from its home market. (The freedoms of the air are defined in Chapter 4.)

Leisure segment   Ideal measures for discretionary purchasers are household income or personal disposable income. In practice, lack of data often requires that per capita GDP is used as a proxy; the assumption is that people's propensity to travel by air will increase as their incomes rise, and there is indeed a strong correlation between per capita GDP and airline trips per capita. One possible problem is that per capita GDP takes no account of income distribution, which in some emerging economies is highly skewed in favour of small elites whose business and leisure travel habits may not be particularly sensitive to changes in income levels. Elsewhere this is less of an issue, and in mature markets predicted growth in nominal GDP might itself serve as a proxy for traffic growth – that is, income-elasticity of demand might be considered to be unity when nominal GDP is used as the income measure (Bowles 1994); some US majors, for example, use forecasted growth in nominal GDP as a proxy for traffic growth.

Alternative measures are used in various countries: in Britain, an index of consumer expenditure is widely used as an accessible measure of income available to consumers. Consumption is arguably a stronger metric than GDP for use in modelling demand in the leisure segment. First, it can accommodate issues arising from some countries' higher than average household savings rates, which are masked in GDP figures but can have a strong effect on patterns of discretionary expenditure. Second, there is little doubt that particularly in Anglophone economies both the wealth effect from rising house prices and stock markets in the early 2000s and the surge in household debt helped fuel consumer expenditure, some of which found its way into air travel demand notwithstanding relatively sluggish growth in real personal incomes.

Income-elasticity calculations in leisure markets are complicated by several issues:

- As we saw earlier in the chapter, there are different subsegments of demand within the leisure segment. These encompass not only different income levels and socio-economic bands, but also different journey purposes – whether weekend break, annual vacation, VFR – and different length of haul. Establishing accurate income-elasticities for each subsegment is difficult and expensive.
- Although most studies of tourism demand assume that it is a function of *current* income, there is debate in the literature regarding whether the focus should instead be on one or both of past income or expected future income. Intertemporal choice theory argues the complexity of real consumer decision processes and, in particular, advances the idea that current consumption is a function of future income expectations – perhaps moderated to some degree by past experiences (Sinclair and Stabler 1997).
- Because leisure air travel is a relatively new form of expenditure, it tends to grow rapidly at first and then more slowly as higher income groups reach a point where the law of diminishing marginal utility sets in (i.e., each additional expenditure on travel yields less utility than the last). Income-elasticities in this segment will therefore change over time, raising doubts about the reliability of forecasts based on historical time-series drawn from an individual market.

Business travel segment GDP forecasts are still widely used as inputs into demand forecasting models for the business travel segment. However, some analysts – particularly those examining air transport demand out of relatively small economies – prefer to substitute income-elasticity calculations with a measure of trade-elasticity, believing trade to have more impact on business travel than any aggregate income figure.

Others now consider business travel to be more dependent upon corporate profits than GDP. Whilst profits and GDP have historically been quite closely correlated, in the United States in 2002 they became significantly disconnected for the first time; the weak airline revenue environment was more in line with the dire performance of the corporate sector than with the positive, if at that time anaemic, trend in GDP. Conversely, by mid-decade the 25-year high in multinational corporations' profitability, measured by return on equity, was being cited as a key driver of continuing strong demand for business travel; in fact, the real drivers underlying the demand-impact of corporate profitability might be the higher capital expenditures and increased volumes of merger and acquisition activity undertaken by corporations around the globe when profits are strong (UBS 2006).

Airfreight markets   Airfreight demand is sensitive to global economic growth generally, and in particular to growth in world merchandise trade; together these are the most significant determinants of airfreight demand. On the whole, growth in world trade tends to be higher than economic growth but also more volatile. The higher growth can be attributed to both the globalisation of manufacturing supply chains and the propensity of the world's consumers, as they become richer, to demand goods sourced from much further afield than in the past (e.g., foodstuffs previously considered exotic or seasonal but now demanded year-round). The volatility, particularly in individual markets, can be attributed to a variety of factors:

- Periodic changes in the economic behaviour of consumers (e.g., the pre-credit-crunch growth in US and UK consumer expenditure fuelled not just by perennially low household savings rates, but also by changes in both the availability of credit and social attitudes to indebtedness).
- Changes in the patterns of demand for goods produced by industries that are heavy users of airfreight in a particular market (e.g., electronic goods in eastbound transpacific markets).
- Shifts in corporate inventories in destination markets, which cause shipments to slow when inventories become too high and accelerate when they drop.
- Plant relocations (e.g., by multinationals, which over the last decade and a half have opened production or assembly plants first in Mexico, Eastern Europe, and South East Asia followed by the eastern seaboard of China and more recently India, Vietnam, and inland China).
- Temporary export promotions, permanent trade agreements, and the relaxation of quotas or duties on specific categories of merchandise that are heavily traded in a particular market.
- In destination countries, a substitution of domestic for imported goods and/or a shift in the structure of imports as the economy develops and per capita income climbs.
- In exporting countries, rising consumer incomes leading to diversion of exports to the local market.

Conclusions

World real GDP growth per annum has broadly fallen within the 2–4 per cent band over the last three decades; this band was breached on the downside in the early years of the 1980s, 1990s, and 2000s and (less dramatically) on the upside in the latter part of the 1970s, 1980s, and 1990s and also the mid-2000s. Traffic growth has been considerably more volatile, but has had a long-term trend close to 5 per cent on the passenger side (RPK growth averaging 4.8 per cent per annum between 1985 and 2005) and 6 per cent for cargo. Both Airbus and Boeing forecast similar rates of traffic growth through 2026 (Boeing 2007, Airbus 2008), implying that the traffic multiplier for real global GDP – growth of which is forecast to be around 3 per cent per annum on average – is approximately two for cargo traffic and somewhat lower for passenger traffic; such multipliers incorporate the effects of both income- and price-elasticities. (Note that if the forecast period is varied, the multiplier would change: because even young markets will gradually mature, the multiplier for shorter forecasts out to a decade ahead or less is likely to be higher.) Being averages, these figures mask the significant year-on-year swings that are evidence of the pronounced demand cyclicality that is characteristic of the air transport industry. Being *global* averages, they mask considerable variation between different regions of the world and different markets:

1. *Different stages of market maturity* RPK growth rate is a function of both the rate of economic growth and the size of the income multiplier (e.g., the GDP–to–RPK multiplier) for the market concerned. As economies mature, rates of economic growth tend to decrease; what happens to the income multiplier in their air transport markets is less deterministic, and can be affected by non-economic variables such as the degree of commercial freedom and entrepreneurial innovation in evidence. For example, Boeing (2007), has forecast average annual real GDP growth of 2.8 and 6.6 per cent in the United States and China respectively over the period 2007–2026, but income multipliers of 1.4 and 1.2 respectively; RPK growth rates therefore come in at just under 4.0 and 8.0 per cent respectively.

   In its forecast for the period from 2008 to 2025, the FAA (2008) saw US scheduled commercial carrier system enplanements rising on average by 3.0 per cent per annum and system RPMs rising by 4.2 per cent per annum on the basis of assumed average annual real GDP growth of 2.7 per cent in the United States and 3.2 per cent globally; international enplanements and RPMs were forecast to grow 4.7 and 5.4 per cent respectively, against domestic figures of 2.8 and 3.7 per cent. Clearly, the domestic market shows more signs of maturity than international markets; this, as well as issues associated with their cost bases relative to short-haul LFAs at home, is why US network carriers have been moving output onto international routes over the last few years.

   In addition to the rate of growth, another relevant aspect of economic development is evolving income distributions. As wealth percolates down to a burgeoning middle class in many developing countries, more income is becoming available for non-essential expenditures such as leisure travel – much of which will be by air because of geography and/or poor ground infrastructure in many of the affected markets (e.g., parts of Asia and Latin America). The income-elasticity of demand for air transport services in many emerging economies will therefore remain consistent with that of a growth industry; indeed, middle-income tourists travelling out of Asian countries are set to become one of the dominant market forces in international leisure travel. Globally, the BRIC countries (Brazil, Russia, India, China) are widely seen as key sources of demand in the decades ahead because of their demographics, their high rates of economic growth, and their relatively liberal operating environments.

   Furthermore, through the 'income effect' of lower fares the expansion of LFAs such as AirAsia and Gol is accelerating the penetration of air transport in markets where economic growth is already raising income levels. Even in the more mature economies of North America and Western Europe, the success of LFAs in making air travel more affordable, bringing it within reach of the most price-sensitive segments of potential demand and also encouraging middle-income groups to fly more frequently, suggests that historical income-elasticity figures will not always be an incontrovertible guide to future traffic levels.

2. *Traffic mix* Income-elasticities can vary significantly on different routes out of the same point of origin. Partly this reflects the predominant purpose for travelling to a particular destination: income-elasticity of demand would be lower in a business market such as London (Heathrow) to Frankfurt or New York to Washington than in leisure markets such as London to Palma or New York to Las Vegas. Whereas the

income-elasticity of leisure travellers can range between 1.5 and 2.5, the figure for business travellers is likely to be lower. Pindyck and Rubinfeld (2001) cite market – as opposed to individual airline – income-elasticities of 1.2, 1.2, and 1.8 for travellers in first class, unrestricted coach, and discounted coach in the US domestic market.

3. *Length of haul* Travelling long distances generally involves a level of expenditure which is less acceptable in difficult economic times than a shorter trip.

In conclusion, the same point needs to be made here as was made in the discussion of price-elasticity: whereas the income multiplier effect is calculated by relating a global, regional, or national income metric to changes in *traffic* (RPMs or RTMs), what actually pays the bills is revenue rather than traffic. Revenue is a product of traffic and yield, so as well as considering traffic growth in response to income changes we also need to look at the yield being earned. We will return to this in Chapter 3.

OTHER DRIVERS OF AIR TRANSPORT DEMAND

Whilst price and income are usually considered to be the most significant elements in a demand function (Battersby and Oczkowski 2001), anything else that affects demand will also have an elasticity associated with it. In principle, but subject in practice to measurement difficulties, it is possible to analyse the impact on demand of any independent variable in a demand function. This section will highlight four of the most important: exchange rates; service attributes; the quality of service delivery; and marketing communications. Some (e.g., design of ground and inflight products) are more likely to impact upon the distribution of market share than absolute demand.

Exchange Rates

Changes in relative exchange rates at either end of an international O&D market can affect demand. For example, a strengthening currency might increase outbound flows of passengers, who now find prices cheaper at their destinations, and soften outbound flows of airfreight, because exports have become more expensive in their overseas markets.

Service Attributes

The design of airline service involves bundling various *attributes* for the purpose of providing *benefits* to targeted customers. Which attributes to incorporate and whether each should be priced into the fare or separately charged is a matter that goes to the heart of a particular airline's competitive strategy: it depends upon which markets and market segments are being served, and where the carrier's cost advantage and/or benefit advantage lie. It underpins design of the business model. For the purpose of this discussion, two sets of attributes can be highlighted: schedule and trip time; and design of ground and inflight products.

1. *Schedule and trip time* Demand for air transport services is affected by the quality of output; we will be looking at this point again in the next section. When elasticity of demand is being considered, two of the key components of quality are normally taken to be schedule convenience and trip time.

- *Schedule convenience* The context within which schedule is assessed is each passenger's 'decision window' – the span between the earliest acceptable departure time and the latest acceptable arrival time (both local, if there is a time-zone change); any combination of departure and arrival times falling within this window should in principle be acceptable (Boeing 1993), but the further these are from preferred timings the greater the 'schedule displacement' – which business travellers in particular want to minimise. Key issues here are frequency and scheduled departure times.
- *Trip time* This will be a function of land access and egress times at origin and destination airports, ground processing times at those airports and any connecting point, directness of the customers' path through the airline's network where connections are required, aircraft type, and the carrier's on-time performance on the route(s) concerned.

Increases in frequency and in non-stop flights may increase demand because they reduce total trip time. Research in the United States by the MITRE Corporation suggests that a 1 per cent decrease in elapsed journey time increases passenger demand by 0.8 per cent (Homan 2000); in other words, *time-elasticity of demand* describes an inverse relationship, such that decreases in total trip time lead to increases in demand and vice versa. The economic reasoning beneath this finding is that time spent travelling carries an opportunity cost that is reduced by shorter journeys and this has a positive effect on demand, reflected in a rightward shift of the carrier's demand curve.

The higher an airline's share of departures in an O&D market and the more direct its routing, the higher the quality of its product relative to competitors (at least in this sense of the word 'quality'). In the business travel segment, these variables (together with on-time performance) are significant airline choice criteria – often more critical than price. The effect of time-elasticity is therefore particularly noticeable in short- and medium-haul markets which have a strong business element in their traffic mix, because opportunity costs are higher in this market segment and because any given change in trip time will form a higher proportion of a short- than a long-haul journey.

However, a word of caution is in order, particularly where new non-stop service is inaugurated by an LFA: a study by Ford (2005) of 82 US domestic markets in which non-stop service was added found that on the whole prices declined, implying that observed stimulation of traffic was likely due to the impact of price-elasticity as well as time-elasticity.

Frequencies in many long-haul markets have yet to be built to the extent that small variations in schedule will have the same competitive impact that they are capable of having in business-oriented short-haul markets (Clark 2001). However, as growing numbers of efficient mid-sized widebody twins enter airline fleets, schedule density will thicken on existing routes and network scope will be broadened by the introduction of non-stops into relatively thin O&D markets currently served by hub connections; time-elasticity will therefore grow in importance as a determinant of demand in the revenue-rich long-haul business segment.

2. *Design of ground and inflight products* Product upgrades and relaunches are more likely to attract or defend market share than to stimulate an outright increase in market demand. In the final analysis, they are investments which need to be evaluated in terms of the returns anticipated relative to costs incurred – much as though they were tangible assets. What can make the mathematics rather difficult is the fact that upgrading 'hard' product features, such as the inflight service environment or the range of amenities offered, may have an unquantifiable but nonetheless positive effect on 'soft' variables, such as

employee morale, motivation, and attitudes. This effect broadens the dimensions across which consumers' experiences are being improved and contributes, through enhanced satisfaction, to higher levels of customer retention and to higher revenues.

Those LFAs such as Virgin Blue and jetBlue which have moved away from the hard-core low-fare model by adding frills (i.e., product attributes) are consciously trying to uncover and exploit marketing elasticities in order to penetrate higher-yielding market segments thought previously to be the preserve of network airlines. Their low cost bases generally allow them to do this profitably, and to the extent they are successful they will put pressure on the yield premia that some established carriers still need to earn in order to cover their own higher costs.

If an airline exercises monopoly power, in which case its demand curve is equivalent to the market demand curve, service enhancements are likely to be reflected in higher prices for the same level of output (Morrison and Winston 1989). The more competitive the market, the more likely they are to be reflected – at least in the short run – in increased sales (Homan op. cit.). Airline managers would therefore clearly benefit from an understanding of the impact that changes in product attributes will have on traffic and revenues. Unfortunately, whilst variations in service attributes can certainly affect demand, the nature and size of the causal relationships have not been widely studied and can be difficult to establish.

Quality Of Service Delivery

The MITRE Corporation has found that a one per cent improvement in on-time performance increases passenger demand by 0.43 per cent (ibid.). By reducing consumer uncertainty, better on-time performance increases the value of the service and shifts the carrier's demand curve to the right. Improvements in other operational metrics such as reduced baggage loss and, in airfreight markets, higher flown-as-booked rates can have a similarly positive effect – although it has to be emphasised that the precise numbers are not well understood.

Investment in remedying service failure (i.e., delivery perceived to be below customers' expectations) also needs to be looked at as expenditure that carries potential revenue implications – in this case future revenue saved. Holloway (2002) discusses service failure at some length. The point as far as the present book is concerned is that each category of recurrent service failure (either across the network or in a specific market) will affect an identifiable number of passengers, a percentage of whom will not repurchase and some of whom will spread adverse word-of-mouth; the cost of remedying the problem by enhancing service design or delivery can therefore be compared against an estimate of revenue preserved. (See Heskett *et al.* [1997, pp. 47–48] for a brief example of some numbers generated by British Airways using this approach.)

Marketing Communications, Frequent Flyer Programmes, And Branding

Advertising has an elasticity of demand associated with it. Airline advertising might be targeted at corporate image enhancement, it might be a price- or destination-oriented market-specific message, or it might focus on targeted segments such as business or leisure travellers irrespective of route. (Note that if price-oriented there is a question whether we are dealing with price-elasticity as well as advertising elasticity, and if destination-oriented there is a danger that some of any stimulated demand will be picked up by competitors.) Whatever form advertising takes, it is important – but usually quite difficult – to establish how much additional traffic (and, ideally, revenue) is generated by every dollar of expenditure. A low advertising elasticity of demand would imply that an airline must spend substantial amounts of money to shift a demand curve in the desired direction (i.e., to the right). In this case, there could possibly be more cost-effective alternatives – such as sports promotion (an approach particularly favoured by Emirates, for example), or offers targeted directly at FFP members.

Studies have found that FFP membership, particularly active membership, can be a significant determinant of airline choice in certain cases (e.g., Proussaloglou and Koppelman 1995). Whether it outweighs schedule convenience in the case of business travellers and price in the case of leisure travellers depends on individual choice processes, but taking these segments as a whole there has to be doubt that it does.

One reason airlines spend money on FFPs, brand image, advertising, and other sources of distinctiveness is to shift the demand curve rightwards and to dampen price-elasticity, particularly amongst high-value customers, by steepening it. The outcome should ideally be an ability to raise prices without having an unduly negative impact on sales. In many markets, of course, there are segments whose members will respond to these non-price determinants of demand only if the carrier concerned is at least matching competitors on price.

Conclusion

The concept of marketing elasticities is closely tied to the distinction drawn by marketers between 'expansible' and 'inexpansible' markets. These models rest at either end of a continuum:

- Expansible markets are sensitive to industry-wide marketing efforts, and within the industry individual market shares will be sensitive to particular airlines' initiatives. In this case, a carrier's revenue forecast will to a considerable extent depend not only on obvious demand determinants such as price and income levels, but also on how much effort and cash it is prepared to invest in non-price elements of the marketing mix. Forecast traffic and revenue is therefore an outgrowth of the marketing plan.
- At the other end of the continuum, an inexpansible market offers little more than an opportunity to push on the proverbial 'piece of string': levels of marketing expenditure will have little direct bearing on demand.

Most airline markets are located closer to the expansible than to the inexpansible end of this continuum. One of commercial management's primary tasks is to identify approximately where – that is, to identify the marketing elasticities it faces – and invest accordingly.

A final point which applies to most types of elasticity is that time is inevitably a consideration. The long-run elasticity of any demand-determining independent variable tends to be greater than its short-run elasticity. This is because there is a time-lag between most types of event likely to affect demand and the materialisation of that effect, while information about the event reaches consumers and is processed. (Major, instantaneous exogenous shocks such as 9/11 are an obvious exception.) Also, the more time that elapses, the greater the likelihood that substitution possibilities will arise.

SUMMARY

What underlies the demand for air transport is people's desire to travel – to be somewhere else in order to gain satisfaction from the experience or from the business done. As desire is impossible to model, demand is analysed relative to determinants which are for the most part more easily accessible and quantifiable. Demand is a function of (i.e., depends upon) several determinants, notably including: price, and the price outlook, in respect of the service concerned and available substitutes; the prices of complementary services such as hotel accommodation and car rental; the number of consumers potentially present in the market; income levels and general economic conditions; the volume and quality of supply (i.e., output offered, whether routings are non-stop, direct, or connecting, and the frequency of service); consumer tastes and preferences; exchange rates (in international markets); and the effect of actively managed non-price marketing mix variables such as product design (including schedules, and ground and inflight products), distribution, advertising, and promotion. Price and income are usually cited as the two most important drivers. Although distinct, the two work in unison. Whereas in 1955 an average Australian would have had to work for 130 weeks to pay for a ticket from Sydney to London, in 2006 it would have taken less than a fortnight to earn the fare; a ticket on Japan Air Lines' inaugural Tokyo–San Francisco service in 1954 cost 100 per cent of the prevailing Japanese annual average wage, whereas 50 years later a discounted ticket could be bought for around 3 per cent of the 2004 average wage (JITI 2006). Huge gains in the efficiency of airframes and powerplants have allowed real airfares to fall, and the positive income effect from this has been reinforced by economic growth contributing to significant gains in actual incomes.

An entrant needs to consider what effect its arrival – specifically, its output, pricing, product design, advertising, and promotional decisions – will have on demand, what reactions this is likely to provoke from incumbents, and how it might choose to respond to incumbents' reactions. (Game theory can be used to help with this type of strategic assessment; see Besanko *et al.* 2000, for example.) In the final analysis, managers have to decide what value they are able to bring to customers in a particular market or segment, how competitors are likely to behave, what revenues can be earned, and whether these revenues will exceed service delivery costs by a sufficient margin to earn an acceptable return. Embedded in this judgement are service and operations management issues that we will be touching upon throughout the book.

V. Characteristics of Air Transport Demand

Air transport demand has several important characteristics: it is a 'derived demand'; it can be strongly influenced by the supply of output; it is prone to marked fluctuations over time; and, in some markets, it is subject to directional imbalances in either the volume or the timing of traffic flows. The following subsections briefly consider each of these characteristics.

DERIVED DEMAND

This chapter opened with a quote from Tom Peters: 'Markets don't buy services – customers do.' In other words, demand in any market is a reflection of the purchase behaviour of many individual customers. Neoclassical microeconomic theory recognises two types of individual demand: direct and derived.

1. *Direct demand* comes from individuals who want to consume goods and services which themselves satisfy needs and wants.
2. *Derived demand* applies in respect of intermediate goods and services acquired for their contribution to some other good or service rather than for their own intrinsic worth. Aside from pleasure flights, demand for air transport is just such an intermediate service. It is derived indirectly from the demand for the final service or purpose to which it contributes – notably business meetings, visits to friends or relatives, vacations, trips to and from educational institutions, or the requirement to ship goods rapidly to wherever they are needed.

Because intermediate services such as air transport are not generally wanted for consumption in their own right, demand will depend on:

*   Demand for the underlying purposes of travel.
*   The costs and benefits offered relative to alternative intermediate inputs – that is, relative to substitutes. For freight shippers, such alternatives might be truck haulage over short or medium distances and sea, sea-land or sea-air combinations to more distant destinations. For business travellers, electronic media are rapidly becoming viable intermediate services for satisfying some of their needs to communicate with colleagues, suppliers, and customers. Vacationers on short-haul routes may have alternative intermediate services available in the form of surface transport modes.
*   The proportion of the cost of the end-product which is accounted for by airfares or freight rates. A large absolute increase in fares would have a greater proportional impact on the overall cost of a short vacation or business trip than on one planned to last considerably longer. Fares are also likely to constitute a higher proportion of expenditure on a VFR trip than on a vacation or a business trip, because VFR passengers generally stay with the friends or relations being visited and so spend relatively little on accommodation.

Unlike many intermediate products which, as far as consumers are concerned, are submerged into the end-product and only get attention if they contribute to a product failure, air transport services are separable and directly experienced in their own right. This presents opportunities:

1. Airlines are free to design, price, distribute, and promote their products so as to maximise the value provided to consumers in much the same way as if they were indeed dealing with direct demand.
2. They are also free to identify the service being offered with the satisfaction of consumers' ultimate needs and wants. This can be done by promoting a leisure destination, for example, or by bundling air transport services into a vacation package (organized either by an in-house unit or by an external packager).

On the other hand, because the demand for seats or cargo space is a derived demand, an airline could offer service which might in many respects represent excellent customer value but still lose traffic if the end product – whether business trips or vacations to a particular destination – is for whatever reason losing popularity. Similarly, airlines might find themselves competing with each other even where there is no route overlap; for example, somebody who wants a break might choose a Ryanair destination over an easyJet destination or vice versa simply because the fare to one is cheaper than the fare to the other at the time she wants to travel (i.e., the destinations are strong substitutes).

THE INFLUENCE OF SUPPLY

Airline managers have limited control over demand, but use of pricing, revenue management, promotional, and loyalty programmes enables them to influence it to a greater extent than has been possible in the past. A more fundamental way to exert influence over demand is through manipulation of supply. 'Supply' in this context means not just raw output, but also the quality of service offered in respect of frequencies, departure and arrival times, seat accessibility, routings (i.e., non-stop, multi-stop or connecting service), and on-time performance. Enhanced supply can stimulate demand. (Note the particular way in which the word 'quality' is used here. When transport economists discuss 'the quality of service' their interest tends primarily to be in the variables listed above. On the other hand, the services management and marketing literatures often measure service quality as the gap between customers' expectations and perceptions of service across a much broader range of benefits – including, for example, amenities, cabin comfort, the style and tone of service delivery, and brand associations. Use of the word 'quality' in this chapter follows the economists' approach. Later in the book we will broaden the discussion of supply/output to encompass different types of ground and inflight product.)

There are many examples of the impact that supply can have on demand. To take just three:

1. Prior to the 1995 United States–Canada Open Transborder Air Services Agreement, passenger traffic between the two countries was growing at around 3 per cent per annum. In the first year of the new agreement – a period during which US carriers still had only limited growth rights at Toronto, Montreal, and Vancouver under negotiated phase-in provisions – traffic expanded by 14 per cent. Between 1995 and 2004, traffic was on average around 3.3 million enplanements per annum greater than had been forecasted in 1994 (InterVISTAS Consulting 2005). This acceleration was largely due to the availability of new, non-stop cross-border routes made possible by market liberalisation.
2. The entry of LFAs onto several hundred previously unserved intra-European routes over the last decade has both responded to and stimulated demand in markets which established carriers had either ignored or served only through connecting hubs.
3. The European Commission has estimated that the open skies agreement which came into effect between the United States and Europe in March 2008 will lead to a 50 per cent increase in transatlantic passenger numbers within 5 years – although quite how the palpable sense of euphoria surrounding announcement of this estimate should sit with the same body's environmental agenda, the implications of which threaten profitable long-term air transport growth, is not clear. (Reitzes and Robyn [2007] provide a comprehensive analysis of the economic impact anticipated from a Transatlantic Open Aviation Area.)

A different but not unrelated point, which was touched upon above in the context of time-elasticity, is that a carrier which expands supply to the extent that it dominates output on a route is widely believed to be able to secure for itself a disproportionately large market share. This is known as the 'S-curve' effect because of the shape of the curve derived from plotting frequencies (on the vertical axis) against market share. (We are assuming here that output dominance arises from offering more, well-timed, departures rather than from flying larger aircraft than competitors.) The rationale is that any wasted time between precisely when a passenger wants to depart and when the scheduled departure nearest to that time allows them to depart detracts from the quality of service being offered. The airline operating the highest frequencies in a market will stand a better chance of having a departure close to the times desired by a greater proportion of potential travellers than will its competitors. It is therefore offering a better quality of service in this important dimension, and so will carry a larger proportion of traffic than its share of aggregate output. In other words, an airline which builds for itself a frequency advantage – whether on a single route or out of a particular airport – will be rewarded with a proportionately greater market share advantage (Fruhan 1972).

Not all observers accept the existence of the S-curve relationship. For example, relatively small competitors with a strong brand image and what is perceived to be a competitive value proposition might be able to retain a market share premium (i.e., a higher percentage share of traffic than of total output offered) without frequency domination – something Virgin quickly achieved after entering the North Atlantic market, for example. Furthermore, some segments of demand are clearly more price-sensitive than time-sensitive – notably the leisure and VFR segments, which if the price is low enough may well be prepared to wait. On the whole, however, there is still a widespread belief in the S-curve relationship; this sometimes leads competitors to over-schedule.

FLUCTUATIONS IN DEMAND

The trend growth rate for global RPKs masks three important facts:

1. Pronounced regional variations in rates of growth: markets to, from, and within Asia have shown particularly strong rates of growth as, for different reasons and off a significantly lower traffic base, have markets to and through the Middle East.
2. Pronounced variations in growth rates between market segments.
3. Pronounced temporal fluctuations: Table 2.2 tracks these since the mid-1980s.

Demand is subject to secular effects and to cyclical, periodic, and irregular fluctuations.

Secular Effects

Although growth has slowed compared to the heady rates of expansion in the 1960s, 1970s, and 1980s, global passenger demand is still projected to expand at an annual average rate of 5 per cent or better over the next two decades (the precise figure depending upon the source of the forecast); air cargo demand is on track to expand at a considerably faster rate. As we have seen, these averages mask regional variations, with markets in some areas of

Table 2.2   Year-on-year traffic growth rates 1985–2006

Scheduled traffic	1985	1986	1987	1988	1989	1990	1991	1992	1993	1994	1995
World airlines (RPK growth %)	7.0	6.2	9.5	7.3	4.0	6.8	-2.6	4.5	1.1	7.7	7.1
US airlines (RPM growth %)	10.2	9.0	10.3	4.6	2.2	5.8	-2.2	6.8	2.3	6.1	4.1
World airlines (FTK growth %)	0.4	8.4	11.9	10.2	7.3	2.9	-0.4	7.0	9.3	12.8	7.7

Scheduled traffic	1996	1997	1998	1999	2000	2001	2002	2003	2004	2005	2006
World airlines (RPK growth %)	8.2	5.8	2.1	6.4	8.6	-2.9	0.5	1.8	14.1	8.0	5.2
US airlines (RPM growth %)	7.0	4.3	2.4	5.5	6.2	-5.9	-1.6	2.5	11.7	6.2	2.3
World airlines (FTK growth %)	7.3	15.3	-1.0	6.7	8.7	-6.2	8.2	4.9	10.5	2.5	5.0

Sources: World airlines – ICAO; US airlines – Air Transport Assocation of America

the world (e.g., US domestic and Western Europe) being more mature than others (e.g., intra-Asia, Europe–Asia, the North Pacific, and Latin America). Generalisations should be treated with caution, however; prior to a pronounced slow-down in demand beginning in 2005, the supposedly mature UK leisure market was explicitly described by the CAA (2005) as 'not near to maturity'.

There is anyway some debate regarding how to define a 'mature' market. Graham (2000, p. 112) identifies three widely used approaches:

- Maturity evidenced by a declining rate of growth in enplanements or RPMs and RTMs.
- Maturity evidenced by declining income-elasticity of demand or, more specifically, by a decline in income-elasticity to unity or below.
- Maturity evidenced by declining growth in air transport revenues as a percentage of nominal GDP. For example, US airline passenger revenue has fallen to around 0.7 per cent of US nominal GDP having trended over 0.9 per cent in the two decades prior to 2000.

As markets mature in more developed economies and the number of first-time flyers as a proportion of annual enplanements in these economies diminishes, further substantial demand growth comes to rely more heavily on encouraging increased usage amongst existing customers rather than attracting new customers to the industry. The number of US citizens that has ever flown, for example, rose rapidly in the 1970s but levelled off in the 70–75 per cent range during the mid-1980s (James 1993). The continuing growth of LFAs is expected to stimulate further demand amongst segments of mature markets that fly irregularly if at all, but incremental demand from customers who already travel reasonably frequently will probably be more important. In less mature markets such as Asia and Latin America, there is still plenty of room for both types of growth.

Cyclical Fluctuations

The airline industry's strong secular growth trend has been marred by pronounced cyclicality, due in large part to the relatively high income-elasticity of demand for air transport services. The effect of demand-, and therefore revenue-, cyclicality on airlines' financial performances is magnified by their generally high short-run operating leverage (i.e., high proportion of fixed to total costs) and financial leverage (i.e., high level of interest-bearing debt as a percentage of total liabilities plus net worth).

The classic industry demand cycle runs though the following stages:

1. Airline revenue growth peaks, buoyed by firm yields and strong traffic, but growth in the wider economy (GDP) begins to slow. Aircraft orders may peak here, but commonly they peak a year or so after the top of the traffic growth cycle.
2. The rate of traffic growth gradually declines over the next 6–9 months as consumer and business confidence are eroded. In a severe recession such as the early 1990s and 2001/2002 demand might actually fall, but in most cases what happens is that the rate of demand growth remains positive whilst dropping below the long-term trend-line. Discretionary travel weakens and companies pay closer attention to the number of trips, the number of people travelling, and the class of service. Business travel tends to lead leisure travel in slowing into a recession. Airline profits quickly come under pressure because high operating and financial leverage continue to generate fixed costs that cannot rapidly be reduced in response to stagnant or declining revenues.
3. Airlines take delivery of aircraft ordered earlier, at the peak of the economic cycle when demand was strong and projections were bullish. (Indeed, the turning point in an equipment cycle has historically been called when aircraft deliveries overtake orders and the airframe manufacturers' backlogs start falling.) Overcapacity is worsened and, if sufficiently severe, results in significant numbers of aircraft being taken out of service – temporarily when new or young, perhaps permanently if fuel-inefficient or expensive to maintain. Some aircraft orders are cancelled or deferred. At the same time, further efforts are made, particularly with regard to labour expenses, to adjust cost structures in line with lower or more slowly growing revenues.
4. The economy bottoms out. Traffic might be holding up reasonably well in response to fare wars as airlines struggle to fill surplus capacity which has not been parked, but yields (i.e., revenue per RPM or RTM) remain weak.
5. Several months after the economy begins to recover, consumer and business confidence pick up across a broader base, traffic growth accelerates, discounts becomes less aggressive and more selective, yields improve somewhat, and load factors rise. Recovery of business traffic may lag the upturn in economic activity; after 9/11, for example, leisure traffic rebounded more strongly than business traffic, particularly in the United States.
6. As the economy nears its peak, profits recover first at the operating level and then on a net basis as rising demand and firmer yields combine with measures taken earlier in the cycle to control costs and capacity. Parked aircraft are brought back into service and orders for new lift begin to materialise. (The 2001/2002 downturn was different insofar as the advanced ages of many of the parked aircraft meant that a high proportion remained permanently grounded.)

Having described the 'textbook' model, there are two caveats:

- Several of the industry's more serious downturns have been due not just to the classic economic or business cycle but to the effect of external shocks such as the oil crises of the 1970s, the Gulf War, the Asian financial crisis of 1997, 9/11, Iraq, and SARS. These events either caused economic downturns or intensified recessions already underway. In each case, but particularly after 9/11, the impact on traffic and yields was felt more quickly than suggested above.
- Many observers believe that the significant growth in demand for air travel forecast for Asia, particularly China and India, over the next two decades will be sufficient to moderate the effect (at a global level) of future cyclical downturns attributable to economic slowdowns in North America or Europe.

There are four points in particular to note with regard to the cyclicality of demand. First, whilst the overall outlook for global economic growth (using indicators such as GDP, trade, industrial output, etc.) is widely seen as positive, periodic economic downturns will continue to punish overinvestment in capacity, unbridled pursuit of market share, and ill-timed corporate acquisitions made at the top of the cycle; by raising the importance of low prices to consumers, downturns also penalise bloated costs and boost the strategic position of LFAs. Because this is still on the whole a growth industry, any given percentage drop in traffic growth implies a larger absolute number than a similar drop would have led to in the past – potentially leading to a correspondingly larger volume of unsold output. The stakes in the capacity management 'game', and the importance of operational flexibility, are therefore rising.

Second, given high short-run fixed costs and attendant volume dependency, the profitability of scheduled airlines is always going to be profoundly sensitive to the effect of economic cycles on their revenue streams.

Third, in international markets the economies at either end might not be experiencing synchronised economic cycles; any resulting imbalance between the sources of originating traffic will have both marketing and currency exposure implications. This points to one possible advantage of having a geographically dispersed portfolio of international routes, as opposed to a purely domestic system. More generally, a wide network broadens the portfolio of market risks; an airline serving a small number of markets or market segments, particularly a network carrier relying on high-yield traffic, will be more adversely affected by a demand downturn in one of them than will a competitor with a better spread of markets to serve.

Finally, the cyclicality of air transport demand has been used as a justification for the diversification strategies implemented by a number of airlines and airline holding companies. Often these are strategies of 'related diversification' intended to leverage resources and capabilities in MRO, catering, ground-handling, and other fields related to the core passenger and/or cargo transportation business. Whilst businesses such as these are themselves exposed to cyclicality in the demand for air transport services, the argument is that they are less exposed than are flying activities and to this extent provide a hedge – albeit an imperfect hedge – to protect corporate revenues in a downturn.

Periodic Fluctuations: Demand Peaking

Annual traffic figures conceal pronounced peaking of seasonal, weekly, and daily demand. When peaks actually occur in any given market depends upon the nature of the market concerned, notably whether it is oriented primarily towards business or leisure segments and whether it is short- or long-haul.

Seasonal peaking   Seasonal peaks in passenger markets are driven by customs and festivals such as Haj, the eids, Christmas or Thanksgiving, and by vacation practices. Charter (i.e., nonscheduled) carriers serving leisure markets face the most intense seasonal peaking problem. The low-season charter market out of the United Kingdom, for example, is rarely more than one-third of the summer peak despite the shifting of capacity from Mediterranean resorts to skiing and long-haul sun destinations. This type of demand fluctuation creates different operational problems from daily or weekly peaks, requiring carriers to employ large numbers of temporary and part-time staff and to work hard each year at deploying surplus aircraft during the low season; some charter carriers have responded by moving aircraft into scheduled service (e.g., airberlin). Neither are scheduled carriers immune from heavy seasonal variations in leisure demand; traffic on North Atlantic routes, for example, usually peaks in the summer at twice the level of the February trough. Because scheduled airlines in the US domestic market carry a higher proportion of leisure traffic than most scheduled European airlines (with the exception of Air Malta, Finnair, and the LFAs), they also experience steep first (calendar) quarter downturns in demand. Canadian carriers face a marked drop-off in demand during the winter which they offset by reallocating aircraft to sun destinations in Mexico and the Caribbean; WestJet has a large winter charter programme, for example. Indeed, demand peaking is such that some northern hemisphere network carriers have at times relied on the third quarter to make sufficient operating profit and generate sufficient cash to carry them through the other quarters.

   Seasonal peaking also occurs in many airfreight markets, with the pre-Christmas surge, the introduction of each new season's clothing lines, and the seasonal bulge in shipments of different types of fresh foodstuffs out of their production areas being three obvious examples.

   When analysing monthly or quarterly traffic figures with a view to looking through seasonal influences for a longer-term trend, there is merit in basing the comparison on the same period in previous years rather than the immediately preceding month or quarter. A year-to-date versus year-to-date comparison would also avoid seasonal bias.

Weekly peaking   Particularly in short-haul business markets, extreme peaking is common on Monday mornings and Friday afternoons/evenings. Traffic in the US domestic system on Fridays is generally around 10 per cent higher than on other weekdays. Conversely, many long-haul markets and short-haul city-break markets peak at the weekend.

Daily peaking   Short-haul business markets tend to have a pronounced morning peak, perhaps a midday mini-peak, and a longer, less-pronounced late-afternoon/early evening peak; the morning and evening peaks are often intensified where day-return business trips are feasible in a particular market. Daily peaking on long-haul flights is usually driven by the effect of time zones, which create preferred departure and arrival 'windows' influenced both by consumer preferences and airport curfews or movement quotas.

Conclusion   The costs of meeting peak demand are high if this entails having capacity lie idle in off-peak periods; capacity-related fixed costs such as lease rentals, depreciation, and insurance have to be charged to the income statement whether or not an aircraft is airborne. The less that aircraft and other assets are used during off-peak periods, the more these and similar fixed costs will have to be recovered from peak-period traffic – perhaps by charging higher fares, or accepting a lower profit, than would be the case were off-peak demand higher. This is a serious management challenge. An airline filling on average, say, 70–75 per cent of its seats will be spilling demand during peak periods and yet still be flying aircraft with little more than half their output sold off-peak. The greater the scope of its network – in terms of both numbers and types of destination – and the wider the range of market segments served, the better able an airline should be to spread utilisation of its aircraft and other resources.

Irregular Fluctuations

Peak/off-peak fluctuations are systemic and reasonably predictable on an average basis. Individual departures, on the other hand, are subject to demand irregularities which make prediction much more difficult. Even if it is known that traffic on a particular departure can be expected to fluctuate by as much as, say, 25 per cent either side of the mean for a given period, managers cannot know with complete confidence what demand will be like for any given flight. Complicating matters further is the fact that random demand variability differs between market segments, with demand from business travellers generally more volatile on a per-departure basis than demand from other segments; this is one reason why cabin planning factors (i.e., target load factors) tend to be lower in business and first class cabins than in coach/economy cabins – the intent being to minimise spill. However, increasingly sophisticated demand analysis tools embedded in revenue management systems are gradually improving predictive capabilities. (Some European network carriers have responded to inter-cabin demand variability by using movable curtains or partitions between business and economy classes.)

Random fluctuations can be particularly marked in airfreight markets. Even in regional, as opposed to city-pair, markets there can be wide fluctuations in year-on-year growth rates which are difficult to predict.

Summary

The demand for a particular flight will vary around a secular trend in response to certain reasonably predictable cyclical and periodic influences and less predictable irregular influences; the effects of the latter can only be estimated stochastically. Demand is generally assumed to be normally distributed, with a mean and a standard deviation which depend on the traffic mix in the market concerned: the greater the business element in a market, the more variable the pattern of demand and the flatter the distribution. Demand fluctuations have to be addressed by a combination of pricing and capacity management such that load factors and yields are acceptable. An 'acceptable' target load factor is one that is not so low as to waste resources producing unsold output, and not so high as to cause unacceptable demand spill; an 'acceptable' yield on traffic carried is one that generates sufficient revenue to cover costs and either achieve or exceed profit and shareholder value objectives. We will revisit these challenges in subsequent chapters.

DIRECTIONALITY

Pure directionality problems are a characteristic of the airfreight business, whereas directionality on the passenger side is more a matter of timing and is closely connected to the peaking problem.

Freight Markets

Flows of freight on any given route are rarely balanced in each direction. This could be because of different levels of commercial activity at either end of the route as a result of the two points being at separate stages of the economic cycle. It might also be because changing relative strengths of the two currencies concerned, if the market is international, affect consumer buying power. For example, the strength or weakness of the dollar against European currencies is one of the determinants of demand directionality in North Atlantic freight markets; dollar strength (or, depending on the point of view, persistent undervaluation of Asian currencies) also tends to intensify eastbound North Pacific flows, which are anyway stronger than westbound flows because of structurally high US consumption of Asian exports.

Another common cause of directionality is the fact that some markets import larger volumes of goods suitable for carriage by air than they export. This is particularly true of countries which import high-value manufactured goods but export bulk commodities. For example, in value terms, Australasia imports almost three times as much by air as it exports.

Passenger Markets

Demand directionality tends to be much less pronounced in passenger markets because most journeys are return. There are three issues of possible importance, however.

1. There can certainly be short-term mismatches in the directional flows of passenger traffic, which cause peaking at different times in different directions on the same route. For example, more people leave the Middle East in June and July than enter it, while the reverse is true in late August and September. More people fly into a leisure destination such as Las Vegas or Reno on a Friday night than leave it, while on Sunday evenings there will be an outbound flow.

    On routes with a high proportion of day-return business traffic, one end might be a stronger originator of outbound morning flows than the other. Even where outbound morning demand is reasonably balanced, it could be that travellers in one direction generally require an earlier departure – perhaps because ground transfer times at their destination are longer and need to be taken into account when planning the working day (Clark 2001). Along with maintenance issues, parking and security costs, and crew scheduling and accommodation costs, these factors will influence where short-haul aircraft are 'stabled' overnight. We will return to this in Chapter 7.
2. The economic circumstances at either end of a route, and particularly relative exchange rates if the route is international, can affect which end generates the most outbound traffic. When the dollar is strong, for example, it is likely that more North Atlantic passengers will originate their journeys in the United States than when

the dollar is weak. Although directional flows are not in this case unbalanced in the sense that they are in many freight markets, which end of a route is the most significant traffic generator might be important from a marketing perspective: an airline based in a strong outbound market can be expected to have a larger marketing organization there than one based elsewhere, and therefore better access to originating traffic.

3. Extending the last point, demand characteristics at either end of a market might be very different. For example, the LA–London return market (i.e., LA-originating demand) is not the same as the London–LA return market. There is a need for good local knowledge of demand at both ends of any city-pair market.

Directional (or timing) imbalances in passenger flows clearly feed through to load factors. Assume, for instance, high demand for an outbound flight from a hub down a spoke to a secondary city at a particular time of day and significantly lower demand for the return flight. Accommodating all the outbound demand implies a low return load factor, whilst operating a smaller aircraft to raise the return load factor will lead to loss of revenue from demand spilled off the outbound leg. This is a problem with several dimensions:

- it is a fleet assignment problem, insofar as we want to operate an aircraft sized to balance the revenue lost from spilled demand on the high-demand flight against the costs of offering too much output for sale on the return leg;
- it is a network management problem insofar as network design which links a spoke or secondary city to more than one hub or other major station can allow aircraft to be flowed across the spoke/secondary city from one hub/major station to another, rather than having to operate a low-demand return leg as part of an out-and-back rotation;
- it is a pricing and revenue management problem insofar as the price and availability of discounted fares will probably have a significant role to play in raising load factors on low-demand return flights.

Generally, a carrier is successfully managing capacity on a route if it is able to consistently achieve a targeted average load factor which balances the revenue spill inherent in operating aircraft that are too small against the higher costs and lower yields inherent in operating aircraft that are too large. We will return to this in Part 3 of the book.

VI. Modelling, Forecasting, and Allocating Air Transport Demand

DEMAND MODELLING

Although the theory of air travel demand is now reasonably well established, relatively few empirical studies of the demand for air travel in specific markets, particularly outside the United States, have been published (Melville 1998; Battersby and Oczkowski 2001). Whilst those models that have been developed often differ with regard to the determinants of demand that they incorporate, Jorge-Calderón (1997) has usefully summarised the demand drivers most widely used (all of which were discussed or referred to above in the section on elasticity).

1. *Geo-economic factors* There are two categories:
    *   *Activity factors* These describe the demographic, commercial, industrial, and cultural characteristics of origin and destination catchment areas; income and population are the most commonly adopted.
    *   *Locational factors* Distance is a key locational factor, but one with a split 'personality'. Demand is generally taken to be negatively associated with increased distance between origin and destination, yet the further apart they are the less intermodal competition there is and so the greater the share of transportation demand that goes to airlines.
        Several studies of air transport demand have relied on various forms of 'gravity model', using activity and locational determinants.
2. *Value* This is usually taken to encompass what are from a customer's perspective the two key aspects of output: quality of the product and price paid.
    *   *Quality* The variables most commonly used for demand modelling have been:
        -   *Frequency* The argument is that 'time costs money', so the greater the number of departures the less variance there is between preferred and actual departure times, the better the quality of service, and the higher demand is likely to be.
        -   *Load factor* High load factors are assumed to be associated with lower seat accessibility (i.e., a lower probability, at any given time a reservation is attempted, of being able to buy a seat in the preferred cabin on the required departure). This increases the risk of 'stochastic delay' (Douglas and Miller 1974a) arising from the non-availability of space.
        -   *Aircraft size and technology* Aircraft size and technology have been found to drive demand insofar as larger aircraft are associated with better inflight comfort, and turbofans are considered more customer-friendly than props.
        Although evidence with regard to the role of load factors is ambiguous, the other determinants in this category have been shown to be significant (Jorge-Calderón op. cit.). On the other hand, Melville (1998) suggests that linking the three in the same model invites multi-collinearity problems, because 'aircraft size × flight frequency × load factor' actually defines demand rather than accounts for it – with the result that using these determinants as independent variables in the demand function simply regresses demand on components of itself (ibid, pp. 316–317).
        What is beyond argument is that the dimensions of service quality used in most economists' models of air transport demand are far less extensive than the range of attributes that airline product and brand managers see as influencing customer purchase behaviour (and which are discussed in Holloway 2002). In part, this is because of the paucity of publicly available information on the impact on demand of 'soft' customer service attributes such as tone and style of service delivery, and even of harder attributes such as cabin configuration or inflight entertainment (IFE) and communication (IFC) facilities; furthermore, some of these attributes might have more impact on individual airlines' market shares and perhaps customer loyalty than on aggregate travel demand. The service quality variable that has in fact received most attention is the time-cost of travel, as reflected in frequencies, routings, and journey times.
    *   *Price* As the neoclassical 'law of demand' suggests it should be, demand has been found to be inversely related to price.

References to empirical research developing demand estimation models that use various combinations of these, and other, determinants can be found in Jorge-Calderón (op. cit., pp. 24–25).

Anecdotally, it appears that although the industry demand function may be reasonably well understood in principle, there are two areas of weakness: first, the precise impact of service attributes on demand has not yet been fully explained; and second, more general demand functions are often, inappropriately, used as proxies for the demand functions of specific individual markets (which may have very different demand characteristics and elasticities). Extending the last point, few empirical studies have endeavoured to model different segments of demand in the markets under consideration; notable exceptions include work on the Australian domestic market by Battersby and Oczkowski (2001).

The role of consumers' attitudes and perceptions is often given scant attention in air transport demand estimation models. Graham (2000), citing Swarbrooke and Horner (1999), distinguishes between factors which make travel feasible (such as economic and social conditions, pricing, schedule, and booking conditions) and factors that influence specific travel decisions (such as an individual consumer's personality, attitude, and perceptions of, for example, different airlines or particular leisure destinations). The latter generally receive more attention in the consumer behaviour, services management, brand management, and general marketing literatures than amongst economists.

DEMAND FORECASTING AND ALLOCATION

Demand forecasting is most commonly used by airlines as part of a two-stage process that also involves demand allocation. Figure 2.3 illustrates the relationship between the two.

Demand Forecasting

Whilst forecasts of aggregate demand at global, inter-regional, and intra-regional levels are important, what matters most to airlines is demand in the O&D city-pair markets that are available for them to serve (either alone or in cooperation with other carriers).

When dropping below the global or regional level of analysis it is important to recall the distinction between a route and a market. Demand on the New York (JFK)–London Heathrow (LHR) route, for example, is driven not only by local traffic but also by traffic originating behind JFK and/or continuing beyond LHR – in other words, by demand in other city-pair markets. Conversely, traffic in the Los Angeles–New York city-pair market might travel on routes originating at any of a number of LA area airports and fly on non-stop routes to any of a number of New York area airports, or it might use routes into and out of intermediate hubs such as Salt Lake City or Denver. The point is that we need to be clear that demand on a route between two airports may be very different from the demand in that same city-pair market – with the difference driven by whether or not the origin and/or destination cities are served by multi-airport systems and, more particularly, by the volume of flow traffic on the route. It is therefore critical that demand is forecast first on an O&D basis rather than a route basis, because traffic on individual routes is a function not just of demand but also of how airlines design their networks.

Demand forecasts are an amalgam of projections and predictions, tempered by judgement: a projection is an extrapolation of past trends into the future, whilst a prediction depends

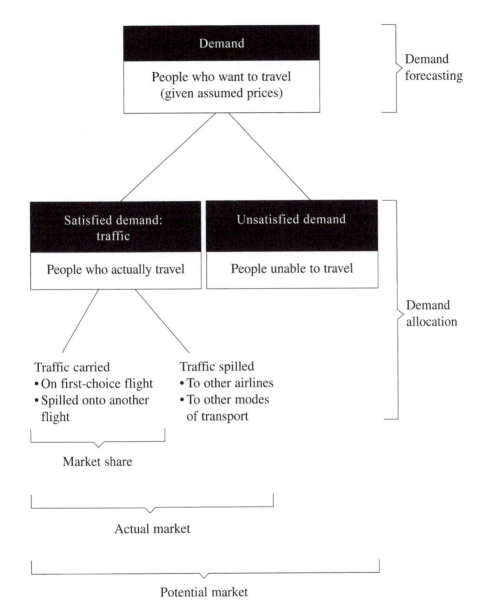

Figure 2.3   Demand forecasting and allocation

upon an assumed linkage between these trends and the underlying independent variables in the demand function that shape them – and a further assumption regarding the future development of those variables. By introducing an entirely new source of 'event risk' that is impossible to forecast yet has enormous human and economic consequences for the industry, 9/11 opened the now ever-present threat that a major discontinuity could arise at any time between historical data and current forecasts. On this latter point, however, it should be noted that although event risk can lead to extreme short-term disruption, the industry as a whole has proven itself to be remarkably resilient over the last several decades in eventually returning to long-term growth trends after externally imposed shocks.

The uses of forecasting   Demand forecasts – together with the market share and traffic forecasts developed from them – are the basis for revenue, cost, profit, and cash-flow forecasts, for managing the marketing mix, and for operational planning. Forecasting can have one or more of several dimensions:

- temporal: short-, medium- or long-term;
- geographical: global, inter-regional, intra-regional, domestic, and/or city-pair demand at an aggregate level;
- product-market: demand in different segments (i.e., for different products) in particular geographical markets over particular time periods.

The uses to which each type of forecast can be put inevitably vary. For example, short-term forecasts assist in scheduling and operational planning (i.e., staff rostering and equipment scheduling), whereas long-term forecasts – particularly as they apply to different geographical levels – are an essential input into network and fleet planning processes. The most useful might combine more than one dimension, such as medium-term forecasts for business class travel on an airline's short-haul international network. However, usefulness ultimately depends upon purpose.

Forecasts clearly have a significant impact on strategic behaviour. They should drive decisions in respect of:

- competitive (i.e., product and geographical) scope – including customer value, brand positioning, and design of ground and inflight services (i.e., design of the attributes intended to deliver expected benefits to targeted customers);
- design of the operating system that will deliver services;
- establishment of tariff structures in each market.

Some of these ideas were touched upon in Chapter 1 when we looked at cost and benefit advantage, the resources underpinning them, and the strategic positions that build upon them. Pricing is the subject of the next chapter. Holloway (2002) provides a comprehensive discussion of all these topics.

Forecasting methods   Choice of forecasting technique should be guided by: the objective(s) of the work; its time horizon; the data, study-time, and resources (financial and human) available; and the risks involved in acting on an incorrect forecast. Data availability in respect of O&D markets can be an issue for start-ups and new entrants in many parts of the world, whereas incumbents have access to proprietary in-house data. This is not a problem in the United States, where DOT data is notably rich (e.g., O&D Survey DB1A/B and T-100 Reports). More generally, any carrier with sufficiently deep pockets can purchase marketing information data tape (MIDT) and ticket control number (TCN) data from the GDSs or third-party providers. These have shortcomings: first, the data does not capture direct bookings made through airline websites and call centres, and this is one reason why it encompasses only around 60 per cent of industry bookings; second, unless the raw data is processed to account for booking irregularities (e.g., duplicate and passive bookings, errors and no-shows) it will be inaccurate. Nonetheless, it is one of the best sources available for the analysis and forecasting of international O&D markets because its geographic coverage is global and its sample size is large. IATA and Airlines Reporting Company (ARC) also provide agency ticketing data from their respective clearing-house operations (the latter relevant to US points of sale only); these sources suffer from geographic limitations.

The following forecasting methods are in common use. (For a more comprehensive and quantitative treatment of the field see Talluri and van Ryzin [2004, Chapter 9].)

1. *Trend analysis* Trend analyses of time-series data are widely used for short-term forecasting, particularly at the O&D market level, and in revenue management systems. Although simple and cheap, trend analysis addresses only one variable – time – and uses this as a proxy for the real underlying influences on demand. Nonetheless, a good number of market forecasts rely on trend analysis (usually moving averages, perhaps exponentially smoothed), supplemented by advance booking data and – particularly in the case of markets critical to a specific airline – manual adjustments based on experience and/or market research into travel intentions. (Note that some airlines use advance booking data as more than just a supplement to trend analysis; several plug this data into complex models which project forward bookings some distance into the future, and they use output from these models to guide capacity and pricing decisions and to forecast traffic and yield – sometimes in preference to more macro-level annual or seasonal forecasts [Robertson 2002].)

2. *Causal analysis* Two types of causal analysis are used:
   - *Econometric modelling* Econometric models are constructed around estimated statistical relationships between a dependent variable such as passenger enplanements or RPMs and several independent (i.e., explanatory) variables such as those discussed earlier in the chapter (e.g., price, income, exchange rates, schedule, etc.); the relationships are derived from time-series data and applied to future projections or predictions of the explanatory variables to arrive at a forecast for the dependent variable. Whether the resulting model is estimated in linear or log-linear form will depend upon the form of equation best fitting the available data, but in the latter case the coefficients estimated for each of the independent variables will be the demand-elasticities of those variables (e.g., income, etc.).

     Used to generate global and regional as well as market-specific forecasts and widely considered one of the more sophisticated techniques available, econometric modelling is hostage to the continuity of the relationships between dependent and independent variables that it seeks to model, and to the accuracy of forecasts in respect of future changes affecting the independent variables. Until redesigned or recalibrated, econometric models are as exposed as trend analyses to discontinuities in historical data relationships caused by events such as a terrorist incident or deregulation affecting a significant market. Judgemental analysis, which is discussed below, may have a role to play here. Also, past relationships between macroeconomic variables and demand in a particular market can be disrupted by the entry of an LFA selling at very low fares.
   - *Gravity models* Referred to earlier in the chapter, these are spatial equilibrium models that work on the assumption that traffic between two points or regions varies directly in response to some economic or demographic measure of their size, perhaps intensified by ethnic or linguistic links, and inversely in relation to the distance between them (although the impact of intervening geographical barriers can distort this latter assumption). Gravity models tend to be more popular for examining demand in respect of modes other than air transport, although they are certainly used in the airline industry (see Bhadra and Kee 2008,

for example). Many are designed more to examine potential traffic movements in general than to forecast actual demand over a specific period of time.

Long-term forecasting undertaken by the world's larger airlines tends to rely heavily on econometric modelling, particularly when a top-down approach is used to analyse global, inter-regional, and intra-regional markets. ICAO, IATA, FAA, and various regional trade associations as well as the major airframe and engine manufacturers also produce aggregate forecasts based on econometric models.

3. *Market research* Market research, notably surveys encompassing interviews and/or questionnaires, can be used to:
    *   track current demand (e.g., segments travelling and their price- and income-elasticity);
    *   forecast future demand (i.e., purchase intentions and willingness to purchase in response to price and other incentives);
    *   investigate the effectiveness of alternative service attributes (e.g., schedule, cabin design, onboard service processes, etc.).

    The three are closely linked. One of the industry's most significant surveys is IATA's Worldwide Traffic Forecast Survey, which annually polls member airlines regarding their 15-year views on traffic in over 2,000 country-pairs.

4. *Judgemental analysis* Judgemental methods include scenario analysis, individual expert judgement, brainstorming, group consensus-building, and the Delphi method. Some are essentially educated guesses. That they are subjective does not necessarily make them more questionable than 'scientific' forecasting techniques, but their worth in practice will depend upon who is involved and whether action based on what is forecast has the backing of sufficiently powerful interests within the airline concerned. There is in fact an argument that uncertain times subject to unforeseeable and potentially significant discontinuities open the door to insightful judgement wider than periods of routine, 'mechanical' growth.

    Market research and judgemental analysis can be particularly useful where historical data is unavailable, as in the case of a newly served market, or is erratic or unreliable, as is often true of airfreight demand in thin markets. They can also be used to forecast subjective variables for which time-series data is unavailable, or the effect of particularly radical developments for which there is no precedent in the data. Their usefulness is enhanced when there are relatively few buyers to consider, which is the case in many airfreight markets, and where research into specific planned developments at one end of a market – such as investment in the air transport or hotel/leisure infrastructure – is likely to provide a more accurate guide to the future than historical data. Finally, both can be used to augment other forecasting methods.

5. *Bayesian methods* Where a set of prior beliefs is held regarding future demand but there is no historical data to support them, Bayesian methods can be used to specify those beliefs and then update them as demand data actually arrives. They link prior subjective judgement to a quantitative analysis of what subsequently happens. An obvious application is entry onto a new route where historical demand data is lacking.

These approaches are not mutually exclusive. For example, in developing its annual long-term forecasts for commercial aviation the FAA takes a blended approach, using trend analysis for the forthcoming year and econometric modelling for the balance of the forecast period; both the forecasts and the assumptions underlying them are also subjected to qualitative assessments of reasonableness by industry experts (FAA 2006).

Returning to Figure 2.3, we can see that whatever demand is forecasted to come forward might be left unsatisfied (e.g., at peak periods), or it might be satisfied – either by the airline undertaking the analysis or by a competitor (including, perhaps, a competing mode of transport). Satisfied demand is referred to as 'traffic'. The decisions underlying all this are part of the 'demand allocation' problem.

Demand Allocation

This section will look first at unconstrained demand and spill – concepts relevant to the topic of demand allocation. It will then turn to demand allocation itself.

Unconstrained demand and spill   Discussing 'demand' so far in this chapter, no distinction has been drawn between unconstrained demand and demand which is constrained by an insufficient supply of output to satisfy it at the time it arises. In fact we need to distinguish between the following:

- Demand – specifically, unconstrained demand – is the total number of passengers willing and able to travel on a particular departure.
- Traffic is that subset of demand – which could be considered 'constrained demand' – that has been able to obtain space and travel.
- Spill is that subset of demand that has been unable to obtain space because demand exceeds available supply. (Spill = demand – traffic.)

Demand for a flight which departs full can only be estimated, because airlines cannot know with certainty how many potential purchasers were unable to travel as a result of the space constraint; spill can therefore only be estimated. Whether or not unconstrained demand can be met will depend upon the decisions which carriers take regarding the volume and timing of output they put into that market. In other words, the source of constraint in a market is the airlines' output decisions – which may not, in tightly regulated markets, be purely commercial.

Estimates of unconstrained demand and spill are particularly important in fleet planning and fleet assignment analyses: if a particular departure (i.e., a series of flights on a route leaving at the same time on the same day of the week throughout a scheduling season) has a high average load factor implying that output is insufficient to satisfy unconstrained demand and some of that demand is being spilled, can profit be raised by purchasing a larger type or assigning one already in the fleet? Spill models – many developed by the leading airframe manufacturers, some by academic institutions (notably MIT), and others by specialised software suppliers – are available to help answer the question. They do this by assuming a normal distribution with the mean and standard deviation estimated on the basis of actual load data drawn from a large sample of flights, never just one flight alone, then applying statistical estimation techniques to generate spill tables (Boeing 1979). Spill costs can be derived from such estimates:

(estimated number of passengers spilled from the flight less the number estimated to have been recaptured by booking on an alternative flight operated by the same airline) × revenue per available seat mile × stage-length.

We will return to this topic in Chapters 7 and 8.

Demand allocation and market share   How much traffic an airline carries in the O&D markets it serves will therefore depend upon several variables: the unconstrained demand coming forward in those markets; the volume and nature of output the airline produces in each; and the volume and nature of output produced by competitors. 'Volume and nature' refers to variables such as the size of aircraft used, the schedule, the routing offered (e.g., non-stop, direct, or connecting), and other relevant variables (e.g., price, brand image, inflight service, FFP benefits, and reliability). Market share is clearly sensitive to how an airline chooses to allocate the unconstrained demand available to it. The choice is reflected in route, schedule, and fleet planning decisions – and its outcome is reflected, inter alia, in achieved load factors.

There are four further points worth noting about demand allocation:

1.   We saw earlier in the chapter that volume and quality of supply have an impact on the demand for air transport services; for example, a conveniently timed non-stop in a short-haul market might stimulate business that an inconveniently timed connecting service would not. Demand allocation decisions can therefore feed back into demand itself.
2.   Demand spilled from one of an airline's flights could be lost entirely as a result of a decision not to travel, it could be lost to competitors, or it might be 'recaptured' through allocation to another of the same airline's flights.
3.   Demand allocation and fleet planning are particularly closely linked. The important point to remember is that whereas demand arises between O&D points (e.g., Wichita and Munich) it is very often served by more than one flight-leg and by alternative paths (e.g., Wichita–Washington Dulles–Munich, or Wichita–Chicago O'Hare–Munich). How a large network carrier chooses to allocate future demand across its network will strongly influence the fleet optimisation process. We will return to this in Part 3 of this book.
4.   Where an area is served by more than one airport and by a reasonable surface infrastructure, demand originating in that area for travel to a particular destination might be allocated over different airport-pairs. For example, people living in the vicinity of Philadelphia might find that city's airport geographically convenient, but for the right incentives could instead be induced to travel from Baltimore-Washington or Newark.

Forecasting Approaches: Top-Down (Macro-Level) And Bottom-Up (Micro-Level) Forecasting

The dependent variable to be forecast might be global traffic, inter-regional or intra-regional traffic, or traffic in a country-pair, city-pair or airport-pair market. Other than at the first and last of these levels, a forecast can be undertaken from the top down or from the bottom up.

1.   A *top-down* forecast involves starting at a higher level of abstraction than that in which the forecast is interested, and cascading down into progressively more focused markets. The metrics of demand used in top-down forecasts will in the first instance be RPMs and FTMs or RPKs and FTKs. At the lower levels of abstraction market share can then be forecast for individual airlines (i.e., demand can be allocated between competitors) on the basis of historical performance adjusted for any planned service quality changes or marketing mix developments likely to affect consumer preferences

– such as pricing initiatives, promotions, product launches, or advertising campaigns. Figure 2.4 illustrates the process.

2. Forecasts can also be built from the *bottom up* by aggregating figures for different O&D markets. The most important metric of demand at this level is the passenger enplanement, and it is met by supplying seats. An important benefit of bottom-up forecasting is that because it is more closely aligned with actual operations than the top-down approach, it plugs more readily into detailed fleet planning and assignment decisions: because different markets or groups of markets have distinct patterns of intra-day, intra-week, and seasonal demand, it is at the individual market level that many short-term operational and marketing decisions have to be taken in practice. More generally, the performance of an airline can owe as much to how it responds to local economic, demographic, and competitive circumstances in its different O&D markets as to the impact of macro-level developments affecting the industry as a whole.

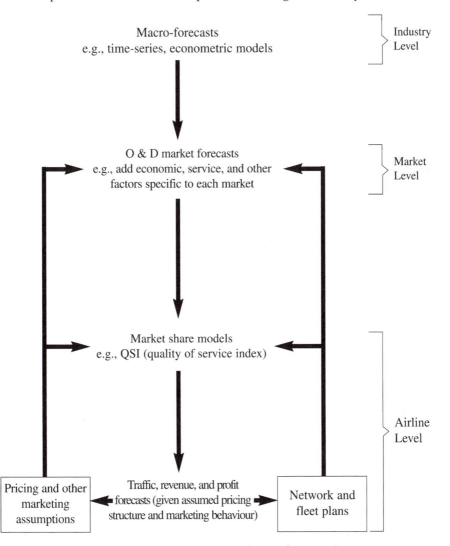

Figure 2.4   A schematic approach to top-down forecasting

The difficulty with bottom-up forecasting is that demand is generally more erratic in individual markets than at a global or systemwide level of aggregation, and so can be reliably forecast only over relatively short periods of time. Furthermore, bottom-up forecasting can be a complex, resource-consuming exercise, particularly for a large network carrier.

An alternative and less fine-grained approach which is also bottom-up in the sense that it deals with disaggregated data is to segment the global market on the basis of journey purpose (usually just business or leisure) and length of haul. As with all disaggregated approaches, this has the advantage of responding to the fact that relationships between traffic and its explanatory variables can differ significantly between segments. On the other hand, it lacks the detail which a carrier with access to proprietary data on individual O&D markets might prefer for planning purposes.

Econometric analysis is often used to generate top-down forecasts, whilst bottom-up forecasts may rely on either or both econometric modelling (where sufficient local data is available) or market research. Trend analysis and judgemental techniques can be applied to either approach. As already noted price, income, and demographics are critical independent variables whatever market is being forecast; the closer the level of abstraction comes down to an individual O&D market, the more significant will be market-specific determinants such as exchange rates, the quality of airline service, availability of substitutes, ethnic and cultural connections, tourist potential, and business links.

Network airlines in particular need O&D market forecasts because they provide critical input for network and fleet planning models as well as scheduling and fleet assignment models. O&D traffic (and revenue) forecasts are in fact the foundation for route and network forecasts:

- *Route forecasts* In a simple point-to-point system these stand by themselves. In a more complex network they will depend in part upon how O&D flows which have more than one potential path are allocated across the network; as we have seen, this is a decision that can itself feed back to O&D demand and market share through the impact of network design and scheduling on customers' purchase behaviour. Route forecasts are built by 'unpeeling' O&D demand and layering it onto alternative flight-legs and routes to create a network of non-stop, one-stop, multi-stop, and connecting services, each perhaps serving a number of different markets simultaneously.
- *Network forecasts* Network forecasts are built by aggregating route forecasts.

Iterations can be driven by different price, marketing, competitive, network design, scheduling, and fleet management assumptions.

The Challenges In Demand Forecasting And Allocation

There are several potential pitfalls which turn straightforward theory into rather difficult practice:

1. The demand characteristics of apparently similar markets can vary markedly because each has a different traffic mix (e.g., a different mix of segments).

2. Even in the same market, different economic and other circumstances at either end might argue for separate models of demand to be used to forecast originating traffic (e.g., one for the US–UK market, and one for the UK–US market).

3. Determination of how each independent variable actually affects demand for passenger or freight service at the O&D market level requires a great deal of historical data upon which to perform regression analysis. A common complication is that price, income, and other independent variables may be difficult to quantify at the individual market level where the fare structure is complex and other figures are unobtainable, unreliable or out of date. Fares might have to be averaged, with the average weighted to reflect traffic mix, for example; the yield earned in a market might be used as a proxy for price. If we bear in mind the importance of price to demand and the fact that in the United States in particular there are tens of thousands of fare changes daily, the difficulties are apparent.

4. Changing relationships between explanatory variables – as when a market gradually matures, for example – may not be captured in the historical data used to specify an econometric model of a demand function. (This problem with multivariate models might ground an argument in favour of univariate time-series even for long-term forecasting. See, for example, the discussion in Grubb and Mason [2001].)

5. Our still imperfect knowledge of consumer choice behaviour means that in addition to price, income and schedule quality there may be qualitative variables (e.g., crowded airports and aircraft) that are difficult to specify but can nonetheless affect demand.

6. It has to be assumed that when customers make their choices of transport mode and carrier they actually have available perfect information about those of the independent variables specified in the model that are believed to impact directly upon consumer behaviour. The reality could be that consumers are simply unaware of changes in marketing mix or other variables which airlines consider, perhaps correctly in principle, should have a profound effect on purchase behaviour and hence demand.

7. It has already been noted that air transport demand is a derived demand because people fly in pursuit of whatever is at the other end of the journey – whether a contract, a suntan or a family visit. If the underlying demand falls, say because there are fewer contracts available, suntans come to be associated with ill-health, or family ties weaken as older generations die out, demand for air services will be affected. The implication is that airlines have to understand and forecast not only the superficially relevant independent variables in their demand functions, but the actual motivations for travel which underlie many of these variables. Such underlying determinants of demand differ from market to market and segment to segment.

8. Aggregate forecasts also have their problems. The industry's income–elasticity of demand inevitably magnifies any errors in GDP forecasts. Furthermore, although demand in large markets is generally more stable and easier to forecast than in small markets, a forecasting error of a similar size will obviously be much more significant in the case of a large market. Taking the industry as a whole and depending upon the precise figures involved from year to year, a 50 basis point error in forecasting growth in global RPMs for the forthcoming year could well be equivalent to the entire annual output of a medium-sized carrier. As the industry grows, any given percentage forecasting error inevitably gets larger in absolute terms – something that has serious capacity management implications.

9. It is vital to remember that a forecast of market demand is not a forecast of what *will* happen. It is a forecast of what will happen if assumptions about how certain

independent variables affect demand, and how these variables will themselves change during the forecast period, turn out to be broadly correct. Similarly, market share forecasts are not forecasts of the demand an airline *will* serve. They are forecasts of what could be achieved assuming market forecasts are correct and, in particular, assuming certain decisions are taken with regard to the marketing mix. If elements of the marketing mix are changed, either by the airline or by its competitors, or if customers respond to one or more elements (such as price or advertising initiatives) differently than predicted, market share will not be as forecast. A forecast is not a plan; it is a planning input.

10. Airlines do not investigate demand functions for individual markets in isolation from an investigation into the costs of meeting forecast demand; implicit in any cost assumption is a level of service consistent with the positioning decisions discussed in Chapter 1. These simultaneous and iterative studies are plugged into decision models, which could range from the intuitive mental model of a small airline's chief executive to the complex econometric models used by well-resourced carriers. The result shapes competitive behaviour insofar as it determines which markets are entered, which continue to be served and at what levels of service, and which will be exited.

11. Finally, it is important to know what if any allowances have been made for the impact of potential infrastructure constraints, which might be significant over a long forecast period. Some publicly available forecasts take this into account (e.g., Boeing), whereas others do not; for example, the FAA (2008, p. 25) notes that its ' ... commercial aviation forecasts are considered unconstrained in that they assume there will be sufficient infrastructure to handle the projected levels of activity'.

However a forecast is derived, the cost of getting it wrong can be high. In a service industry which is not able to inventory unsold output once it has been produced and yet serves customers – particularly high-yield customers – who in many cases cannot or will not wait if output (i.e., space) is unavailable more or less when required, demand forecasting takes on particular significance. If a forecast undershoots the eventual outturn, 'cost' manifests itself in forgone goodwill and revenue (spillage to competitors). If it overshoots, the airline must bear the very real costs of flying under-utilised space – of generating too much output – and often, as a result, having to accept weaker than anticipated yields in order to sell the excess and maintain load factors; underutilised resources other than aircraft – call centres, lounges, gates, and the people who staff them, for example – also carry fixed costs that will not be spread across as many units of output as they otherwise might. Capacity costs, many of which are fixed over the short and medium term, are responsible for a high proportion of any scheduled airline's total operating costs – as we will see in Chapter 5.

VII. Capacity Management: Managing Demand

Traffic (i.e., output *sold*, measured in RPMs or RTMs) and supply (i.e., output *produced*, measured in ASMs or ATMs) are linked by load factor (i.e., the percentage of output *produced* that has been *sold*). One passive way to accommodate increasing demand is therefore to accept a rising load factor: perhaps the best recent example is the US domestic system in 2006–2007, when the majors virtually froze output despite increasing demand driven by a strong economy. The problem with doing this is that beyond a certain level, which will vary depending upon route characteristics and traffic mix, a high load factor will lead to spill – the loss of traffic and therefore revenue. On the other hand, if constraining output forces up yields on the traffic being carried – and if capacity discipline can be maintained across all major competitors which, unusually for this industry, it was in 2006–2007 – spill might not be considered too much of a problem; furthermore, developments in the science of revenue management have allowed historically high load factors to be achieved with less spill than such figures would have generated just a decade ago.

Many airlines do nonetheless still have target load factors keyed-off what they consider to be acceptable spill. It could be argued that a carrier which dominates a route, particularly in terms of frequency, may well find much of any spill being recaptured onto its own alternative services rather than being lost to competitors. On the other hand, no matter how dominant it is on a route, if that route is simply one alternative path between particular origins and destinations which other carriers could as easily connect over different routes on their own networks, then spill to competitors serving these O&D markets may possibly be high.

There are two temporal perspectives on demand management: long-run and short-run.

LONG-RUN DEMAND MANAGEMENT

In the long run, the preferred way to grow demand is to understand available markets and their potential, decide which markets and segments to target, understand the preferences and expectations of the customers in these markets and segments, design service–price offers able to provide the value expected, deliver services to specification, monitor customers' perceptions of service, and adjust service design and delivery to take account of identified service failures and changing consumer preferences and expectations. In other words, invest in the product – including, importantly, the people who deliver it – and understand the payback on product investment. This approach is discussed in much greater depth in Holloway (2002).

If we think back to the 'perceived customer value' diagram in Figure 1.3, the following conclusions can be drawn:

- Improving the product without raising price moves the offer to the left. Important questions are whether this increases production costs, if so how the incremental costs will be addressed (e.g., by higher productivity), and how (as well as how quickly) competitors might respond.
- If the product is allowed to stagnate whilst competitors improve their products, the offer will shift to the right because it embodies lower relative value. A branch of the discipline called evolutionary economics argues that the search for innovative new ways of serving customers is an inevitable dimension of restless, disequilibrating competition, and eventually every competitor must respond in order to stay in the game – unless it is protected by barriers limiting the opportunity for more aggressive competitors to win significant market share. In the short run, of course, downward price adjustments can be made to compensate for product stagnation; in the long run, assuming openly competitive markets, this would at best amount to repositioning in a different (more price-sensitive) segment – and at worst it could be a route to failure.

SHORT-RUN DEMAND MANAGEMENT

Because output is supplied by the plane-load and demand is met by the seat, capacity management in the short run must rely more heavily on managing demand than managing supply (although, as we will see in Chapters 4 and 8, there are effective steps that can be taken to manage supply even in the short run). Short-run capacity management utilises demand-side variables such as pricing, promotion, marketing communications, FFP award variations, and – in markets where they are still relevant – incentives to travel agents in order to absorb excess output on particular departures or routes (perhaps pending a strategic review of the schedule or network). The objective is to smooth predictable peaks by shifting demand to off-peak periods, stimulate increased demand from segments already served and new demand from segments that might otherwise not travel, and at the same time maximise revenues earned from available output.

Demand which turns out to be significantly greater than forecast across an unfolding schedule season raises a different set of issues. Even if aircraft are readily available to satisfy unanticipated demand, the additional slots and gates required to use them at congested airports might not be. In regulated commercial environments, authorisations necessary to add frequencies or larger capacity aircraft may not be forthcoming.

VIII. Summary

This chapter has distinguished between demand and traffic. The importance of understanding and segmenting potentially available markets has been discussed. Demand functions, schedules and elasticity have been considered, as have the drivers of demand, its characteristics, and how it can be modelled, forecasted and allocated across a schedule and a network. Finally, the importance of demand management to wider capacity management efforts, particularly in the short run, has been emphasised.

The nature of demand an airline chooses (or, perhaps, in less liberal environments is constrained) to serve will be reflected in its traffic mix and will have a profound effect on both its revenue and cost streams.

1. *Revenue side* Choice of markets and market segments is reflected in yield. Traffic mix on a network carrier offering more than one class can, if data is available, be broken down into cabin mix and fare mix.
   * *Cabin mix* The distribution of traffic between cabins.
   * *Fare mix* The distribution of traffic travelling on different fares in the same cabin.
2. *Cost side* Choices made regarding which markets and market segments to serve feed through into total cost because they determine product costs, and also because they influence an airline's exposure to the effects of traffic density and demand peaking.
   * *Product costs* Some segments (e.g., most business travellers) are more expensive to serve than others (e.g., most leisure travellers). Business travellers in many markets, particularly international markets, require amongst other things:
     – a higher level of ground and inflight amenities (e.g., airport lounges and spacious premium cabins); and
     – a schedule that has relatively high frequencies and is therefore more expensive to deliver than lower-frequency service operated by larger aircraft having, in all probability, lower seat-mile costs. We will return to this in Chapters 4 and 7.

In summary, service design is a significant cost driver.

- *Traffic density and demand peaking* Traffic density and demand peaking are two important sources of feedback from demand to costs. The higher the traffic density on a route, the more likely it is that a given schedule can be operated by a larger aircraft type (with lower unit costs) than that same schedule would support on a thinner route. The more intense the intra-day and intra-week peaking in particular and the larger the proportion of peak demand that an airline tries to meet, the higher the likelihood that excess off-peak output will have to be sold at a lower yield much closer to the cost of production than might be desirable.

Demand is of course served not by selling the ASMs or ATMs an airline produces, but by delivering a service. The most tangible manifestation of service is a seat on an aircraft or space for cargo in a hold but, as is fully explained in Holloway (2002), this is only one dimension of the airline product. What customers buy is a package of attributes which together provide them with a range of benefits. Each package is part of a value proposition – in effect, a service–price offer (ibid.). The other side of that offer – price – is the subject of the next chapter.

ACCESSIBLE SOURCES OF MACRO-LEVEL TRAFFIC FORECASTS

The following forecasts are available on the Web; new editions are published regularly – in some cases annually. Most cover output as well as demand, and in this respect are also relevant to the discussion in Chapter 4. Where they address yield and the demand for aircraft of different sizes, they are relevant to Chapter 3 and Chapters 6 to 8 respectively.

- Airbus: *Global Market Forecast.*
- Boeing: *Current Market Outlook.*
- Boeing: *World Air Cargo Forecast.*
- Bombardier: *Commercial Aircraft Market Forecast.*
- Embraer: *Market Outlook.*
- Federal Aviation Administration: *FAA Aerospace Forecasts.*
- Rolls-Royce: *Market Outlook.*

APPENDIX 2.1: FARE ELASTICITIES FOUND IN NORTH AMERICAN STUDIES

Study (publication year)	Focus of study	Values
Oum, Zhang and Zhang (1993)*	United and American Airlines' hubs	1.58 to -2.34
Oum, Waters and Yong (1992)†	Trip purpose (business/non-business)	-1.15 to -1.52
	Mixed or unknown	-0.76 to -4.51
Oum, Gillen and Noble (1986)*	First class	-0.58 to -0.82
	Standard economy	-1.23 to -1.36
	Discount economy	-1.50 to -1.98
Royal Commission on National Passenger Transportation (1992)**	Business travel	-1.57 to -3.51
	Non-business travel	-4.38 to -4.50
	Short trip (under 500 miles)	-1.16 to -2.70
	Long trip (over 500 miles)	-1.34 to -2.56
Apogee Research Inc.*	Business travel	-0.59
	Non-business travel	-0.38
Morrison and Winston (1985)*	Non-business	-0.86
Abrahams (1983)*	Transcontinental	-1.81
	Florida vacation city-pairs	-1.98
	Hawaii–West Coast city-pairs	-1.68
	Eastern medium-haul city-pairs	-1.22
Ippolito (1981)*	440-mile trip (one-way)	-0.53
	830-mile trip (one-way)	-1.00
Straszheim (1978)††	First class	-0.65
	Economy, peak period	-1.92
	Economy, average	-1.48
	Economy, standard	-1.12
	Economy, promotional	-2.74
	Economy, high discount	-1.82
De Vany (1983)*	280-mile trip (one-way)	-0.78
	400-mile trip (one-way)	-1.02
	650-mile trip (one-way)	-1.07
	1500-mile trip (one-way)	-1.14
	2500-mile trip (one-way)	-1.17

Gillen, Morrison and Stewart (2002)†¥	Long-haul international business	-0.26
	Long-haul international leisure	-0.99
	Long-haul domestic business	-1.15
	Long-haul domestic leisure	-1.52
	Short-/medium-haul business	-1.39
Brons, Pels, Nijkamp and Rietveld (2002) †¥	Meta-analysis of 204 studies	-1.15
Pickrell (1984)*	Short routes	-2.00
	Business travel	-1.00 to -1.50
Bhadra (2003)*	Less than 250 miles	-0.67
	250–499 miles	-0.56
	500–749 miles	-0.74
	750–999 miles	-1.45
	1000–1249 miles	-1.82
	1250–1499 miles	-0.85
	1500–1749 miles	-1.08
	1750–1999 miles	-0.84
	2000–2249 miles	-1.06
	2250–2499 miles	-1.38
	2500–3000 miles	-0.86

Notes: * US data; ** Canadian data; † Synthesis of previous studies; †† North Atlantic data; †¥ From various international studies.

Reproduced with permission from: Button, Kenneth J. (with the assistance of Henry Vega), *The Taxation of Air Transportation*, Center for Transportation Policy, Operations and Logistics, School of Public Policy, George Mason University, Fairfax, Virginia, April 2005.

3

Yield

Everything should be made as simple as possible, but not simpler.

Albert Einstein

CHAPTER OVERVIEW

Yield is the second of the four elements in the operating performance model around which Part 2 of the book has been structured.

TRAFFIC × YIELD > < OUTPUT × UNIT COST
= OPERATING PERFORMANCE (i.e., PROFIT or LOSS)

This chapter will: discuss price in the context of the airline industry; identify price drivers; explain the use of price as both a strategic and a tactical variable; define the concept of yield; and highlight different sources of operating revenue.

I. Price

Yield, that is revenue earned per RPM or RPK or per RTM or RTK, is the element of the operating performance model upon which this chapter will ultimately focus. But to understand yield we need first to consider pricing, because it is an airline's passenger fare and cargo rate structures together with its traffic mix (i.e., the proportions of traffic moving on each fare and rate basis) that drive system yield.

PRICE DEFINED

Price is here defined as 'monetary cost to customers'. It is not uncommon in the literature for non-monetary costs, measured in terms of time or inconvenience for example, to be embodied in the concept of price. The view taken in this book is that high non-monetary costs are better treated as low-quality service attributes; in this sense, a multi-stop or connecting service 'costs' more time than a non-stop service and so compares unfavourably on this attribute dimension.

Table 3.1 examines which flows of money from a passenger to an airline should be considered part of price and which should not.

Most of the optional purchases listed in the lower part of the table fall into a category now widely known as 'ancillary revenues'; these will be touched upon again towards the

Table 3.1   Elements of 'price'

	Contribute to airline operating revenues	Do not contribute to airline operating revenues
Payment by the customer obligatory: part of 'price'	• Fare • Fuel surcharge (N.B., some airlines account for this as a deduction from fuel cost) • Other charges and fees that the airline is not legally obliged to levy and pay through to an airport or government authority (e.g., insurance surcharge and – where not mandated by the government – security fee)	Taxes, fees, and charges which an airline is legally obliged to levy on its customers and pass through to an airport or government authority (e.g., passenger facility charge, ticket tax, flight-segment tax, and federal security service fee in the United States, and airport departure taxes imposed in most other countries)
Payment by the customer optional: not part of 'price'	Service attributes which have traditionally been bundled into the airline product but for which some carriers now charge if the customer requires them (e.g., desk check-in, seat selection, checked baggage, food and beverages, inflight entertainment)	

end of the chapter. Apart from the fare, there are two significant elements of price which merit brief comment.

1. *Non-mandatory surcharges* Fuel surcharges are particularly common. They are levied by many airlines on both passengers and cargo shippers, sometimes on a per-trip basis and sometimes on a per-segment basis – the latter being a particular issue for passengers connecting over hubs. In principle, it makes no more sense to break fuel out of the income statement for special treatment than, say, senior management bonuses; furthermore, some airlines with significant and effective hedging strategies in place have been just as willing as unhedged competitors to apply surcharges, even though their fuel costs have not risen in the short term. That some airlines account for fuel surcharges as deductions from the cost of fuel rather than as revenue does not weaken the argument.

   Fuel surcharges are part of the ticket price, plain and simple. For example, when on 18 January 2008 American doubled to $40 its domestic round trip fuel surcharge, it exempted many markets where there was LFA competition; given the not unreasonable assumption that fuel was no cheaper in those markets than elsewhere in American's system, the rise can be seen for what it really was – a fare increase keyed off competitive dynamics in the markets concerned. Travel agents in a number of countries (e.g., Australia and the United States) have made this case in law suits arguing fuel surcharges are a commissionable part of the fare. Emirates was one of the first carriers to accept this reality when it began paying commissions on surcharges in April 2006, and then a year later incorporated them into its tariff structure (although at the time of writing it is believed to be giving consideration to separating them out again). Singapore Airlines did the same in late 2007. Other airlines persist in calling part of the price they charge for their services a 'fuel surcharge'. There are two reasons: first, some hope that such labelling might moderate the impact on demand and/or on consumers' perceptions of what is in fact a disguised price increase; second, these and other cash surcharges are levied on travellers redeeming FFP awards just as they are on other passengers, and this not insignificant incremental revenue would be lost were charges bundled into the fare covered by those 'free' tickets.

Similar comments can be made in respect of other non-mandatory surcharges imposed on customers by airlines. Perhaps one of the more astonishing examples was United's decision in April 2007, subsequently followed by several other carriers, to impose a $10 surcharge on flights originating at LAX. It attributed the need for this to a rise in facility rental costs at the airport. Given that United at the time was enplaning close to 5 million passengers a year at LAX and so could expect to generate almost $50 million in incremental revenues to recoup a cost imposed on it by Los Angeles World Airports which on the face of it amounted to no more than $10 million, it is difficult to conclude that this was anything other than a fare increase.

It is in fact now not unusual to find that different airlines operating between the same points impose different 'taxes, fees, and charges' (TFCs). An unavoidable foundation layer is laid down by mandatory government and/or airport TFCs which must be handed over to the authority mandating them, but on top of these many airlines now add non-mandatory fees and charges which flow directly into their revenues. (Technically, ICAO considers a 'tax' to be a levy which contributes generally to central or local government revenues whilst a 'charge' defrays the costs of providing a specific service; terminology is not always used this precisely in practice.) Often TFCs are disclosed on airline websites only after the base fare has been quoted in response to an enquiry, and the impression is left that all TFCs are mandatory; some airlines are better than others at enabling passengers to investigate the nature of, and requirement for, TFCs. If customers are misled into believing that all TFCs are government-imposed, there will be a corollary assumption that they are the same for each airline – implying incorrectly that a comparison of base fares is equivalent to a comparison of final purchase prices. Indeed, one study of airline ticket price transparency found that in a sample of cases as much as 45 per cent of quoted TFCs were non-mandatory – that is, were attributable to commercial decisions taken by airlines to augment their revenue (Steer Davies Gleave 2006). This is a particular problem in those states which do not yet require TFCs to be included in advertised fares.

2. *Government taxes and airport passenger service charges* These have in common the fact that they are compulsory and, because they are passed to other parties, they do not contribute to airline revenues. That they are compulsory means that like airfare and fuel surcharges, but unlike optional purchases a passenger may choose to make, they are part of 'price' and therefore (if large enough) have an effect on demand through the medium of price-elasticity. Because many are fixed amounts rather than percentages of the underlying fare, they often constitute a large share of short-haul ticket prices. In some markets served by LFAs out of the United Kingdom for example, it has been far from unknown for airfares to be virtually free, with taxes accounting for substantially all the price of travel; in the United States, passengers on LFAs might expect to be handing over 15–30 per cent of ticket price in government-mandated taxes or fees of various types, the precise percentage depending upon the airports involved, the routing, and the base fare on the day of travel. (The ATA website http://www.airlines. org lists excise taxes and fees currently imposed in the United States.)

There are strong arguments that users of air transport services should contribute fairly and proportionately towards the economic cost of the infrastructure they use and the cost of developing it for the future, and also towards government revenue generally. On the other hand, governments in some parts of the world quite clearly treat air travel as a cash-cow; sometimes they impose levies to meet expenditures which are unquestionably a central government responsibility and are not imposed on other forms of transport (e.g., security – the United States, international development aid – France), and sometimes they make a general tax-grab under the cloak of environmentalism – as in the United Kingdom and the Netherlands. In many countries, including the United States and several of the larger European states, mandatory TFCs have increased significantly in the last decade – a period during which real yields have continued inexorably downwards (Unisys R2A 2006a, b); almost without exception, aviation has been discriminated against relative to land transport. We will meet this subject again in Chapters 4 and 5.

In the final analysis, when confronted with an outlay – however it is constituted as between base fare, surcharges, and taxes – a potential customer will either choose to travel or choose not to travel. If the choice is not to travel at that price, the airline always has the option of reducing the fare or surcharge (in effect, 'absorbing' some of the taxes) in order to exploit that customer's price-elasticity; alternatively, it could simply forgo the revenue. Taxes eat into operating profits earned from people who do choose to travel: if a given number of passengers are each willing to pay a particular price to fly from A to B, the share of that price that has to be passed on by the airline to the government is revenue that could otherwise have been retained by the airline without affecting demand – it is, in other words, pure profit (or, during economic downturns, perhaps pure loss reduction) that has been forgone. When governments load taxes onto aviation, they are burdening airline shareholders as well as passengers. This is particularly true in markets that are intensely competitive, where the pressure on airlines to absorb part of the tax burden imposed on consumption of their services inevitably increases.

One final point to beware of: the fact that different airlines can choose to account for TFCs in different ways may affect yield and unit cost comparisons. As already noted, for example, fuel surcharges might be treated as either a source of revenue or a deduction from fuel expenses.

DIFFERENT PERSPECTIVES ON THE ROLE OF PRICE

There are several related but separate perspectives on price:

- To an economist, price is a mechanism for bringing supply and demand into balance at a particular level of output. However:
  - Some economists argue that the airline industry is an example of a phenomenon referred to in game theory as an 'empty core' – an oligopolistic market structure unable to arrive at stable equilibrium prices (Button 1996); the foundation of this inherent instability is the fact that output is supplied in expensive indivisible units such as aircraft whilst demand is much more finely grained and comes forward in most cases one seat at a time. The high fixed costs of new capacity introduced ahead of demand lead to unsustainably low pricing to maintain

market share, followed eventually by the exit of capacity, a tightening of supply, and firmer prices. The cycle of instability then starts again.

- Irrespective of whether there is an empty core making air transport markets inherently unstable, there is another fundamental problem facing network carriers in particular: a flight into a hub is jointly supplying output to multiple O&D markets, fares in which are inevitably different because of the different journey lengths involved and, more importantly, the different competitive characteristics of each market. There cannot be a single 'equilibrium price' applicable to that flight because it serves so many distinct O&D markets.

- In the accounting model around which the second part of this book has been structured, price – in the form of yield – is one of four elements in what is usually an unbalanced equation, the balancing item being operating profit or loss.

- To a marketer, price is part of a marketing mix along with service design, service personnel and delivery processes, distribution channels, and the marketing communications mix (i.e., advertising, promotion, public relations, etc.); in principle, all the elements of the marketing mix associated with a particular market should be managed in unison so that it can be approached with an integrated service–price offer. Indeed, price itself has product dimensions beyond its financial meaning. First, *accessibility*: how wide is the range of channels through which a given fare is available, what if any is the incremental cost of using a particular channel other than the Internet, and are all fares down to the last seat available through every channel? Second, *clarity*: how easy is it to uncover what the total price will be for a given service, inclusive of TFCs? Third, *variety*: how many different fares are available on a given departure at a single point in time, and how wide are the same-cabin variations in fares subject to different booking or usage conditions? Fourth, *stability*: does the carrier have an RMS which adjusts prices in response to enquiries and bookings, or does it adopt a more graduated response – for example, raising fares progressively in only three or four steps as departure date approaches?

That price and output decisions are closely linked and that price is integral to a complex marketing mix make it unrealistic to talk about pricing policy in isolation. Furthermore, price is not only one of the most important threads binding the service concept, marketing communications, and distribution strategy into a single, coherent, strategically positioned offer to the marketplace, it is also a tactical variable in the daily cut-and-thrust of liberalised competitive environments. Nonetheless, for the purpose of discussion we will here treat pricing largely as an independent activity.

RESPONSIBILITY FOR PRICING

Although the two functions need to be closely coordinated, at larger airlines there have traditionally been separate pricing and revenue management departments.

- *Pricing* The purpose of a pricing department is to create and administer the passenger fare and freight rate structures applicable to each market. (Freight rates might in practice be set by a separate cargo department, division or subsidiary.) The pricing function also involves establishing 'rules' – conditions subject to which each fare and rate will be offered (with price and conditions together constituting a 'tariff'); rules might encompass advance booking requirements, minimum or maximum stays, Saturday night stay, routing and stopover limitations, rebooking and cancellation restrictions, and restrictions affecting the season, day of week, or particular departure on which the fare is valid. Tariff-setting on alliance routes might, where legal, be coordinated by the partners.

• *Revenue management* The function of revenue management departments is to allocate the physical space available on each individual flight-leg, augmented by overbooking limits, between the different fare and rate bases available for sale on that leg. (We will see in Chapter 9 that there are more advanced revenue management approaches available, but allocation-based methods are still widely used across the industry.) In particular, the purpose of revenue management on the passenger side is to limit the availability of low-yield fares on any departure where unmanaged demand might be expected to fill seats with passengers paying the lowest fares and exclude late-booking passengers prepared to pay more.

At many airlines, a headquarters department is responsible for pricing as well as for the filing and distribution of published tariffs. However, international carriers in particular may grant considerable autonomy to local sales offices, which are free within limits both to respond to other airlines' pricing activities and to negotiate unpublished off-tariff deals with targeted agencies and corporate customers subject to locally agreed conditions. Because of the relatively small number of customers participating in cargo markets (i.e., forwarders, consolidators, and shippers), off-tariff deals are even more common in this sector of the industry.

The fundamental objective of the pricing function is to design a tariff structure for each market that maximises revenue earned from price-inelastic segments of demand, stimulates demand from price-elastic segments to fill space that would otherwise fly empty, and imposes conditions sufficient to limit revenue dilution arising from the diversion of demand from high-yield fare or rate bases targeted at price-inelastic segments to lower fares or rates targeted at price-elastic segments. This latter task has become more challenging for network carriers in short-haul markets as competition from LFAs has increasingly required them to drop onerous conditions often attached to deeply discounted fares – conditions such as return trips only and Saturday night or minimum-period stays.

Looking at passenger fares, it can be helpful to treat the fully flexible, refundable, unrestricted fare applied for travel in a particular cabin (economy/coach, business, or first class) in a given market as the strategic 'price platform' for the service concept of which the cabin concerned is a part; this is what will be meant when the expressions 'full fare' or 'unrestricted fare' are used in the rest of the book. A series of lower fares (published and off-tariff or private) can be developed from any price platform to tap into the price elasticities of different segments of demand identified by reference to their willingness to pay to travel in the cabin concerned, in the market concerned, at particular times. In highly competitive markets, these fare structures will be fine-tuned on an ongoing basis; hundreds of thousands of changes are filed every day in the US domestic market, for example. The notion of a price platform is perhaps less applicable to LFAs, whose highest (walk-up) fares might not be fully unrestricted, and which offer a relatively small menu of discounts – usually dependent upon time of booking rather than willingness to accept conditions.

INFLUENCE OF PRICING

Influence On Demand

Demand does not just exist; it exists at a price. We saw in Chapter 2 that price is one of the most important determinants of demand. It was also shown that there is an elasticity associated with price, as there is with other important independent variables in the demand function; prices influence both traffic generated and the yield earned from that traffic. Liberalisation and deregulation allow carriers to manage traffic and yield more proactively than when price structures are imposed by airline cartels and/or governments, and this is what has been happening in a growing number of the world's most significant air transport markets since the late 1970s. Of course, for airline managers to be able to use price as an effective demand management tool it is necessary that they have some feel for the shape and slope of the demand curves faced by their services at different points in time (e.g., off-peak, shoulder, and peak, or weekdays and weekends, or morning, midday, and late afternoon/early evening). This will allow them to estimate the impact a price change will have on the quantity of service demanded.

Complicating the task, however, is the fact that different segments of the market will probably have different demand curves at different times. The need to exploit these differences to maximise revenue underlay the complex tariff structures that most network carriers created. Under pressure from the simpler pricing models offered by LFAs in their short-haul markets and also the leisure market shift away from distribution through travel agents (who could explain restrictions associated with each fare alternative) and towards reliance on the Internet (which demands clarity and brevity), North American and European network carriers in particular have had to reduce the complexity of their short-haul pricing structures by cutting back on the number of fares, eliminating many of the conditions previously imposed, and keying variations to a greater extent off the advance purchase period.

Another complication arises from the fact that many airline markets tend towards oligopolistic structures, with the result that price changes initiated by any one of the small number of competitors present are likely to garner a reaction from the others – leading to shifts in their initial demand curves. (We will look at oligopoly in Chapter 4.)

Influence On Supply And Costs

By influencing demand, price drives revenue. The volume and nature of demand an airline chooses to supply with output in turn drives costs. For example, by offering a tiered fare structure in response to the price-elasticities of people willing to travel only on discounted fares, an airline is not just striving to maximise its own revenues but is also increasing the density of traffic in the markets concerned. This increased density will have two immediate effects on costs:

1. Capacity costs, the costs of generating output by flying aircraft and operating a ground infrastructure, may or may not rise:
    - They will rise in an absolute sense if additional capacity is required to accommodate the increased traffic. However, unit cost – that is, cost per unit of output produced (e.g., per available seat-mile) – may fall if the higher traffic density allows larger aircraft with lower seat-mile costs to be operated than would otherwise have been the case. We will return to this in Chapters 4 and 5.

- They will remain largely unchanged if increased traffic can be accommodated within the existing system (e.g., by accepting higher load factors).
2. Traffic costs, the costs of handling and flying passengers, will rise as traffic density increases – irrespective of whether or not capacity has had to be boosted.

Much therefore depends upon how changes in absolute costs develop in response to increased traffic moving on the discounted fares concerned. This, in turn, will depend upon the structure of the particular carrier's operating system and cost base.

Through the demand it creates, pricing can therefore affect different types of cost:

- *Variable costs* If a pricing initiative generates incremental demand, what will be the extra costs of serving that demand?
- *Fixed costs* Can incremental demand be served by the existing fleet and infrastructure, or must more capacity – and therefore more fixed costs – be added?
- *Unit costs* What will be the impact of higher throughput on unit costs? The answer to this will be shaped by answers to the two preceding questions, by the size of any economies of scale, density, and scope available to a particular airline, and by the precise nature and geography of the incremental demand.

We will be looking at these different types of cost and at economies of scale, density, and scope in Chapter 5.

Pricing can have an even more direct and immediate impact on costs. For example, a simple and stable fare structure may contribute to lower distribution costs by reducing sales training requirements, shortening reservations calls (so raising the productivity of reservations staff), and lessening the perceived need amongst passengers to rely on travel agents for current fare information; simplicity can also help encourage use of Internet distribution channels. Unfortunately, market liberalisation tends to reduce the predictability of fares from the customer's perspective, and can lead to volatility in both fares and the conditions attached to them.

Influence On Profit, Market Share, And Cash Flow

We have seen that price is an important driver of both revenues and costs. However, the influence is not proportional. This means that a pricing strategy intended to maximise revenue will not necessarily maximise the difference between revenue and costs – that is, profit. There have been quite a few cases over the last two decades of airlines in financial difficulties pricing to generate cash, with carriers reorganising under the protection of Chapter 11 bankruptcy laws in the United States providing a number of high-profile examples, along with state-subsidised 'flag carriers' elsewhere in the world. What an airline sets out to achieve through its pricing policy with regard to revenue, profitability, market share, and cash flow should be driven by wider corporate and marketing objectives.

Influence On Market Positioning

Market positioning essentially defines the location of a service relative to competing services in customers' perceptions (and is therefore slightly different from strategic positioning which, as we saw in Chapter 1, is a supply-side concept used to define an airline's approach to its markets). Price is a vital piece of the information 'jig-saw' assembled by customers. This is true for most products, but especially so for services because their intangibility makes pre-delivery evaluation more subjective (Holloway 2002). The positioning of a first or business class service, for example, might constrain pricing insofar as it can be highly damaging to the image of a premium product for it to be heavily discounted.

PRICING AND MARKET SEGMENTATION

This section will look at three approaches to pricing: uniform, discriminatory, and differential. The discussion here is oriented primarily to the pricing of passenger fares; freight rates are discussed later in the chapter.

Uniform Pricing

Figure 3.1(a) illustrates a uniform pricing structure, which has every buyer paying the same price for a given product; Figure 3.1(b) illustrates a situation in which a uniform price is set at $250 – equivalent to the value placed on the service by Consumer 3, but lower than the maximum amounts that Consumers 1 and 2 would have been prepared to pay.

In Chapter 1 consumer surplus was defined as the value placed by a particular consumer on the benefits received from a service package, less the monetary price paid for that package; in other words, consumer surplus is what a consumer would in principle be prepared to pay for a service less the price actually paid. In Figure 3.1(b), Consumer 1 would be prepared to pay $500 for a ticket that is in fact priced at $250, therefore 'earning' a surplus of $250; similarly, Consumer 2 would have been prepared to pay $400 for the ticket, and so has a surplus of $150. Consumer 3, on the other hand, values the ticket at its market price and so gains no surplus.

On an aggregate level, the surplus from which all consumers as a whole benefit is the shaded area beneath the demand curve and above the market price line at $250. From an airline's perspective, this area represents lost revenue. Although simple and apparently equitable, uniform pricing is rarely a feasible pricing structure. Assuming first that the single price is relatively high, it is likely to leave some consumers still paying less than they would be willing to pay – that is, paying a lower amount than the value they place on the air transport service bought (so benefiting from a substantial consumer surplus) – and a large number of other, more price-sensitive, travellers excluded from the market altogether. When this happens, economies of density are reduced below what they might otherwise have been had more demand been able to come forward, with the result that unit costs will be higher – because of having to operate smaller aircraft with less attractive seat-mile costs, for example. This is likely to cause those who do travel to face higher fares. Furthermore, the high frequencies and wide network coverage particularly valued by the business travellers who will probably constitute a large proportion of those remaining in any market served at a high uniform price might be difficult to sustain on the basis of the lower level of demand attracted by that single price.

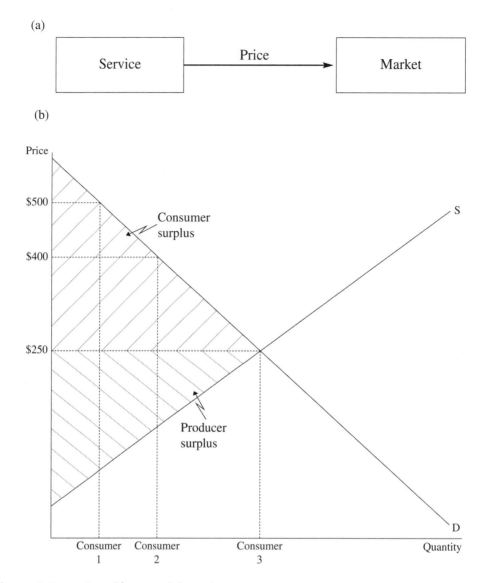

Figure 3.1   A uniform pricing structure

Conversely, if the uniform price is low enough, substantial traffic might indeed be carried. In this case, however, an even higher proportion of passengers would probably be travelling at fares significantly below the value they place on the service, and unless the airline concerned has its production costs well under control profits might prove elusive.

Uniform pricing is rare, although it is increasingly common for just a single fare to be sold *at any one time* for a particular flight – that fare changing, usually rising, as departure date approaches. A particularly extreme example of uniform pricing was provided several years ago by Australian start-up Impulse, which briefly offered a flat fare that applied to all flights across its entire (but admittedly limited) network. In most cases, airlines use more subtle pricing structures based on market segmentation to redistribute in their own favour those parts of consumer surplus above the market price line in Figure 3.1(b) and within the vertical boxes. Most are examples of either discriminatory or differential pricing.

Discriminatory And Differential Pricing

Definitions This subsection begins by defining the two concepts, then goes on to explore their significance in the context of airline pricing. It is a topic that will be touched on again when revenue management is discussed in Chapter 9.

1. *Price discrimination* Price discrimination occurs when buyers of the same service pay different prices which are attributable not to different marginal costs of production but are instead dependent upon their different willingness to pay; in other words, customers who cost more or less the same to serve are nonetheless paying different prices. Because the firm is setting prices by reference to demand rather than marginal cost, there is in theory an implication that it is exerting some degree of monopoly power.
2. *Price differentiation* Differential pricing arises when different prices are charged for different products which have different costs of production.

If essentially the same service package is targeted at multiple segments and priced differently for each despite production costs being largely similar, there is a *discriminatory* pricing structure; if, on the other hand, separate service packages with different costs are specifically designed and priced for different segments, there is a *differential* pricing structure. The obvious question is therefore, 'What constitutes a "product" in this particular context, and having identified the different products being sold can it be asserted that their different costs of production justify their different prices?' We will return to this question in a moment, after first taking a closer look at the topic of price discrimination.

Price discrimination The primary purposes of a discriminatory price structure are:

*   to capture as much consumer surplus as possible from customers present in the market;
*   to attract into the market customers whose willingness to pay is so low that they might otherwise be excluded were only a single uniform fare offered;
*   to redirect the demand of customers with weak time-preferences and high price-elasticity away from peak periods and towards more lightly loaded flights.

Three types of price discrimination are recognised in the literature (Pigou 1920):

1. *First-degree (or 'perfect') discrimination* To maximise revenue by tapping into the consumer surplus that eludes it under a uniform pricing structure, an airline ideally needs to know each potential customer's 'reservation price' – that is, the maximum that each customer is willing to pay given the value that they place on obtaining a seat on a particular flight. This theoretical abstraction is called 'first-degree discrimination'.
2. *Second-degree (or 'indirect') discrimination* Because first-degree discrimination is unattainable in the airline business, carriers have typically clustered customers into a limited number of segments. Members of each segment should be broadly similar in terms of their willingness to pay – something which itself will be driven by the strength of their time-preference for a particular flight and their ability to abide by conditions attached to differently priced tickets. The problem is that the identities of segment members and their willingness to pay to be on a particular flight is impossible to know in advance with any certainty. So carriers offer multiple versions of what is essentially the same service, each version comprising a seat in a particular cabin and

a set of different restrictions on purchase or usage; individual customers then self-select the version that best suits their own price-elasticity, time-preference, and ability to abide by restrictions. ('Versioning' can also segment passengers according to their location, choice of distribution channel, FFP status, or any one of several other criteria.) Second-degree price discrimination therefore targets customers' *behaviour*. Figure 3.2(a) illustrates the approach, whilst Figure 3.2(b) adapts Figure 3.1(b) to show how an airline might target three separate segments with three different prices ($250, $400, and $500) in order to expand producer surplus by tapping into consumer surplus.

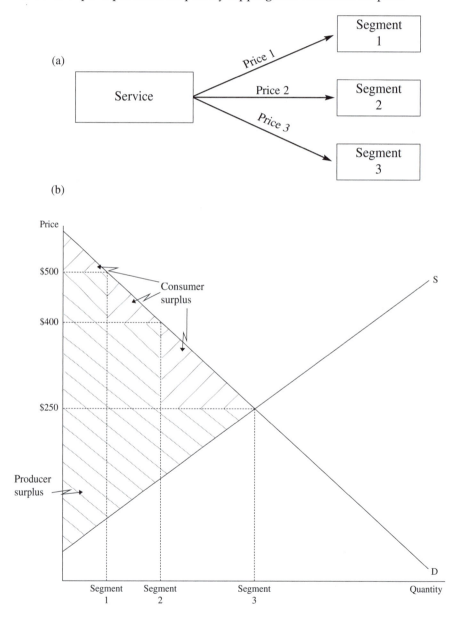

Figure 3.2   A discriminatory pricing structure under a single demand curve

3. *Third-degree (or 'direct') discrimination* This involves discriminating on the basis of verifiable *identity*. Discrimination based on identity uses sorting mechanisms such as age, military or government employment status, or group membership. These essentially descriptive characteristics are generally a poor proxy for price-elasticity, but they do have the advantage of making the segments concerned easy to target.

For a discriminatory pricing structure to be effective in maximising revenue, several requirements have to be met:

1. The market concerned must be divisible into segments that are sufficiently identifiable, large, and distinct in respect of their different price-elasticities, time-preferences, and sensitivities to ticket restrictions to be accessible. Price discrimination is therefore more likely in markets that have a significant traffic volume and a well-dispersed mix of travellers with different preferences (Stavins 1996).
2. The cost of supplying an additional unit of output within existing capacity constraints must be low (i.e., fixed costs must account for a high proportion of total costs).
3. Diversion of traffic from high-yield to low-yield fares must be controllable in order to minimise revenue dilution – the purpose of the restrictions mentioned above.
4. Purchasers must not be able to onsell their tickets – something airlines prohibit contractually.
5. The incremental cost of administering the fare structure must not exceed the incremental revenue it generates – which some LFAs (e.g., easyJet) have claimed is not the case in respect of network carriers' complex fare structures (CAA 2003).
6. Consumers should be neither confused nor alienated by the pricing structure – a requirement that network carriers have not, on the whole, been successful in meeting.

With regard to the sixth point, something which gained a lot of negative publicity in US domestic markets in particular during the late 1990s was the extreme 'price dispersion' in evidence – that is, the large gap between the full coach fare in a market and the deepest discounted fare. Multiples of eight or even higher were not unusual at the time, which meant that a business traveller constrained to book late and pay the highest fare could be sitting next to a leisure traveller who had booked early and paid perhaps one-eighth of that fare for the same ground and inflight product. Since then the expansion of LFAs imposing fewer conditions on ticket usage, the greatly increased price transparency offered by the Internet, and the mounting unwillingness of companies to be 'gouged' (as many saw it) has forced down the highest fares and led to reduced fare dispersion and a simpler overall fare structure in markets where there is strong competition. This compression of the spread between highest and lowest fares – in other words, reduction in price discrimination – in turn contributed to record load factors in mid-decade (FAA 2007a).

How many demand curves are there? The essence of price discrimination is therefore to offer several versions of the same product to different segments of an overall market that it is assumed can be described by a single demand curve. It is indeed the case that segments that are not too dissimilar in terms of price-elasticity will have similar demand curves, assuming other determinants of demand are broadly the same. On the other hand, segments that place very different values on a given service will also have very different demand curves. Figure 3.3 illustrates the hypothetical case of business and leisure segments – the latter price-elastic, the former generally much less so – both travelling in the same cabin but paying different prices; their different price-elasticities are reflected in the shapes of the two demand curves.

Because both segments are served by the same product when they travel in the same cabin, the airline's marginal cost is shown as unchanged between the segments – something which, as we will see shortly, is not a point of view shared by all economists. (The horizontal marginal cost curve is purely illustrative; in practice, marginal cost is likely to vary with output.) If output is set where marginal cost and marginal revenue are equal, as theoretically it should be when profit maximisation is a corporate objective and a market is competitive, the prices that this implies for each segment are different because of the different shapes of their demand curves.

However, introducing the idea that more than one demand function and demand curve exists in respect of different segments travelling in the same cabin is problematic. If it is argued that different tariffs (i.e., combinations of price and booking restrictions) offered for travel in the same cabin are in fact different 'fare products', each with its own demand curve and distinct (albeit not always easily separable) costs of production, pricing differences between them would – because of those different costs – represent differential rather than discriminatory pricing. Why this might matter is considered shortly, but before that the next subsection discusses some of the arguments.

Discriminatory and differential pricing: the arguments Broadly speaking, three arguments can be identified:

1. Each flight, irrespective of the number of different cabins offered, is making available just one product. Because different passengers, even though they may be in separate cabins, are charged fares keyed not off costs but off their willingness to pay for a particular version of what in essence is a single product, this is an example of discriminatory pricing under a single demand curve.
2. Each flight offers as many different products as there are classes of service onboard. Price differences *between* cabins represent differential pricing with a separate demand curve for each cabin, whilst price differences *within* cabins represent discriminatory pricing under the single demand curve for the cabin concerned. Differential pricing provides price platforms for each cabin (i.e., the full, unrestricted fare), whilst discriminatory pricing is used tactically to manage revenue earned from each individual cabin – particularly, but not exclusively, from the economy/coach cabin – by selling space in the same cabin to different customers at different price points. This is illustrated in Figure 3.4.
3. Each flight offers as many different products as there are tariffs. Price differences between cabins represent differential pricing under different demand curves, and so do differences within cabins – in the latter case because each tariff is a different 'fare product' by virtue of its particular conditions and restrictions. These conditions and restrictions are not just 'fences' which prevent diversion of customers to cheaper tariffs, they are also 'product attributes' helping to define customer value and imposing different sets of costs on the airline producing them.

If we take the case of a particular flight, everybody on the aircraft is sharing certain service attributes: the airline's network, schedule, punctuality, safety, and – perhaps less uniformly – whatever benefits might be derived from its brand image. But there are

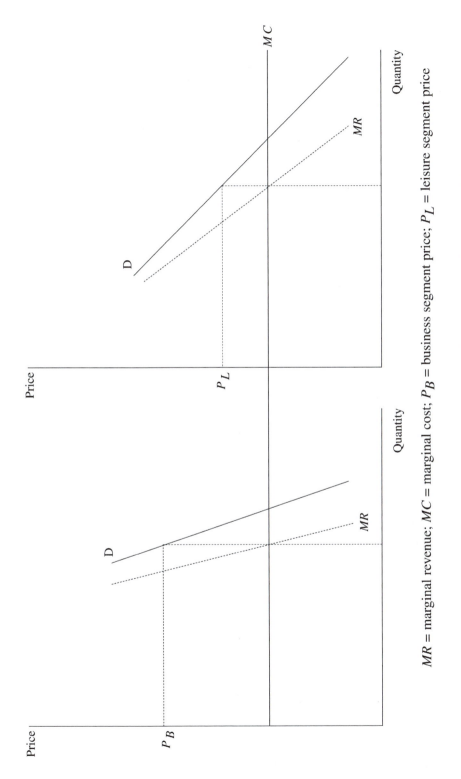

Price

Price

D

P_B

MR

Quantity

MC

D

MR

P_L

Quantity

MR = marginal revenue; MC = marginal cost; P_B = business segment price; P_L = leisure segment price

Figure 3.3   Price discrimination between two segments served together in the same cabin

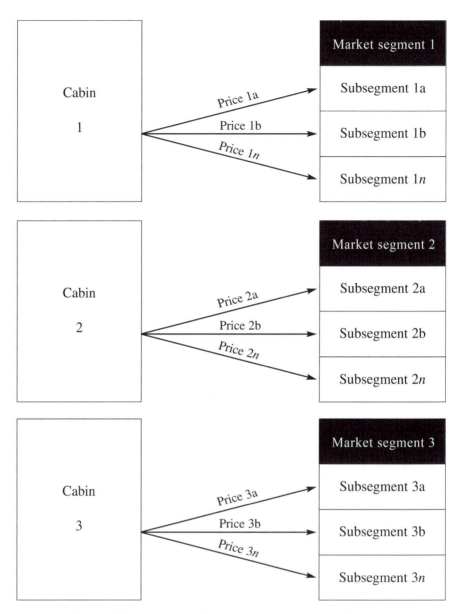

Figure 3.4   Price differentiation between segments of demand, augmented by price discrimination within segments

also product differences to consider. The arguments outlined above can be developed as follows:

1. *Pricing differences between cabins*
    -   Some observers see the quality differentials inherent in different onboard classes as 'relatively minor', and argue that higher production costs in business and first class cabins are to an extent mitigated by economies of scope (Button 1993; Button and Stough 2000).

- An alternative view is that production costs associated with low-density onboard cabins, high standards of inflight service, and associated ground attributes (such as limousine service, valet parking, priority check-in and baggage claim, or lounge access) are so much higher – particularly on medium- and long-haul flights – that pricing distinctions between cabins can be treated as examples of differential pricing.

2. *Pricing differences within cabins*   Most airlines now use revenue management systems (RMSs) which allocate seats within each cabin (or within the single cabin of a one-class service) to different booking (or fare) classes: the highest booking classes (at least on network carriers) usually contain full, on-demand, unrestricted fares, whilst lower booking classes contain discounted fares which have typically been offered subject to progressively tighter restrictions as the depth of the discount increases (although, as noted, conditionality has been relaxed in many competitive short-haul markets). The question is whether different fares in the same cabin carrying different booking conditions or usage restrictions do indeed represent different products with different production costs – that is, whether we are dealing with discriminatory or differential pricing.

   - There is a widely held opinion that the practice of charging different fares to passengers travelling in the same cabin is an example of 'discriminatory pricing' (Kimes 1997), because consumers are being charged different prices for what is essentially the same product with the same production costs. This view accepts that customers travelling on restricted fares can cost less to carry in the same cabin than those travelling on full fares, for reasons outlined below, but the size of discount off full fare is in many cases considerably greater than any reasonably arguable saving in costs; discounted fares are accordingly, on the whole, discriminatory.

   - The alternative view is that if ticket conditions which restrict passengers' booking and/or travel behaviour are characterised as 'negative service attributes' it can be argued that an unrestricted fare is a substantially different product from a highly restricted discount fare; significantly, it offers 'flexibility' as a product attribute that is unavailable to restricted fare classes. Many academics and practitioners use this argument to characterise within-cabin price segmentation as 'differential pricing' (Belobaba 1998b). The argument is that fully flexible 'fare products' do not cost 'essentially the same' to produce as low-yield fare products. On a relatively trivial level, processing costs arise in respect of unrestricted fares when there are schedule changes, re-routings, and cancellations that would not be permissible in respect of restricted tickets; handling costs arise from stopovers (which are freely allowed in the case of unrestricted tickets, subject only to the maximum permitted mileage stipulated for the market concerned). These tickets are also more exposed to prorate dilution, which is discussed later in the chapter, wherever interlining is allowable. More significantly, the real cost of providing flexibility to make reservations late in the booking cycle and to make short-notice itinerary changes can be argued to arise from two capacity variables: the provision of high seat accessibility (i.e., protecting seats for late-bookers and perhaps therefore achieving lower load factors than might otherwise have been the case); and the provision of a high-frequency schedule to offer wide booking and rebooking options.

     In summary, this view takes exception on two related grounds to the argument that within-cabin fare differences are examples of discriminatory pricing under a single demand curve. First, flexibility – to book late, for example – is a service attribute and although people might moan about paying for it, it is a valuable source of product differentiation – and, for the airline, a source of meaningful additional costs. Tickets that provide it are therefore fare products distinct from tickets that do not – fare products which have their own demand curves. Second, important but often overlooked marginal costs of serving high-yield segments include the cost of operating the large network and high frequencies that customers in these segments expect (ibid.), and the cost (in terms of lower load factors) of providing adequate seat-accessibility for passengers booking late or wanting to change itinerary at the last minute.

Developing the latter argument, Botimer (1993) has suggested that each fare represents a different product, defined in part by the flexibility associated with it, and that each has meaningfully different marginal costs of production. Rather than there being just a single demand curve for travel in a given cabin on a particular flight, there are multiple demand functions and demand curves attributable to the multiple segments comprised of people who place different values on different levels of ticket conditionality; importantly, there are also multiple marginal cost curves. According to this argument, the simple models of price discrimination illustrated in Figures 3.2 and 3.3 are inappropriate – despite adopting an analytical approach that is widespread in the industry.

Why the distinction matters   The reason why this matters is that optimal capacity and revenue management decisions cannot be made if we are working on incorrect demand curve assumptions. Furthermore, not only might pricing structures fail to reflect an accurate understanding of the demand curves or the segment elasticities that different prices are designed to tap, neither might they reflect the true marginal costs of serving different segments.

Conclusion   In principle, the debate can be resolved by looking at relativities between price and cost. Discrimination occurs where different customers are charged different fares for products which cost the same to produce (e.g., fare differences within economy/ coach) or, alternatively, where the cost of serving one customer is indeed higher than the cost of serving another but the additional price charged is significantly higher than the additional cost (e.g., fare differences between premium cabins and economy/coach). Some observers argue that airlines only ever apply discriminatory pricing under a single demand curve; others argue that cost, particularly in a network context, is too imprecise a concept to use for this purpose and that it cannot be correct to assume that passengers making last-minute bookings in a premium cabin have the same demand curve as passengers booking months in advance for travel in economy/coach. Whilst it is worth understanding the debate and the reasons for disagreement, it is vital to remain grounded in reality: most airlines still have relatively little insight into price-elasticity and willingness to pay, and their pricing decision support tools focus primarily on monitoring and matching competitors' fare changes – with optimal pricing capabilities to achieve a balance between stimulation and diversion of demand still at an early stage of development (Vinod 2005). Any knowledge regarding willingness to pay at a particular point in time is more likely to be reflected in decisions taken by an RMS than to be embedded in a tariff structure – which is one reason we will refer to this debate again in Chapter 9.

II. Tariff Structures

'Fare structure' is a term encompassing the many different passenger fares that may be offered in a market at any point in time, whilst a 'rate structure' applies to freight traffic. Fares, and rates, together with the specific rules applied to each comprise 'tariff structures'. A tariff structure should be clear and straightforward enough to be easily understood, particularly by travel agents and others in external distribution channels, and yet also sufficiently layered to tap into the various levels of willingness to pay that exist in different segments; in fact, many tariff structures offered by network carriers have over time become complex and arcane. In principle, they should be driven by insight into the service expectations and price-elasticities of different segments of demand; in practice what actually happens is that structures evolve, sometimes haphazardly, in response to incremental market learning (Garvett and Michaels 1998).

PASSENGER TARIFF STRUCTURES

Pressures Shaping Passenger Tariff Structures

Two pressures in particular have contributed to increasingly complex tariff structures and price volatility:

1. Liberalisation and deregulation: airline managers have taken the opportunity to use price proactively as part of both tactical and strategic adjustments to the marketing mix.
2. The use of revenue management systems (RMSs) to micromanage seat availability at different prices: pricing and revenue management have increasingly been used together to maximise revenue capture on a departure-by-departure basis by 'ring-fencing' different market segments with ticket conditions and constrained seat availability in an attempt to prevent price-inelastic customers buying fares set below their willingness to pay. We will return to this in Chapter 9.

Conversely, two pressures have more recently contributed to a simplification of tariff structures, most notably in short-haul markets:

1. The growing market reach of LFAs, which on the whole prefer relatively simple structures that are cheap to administer and easily accessible to customers.
2. The penetration of the Internet, particularly in North America and Europe. This has freed customers from the stranglehold that airlines and their agents had long held on tariff information, allowing almost instantaneous price comparisons. It has also required airlines wanting customers to move away from other, more costly, distribution channels to simplify their tariff structures; fares and conditions must be visually understandable by the public without explanation from a travel agent or call centre employee.

Analysing Passenger Tariff Structures

We have seen that the word 'tariff' refers to a combination of fare and rules, and that the expression 'tariff structure' refers to the different tariffs available in a particular market. Each tariff ('fare basis') can be identified by a fare basis code; depending upon the circumstances in a particular market and the pricing philosophy of the carrier concerned, several dozen fare bases could be in use across the cabins of a network airline on a single departure – particularly in long-haul markets yet to be affected by the pressure for simplification that LFAs have brought to many short-haul markets. To facilitate reservations and revenue management, fare bases are usually grouped into one of a smaller number of booking classes. Variances between fares within a booking class should as far as possible be minimised, whilst variances between those in different booking classes should be maximised; the fares offered within a booking class should average out at the target discount off full-fare for the cabin that has been established by the pricing department. Whether or not a particular fare is available on request therefore depends not only upon whether its conditions (e.g., in respect of advance purchase) can be met, but also upon whether the relevant booking class is open.

In markets – particularly international markets – still subject to a degree of commercial regulation, tariff structures can be relatively rigid; in liberalised or fully deregulated markets they are likely to be dynamic. Fares on offer might be published or unpublished.

Published fares   These are *public fares* that are published to the world at large through industry-standard channels, notably the Airline Tariff Publishing Company (ATPCO) and SITA. They can be broken down into 'normal' and 'special' fares.

1. *Normal (or full, basic or standard) fare*   This is the unrestricted, on-demand or walk-up fare charged for travel in a particular cabin (i.e., first, business, or economy/coach) in a market at any given time. (A few carriers have a separate 'premium economy' cabin for full-fare economy class passengers on long-haul routes, keeping the economy cabin for others travelling on a range of discounted fares; on a small number of carriers, long-haul passengers paying full economy are carried in the business class cabin.) As noted earlier in the chapter, the normal fare can be looked upon as the 'price platform' for a carrier's service–price offers in a particular cabin in a given market. It is associated with booking classes such as: P (long-haul first class) and F (primarily short-/medium-haul first class); J (long-haul business class) and C (primarily short-/medium-haul business class); and Y (coach in the United States and economy elsewhere).

2. *Special (or discounted) fares*   These are fares discounted off the price platform in each cabin and are available, either seasonally or year-round, subject to restrictions on booking (e.g., advance purchase) and/or usage (e.g., minimum or maximum stays at destination); they are associated with alphanumeric codes that vary widely from market to market. Airlines also offer:

    •   Shorter-duration 'promotional' fares. It is common for short-term capacity-controlled offers ('fare sales' or 'seat sales') to be made to promote a particular service or destination, to stimulate low-season demand, or to offload 'distressed' inventory. British Airways has branded periodic sales as 'World Offers', whereas American offers 'MaxSaver' and 'SuperSaver'.

    •   'Preferential' fares available by reference to factors such as age or employment status (e.g., whether over 60 or in military service).

    Promotional fares segment the market on the basis of customers' willingness to modify their *behaviour* to suit the airline's cost and revenue management objectives by meeting the conditions imposed, whilst preferential fares segment on the basis of *identity*. There is no doubting that preferential fares are discriminatory in the economists' sense of the word; as we have seen, whether different promotional fares offered for travel in any one cabin are examples of discriminatory pricing (under one demand curve) or differential pricing (in which case we need to be thinking in terms of several demand curves and different marginal costs of production) is open to debate.

A tiered structure of full and special or discounted fares is now a permanent feature of most long-haul markets, where the margin between the highest and lowest fares available on individual two-, three-, and four-class departures can still be significant. For example, a British Airways long-haul market out of London randomly chosen on the day of writing had 21 published fares with the cheapest economy ticket on sale at one-seventh of the fully flexible, interlineable economy fare and one-twentieth of the fully flexible interlineable first class fare. In short-haul markets penetrated by LFAs, both the LFAs and their competitors generally use a fare structure marked by fewer fare bases, less dispersion between lowest and highest fares (i.e., a more compressed fare structure), and fewer conditions. Many LFAs subject fares only to change and cancellation restrictions, eschewing altogether both fully flexible and highly restricted tariffs; prices vary solely in response to the advance booking period, and can spike quite noticeably close to departure. However, in order to attract higher-yield business travellers, some LFAs (e.g., jetBlue) have recently introduced fully refundable fares.

Finally, where an airline has a weaker presence at one end of a market than the other, it might offer lower fares for journeys originating at the weaker end (i.e., directional fares).

Unpublished fares   These are individually negotiated *private fares* made available to specific agencies or corporate clients, offering prices and/or terms unavailable through other channels. Once they have been negotiated, some are then accessible only direct from the airline but often they can be bought through GDSs via code-restricted access.

The use of unpublished tariffs by agencies owes something to the history of airline pricing and distribution practices. In some (particularly long-haul international) markets where fares were tightly regulated and airlines were unable to compete openly on price, a complex multi-tiered distribution system evolved comprising different types of agencies (e.g., general sales agents (GSAs), consolidators, and 'bucket shops'); within this 'grey market', tickets are wholesaled and retailed at unpublished fares. This was the only way to establish anything close to a market-clearing price structure in many regulated markets, and to the extent that it transferred the risks inherent in price competition to the agencies involved it had attractive aspects from an airline's standpoint – although control over pricing was clearly not one of them.

In liberalised markets, however, airlines have the freedom to adopt a more complex structure of published fares and to use RMSs to ration space availability at each of these different fares. Many have also been encouraging customers to migrate from agency channels towards their own website(s). Unpublished fares do nonetheless remain significant in many liberalised and deregulated markets:

1. *Net fares*   These are a feature of some international markets in particular, and are notably important in Asia. A 'net' fare in this context is the gross fare for a block of seats sold to an agency or travel wholesaler (possibly the normal fare or perhaps a group inclusive tour [GIT] fare) less standard commission and any other fare adjustment typically applied in the market concerned; 'adjustments' could include travel agency commission overrides (TACOs), which are volume- or market-share-

dependent supplemental incentives offered by the airline to a particular agency with which it has targeted a special relationship. The airline receives the net fare, and instead of a commission and other incentives the agency receives whatever mark-up over the net fare it is able to obtain from its retail customers. The lower the net fare available to an agency, the lower the price it is able to charge retail consumers (or the higher the profit margin it can earn). Agencies which are offered net fares sometimes subcontract with smaller retail outlets, as described above, to broaden distribution and help them retain and increase volume incentives available from the airline – although the development of Internet distribution has eroded this structure in many markets.

(The following usages are worth noting: internally, airlines might use the expression 'net fare' either to describe revenue earned after commission has been paid, or revenue earned from a ticket sold net of commission on the basis described in the last paragraph; a 'net net fare' is net fare less any prorate dilution arising from the airline having to share revenue from a sale with another carrier used by the passenger on the same journey – although it is also sometimes used to describe revenue net of commission and net of TACOs or other supplementary incentives.)

2. *Other off-tariff arrangements* Corporate (including government) and group deals are broadly self-explanatory. Individually negotiated corporate arrangements, also widely referred to as net fares because they are sold net of agency commissions, might involve discounts off the prevailing published fare, relaxation of booking and usage conditions (which itself amounts to a price break), and/or free upgrades; in the US market, negotiated flat or fixed-price fares and also prepaid bulk purchases are common. Alternatively, an end-of-period rebate might be payable by an airline to a corporate client subject to attainment of agreed sales thresholds, applied either to absolute levels of expenditure or to the number of journeys made on a specific group of routes or the network as a whole. A number of large corporations have negotiated deals with airline alliances, but antitrust/competition law can be a barrier to this type of pricing coordination between carriers in many jurisdictions unless the alliance has been 'immunised'. Furthermore, there is anecdotal evidence from corporate travel buyers that some alliance members are less than wholehearted in their commitment to multi-party price negotiations.

Large carriers with extensive network coverage are in a strong position to offer favourable contracts to corporate customers. Airlines with wide networks emanating from a dominated hub or national market, perhaps augmented by relationships with alliance partners, clearly have more to offer local companies because any one competitor is likely to be strong – if at all – in only a small number of those markets and so be unable to offer the scope of coverage probably required by a corporation generating trips to a wide range of destinations. However, this is not the sole preserve of network airlines. Amongst LFAs, Southwest added to its (admittedly quite small) corporate sales force in 2007, whilst WestJet went from having no corporate deals in early 2006 to having over 800 just 18 months later.

Separately, airlines with FFPs frequently target late-available unsold seats at members who sign up for email offers. Not only is this a useful outlet for distressed inventory, but it also provides an opportunity to learn about different customers' responses to different offers – and perhaps to build a deeper brand relationship with customers than can be achieved by using other distribution channels.

To the extent that agency and corporate price breaks and rebates are discontinuous rather than linear, being triggered by the attainment of agreed volume thresholds, they offer discounts that are not based on volume economics. This could in principle ground an argument that they are anti-competitive, in the sense that they are designed to bind customers to the supplying airline rather than to pass on volume-driven cost savings.

Conclusion In order to make sense of sometimes highly complex passenger tariff structures, it is helpful to use five analytical dimensions: class of service; time of travel; ticket conditionality; bundling; and distribution channel.

1. *Class of service* This dimension corresponds to onboard cabins and associated ground and inflight amenities.
2. *Time of travel* Time-dependency manifests itself in two ways:
    * *Peak-/off-peak pricing* Whilst the use of peak-period surcharges on normal fares is not unknown, neither is it particularly common. Off-peak discounting, most notably in coach/economy cabins, is a widespread feature of the industry.
    * *Inventory allocation* Another widely used approach is to rely on an RMS to allocate most seats on peak departures to high-yield booking classes, so limiting the availability of lower fares. This in effect protects more seats for customers who have strong time-preferences that make them willing to pay higher fares to travel on peak departures, and restricts availability for lower-yield demand with weaker time-preferences – spilling the latter onto off-peak departures (or the peak departures of less yield-sensitive competitors).
3. *Booking restrictions* We saw earlier in the chapter that in order to target identified segments of demand and/or respond to competitive conditions in particular markets, an airline will offer a range of different fares for travel in each cabin – particularly the economy/coach cabin. Full fares are usually unrestricted insofar as they can be used for travel at any time within 12 months, can be rebooked or rerouted (subject to maximum permitted mileage restrictions), and refunded if unused. Fares discounted off the full-fare price platform for travel in a particular cabin in a particular market in order to stimulate demand from price-sensitive segments are, as already noted, subject to conditions intended to minimise the diversion of time-sensitive, price-insensitive traffic to low-yield fares.
4. *Bundling* In some leisure markets airfares are commonly bundled together with surface arrangements such as airport transfers, car hire, and accommodation to produce an inclusive product. Most frequently this bundling has been done by tour operators to which airlines sell heavily discounted space. Interestingly, there are now two distinct trends with regard to bundling: first, in countries where Internet penetration is high, customers are increasingly choosing to 'unbundle' by selecting and packaging for themselves each separate travel product – hence the challenges facing Europe's inclusive tour industry; conversely, although in most cases explicitly not acting as packagers or tour operators in this regard, many airlines – notably including LFAs – are keen to sell other suppliers' travel services through their own websites (the components at present being individually priced, but with fully bundled 'dynamic packaging' under development). Bundled packages are therefore being transformed with regard to who is offering them and how they are priced.
5. *Distribution channel* Demand presents itself, and products are sold, through many different distribution channels: airline call centres, airline websites, online travel

portals, travel agents (online and 'bricks and mortar'), consolidators, tour operators, cruise lines, corporate accounts (direct and through TMCs), and partner airlines. Pricing of space on any given departure can vary between these channels.

The average fare on a flight, in a market, or across a network is total revenue divided by the number of originating passengers. Yield, as we will see later in the chapter, is a distance-weighted metric calculated by dividing RPMs (or FTMs) into total revenue. Because total revenue is a function of the different fares available and the number of customers buying each of them, both average fare and yield will be sensitive to tariff structures.

What Has Been Happening In Practice

The liberalisation and deregulation of progressively more markets over the last several decades has allowed carriers to practice much more finely grained pricing than was possible under the relatively static and simple price structures associated with most regulated markets. One significant outcome has been a reduction in real average fares in many markets as stiff increases in full fares have been outweighed by the wider availability and deeper discounts associated with other fares; this accounts to a significant extent for rapid traffic growth, and declining real yields, in deregulated and liberalised markets (Pickrell 1991).

However, selling a large proportion of output at deeply discounted prices is viable for an airline with a traditional cost model only if time-sensitive passengers who book late, primarily business travellers, are prepared to pay high walk-up fares to make up the revenue shortfall. In the United States it became clear from 2000 onwards that the price-inelasticity taken for granted in this segment was unravelling. Revenue models built around exploiting the price-inelasticity of business travellers, and the willingness of others to accept restrictions in return for discounts, have been undermined by:

- corporate customers' reassessment of business travel budgets and practices;
- the inexorable growth of Southwest and other LFAs offering consistently low and simple pricing alternatives based on single flight-legs rather than return journeys;
- much greater price transparency resulting from the shift to Internet distribution.

Network carriers were slow to accept that their revenue model was permanently broken. First America West and Alaska, then in January 2005 Delta with its 'Simplifares', eventually responded by restructuring their tariffs (although Delta subsequently reintroduced complexity into some of its less competitive markets and dropped internal use of the SimpliFares name). This response is now typical of the reaction of network carriers in North America and Europe faced with LFA competition. Tariffs have been simplified by reducing the number and dispersion of fares on offer and by eliminating Saturday night stays and mandatory return bookings. Having said that, several US network carriers began in late 2007 to reintroduce minimum and/or Saturday night stay requirements in markets where they do not face LFA competition. The objective, as always, is to compel business travellers to purchase more expensive, less restricted fares.

The most noteworthy conditions associated with fares other than fully flexible fares tend now to be restrictions on rebooking and cancellation. The result has generally been that although RMSs continue to control release of space in different booking classes, the relaxation of conditionality has allowed widespread diversion of passengers to less expensive fares, leading to higher load factors but pressure on revenues. This is why, as highlighted in Chapter 1, network airline cost models have had to change.

In some markets the change in approach to pricing has been sufficiently radical to represent a new paradigm:

- *Old model* The airline 'sells down': hallmarked by high unrestricted fares, and other fares offered at increasingly deeper discounts as restrictions on purchase and usage are added.
- *New model* The passenger 'buys up': hallmarked by low basic fares, perhaps rising as the departure date approaches, with incremental charges for additional product features (e.g., seat assignment, priority check-in and boarding, checked baggage, or inflight catering).

Air Canada was one of the first airlines to make a clean break with the traditional pricing structure by offering five branded fares: Tango, Tango Plus, Latitude, Latitude Plus, and Executive (business class). None is subject to advance purchase requirements but each offers different combinations of service attributes (e.g., seat selection, mileage accrual, lounge access) – thereby providing customers with distinct service–price choices. It has already been noted that many LFAs and a growing number of network carriers are now unbundling the air transport product to offer previously free attributes such as seat selection and baggage checking for an additional charge; what Air Canada did was leap-frog that unbundling stage by repackaging attributes and charging differentially for the package rather than individual attributes alone. It then went even further by offering Web-only unlimited travel passes for a flat monthly fee, with the price differentiated according to which of the above five fare products is bought and which of several alternative geographic zones and time periods is accessed. Icelandair is just one of several carriers that have subsequently followed Air Canada to a bundled approach, offering different service attributes in each of four fare categories (which are combinable in different directions of travel): Best Price, Economy, Economy Flex, and Saga.

A challenge facing airlines wanting to package different combinations of product attribute into separate, branded products has been the inability of GDSs to accommodate this type of differentiation. However, the GDSs have been addressing the matter, and tools such as Sabre Branded Fares and Amadeus' Airline Retailing Platform are becoming more widely available.

Tariff Setting And Filing

Domestic markets   In the US domestic market, airlines set fares as they wish and transmit them to the Airline Tariff Publishing Company (ATPCO), from where they are distributed directly to travel intermediaries, to GDSs, and to other airlines' computer reservations systems (CRSs). Hundreds of thousands of daily amendments pass through ATPCO. In other domestic markets the level of government intervention in tariff setting varies widely, and many countries still require tariffs to be filed. On public policy grounds some national authorities (e.g., Venezuela and Libya) have imposed price ceilings to maintain low domestic airfares, whereas others keep prices artificially high to protect inefficient national carriers. In China, the government tried for many years to limit discounting – albeit with relatively modest success. But on the whole, carriers now have a great deal more pricing freedom than they had in the relatively recent past (e.g., within Europe, Canada, Australasia, and most Latin American countries); the requirement to file domestic fares with governments is also less widespread.

International markets   In many international markets SITA is a commonly used channel for uploading fares into the distribution system. The established practice in regulated markets was historically for a scheduled service tariff structure to be agreed at semi-annual IATA regional traffic conferences, filed with the appropriate governments as required under the terms of the bilateral air services agreement (ASA) in force between the countries concerned, and then published. This subsection will look first at IATA's role in price-setting, then at different tariff-approval mechanisms found in ASAs.

The purpose of IATA's involvement was originally to enforce pricing discipline amongst members of what was in some respects an international cartel. In recent decades the purpose has simply been to ensure that a system of multilaterally agreed, fully flexible fares exists to permit passengers both to interline and to buy tickets endorsable from one airline to another. Three forces have undermined IATA's former role in tariff-setting:

1. The availability of discounted fares below agreed interlineable fares has been progressively liberalised since the 1970s. In many markets this has resulted in a complex structure of discounted fares or fare bands being developed and filed by airlines acting either alone or, where permitted by competition authorities, jointly with other carriers designated by their governments to serve the market concerned. Most of these discounted fares are ineligible for interlining or for endorsement to another carrier.
2. The growth of global alliances has resulted in a decline in the number of passengers making interline connections between non-allied carriers. Alliance partners will often negotiate joint fares in a market – particularly a highly competitive market – rather than sell the full 'IATA' fare, which therefore has declining relevance.
3. Competition authorities are innately suspicious of the opportunity for collusion presented by multilateral price-setting. The United States has long been unfavourably disposed towards IATA tariff-setting, although in 1985 it did immunise the practice from challenge under antitrust law; DOT has partially overcome its philosophical objection by choosing to view IATA rates as advisory rather than binding. Several other jurisdictions, notably the EU and Australia, have tolerated IATA tariff-setting in recent years only through time-limited exemptions from competition law. However, in its Regulation 1459/2006 of 28 September 2006 the European Commission:
    *   eliminated the 1993 block exemption for tariff coordination on intra-European flights with effect from 30 June 2007; and
    *   extended the block exemption in respect of flights departing from or destined to airports outside Europe, but subject to a further review which, in the event, led to its termination from 31 October 2007.

IATA has responded to the EU rule, and to the progressive elimination of 'IATA fares' generally, by introducing a new system of interlineable and endorsable 'flex-fares' recalculated semi-annually for each market as an average of the full, unrestricted fares charged in that market, plus a premium for the added flexibility of being able to interline.

Bilateral ASAs usually incorporate one of several tariff approval mechanisms. In increasing order of liberalism these are:

- dual approval: both governments must approve every filing;
- single disapproval: tariffs enter into force unless one government explicitly disapproves;
- country of origin: each government's right to disapprove lies only in respect of tariffs outbound from its jurisdiction, one way or return, and there is no power to disapprove inbound tariffs;
- double disapproval: both governments must disapprove any filing in order to prevent it coming into effect.

A less common variant is the 'designated carrier' approach, which gives each government the right to approve or disapprove only filings by its own designated carrier(s), irrespective of the country in which travel originates. Separately, some bilaterals allow for automatic approval of tariffs within specified tariff zones around predetermined reference levels. Different zones might, for example, be defined for first class, business class, full economy/coach, discount, and deep discount tariffs. Filings outside these zones would be dealt with by the normal method required under the terms of the bilateral concerned (i.e., double approval, country of origin, etc.).

Where open skies bilaterals or agreements having a similar effect have been entered into, either double disapproval or automatic approval might be agreed. The result in the latter case is that neither government has any right to disallow a tariff filing unless – perhaps – it is by some standard determined to be excessively high (and possibly therefore an abuse of dominant position), artificially low (and therefore perhaps predatory), or unreasonably discriminatory. Not all ASAs in fact require fares to be filed, although where filing is not required the governments concerned may nonetheless retain oversight powers for use if they consider fares predatory or unreasonably discriminatory.

Tariffs governing nonscheduled services have typically been subject to unilateral state control; many countries continue to ban inbound charters in order to protect their national airlines' scheduled services, whereas others take a liberal attitude to support the domestic tourism industry. However, an increasing number of bilaterals now incorporate clauses in respect of nonscheduled operations, and where this is the case 'country of origin' tariff approval tends to be the rule.

FREIGHT RATE STRUCTURES

Until the early 1980s, international freight rates were largely regulated in much the same way as passenger fares. Nominal competitors agreed rates within the IATA framework and submitted them for rubber-stamping by their governments under the terms of bilateral ASAs. Since then rates have become a very much more active element in the marketing mix on most international routes and there is now considerable price competition, particularly for the business of shippers and forwarders moving large quantities. Indeed, rates in most major markets are effectively deregulated.

An increasingly complex rate structure evolved during the decades before the 1980s. Box 3.1 summarises this structure.

Box 3.1: The Freight Rate Structure

Subject to some variation between markets, the following structure and terminology came into widespread use:

General cargo or commodity rate   This became the baseline, 'normal' rate for movements in a particular market (with different rates likely to be applicable in different directions). 'Class rates' are upward or downward adjustments to the general rate in respect of certain categories of goods; an example of an upward adjustment, referred to as an 'exception rate' in the United States, is the carriage of live animals or other shipments that need special handling. The general rate would be subject to quantity discounts, escalating at each of several break-points, to encourage consolidation; the amount of the reduction in price per kilo at a given break-point is known as the 'rate differential'. Although the situation varies depending upon the level of competition on any given route, only difficult, emergency or very small shipments would move at or close to the general rate.

Specific commodity rates   These were introduced into various markets and applied to goods relevant to the city-pair concerned, with the objective of countering weak or erratic demand or perhaps just stimulating the market generally – often to help fill burgeoning belly-hold capacity on passenger widebodies. They are numerous, and are intended specifically to stimulate the use of airfreight by shippers of targeted commodities rather than simply being a figure keyed-off the general rate and adjusted to reflect differential costs. Specific commodity rates became dominant in some markets, much as discounted fares have become in many passenger markets. They proliferated and became extremely complex in their application, both because of wide variations in practice between different markets and because precise definitions of the qualifying commodities proved cumbersome. Again, weight-breaks usually determine the size of any discounts; minimum charges have tended to be higher than in respect of the general rate. Specific commodity rates nonetheless contributed substantially to declining cargo yields in some markets.

The traditional rate structure has now been largely superseded in most important markets by a cocktail of standard retail rates, frequently based on bulk unitisation, and directly negotiated contract rates.

Bulk unitisation   Another by-product of the rapidly increasing availability of belly-hold capacity aboard growing numbers of new widebodied aircraft in the 1970s and 1980s was the introduction of lower rates for shipments prepacked onto or into unit load devices (ULDs) – irrespective of the commodity(ies) concerned. The advantage of ULDs for airlines is that they involve lower handling costs because they are ready to load. The usual practice would be to levy a minimum charge per kilo in respect of each pallet or container on the assumption that the weight of the shipment is equivalent to a certain pivot weight; if the actual weight turns out to be in excess of the pivot weight, any difference would be charged at a rate more favourable than the general rate. The disadvantage of bulk unitisation is that airlines cede control over their markets to large forwarders able to consolidate shipments from a wide range of shippers and smaller forwarders.

Contract rates   Because the role of forwarders is to consolidate into larger shipments the freight despatched by multiple shippers, their profitability has historically depended upon the airlines' pattern of rate break-points and the size of rate differentials (see above). More recently, large forwarders able to commit to significant tonnages have been able to negotiate special contract rates irrespective of commodity type or ULD usage – although ULDs often still benefit from price incentives. Such contract rates are sometimes referred to as freight-all-kinds (FAK) rates, indicating that they are not tied to a specific commodity. The strongest forwarders have even been able in some markets to negotiate commissions from airlines, much as travel agencies have historically done. Similarly, significant shippers can usually negotiate attractive contract rates directly with airlines, and some do; others, however, prefer not to enter into long-term commitments – despite peak-period shortages of space in many key markets – in the hope that they can benefit most of the year from cheaper spot prices.

To this structure might be added special seasonal and promotional rates, higher rates for reserved space on a specific flight, express rates for time-definite delivery (a segment now almost totally dominated by the integrators), and also ad hoc 'spot' rates for late-booking shipments on lightly loaded departures.

In addition to the effect of prevailing economic conditions on airfreight demand generally, a number of other structural factors within the industry are combining to affect pricing:

1. *Downward pressures* There are several downward pressures at work:
   - In many medium- and long-haul markets freight rates can be even more volatile than passenger fares where substantial volumes of belly-hold capacity are available on passenger aircraft relative to off-peak demand in the freight market concerned. This is particularly true when widebody twins are operated at a high frequency, and when fifth and sixth-freedom carriers with by-product approaches to airfreight costing have to price aggressively to win business from better established third- and fourth-freedom airlines. (Freedoms of the air and different approaches to costing will be discussed in Chapters 4 and 5 respectively.)
   - The intense demand directionality highlighted in Chapter 2 means that in many markets the supply of space required in the high-demand direction (e.g., eastbound on the North Pacific) exceeds what can be sold profitably in the opposite direction.
   - The negotiation of discounts below retail levels for individual high-volume shippers and forwarders is now widespread. Most airlines still rely heavily on forwarders to generate traffic, and having to deal with this relatively small number of buyers inevitably weakens their control over pricing. The situation is becoming more acute as the forwarding industry consolidates, with close to half the world's airfreight now being shipped by around a dozen intermediaries.
2. *Upward pressure* Integrated carriers offer simple but relatively high-yield rate structures based on time-definite door-to-door service and real-time tracking. The standard of service provided by the integrators, and particularly their use of time and value-added on the ground rather than the nature of shipped commodities as a basis for pricing (unless special handling is required), have changed customer expectations in many airfreight markets. Some all-cargo airlines and combination carriers (i.e., airlines which fly freight as well as passengers) have responded, but most remain committed to traditional, low-yield, airport-to-airport line-haul services targeted primarily at forwarders.

   The number of carriers that have tried offering a range of high-yield 'branded' time-definite door-to-door services in addition to straightforward airport-to-airport haulage is small; in some cases these products have been offered in partnership with preferred forwarders – the intention being to create a 'virtual' network capable of competing with integrated carriers such as FedEx and UPS. Success in this endeavour has been mixed, in large part because most combination carriers and all-cargo airlines have neither the geographic scope to compete with the largest integrators nor the throughput volume to justify IT and handling investments on the scale necessary to deliver the quality of service provided by them. In other words, the airlines face significant barriers to entry into this type of market because they lack adequate scope and scale; we will look at economies of scope and scale in Chapter 5.

The Payload–Volume Trade-Off

An aspect of freight pricing not met on the passenger side of the industry is the need to optimise the payload–volume trade-off such that revenue from available cargo capacity is maximised given the type of aircraft operating a service. Every aircraft has a fixed volumetric capacity for the carriage of freight, as well as a payload capacity that will vary depending upon the weight of fuel and (where relevant) passengers carried on a particular departure. Clearly, there is no merit in filling (i.e., 'cubing out') available space with a light-weight commodity and then charging shipment on the basis of weight; at the other extreme, neither is there merit in carrying maximum payload in the form of a dense commodity and then charging on the basis of volume. Airfreight pricing structures have to be designed to maximise revenue by carefully managing charges for weight carried and volume taken-up.

Applying a minimum charge based on assumed weight per unit of cubic capacity (i.e., 'dimensional weight') is one way of managing this trade-off. A commonly used approach is to assume a dimensional weight of 166.67 kilograms per cubic metre and assess the chargeable weight as the higher of dimensional or actual weight. (The figure 166.67 is one-sixth of a metric ton, hence this rule is sometimes referred to as the '1/6th rule'.) In respect of smaller packages a common approach is to calculate dimensional weight as the sum of the three dimensions divided by 6000, then compare this with actual weight (an approach used by UPS, for example).

III. Price Drivers

What drives pricing? To help answer this question, it is useful to assume floor and ceiling prices: the floor is set by airline costs, because rational producers do not sell below cost; the ceiling is defined by whatever value customers place on the service being bought (i.e., their willingness to pay). That this is an idealised model of reality is borne out by the following quotation:

> Every thriving businessperson knows that you have to sell a product for more than it costs to make. But there is more to this simple-sounding concept than meets the eye. How should costs be defined? Fully-allocated versus marginal? Short-run versus long run? Tangible versus opportunity? Once this dilemma is addressed, rational pricers learn that the basic rule is true only on average. Prices may be below average costs in off-peak times and significantly above in peak times. Prices may be below average costs for elastic leisure and VFR passengers and above average costs for inelastic commercial customers. Customers may pay different amounts based on their relative negotiating leverage.

> Thus it becomes clear that pricing occurs in both the world of cost and the world of demand. As a result, skilled pricers will consider cost factors as constraints and demand factors as a primary driver.

> (Garvett and Michaels 1998, p. 335).

The fact is that there can be sound competitive reasons for pricing below one or other definition of cost, especially in the short run. The image of a floor and ceiling is nonetheless helpful because it opens the idea of a space within which competitive forces play out to determine how much of the value created by a service is captured by consumers, as consumer surplus, and how much by the airline providing it.

COSTS

On a system-wide basis, there is certainly evidence that costs can feed directly into prices. We see this with fuel surcharges when the price of oil spikes. Another example came in late 2000 when United followed-up a handsomely rewarding contract for its pilots by increasing unrestricted domestic fares by 10 per cent – arguably the final flourish of the now-obsolete US domestic network carrier revenue model. Using a market-specific frame of reference, however, it is generally true that fares owe more to customers' willingness to pay for what is offered than to the costs of offering it (Smith *et al.* 1998).

There are in fact plenty of 'disconnects' between airline costs and individual fares:

1. Many airline services are characterised by 'production interrelatedness' – in other words, 'joint products' are produced as an inseparable consequence of a single production process. For example:
   - It can be argued that below-deck cargo output is simply a *by-product* of passenger service.
     - Many airlines do indeed price belly-hold freight on a by-product basis. They expect freight revenue to cover direct ground-handling costs, incremental fuel-burn, and sales and administration overhead, and beyond this to make a positive contribution to the rest of the airline's income statement – but they do not expect it to cover an allocated share of other operating and nonoperating costs that are not directly attributable to the carriage of freight.
     - Conversely, some carriers – particularly those that have spun cargo operations off into separate subsidiaries or profit centres – expect cargo revenues at least to cover fully allocated costs: direct operating costs of a combination flight not specific to cargo (e.g., pilots' salaries and flight dispatch costs) might, for example, be allocated between passenger and cargo products on the basis of aircraft volume; corporate overhead could be allocated to cargo and passenger products proportionate to their share of direct costs, both specific and allocated.

     Clearly, the use of a by-product approach as a pricing input is likely to lead to lower cargo rates than fully allocated costing – a point that can become particularly knotty when it comes to interlining freight between alliance partners who take different approaches to costing and pricing.
   - A more complex example is joint production of cargo and passenger space on a combi aircraft that has both types of capacity on its main deck. Here, output in the two categories is produced deliberately rather than one being a by-product of the other. The complication in this case arises from the opportunity that exists to vary the capacity of each category, unlike belly-hold cargo space which is largely fixed (subject, on some aircraft types, to options to locate galleys and/or crew rest areas below deck). Another example of joint production arises when

passengers travelling from and to a number of different origins and destinations share a particular flight as part of their respective journeys over a hub or other transfer point. And, of course, on any one flight the output associated with different cabins is jointly produced.

Some airlines use complex cost attribution formulas, whereas others either cannot or choose not to be precise in linking costs to specific fares and freight rates. There is a strong argument that the further a network carrier moves away from total cost, the deeper it is venturing into the realm of opinion. This does not mean that efforts to cost the delivery of specific services to specific market segments on specific flight-legs are pointless; what it does suggest is that efforts to argue a tight linkage between these costs and individual fares or freight rates are open to question.

2. When an airline serves a given route with very different aircraft types, each having different seat-mile costs, this is not reflected in fares. Indeed, it might be that low off-peak fares are offered on flights which – because of weak demand at the times concerned – are operated by smaller aircraft having higher seat-mile costs than larger aircraft scheduled onto the route at other times to accommodate peak demand. In the freight sector, rates do not distinguish between aircraft used (e.g., passenger, combi or freighter), or the circuity of the route taken between origin and destination, despite very different costs.

3. Passenger fares and freight rates generally taper with distance so that the monetary amount paid per mile for a short journey will tend to be higher than the amount per mile for a significantly longer trip. The reason for this is that operating costs – unit costs or cost per ASM (CASM) – decline as stage-lengths increase. To understand why, consider two categories of cost:
    *   *terminal costs*: these arise from handling passengers, freight, and aircraft, as well as from reservations and sales activities;
    *   *line-haul costs*: these encompass the costs of operating a flight from gate to gate (i.e., doors closed to doors open).

    CASM declines as stage-length increases because: first, terminal costs associated with each departure and arrival are spread over a greater output of ASMs than would be the case were the flight-leg shorter; second, costs associated with taking off and manoeuvring to land – both significant elements of line-haul cost – are also spread over a greater output of ASMs on a long flight-leg. However, fares tend to taper less than costs, in part because of the lack of intermodal competition on medium- and long-haul routes. Furthermore, the rate at which fares taper is inconsistent across different routes of similar length operated by the same airline using a given aircraft type – with the rate of taper appearing to owe more to the intensity of competition than to airline costs.

4. It is not uncommon for point-to-point fares into a hub from a given origin to be more expensive than fares for connecting services from the same origin to a destination beyond the hub. This type of pricing across international hubs is far from unusual, and neither is it unknown across US domestic hubs. It can be justifiable where carriers have to respond in their flow markets to the fact that consumers generally value connecting services less than non-stop (or even direct) services.

    Where demand arising in an O&D market is met by output supplied using two or more flight-legs over a hub, the characteristics of the demand arising in that particular market are likely to be stronger price drivers than flight-leg costs (or the costs associated with operating the hub). Conversely, where market conditions require it, an airline might price fares in an O&D market over its hub higher than competing non-stops in order to preserve space on flight-legs into and out of the hub for higher-yielding local traffic (or even higher-yielding flow traffic in other connecting markets). There is no general rule: if we take an airline such as Emirates and compare fares in sixth-freedom markets connected over its Dubai hub with fares offered by third- and fourth-freedom carriers serving the same markets non-stop or direct, sometimes Emirates is a price leader and sometimes it is not. Pricing multiple markets served across a hub by joint supply is clearly a complex task which has as much to do with comparative available yields as with the production costs arising from any individual flight-leg; where multi-hub networks are involved, the task becomes even more complex.

5. Directional fare differentials exist in a number of long-haul markets. Sometimes these are attributable to currency exchange rates, but often they are not. Directional fare differentials (and freight rate differentials) have been particularly marked over the North Pacific, with passengers originating in Asia historically paying more than passengers travelling between the same city-pairs but originating in North America.

6. Airlines frequently sell seats at different fares depending on whether they are bought in the country from which the service originates or in another country.

Notwithstanding that it was broadly used as the basis for setting US domestic fares prior to deregulation, cost-plus pricing is difficult to apply in practice because there are so many different ways to define the airline 'product' and – as is explained in Chapter 5 – so many possible definitions of 'cost' and methods of cost allocation. It is now some way from being the norm, although the smaller an airline is and the more simple its network the easier a linkage between costs and prices should in principle be to establish: for example, an LFA flying entirely point-to-point and selling only on the basis of one-way flight-segments is clearly in a stronger position to understand the costs associated with carrying a given load on a given flight than would be the case for a network carrier feeding the same flight into a hub. There is anyway an argument that prices should drive costs, rather than the other way around: the sequence (known as 'target costing') is to design service–price offers suitable for the markets and segments being targeted, then get costs down to ensure that forecasted demand can be served profitably.

In the final analysis, customers' willingness to pay for a service is based on the value they place on the package of benefits offered by that service; what it costs the airline concerned to assemble and deliver the package is irrelevant to the customer. How far an airline can eat into consumer surplus by charging a price as close as possible to the value that targeted customers place on the perceived benefits offered by the service concerned will depend upon the degree of 'monopoly power' the carrier is able to exercise.

MONOPOLY POWER

An airline does not need to be a pure monopolist (i.e., a sole supplier) to have monopoly power in a market. The degree to which an airline is able to exploit monopoly power in its pricing decisions is reflected in the price–cost margin (i.e., (price – cost)/price): a ratio of zero implies a perfectly competitive market, whereas the further the ratio rises above zero the greater the airline's monopoly power can be said to be. Whether monopoly power exists will depend in large measure on price-elasticity in the market concerned and on whether products are differentiated.

Price-Elasticity Of Demand

The price-elasticity of demand faced by any airline is a function of three factors: the price-elasticity of market demand; the number of competitors in the market; and competitive interaction among carriers (Pindyck and Rubinfeld 2001).

The price-elasticity of market demand   The price-elasticity of demand places a limit on a carrier's potential monopoly power. The more price-elastic a demand curve, the less monopoly power the carrier can be said to have. If the proportion of global traffic that is travelling for leisure purposes continues to grow as forecast, it can be expected that the generally higher price-elasticity of this segment will contribute to progressively higher aggregate price-elasticity for the industry as well as for many individual O&D markets.

The number of competitors present in the market   If we take the global air transport market as a whole, there is a large number of airlines providing output. If instead we look at individual city-pair markets, the number of competitors is invariably much smaller. A widely used technique for estimating the level of concentration in a market is the Herfindahl-Hirschman Index (HHI), which is calculated by squaring each competitor's market share; as the result moves from zero (the baseline of perfect competition attainable only in theory) towards 10,000 (i.e., 100^2 – pure monopoly) the level of concentration increases, and in principle the intensity of competition might be expected to weaken. The US Department of Justice (DOJ) considers results below 1000 to imply a competitive market, results between 1000 and 1800 to indicate moderate concentration, and results over 1800 to suggest a highly concentrated market.
   Just how many airlines are present in any one market will depend upon:

- regulation – whether or not there are route licensing, designation or similar barriers to entry;
- other barriers to entry – notably infrastructural constraints, but also the presence of a dominant incumbent (or allied pair of incumbents);
- geography – whether the origin and destination are far enough apart to allow connecting services over one or more intermediate hubs to compete with direct and/or non-stop services (and, if the market is international, what pricing and capacity rights the sixth-freedom carriers have with regard to flow traffic);
- economic attractiveness – whether the density and/or traffic mix appeal to potential entrants.

   A persistent issue of debate has been whether or not carriers that dominate 'fortress hubs' are able to charge a 'hub premium' by exerting monopoly power over local traffic originating at, or destined for, these hubs. The primary source of power would be high market share concentration, augmented by the attractiveness of the hub carrier's frequent flyer, corporate discount, and (where relevant) agency incentive programmes given that it serves a far wider range of destinations from the hub than any single competing carrier; as we saw in Chapter 2, the effect of these might be to shift the demand curve to the right and so allow a higher price to be charged for a given volume of output. It is anecdotally interesting that dominated hubs usually take the top spots in US Department of Transportation (DOT) surveys of the most expensive airports to fly from, with Cincinnati having spent several quarters 'on the podium' at the time of writing. Furthermore, although since the 1980s various studies have come down on both sides of the argument (e.g., Graham *et al.* 1983; Bailey *et al.* 1985; Call and Keeler 1985; Morrison and Winston 1987; Bamberger and Carlton 2002), and some observers consider academic evidence on the existence and size of hub premia to be 'mixed' (Ben-Yosef 2005), there has been reasonably broad agreement that hub premia do exist in US domestic markets. For example:

- Several US government studies have found that average fares at concentrated hubs are substantially higher than at non-hub airports (DOT 1990, 2001; Transportation Research Board 1999; GAO 1990, 1999).
- Work by Morrison and Winston (1995, 2000), Borenstein (1989), and Evans and Kessides (1993) has reached broadly the same conclusion; the latter found that an airline's ability to charge higher fares out of a hub owes more to hub dominance than route dominance.
- Borenstein (2005) has concluded that there are significantly higher prices at hubs that have not been strongly contested by LFAs.

On the other hand, Borenstein (ibid.) also noted that where hub premia do exist they declined somewhat between 1995 and 2004. It is also worth noting that many studies do not control for traffic mix. Lee and Luengo-Prado (2005) argued that whilst average fare per mile to and from their hubs does tend to be higher than elsewhere in each US network carrier's system, part of the difference is attributable not to market dominance but to a greater than average percentage of high-yield business travellers in the hub traffic mix than on non-hub routes. Although this last point may well be true, however, a corollary would be that the local strength of the dominant carrier's FFP would probably influence pricing; Lederman (2008) has established a link between FFPs and hub premia.

Outside the deregulated US domestic market, academic evidence is certainly less clear. For example, Marin (1995) found that an airport dominance effect was absent in regulated European markets and negative (i.e., the reverse of US experience) in deregulated markets. On the other hand, Bilotkach (2007) identified a hub premium for Continental on specific transatlantic routes out of Newark.

More generally, there is intuitive appeal in the view that the higher the concentration ratio in a market, the more monopoly power incumbents are likely to exercise. Conversely, as markets become progressively more open and competitive their price-elasticities increase in response to the greater availability of substitutes and firms are able to exert less monopoly power. There is therefore a continuum of pricing possibilities dependent in part upon the number of competitors in a market. Neoclassical microeconomics identifies four idealised market structure models along this continuum: perfect competition, monopolistic competition, oligopoly, and monopoly. We will look at these models in the next chapter. What they pay relatively little attention to, however, is behavioural influences on competitive interaction.

Competitive interaction among carriers In the past, markets dominated by just two carriers have frequently been at best arenas of competitive inertia and at worst of tacit, sometimes even explicit, collusion. Similarly, if two airlines that formerly competed on a route decide to enter into an alliance, it is quite possible that prices will move away from a competitive level and begin to squeeze consumer surplus. However, there are three reasons why an alliance might not in fact lead to higher fares:

1. It can be argued that if an alliance results in lower marginal costs, the post-alliance exploitation of monopoly power might not inevitably mean that prices are any higher than before the alliance. For example, if a merger or alliance generates efficiencies which lead to lower marginal costs a price–cost margin can widen, implying greater monopoly power but without any rise in prices (Williamson 1968).
2. In a contestable market freely accessible to potential competitors, supernormal profits should – in principle – attract challengers.
3. Excessive profits could provoke scrutiny from competition authorities.

If we move the level of abstraction from alliances down to individual carriers, it is feasible that management might pursue pricing objectives other than profit maximisation. Pricing might, for example, be intended to expand market share and/or drive out competitors with less financial staying power. Alternatively, if a carrier is in financial difficulties low prices which are unsustainable in the long run could be justifiable to generate cash.

Despite the 'antiquity' of the example, this behavioural dimension is well illustrated by Northwest's aggressive price-cutting in the spring of 1992 (Gertner 1993). The crucial driver in this case was management's response to perceived competitive asymmetries. With a relatively weak domestic route network and a poor service image, the only way for Northwest to boost traffic substantially and generate cash in the teeth of a recession was seen to be to force an industry price cut so deep that at least some of the significant amount of incremental traffic entering the market would inevitably be spilled from stronger competitors onto its own services. Northwest's choice of timing was driven by the fact that summer is the peak period for discretionary travel and that demand from discretionary travellers is more price-elastic and less quality-sensitive than other types of demand. (In the event, American responded with a 50 per cent discount offer and Northwest's initiative lost it around $40 million through fare-matching. The blood-letting did not stop Northwest trying again the following winter, however, and neither did it stop American and others responding once again.)

Clearly, the cost structures, attitudes and behaviours of suppliers present in a market – rather than just their raw number – are critical influences on pricing. This explains why 'intensity of competitive rivalry' is central to Porter's (1980, 1985) popular five-forces model of market structure.

Product Differentiation

Through innovative product design, the development of a strong brand image, and the nurturing of a loyal customer base a carrier might be able to differentiate its services – thereby creating a quasi-monopoly within the market(s) or segment(s) concerned. In this situation the airline could possibly sustain a price premium, at least until competitors make a preferable offer; the more price-elastic the segment concerned, however, the less viable this strategy will tend to be.

The feasibility of premium pricing is subject to three influences:

1. *Economic conditions* During economic upturns, passengers' and shippers' willingness to pay tends to increase; service-sensitivity also rises, although significant segments

of most markets do still remain price-sensitive. Towards the top of the cycle in 2006 Singapore Airlines began charging a premium for travel in first and business classes on its newly introduced B777-300ERs, which offered significantly upgraded inflight comfort and amenities. The same carrier also charged a 15 per cent premium for travel on A380 services to Australia, introduced in October 2007.

2. *Competition* In due course, 'fast followers' will catch an innovator. The question then is whether any premium price established in a particular market will become the new price platform for the cabin concerned in that market, or whether it will be eroded by competitors charging 'less for more'. It is not unusual for airlines with strong service reputations to invest upwards of $200 million on long-haul business and first class cabin upgrades, only to have to do the same again in 4 or 5 years; whether they can earn an incremental return on this investment over its relatively short life or whether it simply serves to protect their existing revenue stream depends upon the competitive dynamics of the markets into which the product is deployed. Given that Emirates has committed not to introduce an A380 premium, it will be interesting to see how long Singapore Airlines' premium survives in UK–Australia markets where the two compete directly.

3. *Customers' perceptions of value* Customers must feel that the product offers sufficient incremental value to justify a higher price.

CUSTOMER VALUE

The ceiling in our simple model of cost drivers is set by customer value. Referring back to Chapter 1, where customer value was discussed in a strategic context, we can recall that it has four elements (Figure 1.2): perceived benefit offered by a service (in the minds of customers); value created (perceived benefit less all input costs); consumer surplus (perceived benefit less the monetary price paid by customers); and seller's profit (monetary price paid by customers less input costs). The difference between value-based pricing and a cost-plus approach is that the latter starts with costs and then turns to the market, whereas the former looks first to the market – the assumption being that in liberalised or deregulated environments it is the market that decides what can be charged for a given level of service.

A value-based approach to pricing endeavours to pitch price at a level that is above costs and as close as possible to the amount that the customer is willing to pay given their perception of the benefits offered by a particular service package. This perception is to a large extent moulded by the manner in which service design and the other marketing mix variables are managed in order to build value in customers' minds. (A product's perceived benefits and the value placed on them by customers are inevitably very difficult to measure with precision; techniques used in some industries include the reservation price method, the attribute rating method, conjoint analysis, and hedonic pricing analysis, all of which are briefly explained in Besanko *et al.* [2000] and are at least touched upon in modern marketing texts. They are not widely used by airlines.)

Some carriers offer relatively low levels of perceived benefit, but compensate for this with low prices – prices that are nonetheless profitable because of these carriers' low input costs and/or high resource productivity; this is the strategic path chosen by most LFAs and European charter airlines. Others concentrate on maximising perceived benefits, particularly for segments of demand prepared to pay higher prices in return for those benefits; this approach underlies the continuous cycle of product upgrades and relaunches in long-haul business and first class cabins.

One of management's most important tasks is therefore to decide on the level of service to be offered, and then provide it at a cost lower than the price the market is prepared to pay – bearing in mind that we are here talking averages, because what price the market will pay for a service is variable not only between different segments but across a network and in response to daily, weekly, and seasonal demand peaks. If competitors can produce a similar service package more cheaply and choose to reflect this in their prices, or if competitors with a lower cost base can profitably offer a better service package at the same price, an airline will find the loyalty of its customers tested.

It is a clever trick, of course, to assess correctly the needs of each targeted segment, design a service that satisfies those needs and is perceived by consumers to meet their expectations, and then pitch the tariff structure correctly in the context of other marketing mix variables and rather imprecisely estimated elasticities. Nonetheless, there is strong theoretical appeal in value-based pricing insofar as it is keyed off demand, elasticities, and market positioning rather than costs – and the closer an airline can get to charging a fare that equates to the maximum that target customers would be willing to pay, the more of the added value in an air transport service it is capturing for itself.

CONCLUSION

As markets are progressively freed from tight commercial regulation, prices are increasingly being set by reference to estimations of customer value and in response to the interplay of competitive forces. It is therefore up to airlines to ensure that their costs allow profitable production of the services they choose to deliver at prices customers are prepared to pay. Of course, market structure is clearly an important influence on prices even in liberalised and deregulated markets. Despite all the talk of consolidation and globalisation, the airline industry remains fragmented. Carriers operate in multiple O&D markets that are each differently affected by competition and by the varying demand elasticities of the particular types of traffic that predominate. The same airline's pricing behaviour will therefore not necessarily be consistent between a market dominated by business traffic in which it faces little or no competition, and may therefore have significant monopoly power, and a highly competitive leisure market.

In practice, the management time spent on pricing has often been much less than that spent on other marketing mix variables. This is in part because the industry has a long history of setting prices in a non-competitive commercial environment which allowed costs (identifiable at a system-wide level, less accurately on a leg- or product-specific basis) to be passed on to customers relatively freely. It is also because much of the information that economists like to assume is available for plugging into pricing models is, in reality, hard to come by and often of dubious efficacy. More fundamentally, it is very difficult for any airline to assess in monetary terms the benefits and sacrifices embedded in the products being offered to each of its targeted markets and segments.

Some airlines and their consultants are nonetheless working on systems designed to predict what different market segments are prepared to pay for specific services at particular times. Several carriers have been developing automated systems able to make pricing decisions that respond to the quality of their services (which might vary from market to market depending upon routing and schedule, for example) relative to what is offered by direct competitors; demand elasticities associated with different service attributes are also factored in. The goal of interactive automation efforts is to encompass product design (including schedule and routing), segment demand elasticities in respect of price and various service attributes, competitors' offers, and both the cost and revenue outcomes of different pricing and distribution alternatives within a single marketing decision support system.

This sort of capability remains a distant prospect for most airlines, and for some – notably LFAs – a costly irrelevance. It is nonetheless true that in most parts of the world price is becoming an ever more sensitive element in the industry's marketing mix. Price is now both a strategic variable – a platform that helps define the positioning of different services – and a tactical variable used, in conjunction with RMSs, to respond to and help manage short-run demand fluctuations in individual markets.

IV. Tactical Pricing

Scheduling and pricing are symbiotic activities – the same coin with different questions on either side depending upon the direction from which it is approached: given the pricing structure in this market, how much output should be produced and when? Given the schedule we have published for this market, what is the best pricing structure to maximise revenue? This section of the chapter will take the second perspective, looking at how pricing structures can be used to maximise revenue from a given schedule (and therefore setting the scene for consideration of revenue management in Chapter 9). We will look at the use of pricing as a tactical tool under different-shaped demand curves and then at the difficult topic of marginal cost pricing, before turning to a discussion of issues that need to be addressed when introducing and responding to fare changes.

PRICING AS A TACTICAL TOOL

Tactical pricing involves the manipulation of three variables: fares, conditions of sale, and the amount of space allocated to each of the fares available on a particular departure. We will concentrate largely on fares.

Price is a valuable tactical tool because it is quicker and easier to change a fare or freight rate than to redesign a product or reorient a marketing communications programme. Indeed, in the United States most majors have automated pricing systems that identify competitors' price changes as they are filed with ATPCO, apply various algorithms, and in 70–80 per cent of cases decide how to respond without human intervention.

The use of price to manage demand for tactical purposes should in principle be based on knowledge of the demand curves an airline faces in different segments of each of its markets, and therefore on knowledge of the elasticities available to be exploited. If a market is price-elastic, total revenue will decline in response to a fare increase and rise in response to a reduction – by amounts that depend on the magnitudes of the fare changes and the degrees of elasticity involved. The problem is that elasticities change over time, and it is today's rather than yesterday's that matter. Furthermore, it is optimistic to assume too much regarding how accurately any market can be segmented and its elasticities measured: relatively few airlines have detailed knowledge of the shapes of the demand curves for their products or of the various elasticities in their demand functions across all the many different city-pair markets they serve, and the market research required to uncover them is time-consuming and expensive. Elasticity information, even if imperfect, can nonetheless be a useful competitive weapon for network carriers.

In Figure 3.5, a reduction in fare from P_1 to P_2 leads to an increase in the quantity demanded from Q_1 to Q_2; however, the impact on revenue is unfavourable, as is implied by the fact that Area 2 (representing additional revenue earned from the incremental demand) is smaller than Area 1 (which represents revenue lost from existing traffic). In Figure 3.6, the slope of the demand curve is considerably more shallow, with the result that the same reduction in fare will lead to a gain in total revenue – as suggested by Area 2 now being larger than Area 1.

Before leaving Figures 3.5 and 3.6, we can put them to another illustrative purpose. Thinking back to the discussion of discriminatory pricing above, assume now that two different fares P_1 and P_2 are offered to distinct market segments – so that instead of considering a price change from P_1 to P_2 we are now looking at two quite separate prices. Further assuming that fare rules are imposed to prevent passengers willing to pay P_1 buying tickets at P_2 instead, we can make the following observations:

- if only fare P_1 is offered, total revenue will be P_1Q_1;
- if fares P_1 and P_2 are both offered and the targeted segments are kept apart (i.e., passengers willing to pay P_1 are unable to meet conditions required for the purchase and use of fare P_2), total revenue increases to $P_1Q_1 + P_2(Q_2-Q_1)$;

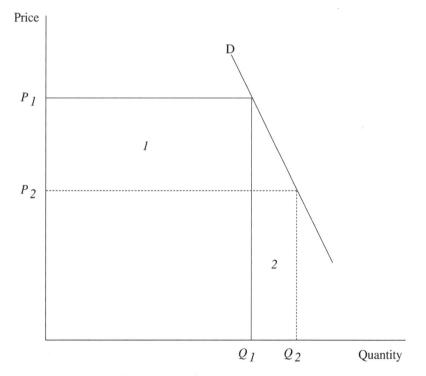

Figure 3.5   **Pricing under a steep demand curve evidencing low price elasticity**

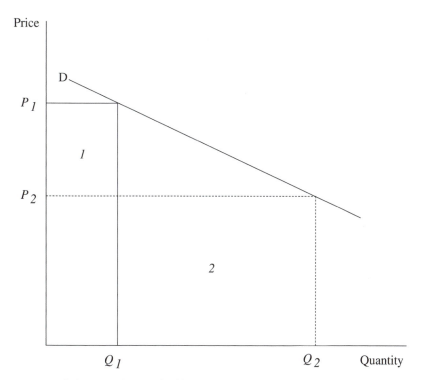

Figure 3.6   Pricing under a shallow demand curve evidencing high price elasticity

- the higher the price-elasticity (as illustrated in Figure 3.6 as opposed to Figure 3.5), the greater will be the revenue gain from identifying a more price-sensitive segment and offering to it fare P_2.

These observations are central to revenue management, as we will see in Chapter 9. Analysis of this type also underpins the complex tariff structures that still apply in many air transport markets. A potentially difficult question to which such structures give rise is how low the lowest discounted fare should be. This leads to the thorny question of marginal cost pricing.

MARGINAL COST PRICING

As soon as an airline commits to a schedule, a high proportion of its total costs can be considered fixed and the variable costs of carrying additional passengers on a flight expected to depart with empty seats can seem very low. There is an ever-present temptation in the airline business to argue that once a schedule has been published the 'marginal' cost of filling an otherwise empty seat is low and therefore justifies low marginal cost pricing of perishable inventory for fill-up purposes. This argument is not necessarily incorrect, but it does introduce some significant definitional issues.

Marginal, Fixed, And Variable Costs

It is important when discussing 'marginal cost pricing' to understand the following distinctions. (We will revisit these topics in Chapter 5.)

1. *Output and capacity costs, traffic and traffic costs*   For the limited purpose of this discussion, airlines can be said to do two things:
   - They generate output by flying seats; doing this imposes 'capacity costs' – the costs involved in generating output, irrespective of whether or not that output is sold. These costs account for a high proportion of any airline's total cost. Marginal cost is the increase (or decrease) in cost associated with producing one more (or one less) unit of output.
   - Airlines also sell the output they produce. When they do this they carry traffic, and traffic imposes traffic costs – such as distribution, handling, catering, incremental fuel-burn, and so on. Traffic costs are not insubstantial, but are generally small relative to capacity costs.

   The traditional neoclassical equilibrium models found in most economics textbooks assume that all output produced is sold (at the market-clearing price). In the airline business, however, this is not the case; if it were, load factors would be 100 per cent all of the time. We therefore need to be careful when talking about marginal cost in the airline industry to distinguish between the marginal cost of *producing* one additional unit of output (which is a capacity cost), and the marginal cost of carrying one additional passenger by *selling* another unit of output (which is a traffic cost). We also need to distinguish between 'marginal' and 'variable' costs.

2. *Marginal cost*   This is an economic concept oriented to the present and the future. Marginal cost can be taken here to be the cost of producing and/or selling an additional unit of output; it is avoidable if that output is not produced or sold. There are two types of marginal cost:
   - *Short-run marginal cost (SRMC)*   If extra units of output can be produced by adding a flight within the existing range of capacity (e.g., by improving aircraft utilisation and without adding to the fleet), the SRMC of those units will be very close to the variable costs associated with producing them (e.g., fuel and other flight-related costs, but none of the fixed costs that would arise if capacity had to be added – that is, if another aircraft had to be acquired to operate the flight). Similarly, the sale of an extra seat on an aircraft already committed to a schedule will carry marginal traffic costs equivalent to the variable traffic costs involved – agency commission, GDS fees and ticketing costs, administration, handling and catering costs, for example. If, on the other hand, producing an extra unit of output requires additional capacity or selling an extra unit requires additional output (using existing capacity), SRMC will in both cases be higher because marginal capacity costs have to be taken into account.

      Crandall (1995) has suggested a generalised SRMC figure, depending upon load factor, in the region of 25 per cent of full costs – although this figure should now probably be higher because system load factors have risen significantly in the intervening years. The marginal cost involved in adding traffic to a system experiencing low load factors is lower than when high load factors imply that many flights are already facing an overdemand situation and output would need to be increased to accommodate additional traffic. In the latter case, the marginal

cost of carrying one more passenger might theoretically encompass not just variable traffic costs, but also the marginal (capacity) costs of adding output to accommodate that passenger.

- *Long-run marginal cost (LRMC)* This encompasses SRMC, but also adds one or both of two additional costs: the cost of replacing existing capacity when this becomes necessary in order to maintain service; and the cost of adding capacity to meet future demand growth.

  Whereas SRMC pricing takes no account of future investment needs, LRMC pricing is higher in order to accommodate these requirements. SRMC pricing may distort signals from the market that can otherwise help map out future resource requirements. It is not unknown for airlines facing high demand generated by aggressive discounting to meet it with additional output. However, what might have been sound marginal cost pricing on the original flight may quite possibly represent unattractive, below-cost pricing on the supplementary flight.

3. *Fixed and variable costs* These are concepts met in both economics and accounting. They are oriented to the present and the past:
   - *Variable costs* Variable costs increase or decrease in response to changes in the volume of output produced (variable capacity costs) or sold (variable traffic costs). When output is increased within the current range of a system's capacity or when additional sales are made from an existing schedule (i.e., an established commitment of output), variable costs and SRMCs are likely to be very similar. (Where an airline declines to pay agency commissions or GDS fees and charges for any catering it supplies, variable traffic costs will be particularly low.)
   - *Fixed costs* Fixed costs include accounting line items that are either spread arbitrarily over the assumed life of an asset (e.g., depreciation of aircraft and maintenance facilities) or charged more or less as paid-for (e.g., hull insurance). Although they are costs attributable to acquiring and sustaining the assets required to generate output, they do not vary with output or traffic as long as output remains within the current capacity range. However, if an increase in output requires additional capacity (e.g., more aircraft), fixed costs will rise because the fixed costs of the new capacity have to be taken into account along with those attributable to existing capacity. Whilst the LRMC concept treats historic costs of acquired capacity as sunk and looks instead at the need for future replacement and expansion, fixed costs arise only once capacity has been acquired; in this sense fixed costs are backward-looking whereas LRMC is forward-looking.

     Variable cost pricing of incremental output covers only the variable costs associated with that output. Pricing on the basis of fully allocated costs, on the other hand, covers both variable costs and the share of fixed costs allocated to the output concerned (and should also include a profit margin). Box 3.2 briefly introduces the topic of cost allocation – a topic we will look at again in Chapter 5.

When discussing marginal cost pricing in the airline business it is not uncommon for the concepts of marginal, variable, and fixed cost to become intertwined. The fundamental points to remember are these:

- Many economists recognise welfare benefits in LRMC pricing because it relates future investments in replacement or growth capacity to current users' willingness to pay for that capacity, whilst SRMC pricing offers no evaluation of future

---

Box 3.2: Cost Allocation

Once a schedule has been established, the first seat sold on each departure notionally bears all the fixed costs associated with that flight and every other seat bears only variable costs and is therefore ripe for (short-run) marginal cost pricing. Of course, this extreme view is never reflected in pricing practice but it does underline a fundamental question: at what point between selling the first seat and the last seat on a given departure should we treat all fixed costs as fully allocated and so switch comfortably to marginal cost pricing without having to worry further about whether sales cover average total cost? There is no formulaic answer. Everything depends upon the traffic mix and fare structure in markets served by a given flight-leg. If there is plenty of high-yield traffic and a fare structure able to tap into consumer surplus in this segment, then the high contribution (i.e., revenue net of variable costs) made by that traffic will cover fixed costs relatively quickly, and SRMC pricing can be justified in respect of a significant proportion of remaining seats; in markets unsupported by the large contribution margins of high-yield traffic, low-yield sales will have to bear a greater share of the contribution to fixed costs and exceptionally low fares will only be sustainable by an airline with exceptionally low costs (e.g., LFAs and nonscheduled/charter carriers).

As we will see in Chapter 5, it can be argued that there is no such thing as 'the' cost. For example, if each unit of output up to a certain level can be priced to exceed average cost (i.e., (total variable costs + total fixed costs)/output) and then sold, it might be perfectly rational to argue that 'the' cost of any incremental output is equivalent to its variable costs alone – assuming that fixed costs, which have already been covered in the price of existing output, do not have to be increased. Conversely, we might argue that 'the' cost is the average cost of all output – existing and new. Both perspectives are defensible, but which is the most appropriate will depend upon the nature of the decision for which cost data are required.

---

requirements. (There is a related point relevant to airlines both as suppliers of output for which demand experiences notable peaks and troughs, and as users of airport and airspace infrastructure which also experiences heavy peaking. Peak-period users of any system place more strain on resources than off-peak users, and therefore contribute more to the eventual need to replace and/or expand existing capacity; this being the case, whilst SRMC pricing of off-peak output can be rational, peak output should in principle be subjected to LRMC pricing. Although such 'scientific' approaches to pricing are seldom met in practice, airlines do use RMSs to ensure that revenue is maximised from high-demand flights; on the other hand, they resist the idea of congestion- or peak-charging at airports – for reasons that will be discussed in Chapter 5.)

- The perishability of airline seats once the doors close, together with the need to cover the high fixed costs associated with scheduled airline operations, put a great deal of pressure on carriers to sell close to variable cost (which is often referred to in this context as marginal cost). Because marginal revenues even from deeply discounted fares tend to exceed variable traffic costs, additional sales of output produced within a given capacity range will usually make some level of contribution to fixed (capacity and traffic) costs.
- Pricing some sales at little over variable cost fails to cover fixed costs, and so in the long run can only be sustainable if other passengers (i.e., those travelling on higher-yield fares) are paying sufficiently dearly to make up the revenue shortfall. The argument often used to justify deeply discounted fares and so encourage fill-up traffic is that the business they generate is better than empty seats, provided

there is a difference between marginal revenue and variable (traffic) costs that can make a contribution – however small – to fixed costs and profits; this is fine as long as these fares are capacity-controlled and there is other, higher-yielding traffic to make a more significant contribution to fixed costs and profits.

- Variable (or marginal) cost pricing will seldom cover average costs – because the latter average fixed as well as variable costs. Average cost pricing is helpful in recovering the costs associated with past investments because it includes an allocation of fixed costs, but it does not help arrive at future investment decisions based on consumers' willingness to pay, and neither does it impose the highest prices on those whose pressure on the system actually generates the most need for future investment – that is, peak-period users. Furthermore, charging average cost prices to one set of users is a recipe to do no better than break even unless higher prices are being charged to other users.
- SRMC pricing and variable cost pricing diverge if the output being priced relies on incremental capacity to generate it – because SRMCs would encompass the immediate acquisition costs involved whilst variable costs would not. The use of variable cost pricing not on a fill-up basis but in respect of output produced by incremental capacity is short-sighted from a longer term capacity management perspective. Of course, in practice an airline will not add a frequency or schedule a larger aircraft to accommodate a single passenger. But at some point in time growing demand will force the decision to increase output, and at this point it is important to know whether that demand is coming forward in response to economically sustainable pricing.
- There can sometimes be a tendency to accept as fixed the costs associated with overcapacity, rather than acting to rationalise that capacity and hopefully underpin firmer prices.

Marginal Cost Pricing In Practice

The apparently low cost of filling an otherwise empty seat makes aggressive pricing attractive at the margin. The problem is that although such aggression might be sound in the short run, it fails to pick up the 'tab' for past investments or to send accurate signals about future resource requirements. Marginal cost pricing can therefore be an invaluable demand and revenue management tool, but there are traps associated with its use that require adherence to the following best practice:

1. Understand the demand curve and, particularly, the price-elasticity of any market segment at which discounted prices are to be targeted. Where either or both detailed statistics or analytical resources are in short supply, this is not necessarily straightforward.
2. Control discounting closely.
   - On a tactical level, this means:
     - Using RMSs to monitor the release of space at various discounts to ensure seat accessibility is maintained for high-yield passengers: RMSs are critical tools for network carriers wanting to ensure that the accessibility of seats on high-demand flights to late-booking, full-fare passengers is not inhibited by early release of too much space at lower-yielding, discounted fares.

- – Using purchase and usage restrictions to ensure that revenue dilution is minimised: revenue dilution occurs when a passenger travels at a fare lower than the highest amount she would otherwise have been prepared to pay in order to fly.
- On a strategic level, control means not letting a surge of traffic in response to loosely monitored discounting form a base for output expansion. Selective use of discounts to fill scheduled capacity on a base-load of higher-yielding passengers might be economically justifiable, but building expansion plans on the basis of demand from such incremental traffic – which will probably be paying less than the airline's long-run average cost – is not.

3. Understand competitors' probable reactions. If competitors have in the past acted, or are now signalling an intention to act, in a manner suggesting they will respond in kind to any further discounting within the established tariff structure, it is quite possible that a fare war will develop. The airlines involved are then likely to fall short of achieving their tactical demand management goals and, at the same time, will probably suffer declining yields. (This links to the discussion of oligopolistic market behaviour in Chapter 4, and is a decision field addressed in recent years by game theory.)

Together, the impact of nonscheduled airlines in highly visible markets such as the North Atlantic during the late 1960s, the scheduled airlines' need to fill new widebodies arriving amidst the economic uncertainties of the mid-1970s, the deregulation of US domestic passenger air transport and then other markets from 1978 onwards, and the more recent growth of LFAs in short-haul markets have set in motion an avalanche of consumer expectations with regard to the availability of discounts off normal or full fares. Today, a wide range of fares below the highest fare applicable for travel in each cabin is offered in most truly competitive markets, and even in markets that remain regulated or for some other reason lack intense price competition there are usually discounts available – either as part of the established fare structure, in conjunction with limited-period promotions, or in the grey market. Indeed, so entrenched have consumer expectations become, the word 'discount' is now something of an anachronism. From an airline's perspective, offering a broadly based structure of fares below the highest fare in each market is a critical demand and revenue management tool. Going down to marginal cost, however, can be justifiable in certain circumstances but has pitfalls that need to be understood.

Marginal Cost Pricing Of Freight

As we saw above, it is sometimes argued that because combination carriers exist in most cases primarily to serve passengers, belly-hold freight output on passenger aircraft is essentially a 'free' by-product – aside from marketing, documentation, surface transport, warehousing, and handling expenses, and the cost of incremental fuel required. Marginal cost (or 'by-product') pricing is entirely appropriate based on this argument. (Ground-handling, incidentally, accounts for a very much higher proportion of freight transportation costs than is the case in respect of passengers.)

The alternative view is that freight capacity made available on passenger flights should also bear a share of allocated capacity costs. Airlines relying on freight for a significant proportion of their revenues, particularly carriers that operate freighters, are more likely to cost on a fully allocated basis than those looking on freight as a simple by-product of passenger output. But in either case, the pressure to use something close to marginal cost pricing in order to fill unsold space and to boost load factors and revenues on lightly loaded departures is as real as it is on the passenger side of the industry.

One airline's decisions with regard to its approach to freight pricing can clearly have a profound impact on competition. For many years, several carriers flew freighters from the US west coast to Australia with high load factors and reasonable yields, onwards to Hong Kong at low load factors and low yields, and then back across the Pacific at high load factors and strong yields. In aggregate, this triangular routing produced acceptable returns to the operators concerned, but local competitors in the Australia–Hong Kong market suffered from the effects of both the incremental output and marginal cost prices brought into that market (Walker 2002). Multilateral deregulation of airfreight markets, a long-running proposal likely to gain momentum as the proportion of cargo carried in freighters (as opposed to the belly-holds of passenger aircraft) increases in the years ahead, would inevitably lead to many more such examples in the future.

INTRODUCING A FARE CHANGE

Fare changes can be system-wide (e.g., flat dollar amount increases or decreases applicable to all itineraries), route-specific (e.g., off-peak fare sales), or departure-specific – although given the oligopolistic structure and multi-market contact characteristic of the industry, a route-specific change may well ripple, via competitors' reactions, across other parts of a wider network. The following considerations apply when initiating a fare change:

- *The traffic, revenue, load factor, production cost, and profit changes anticipated given assumed price-elasticities* When prices are reduced, traffic volume should rise: can this increase be accommodated within the range of existing output (i.e., through higher aircraft utilisation and/or load factors)? If not, can additional output be produced profitably given the cost base? In either case, will revenue from incremental traffic attracted by the price reductions more than compensate for any revenue forgone by levying the lower price on traffic that would have been carried anyway at the original price? If prices are raised, traffic may fall or it might continue to rise but more slowly than had fares remained unchanged: If traffic falls, will the airline be left with too much capacity bearing high fixed costs? Will the increase in revenue from traffic still carried more than compensate for the loss of revenue from passengers spilled to competitors?
- *The traffic and revenue changes anticipated within the carrier's own portfolio of services given demand interrelatedness within that portfolio and the attendant risk of traffic diversion arising from cross-price elasticities* We saw in the last chapter that demand interrelatedness arises when an airline has a portfolio of service packages that are possible substitutes for each other.
- *The traffic and revenue impact of competitors' likely reactions – and the carrier's own subsequent response to those reactions* If a carrier is a major supplier of output in the market(s) concerned, its price initiatives – particularly reductions – will probably be matched; if it is not, the likely response of any dominant carrier is best judged by reference to past behaviour.

The remainder of this section will look at three contexts within which these considerations might have to be weighed: network context; market entry; and product life cycle.

Pricing In A Network Context

In Chapter 2 we alluded to a problem facing network carriers in particular which can make it difficult to apply even the most basic economics of demand, supply, and pricing to their businesses: whilst demand arises in O&D markets, any O&D market might be served by supply produced by aircraft that are at the same time supplying other markets. Thus, an American flight from Miami to Dallas will be supplying output not only to the Miami–Dallas market, but also to O&D markets between points behind Miami and beyond Dallas.

There are two particularly important issues to highlight here:

1. *Displacement of local traffic by connecting passengers* Any airline carrying a significant number of passengers connecting online over one of its hubs will need to give particular attention to tactical pricing. The reason is that the revenue earned off a passenger carried from origin O to hub H and on to destination D may well be less than the sum of the revenue that could be earned from two 'local' passengers using those same seats to travel from O to H and from H to D respectively. This can happen when passengers in O can choose from competing carriers' hub-and-spoke systems to get them to D, whilst those only travelling to or from fortress hub H are subject to the dominant carrier's market power at that hub. Similar considerations can also arise on a linear multi-stop routing where the sum of local fares for intermediate segments exceeds the end-to-end fare (because of the effect of price tapering).

2. *Pricing over a hub as a competitive weapon* Depending upon the location of its hub(s), a network carrier might be able to attack price-sensitive segments of a competitor's non-stop markets by offering a range of discounted fares to draw traffic over the hub; to avoid displacing its own local traffic to and from the hub, over which more market power can be exercised, these lower through-fares should be capacity-controlled. Although low fares may not influence time-sensitive, price-inelastic segments of demand, it seems to be the case that price-elastic segments in US domestic markets, for example, treat connecting services as a reasonable substitute for non-stops (Berdy 1998). (Another possibility might be to boost frequencies on the connecting routes O–H and H–D in order to offer more departures from O to D than the competitor is able to mount with non-stop O–D service, thereby offering a better quality schedule to compensate for the inconvenience and time penalty of having to connect at the hub; this, of course, requires the reassignment of resources – people, ground equipment, aircraft, gates, and (where relevant) slots – from other network activities, which will have opportunity cost implications. Much depends upon prevailing load factors and system capacity. We will return to this in Chapters 6 and 7.)

Pricing For Market Entry

Pricing for market entry depends heavily upon existing market structure. It will here be assumed that the market being entered already has one or more incumbents in place.

We will look beyond any promotional introductory pricing offered for an initial period (and likely to be matched by the incumbent if available in sufficient volumes to cause a significant loss of market share).

An airline choosing to enter a market with a similar fare structure to the incumbent(s) will need to offer something else in order to attract traffic – a superior brand image, a more generous FFP (perhaps augmented by bonus awards during the initial promotional period), a wider network, and/or fewer booking conditions at a given fare level. Higher frequencies than incumbents are offering might be required to attract business travellers – but these would be expensive to produce, particularly for a start-up or small carrier, and could lead to excess output in the market.

The case of a small entrant challenging a larger incumbent   A small carrier challenging a large incumbent on the basis of lower fares, similar fares but fewer restrictions, or similar fares with better service has essentially three choices:

1. To target relatively low-density 'niche' routes and try to avoid aggravating the incumbent with too many frequencies. This was ValuJet's early approach at Atlanta after start-up in 1993, and it was broadly successful until 1996. (Game theorists refer to it as 'the puppy dog ploy'.)
2. To choose relatively dense routes with sufficient volume to allow diversion of enough traffic from incumbents to generate sound operating economics for the aircraft type(s) being put into the market without inevitably provoking a fare war. This was Virgin Atlantic's approach in its early years.
3. To target overpriced and/or underserved markets and rely on price-elasticity to generate increases in traffic volume. This was the initial approach of Frontier at Denver, and has been the hallmark of most European LFAs.

A challenger sometimes has no alternative other than to price aggressively in order to counter the network and marketing (e.g., FFP, brand, advertising, and general market presence) strengths of a larger incumbent. An unsubsidised entrant choosing to compete on price must have a sustainable cost advantage for the strategy to be viable in the medium and long term.

The case of a large airline challenging a smaller incumbent   For the large airline, addition of an extra route may not add greatly to total costs – particularly if under-utilised, off-peak capacity can be deployed. Pricing at little over variable costs can therefore seem a commercially attractive proposition, especially when it generates incremental network feed. However, the same route may account for a significant proportion of the small incumbent's revenues, and therefore not only must it cover variable costs but a substantial contribution to fixed costs also has to be made.

It is seldom advantageous for small incumbents to prolong confrontation with a larger entrant under this type of circumstance unless they have a meaningful cost advantage. Even then, it is quite possible that the resources of the larger carrier may better enable it to sustain a protracted fare war. Amongst these resources will often be a greater scope to cross-subsidise heavily contested markets from other, less competitive markets. (However, in the absence of barriers to entry an airline cross-subsidising low fares in one market, or segment, with profits from others may be vulnerable to attack in its high-margin markets.)

Stage In The Product Life-Cycle

When an established inflight product has reached maturity and is no longer providing value equivalent to competitors' similarly priced but more recently introduced alternatives there is an argument (often ignored) in favour of downwardly flexible pricing. This might happen, for example, when a competitor significantly raises the standards of inflight comfort, entertainment, and service available in its long-haul business class, as several carriers now do on a regular basis. Clearly, airlines which do not respond with their own improvements are offering more mature products. Some choose to deal with this by lowering their prices. Others prefer not to respond directly because they perceive themselves as having other advantages, such as a strong brand image, perhaps reinforced by an attractive FFP and wide network scope; or they might not respond because the innovator has only sufficient capacity to take a small share of the market.

RESPONDING TO COMPETITORS' PRICING

The following considerations apply when responding to a competitor's pricing initiative:

- *Identification* Given thousands of daily fare changes, particularly in US domestic markets, the first task is to identify those that matter (i.e., significant changes in significant markets – changes that might shift share in one of the carrier's core markets).
- *Impact evaluation* The next task is to assess the traffic, revenue, and profit impacts the identified changes are likely to have. In a volatile pricing environment, airline managers have to decide quickly which of their competitors' initiatives should be matched.
- *Response* Some airlines have processes that allow them to respond very quickly, whilst others are more ponderous. In either case, the response must consider very much the same issues that were raised above in the section on initiating a fare change.

Many larger airlines have automated this process. Assuming human intervention, we will briefly look at responses in two possible situations: price changes initiated by an existing competitor; and the entry of a new competitor.

Responding To An Existing Competitor's Pricing Tactics

If a competitor changes its prices an airline must consider:

- why (e.g., to increase market share, raise load factors, pass on cost increases, generate cash under conditions of financial distress, or stimulate a market-wide price change);
- whether the move is tactical or a strategic commitment;
- the likely reactions of any other competitors.

It must also consider the alternative responses open to it, the counter-responses each of these might provoke from competitors, and the probable impact on market share and profits under each of the available response and non-response scenarios. Contingency plans should ideally have been drawn up because whereas a competitor's action might have been planned over a long period, the time available for reaction is usually short.

Responding to price rises   When another carrier raises its fares in an inelastic market, serious consideration should be given to doing the same. Any price advantage gained by failing to respond is likely to be temporary because the probability is high that an unmatched fare increase will be reversed once its initiator starts to lose market share; in the US domestic market, airlines typically rescind price increases that competitors do not match. Much depends on the different parties' views of segment price-elasticity and the likely impact on revenue of the new, higher fare.

An airline's strategic position can also be a significant consideration in shaping its price response. LFAs are in general disinclined to increase fares simply because others have raised them, as was seen when most in Europe declined to impose fuel surcharges in 2004–2008 at a time when network carriers were using these to increase their prices. On the other hand, Southwest was often a willing participant – and occasionally an initiator – when airfares were raised across the US industry on multiple occasions in 2005–2008.

Responding to price reductions   Prices do not fall autonomously; they fall because at least one participant in a market believes it will gain market share by reducing them, and others then follow. Downward pressure on fares is particularly likely where:

- there are large numbers of competitors present, because the larger the number the more likely it is that one will break ranks;
- there is excess capacity;
- competitors have different cost bases, and those with low costs are committed to low fares as part of their strategic positioning and/or believe they can drive high-cost competitors from the market by sacrificing current margins to build market share;
- products are perceived as largely undifferentiated and customers have low switching costs;
- there are strong exit barriers keeping capacity in the market, such as Chapter 11 bankruptcy protection or the support of state shareholders (Besanko *et al.* 2000).

Competitors must decide whether they want to match a reduction; in practice, airlines are often quick to do this. In complex networks where many different O&D markets are served by joint supply over one or more hubs, it is often simpler to respond quickly in defence of market share than to go through the (questionably accurate) process of evaluating demand responses in all the different markets that might be affected.

Sometimes, however, a carrier with high market share might instead prefer to exploit its relatively strong position by resisting pressure for widespread discounting, and turn instead to non-price responses such as improving product quality (e.g., enhanced inflight service), relaxing ticket conditionality, and promoting customer loyalty (e.g., reinforcing brand positioning and/or boosting FFP awards). These responses are not likely to impress the most price-elastic segments, but may have an impact further up the yield structure.

Conclusion   Responses to an existing competitor's tactical pricing initiatives should be shaped by the price-elasticity and value sensitivity of the market(s) affected, the current positioning and life-cycle stages of the product(s) concerned and their significance in the airline's overall product portfolio, the strength and likely objectives of the competitor, and the behaviour of costs in response to volume changes.

Tactical Pricing In Response To Market Entry

Much will depend upon the size of the affected market and its significance to the incumbent's overall network, as well as upon the volume of output being offered by the challenger, the number of frequencies operated, the level of fares and the nature of associated restrictions, and the threat potentially posed by the challenger to the incumbent's market share once any introductory promotion ends.

Response to the threat of attack   A well-publicised price reduction in response to potential market entry might have the two benefits of generating positive PR and conveying to the prospective competitor a message that their revenue projections will come under pressure if they do enter. Air New Zealand has used this tactic more than once to discourage committed entry into its domestic markets by prospective competitors. Of course, when the incumbent is a network carrier with relatively high costs and the potential entrant is a large LFA with staying power, deterrence is unlikely to be effective.

Response to a limited attack   If a market entrant is a start-up or perhaps a minor player it will lack the brand recognition, resources, network scope (and opportunity to cross-subsidise markets), FFP coverage, and strength across a broad range of distribution channels that an incumbent typically possesses; the only competitive dimension open to it is likely to be price. Particularly if the entrant is producing only limited output and the incumbent can offer significant non-price benefits to customers, existing market share might not be sufficiently threatened to warrant the revenue dilution likely to follow from a robust response in the tactical pricing arena. This was the approach taken by British Airways when premium-only carriers arrived in the UK–US market in 2005. On the other hand, complacency can be dangerous; Southwest was once a minor challenger.

One final point that will be picked up again in Chapter 4 is that large incumbents might sometimes feel constrained by the oversight of competition authorities from responding too aggressively to market entry by a small challenger. Having said that, we will also be noting in Chapter 4 that predatory pricing is difficult to prove and has a long history of going unpunished in the airline industry.

Response to a more serious threat   An attack on a core market or an attack on the integrity of a network sufficient to erode the flow of connecting traffic over an incumbent's hub is likely to be met by lower fares and, perhaps, by higher frequencies and aggressive marketing communications. A common reaction from incumbents attacked in a core market is to offer discounted fares on a capacity-controlled basis, in order to facilitate a counter-attack without unduly diluting the revenue stream. However, most airlines do try to maintain price leadership if one of their core markets is seriously threatened and in certain circumstances a more draconian response might be warranted. When in July 2004 AirTran launched two daily flights to LAX from American's DFW hub, American responded not simply by matching fares to LAX but doing so on 39 daily departures to

5 Southern California airports. Consumer surplus certainly went up, but 18 months later AirTran had left the market.

More generally, incumbents might face two potentially troublesome situations where:

- the challenger has significantly lower costs that it is willing to use to sustain an indefinite attack; or
- a core market priced by the incumbent on the basis of fully allocated costs is attacked by an entrant using it to absorb surplus (e.g., off-peak) capacity and so willing to price closer to marginal cost.

Looking at the former – and increasingly widespread – situation, the question is who has the deepest pockets. Whilst incumbent US majors were able to deploy their network scope, marketing prowess, and command of mainframe computer technology to dispose of many of the first wave of undercapitalised start-ups which challenged them in deregulated short-haul markets during the 1980s, they had less initial success dealing with Southwest or with the well-resourced subsequent wave of LFA start-ups able to tap into Internet distribution and new business design concepts. It is now clear that the historic revenue model based on imposing extremely high fares on late-booking and supposedly price-inelastic business travellers to subsidise deeply discounted leisure fares is unsustainable in short- and medium-haul markets attacked by LFAs able profitably and reliably to offer lower average fares with relatively few usage restrictions.

An incumbent challenged by sustainable low-fare entry in its core market has broadly three alternatives:

1. *Match fares* The problem with doing this is that not only will fares have to be matched, but also booking and usage restrictions. If the latter are relaxed to match those of the LFA, there will inevitably be some trading down into lower-priced booking classes by potentially high-yield traffic. Even if it tries to match on a capacity-controlled basis, the incumbent can therefore expect a revenue hit.
2. *Establish a low-fare operation* Although some appear at the time of writing to be meeting their parents' strategic objectives (e.g., Jetstar), carving cost-efficient new processes and an intensely cost-focused new culture out of an existing airline is exceptionally difficult and establishing a completely separate new subsidiary for the purpose is only slightly easier. The track record of this type of response is not encouraging, as has already been noted.
3. *Redefine and simplify the business model* We saw in Chapter 1 that, eventually, all North American and many European network carriers chose to respond to LFA entry in this way. Whether they have yet done enough to preserve their remaining short-haul market share on a long-term basis remains to be seen.

Separately, where a challenger has a more established market presence at one end of a city-pair market than the other, the incumbent might compete more robustly for traffic originating at the challenger's stronger end, relying on its own better-established market presence to counterbalance any price disadvantage at the other end of the market. This was a situation faced by British Midland (subsequently bmi) when it entered short-haul markets between London and several continental European cities in the 1990s: British Airways responded more aggressively at the London end of each new route than at the corresponding European end, because British Midland at the time had a much less developed market presence in mainland Europe than in London.

Conclusions On Tactical Pricing

Tactical pricing decisions require knowledge of demand curves, segment elasticities, and competitors' actions and likely reactions. They should be taken with a full understanding of their cost and revenue implications. The availability of information necessary to make informed tactical pricing decisions has therefore become one of the factors critical to success in the contemporary airline industry – certainly as far as the larger network carriers are concerned. However, any airline operating a hub-and-spoke system with a significant number of stations served by flights that can be distinguished according to time of departure, day and season of operation, and which serve different segments of demand each with their own demand functions will have a highly complex tariff structure – and hundreds of thousands of pricing decisions to make and subsequently amend as both customers and competitors act and react in response to what is on offer. Clearly, pricing on this scale has to mix experience and judgement with effective automation. It also, inevitably, involves decision-making on the basis of volatile and often imperfect information.

Whenever a fare or cargo rate is reduced with the intention of stimulating traffic, there are two critical questions:

1. Does the incremental revenue from new traffic exceed revenue lost from passengers or cargo moving at the new, lower price that would otherwise have been carried at the old, higher price?
2. Does the incremental revenue from new traffic exceed the incremental cost of carrying it? (The challenge here, as we have seen already and will see again in Chapter 5, is how to define 'cost'.)

One final point: despite all the references above to price-matching, and despite its widespread use as a competitive tool throughout the industry, it would be wrong to conclude that all competitors in liberalised and deregulated markets invariably charge comparable prices for comparable products. A quick search of fares in major markets to/from and within Europe will confirm this.

V. Yield

YIELD DEFINED

Having discussed price in general and what drives it, we now turn to consideration of the average price per (distance-weighted) unit of output sold – that is, per RPM or RTM. This is 'yield', and yield – rather than price – is the component of interest in the context of the operating performance model around which this second part of the book has been structured.

Yield per RTM is the average revenue earned from each ton of payload carried one mile, and similarly yield per RPM is the average revenue generated by carrying one passenger one mile. Yield may be split into: gross yield (i.e., operating revenue ÷ RPMs or RTMs); net yield (i.e., operating revenue net of agency commissions ÷ RPM or RTM); and net net yield (i.e., operating revenue net of commissions, TACOs, and other agency incentives ÷ RPMs or RTMs). In this book, 'yield' refers to gross yield. Yield is not the same as 'average fare', which is: operating revenue ÷ number of originating passengers; yield is distance-weighted whilst average fare is not.

Yield can be calculated across the spectrum of an airline's operations, encompassing all the products offered over its entire network. Alternatively, if accounting capabilities permit, calculations can focus on a particular product – say, first or business class yield system-wide – or on a market, route, or flight-leg. (Revenue dilution in any class/cabin, taken here as a proxy for 'product', can be assessed by calculating actual yield as a percentage of the yield that could have been earned had all tickets in the class/cabin concerned been sold at full fare.)

Any two airlines might generate similar revenue figures whilst having quite dissimilar traffic and yield structures. We will look at the relationship between traffic and yield in Chapter 10, but at this point it is worth bearing in mind the following:

1. Traffic and yield tend to trade-off against each other. The extent to which this is the case depends upon the price-elasticity (and, where relevant, the cross-price elasticity) of demand in the market(s) concerned. They also bear different relationships to cost: in the absence of major product upgrades (e.g., better seat accessibility or lower seating densities) or expensive marketing communications programmes, increases in yield can be largely cost-free; increases in traffic (i.e., RPMs and RTMs), whilst not as expensive as increases in output (i.e., ASMs and ATMs), are never cost-free.
2. Because yield is an average of revenue earned per unit of output sold, different airlines will have yield structures which reflect the different source(s) of their revenues – that is, their different traffic mixes. Specifically, these structures respond to the nature of demand being met in the markets from which revenue is being earned. They need to be related to the costs incurred meeting that demand given the positioning of a particular airline's product(s) within the markets concerned:
   • High-yield passengers will often require greater product-related expenditures than low-yield passengers, notably in respect of higher frequencies and, where they occupy separate cabins, more onboard space.
   • Conventional wisdom holds that high yields might to some extent compensate for high costs. This could be true in the short term, but it is not a comfort which is without danger; high-yield traffic can evaporate in a recession, and is at any time vulnerable to a competitor with lower costs able to offer the same or better service standards at lower prices. Furthermore, there is the downward secular trend in industry (real) yields to be concerned about.
3. Low-yield traffic may contribute unseen value to high-yield passengers in some markets. It can do this in several ways:
   • Low-yield traffic may add density to a route sufficient to enable the use of larger aircraft than high-yield traffic alone can justify. As we will see in Chapter 5, any aircraft of a given technological generation is likely to have lower seat-mile costs than a smaller type of the same generation. These lower unit costs might be reflected in lower high-yield fares than would otherwise have been the case.

(However, we will also see that larger aircraft have higher trip costs, so the aggregate revenue earned from incremental low-yield traffic must be sufficient to at least cover these – otherwise, the unit cost advantage will count for little.)

- Corporate overhead that would exist whether or not the incremental low-yield traffic is carried can be spread over a larger output of available seat-miles. This can also contribute to a reduction in unit costs (i.e., cost per ASM).
- The presence of low-yield traffic may permit more frequencies to be mounted across a broader network than high-yield traffic alone could support (Shaw 1999).

One certainty that should always be borne in mind is that movements in yield and in profit do not necessarily track each other. It is quite possible for profits to rise at a time when yields are falling and vice versa.

RECENT YIELD TRENDS

Before considering recent yield trends, it is worth reiterating a couple of key relationships:

$$\text{Operating revenue} \div \text{traffic} = \text{yield}$$

If traffic grows faster than revenue, yield will decline; this has been a common feature of the airline industry.

$$\text{Traffic} \times \text{yield} = \text{operating revenue}$$

Operating revenue can rise even if yield is falling, provided that traffic grows faster than yield declines; this has also been common, and it explains why if costs are well-managed profits can in principle rise despite falling yields. Rising traffic, of course, does tend to put upward pressure on costs.

These relationships should be kept in mind when reading the following paragraphs. However, be careful about causality: it is sometimes reported that an airline's revenue has risen *because* of stronger yields, but yield is simply a number which reflects other numbers – specifically, traffic and revenue – and in itself drives nothing. Changes in yield do not drive changes in revenue. On the contrary, it is differential movements in revenue and traffic that drive changes in yield. The 'traffic × yield = revenue' relationship is nonetheless helpful for the purpose of modelling financial performance, which is why it has been used in this book.

Globally, average real passenger yield fell 2.6 per cent per annum between 1975 and 2005, whilst real freight and mail yield fell 3.5 per cent per annum (ICAO 2007b); real operating cost per ATK, on the other hand, declined by only 2.0 per cent per annum (ibid.). ICAO figures for the years 2000–2005 tell an even more sobering story when world real economic growth percentages are compared with changes in global airline real yield (the latter in parentheses):

2000: 4.7 (-3.0);
2001: 1.6 (-2.6);
2002: 1.7 (-4.6);
2003: 2.6 (-4.9);
2004: 4.1 (-2.6);
2005: 3.6 (-1.3).

We have seen that because yield is calculated by dividing RPMs into operating revenue, changes in yield are shaped by differential movements in revenue and (distance-weighted) traffic. What explains the figures above is that global traffic has been growing more rapidly than real (i.e., inflation-adjusted) revenue, with the result that real yield across the industry has been falling. Linking traffic and revenue in this context is the fact that in both passenger and freight sectors, price stimuli have been major contributors to the rapid growth in traffic seen over the last several decades.

An excellent place to get a feel for the development of US airline yields is the ATA website (http://www.airlines.org/economics/finance), which provides figures back to the 1920s. Just a small sample of these figures reveals the essence of the story: in 1978, the year US domestic passenger markets were deregulated, nominal (i.e., current-dollar) system yield was 8.29 cents; in 2005 the nominal yield was 12.00 cents, but the yield expressed in 1978 dollars was just 4.00 cents. In 2005, which was a strong year for US airlines given a firm domestic economy and the network carriers' restraint in adding capacity, nominal system-wide yield rose 2.8 per cent but after adjusting for inflation real yield was down by 0.6 per cent; real yield earned by the majors as a group was 18 per cent lower in 2005 than in 2000. The story these figures tell has not unfolded uniformly across all markets, however: according to GAO figures (2006) there was a 40 per cent fall in the overall median US domestic airfare between 1980 and 2005, expressed in 2005 dollars, but fares declined by significantly less than this in shorter and thinner markets (i.e., those of 250 miles or less and in the bottom 20 per cent of traffic-generators).

The Air Transport Association (2006, p. 12) also provides a stunning insight into the weakness of the US domestic revenue environment, and therefore the weakness of yields, relative to other products. Nominal US domestic airfares (i.e., unadjusted for inflation) rose 45 per cent from deregulation in 1978 through 2005, 'while the price of milk has risen 133 percent, single-family homes 326 percent, new vehicles 339 percent, prescription drugs 467 percent and public college tuition 698 percent'. In this type of revenue environment, it is not surprising that traffic has reacted strongly to the price stimulus.

Having set the scene, it needs to be pointed out that in cyclically strong markets where robust demand presses against restrained growth in output, yields can perform well – albeit perhaps briefly. For instance, US domestic mainline yield rose 8.5 per cent nominal in 2006 and 4.7 per cent in real terms. However, the spike was reversed to 1.0 per cent nominal and -1.3 per cent real in 2007; this helps explain the enthusiasm of network carriers for shifting growth to international markets, where their real yield that year was up 4.2 per cent (FAA 2008). The FAA forecast for the period 2009–2025 (ibid.), sees mainline domestic yield changing at annual average rates of 1.6 per cent nominal and -0.7 per cent real, and international yield changing by 1.2 per cent nominal and -1.0 per cent real.

There are several reasons why real yields globally have been widely expected to continue their secular downward trend (although whether this expectation will be fulfilled should oil prices continue the sustained rise that began in 2005 and accelerated in 2007–2008 is an open question):

1. Price-sensitive leisure travel is growing much more rapidly than business travel.
2. LFAs are continuing to expand their market share, which in turn mandates pricing responses from incumbents.
3. The transparency of the Internet has shifted the balance of power from revenue-managing airlines to price-managing consumers.

4. Long-haul journeys, which are generally lower-yielding than short-haul trips, are growing as a proportion of total journeys.
5. Trading down has led over time to a growing proportion of business travellers in particular 'migrating' from premium cabins and, where possible, from unrestricted fares. Between the first quarter of 2000 and the final quarter of 2005, the percentage of US passengers travelling on business fares (i.e., first class, business class or unrestricted economy fare codes) fell from 21 per cent to 10 per cent (DOT 2006b). In international markets the picture has been more mixed: several airlines have eliminated first class service and a number have introduced premium economy cabins to accommodate business travellers who might previously have flown in business class, yet in some markets (e.g., Europe–Asia) demand for premium cabin space has been strong.
6. Increasing competition keeps airlines under relentless pressure to share with customers the cost savings which flow from new technologies and remodelled business processes.
7. Each new generation of aircraft will continue to be more efficient than its predecessors, and the history of the industry suggests that productivity improvements tend in large measure to be passed through to passengers. The same can be said with regard to efficiency improvements stemming from areas of the business other than flight operations. (On the other hand, airlines may in future find ways to appropriate for themselves a greater share of the benefits from efficiency gains should the industry consolidate as many now expect and should airport congestion prove an insurmountable barrier to entry by challengers into progressively more hub markets.)

Given persistently declining real yields, it is not surprising that costs have come under the strategic microscope in recent years and will have to remain there notwithstanding the cyclical firming in yields that inevitably takes place in some markets from time to time. Unfortunately, real unit costs have in many cases been declining more slowly than yields.

It is worth noting, however, that falling yields do not inevitably imply lower average fares in a given market. For example, assume that a fare between points O and D remains unchanged when the current non-stop service is replaced by a connection routed over hub H. Further assuming that H does not lie directly en route between O and D, the airline carrying passengers from O to D via H is now generating more RPMs to perform the same journey that was previously accomplished non-stop. Given that yield is revenue per RPM and assuming that revenue (i.e., the fare) is unchanged whilst RPMs have risen, yield from carrying the existing traffic (i.e., ignoring any additional traffic generated by the network connectivity benefits of hubbing over H) must decline. In the real world, fares and traffic would probably, and costs would certainly, change under this type of circumstance; nonetheless, it illustrates the point. Because it is based on price, numbers of passengers or amounts of freight carried, and the distance of carriage, a change in yield does not always tell the story it might at first appear to be telling.

Comparisons between carriers therefore need to be made with an understanding of the factors that influence yield.

FACTORS INFLUENCING YIELD

Passenger Yields

The following factors affect passenger yields: fare structure; traffic mix; length of haul; intensity of competition; and network design.

Fare structure   The different levels of fare available in a market provide the foundation on which yields are built.

Traffic mix   An airline's traffic mix, the proportion of traffic travelling at each different price on offer within the given fare structure in each market, has a fundamental influence on its yield. Traffic mix is a function of three factors:

1. Demand characteristics – for example, the relative proportions of business and leisure traffic present in a market.
2. The effectiveness of conditions imposed within the tariff structure to prevent diversion of relatively time-sensitive and price-inelastic customers to products designed for the more time insensitive and price-elastic segment(s) being targeted by lower fares.
3. The effectiveness of the carrier's RMS in protecting space on high-demand flights for late-booking, high-yield passengers. (However, we will see in Chapter 9 that revenue maximisation and yield maximisation are not synonymous, and that the task of an RMS is to maximise revenue rather than yield – because it is revenue that pays the bills, whereas yield is just a number.)

These factors are clearly influenced by the manner in which an airline positions its products to tap targeted demand, and the sophistication with which it manages the relationship between product quality, the price-elasticity of different market segments, and the release of space. In this sense, yield is to a large extent a reflection of the interaction between product design and pricing activities, because it is these which position a carrier in its markets and shape the traffic mix. However, an airline's control over such variables is never absolute in competitive markets.

Length of haul   As noted, fares per mile are generally lower for long-haul than short-haul routes because unit costs taper as stage-length increases. Other things being equal, which they seldom are of course, a carrier whose average passenger journey is significantly longer than another carrier's average will probably earn a lower yield. (We look at average journey length here rather than the average stage-length on the airline's network because average stage-length tells us nothing about the volume of traffic carried on flights of different lengths; for example, a predominantly short-haul carrier might have its average stage-length boosted by a few long-haul routes operated at such low frequencies that they carry only a small proportion of total traffic and have little impact on system-wide yield.) There are therefore two contrary influences to consider when comparing short-haul yields generated by network carriers against those generated by LFAs:

1. Traffic moving at low fares in long-haul O&D markets can depress network carrier yields on short-haul routes into and out of hubs – possibly to the point where they are below corresponding LFA yields.

2.   Conversely, network carriers benefit from having business and first class cabins which – provided they are not filled with non-revenue passengers – can generate firm yields.

The correlation between distance and yield is not perfect, however. Regionals have certainly tended to generate higher yields than other categories of US carrier, as might be expected given the shorter average journey lengths of their passengers, but at the time of writing – and contrary to what might be expected – the yield generated by the six largest network carriers from their domestic systems is slightly below the yield being earned from (longer range) Latin American operations. Competitive circumstances, in this case the influence LFAs are having on domestic market pricing, can clearly distort the relationship between journey length and yield.

Intensity of competition   The more monopoly power a carrier benefits from, the stronger in general its yields will be. Conversely, increased price competition puts downward pressure on yields. (Non-price competition, on the other hand, tends to put upward pressure on costs – associated with product improvement or advertising, for example – but may leave yields relatively unscathed.)

Network design   One important variable under this heading is whether we are dealing predominantly with a hub-and-spoke or a point-to-point system. As noted above, this affects yields insofar as it determines the distance flown in each O&D market; the greater the distance covered in serving a market the lower the yield at any given fare because the revenue from that fare must be spread over more RPMs. Another variable is the extent to which an airline's network and scheduling lead it to interline passengers with other carriers; this can influence prorate dilution and therefore yield, and is explored in Box 3.3.

Box 3.3: Prorate Dilution

When a passenger buys a ticket from A to B on one airline and then onwards to C on another (whether an alliance partner or not), the fare paid for the entire journey from A to C can, for the purpose of this discussion, be assumed to be calculated in one of two ways:

1.   On a sum-of-sectors basis: the two local fares are simply summed. A short-haul carrier prepared to take on the costs and complications associated with interlining is likely to prefer this approach because it earns the same yield from a connecting long-haul passenger as it could have earned from any local short-haul passenger who was displaced.
2.   On a through-fare basis: the through-fare will normally be less than the sum of local fares from A to B and from B to C. This is because, as noted above, prices generally taper with distance (i.e., the average price paid per mile falls as trip distance rises).

Our concern here is with through-fares and the consequent need to prorate them between two (or possibly more) carriers.

The agency making a booking, or the passenger if buying direct, pays the entire fare to the airline flown on the first part of the journey, and this airline passes on part of the revenue to the second carrier either through some local arrangement or through the IATA Clearing House. Each carrier therefore experiences 'prorate dilution' as a result of the fact that more could have been earned carrying a local passenger than an interline passenger; the actual cash difference between the local fare and the revenue actually earned is 'prorate absorption'. A desire to avoid both prorate dilution and costs such as baggage transfer and accommodating passengers who have missed connections is why LFAs, with some notable exceptions, choose not to negotiate interline agreements with other carriers.

Returning to the above example, the two airlines flying a passenger from A to B and then B to C respectively have to agree on how they will prorate (i.e., divide between themselves) the through-fare bought from A to C. There are two multilateral prorate agreements (MPAs), each open to any scheduled airline; one covers cargo rates, the other deals with passenger fares. In addition, carriers (including regionals code-sharing with majors) very often negotiate their own bilateral special prorate agreements (SPAs) under which each party specifies the minimum amount it requires to carry a passenger on its portion of the route concerned; these are often the basis for joint fares below the full interlineable 'IATA' fare. The following are the most common of the basic approaches used in prorating:

1. *Straight prorate* This method applies prorate factors based on fares or distance.
    *   *Fare prorating* The O&D fare is split according to the percentage of aggregate local fares accounted for by each individual local fare. For example, assume the local fares from A to B and B to C are $100 and $150 respectively whilst the A to C through-fare is $200; if Carrier 1 flies the passenger from A to B it will earn 100/250 × 200 = $80, whilst Carrier 2 flying the passenger from B to C will earn 150/250 × 200 = $120.
    *   *Mileage prorating* The calculation is the same, except that miles (or sometimes the square root of miles) flown by each carrier are used instead.
    Weighted adjustments are commonly applied to take into account the fact that operating costs for short-haul flights are likely to represent a disproportionately high percentage of aggregate operating costs for any journey comprising both short- and long-haul sectors. (The reason why this is so will be explained in Chapter 5.) Different adjustments are used for cargo and for passengers.

2. *Prorate factoring with provisos* Even after weighting adjustments, mileage prorating in particular can be unfavourable to short-haul operators interlining traffic onto long-haul routes; for example, Lufthansa will most probably have very little use for, say, ten per cent of a $500 Düsseldorf–Manchester–New York fare as reward for carrying a passenger from Düsseldorf to Manchester in order to interline onto a transatlantic flight – particularly if that seat could instead have been sold to a higher-yielding local Düsseldorf –Manchester passenger. (On the day this was written, the lowest return fare quoted by Lufthansa on its UK website for outbound travel on this 90-minute route in the next four days was £193 and the highest was £1077.) Fare prorating is somewhat more favourable to the short-haul carrier insofar as the local fare on a short-haul journey is likely to comprise a higher percentage of the O&D fare than short-haul mileage comprises of the total journey length. Nonetheless, it is not uncommon for prorate factors to be used subject to provisos filed by individual airlines requiring either specified percentages of each fare or absolute amounts of money to be 'ring-fenced' before prorating begins.

Short-haul carriers in particular therefore tend to negotiate interline agreements which specifically give them a more favourable share of any constructed or agreed joint fare. A significant number of domestic operators insist on full or nearly full payment of the local fare as an 'add-on' in preference to prorating; if we look upon such add-ons as deductions from the O&D fare, the result can be serious revenue dilution for international carriers that interline significant volumes of traffic under such arrangements. As an alternative to prorating, some independent regionals in the United States and to a lesser extent elsewhere have signed 'fee-per-departure' or 'fee-per-ASM flown' agreements with their major code-share partners; the regional benefits from improved cash flow predictability, whilst the major gains control over network management (i.e., points served, routing, schedule), pricing, seat inventory, and revenue management.

The fact that a large and growing proportion of the industry's passengers travel on restricted fares which are in most cases only good for use on the issuing carrier has tended to reduce the prorate problem. It has not gone away, however, because the growth of alliances is pushing in the opposite direction by creating networks expressly designed to flow traffic between partners.

To the extent that an airline can retain passengers online, clearly an easier prospect for carriers with large networks, prorate dilution will have less impact on yields. In the US domestic market, only a very small percentage of passengers interline between unaffiliated carriers. On the other hand, some African operators with limited networks interline over half their long-haul passengers. This disadvantage is compounded by the severe directional imbalance of fares in many of the markets they serve, with northbound prices often consistently lower than southbound. They are therefore left with little room to negotiate favourable prorates with transatlantic or European domestic airlines in respect of passengers originating from Africa and continuing their onward journeys offline. Furthermore, exchange rate effects can either magnify or reduce the impact of prorate dilution on revenues denominated in the home currency – particularly where prorated traffic originates overseas and pays in a foreign currency.

Yields will also suffer if an airline books or carries significant volumes of interline traffic and is inefficient at checking its monthly billings through the IATA Clearing House. This is sometimes a particular problem for those small airlines which, because of the impact of their route structures on the proportion of online to offline revenue ticketed, tend to be net creditors in the clearing system. As far as net debtors are concerned, verifying the accuracy of prorate billing can be burdensome for airlines with thinly stretched resources – but overcharging through incorrect prorate claims is not infrequent and can prove even more burdensome.

One final point relevant to the impact of network design on yield is that a carrier with a network covering a good spread of O&D markets and having the freedom to reallocate capacity may well be able to compensate for a softening of yields in one market by withdrawing and reallocating aircraft or by varying its planned rate of output growth. This assumes that profit maximisation is a stronger objective than market share. Emirates, for example, could deal with softening yields between the UK and Australia by slowing output growth and reallocating planned capacity to alternative markets with stronger yields.

Freight Yields

In some cases, similar influences also affect freight yields – which, other than for the purposes of comparison with passenger yields, are generally calculated per FTK (i.e., revenue from scheduled freight divided by FTKs).

Although the generalisation might not hold in a particular market at a particular time, it is often the case that freight yields per RTM are below passenger yields calculated on the same basis. There are several reasons for this:

- Particularly in international markets, a high proportion of freight output is sold in bulk through distribution channels in which buying power is concentrated in the hands of a relatively small number of powerful forwarders.
- The directionality of freight flows, met in Chapter 2, leads to weak demand and therefore soft yields in one direction on many routes.

- Output of freight space in most long-haul markets is paced more by the demand for passenger services than by demand from shippers. Long-haul widebodies have significant belly-hold capacity, so when passenger demand and market liberalisation lead to increased frequencies being operated there is an inevitable increase in freight space – whether the market needs it at the time or not.
- Looked at as a whole, airfreight is primarily a medium- and long-haul product – something that is being compounded by the growing proportion of global airfreight accounted for by shipments from Asia to destinations in Europe and the Americas (Taneja 2002). Long-haul traffic, as we have seen, tends to generate lower yields than short-haul traffic.

Yields on time-definite express documents and parcels are of course higher than the average for freight as a whole, and have been steadily increasing.

VI. Operating Revenue

COMPONENTS OF OPERATING REVENUE

Although airline accounting practices vary widely, it is broadly the case that operating revenue can be broken out into traffic revenue, ancillary revenue earned from passengers, and other transport-related revenue.

Traffic Revenue

Traffic revenue is revenue earned directly from passenger airfares (i.e., ticket sales) and from the shipment of cargo, net of taxes and charges which are collected by the airline from its customers but must be passed through to governments or airport authorities. It includes fuel surcharges and other journey- or shipment-related fees or charges levied on customers, whatever they might be called, which are not mandated by a government or airport authority and do not have to be passed on by the airline to such authority. On average, cargo revenue represents approximately 15 per cent of the industry's traffic revenue. For several network carriers, notably based in Europe and Asia, the percentage is very much higher; the average for members of the Association of Asia-Pacific Airlines, for example, is closer to 25 per cent, and both EVA Air and China Airlines generate more than 40 per cent of their revenue from cargo. On the other hand, cargo contributes less than 4 per cent of revenue at American, Delta, and United.

Two initiatives aimed at stemming revenue leakage estimated to amount to as much as $12 billion per annum across the industry as a whole (Arinbjarnarson 2007) have become increasingly widespread in recent years:

1. *Revenue integrity* The objective is to maximise the percentage of bookings that turn into flown revenue by reducing:
   - duplicate passenger name records (PNRs);
   - speculative or erroneous bookings;
   - breached ticketing time limits (TTLs).

2. *Revenue protection* The objective is to reduce revenue leakage and increase revenue recovery by carefully auditing agency transactions to ensure:
    *   rules associated with both published and unpublished fares have been complied with;
    *   TFC calculations are correct;
    *   commission and incentive payment calculations are correct.

Fees levied on passengers for reservation changes or cancellations are commonly treated as traffic revenue, but may instead be accounted for as ancillary.

Ancillary Revenue

Ancillary (i.e., non-ticket) revenue is an increasingly important part of many airlines' revenue streams; Ryanair, for example, earns approximately 18 per cent of its total operating revenue from this category, Spirit around 20 per cent, and on some definitions easyJet's figure could be over 25 per cent. LFAs such as Ryanair and easyJet rely particularly heavily upon ancillary revenues. In its 2006 financial year, the €259 million in ancillary revenues earned by Ryanair was equivalent to almost 70 per cent of the carrier's total operating profit; in a similar vein, the Chief Executive of easyJet has been quoted as saying, 'We fly people virtually for free. Ancillaries are essential to our profit' (*Business Travel World*, March 2007, p. 30). In 2007 Southwest set an objective of earning an incremental $1 billion per annum from ancillaries, notably the sale of more vacations, hotel rooms, and car rentals through its website, and the sale of preferred treatment such as priority boarding, bonus frequent flyer miles, and onboard cocktails. Across the industry as a whole these still remain relatively extreme examples, but an increasing number of airlines – particularly those operating in highly competitive short-haul markets – are coming to rely on growing ancillary revenues to combat perennially weak real yields. Figures in excess of $10 per passenger are now not unusual, with Allegiant apparently leading the field with closer to $20 – although direct comparisons are complicated by different carriers having their own definitions of 'ancillary' and some being unwilling to provide a breakdown of revenue sources. Business plans for long-haul LFAs also place heavy reliance on revenues from the sale of catering, IFE, and duty-free sales.

An important source of attraction in ancillary revenues, particularly for some LFAs, is that margins are high compared with margins on ticket sales. They are earned from two primary activities:

1. *Unbundling the traditional airline product and charging for product attributes that were formerly encompassed within the ticket price or were available only to travellers in premium cabins* Examples include charges for: using distribution channels which cost the airline more than Internet bookings (e.g., call centres); credit card fees; airport check-in; priority check-in; seat allocation (both in general and for preferred seating such as seats with extra legroom); checked baggage; lounge access; priority boarding; catering; and IFE. It should be noted that whilst airlines are able to redesign their own websites to sell unbundled product attributes at the optimum time, which is the time a reservation is made, when bookings come through other distribution channels relying on GDS mainframes the relative lack of flexibility inherent in these systems can pose a problem; however, this is in the process of being solved (e.g., Sabre's Distribution Merchandising Suite).

   In the United States, Spirit was amongst the first to move to a fully unbundled pricing structure, selling just the seat and then offering other attributes for sale 'à la carte'. On the other hand, when network carriers unbundle their short- and medium-haul products, either by eliminating attributes altogether or charging for what was previously 'free' (e.g., United's baggage charges introduced in May 2008), they are arguably stripping away one source of what differentiates them from LFAs. Many need the incremental revenue. However, quite a few also still need to earn a yield premium to accommodate cost bases which, despite remodelling, remain in some cases uncompetitive against those of LFAs. If they are to be sustainable in the long term, yield premiums have to be supported by some form of differentiation. Yet if all competitors, both network carriers and LFAs, are offering similarly unbundled products in short-haul markets where they compete, the former have little left to differentiate them in support of yield premiums – except perhaps the scope of their networks. One approach, taken by bmi, is to allow high-tier members of the FFP free access to attributes such as inflight catering.

2. *Adding and charging for additional services beyond the core air transport product* Examples include travel insurance, airport parking, car hire, bus and train tickets from destination airports, and hotels. Some of these are offered as carrier-branded 'add-ons' (e.g., ryanairhotels.com's deal with Expedia Private Label, and the availability of flexible flight plus hotel packages from easyJetHolidays), whilst others are offered as commissionable 'click-throughs' to suppliers' own websites (e.g., Lufthansa's link to Octopus Travel's site for car hire). The ultimate goal is felt by some in the industry to be 'dynamic packaging' – a capability which allows an airline to sell revenue-managed (i.e., continuously repriced) packages including both airfare and other services for a single amount without revealing the price point of each element.

   Some airlines also earn fees from the booking of tickets on partner airlines; particularly where the carriers involved are LFAs this might allow purchasers to create an 'interlined' itinerary. Another important source of revenue for many LFAs is the inflight sale of general merchandise.

Airlines are therefore increasingly exploiting two arenas as distribution channels in what are rapidly expanding retail strategies intended in part to de-link revenue growth from growth in output:

- their websites, which are being used for more intensive point-of-sale merchandising;
- their aircraft cabins, which some airlines – particularly LFAs – are now exploiting for more intensive point-of-use merchandising and also for advertising.

What may appear to be imaginative opportunism is actually supported by a body of academic work known as 'Prospect Theory', which argues inter alia that once consumers have committed to spend money they have a greater inclination than previously to spend more (Kahneman and Tversky 1979; Shoemaker 2005). On the other hand, there is an argument that although airlines might be able both to sell more effectively through their websites and to 'train' customers to pay for service attributes that were previously free, there could ultimately be resistance to the constant 'hawking' that has already become a feature of flights on some European LFAs. Be that as it may, where an airline needs revenue growth in order to remain profitable in the face of rapidly rising input costs but cannot substantially increase fares or add fuel surcharges without damaging its brand and undermining the credibility of its business model – broadly the situation that Ryanair finds itself in, for example – ancillaries become critical.

Other Transport-Related Revenues

Many carriers, particularly in the United States, earn substantial revenues from co-branded credit cards and from the sale of miles to other suppliers who then offer them as incentives to their own customers (i.e., independently of any purchase of air travel). US carriers generate in excess of $3 billion each year from selling FFP mileage.

Separately, some airlines also earn revenue from activities such as third-party MRO and ground-handling contracts, and from the leasing or subleasing out of gates and other airport facilities (where these are owned or leased by the airline concerned). As explained in Chapter 1, these are not revenue sources with which this book is directly concerned.

THE RELATIONSHIP BETWEEN REVENUE AND GDP

Airline revenues are almost invariably expressed in nominal terms (i.e., in current-year dollars, euros, or other reporting currency); both national and global GDP figures are also commonly reported in nominal terms. On the other hand, whilst airline revenue *growth rates* from year to year are quoted in nominal terms (i.e., the growth of one year's nominal figure over the preceding year's nominal figure), GDP *growth rates* are most frequently cited in real terms (i.e., after downward adjustment to take into account the impact of inflation). It is therefore important to be aware that when comparing revenue growth with GDP growth some commentators do not necessarily compare like with like.

Growth in global airline nominal operating revenue has historically been faster than growth in global real GDP; in other words, there appears to be a positive income-elasticity of demand between GDP growth and revenue growth, just as there is between GDP growth and traffic (as we saw in Chapter 2). On the other hand, Sentance (2001) has observed that if nominal airline revenues are deflated to transform them into real revenues their growth rate relative to growth in real GDP shows a very different picture: on the basis of figures current at the time he was writing, real revenues had been growing at a rate broadly similar to the growth of real GDP. Notwithstanding the exceptionally strong revenue environment in 2004 and 2005, there is reason to believe that on average over the course of an economic cycle the income-elasticity of the industry's inflation-adjusted revenue growth might be closer to unity than buoyant growth in both traffic and nominal revenues suggest. In other words, the income multiplier in respect of real revenue is not as encouraging as its more widely cited counterparts in respect of nominal revenue and traffic.

In the United States the income multiplier in respect of revenue (as different from traffic) appears to be below unity. Between 1990 and 2005, nominal GDP grew 115.18 per cent but airline operating revenue grew 83 per cent. In 1990 passenger revenue was equivalent to 1.01 per cent of nominal GDP, whilst 15 years later it was equivalent to just 0.73 per cent. Put another way, an amount of money equivalent to around 0.28 per cent of US GDP (approximately $35 billion in 2005) which might in the past have been spent on air travel and related activities was being spent in some other way.

VII. Summary

This chapter opened by defining 'price', summarising influences on airline pricing decisions, and considering uniform, discriminatory, and differential pricing, before moving on to look at passenger and freight tariff structures. The degree of monopoly power exerted by a carrier was identified as an important price driver, bracketed by costs on the downside and customer value on the upside. The use of pricing as a tactical tool was considered, with particular attention paid to marginal cost pricing, the introduction of fare changes, and possible responses to competitors' pricing initiatives. We then looked at yield – the element of the operating performance model around which the second part of the book has been structured; we saw that pricing is a fundamental determinant of yield, but that there are also other important influences. Finally, the discussions of traffic in Chapter 2 and yield in the present chapter were brought together in the penultimate section, which looked at airline revenues as a whole. The point was made several times throughout the chapter that although an understanding of price theory and the components of yield is critically important, managers often have to make pricing decisions on the basis of imperfect data derived from an intensely volatile competitive environment.

4

Output

Give a man a fish and he'll eat for a day. Teach a man to fish and he'll eat for a lifetime. Teach a man to create an artificial shortage of fish and he'll eat steak.

Jay Leno

CHAPTER OVERVIEW

Supply of output is the third of four elements in the operating performance model around which Part 2 of the book has been structured:

TRAFFIC × YIELD > < OUTPUT × UNIT COST
= OPERATING PERFORMANCE (i.e., PROFIT or LOSS)

This chapter will define supply, look briefly at the economics of supply, and summarise the supply-side characteristics of the airline industry. Market structure, barriers to entry, and competition policy will be considered, and the threat to future output growth posed by environmental issues will be touched upon. Finally, the supply-side of capacity management will be discussed ahead of more detailed treatment in Part 3 of the book.

I. Definitions

OUTPUT

The output produced by an airline can be analysed in respect of a single aircraft, a subfleet, or an entire fleet, on a particular route, across a route group (e.g., US domestic, Atlantic, Pacific, and Latin America) or across an entire network. It may be expressed as the number of seats offered for sale in a period of time. Using this metric, the seat-share of LFAs is now significant in most major regions: 30 per cent in Europe, 28 per cent in North America, 20 per cent in Latin America, and 12 per cent in Asia (Airbus 2008). Alternatively, a distance-weighted measure can be calculated by multiplying a unit of seating or payload by distance flown:

1. Available seat-miles (ASMs) or available seat-kilometres (ASKs), each of which represents one seat (irrespective of whether or not it is occupied) carried one mile or kilometre respectively.

2. Available ton-miles (ATMs) or available tonne-kilometres (ATKs), which represent one ton of payload potential (again, irrespective of whether it has been *sold* to passengers or cargo shippers) carried one mile, or one tonne carried one kilometre. Available freight tonnage is calculated by taking the freight volume available on the type concerned after allowing space for passenger baggage at 100 per cent seat factor, then applying an assumed freight density figure (e.g., 10 or 11 lbs per cubic foot of remaining available space). (This method can in fact result in a freight load factor in excess of 100 per cent where the passenger load, and hence accompanied baggage, is light and freight actually carried has a higher density than assumed (Robertson 2008)). Potential passenger payload is converted to ATMs and ATKs using an assumed weight per passenger and baggage (commonly 100 kg, and more than that on certain routes – such as transpacific on Qantas, where the figure is 105 kg). These measures of output are particularly favoured by airlines with substantial cargo operations. (For analytical purposes cargo is widely defined as freight plus unaccompanied baggage, and is distinct from mail; ICAO, it should be noted, omits unaccompanied baggage from its definition of cargo – leaving the latter more or less synonymous with 'freight'. Colloquially, cargo is often used as a catch-all encompassing freight, unaccompanied baggage, and mail.)

CAPACITY, UTILISATION, AND OUTPUT

This book refers to 'capacity' as a fleet's potential output if fully utilised, and 'output' as the ASMs or ASKs and ATMs or ATKs actually supplied to the market. (RPMs or RPKs and RTMs or RTKs, on the other hand, are a measure of output that has been *sold* – that is, of 'traffic'.) An aircraft or fleet, or any other productive resource, has the *capacity* in principle to produce a finite amount of output if fully utilised (subject to maintenance requirements); the extent to which an aircraft or fleet is in fact *utilised* determines the volume of *output* it actually produces. Clearly, an airline will in most cases want to get output as close to capacity as possible by maximising utilisation in order to ensure that fixed costs (e.g., depreciation, insurance, lease rentals) are spread over as many units of output as possible and therefore are averaged down. A notable exception is the short-haul overnight feeder services flown by FedEx and other integrators; these tend to involve low aircraft utilisation, in part because daytime operations are unattractive due to the risk that they might leave aircraft out of position and so disrupt the core high-yield night services. Their output therefore falls well short of theoretical capacity. The answer in this case has to be to use aircraft with very low ownership costs – such as low-cost single turboprops on thin routes, and relatively old passenger conversions on denser routes.

The problem is, of course, that as far as aircraft are concerned their capacity to produce output over a given period of time is a notional figure rather than an incontrovertible fact. The capacity of any given type of aircraft to produce ASMs (or ATMs) per day or per year will depend to a considerable extent upon the nature of the airline operating system within which it is deployed. In particular, it will depend upon:

*   average stage-length – because, other things being equal, longer stage-lengths generally permit more output to be produced in a given time by a given type;
*   the nature of the airline's product – because, other things being equal, more complex inflight products require longer transit and turnaround times between flight-legs (e.g., to restock galleys);

- network design – because hub congestion and the need to buffer schedules to 'assure' connections generally make it impossible to extract as much utilisation from a given type operating within a hub-and-spoke network as from the same type flying similar stage-lengths on a point-to-point basis.

For example, a B737 operated by a network carrier offering an attribute-rich inflight product will be able to produce less output (i.e., will have less capacity even if efficiently utilised) than one operated by an LFA flying point-to-point; similarly, a B737 operated by a charter airline serving the Mediterranean from Northern Europe will generate high levels of output during the peak summer period because it can be – and usually will be – flown day and night. Even when airlines achieve similar levels of utilisation from a given type in terms of hours per year, output of ASMs will vary to the extent that they choose different seating configurations – essentially a service design decision. For example, Emirates flies its A340-500s and its various models of B777 with higher seating densities than Singapore Airlines, so generating more output per block-hour.

Table 4.1 traces the development of distance-weighted scheduled airline output from 1990 to 2006.

A regional breakdown of global output figures reveals strong disparities. Whereas North American carriers produce over 3000 ASMs per head of population each year and European airlines produce in excess of 1000, the corresponding figures for Latin America and Asia are under 400 and 300 respectively; according to Eclat Consulting (2007), China produces 198.71 ASMs per person and India just 61.01. Given the rising incomes forecast for these regions in the decades ahead, particularly in Asia, it is clear why rapid output growth is anticipated for airlines serving them. However, uncertainties regarding the cost of jet fuel, and therefore the sustainability of stimulatively low fares, in the years ahead make it unwise to assume that emerging markets will inevitably attain the levels of output per person that have been achieved in the United States and Europe under profoundly different economic circumstances.

OVERCAPACITY, EXCESS OUTPUT, AND SPOILAGE

Particularly when looking at capacity management in Part 3 of the book, it can be helpful to distinguish between the following three ideas:

1. *Overcapacity* This arises when aircraft are not being as fully utilised as they might be, given the nature of a particular airline's operating system. Broadly, it can be equated with having more aircraft than required to produce the amount of output being produced; however, as we will see when looking at network and fleet management in Chapters 6 to 8, the complexities of network design and scheduling and of fleet assignment mean that overcapacity is not necessarily simple to identify in practice.

Table 4.1   World airline scheduled output 1990–2006

	1990	1995	2000	2001	2002	2003	2004	2005	2006[1]
ASKs (billions)	2801	3359	4286	4272	4167	4228	4705	4976	5197
% change		19.9	27.6	-0.3	-2.5	1.5	11.3	5.7	4.4

[1] Preliminary figures.

Sources: ICAO and IATA

2. *Excess output* This is evident when more output is available than the demand coming forward to purchase it at a given price. Load factor, the percentage of output that has been sold, is a commonly used indicator. When there is excess output, the result is normally the same as in any other industry where supply exceeds demand: price competition intensifies and yields suffer. This happened in India in both the early 1990s and from 2003 onwards, for example, when liberalisation freed existing carriers and start-ups to pour output into the market.

   However, enough has been said about the peaking characteristics of air transport demand (in Chapter 2) and the complexities of pricing (in Chapter 3) to make two things very clear:

   - Although individual flights frequently operate with all their output sold, an entire system never can. Airlines inevitably produce more output than they sell, but the extent to which this unsold output is 'excess' will always be subject to debate. As we will see later in this chapter and in Parts 3 and 4, much depends upon the nature of a particular airline's operating system.
   - If an operating profit is to be earned, excess output (i.e., unsold output) has to be paid for out of the revenue earned from output that has been sold. We will return to the linkage between output and price in a moment, and revisit the point later in the book.

   Japan Airlines recognised in 2006 that it was producing excess output on many European routes as a result of having too many B747s in its fleet; these had originally been bought at a time when there were no smaller aircraft available that were capable of serving long-haul non-stop routes to and from Japan. They were inappropriately sized for the nature of the demand now being served and were therefore replaced by B777-300ERs on the routes concerned.

3. *Spoilage* Spoilage occurs where seats fly empty despite there being sufficient demand, at a given price, to have filled them. This can happen, for example, when flights are fully booked, reservation requests are refused, but seats nonetheless remain available at departure because of late cancellations and no-shows. As we will see in Chapter 9, overbooking is used to limit spoilage – particularly in respect of refundable fares; on the other hand, where a seat is sold on a non-changeable, non-refundable basis there should be no lost revenue should that seat depart empty.

   Excess output and spoilage are similar but distinct concepts: where there is excess output space flies empty because of insufficient demand at the price(s) offered, whereas spoilage occurs where demand is sufficient to absorb output but for some reason fails to materialise as booked.

It should be noted that although these definitions are technically correct and are adhered to in this book, it is not uncommon in practice to see 'overcapacity' used as a catch-all for both too much capacity and too much output, and to see 'spoilage' used to refer to empty space at departure regardless of whether or not there ever was demand for it.

Irrespective of what definitions are used, the following critical observation will re-emerge at various points throughout the remainder of the book: whilst it is necessary to maximise resource utilisation in order to produce as much output as possible over which to spread fixed costs and so average down unit cost, it is also vital to be sure that the incremental output can be sold – and can be sold at a profit. The discussions of cost allocation later in this chapter and in Chapter 5 will show how complex the implications of this very obvious statement can be in practice, and Part 3 of the book will explain that it lies at the heart of the airline capacity management challenge.

II. The Modelling of Supply: A Brief Refresher

This section will look at the close relationship between output and price. Subsequent sections will consider the heterogeneity of airline output, and the more important supply-side characteristics of the industry. Detailed consideration of costs is held over to the next chapter.

OUTPUT AND PRICE

'Supply' is the amount of a product that producers are willing and able to make available during a given time period and subject to a given set of determinant (independent) variables. Market supply is the aggregate of each firm's individual supply decisions.

1. A *supply function* is a table that relates the current states of various supply-determining independent variables, notably input cost and output price, to a particular quantity of product supplied (the dependent variable).
2. A *supply schedule* is a table relating a series of possible prices to the quantity supplied at each price if all other supply-determining variables remain unchanged. In other words, quantity of output supplied (q) is treated here as a function of price (p).
3. A *supply curve* is a graphical representation of a supply schedule. With price again on the vertical axis and quantity on the horizontal, the curve will be upward-sloping from left to right – illustrating that in most cases 'q' will fall as 'p' declines, and vice versa, assuming all other things remain constant.

That 'things' in fact do not always remain constant leads to the following distinction:

- *Change in quantity supplied* This is marked by movement up or down a given supply curve. The 'law of supply' states that there is a direct relationship between price and quantity supplied; all other things being equal, if price rises so will the quantity supplied and vice versa. Everything else that might affect supply – such as falling input costs or the introduction of productivity-enhancing new technology, either of which could hold out the prospect of increased profits and so motivate producers to supply more output – is assumed to remain unchanged. (The 'law of demand' that we met in Chapter 2 states that as price rises quantity demanded falls; it is these contrary movements up and down demand and supply curves that bring markets into short-run equilibrium at a particular price.)
- *Change in supply* In this case, one of the non-price determinants of supplier behaviour has shifted the supply curve right or left of its original position and so changed the quantity supplied at each given price. A rightward (or downward) shift in the supply curve increases the quantity that producers are prepared to sell at any given price; an upward or leftward shift implies that producers require a higher price for each unit brought to market (perhaps, for example, because input costs have risen).

The percentage change in output (the dependent variable) that occurs in response to a 1 per cent change in an independent variable is known as the *elasticity of supply*. The most commonly used independent variable is price (i.e., the 'price-elasticity of supply'); others include interest rates, wage rates, and non-labour input costs. Supply is generally more elastic in the long run than the short run because most firms face capacity constraints that require time to overcome – although the truth of this generalisation depends upon the nature of the product and, in particular, the production process.

A profit-maximising firm should produce output at the level which maximises the difference between total revenue and total cost. This is found where marginal revenue (*MR*) is equal to marginal cost (*MC*): if *MR* exceeds *MC*, profit can be increased by selling more and to achieve this price should be lowered; if *MR* is less than *MC*, profit can be increased by selling less and to achieve this price should be raised; if *MR* and *MC* are equal, profit cannot be increased by raising or lowering output and so both output and price are optimal.

This is sound economic theory, but there are several 'disconnects' that separate it from the practical world:

1. It is doubtful that decision-makers ever know their marginal costs or, indeed, the details of their demand and supply functions (Bowman and Ambrosini 1998). (Economists have developed various methods for estimating their way around such problems, but these methods are less than perfect and are anyway beyond the scope of the present discussion.) Analysis is also complicated by the distinction between SRMC and LRMC met in the last chapter.

2. As just noted above, airlines inevitably produce excess output (reflected in load factors below 100 per cent). There are two principal reasons:
    *   The sometimes extreme demand peaking experienced in the industry, exacerbated by an inability to inventory output, means that any level of capacity capable of meeting a substantial proportion of peak demand will – if reasonably fully utilised at other times – inevitably lead to the production of excess off-peak output.
    *   Some market segments (notably business travellers) are responsible for significant random demand variation (on a departure-by-departure basis), yet also require the late availability of space (i.e., high 'seat accessibility') to accommodate their last-minute travel purchase behaviour. (Seat accessibility has in fact been progressively eroded in many markets by load factors rising to historically high levels.)
    This is part of the cost of doing business in the airline industry, but it is something that does not sit comfortably with the structure of traditional economic models.

3. Recall from chapter three that a price–cost margin (i.e., (price – marginal cost)/price) of zero is evidence of perfect competition (where $P = MC = MR$); the closer the price–cost margin comes to unity, the greater is the monopoly power of the firm concerned. Whilst the idea that output and price are optimised where $P = MR = MC$ might be appropriate to the baseline theoretical model of perfect competition, most airline markets are to a greater or lesser extent imperfect. In imperfect markets firms will try to exploit whatever opportunity they are given (e.g., by a government dispensing route designations in a regulated market) or are able to create (e.g., by building a fortress hub) to price above *MC*.

4. Price is anyway not necessarily a single, discernible figure; at any one time there can be many different prices charged for essentially similar products in the same marketplace. Price is a highly complex concept in an industry such as the airline business where differential and discriminatory pricing are widespread and output is actively revenue-managed. Furthermore, the fact that demand arises in O&D markets whilst output is supplied by individual flight-legs means that for network carriers it is very difficult to compare demand and supply at the market level or establish market-clearing prices.

5. The last point underlines that even what is meant by 'product' and 'marketplace' is open to question, to the extent that a flight departing from point A en route to point B, which in one sense is itself a 'product' by virtue of its schedule and routing, can also be argued to be offering a number of different products in several different markets: different products might be defined by inflight amenities in the separate cabins or by the various conditions applied to tickets purchased by individual travellers in any one cabin; furthermore, the flight could be carrying not only local passengers travelling from A to B, but also passengers who started their journeys somewhere behind A and/ or will continue beyond B – that is, passengers whose journeys constitute purchase decisions made in numerous different city-pair markets.

The assumption made by neoclassical economic models that output, in this case airline output, is homogeneous is therefore open to serious doubt. We will look at this next.

III. Airline Output

THE HETEROGENEITY OF AIRLINE OUTPUT

Different airlines produce very different mixes of cargo and passenger output. These can be broken down into narrower categories such as scheduled passenger, scheduled freight and mail, nonscheduled passenger, and nonscheduled freight output. Furthermore, although airlines produce ASMs and ATMs, customers each buy a service package comprised of attributes designed to deliver certain benefits. The core of each package is safe, reliable transportation for themselves or their goods, but there is much more to any package than just this core (see Holloway 2002).

Passenger Output

'ASM' and 'ATM' are metrics that measure aggregate output but tell us nothing about the nature of that output. General Motors produces X million cars each year and Delta flies Y billion ASMs – but what sort of cars for which markets, and what sort of air transport services delivered in what types of market? If we accept that demand is heterogeneous, as argued in Chapters 1 and 2 and reflected by the efforts of marketers to divide markets into segments having different demand curves, then supply must also be heterogeneous wherever producers are actually trying to satisfy consumer demand.

In this there are cost implications. One ASM generated by Southwest is pretty much the same as another; any differences in the production costs associated with the output of different ASMs are largely attributable to different stage-lengths (and to a much lesser extent station costs), because the aircraft type and the onboard product are standard across the network. (This is not strictly true given the different series of B737s operated and the slightly higher standard of service offered to purchasers of Business Select fares, but the point holds well enough for the purposes of the present argument.) At American, in contrast, the network output of ASMs is an average that masks considerable differences in the nature, and costs, of the different types of output being produced; because American's fleet contains numerous aircraft types and its service portfolio encompasses much broader geographic and product scope than is the case at Southwest, it is fairly obvious that the larger carrier produces ASMs in many more different ways. The point here is that the raw number of ASMs supplied by an airline tells us only so much. A more complete understanding comes from familiarity with the markets in which it has chosen to generate ASMs and the service(s) it has decided to offer into those markets. This is particularly true now that, as we saw in Chapter 1, the growing number of different business models being implemented is creating a more varied range of output than has been seen before. (See Holloway [2002] for a comprehensive discussion of passenger service attributes.)

Cargo Output

Airlines differ substantially in the amount of cargo output they generate. This section will first consider the different ways in which cargo output can be produced, and then briefly note the types of product offered to the market.

The production of cargo output Scheduled airlines producing cargo output fall into two categories:

1. *Scheduled combination carriers* These are airlines which carry both passengers and freight within a scheduled system. There are three subcategories:
   - Many airlines, including some which are active in cargo markets, rely solely on belly-hold capacity and do not operate freighters. A short-haul scheduled passenger carrier competing against well-developed surface modes might carry mail, but is unlikely to need capacity for substantial volumes of freight; many LFAs do not use belly-holds for anything other than baggage because cargo-handling is seen as a threat to the fast turnaround times essential to high aircraft utilisation. The output of saleable freight ton-miles increases dramatically when a carrier operates medium- and long-haul widebodies with large belly-holds; indeed, cargo operations make significant contributions to the profitability of many long-haul routes, particularly where passenger demand is intensely seasonal. (Interestingly, because of its high passenger baggage load the belly-hold cargo capacity on an A380 operation may be below what it could have been had one of the larger widebody twins flown the service.)
   - A small number of airlines supplement the capacity available in their passenger fleets by using combis (i.e., aircraft carrying both passengers and cargo on their main decks, as well as cargo in their belly-holds).
   - Several airlines, particularly in Asia, Europe, and increasingly the Middle East operate freighters alongside passenger fleets. Although their number is still relatively small in the context of the global airline industry as a whole, these carriers are responsible for somewhat over half of international air cargo output (but much less if the US domestic market is included, because this is dominated by the integrators).
      (Different types of in-house lift might be supplemented by wet-leased freighters, either from time to time or on a long-term basis.)
2. *Scheduled all-cargo carriers* There are relatively few scheduled all-cargo airlines, with Cargolux and Nippon Cargo being two obvious examples. A special case is the integrated carriers, notably Deutsche Post World Net, Fedex, TNT, and UPS, which offer time-definite door-to-door services. Several joint venture cargo operators have emerged in China recently; most link local and foreign airlines (e.g., Jade Cargo, formed by Shenzen Airlines and Lufthansa), but Korean Air chose instead to team with logistics company Sinotrans.

Some European airlines make extensive use of cross-border rail and, particularly, road transport to feed long-haul services, so producing ASMs on the ground. Within North America, much of the freight shipped by integrated carriers now goes by truck.

There is also a large number of nonscheduled (i.e., charter) cargo airlines, some offering general capacity and others specialising in the transportation of loads which by virtue of their size or the nature of the commodities involved require special handling (e.g., perishable products, live animals, or outsize loads). Because aircraft utilisation tends to be lower than on the scheduled side of the industry, these carriers generally operate older aircraft with lower ownership costs; the price they have to pay for this is higher fuel and maintenance costs – a point we will return to in Chapter 8.

Freighters, both scheduled and nonscheduled, account for around half of global cargo output. Many are conversions of mid-life passenger aircraft, but there has also been strong demand for fuel-efficient new-build widebodied freighters. Because freight traffic is forecast to grow more rapidly than passenger traffic over the next 20 years, the role of freighters will expand.

However, perhaps the most interesting point to come from this discussion takes us back to a comment made in the last chapter regarding the 'disconnect' between airline costs and prices: with so many different types of cargo lift – each having different operating costs – competing in the same markets, and with some combination carriers costing belly-hold space on a by-product basis, linkages between market price and production costs are always going to be tenuous at best.

Types of cargo output Very broadly, we can distinguish the following different approaches to the design of cargo products:

1. *Airport-to-airport line-haul* Although a growing number of combination carriers are now offering time-definite products in international markets, some of which are standardised across alliances as in the case of SkyTeam Cargo, most are still primarily engaged in relatively low-yield airport-to-airport line-haul – sometimes on a space-available rather than firm-space basis. The fundamental issues in this case are sales channel design and airline brand visibility amongst shippers.

    Relatively few carriers offer effectively branded cargo services or maintain significant direct relationships with shippers. Those that do not are essentially selling line-haul products to forwarders and consolidators who can shop around for the cheapest rates because, subject to reliable service, shippers on the whole are not carrier-sensitive. Cargo sales departments at such airlines are filling space rather than developing markets for their output. To overcome this problem, some carriers are building closer relationships with key forwarders to offer time-definite, 'virtually integrated' door-to-door service in competition with integrated carriers and even, for the largest shippers, an integrated logistics product. This latter trend involves relatively few airlines, and some that have attempted it have pulled back; forwarders are generally very protective of their customer relationships and need compelling reasons to become involved in joint ventures with airlines. However, it seems likely that the integrated carriers will continue to make inroads into high-yield segments of international freight, including heavy freight, markets; this might in time stimulate greater cooperation between airlines and forwarders.

    Smaller airlines generating only limited cargo revenue (under, say, $150 million a year) sometimes prefer to pass their entire output either to a cargo wholesaler or to an alliance partner which has a better-developed marketing organization capable of selling more output than it has available in-house. Amongst other benefits, this relieves the smaller airline of the need for warehouse space in which to build-up and break-down containers and pallets – requiring instead just through-flow facilities.

2. *Branded products* The archetypal branded cargo product is a time-definite door-to-door service offered by an integrated carrier. Focusing at first on small packages and still known as 'express' in some markets, time-definite products have come to encompass the full spectrum of weights and air-shippable commodities. Indeed, Boeing (2006b) has observed that as traditional cargo airlines expand their range of time-definite product offerings and as they and integrators penetrate deeper into supply chain logistics management, the distinction between express and general cargo is continuing to blur. Integrated carriers still dominate the market for branded products, however, and are benefiting in their international operations from the type of double-digit growth which was generated in US domestic markets during the 1980s and 1990s. Amongst combination carriers, British Airways provides an example of one which has invested heavily in branded time-definite products: BA World Cargo has opened its 77,000 square feet Premia facility at London Heathrow to handle the 10 per cent of business accounted for by three premium products – Prioritize (a time-definite service for freight of any size or weight), Control Climate, and Airmail.

    Figure 4.1 illustrates some of the key differences between line-haul and integrated products.

3. *Outbound wet-leasing of freighters* Before later starting to diversify, Atlas Air created a niche in the 1990s by leasing out freighters on an aircraft, crew, maintenance, and insurance (ACMI) basis, with lessees paying rentals, providing traffic rights, and meeting cash operating costs. There are several other carriers which generate cargo output indirectly in this way; most, although not all, specialise in long-haul widebodies. The product offers lessees an opportunity to test new markets without committing to a long-term fleet expansion and to augment output in established market (perhaps on a seasonal basis). Whilst this flexibility benefits lessees, the ACMI business model is not without its challenges for lessors: first, it can be volatile – expanding rapidly when demand is high and capacity is constrained but dropping steeply when cargo markets turn down and lessees cut leased-in capacity rather than in-house lift (as in 2001–2003); second, there are relatively few barriers to entry.

    Despite average annual growth of 18.6 per cent from 1990 to 2005 and growth rates in excess of 19 per cent in both 2004 and 2005, ACMI lift carried only 6.2 per cent of world air cargo in 2005 (ibid.).

    As is the case with passenger products, cargo services can be characterised as being comprised of bundles of attributes targeted at segments of shippers and forwarders with different requirements. A survey of shippers by Mercer Management Consulting suggests that key attributes in order of priority are: reliability; transit times; price; real-time shipment tracking; ease of documentation; guaranteed pick-up/drop-off times; specialised freight-handling capabilities; strong global network; and electronic data interchange (EDI) capabilities (Shields 1998). Cargo output, therefore, need not be a homogeneous block of ATMs or FTKs; by making explicit service design decisions airlines can pitch their output at specific shipper and forwarder requirements, target specific types of heavy freight and/or express (document and small parcel) shipment, and position themselves strategically on a continuum stretching from pure capacity provision to value-adding service partner.

	Integrated Product	Traditional Line-Haul
Advantages	• Transparent total pricing • Single-party door-to-door control over the shipment (subject to exceptions in some markets) • Real-time tracking • Straightforward documentation • Range of guaranteed time-definite services • Growing availability of value-added warehousing, assembly, and distribution services • Reliability • High standards of customer service • Strong brand image	• Strong existing links with forwarders • Inter-modal flexibility (e.g., sea/air services) • Ability to accommodate a broader range of commodities, weights, and sizes • Lower costs
Disadvantages	• High costs (driven in part by the high levels of operational support required) • Some weight, size, and commodity limitations	• Sometimes opaque pricing • Unclear brand image as perceived by shippers (leading to heavy reliance on forwarders) • Hand-offs between forwarders, airlines, customs agents, warehouse operators, and/or ground transportation firms can impair security, complicate documentation, and increase cargo dwell times • Patchy customer service • Limited (but improving) tracking capabilities

Figure 4.1   A summary of advantages and disadvantages of integrated and traditional line-haul airfreight products

Source: Virtual Aviation College (www.virtualaviationcollege.org)

THE SUPPLY-SIDE CHARACTERISTICS OF AIRLINE SERVICE

Heterogeneous though it is, there are certain common characteristics of all airline output that flow directly from the nature of the air transport industry (Rispoli 1996, Holloway 2002). The points which follow are framed with reference to the passenger side of the industry, but most can be extended to cargo output.

1. It is a feature of airline economics that adding output improves product quality as perceived by customers. This manifests itself in two ways:
    *   Empty airline seats are not necessarily evidence of oversupply – they are also part of a product. Certain types of passenger, notably those travelling on business, tend to book quite close to departure and also to change their travel plans after booking or once a journey has begun. Such passengers usually must pay the highest fares chargeable in the chosen class of travel in order to obtain this flexibility, and the revenue they generate is therefore particularly important for many scheduled airlines. Fully booked airplanes inhibit such flexibility and, whilst being beneficial to airline revenues in the short term, might have negative long-term repercussions if the brand loyalty of these customers is eroded by frequent inability to make or change bookings at short notice.
        To ensure this does not happen to an unacceptable extent, airlines have typically tried to build seat accessibility into their full-fare products (i.e., to build-in a high probability of being able to obtain a booking on the required flight in the preferred class whenever a reservation is attempted); high accessibility is achieved by ensuring seats remain available for this important category of passenger until very close to departure. This means that, particularly in first and business classes, although an airplane might depart with some empty seats there is not necessarily an oversupply problem.
    *   Additional frequencies improve choice of departure time. Frequency competition is a key dynamic in many liberalised markets, especially when the business segment is being targeted; operating smaller aircraft at higher frequencies than before need not inevitably boost aggregate output in a market, but on the whole the recent history of the industry has seen increased frequencies putting upward pressure on output (Wells 1999).
2. Consumers (i.e., end-users of the service, who may or may not also be the customers who make actual purchase decisions) need to be physically present to receive the core transportation service. This means that unsold output is lost at the point of production because it cannot be inventoried; in other words, the product is highly perishable.
3. We have seen that transportation is an experience derived from a mix of tangible and intangible elements that can be identified as separate service attributes (Holloway 2002). Different packages of attributes can be assembled pursuant to different service concepts, and this is what makes output heterogeneous; the more service concepts an airline has in its portfolio, the more heterogeneous its output. Different packages have different production costs. (Another effect of intangibility is that the complexity of their price–quality relationship makes services difficult to price.)
4. Because production and consumption of the service can only occur simultaneously, there is a high level of contact between consumers on the one hand and an airline's operational staff, facilities, equipment, and processes on the other. Interpersonal contacts between consumers and service providers (i.e., an airline's front-line staff) are therefore a significant part of the service experience and are highly significant service attributes. This places the marketing and operations functions into particularly close proximity with each other.
5. Front-line personnel in direct contact with consumers can have a profound impact on the quality of service delivered, but often have little influence over the design of that service.

6. Many airlines have transactional dealings with an overwhelming majority of their customers, but relationship dealings with a relatively small number of frequent (primarily business) travellers who generate a disproportionately high percentage of their revenues.

7. The level of output customisation airlines are able to offer even to their high-value customers is relatively limited, with the result that the style and tone of service delivery are often all that prevent a consumer feeling they are being anonymously processed.

8. As well as being people-intensive, airline service is also equipment-intensive and information-intensive, with the result that service delivery depends heavily on the effective management of both people and technology.

9. Airline operations exhibit a great deal of short-run rigidity:
   - Whilst some airlines now manage their fleets much more flexibly than in the past (making late substitutions of different-sized variants within families such as the B737 and A320 series, for example), output (i.e., ASMs and ATMs) remains difficult to adjust on any significant scale over a short period of time – with upper limits imposed by capacity at full utilisation, and lower limits set by the sustainability of fixed costs associated with an underutilised fleet. A countervailing advantage is that because aircraft are mobile, they can be quickly reallocated in response to demand fluctuations in different markets. (We saw in 1991 and, more acutely, in 2001 and 2008 that airlines willing to take drastic action can in fact make swift and substantial cuts in output; however, unless aircraft that are parked are fully depreciated, their ownership costs will remain a burden and a longer-term solution must be found.)
   - It is difficult and expensive to upgrade service quality levels quickly because heavy investments are likely to be needed in facilities and equipment and, particularly, in staff training.

10. The fact that a system comprised of capital equipment and highly trained people has to be in place to offer service on any significant scale means that fixed costs are high; this in turn puts airlines under pressure to adopt a volume-oriented approach to their business, which then exerts pressure to engage in marginal cost pricing whenever this is what it takes to maintain traffic volume. The impact may be reflected in weak yields, particularly when new capacity is added to a market or when the economy turns down but capacity is left in place.

11. Output decisions in many, albeit a declining number of, international markets remain constrained by the terms of bilateral air services agreements (see below).

12. In some jurisdictions, competition authorities can influence output decisions which are deemed, for example, to be predatory or an abuse of dominant position.

Picking up on the last point, the next section will discuss market structure using the traditional neoclassical models, and will then briefly touch on competition policy.

IV. Market Structure and Competition

Competitive strategy is driven by both internal, firm-specific considerations and by the structure of external markets. In this section of the chapter we will look at what neoclassical theory has to say about market structure, and relate the models proposed to what is happening in air transport markets. A brief introduction to the evolving role of competition policy will follow.

DETERMINANTS OF MARKET STRUCTURE

The neoclassical approach characterises firms as technology-driven production functions within which inputs are transformed into outputs of goods and services; once an objective function such as profit maximisation has been assigned, the level and price of output can be set and varied in response to changes in input prices, production efficiency, and demand. The precise nature of this interaction will be heavily influenced by the structure of the market in which the firm is operating. Market structure provides a context for management behaviour and so can help explain conduct (i.e., the competitive decisions taken by airline managers) and performance (i.e., how efficient the price and output decisions at which they actually arrive are in allocating scarce resources).

Because a market is comprised of buyers, sellers, and a product, the structure of that market will depend upon the numbers and relative power of buyers and sellers, the defining attributes of the product concerned, and how much information the parties have.

The Numbers Of Buyers And Sellers, And Their Respective Power

Most passenger markets have a large number of buyers; airfreight markets have relatively fewer, particularly given recent consolidation in the forwarding industry, but rapid growth of the express parcel business has significantly expanded the number by creating a 'retail' market. How many sellers are present varies widely between city-pair markets. And here we have the first hint of a truism often overlooked: there is no such thing as *the* air transport market, but instead thousands of individual city-pair markets. In most of these there are substantial numbers of buyers, whereas the numbers of sellers might range upwards from one to quite a few depending upon the regulatory environment and the geography of the market (for example, whether there are competing hubs situated between the origin and destination). Where power lies in a particular market will depend on the impact of any commercial regulations affecting that market, the number of sellers present in it, and the appetite each seller has for real competition. Another variable, to which we will return shortly in the context of contestability theory, is the impact of *potential* market entrants on the supply side. Finally, some competing suppliers might be outside the airline industry – that is, might be producers of substitute products (e.g., videoconferencing).

Ease Of Market Entry, Mobility, And Exit

Buyers are largely free to enter or leave air transport markets, although some business travellers and freight shippers have less choice in this regard than discretionary users; sellers do not always have the same degree of flexibility. Barriers to entry are characteristics of an industry which place incumbents at an advantage over new entrants. Barriers to mobility are characteristics that limit mobility within an industry insofar as they constrain incumbents wanting to embark on a significant change in strategy. Barriers to exit are industry characteristics which militate against redeployment of assets. We will look at these different barriers later in the chapter.

The Extent Of Product Differentiation Or Distinctiveness

We saw in Chapter 1 that 'differentiation' exists when one of two or more competing products is perceived by customers to offer differences sufficient to justify payment of a price premium; perceived differences between products can also give rise to what the brand management literature refers to as 'distinctiveness', but in this case although they might stimulate a preference and a purchase they will not generate a price premium. Either differentiation or distinctiveness can be attributable to any of the benefits offered by a particular service package (Holloway 2002). The purpose of both is to turn other products into weaker substitutes for the product in question than would otherwise be the case. Substitutes enhance competition.

It is commonly argued that airline seats are commodities. This is debatable. It is certainly true that the number of ways available to make the attributes of a service package truly different is limited, and that differences in the 'hard' attributes derived from facilities and equipment can in many cases be readily imitated. On the other hand, brand image and service style, both underpinned by a strong service culture, are not as easily imitable – and this is often where true distinctiveness, if not necessarily differentiation, lies (ibid.). Southwest, for example, has an image and corporate personality which make it stand out; an airline that appears to be selling a commodity service largely on price is in fact selling a distinct combination of service attributes (frequency, schedule, reliability, and service style, for example, as well as the more visible attributes embedded in cabin configuration) – all of which are priced to offer a particular type of customer value reflecting a service concept distinct from any of the concepts offered by, say, American.

The Availability And Cost Of Information

This is another important determinant of market structure according to the neoclassical model. The cheaper and more readily accessible information about alternative products and their prices is, the more competitive a market will usually be. The Internet has made it easy and cheap in principle for buyers to tap information about product availability, price, and quality. From the industry's side, even start-ups and small carriers now have access to global distribution channels which would have been unavailable or prohibitively expensive just a few years ago. (Distribution will be discussed in Chapter 5.)

GENERIC MODELS OF MARKET STRUCTURE

To analyse the structure of a market, we can use:

- The neoclassical microeconomic model, which recognises monopolistic, oligopolistic, imperfectly competitive, and perfectly competitive markets.
- Porter's widely adopted five-forces model (1980, 1985). A more fine-grained development of the neoclassical approach (Sinclair and Stabler 1997), this recognises as key variables in any market's structure the degree of rivalry between existing competitors, the threat of market entry, the threat from substitute products, and

the power of buyers and suppliers. Market size is also important. A market may be structurally attractive but too small to justify entry by a carrier with a wide-market strategic position; it might, on the other hand, be attractive to a niche operator.

The purpose of both is to assess the impact of market structure on output and pricing decisions and on likely profitability.

The four models of market structure found in neoclassical microeconomic analysis are outlined below, along with some of their implications for the air transport industry.

Perfect Competition

The key assumptions of this model are as follows:

1. Large numbers of small producers and consumers are present, none of whom is able to influence market price. Producers are therefore 'price-takers' whose individual pricing and output decisions have no impact on market price; none has market power. Indeed, there is no actual *competition* under conditions of perfect competition because by definition no firm can influence the market through its choice of strategic conduct. *Short-run* equilibrium is established by firms varying output in an effort to maximise profitability given their individual cost structures and the price they have to accept for their products. Output is set where the marginal cost of producing the next unit is equal to the price being imposed by the market. In fact, very few air transport markets have large numbers of producers; also, the fact that airlines have to pre-commit output and then choose to use revenue management systems to control its sale means that there is seldom a single price, even within the same aircraft cabin, throughout the period between committing production capacity (i.e., announcing a schedule) and closing a flight.

2. Products are commodities – that is, perfect substitutes for each other giving rise to an absence of consumer preference as between suppliers – with the result that no firm can raise its price without losing all of its business. The assumption of product homogeneity means that there is a single market price for the industry's output. In fact, there is no single market for the output of the air transport industry and neither is there a single commoditised product; there are thousands of city-pair markets, and in many of these will be separate groups of consumers demanding particular types of output and separate airlines competing to provide these different segments with what they are demanding. There is no single industry cost curve, and no single market-clearing equilibrium price for air transport services.

3. Information is 'perfect' in the sense that it is costless and freely available to all market participants. In fact, consumers do not have *perfect* information. Although the availability of price- and product-comparison websites certainly provides greater transparency than before in markets where Internet penetration is high, even here information-seeking does still involve 'search costs'. One purpose of investing in a strong brand image is to distinguish the airline concerned and so reduce consumer uncertainty with regard to service availability, quality, and consistency – something that is anathema to perfect competition.

4. Innovation is entirely exogenous (i.e., from sources external to the market), making firms perforce reactive rather than proactive. The air transport industry in fact has a long history of endogenous (i.e., internally generated) technical and commercial innovation.

5. Consumers face no switching costs. In fact, airlines use a variety of techniques – with varying degrees of success – to raise switching costs. The most obvious example is FFPs, which should in principle be designed to retain the most profitable (i.e., frequent and high-yield) customers; brand-building has the same objective, albeit at a more general level. Within agency distribution channels, TACOs and other forms of incentive are intended to raise agents' switching costs.

6. Barriers to entry and exit are absent, allowing perfect mobility in markets for both factor inputs and the product being produced. This is important because when supernormal profits are being earned it is necessary for challengers to be able freely to respond to the price incentive by entering and competing those profits back down to normal levels; *long-run* equilibrium is established by the entry and exit of firms in response to the presence or absence of opportunities to earn (economic) profit. In fact, there is no shortage of entry barriers in the air transport industry – as we will shortly see.

Bearing on the last point, a key question is whether *actual* market entry is required in order to put downward pressure on equilibrium prices, or whether *threat* of entry is sufficient. Contestability theory argues that the market efficiencies associated with perfect competition can be generated as readily by the threat of market entry as by actual entry.

Contestability theory   Airline deregulation in the United States was the outcome of three sets of pressures – two academic and one consumerist:

1. A body of research was accumulated during the 1960s and 1970s suggesting that regulation resulted in unnecessarily high service quality (i.e., flight frequencies) and correspondingly low load factors sustained by high fares. (See, for example: Levine 1965; Jordan 1970; Kahn 1971; Keeler 1972; Douglas and Miller 1974b.) The particular concern of many leading US economists was that regulation was causing prices to diverge from the welfare-maximising level established by LRMC (Button 1993).

2. With the University of Chicago in the vanguard, a view gained momentum that regulation was incompatible with the public interest. The heart of the problem was thought to be 'regulatory capture': regulated firms, in this case airlines, were argued to have undue influence over regulatory agencies both because these agencies rely on the firms for cost data and also because of the firms' lobbying power. (This problem has since arisen in respect of many of the previously state-owned monopolies privatised throughout the world since the early 1980s – notably including airports.)

3. Air travellers were able to see palpable differences between low fares in the deregulated California and Texas intrastate markets and higher prices in federally regulated interstate markets.

A theory which shaped the deregulation debate but which was in fact most fully developed in the immediate post-deregulation years and used both as an *ex post* justification (ibid.) and as an argument for adopting a relaxed attitude towards the wave of airline mergers in the 1980s was contestability theory (Bain 1949; Bailey and Panzar 1981; Baumol *et al.* 1982). Instead of the large number of *actual* competitors required by the perfect competition model, contestability theory is content with the presence of just a threat of entry from *potential* competitors – all other requirements of the model remaining more or less unchanged. It was argued that under certain conditions many of the benefits of perfectly competitive markets (notably improvements in consumer welfare in respect of price and service quality) could be 'simulated' whenever a plausible competitor was potentially free to attack, if only on a hit-and-run basis, a market in which excessive profits were being made by one or more incumbents.

Hit-and-run entry, it was argued, can be remunerative provided that the entrant is able to establish a sufficiently high price for long enough to permit earnings to at least compensate for the sunk (i.e., unavoidable and irrecoverable) costs arising from entry; the lower these sunk costs are the more appealing such a strategy could be, and in the case of the airline industry they were held to be low because infrastructure such as airports and airways is provided by other parties and aircraft are not market-specific. The threat of entry alone would be sufficient to influence prices charged by incumbents, and actual market entry would be unnecessary. In this way, resources would be efficiently allocated, monopoly profits would be unsustainable in the long run, and the industry would produce optimum output at minimum cost.

If contestability theory holds true, it should be possible to identify certain characteristics in a deregulated market (Button op. cit.):

- active entry and exit affecting both the industry as a whole and individual city-pairs;
- pronounced efforts to minimise costs;
- absence of sustained supernormal profits;
- pricing behaviour that is not primarily driven by the numbers or sizes of actual competitors.

In the post-deregulation United States, the first two predictions have been satisfied only to a limited extent: whilst entry and exit have been active at the industry level and in respect of many domestic city-pair markets, non-regulatory barriers to entry have arisen in some important non-stop markets (e.g., those with a fortress hub at one end); with regard to cost discipline, this was slow in coming to a number of incumbents and despite painful efforts in the 1990s arguably started to bite only in the post-9/11 downturn. The presence of supernormal profits is difficult to determine because derivation of economic profit from financial accounting presentations is not a straightforward task. Empirical studies have therefore focused largely on airline pricing, and the weight of evidence suggests that contestability – at least in its purest form – is not an adequate predictor of competitive behaviour in deregulated airline markets (Graham *et al.* 1983; Meyer and Oster 1984; Bailey *et al.* 1985; Baumol and Willig 1986; Moore 1986; Bailey and Williams 1988).

On the other hand, Morrison and Winston (1986) have argued that there is support for what they call 'imperfect contestability', if not for 'pure' contestability. Were a market perfectly contestable, fares would be independent of the level of concentration amongst producers; Borenstein (1989) found this not to be the case in the US domestic air transport markets studied, but did find that fares on monopoly routes are reduced – albeit not to competitive levels – when another carrier is already operating at one or both ends of the route. Other studies have also found that potential entry constrains fares (Evans and Kessides 1993). One important consideration, though, is how to identify potential entrants when trying to assess their influence: whilst it is common to assume that airlines already serving both endpoints of a route are potential entrants, there are researchers who consider carriers to be potential entrants only if they are not at a significant disadvantage to the incumbent(s) in generating connecting traffic (Hurdel *et al.* 1989).

On the whole, it is fair to assume that a majority of observers concur with the findings of Borenstein (1992) and Hurdel *et al.* (op. cit.) that the impact on ticket prices of the number of *potential* competitors is considerably less significant than the impact of the number of carriers actually operating in a market. In fact, some of the fundamental assumptions underlying contestability theory have come under attack in the literature, most notably:

1. *The absence of barriers to entry* A barrier to entry is anything that physically prevents a challenger from entering a market (e.g., lack of traffic rights or slots) or economically disadvantages the new entrant by imposing upon it higher costs than are faced by the incumbent (e.g., economies of scope or density – both discussed in Chapter 5). We will look at barriers to entry in a moment, but it is safe to say that few observers now deny that they pose problems in many important air transport markets (Button and Nijkamp 2003). (Schnell [2005] presents a critique of studies that have identified the existence of barriers to entry, argues that managers' perceptions of their presence can have as profound an effect on market entry as their actual presence, and describes the results of a survey of perceptions.)

2. *Low sunk costs confronting entrants* Whilst it is true that aircraft are highly mobile and therefore rarely become 'sunk' into a particular market, the same is not true of advertising and route development costs – or of the early post-launch losses often incurred when a new market is entered. That said, the size and significance of sunk costs involved in entering a given market will depend upon the identity of the entrant. For example:
   - market entry *might* impose on a large and well-established airline fewer absolute sunk costs than a start-up insofar as it already benefits from a corporate infrastructure with the experience and capacity to launch new routes and, importantly, it may well have an established brand image that is recognised in the market being entered;
   - even if the sunk costs encountered are the same, they are likely to be proportionately less significant to an established carrier than to a start-up.
   Airlines certainly do enter markets opportunistically and/or experimentally (e.g., Allegiant), but 'hit-and-run' network strategies are still relatively rare on the scheduled side of the industry as a whole; in particular, hubs and other major centres of operation impose high location-specific sunk costs. (Baumol [2002] has in fact proposed a theory which attempts to reconcile high fixed and sunk costs with ease of entry and competitive pricing. He makes two primary arguments: first, sunk costs are indeed substantial, but to the extent that they must be borne not only by entrants but also by incumbents – who need to innovate and to invest in order to maintain their networks – they may not constitute real barriers to entry; second, even where sunk costs are high enough to prevent wide-market entry, there may exist the potential for niche entry.)

3. *Incumbents' inability to respond rapidly to entrants' lower prices* The assumption that incumbents will keep their prices down to avoid provoking potential entry also runs counter to much recent experience. More often an incumbent will price as high as a market will bear and then respond aggressively to any new entrant that does in fact materialise. Potential entrants now know from their own and others' experiences that in many cases apparent profit opportunities can whither away the instant they enter, because incumbents have the ability to respond immediately with aggressive capacity-controlled discounting. Certainly, the requirement of the theory that consumers are able to respond more rapidly to an entrant's low prices than is

an incumbent, so diverting business almost instantaneously to anybody flying in to attack the incumbent's supernormal profits, is unlikely to be met. An incumbent able to lower prices more rapidly than a new entrant is able to establish itself in a market is less likely to be concerned about the dangers of keeping prices high prior to – and under threat of – entry than about keeping costs low, so that it can better sustain a fare war if one were to develop as a result of that threat of entry materialising.

Whatever the perceived merits or shortcomings of contestability theory as a justification for deregulation or liberalisation, there are forces at work in some markets which make it increasingly difficult for potential entrants to turn threat into reality. Even where regulators have backed away, there are other barriers that can inhibit market entry – particularly by start-ups and small carriers, but also by larger airlines as well in some cases. We will look at these shortly.

Conclusion   Whilst some financial and commodity markets do approximate the ideal of perfect competition, most – including air transport markets – do not. Few markets are as frictionless as the ideal modelled by perfect competition, and the real use of the model is less as a realistic goal than as a benchmark against which to compare prevailing reality. Perfect competition in fact models an idealised 'limiting case' at the opposite end of the spectrum from monopoly; put simply, what distinguishes the two is whether or not a producer has the power to set prices.

Monopoly

Monopoly is characterised by one seller, high (perhaps insurmountable) barriers to market entry, the unavailability of close substitutes, and a poor flow of information to consumers. A monopolist's demand curve and the market demand curve are identical.

Monopolies might be economically efficient in industries with very high fixed costs wherein scale brings to the production process such benefits that average cost can be minimised only by serving the entire market, or where – as in the case of air traffic control – there can only be one provider (circumstances referred to as a 'natural monopoly'). Where unregulated or benignly regulated, however, monopolists tend to offer less and lower quality output or to sell at higher prices than would prevail in a competitive market; supernormal profits are in principle attainable – something of which a number of privatised airport operators stand accused.

Monopoly power   Although pure or perfect monopoly is relatively rare in air transport markets because substitutes tend to be available (Button 1993), it is not unusual for markets to have few competitors. Where these firms are able to influence price, and in particular sustain a price above marginal cost, they have a degree of monopoly power. (This observation has already been made in Chapter 3 where monopoly power, reflected in the size of a firm's price–cost margin, was characterised as one of several possible price drivers.) We will shortly look at market situations that might lead to monopoly power either narrowly within specific niches (e.g., monopolistic competition) or more broadly across an industry (e.g., a collusive oligopoly). The point here is that monopoly (i.e., a single supplier) and monopoly power (i.e., an ability to influence price and earn supernormal profit) are not necessarily synonymous.

Monopolistic Competition

The advantage of monopoly power is, as we have seen, the opportunity it confers to earn supernormal profits. Neoclassical microeconomics proposes models of market structure other than pure monopoly under which despite several producers being present in the market, one or more of them has at least some degree of monopoly power (Pindyck and Rubinfeld 2001): we will look first at monopolistic competition, then at oligopoly.

The theory of monopolistic competition was put forward by Chamberlin (1933). The model has less strict defining conditions than perfect competition, notably that apparently similar products may be perceived by consumers to have important differentiating attributes: competing products might therefore be substitutes for each other but not perfect substitutes, so their cross-price elasticities of demand would be significant without being infinite. This gives sellers, who must according to the model be large in number, somewhat greater control over prices than in markets with structures closer to perfect competition. Neither will a price change by one firm lead inevitably to a change in price by others, as it would in an oligopolistic market. The extent to which a firm can translate consumers' perceptions of a product's differential advantage into additional profits depends in part upon just how different the product is perceived to be, and in part upon how important that difference is to consumers; in other words, it will depend upon the elasticity of the demand curve that the firm has been able to create by differentiating its product.

Whether monopolistic competition can exist depends therefore on the ability of firms in an industry to differentiate their products, and whether there is free entry and exit. Whereas in perfectly competitive markets each firm faces its own horizontal demand curve and only the market demand curve is downward sloping, firms under monopolistic competition face downward-sloping individual demand curves; this gives them some monopoly power, but not necessarily free rein to earn substantial profits. Something close to a limited monopoly might be achievable in the short run, but in the long run supernormal profits will be competed away by the arrival of competitors and economic profit will revert to zero. Firms use branding, product design, FFPs, and other loyalty-generators to 'lengthen' the short run. Indeed, any barrier that prevents or deters market entry by a potential competitor can serve to lengthen the short run.

Monopolistic competition is considered less economically efficient than the ideal of perfect competition because it tends to generate excess capacity, and firms produce at output levels other than those that minimise average costs. On the other hand, monopolistic competition can have the redeeming virtue of offering consumers greater choice insofar as they perceive each producer's offer to be at least somewhat different from other offers. Just how economically inefficient a monopolistically competitive market is relative to the perfect ideal will depend upon the market power of firms within it, which in turn depends upon their number, their attitude towards competition, and how substitutable consumers consider their products to be.

Monopolistic competition and market segmentation Although it took over two decades and several refinements, the concept of monopolistic competition was perhaps more warmly received amongst marketing practitioners than by traditional economists. Alderson (1957) developed from it the idea that firms 'compete for differential advantage' in markets where products are not necessarily homogeneous and which can therefore be segmented (ibid., p. 101). 'No-one,' he argued, 'enters business except in the expectation of some degree of differential advantage in serving his customers, and ... competition consists of the constant struggle to develop, maintain, or increase such advantages' (ibid., p. 106).

We can see in this argument, and in the quotation that follows, a significant early step away from the neoclassical assumption of homogeneous firms competing in homogeneous product markets and towards what became the resource-based theory of competitive strategy – which holds that firms apply heterogeneous resources in pursuit of advantage.

> Every business firm occupies a position which is in some respects unique. Its location, the product it sells, its operating methods, or the customers it serves tend to set it off to some degree from every other firm. Each firm competes by making the most of its individuality and its special character. It is constantly seeking to establish some competitive advantage ... [because] an advanced method of operation is not enough if all competitors live up to the same high standards. What is important in competition is differential advantage, which can give a firm an edge over what others in the field are offering (ibid., pp. 101–102).

The vehicle for differential advantage is identification of unserved or poorly served market segments and the development of service–price offers that will appeal more to constituents of a specific segment than will competing offers. Putting this into the terminology of the resource-based theory of competitive strategy, Hunt (2000, p. 64) argues that 'firms pursue comparative advantage in resources that will yield marketplace positions of competitive advantage and, thereby, superior financial performance'. (In using the expression 'comparative advantage', he is drawing on international trade theory to help understand sources of *competitive* advantage.) Although rarely acknowledged, there is a striking resemblance between, on the one hand, the notion of differential advantage that grew from seeds sown by Chamberlin in the 1930s, and on the other the idea of competitive advantage popularised in the strategy literature since the late 1970s.

Conclusion   The argument has been put forward in recent years that the air transport product has become commoditised – that is, has become a homogeneous, undifferentiated product in the sense of the word 'commodity' as used by economists. A very different argument is put forward in Holloway (2002). There is undoubtedly considerable homogenisation of 'hard' or functional product attributes in markets characterised by similar stage-lengths; for example, in any given cabin class there is often broad similarity between different carriers' products within, say, US domestic markets or intercontinental markets. Nonetheless, functional attributes – particularly in long-haul markets – are not universally the same, and a growing number of carriers are also expending a great deal of effort developing distinctive soft attributes founded on their different corporate cultures, tone and style of service delivery, and brand images.

It is therefore reasonable to characterise at least some air transport markets as monopolistically competitive (Stavins 1996). The problem is that whilst efforts to make a carrier's service distinctive might generate a brand preference for that carrier when price is broadly comparable with competitors' prices, demand curves in many segments are sufficiently elastic to make premium pricing difficult or impossible to sustain. The real difficulty, however, lies in the long run. To see monopolistic competition in the air transport industry it is necessary to accept contestability theory, because there are few markets in which the defining requirement for a large number of sellers is actually (as opposed to potentially) present, and to take a relaxed view on the impediment posed by barriers to entry – which we will look at below. In a growing number of markets, both propositions are questionable.

Oligopoly

Oligopoly is characterised by few sellers ('duopoly' being the special case of just two sellers), products which may be either commoditised or differentiated (if only, in the latter case, by heavy advertising), high barriers to entry and exit, and limited consumer access to price, product quality, and cost information. The small number of sellers means that actions taken by one can affect demand in the market as a whole, and this results in a high degree of strategic interaction between firms because moves will characteristically be countered. Oligopolistic structures arise not only through internal growth but, characteristically, as a result of mergers and alliances. Many observers consider that the deregulated airline industry tends naturally towards oligopoly (Ben-Yosef 2005).

One of the defining characteristics of oligopolistic markets is the high level of interrelatedness between the actions and reactions of sellers; for example, very frequently a price reduction by one firm will be matched by others – leading, perhaps, to a price war. According to neoclassical theory, a firm's demand curve relates quantity to price, *holding constant all other demand-determining variables*. Thus, its demand curve will shift if the firm lowers its prices in an oligopolistic market because such a change is highly likely to lead to reactive price moves by competitors – in which case other demand-determining variables (i.e., in this case, competitors' prices) are no longer being held constant. This has to be factored into managerial decision-making.

> Managing an oligopolistic firm is complicated because pricing, output, advertising, and investment decisions involve important strategic considerations. Because only a few firms are competing, each firm must carefully consider how its actions will affect its rivals, and how its rivals are likely to react [in response, say, to a price cut intended to stimulate sluggish sales] … These strategic considerations can be complex. When making decisions, each firm must weigh its competitors' reactions, knowing that those competitors will also weigh *its* reactions to *their* decisions. Furthermore, decisions, reactions, reactions to reactions, and so forth are dynamic, evolving over time. When the managers of a firm evaluate the potential consequences of their decisions, they must assume that their competitors are as rational as they are. They must put themselves in their competitors' place and consider how they would react (Pindyck and Rubinfeld 2001, p. 429; parentheses and italics in the original).

Game theory has increasingly been used by economists and strategic management researchers to help understand decision dynamics under oligopolistic and quasi-oligopolistic market structures. The necessity to engage in strategic gaming – that is, to consider how others might react in response to a decision – is characteristic of oligopolistic markets, and sets them apart from the idealised world of perfectly competitive markets where strategic behaviour is irrelevant. The monopoly power held by oligopolists and the profitability of oligopolistic industries depend in large measure upon how players interact when making output and pricing decisions – particularly whether they are prone to cooperate or to compete aggressively. Cooperation might, for example, allow firms to charge prices significantly above marginal cost and earn substantial short-run profits whilst at the same time ensuring that entry barriers are kept as high as possible in order to maintain profits in the long run.

Non-cooperative oligopolistic behaviour   Non-price competition – based on product attributes (e.g., network scope, schedule, onboard service), heavy advertising, loyalty schemes or brand image, for example – is common in oligopolistic markets. This is because, as noted above, there is under normal circumstances a considerable amount of price interdependence amongst oligopolists. They generally believe that any price decrease will be matched, causing a decline in profits, and that in normal markets (i.e., excluding circumstances such as the run-up in jet fuel prices in 2007–2008) any increase may fail to stick due to competitors' reluctance to follow suit, causing a decline in market share. What they try to do instead, therefore, is shift the demand curve for their products to the right; the objective is to allow more output to be sold at an unchanged price, and although competitors may ultimately react, the response is likely to be less direct or damaging than a response to a price cut. Nonetheless, when rapidly rising output and/or stagnant demand lead to oversupply, price competition can become intense even in oligopolistic markets – particularly where, as in the case of the airline business, the product is perishable; conversely, when demand is strong and output growth restrained, as in many US domestic markets during 2005–2007, price increases will be matched and are likely to stick.

Although non-cooperative oligopolistic behaviour is perfectly legal in most countries, notwithstanding that it might lead to anti-competitive outcomes and economic inefficiency, oligopolistic market structures are often perceived as being susceptible to price- and/ or output-fixing by producers who either get together openly (sometimes with official blessing) to form a cartel, or collude in secret – the purpose being to create and then benefit from monopoly power.

Cooperative oligopolistic behaviour   The objective of acting together is to maintain prices at a level that maximises the aggregate profits of all producers by simulating the behaviour of a monopolist. Three broad categories of cooperative strategy can be identified: cartelisation; collusion; and strategic alliances. The first and second are illegal in many jurisdictions. Legality aside, the three categories are not mutually exclusive.

1. *Cartelisation* Cartels exist where producers formally and openly agree on pricing and/ or output levels. Not all producers of a particular product need necessarily be members of a cartel, but if it is to be effective it must embrace producers responsible in aggregate for a significant share of industry output. For a cartel to be successful in driving prices significantly above competitive levels, market demand must be relatively inelastic.

    Cartels are illegal in many developed commercial jurisdictions, although some might be explicitly permitted under the terms of a specific exemption to otherwise applicable antitrust/competition laws. Even when they are legal, cartels face two significant challenges: first, getting initial agreement from members perhaps having different cost structures, market projections, and strategic objectives is not necessarily easy; second, the temptation to 'cheat' by lowering price or increasing output to gain market share is ever-present. Only if potential gains from coming together to exert monopoly power unavailable to a member acting individually are sufficiently attractive will the challenges be overcome in the long run. Even then, there remains the question of what impact the pricing and output decisions of non-members might have.

Cartelisation is not an unfamiliar form of competitive strategy in the airline industry. Until cracks began to appear in the 1970s, the post-war regime governing international air transport – founded on the Chicago system of bilateral ASAs between governments and multilateral tariff coordination amongst airlines – was in essence a cartel. (Note that whilst the international aeropolitical system in its entirety functioned as a cartel, IATA itself never strictly speaking did; IATA membership was freely open to any carrier operating international services and even at the peak of its power the Association controlled prices in international markets but not levels of output.)

2. *Collusion* Less formal than a cartel, collusive strategies involve airlines cooperating on output and/or pricing decisions. Collusion in its strongest form might involve output restraint in order to keep prices above competitive levels. A weaker case sometimes referred to as 'semi-collusion' might, for example, involve cooperation on prices but competition in output volume (Fershtam and Muller 1986); the temptation to engage in marginal cost pricing to fill perishable seats makes this type of collusion difficult to sustain in many airline markets, although it can work if demand growth is strong.

Collusion might be explicit or tacit. Although *explicit* collusion through open communication still exists in some markets, it is broadly illegal in the United States, the European Union, and other countries with well-developed bodies of competition law; an exception to this generalisation is the US practice of granting antitrust immunity to alliances between US carriers and partners from countries that have signed open skies bilaterals with the United States. Despite its illegality, several examples came to light in 2006/07: the UK Office of Fair Trading and the US DOJ launched independent investigations into the alleged fixing of transatlantic passenger fuel surcharges by British Airways and Virgin Atlantic; parallel investigations into collusion with regard to fuel, insurance, and security surcharges in freight markets involving as many as 30 airlines were initiated by the European Commission (EC), the DOJ, and competition agencies in several countries; and Lufthansa agreed to pay $85 million to settle related class action lawsuits arising from allegations of price-fixing made by freight forwarders. In March 2008 the EC launched an investigation into collusion on routes between Europe and Japan, and in May a former Qantas freight executive was jailed in the United States.

Tacit collusion exists where output and/or pricing decisions are coordinated other than through direct communication; the usual means is through forms of 'signalling', which might be recognised within the industry but not easily spotted by outsiders. Signalling could, for example, involve providing advance notice of fare or output plans to give time for competitors to indicate how they will react; where competing networks overlap and there is 'multi-market contact', an airline might signal its displeasure at a competitor's initiative in one market by responding aggressively in another, with the intention of getting the initiator to make a connection and reverse the initiative. For instance, the US DOJ reached a settlement in the mid-1990s with ATPCO – a joint venture owned by several carriers and used as an electronic clearing house for current and proposed fares – in respect of allegations that fare postings were often used as a medium for 'negotiation' of prices (Havel 1997). Tacit collusion in a multi-point competitive environment is referred to in the strategic management literature as 'mutual forbearance': the greater the market overlap, the greater the impetus towards forbearance (i.e., competing less intensely than would otherwise be the case) (Gimeno 1999).

Another form of tacit collusion is 'parallel conduct', which can be defined as an implicit understanding that one firm's output and/or pricing decisions will follow those of another irrespective of whether or not such conduct is consistent with what would be expected in a fully competitive market. 'Price leadership', where firms follow the pricing decisions of a tacitly recognised 'leader', is a particularly common feature of oligopolistic markets; American has in the past sometimes worn this mantle in US domestic markets – although, as the 'value pricing' debacle of 1992 well illustrates, followers cannot always be relied upon to follow when market conditions are difficult.

Tacit collusion is often a fragile strategy in the long term: first, it is open to cheating; second, any market accessible by a competitor prepared to exploit differentiation or cost advantages will in all likelihood eventually attract just such a competitor. That the airline industry has periodic difficulty balancing output with demand and also faces perennial pressure to dispose of a perishable inventory makes tacit collusion a difficult strategy to maintain. In principle, the fewer competitors there are in a market, the easier it should be to tacitly collude; much, however, depends upon the attitudes and competitive instincts of the competitors concerned, as the likes of Southwest and Ryanair have shown.

Although no longer institutionalised, the tendency towards collusion within the global air transport industry is deeply rooted and should be kept in mind by competition authorities tasked with evaluating further consolidation within the industry.

3. *Strategic alliances* This type of cooperative strategy exists when firms explicitly and formally collaborate. Their purposes could include consultation on pricing and output decisions where this is legal, but are usually much broader – covering a range of initiatives on both the cost and revenue sides of partners' income statements (Barney 1997; Dussauge and Garrette 1995). Whereas collusion tends to be a horizontal strategy within a single industry, strategic alliances can also occur vertically within a value chain and across industry boundaries. They cover forms such as equity and non-equity alliances (e.g., airlines investing in other airlines or airlines entering into long-term supply agreements with third-party maintenance providers), joint ventures, and franchising, for example. Separately incorporated joint ventures are the exception rather than the rule as far as actual airline operations are concerned – SAS being a noteworthy example, as are the Chinese cargo ventures referred to above; however, they are becoming increasingly common frameworks for cooperative relationships between airlines and other types of organization (e.g., engine manufacturers in the aftermarket business).

    Most horizontal alliances between airlines are based on contractual agreements of one form or another; sometimes a hybrid approach is adopted, wherein certain clearly defined activities are housed in a separately constituted joint venture whilst the rest of the alliance relationship is structured around contract law rather than company law (e.g., the now largely inactive WOW cargo venture formed by Star Alliance members Lufthansa, SAS, and Singapore Airlines – and subsequently joined by non-member Japan Air Lines). In economic terms, airlines 'have an incentive to co-operate in strategic alliances when the value of their resources and assets combined is greater than the value of their resources and assets separately' (Barney 1997, p. 386). Specific motivations for entering into a strategic alliance might be to exploit economies of scope or scale, share costs, share complementary resources and capabilities, learn from partners, better manage risk and uncertainty, facilitate legally permissible collusive practices, and/or access new markets or segments that otherwise could not be served either at all or as cost-effectively.

Although alliances between airlines can lead to an increase in monopoly power in inter-hub/inter-gateway markets, the research evidence seems to point to a positive impact on consumer surplus – particularly where the partners' networks are complementary rather than overlapping; this can be attributed to a share of the cost savings that arise from cooperation being passed on to consumers. (Recent empirical support for this generalisation comes from Brueckner and Whalen [1998], and Oum *et al.* [2000]; see Pels [2001] for an overview of the evidence.) Nonetheless, competition authorities have shown themselves willing to act where the threat to competition posed by a planned alliance is deemed too great: Air New Zealand and Qantas tried for many years to cooperate both broadly and, after that was rejected, on (low-yielding and arguably oversupplied) trans-Tasman routes – but in November 2006 the Australian Competition and Consumer Commission emphatically rejected a proposal to code-share and to fix prices and output in markets between the two countries.

An important motivation for many alliances is the overcoming of barriers to market entry. Another motivation may well be to create them. We will look at barriers to entry in a moment. First, the increasingly important role of competition/antitrust law in policing cooperative oligopolistic behaviour will be briefly considered.

COMPETITION POLICY

Commercial regulation of air transport services is generally intended to achieve public policy goals that it is felt would not be realised through the operation of free market forces. It normally focuses on one or more of:

- market access (i.e., route entry and exit);
- output levels (i.e., frequency of service and/or size of aircraft used);
- pricing and conditions of purchase (i.e., tariffs).

Air transport has historically been regulated by industry-specific commercial rules and processes, which in many cases have overridden more generally applicable competition laws. For example, Japan's Civil Aviation Law has precluded application of the country's Anti-Monopoly Law in respect of activities approved by the Ministry of Transport, and the US DOT still has authority to immunise agreements between US and foreign airlines against the application of antitrust laws by DOJ. Indeed, one of the most significant practical benefits of open skies agreements has been the immunity granted to US carriers and their overseas partners from the countries that have signed them. Immunity allows considerably more joint capacity planning, fare-setting, inventory and revenue management, and selling than is permissible under a standard marketing alliance or code-share agreement without immunity.

Nonetheless, as commercial liberalisation and deregulation have spread since the late 1970s, general competition laws have come to play an increasingly influential role in several important markets (e.g., US domestic, intra-European, and Australian domestic).

The Purpose Of Competition Law

Bodies of competition law exist in over 50 countries. They vary in the breadth of their coverage and the diligence with which they are enforced, but most are intended to encourage economic efficiency (i.e., efficient resource allocation) where the market fails to do this and/or to protect consumers by encouraging competition and maintaining a level playing field amongst competitors. Inevitably, many countries have other (often social) items on their agendas as well as or instead of these two. If this were not the case, microeconomic analysis would be the lingua franca of competition policies everywhere and competition laws would be broadly the same – which, despite the efforts of ICAO and the International Competition Network (a forum created by several antitrust agencies to promote multilateral cooperation), they manifestly are not. Differences notwithstanding, we can generalise that competition laws typically address one or both of the following:

1. *Market structure* The policing of market structure attempts to control alliance formation, mergers, and other forms of consolidation that could lead to market dominance.
2. *Market conduct* The policing of conduct addresses areas such as:
   • abuse of dominant market position (e.g., price fixing, market allocation, and/or output restriction);
   • predatory pricing;
   • insistence that entry by a dominant party into one type of exchange relationship (e.g., an interline agreement) should be predicated on the willingness of the other party to enter into another type of relationship (e.g., purchase of the dominant party's ground-handling services);
   • impediments to the flow of product information to consumers;
   • interference with competition in downstream markets or distribution channels by practices such as tied selling;
   • interference with competition in upstream markets, such as vertical integration to obtain control over key resources.
   Competition authorities have also intermittently, and inconsistently, addressed problems arising from the 'spatial pre-emption' of airport slots and gates by grandfathered incumbents.

The Issues

The key issues are summarised below. Many could equally apply to a market dominated by one carrier or by a small group of colluding oligopolists.

Abuse of a dominant position   FFPs, negotiated corporate deals, and incentives aimed at targeted members of distribution channels (particularly incentives with nonlinear reward structures that offer disproportionately higher benefits as successive sales thresholds are crossed) might be manipulated by a locally dominant carrier to consolidate market dominance and erect effective barriers to entry. In late 2006, for example, the South African Competition Commission fined South African Airways for abusing its dominant position in domestic markets by agreeing special incentives for travel agents intended to further exclude competitors from those markets.

A key question, of course, is how a 'dominant position' should be defined. One argument is that a dominant position exists when a carrier has the power to weaken competition, and that it is being abused when that power is exercised (Kyrou 2000, following the European Court of Justice).

Market access   The question here is who can become a competitor. There are two sub-issues. First, structural barriers to market entry might exist or be created (e.g., airport congestion, or the economies of scope available to carriers having large, integrated networks); these will be considered later in the chapter. Second, predatory strategies could be pursued by incumbents intending to deter competition or eliminate it if it does materialise. Predation involves forgoing short-term profits in the expectation that this will 'buy' market power and the opportunity to earn greater long-term profits (expressed in terms of net present value). It is discussed in Box 4.1.

Box 4.1: Predatory Conduct

Predatory pricing is tactical pricing by a dominant carrier at levels which are either below cost or substantially lower than what the market will bear, with the intention of disciplining or driving out more efficient competitors and subsequently seeking to earn monopoly profits by charging prices higher than they would otherwise be. 'Cost' in this case is usually taken to mean SRMC. In a perfectly competitive market, price and SRMC should be equal; if price exceeds SRMC this is an indication of some degree of monopoly power, and if it is below SRMC there is a presumption of a predatory motive.

Although courts in different jurisdictions apply different tests to establish predatory pricing, average variable cost (AVC) is often used as a proxy for SRMC, because defining both the marginal unit of output and the cost of that unit can be impossible (Areeda and Turner 1975). In the EU, for example, the European Commission applies a two-tier cost test pursuant to several decisions made by the European Court of Justice:

1. First, a dominant airline setting a fare below AVC would be guilty of abusing its dominant position.
2. Second, even were a dominant airline to price above AVC, its behaviour could be considered an abuse were prices set lower than average total cost and established in the context of a plan to eliminate competition from the market concerned. Going one step further, there is an argument that pricing does not have to be below average total cost to be predatory – the sole criterion for predation being a willingness to accept lower profits than might otherwise be earned in order to deter or eliminate competition (Joskow and Klevorick 1979).

However, even an apparently simple concept such as AVC is muddied by the inevitably arbitrary way in which common costs on a particular departure have to be allocated between products and fare types (e.g., On the basis of cabin floorspace available to each? On the basis of load factor? On the basis of relative service levels?). Thus, whilst determining the AVC for a particular flight is reasonably straightforward, obtaining a meaningful cost figure for different products or booking classes is not. More fundamentally, we have already seen that airline prices are set in respect of individual journeys in O&D markets whereas a high proportion of costs are incurred operating aircraft on flight-legs (which may or may not correspond to an O&D market); the fact that output may be jointly supplied to multiple O&D markets and is certainly delivered in units larger than the individual journey makes any comparison between price and cost, whether SRMC or AVC, fraught with difficulty. Furthermore, there are theoretical objections to the use of AVC: first, pricing below AVC need not necessarily be predatory (in the sense that it diminishes welfare); second, SRMC can exceed AVC as, for example, when capacity has to be added (and incorporated into SRMC) in order to accommodate traffic stimulated by a price decrease (Edwards 2002).

The intent of predatory pricing is usually to drive competitors from the market and, presumably, thereafter open the opportunity for prices to be raised again and supernormal profits to be earned. When an airline operates in multiple city-pair markets, cross-subsidisation to support predatory pricing is entirely feasible. Alternatively, the objective might be to deter market entry by using 'limit pricing' selectively in respect of certain segments of demand; the purpose here would be to demonstrate to potential challengers that their prospective profitability will be limited by lower revenues than might otherwise have been expected from these segments, and possibly also from the market as a whole if such predation is taken as a signal of intent by the incumbent to mount a more wide-ranging price response should entry materialise. (Such signalling need not in practice require the introduction of low fares – announcement of an intention to do so, perhaps via a GDS, might be enough to deter market entry. Similarly, as noted earlier, if an existing competitor announces fare reductions, a signal can be sent threatening to match such reductions not only in the market concerned but also in other markets where the two compete; this would amount to illegal price collusion in some jurisdictions.)

Predation can be difficult to establish in any industry, but particularly so in the airline business. The facts that airlines generally have high short-run fixed costs and low SRMCs and AVCs, and that their basic transportation product is perishable, make the distinction between marginal cost pricing and predatory pricing largely one of intent. It is not prima facie unreasonable to argue that pricing only slightly above AVC is rational in respect of a flight or a series of flights if revenue generated covers variable costs and makes a contribution to fixed costs; the longer such behaviour persists, however, the less reasonable the argument becomes because it is evident that some motive other than profit maximisation underlies the pricing decision.

There are other complications:

- A static short-run price–versus–cost analysis ignores the fact that airline pricing decisions are made in a fluid intertemporal context and have outcomes discernible only in the long term.
- There is also a network context, with pricing in a local market into or out of a hub possibly having much to do with competitive conditions in flow markets which are being jointly supplied with output by the local flight.
- Even pricing well above AVC can be predatory where the resources required to generate output are retained in a market solely for predatory reasons and despite there being an opportunity cost involved in not moving them to more profitable uses. Predatory intent might in this case be identified in a carrier's willingness to bear economic losses even though accounting results from the operation concerned show a profit (Oster and Strong 2001, citing Comanor and Frech 1993).
- Revenue management systems can be used to disguise predation. Without lowering the deepest discounted fare already offered in a market affected by low-fare entry, an incumbent can engage in predation by aggressively expanding the allocation of seats available to that fare (and perhaps also loosening applicable booking and/or usage restrictions); it appears that some Asian network carriers are using capacity at the back of their widebodies in this way to match the volume and availability of low fares put into the market by LFAs that have entered short- and medium-haul trunk routes with lower-capacity narrowbodies. Similarly, a significant increase in output on a route is likely to lead to a higher proportion of total seats going into low-yield booking classes, as the RMS copes more or less automatically with the implications of having a fresh supply of seats to sell.
- Incumbents might try to introduce predatory pricing indirectly by establishing a low-fare subsidiary or division. Unless there is a high degree of financial independence, competition authorities could look through the 'corporate veil' and characterise even the

pricing decisions of a wholly separate subsidiary as an extension of the incumbent's strategic behaviour.

Distinguishing between predation and well-targeted price competition is not necessarily straightforward for outsiders without knowledge of managerial intent. Furthermore, given the burden of proof under the tests for predation imposed in some jurisdictions and the expense of litigation (both exceptionally high in the United States, for example), the threat of an incumbent being convicted of predatory pricing is relatively low relative to the frequency with which complaints are voiced.

Predation is anyway often less readily discernible in prices than in non-price exclusionary behaviour. Examples of the latter could include:

- dominating slots at congested airports;
- capacity dumping (i.e., expanding output such that incremental revenues fail to cover incremental costs or, alternatively, such that profit-optimising opportunities elsewhere are forgone). This might involve either or both:
  - 'swamping' a route with larger aircraft (i.e., capacity swamping);
  - adding frequencies (i.e., overscheduling).
  (One objective of capacity swamping and overscheduling is to benefit from the S-curve effect and maintain a market share premium [Beyer 1999].)
- 'sandwiching' or 'bracketing' a low-frequency competitor's departures or scheduling away from a competitor's connections (i.e., predatory scheduling);
- refusing to interline, or imposing discriminatory conditions on access to ground services such as passenger-handling or ramp and maintenance support;
- monopolisation of traffic feed;
- monopolisation of access to infrastructure;
- predatory use of corporate rebates, TACOs, and FFP awards by targeting abnormal benefits at markets challenged by new entrants;
- 'route overlay' – the duplication by an incumbent of all or a major part of a small challenger's network, as Northwest is alleged to have done to Reno Air in the early 1990s.

More subtly, the fact that many airlines compete across networks rather than just in individual city-pairs opens the possibility that predatory behaviour in response to market entry might not be targeted at the city-pair concerned; a carrier threatened by entry in one of its core markets might retaliate – or signal potential retaliation – by adjusting prices, frequencies, aircraft capacities, and/or routings in other markets where the same two airlines compete. These 'network effects' arising from multi-market contact between network carriers can be particularly difficult to uncover and police.

The distinction between fair competition on the one hand and predation on the other is not always easy for the untrained eye to discern. The more liberal or deregulated the market, the more likely predation is to occur and the more important the rigorous application of general competition law becomes. The problem is that the airline business is a network industry which sells highly perishable services and uses mobile assets to produce those services. In circumstances such as these, most bodies of competition law are ill-equipped to distinguish between predation on the one hand and sound marketing or network management on the other. This is why very few allegations of predatory behaviour in the industry have found judicial favour. The complex nature of the airline business and the voluminous data required can make it practically impossible to prove unequivocally that an incumbent's actions alone have turned a potentially profitable entry opportunity for a challenger into an unprofitable one (OECD 1997). Furthermore, the judicial process might outlast the financial endurance of a small or under-capitalised challenger.

(Forsyth et al. [2005] provides accessible and comprehensive coverage of predation in aviation markets.)

Even more difficult to control than overtly predatory behaviour is the latent threat of predation. When a particular carrier builds a reputation for predatory behaviour it might, without having to take any overt action, be able to discourage market entry by more efficient potential competitors who have insufficiently deep pockets to sustain the negative impact on their profits that a predatory response usually implies. The end result of both actual and latent predation is likely to be the same: economic inefficiency and the elimination of price and/or service choices that would otherwise have been available.

Capacity fixing   Continuing this brief review of some of the key issues addressed by competition law, the questions in respect of capacity are who determines the level of output in a market, and how. Protectionist bilaterals regulate capacity as well as entry in some international markets. Inter-airline 'pooling' agreements between nominally competing carriers have historically been used to fix market shares as well as cost and/or revenue apportionments. Although they appear anti-competitive in intent, there is an argument that some of these arrangements do serve consumers' interests by spreading output to off-peak periods which would otherwise be ignored by carriers interested only in competing for more lucrative peak business. The same argument is now frequently heard to justify joint services or joint scheduling by code-share partners. The counter-argument is that such activities deprive consumers of choice and might also artificially restrain market growth. Arguments of this nature need to be assessed on a case-by-case basis.

Tariff-setting   The issue here is how the price of output is determined, and what if any conditions should be attached to tickets sold at various different price levels. As we saw in Chapter 3, tariff-setting has historically been an institutionalised part of the Chicago system of international aeropolitical relations: semi-annual IATA traffic conferences set fares and conditions, to be submitted for government approval under the terms of applicable bilateral ASAs. This was the predominant method for establishing prices until the 1970s. It runs counter to the spirit if not the letter of competition laws in most jurisdictions that have them, but in many countries these have either been held not to apply to a government-regulated industry such as air transport or specific exemptions have been agreed. These exemptions are gradually being removed and the 'IATA fare' is sliding into history. The challenge for competition authorities will be to ensure that institutionalised tariff-setting is not replaced by collusive tariff-fixing.

Distribution   The question in this case is how information about output and prices is distributed. For a competitive market to function properly, information on available products and prices must be freely and cheaply accessible to customers. According to neoclassical theory, only if information is openly available and fully incorporated into a price can that price work as an efficient mechanism for coordinating supply and demand. However, it is not uncommon for sellers to work simultaneously both to overcome and to deepen information asymmetries: brand images are in part a tool used to convey information about what buyers can expect from a purchase and to reduce consumers' uncertainty and search costs; on the other hand, some carriers hide behind non-mandatory fees and charges to disguise their true base fares and present their offers in a favourable light relative to competitors whose pricing is more transparent.

Potentially predatory practices such as the use of TACOs, intended to encourage travel agents to channel business to preferred carriers, have already been mentioned and remain of concern in some international markets where Internet penetration is low and/or reliance on agents remains high. An even stronger concern of competition authorities in the United States and the EU in particular over the last two decades has been the use of GDSs to manipulate markets by biasing information flows. Market power has been achievable through a variety of means, including the biasing of screen displays in favour of an owner, and using system data to gain early warning of competitors' marketing initiatives – or to analyse the outcome of initiatives so that counterattacks can be formulated. These threats to competition have diminished significantly as airline shareholdings in GDSs have been sold and, in particular, as the availability and significance of alternative booking channels on the Internet have expanded.

Conclusion On Competition Law

Arguably the most significant challenge facing decision-makers concerned with the application of competition law to the air transport industry in the years ahead will be how to deal with industry consolidation. Particularly where cross-border consolidation occurs in the context of liberalised access to different countries' air transport markets, this will require some degree of convergence between those countries' competition/antitrust laws. (Lu [2003] provides insight into the legal issues involved, looking specifically at the different approaches to airline alliances adopted by European competition law and US antitrust law.)

CONCLUSION WITH REGARD TO MARKET STRUCTURE

Some observers believe that the airline industry tends inevitably towards oligopoly. Proponents of deregulation in the United States disputed this, arguing that the absence of substantial economies of scale in the industry removes a fundamental motivation for airline mergers by denying large firms a meaningful cost advantage over small competitors. Using contestability theory, they suggested that threat of market entry was anyway sufficient to keep potential oligopolists from exploiting monopoly power in a deregulated environment. Consolidation at the industry level and the domination of fortress hubs by individual carriers seem to suggest this optimism was misplaced. Furthermore, and contrary to the assumptions underlying contestability theory, numerous studies of the US domestic market have confirmed what might be intuitively expected: average prices, adjusted for stage-length, tend to rise as the number of competitors in a market decreases (Stavins 1996; Transportation Research Board 1999).

The smaller the number of major players left in the industry, the more multi-market contact there is likely to be amongst remaining competitors, and the greater is the danger of tacit collusion – particularly during periods of strong economic growth, when demand is robust and load factors are high. There are, however, two other variables that need to be considered, at least as far as price competition is concerned: behaviour and geography.

Competitive Behaviour

Actual behaviour in apparently oligopolistic markets will not always be deterministically anti-competitive. There are two reasons for this. First, the fact that the industry faces significant challenges in profitably aligning output and demand on a departure-by-departure basis, together with the innate perishability of its output, mean that price competition is unlikely ever to disappear. Second, LFAs have successfully staked-out strategic positions in short-/medium-haul and medium-/high-density markets, and where these carriers are present price competition seems likely to remain robust.

Geography

Competition in the airline industry can be considered on four geographical levels: region-to-region (e.g., North America–Europe), country-to-country (e.g., USA–UK), city-to-city (e.g., New York–London), and airport-to-airport (e.g., JFK–LHR). Choosing the correct geographical frame of reference is critical when competition is being analysed. Commercial liberalisation is allowing international hub-and-spoke networks in general, and multi-hub alliances in particular, to reorient the arena of inter-airline competition away from the individual route towards the network. Airlines have an interest in defining markets as widely as possible – making a case, in the extreme, that it is network versus network competition that matters rather than what happens on any one route. Whilst this argument has strategic merit, it offers little consolation to consumers in individual markets subject to an abuse of dominant position: what happens on specific routes and in specific O&D markets should remain of primary concern both to consumers and to competition authorities.

The geography of competition is complicated by the fact, already mentioned in several different contexts, that 'route' and 'market' are not necessarily synonymous. A city-pair market connecting origin O to destination D might be served by a non-stop route, a multi-stop (same-plane or 'direct') route, and/or by separate routes connecting over one or more airlines' different hubs. One result could be that even though neither the non-stop O–D route nor individual routes to and from each hub are themselves highly competitive, the city-pair market between O and D is. Different routes can be part of the same market if demand on one is a substitute for demand on the other(s). Much therefore depends on the impact that geography and the design of competing networks have on the availability to consumers of alternative paths between O and D.

The prospects for price competition in markets which for whatever reason fail to attract competing non-stop or through-plane service can still be reasonable where the origin and destination are far enough apart to be connected over two or more competing hubs. This applies in the US domestic market, and also in international markets. If the global industry does consolidate further, as is widely anticipated, much will depend upon how actively the resulting networks compete for behind/beyond flow traffic over their respective hubs. However, intervening hubs are not always in an ideal position when competing against non-stop service:

1. *Short-/medium-haul markets* Intervening hubs are unlikely to be competitive against non-stops taking less than, say, 2 hours because even a conveniently timed hub transfer of 30–40 minutes would increase O&D journey time by a much higher percentage than would be the case were the stage-lengths significantly longer. Price-elastic, non-time-sensitive customers might accept a 25–33 per cent increase in journey time to save money, but most business travellers will not.
2. *Medium-/long-haul markets* Similarly, intervening hubs (e.g., London) are unlikely to provide serious competition in respect of high-yield O&D traffic travelling in another carrier's or alliance's non-stop inter-hub markets (e.g., Frankfurt–Washington Dulles).

This is why high-yield segments of local inter-hub markets have often been 'carved out' of antitrust immunities granted by the US DOT to transatlantic alliances. On the other hand, route deviation and a hub transfer might matter less to discretionary travellers provided they are given sufficient price incentive.

Where an O&D market is such a long haul that non-stop service is impossible (e.g., London–Sydney), sixth-freedom carriers with well-located hubs astride the traffic flow (e.g., Emirates and Singapore Airlines) can compete with third- and fourth-freedom through-plane services (e.g., British Airways and Qantas) without imposing a significant time penalty. More effective scheduling over sixth-freedom hubs has greatly increased the number of service–price choices available to passengers, shippers, and forwarders in some international markets (e.g., Europe–Australasia). Elsewhere, frequency and routing disadvantages combined with a lower market profile in originating countries may restrict sixth-freedom carriers to relatively small market shares; nonetheless, even here they can provide valuable competition for price-sensitive traffic.

Conclusion

The presence of fewer competitors globally and the concentration of higher percentages of global output into fewer hands need not necessarily imply reduced competition, because it is in individual city-pair markets that airlines physically compete for revenue – not in 'the global market'. Furthermore, competition in any marketplace is sometimes as much a reflection of intent as of the raw number of competitors present. However, global alliances can easily become quasi-monopolies on routes linking their partners' major hubs. Arrangements between alliance partners such as the cost- and revenue-pooling agreements entered into by Lufthansa on the one hand and both Thai and United on the other in respect of routes between their respective hubs at best point to the anti-competitive potential of alliances, and at worst evoke memories of the pre-deregulation European flag carrier duopolies.

More generally, the following types of market are particularly vulnerable to anti-competitive behaviour:

- markets at one end of which is a hub where the carrier surviving after a merger or acquisition is significantly more dominant than was previously the case;
- markets connecting two hubs, each dominated by the same carrier or by partners in a single alliance;
- markets in which code-sharing eliminates active competition;
- thin markets served over a hub by a sizeable network carrier where there is no possibility of rerouting traffic flows over another airline's competing hub or network, in which there is inadequate local traffic to support a competing non-stop, and where the incumbent's network is large enough to offer economies of scope sufficient to exclude existing or potential competitors.

Whereas some airlines would undoubtedly prefer regulators to limit their oversight to the 'big picture' issue of network-to-network inter-regional competition, it is in consumers' interests for competition law to be applied where it matters most – in O&D city-pair markets.

V. Restraints on Output

This section will look first, and in most detail, at barriers to entry. It will then turn briefly to an issue of rapidly growing strategic significance in Europe and, increasingly, North America: environmental pressures. Finally, the threat from pilot shortages will be considered.

BARRIERS TO ENTRY

According to microeconomic theory, firms in perfectly competitive industries are unable to sustain above-normal returns because these would quickly be competed away by new entrants attracted to the industry. In contrast, firms in industries where conditions of monopolistic competition, oligopoly or monopoly prevail are in principle able to earn above-normal returns; for example, the GAO (1991) has modelled a direct linkage between barriers to market entry and higher airfares in US domestic markets. The size and duration of any advantage will depend in part upon the nature of whatever barriers are constraining contestability (i.e., preventing entrants from moving in immediately in response to price signals).

A barrier to entry is something which favours incumbents already present in a market (GAO 2001). As already noted, it might be externally imposed (e.g., government unwillingness to licence start-up airlines or grant additional route designations to existing carriers), it might grow over time through force of circumstance (e.g., slot constraints), or it might be deliberately created by the strategic behaviour of an incumbent (e.g., network, brand, or distribution strengths, or a reputation for responding aggressively to new entrants). The effect of a barrier might be to make entry:

1. Impossible in a practical sense – for example, non-availability of slots or control by an incumbent of gates and other critical resources.
2. Less profitable than would otherwise be the case, by:
   - raising entrants' costs (e.g., charging high rents for gate subleases); and/or
   - reducing their revenues, most obviously by lowering prices either:
     - prior to entry (a response referred to as 'limit pricing'); or
     - after entry (a response which might be deemed to amount to predatory pricing).

   Higher costs suggest not only a weaker competitive position but a greater risk of commercial failure, and this perceived risk in itself is often sufficient to deter entry.

It will be recalled that one of the assumptions underlying contestability theory is that the sunk cost of entry is low. In principle it should be relatively easy to enter the airline industry because: some of the largest sunk costs arising in the business – for provision of airport and airway facilities – are met in most countries by government authorities or other parties, and paid for in line with usage (at rates that may fall well below true cost); aircraft can be leased-in and rentals paid out of current revenue; and in a lot of countries many of the services required to run an airline can be outsourced from third parties. Of course, the other – not insubstantial – sunk costs already discussed in the context of contestability theory, notably marketing communications together with any irrecoverable route entry costs and operating losses, do have to be absorbed. Nonetheless, relative to the capital intensity of the industry, it still looks fairly easy on paper to get into the air.

Reasons why this is frequently not the case are listed in the subsections below. The discussion relates in general to the scheduled passenger side of the business. Cargo and nonscheduled passenger airlines are widely considered to face fewer barriers to entry, and in many cases it is true that these sectors of the industry are more readily contestable. However, if the European passenger charter market is taken as an example, it can be seen that barriers to entry may in fact be quite high. In the United Kingdom and Germany, for instance, a considerable degree of vertical integration has emerged between tour operators, the airlines serving them, and the retail travel agencies which sell their leisure products; airline output within the inclusive tour value chain is also becoming more concentrated. This is not an easy business for an independent start-up carrier to penetrate other than on the periphery, supplementing base-load capacity flown by the major groups' in-house airlines and perhaps also serving smaller tour operators that do not have their own affiliated carriers. Furthermore, the challenge of finding remunerative employment for aircraft during off-peak periods is always present and makes entry into this market segment on any significant scale a high-risk venture.

Similarly, there are parts of the cargo business – notably airport-to-airport line-haul and ACMI leasing – that are in principle not expensive to enter. However, any carrier wanting to compete with the time-definite, door-to-door services offered by integrators such as FedEx would face heavy, possibly insurmountable, capital expenditures in order to build a competitive network and the necessary IT infrastructure.

Bain (1956) identifies three situations that might confront an entrant:

- *Blockaded entry* Entry is blockaded when barriers exist without incumbents having to act. Barriers in this case will be 'structural'.
- *Deterred entry* Entry is deterred when incumbents successfully engage in entry-deterring strategic behaviour.
- *Accommodated entry* Entry is accommodated when structural barriers are low and when entry-deterring strategies available to incumbents are likely to be either ineffective or too expensive to sustain.

We will look briefly at *structural barriers* to entry and at *entry-deterring strategies*. The most important structural barriers to entry are: government policy, spatial pre-emption, and commercial barriers.

Government Policy

One of the principal reasons why an industry with such global reach remains fragmented relative to most other industries of its size is that governments have historically imposed barriers to entry into the industry itself and into particular markets. They have done this on a variety of grounds, some explicit (e.g., the economic significance of the industry being too important to leave to the vagaries of market forces) and others clear but unspoken (e.g., national prestige and preservation of ministerial power and patronage). Regulations restricting access both to the industry and to specific markets have in fact historically been the most significant of the barriers to entry constraining airline output.

Barriers to entry into the industry: licensing, and restrictions on foreign ownership and control   To operate an airline it is necessary in most countries to obtain, inter alia, an operating licence (or in the United States make a showing of 'fitness' satisfactory to the DOT) and an air operator's certificate (AOC – issued in the United States by the FAA). The operating licence requires certain financial and other commercial criteria to be met. The AOC certifies compliance with relevant technical competence and safety requirements. (Depending upon national regulations, it may be possible for a start-up to use an existing carrier's AOC pending receipt of its own; easyJet operated for its first two years under Air Foyle and GB Airways licences, for example.)

Licences have historically been issued by the country in which the airline concerned has its registered office (or 'seat' in some civil law countries), and limited by domestic legislation to carriers majority-owned by citizens of that country; other factors might be taken into consideration as well – notably the nationality of any parties deemed to be in 'effective control' of the airline, the nationalities of directors and senior managers, the company's principal place of business, and its centre of operations. Legislation in nearly all countries limits ownership of airlines by non-citizens to 49 per cent or less; tighter limits are sometimes imposed in respect of voting rights. Most countries will therefore license only airlines which satisfy nationality requirements laid down in domestic statutes: thus, the nationality of several US start-ups – most recently Virgin America – has been challenged by competitors on the grounds that they are not effectively controlled by US persons. However, there are some notable exceptions. For example:

- As we will see below, nationality has been superseded by the concept of community air carrier in the European Common Aviation Area (ECAA).
- Australia will license wholly or majority foreign-owned carriers to fly domestically (e.g., Tiger Airways Australia). (However, it will not allow them to fly internationally, so a foreign party wanting its Australian airline to be designated for international service must own less than 50 per cent – which was Lion Air's approach when its intentions were announced in early 2008.)
- New Zealand will license foreign-owned airlines to fly domestically or internationally.
- Certain Latin American countries (e.g., Ecuador, Chile, and Argentina) have been willing to license foreign-owned carriers.

But on the whole the bar to foreign ownership and control of airlines remains in place. If applicable limits are breached (e.g., by a cross-border acquisition) the nationality of the acquired airline will be compromised, with two possible effects:

- it may no longer qualify for its operating licence, AOC, and domestic route licenses (if required);
- foreign countries may be entitled, under the terms of bilateral ASAs, to reject its designation by the country of its purported nationality – an issue we will explore in greater depth below.

Barriers to entry into specific markets: route authority and designation In a commercially regulated environment, an airline will most probably need to apply for a licence or other form of authority to operate each route it wishes to fly. We can distinguish:

1. *Entry into domestic markets* Once it has the required operating license and AOC, or local equivalents, an airline might still have to apply for individual route authorities even if it only wishes to operate in domestic markets. However, since the US

Airline Deregulation Act 1978, the trend towards liberalisation of domestic market entry has gradually built momentum elsewhere in the world: the European Union created the Single European Aviation Market in three stages between 1987 and 1997 by eliminating, subject to some very minor exceptions, regulation of market entry, output, and pricing; this single market has since been broadened by the EU joining together with several neighbouring countries to form the ECAA; Canada, Australia, and New Zealand also deregulated their domestic markets during this period, and since then many other countries have to varying degrees done the same – including most notably Brazil, Mexico, and India. China has set a target date of 2010 for the complete liberalisation of domestic route entry; given systemic pressures created by consistently rapid growth, and a lingering proclivity to protect the 'big three' incumbents, this may prove overambitious.

Removing government-imposed barriers to domestic operations has in several cases had a profound impact on airline output. The number of intra-ECAA routes grew 145 per cent in the 15 years after the third package of liberalisation measures was signed in 1992, for example, and during the same period the number of routes with two or more competitors grew in excess of 300 per cent (Geil 2006); much of this growth was due to the rapid expansion of LFAs, many of which entered non-traditional city-pair markets. Similarly, rapid growth of output in India after a second wave of market entry began in 2003 put downward pressure on fares – despite the enormous pent-up demand which had for decades been left unsatisfied as a result of regulatory barriers to entry limiting the country's domestic (and international) airline output.

2. *Entry into international markets* Although something of an oversimplification, three conditions must be satisfied before an airline may operate an international route where commercial regulation of entry is in place:
    *   the airline's country of registration must negotiate a bilateral ASA with the government of the other country which, inter alia, permits traffic rights to be exercised on the route concerned;
    *   the airline must be designated by its own government to operate the route;
    *   that designation must be accepted by the other government.

    Currently in a transitional phase towards more liberal market entry, the regulatory regime governing international air transport services nonetheless remains rooted in the institutions and practices of the 'Chicago system'. The following paragraphs will explain the core elements of this system, and both why and how it is changing.

The Convention on International Civil Aviation 1944 (the Chicago Convention) shaped the post-war aeropolitical system by first confirming the principle of state sovereignty over airspace, but then failing to agree on a multilateral disposition of rights to the use of that airspace. The outcome was that freedom to exploit it commercially became a privilege subject to bilateral negotiation within the context of different countries' public policy objectives and, importantly, subject to the principle of reciprocity: market access was not to be granted to another state's carrier(s) without receipt of a corresponding benefit. A standard form was agreed at Chicago and what was to become the detailed template for most future bilateral ASAs was negotiated between the United Kingdom and the United States at Bermuda in 1947; now known as Bermuda I, by virtue of the fact that the two countries signed a second bilateral on the same island three decades later, this became the model for thousands of subsequent ASAs. There are now estimated to be in excess of

4000 bilateral ASAs in force between the world's states (all of which should be, but not all of which in fact are, deposited with ICAO in Montreal). The following paragraphs will briefly outline the fundamentals of an ASA, before going on to discuss changes both in the approach to bilateral negotiations and in the Chicago System which are gradually lowering barriers to entry into international markets.

Bilaterals are individually negotiated. They follow a fairly standard format in the main body of the text, with matters specific to the particular agreement often appended in annexes or subsequent memoranda of understanding which specify the commercial details of what has been agreed; even where the countries involved make their ASAs publicly available, some or all of the annexes and memoranda might remain confidential. For the purposes of the present discussion, the following elements are significant:

1. *Market access* One or more of several 'freedoms' might be on the table at any bilateral negotiation. (Note that only the first five are technically 'freedoms' as defined at Chicago; the other three were not contemplated given the structure of the industry at that time. Note also that only freedoms three to eight give rise to traffic rights.)
   - First freedom: an overflight right.
   - Second freedom: a right permitting technical, non-traffic stops.

   The first and second freedoms are covered by the multilateral International Air Services Transit Agreement 1944 – the 'Two Freedoms Agreement'. This means that they do not have to be bilaterally negotiated where the two parties are both signatories. However, some large and strategically located countries have not signed (e.g., Russia, Kazakhstan, Brazil, Canada, Indonesia, Saudi Arabia, and several African countries); where a state wishes to exercise one of these freedoms vis-à-vis a non-signatory, the right must be bilaterally negotiated – and perhaps, as famously in the case of Russia, paid for.
   - Third freedom: a right allowing an airline to uplift traffic (passengers and/or cargo) from its state of registration and transport it to a destination in the other state (e.g., Delta flying Atlanta–London).
   - Fourth freedom: a right allowing an airline to uplift traffic from the other state and transport it to its state of registration (e.g., Delta operating London–Atlanta).
   - Fifth freedom: a right allowing an airline to uplift traffic from one foreign state and transport it to another state along a route which originates or terminates in that airline's state of registration (e.g., Northwest uplifting traffic in Tokyo destined for Seoul on a Los Angeles–Tokyo–Seoul service). A 'change of gauge' might be involved if aircraft of different sizes are used on different sectors. Fifth-freedom rights are sometimes restricted to a carrier's own stopover traffic (i.e., 'blind sector' rights). Airlines using fifth- (and occasionally also sixth) freedom rights might be required to pay either a 'per passenger' or a 'percentage of revenue' royalty to third- and/or fourth-freedom carriers; they are also sometimes forbidden from exercising price leadership in the fifth-freedom market.

   There are two types of fifth-freedom right. When Air China carries traffic between Madrid and São Paulo on a service originating in China it is exercising 'intermediate' rights granted by Brazil in the China–Brazil ASA; at the same time it is exercising 'beyond rights' granted by Spain in the China–Spain ASA. Fifth-freedom rights therefore involve a minimum of three countries and two ASAs (possibly three if the bilateral between the two foreign states – in this case Spain and Brazil – were to limit fifth-freedom services by other countries' airlines); the more points involved, the more complex matters become. However, now that there is a wide variety of long-haul aircraft available across a range of capacities, fifth-freedom rights are becoming somewhat less relevant than they were when intercontinental routes had to be operated by medium-haul aircraft which required en route stops, as in the early post-war decades, or by B747s which were too large for some non-stop markets and needed intermediate fill-up traffic, as in the period from the early 1970s until the advent of smaller long-range twins.

The first five freedoms were incorporated into the International Air Transport Agreement 1944 – the 'Five Freedoms Agreement'. However, fewer than a dozen states signed it, and this first attempt at commercial multilateralism failed; instead, states took to entering into bilateral agreements.

- Sixth freedom: a combination of fourth and then third-freedom rights resulting in the ability of an airline to uplift traffic from a foreign state and transport it to another foreign state via an intermediate stop – probably involving a change of plane and/or flight number – in its state of registration (e.g., American carrying traffic from London to Lima over its Miami hub). A possible constraint in some sixth-freedom markets is the question of traffic rights and pricing freedom. Whether or not this is an issue will depend upon the terms of the ASAs negotiated by the intervening (i.e., sixth freedom) state with the origin and destination states; some ASAs specifically address sixth-freedom services, some treat them as de facto fifth freedoms and limit them in this way, whilst others ignore them altogether.

- Seventh freedom: a right granted to an airline permitted to carry traffic between two foreign countries on a route that does not begin or end in its state of registration (which would be fifth-freedom traffic) or make an intermediate stop in its home country (which would be sixth-freedom traffic). Seventh-freedom rights have seldom been granted for passenger services; one of the very rare exceptions arose in the early 1990s when British Airways received US rights to operate transatlantic flights from a number of mainland European points – but corresponding rights at the European end were unavailable at that time, so services were never introduced. Transatlantic seventh-freedom services operated by European airlines are now feasible under the US–EU open skies agreement which entered into force in March 2008.

  With regard to cargo, seventh-freedom rights have typically been easier to come by – and, given the directional imbalance of traffic flows discussed in Chapter 2, have been essential to the viability of some services. Particularly striking examples have been the opening of hubs outside the United States by FedEx and UPS. The United States now negotiates for the inclusion of seventh-freedom cargo rights in its open skies agreements.

- Eighth freedom/cabotage: 'cabotage' is a right granted to an airline permitting it to carry traffic between two points within a single foreign country. It also is rarely granted. 'Consecutive cabotage' would allow an airline to uplift local (as opposed to 'own stopover') traffic between the first gateway at which a service arrives in the foreign country (e.g., Honolulu) and a subsequent destination in the same country (e.g., Los Angeles) or vice versa. 'Full cabotage' (occasionally referred to as the ninth freedom) is operation by an airline of services which originate and terminate wholly within a single foreign country; an alternative to full cabotage would be the establishment of a locally incorporated, majority- or wholly-owned subsidiary to operate in the foreign country – but, as noted above, the domestic laws of most countries preclude this.

Within the conceptual framework provided by these freedoms of the air, ASAs traditionally have imposed three specific barriers constraining market access: they specify which freedoms may be exercised; they specify which points in the countries concerned can be served (thereby confining services to identified gateway cities); and they specify how many carriers from each side are permitted to fly each route. Originally, it was normal for each party to an ASA to designate just one carrier. Gradually, dual designation became more normal – although outside the United States relatively few countries have until recently had more than one international carrier. Where designations remain limited in number but a country has more than the permitted number of airlines interested in flying a particular route, licensing criteria and procedures have to be followed – as exemplified by the hot pursuit of routes to China by various US airlines when additional authorities have become available.

2. *Ownership and control* It has been the norm in ASAs for 'nationality clauses' to specify that 'substantial ownership and effective control' of carriers designated under the agreement be in the hands of citizens of the designating state. There is no internationally accepted definition of 'substantial ownership' or 'effective control'. The need for designated airlines to be substantially owned and effectively controlled by the state designating them under the terms of a bilateral, or by nationals of that state, has been a significant impediment to cross-border airline mergers or acquisitions: if an airline domiciled in country A takes ownership or effective control of an airline domiciled in country B, even though the authorities in country B have no objection it is possible that B's bilateral partners (other than country A) might deprive the acquired carrier of traffic rights (or impose restrictions) on the grounds that it is no longer owned and effectively controlled by citizens of the designating country – that is, country B.

3. *Output* Not only have ASAs typically specified the markets available for entry and the number of carriers permitted to enter, most have also either specified limits on permitted output or incorporated mechanisms allowing *ex post* imposition of controls on output if required. Control can be achieved by reference to one or more of frequency, aircraft type, and total seats per week. In increasing order of liberalism the three most common approaches have been:
    *   predetermination: output must be agreed before services begin;
    *   a posteriori review: the Bermuda I approach, designated airlines match output to demand but their decisions may subsequently be reversed if they are deemed to be oversupplying the market;
    *   free determination: each designated airline is free to decide its own frequencies and aircraft types.

4. *Tariffs* We saw in Chapter 3 that ASAs have traditionally sought to restrict pricing freedom in one of a variety of ways. In increasing order of liberalism these are:
    *   dual approval: the Bermuda I approach, both governments must approve every filing;
    *   single disapproval: tariffs enter into force unless one government explicitly disapproves;
    *   country of origin: each government's right to disapprove lies only in respect of tariffs outbound from its jurisdiction, one way or return, and there is no power to disapprove inbound tariffs;
    *   double disapproval: both governments must disapprove any filing in order to prevent it coming into effect.

Note that not all ASAs require fares to be filed; where filing is not mandatory, the governments concerned may nonetheless retain oversight powers for use if they deem it necessary. In some cases 'tariff zones' are established with the effect that neither country has a right to disapprove fares falling within them.

Whilst a majority by number of the world's bilaterals remain at least to some extent restrictive and therefore present significant barriers to entry, many of the countries whose markets encompass the highest density international traffic flows have chosen to take a more liberal approach. The following paragraphs will look at why it is that the Chicago System has been coming under pressure and then outline some of the more significant changes that have been taking place.

Since the late 1980s pressure for fundamental change in the Chicago regime (i.e., the Chicago convention and the system of bilaterals to which it has given rise) has been building as a result of the following factors:

1. There has been a shift in public policy priorities in several aeropolitically important countries – specifically, a move away from protecting their airlines and towards:
    *   promoting competition, both to make airlines more economically efficient and to encourage a wider range of service–price offers to air transport users;
    *   widening market access to facilitate economic growth through tourism, trade, and investment.

    Several studies were cited at the beginning of Chapter 1 which provide quantitative evidence of the benefits arising from air service availability, and recent studies by InterVISTAS Consulting (2005) and InterVISTAS-ga[2] (2006) have advanced the argument in favour of liberalisation of international markets.
2. US aeropolitical policy since the late 1980s has been aggressively liberal – at least in respect of traffic rights, if not ownership and control. This has resulted in the pursuit wherever possible of open skies agreements. Whilst there is no single definition of 'open skies', the influential US interpretation outlined in 1992 (DOT Order 92-8-13) embodied the following elements: open access to all potential city-pairs between the contracting states and unrestricted traffic rights with no need to apply for designation (subject to the important exclusion of cabotage – a highly sensitive area for US airline unions); unrestricted code-sharing; double disapproval pricing; liberal regimes governing nonscheduled and cargo operations; and pro-competitive provisions in related areas such as ground-handling (i.e., the right to self-handle), reservations systems, and remittance of foreign currency earnings. Since 1992 the United States has had growing success in securing open skies agreements, of which it has now concluded close to 80, and several other countries (e.g., Singapore, Morocco, and Chile) have shown a similar inclination. (Dubai had an open access policy long before the expression 'open skies' came into vogue.)
3. A global multilateral approach to aeropolitical relations was on the agenda at Chicago in 1944 but never materialised. With Europe leading the way, regional multilateralism has gained momentum since the 1980s and has the potential – albeit over a long time-horizon – to act as a catalyst for change in the bilateral system.
4. Pressure has been growing from within the industry to be permitted to build global networks. Many observers argue that it is anachronistic to regulate air services on the basis of a balance of benefits derived by national carriers from serving traffic flows between their respective states when network redesign and increased hubbing

by international airlines now frequently lead to diversion of these flows over one or more third countries. This pressure for greater freedom to deploy their resources and manage their operations without regard to bilateral restraints rooted in another era is paralleled by pressure to remove constraints on ownership and control so that capital can be more efficiently sourced from global markets.

5. Finally, the embedding of a broadly liberal multilateral trading regime into non-aviation sectors of the world economy, together with the globalisation of ownership and output in industries which were also formerly considered 'strategic' and dominated by 'national champions', has made the argument that aviation should be treated differently more difficult to sustain. The financial volatility of the airline business, some (but by no means all) of which can be attributed to operational inefficiencies imposed by commercial regulations, has been used as evidence of the need for structural change.

That the Chicago System is on the cusp of change cannot be doubted. Evidence of change can be seen in the following:

1. *More liberal bilaterals* Since the 1980s, the tide has been flowing in the direction of more liberal bilaterals; early examples were ASAs between the UK and Ireland and the UK and the Netherlands. As noted, the United States has actively promoted its version of open skies, and a growing number of other countries have moved in the same direction; by late 2007 there were 131 open skies bilaterals, of which the United States was party to 77. An extremely liberal example is the Single Aviation Market created by Australia and New Zealand between 1996 and 2002. Even where open skies have not been achievable, many countries have been willing to renegotiate bilaterals or amend them through memoranda of understanding in order to loosen or even eliminate restrictions on market entry, output, and pricing freedom in respect of allowable routes. India provides a significant recent example. More restrictively, some countries have adopted a liberal approach towards international service into points other than their capital or principal commercial gateway (e.g., Egypt and Japan).

    On the other hand, illiberal instincts are far from dead. Germany and the Netherlands, for example, have in recent years tightened bilateral restrictions in their ASAs with certain countries (e.g., Pakistan). In 2006, Australia – generally one of the world's more aeropolitically liberal countries – decided to protect Qantas by denying Singapore Airlines access to US–Australia markets. The decision resulted from a formal (if procedurally rather opaque) review of international air services policy, the outcome of which was publicised in what, under the circumstances, might be considered a curiously titled media release: 'Australia to Continue Liberalisation of International Air Services' (DOTARS 2006).

2. *The spread of multilateralism* It was noted above that in the period 1987–1997 markets within the EU were combined and, from a commercial perspective, almost entirely deregulated. Not only has this had a profound impact on the countries directly and immediately involved, it has more recently begun to affect aeropolitical relations with other countries and, as a result, undermine the Chicago System. Two outcomes of the EU's internal multilateralism deserve particular attention:

    • *Creation of the single market* The fact that ECAA countries (with limited exceptions in the case of Switzerland) together constitute a single market means that if, say, an Asian or US carrier operates from one ECAA country to another this is cabotage – in commercial fact, if not in international air law. (That the EU–US agreement in effect since March 2008 permits US carriers to operate cross-border services within the ECAA but does not allow European carriers access to cabotage routes within the United States implies a lack of balance – albeit one mitigated by the widespread use of code-sharing.)

- *Creation of the concept of 'community air carrier'* As a result of the European Council's Regulation 2407/92, carriers licensed by Member States are considered not to have the nationality of that state but to be community air carriers – the purpose being to facilitate a single market free of the impediment of nationality for any airline with its principal place of business and registered office in the Community and which is majority-owned and effectively controlled by nationals of a Member State.

Box 4.2 examines the external effect of EU aviation policy.

Box 4.2: The External Effect of EU Aviation Policy

The EU single market is founded on freedom of establishment (i.e., any EU national may establish business in any member state) and on the free domestic and cross-border movement of people, capital, goods, and services; it is provided with teeth by the primacy of European over national law. To give (belated) effect to these principles and eliminate fragmented and protected national air transport markets, three packages of reforms were introduced in the 1980s and 1990s culminating in a single aviation market in 1997. However, EU aviation policy is more encompassing than 'just' the creation and enforcement of a commercially open single market: it also addresses infrastructural impediments to open competition through initiatives targeted at airport access (slots and ground-handling), airport charges, airway capacity, consumer protection, and safety. All are important but the latter particularly so in the context of the present discussion. One of the arguments often mounted against moving from a bilateral to a multilateral aeropolitical regime is that once airlines are free to operate anywhere within a borderless open market they will engage in 'regulatory arbitrage' by establishing their principal place of business in whichever country within that open market exercises the least intrusive licensing and safety oversight regime: the development of a multilateral approach, and the avoidance of a 'flag of convenience' situation, clearly requires convergence of licensing and oversight standards and practices.

Although since 1997 EU governments have not been free to discriminate in favour of their own airlines with regard to services within the single market (notwithstanding that a small number have tried), each continued to sign bilateral ASAs with non-member states which committed them to designating only carriers 'substantially owned' and 'effectively controlled' by their own nationals. There was an argument that these nationality clauses were discriminatory, and so in breach of the right of establishment (Article 43 of the EC Treaty), because they give the non-EU party to an ASA the right to refuse designation of a community air carrier owned or controlled by citizens of a different member state on the grounds of its nationality – thereby depriving it of legitimate market access. On 5 November 2002 the European Court of Justice confirmed this: amongst other things, the Court held that not only should EU governments not be restricting designation to their own carriers on routes outside the EU, but the negotiation of bilaterals was itself something in respect of which the European Commission shared competence with individual governments. This decision was a catalyst for a new approach in the EU's external aviation policy, resting on three pillars (Geil 2006):

1.   Bringing member states' existing bilateral arrangements into conformity with Community law (pending the eventual renegotiation of all bilaterals by the European Commission). This has involved two initiatives:

- Council Regulation 847/2004 granted the European Commission a mandate to enter negotiations with non-member countries for the purpose of replacing nationality clauses in those countries' separate bilateral agreements with individual member states; a single 'horizontal' agreement is entered into between the EU and the non-member whereby the nationality clauses in each of the latter's individual ASAs with Member States are overridden by an agreement to permit designation by the Member State not just of its own carriers but of any community air carrier. The bilaterals themselves are not replaced, but their nationality clauses (along with certain other provisions) are amended to bring them into conformity with Community law by providing non-discriminatory access for all community air carriers into markets between the two countries.
- Subject to notifying and receiving no objection from the European Commission, individual member states might also negotiate similar amendments if bilateral negotiations with a non-member arise before the Commission has had an opportunity to negotiate a 'horizontal agreement' with the partner concerned.

By the end of 2007 more than 70 non-member states had agreed to Community designation. Where one of these countries has a bilateral ASA with an EU member state it will therefore accept designation by that state of a carrier owned, controlled, and based in a different member state – thereby allowing what might in effect be fifth- or seventh-freedom services to be approved as though they were third and fourth freedom. Of course, whether a particular EU state, say France, would designate a carrier based in another member state, say British Airways, to operate between its territory and a non-member state on routes where the number of designated carriers and/or output remain limited under the terms of a traditional bilateral is open to question; however, were the bilateral concerned to be an open skies agreement, then designation no longer applies and any EU carrier could fly between the Member State and its bilateral partner. Furthermore, when a community air carrier makes a cross-border acquisition of another community air carrier, the acquired carrier should not lose its traffic rights to non-member countries with which an amended ASA is now in place.

2. Creating a common aviation area with neighbouring countries. An early example was the Euro-Mediterranean Agreement signed in 2006 by the EU and Morocco; other states on the southern littoral are expected eventually to join – a process known as 'plurilateralism', which involves the coming together of like-minded states to negotiate liberal agreements which others can join at a later stage. The objective of the EU's 'European Neighbourhood Policy' is to create a single European Common Aviation Area incorporating states already in the single aviation market by virtue of being members of the European Economic Area (EEA – a free-trade area comprised of EU member states plus Iceland, Norway, Liechtenstein, and Switzerland), together with neighbouring non-members to the east and south of the EU. Accession requires not simply entry into the single market, but phased convergence of domestic safety, consumer protection, and competition laws with EU norms to create a level playing field.

3. Concluding liberal agreements between the EU and key partners (notably the United States, but also Russia, China, India, and Australia) to supersede existing bilaterals between those countries and individual Member States. This pillar led to the EU–US open skies agreement of 2007 (effective March 2008), which may eventually prove to have been a catalyst for at least partial industry consolidation because of two particular provisions:
- The replacement of national designation by Community designation means that any community air carrier is free to operate between any point in the Community and any point in the United States. Seventh-freedom services (e.g., British Airways operating, itself or through a subsidiary, between Paris and New York) are therefore possible without the airline concerned having to apply for designation – a hurdle which disappears from transatlantic markets. (This applies also to non-EU states within the ECAA.)
- The United States has agreed not to reject on nationality grounds an airline designated by one of almost 30 named non-EU countries where the airline concerned is owned and controlled by EU nationals.

The European airline industry is considerably more fragmented than is the case in the United States, and this agreement opens the way to further consolidation within Europe without risk of losing US traffic rights on nationality grounds. However, one serious impediment remains to consolidation at a global level: the refusal of the United States to allow foreign control of US carriers. Until this policy is reversed, industry consolidation can proceed regionally and perhaps in a few cases between continents, but it will not become truly global. Even for consolidation to proceed outside the United States, there must be continued relaxation of designation criteria, both de jure (as in the EU's horizontal agreements) and de facto.

(Bartlik [2007] provides a comprehensive review of the impact of EU law on ASAs. In particular, he looks at how air traffic rights might be distributed between EU airlines seeking designation under ASAs between EU and non-EU states which are not open skies agreements and therefore do not permit free market entry by any EU airline.)

Although the EU has been in the vanguard of regional multilateralism, in large part because it benefits from a strong central authority, other initiatives are underway. There are several in Latin America, South East Asia, and Africa. None is as comprehensive as the EU single market – and some do not work at all (e.g., the Yammassoukro Declaration of 1988). But a few have made headway in opening fifth freedom services (e.g., the Fortaleza Agreement between Mercosur states Brazil, Paraguay, Uruguay, Argentina, Chile, and Bolivia) or services between secondary cities previously not served by international routes (e.g., the BIMP East ASEAN Growth Area incorporating Brunei, Indonesia, Malaysia, and the Philippines); ASEAN (the Association of Southeast Asian Nations) has a 2015 target for full open skies. A noteworthy plurilateral open skies agreement, under the auspices of APEC, is the Multilateral Agreement on the Liberalisation of International Air Transportation (the MALIAT or Kona Agreement) signed in 2001 and encompassing Brunei, Chile, the Cook Islands, New Zealand, Samoa, Singapore, Tonga, and the United States (Peru having joined in 2002 but left in 2005). MALIAT covers first to sixth-freedom rights, and there is a subsequent Protocol entitling signatories to agree exchange of seventh and eighth freedoms – the latter perhaps mainly symbolic given the restrictive US attitude towards cabotage and the small domestic markets of the other signatories; there are no limits on output (i.e., frequency or aircraft type), and the requirement for substantial ownership (but not the requirement for effective control) by nationals has been eliminated. (Australia participated in the MALIAT negotiations but refused to sign.)

At a global rather than regional level, the General Agreement on Trade in Services (GATS) – a treaty entered into by members of the World Trade Organization to extend multilateral trade liberalisation from goods to services – includes an Annex on Air Transport Services. As originally formulated this covers MRO, CRSs, marketing and certain other 'soft' rights but excludes 'hard' traffic rights and services related to the exercise of those rights. However, the Annex is subject to review at least every 5 years and there has been support (e.g., from Australia) for allowing it to develop as a plurilateral vehicle for gradually extending open skies and removing nationality restrictions (see Lyle 2006 for a summary of the arguments). On the other hand, that this might also prove to be a rocky road is evident in the lengthy disagreement between some signatories as to whether ground-handling is excluded from the Annex on the basis of it being a 'service directly related to the exercise of traffic rights'.

3. *De facto relaxation of nationality criteria* Concerns that KLM might lose its traffic rights if the Netherlands' bilateral partners deemed it to be no longer Dutch, and therefore no longer eligible for designation by the Netherlands, were in part behind the convoluted structure and carefully chosen language which accompanied the carrier's acquisition by Air France. In fact, many countries now turn a blind eye to the ownership and control of other countries' designated carriers. KLM has not lost any traffic rights since being acquired by Air France, nor has Swiss lost any since becoming a subsidiary of Lufthansa. Neither has there been any objection to Aerolineas Argentinas being controlled by Spain's Grupo Marsans (albeit through an Argentinian vehicle). On the other hand, the matter is not yet entirely moot; whereas US airlines apparently have no objection to Aerolineas Argentinas being beneficially owned by foreigners, some took exception to LanEcuador's Chilean parentage – perhaps because LanChile is a tougher competitor. (Lelieur [2003] provides a scholarly analysis of the topic, whilst the UK CAA [2006c] has produced an excellent discussion of issues arising from the liberalisation of ownership and control and how they might be resolved.)

Given the momentum behind liberalisation and the fact that barriers to market entry have disappeared, or are in the process of disappearing, in many of the world's densest markets, it is easy to overlook the fact that a primary reason why the Chicago System has survived for over half a century is that whilst some people see it as no longer fit for purpose, others see in it an effective mechanism for protecting national interests. Sometimes those interests run no further than cosseting an inefficient state-owned flag-carrier; on the other hand, there are countries which perceive themselves as having both a right and a vital interest in participating in a global air transport industry which might have no room for them if completely deregulated. The Chicago System has given effect to this right and facilitated participation. Despite headline grabbing initiatives of undoubted importance from the EU and the United States and other aeropolitically liberal actors such as Australia, Chile, New Zealand, and Singapore, the world's air transport system remains to a large degree locked within a bilateral structure dating back to the 1940s and hallmarked by ASAs which, at least by number, are overwhelmingly 'traditional' (ibid.).

The prevailing system is, if nothing else, highly complex. Taking the relatively simple example of New Zealand, at the end of 2006 the country had: a horizontal agreement with the EU; membership of MALIAT; bilateral relations with 43 states, 12 of which had been partly overridden by the EU agreement and 6 of which had been suspended as a result of having joined MALIAT; and a non-governmental agreement covering Taiwan.

Conclusions The last two subsections have examined government policy as a barrier to entry and therefore a constraint on airline output. It is the most important impediment to an economically rational reorganization of the way in which capital is sourced and deployed in the airline industry. The purpose of liberalisation, and ultimately deregulation, is to remove commercial barriers to entry in order to promote competition, thereby stimulating improved efficiency and productivity, lower prices, and better service – which should in turn enhance economic welfare, for the economy in general and for consumers in particular.

The inevitability of change is unquestionable; on the other hand, the Chicago System has survived more or less intact since the 1940s, and the reason for this is that its practices suit significant numbers of states and airlines. If change is inevitable, so is resistance. ICAO's 'Declaration of Global Principles for the Liberalization of International Air Transport', issued in March 2003, espouses liberalisation of the aeropolitical regime and relaxation of controls on cross-border ownership and control; however, there are also references to the rights of countries to proceed at their own desired pace and to continue benefiting from participation in the international air transport system on the basis of fair and equal opportunity. Decoded, this means that the bilateral system is alive and well.

Two tentative conclusions can be drawn:

1. *Traffic rights* The bilateral system will survive, simply because it suits a large number of international actors. Particularly in parts of Asia, bilaterals are still relatively protective of 'flag carriers' – even where the airlines concerned are no longer state-owned; the instinct to protect airlines rather than advance the wider national economic interest remains an impediment to liberalisation in many countries. Nonetheless:
    *   The trend towards liberal and even open skies bilaterals has momentum and will continue to build, encompassing a number of ASAs which remains small relative to the total number in existence but significant given the importance of markets covered.
    *   Multilateralism has made considerable progress, notably in Europe but also in the Asia-Pacific region and certain parts of Latin America and the Caribbean, and can be expected to develop further. However:
        –   whilst on balance highly positive for the liberal cause, too many multilaterals would not necessarily be what the industry needs given that even though each might be liberal in its own way their painstakingly negotiated terms are likely to be sufficiently different to slow the progress towards a single, global multilateral arrangement;
        –   given that ICAO's mandate is essentially technical rather than commercial, any global multilateral arrangement will most probably be negotiated through GATS – not invariably the swiftest of forums within which to fashion consensus and bring about change.

2. *Ownership and control* Even where a country is prepared to accept the designation of an airline that is not a national of the designating bilateral party (e.g., US willingness, in the 2007 US–EU open skies agreement, to accept designation of community air carriers irrespective of nationality), it may not necessarily be willing to allow its own airlines to be majority-owned or controlled by non-citizens (e.g., US refusal to agree to EU citizens owning and controlling US carriers). This is true throughout the world, subject only to the limited exceptions noted above. As this chapter is being written it seems that a small number of private equity interests are attempting to build portfolios of airlines in different countries; it will be interesting to see whether these investors are content with a portfolio approach or will, at some point, want to bring their undoubted influence to bear on legal barriers which prevent cross-border consolidation. (LFAs have already been successful in pushing for greater harmonisation of safety regulations within parts of South East Asia, for example, thereby easing the cross-border assignment of aircraft between affiliated carriers.) On the whole, however, restrictions on cross-border ownership and control of airlines seem likely to stand in the way of a truly globalised air transport industry for several – perhaps many – years to come; in particular, truly global consolidation of the industry will have to await a change in US restrictions on foreign ownership of that country's airlines. When in May 2008 the United States proposed (albeit in very general terms) a multilateral treaty that initially would encompass most of the

countries with which it had already negotiated open skies agreements and do away with nationality clauses, the response of some in Europe was that this would yet again primarily benefit US carriers without providing others with reciprocal access to US domestic markets.

Constrained Access To Airports And Airspace

A structural barrier to entry clearly exists where a potential entrant does not have access to essential production inputs on an equal basis with incumbents. Ultimately, incumbents may be able to extract high economic rents from these constrained factors of production. In the airline industry, spatial constraints exist at certain points in the system and at certain peak times in respect of air traffic control capacity, runway slots, gates, stands, baggage-handling facilities, counter space, and even lounges. Airport and airspace supply constraints arise when demand exceeds some defined measure of capacity and are attributable to one or more of poor planning, inadequate funding for necessary expansion, inefficient operations (perhaps exacerbated by noise abatement controls and procedures) or successful opposition to growth. An incumbent able to build sufficient scale as a user of airport slots and facilities can implement a deliberate strategy of 'spatial pre-emption' in order to exclude potential competitors.

The following subsections will look very briefly at current and prospective shortages of airport and airspace capacity as barriers to entry. The emphasis is on threats posed to the industry's projected output growth; consideration of cost issues arising from congestion and suboptimal access is left until the next chapter.

Access to airports   'Air traffic demand [measured in RPKs] will double in the next 15 years. Airport capacity will not' (Airbus 2008, p. 64). Globally, the more than 2.2 billion passenger journeys estimated to have been made in 2007 represent a half billion increase over 2002. The number of passengers travelling in the United States is forecast to treble between 2005 and 2025, whilst in Europe the growth multiple is expected to be 2.5 over the same period. By 2015, the Los Angeles, San Francisco, and Philadelphia metropolitan areas are considered likely by the FAA to join New York in lacking the capacity required to accommodate forecast growth (even if current projects are completed), and Chicago (where a third airport is under consideration), Phoenix and Las Vegas are at risk of joining them (FAA 2007b). In Europe, London Heathrow and Gatwick, Paris Orly, Frankfurt Main, Düsseldorf and Milan Linate face excess demand through most or all of the operating day, and by 2025 another 20 airports will join them and an additional 40 will be congested during peak periods. ECAC (2004) has estimated that without action some 17 per cent of demand will go unmet by 2025, and even if 60 per cent capacity growth is assumed over the period more than 60 airports will be congested and 20 will be saturated much of the day. It is usually runway access that is the most serious constraint on output at congested airports. (The special case of 'perimeter rules' applied to cap stage-lengths on flights serving Washington National, New York La Guardia, and Dallas Love Field is not considered here.)

IATA guidelines recognise three categories of airport:

1.   *Level 1* Airports at which schedule coordination is not required.
2.   *Level 2* Airports not sufficiently congested to be designated as 'coordinated' but which nonetheless face periodic overdemand, and at which airlines voluntarily discuss

scheduling with a designated facilitator – hence reference to 'schedules facilitated airports'.

3. *Level 3* Airports where voluntary schedule coordination has been insufficient to deal with congestion, and at which an appointed coordinator allocates slots – hence reference to 'coordinated airports'. When national regulators designate a congested airport as 'coordinated', slots are allocated in accordance with rules and guidelines established by IATA and reflected in national regulations such as the EU's Regulation 95/93 (as amended by Regulation 793/2004): slots are allocated by an independent coordinator in a transparent and non-discriminatory procedure and incumbents' rights to exercise them are grandfathered from one schedule season to the next; there is an 80 per cent 'use-it-or-lose-it' rule; slots which are underused or explicitly vacated are returned to a slot pool, 50 per cent of which is allocated to new entrants and 50 per cent to incumbents on a waiting list. The integration of slot allocations at different airports required to create viable schedules for the airlines holding them is managed at semi-annual IATA schedules conferences.

IATA has identified 93 airports which are already capacity-constrained and unlikely to benefit from near-term relief. According to Airbus (2008, p. 65), these airports 'accommodate 64 per cent of world traffic'.

Most airports in the United States, including several that are periodically congested, operate on a first-come-first served basis. Restrictions have, however, been applied by the FAA at the country's worst-affected facilities. The 'High-Density Rule' introduced in 1969 imposing slot constraints at JFK, La Guardia, O'Hare, and Washington National has been phased out pursuant to the Air-21 FAA reauthorization legislation in 2000, but by mid-2008 worsening congestion had led to movement caps being introduced at JFK, La Guardia, and Newark; voluntary schedule reductions and hub depeaking saved O'Hare from similar restrictions, although de facto slot regulation is a fact of life there as well. In addition to supply management, it is increasingly likely that the demand side will also be targeted: in January 2008, DOT issued a Notice of Proposed Rulemaking that would permit US airports to consider the time of day and traffic carried (rather than just aircraft weight) when calculating charges – apparently opening the door to congestion pricing.

Slot shortages confronting prospective entrants at key airports can be addressed in one or more of the following ways:

1. *Building new runways at new and existing airports* There are two sides to this story:
    *   On the negative side (from the industry's perspective) is the fact that in many countries both options are likely to encounter opposition from local communities and environmentalists, and to face long planning lead times; this can be particularly true in respect of airports serving densely populated metropolitan areas where new capacity is needed most. For example, Frankfurt's fourth runway and third terminal have been long-delayed, whilst Tokyo Narita has managed no more than an extension to a short second runway after decades of trying; BAA's plans to increase capacity at its London area airports have encountered predictable community opposition as well as Britain's legendary planning marathon. (The same week in January 2008 that British Airways showed off its new Heathrow Terminal 5 to the press ahead of a March opening, *Flight International* (22–28 January, p. 34) carried a '25 years ago' piece marking launch of the carrier's campaign for the terminal to be built.) In the United States,

despite close to 30 new runways having been constructed at major airports in the 16 years to 2008 and more being in the pipeline, just two significant new hubs (at Dallas-Fort Worth and Denver) have opened in the last four decades and no others are at present firmly planned.

- On the positive side, Berlin and Frankfurt are expanding somewhat, Paris CDG has ample room for growth, a new 3-million passenger airport is planned for Nantes in the West of France, and Lisbon may get a new airport – although almost certainly not within the next decade; also, European LFAs are opening up previously underused secondary and tertiary facilities across the continent, and in doing this bringing 'new' capacity into the system. Notwithstanding its near-simultaneous release of the Stern Report on climate change and public championing of an ostensibly green platform, the UK government in late 2006 conceded the imperative of increasing the country's airport capacity to accommodate a trebling of flights by 2030. Over $20 billion has been earmarked for Gulf airports in the next decade, with an ultimate planned capacity of 220 million passengers per annum (120 million at Dubai's Al Maktoum International alone). China's 2006–2010 5-year plan allocated $17 billion for 44 airport upgrades and 42 greenfield projects; in early 2008 the Chinese government went even further by announcing a plan to spend up to $64 billion building 97 new airports by 2020. In Japan, Tokyo Haneda's long-awaited fourth runway will from 2010 boost annual slot numbers from 285,000 to over 400,000; however, some of this increment will be eliminated by ANA and JAL decisions to downsize their widebody fleets and meet demand growth through higher frequencies – strategic choices which mirror those taken after deregulation in the United States and Europe.

  In India, the situation became so bad as a result of 25 per cent per annum traffic growth in response to market liberalisation that in 2006 the government talked about limiting aircraft orders until the nation's infrastructure caught up. However, up to $10 billion will have been invested in the four years to 2010 in order to upgrade Delhi and Mumbai airports and to build new facilities at Bangalore and Hyderabad; at least two other new airports and more than 30 upgrades are also being planned. The backlog of aircraft orders may nonetheless place strain on India's aviation infrastructure.

2. *Improving the management of aircraft movements* This option offers considerable scope for the future using new technologies, more efficient procedures, better monitoring of surface movements, and restructured airspace. For example, the UK's NATS is exploiting the precision area navigation (P-RNAV) capabilities of modern aircraft to help restructure terminal airspace north of London and make access to the region's runways more efficient.

3. *Redistribution of available slots* There is debate regarding whether slots are legally owned by incumbents; nonetheless, in the United States they are openly marketable assets and in several other countries, such as the UK, they are actively traded (albeit with little price transparency). Beyond this not insignificant uncertainty, redistribution raises at least two questions:

- How should redistributed slots be sourced? Many of Europe's congested airports are dominated by an incumbent, and the pattern over time has been for these incumbents gradually to increase their slot holdings – as British Airways has done over several years at Heathrow (although it did significantly reduce its Gatwick slot inventory after a shift in strategy began in 2002). Slots that do become available usually fall far short of what is needed to mount a serious competitive attack – particularly during peak periods. In the United States, majors have often been accused, not least by the FAA, of using regional partners to 'babysit' otherwise surplus slots at La Guardia in particular.

If voluntary releases are unlikely, then confiscation could in principle be an option; however, not only would this be politically unpalatable in many countries, it would introduce an unacceptable degree of instability into air service provision were it to be done on a scale sufficiently meaningful to benefit new entrants. When a network carrier loses slots, its position is likely to be weakened not just by the arrival in specific markets of the new competitors who take over those slots but also by possible loss of more generalised network synergies vis-à-vis other network carriers. In April and May 2008 the US DOT nonetheless floated alternative proposals for gradually withdrawing a proportion of La Guardia, JFK, and Newark slots from incumbents and auctioning them.

- How should available slots be distributed? It has long been common practice for airlines to exchange slots, sometimes along with monetary payments, in the process of fine-tuning a season's schedules – although who actually owns the slots and whether cash sales are legal has not been universally agreed. Since 1986 the sale, leasing, and mortgaging of slots has been permitted in the United States; how the implication of ownership implied by this fact (and extensive case law) sits with the DOT's above-mentioned proposal to withdraw and auction New York slots and reinvest sale proceeds in airspace capacity upgrades is not entirely clear, but the FAA appears to consider slots to be its property which it has the power to reclaim and then lease-out via auctions (*Aviation Week & Space Technology* May 26, 2008, p. 59). The UK government and CAA are also in favour of market mechanisms such as sealed bids or secondary slot auctions, and at Heathrow the number of slots bought and sold in the grey market each year normally outstrips the number allocated from the slot pool; indeed, the deregulation of transatlantic access to Heathrow from March 2008 as a result of the US–EU open skies agreement led to a flurry of slot acquisitions by carriers intent on opening service. (Continental has stated in an SEC filing that it paid $209 million for four pairs of Heathrow slots in late 2007; the carrier's SkyTeam partners Air France and Alitalia are believed to have sold a pair each.) After years of holding that slots could be swapped but could not be bought and sold, the European Commission in May 2008 accepted that cash transactions are legal and dropped its threatened investigation of UK practices. At the same time the Commission called for trading to be transparent and non-discriminatory, and announced that it was looking into additional mechanisms to ensure new entrants have sufficient access to whatever slots become available. (Shortly afterwards, bmi added £770 million to its balance sheet to reflect the assumed value of Heathrow slots, arguing that this was justified by the existence of an active market; were British Airways to adopt the same approach, its net assets would be inflated by an amount not far short of the company's entire market capitalisation at end-May 2008 share prices.)

Arguments in favour of more widespread secondary market trading highlight economic efficiency, whilst arguments against tend to focus on one or both of the windfall benefits accruing to grandfathered carriers and the likelihood of predation by these carriers accumulating unwanted slots simply to exclude new entrants. (See Starkie [1998] and DotEcon [2006] for discussion of the issues.)

Another administrative approach to the rationing of runway access is to impose *traffic distribution rules* across a multi-airport system which either exclude or restrict to off-peak periods certain types of movement, such as all-cargo, nonscheduled, or general aviation, at specified airports within that system. Alternatively, the design of an airport's *pricing structure* might have the effect of constraining access by certain types of traffic, as at London Heathrow where the operation of the smallest regional aircraft has long been uneconomic because of what amount to high per-seat charges for these types.

Slot availability at the most congested hubs worldwide is now often limited to unattractive times of day, and the chances of an entrant being able to obtain sufficient resources – in terms of slots, apron or gate space, counters, and access to other common-user equipment and facilities – to establish competitive frequencies on short-haul routes in particular are poor. Indeed, EU Regulation 793/2004 has broadened the definition of 'slot' from a scheduled time of arrival or departure (Regulation 95/93) to a permission to use the full range of airport infrastructure necessary to support a flight. A problem of some significance in the United States is that airlines at several important airports hold long leases on terminals and other facilities which, through 'majority in interest' or 'exclusive use' clauses, give them power to veto capacity expansion. They also have the right to refuse to sublet or, if they do sublet, to charge mark-ups which impose a substantial cost disadvantage on potential competitors; it is not unheard-of for gate subleases to come with surcharges as high as 20–25 per cent.

Clearly, access to facilities at a steadily growing number of airports has the potential to constrain the output of airlines based at these hubs and of airlines whose network strategies demand access to the markets they serve. In the final analysis, the industry's demand forecasts imply that there will be at least twice as much output in 2020 as in 2005. Notwithstanding that existing resources could be – and gradually are being – better used as new technologies and procedures are introduced, the present ground infrastructure cannot accommodate projected growth. Unless it is significantly expanded, output will be constrained and capacity will increasingly have to be rationed at key hubs.

Access to airspace   Output will also be constrained, certainly in parts of North America and most of Europe, unless there is a marked improvement in the efficiency with which en route and terminal area airspace is used. This is a complex topic that is largely beyond the scope of the present book; comprehensive coverage of the issues raised can be found in Sudarshan (2003) and, in respect of Europe, Cook (2007b). However, the issue can be encapsulated in two statements:

1. *Technology is not a problem, although funding it might be* Much of the communication, navigation, and surveillance (CNS) technology essential to development of air traffic management (ATM) capabilities over the next 20 years is either available now or reasonably advanced in its development. That is not to say that there is anything other than a lot of work to be done on development and deployment, and a lot of money to be spent on both; however, the most daunting challenges are political and institutional.
2. *Political and institutional challenges are formidable* These can be summarised by making a globally applicable comment, and then by commenting briefly on the specific situations in the United States and Europe:
    *   Globally, the challenge is to fashion a seamless air traffic system hallmarked by compatible technologies and procedures, airspace blocks designed and optimised for users, and interoperable airborne equipment. Despite work done in the context of ICAO's FANS (future air navigation system) initiative and more

recently IATA's (2004b) roadmap for implementation of a globally harmonised ATM system, the current position remains one of institutional and technological fragmentation. Change is being embraced in some countries and regions more rapidly than in others.

- In Europe 47 ATC providers (civil and military) operate 58 ATC centres using 22 operating systems and 30 programming languages. To deal with the inadequacy of this system the EU implemented the Single European Sky (SES) legislative package in Regulations 549–552/2004, which established an institutional structure and a set of broad objectives. The most significant outcomes were to involve: redesign of the continent's airspace into more rational 'functional airspace blocks' (FABs) shaped by reference to traffic flows rather than national boundaries; more flexible use of airspace in cooperation with military authorities; and the development of next-generation ATM technology. The technological dimension was to be defined by SESAR (Single European Sky ATM Research) in a European ATM Master Plan delivered in 2008, then developed and deployed pursuant to sequential 5-year Work Programmes implemented in three stages to 2020. Both the Master Plan and the 2008–2013 work programme have been delivered, and implementation is being undertaken through a joint group of stakeholders (SESAR-JU). There are certainly technological and financial challenges ahead, but the most worrying threats to airline output are political: the unwillingness of some governments to forgo what they see as sovereignty over their airspace, and the unwillingness of air traffic controllers to accept the consequences of cross-border rationalisation for their employers and their jobs. A second package of SES measures was therefore introduced in 2008 to address these and other issues.

- Similarly, the challenge facing the US National Airspace System (NAS) over the next two decades is less technological than institutional. There are two issues. The first relates to governance: should the FAA continue to act as both regulator and air navigation services provider (ANSP), or should its recently created Air Traffic Organization be entirely independent to operate free of congressional micromanagement, the federal appropriations process, and the civil service culture? The second relates to the size and predictability of funding: the current system relies too heavily on unpredictable excise taxes on air transport revenues, but – as the 2007/08 FAA funding reauthorization debate clearly illustrates – any move away from tax-based funding towards the arguably more stable and predictable user-fee system preferred by airlines pits carriers against the lobbying power of business and general aviation. (The outcome of this debate is still unclear at the time of writing in spring 2008; GAO [2007c] provides an excellent summary of the arguments on both sides.)

   The Century of Aviation Act 2003 mandated efforts towards creating a performance-based Next Generation Air Transport System (NGATS or 'NextGen') by 2025, and established the interagency Joint Planning and Development Office (JPDO) within the FAA to act as a focal point for research, planning, and transition. Imperfect though some argue the process to have been so far, this initiative clearly recognised the now critical need to address capacity constraints. (See GAO [2007b] for an initial assessment of the process.) Nonetheless, although technology and cost are not unimportant issues, the key variable lies in the public policy domain: that variable is the political will to change – specifically, the political will to manage and fund change in a rational, stable way.

The postwar ATC system has for more than half a century been based on voice communication, navigation by reference to fixed ground-based aids, and surveillance by primary and secondary radar or – in its absence – adherence to procedural separation. The ATM system 20 years from now must be one in which aircraft equipped with modern satellite-based CNS technologies are able to fully exploit their navigational performance capabilities. Using the full potential of techniques such RNAV-RNP (area navigation and required navigation performance) and 4-D trajectory operations both en route and down to the bottom of a continuous descent approach (CDA) will be a major part of what is required to ensure that airspace constraints do not impose limits on airline output well below forecast demand. Technology seems likely to be capable of playing its part in a move towards a seamless, rationally structured performance-based CNS/ATM system; at the present time, it is less easy to be sanguine about the comprehension and foresight of some US and European politicians.

Conclusion   Although the precise situation varies across the global system, there are two overriding challenges facing the industry in respect of both airports and ATM:

1. *Unlocking latent capacity in the system as presently structured*   This has been, and continues to be, done by introducing new CNS technologies (e.g., ADS-B) and new ATM procedures (e.g., RVSM, RNAV, and RNP); introduction of an RNAV standard instrument departure (SID) at Dallas-Fort Worth is estimated to have increased capacity by 7–8 per cent, for example. Broader efforts include Europe's Dynamic Management of the European Airspace Network (DMEAN) programme and the FAA's collaborative decision-making (CDM) initiative, both intended inter alia to improve information exchange between ANSPs and airlines as an aid to better real-time flow management and the release of additional capacity.
2. *Investing in new capacity*   This will require:
    *   investment in new runways and airports – something which will create a great deal of opposition in many countries;
    *   investment in the development and deployment of new technologies to transition CNS/ATM from its current mid-twentieth-century model to a performance-based system which leverages the capabilities of satellites and modern avionics;
    *   willingness amongst stakeholders, notably governments and unions, to accept new institutional arrangements for the funding and operation of what must become a more globally seamless and interoperable air transport system.

ICAO believes that commercial aircraft departures will have risen from 24.9 million in 2005 to 50.5 million by 2025. It remains to be seen whether the global air transport system as a whole will prove as scaleable as such forecasts suggest it will need to be.

Commercial Barriers

This section looks at barriers to entry posed by start-up costs, production costs, incumbents' reputation, and exit barriers.

Start-up costs   Significant capital costs are a structural barrier to entry into any industry, particularly when a high proportion represent sunk costs that are irrecoverable should the entrant quickly decide to leave the market. We have already seen that the existing provision of infrastructure and the availability of leased aircraft and outsourced services in principle reduce sunk entry costs into the airline industry. Nonetheless, initial certification, systems establishment and provisioning, and also training and marketing costs are not necessarily insubstantial; early losses are also sunk. Any effort to build a sizeable integrated hub will involve heavy expenditure on resources.

Poor risk-adjusted rates of return across the industry as a whole make investment in any new airline a somewhat sporty prospect (Newhouse 1988), and the raising of sufficient capital can be correspondingly difficult, other than in times of extraordinary capital market liquidity such as the period beginning in 2002/2003. In the United States, initial funding in the $100–150 million range has been considered comfortable but not excessive for start-ups such as jetBlue and Skybus; the latter failed notwithstanding 'comfortable' initial capitalisation. Inability to access follow-on tranches of capital was part of the problem underlying the failures of all-premium transatlantic carriers in 2007/2008.

Of course, if an entrant into an individual market is already in the industry, these problems are greatly reduced: it might have the necessary resources and expertise in place, and also be able to benefit more generally from spreading over a large existing output those of its costs that are common to the existing and new services. When a start-up or small established airline enters a market with the sort of schedule likely to be necessary to generate credibility amongst customers and external distribution channels (assuming it to be relying on agencies), it is making a commitment which risks proportionately far more of its net worth than a large carrier risks when launching just one more route. Once the service is running, the larger airline might also feel better able to engage in short-run marginal cost pricing provided there is strategic justification in the context of the network as a whole and that a contribution is being made to fixed costs. A smaller entrant, on the other hand, will need to be covering full costs on most or all of its routes.

Production costs   Once operating, any small carrier will face structural cost disadvantages associated with the economics of the industry – notably economies of scale, scope, and density – which in principle make it cheaper for an incumbent to add output than for a small challenger to do the same. Briefly, whereas economies of scale benefit an incumbent when average cost falls as output increases, economies of scope arise where joint production of two or more related services can be achieved at lower unit cost than when both services are produced separately; hub-and-spoke networks, which are designed to produce multiple products in multiple city-pair markets, can generate significant economies of scope (as well as certain diseconomies, which will be examined in Chapter 6). Economies of density arise when it is cheaper for an incumbent to increase output on an existing network than for a challenger to enter the same routes. Any entrant taking on an established network carrier will face substantial structural cost barriers that have to be compensated for by higher resource productivity and, where possible, lower input costs.

Reputation   A strong brand image supporting a loyal customer base and a dominant market share might be difficult to sell against unless a new entrant is offering something a segment of the market values and is not receiving (e.g., consistently lower prices or more reliable service), and has sufficient inimitable resources to sustain the offer against retaliation. Some new entrants have been successful establishing awareness through astute PR campaigns alongside paid advertising; the early years of Emirates, Virgin Atlantic, Morris Air (since absorbed by Southwest), jetBlue, and easyJet provide examples. Existing recognition of the Virgin brand in Australia made the barrier imposed by Qantas' formidable local reputation lower for Virgin Blue than for other start-ups such as Compass and Impulse – although having a feasible strategy also helped.

On the whole, however, the requirement for heavy advertising and promotional spending can be a barrier to entry. Furthermore, challengers have to overcome any consumer loyalty from which incumbents might benefit in respect of either their brand in general or specific, unique service attributes in particular; the practical effect of consumer loyalty, whether it reflects 'genuine' commitment or is simply a result of high switching costs imposed by FFPs, is to steepen the incumbent's demand curve. That these barriers can be overcome is evidenced by the success of the carriers named above as well as several others; that they are nonetheless on the whole difficult to surmount is evidenced by the very high failure rate amongst start-ups generally.

Exit barriers   These are economic, institutional or emotional considerations which keep airlines on certain routes, or indeed in the industry, when for one reason or another they are earning subnormal returns. Shrinking a large airline can anyway be a slow and expensive process. Where exit barriers are high there tends to be overcapacity, excess output, and downward pressure on yields. Perversely, exit barriers – such as state aid and US Chapter 11 bankruptcy protection – can also be barriers to entry when, for example, they sustain in a market carriers that are in some way being subsidised and so have opportunities to cause market distortions. (See Schnell [2001] for one of the few studies of exit barriers in the airline industry.)

Chapter 11 of the US Bankruptcy Code provides an interesting and contentious example of a barrier to exit. The argument in favour of reorganization provisions is that they preserve salvageable companies to the benefit of employees, creditors, and – arguably – the nation as a whole; the legislative history of the Code indicates that this was the intention of Congress. Arguments against are that they: distort the free enterprise system; disadvantage competitors (such as American and Southwest) which stay out of bankruptcy and instead honour their financial obligations in full; and preserve output which the market has deemed uneconomic. Perhaps surprisingly, the GAO (2005, p. 3) has observed that, 'The available evidence does not suggest that airlines in bankruptcy contribute to industry overcapacity or that bankrupt airlines harm competitors by reducing fares below what other airlines are charging.' The following year it again noted that there was '... no evidence that bankruptcy harmed the airline industry by contributing to overcapacity or underpricing' (GAO 2006, p. 180). However, notwithstanding the significant cuts in output made by US Airways, United, Northwest, and Delta during their various bankruptcies – some in excess of 30 per cent – it is irrefutable that these carriers remained in business producing output some of which, under a truly free-enterprise system, might instead have been produced by start-ups with newer and more efficient business models. At one point in 2005, almost half the ASMs being produced by mainline jets in US domestic service were being generated by carriers in or recently out of Chapter 11 protection. Like all exit barriers, Chapter 11 is also a barrier to entry.

Entry-Deterring Strategies

An incumbent with a history of responding vigorously to competitive inroads (e.g., by lowering prices, boosting output or increasing promotional expenditures) might present enough of a 'credible threat' to deter future entry. Bear in mind that it is not airlines which respond, but decision-makers; if one or more key decision-makers change at an incumbent, so might a potential new entrant's evaluation of the likelihood of a robust response. Entry-deterring strategies usually involve one or more of the following: price, output and capacity, access to distribution channels, corporate contracts, and FFPs.

Price   The most obvious tactic is to reduce prices in response to entry. Because air transport is a multi-product industry producing output over a network, and because start-ups are unlikely to be able to duplicate the network of a large, well-established incumbent, there is widespread opportunity to respond to a competitive challenge by engaging in cross-subsidisation. This could take one or more of several forms. For example, profits from long-haul routes could be used to subsidise aggressive short-haul pricing; profits attributable to economic rents earned from local traffic to and from a dominated hub could subsidise more competitive routes; or profits from routes still subject to commercial regulation of entry, output, and/or pricing could subsidise competition in liberalised markets. Similarly, profits from high-yield fares in one market could be used to subsidise discounting of coach/economy tickets in the same or different markets.

Output and capacity   An incumbent's capacity to produce output can create a barrier to entry from two perspectives. First, there is a tendency for airlines that dominate frequencies in a given market to carry a disproportionately high share of traffic; this is the S-curve effect that we met in Chapter 2. Second, although 'capacity' and 'spare capacity' are not necessarily the same, the more capacity an incumbent has available in its system the greater the likelihood that it could redirect some of it to match, sandwich, or swamp an entrant's frequencies – provided it has sufficiently deep pockets to live with the negative impact on yields and/or load factors that excess output might cause. If the battleground is a hub dominated by the incumbent, it will also have far more flexibility to juggle slots and adjust frequencies in response to entry than the entrant will have to counter the response.

Access to distribution channels   Although the situation does vary in different parts of the world, incumbents' ability to use influence over distribution channels to deter entry has diminished greatly over the last few years. First, start-ups – particularly in Europe and North America – now generally rely on direct distribution over the Internet (and perhaps through call centres) rather than agency channels which might, in the past, have been incentivised to direct business to larger incumbents. Second, airlines in Europe and North America have divested their interests in GDSs, with the partial exception of Amadeus, so start-ups distributing through agency channels and putting their inventory onto GDSs no longer need be as concerned about issues such as screen bias as would have been the case a decade ago.

Nonetheless, where agency distribution is necessary to an entrant's marketing strategy, as it still is in many international markets, incumbents can create barriers to entry by encouraging agents to favour them – using allocations of cheap tickets, TACOs, or other forms of incentive. Less well-established carriers are likely to have to pay larger overrides or to make a higher proportion of their agency business eligible for overrides.

Corporate contracts   Large airlines with extensive network coverage are in a strong position to offer attractive deals to significant corporate customers. These could include one or more of price breaks, rebates, free upgrades, or the waiving of conditions normally applied to discounted fares.

Frequent flyer programmes   A primary objective of an FFP is to give customers an incentive to remain loyal, thereby raising their switching costs and reducing the pool of potential revenue available to competitors.

Conclusion On Barriers To Entry

Dozens of carriers enter the airline business each year. Because this is a network industry comprised of literally thousands of individual city-pair markets, it would be surprising if there were not regular entry and if on occasion entrants did not meet with success – simply because by astutely targeting markets where identified opportunities exist and which they are suited to serve effectively and efficiently, some will inevitably be able to succeed in 'walking between the raindrops'. As a whole, however, this is an industry in which size matters and in which there are some very real barriers standing in the way of challengers wanting to take on established incumbents.

Readers who doubt this could point to Emirates, Ryanair, and easyJet – the first two dating from the mid-1980s and the latter from the mid-1990s, but all now major producers by any standard. What marks these three out, however, is that they each exploited unusual opportunities with well-conceived and well-executed strategies: Emirates' growth spurt began in the early 1990s when its focus on a high-quality inflight product separated it from many other recession-struck long-haul carriers intent on cutting costs, and when the first signs of the international market liberalisation necessary to build an extensive sixth freedom hub-and-spoke network were beginning to appear. More recent competitors Etihad and Qatar Airways must find a way to grow profitably alongside what is now a very large and powerful competitor. The rapid growth path followed by Ryanair and easyJet, which began after the Third Package of EU deregulation measures came fully into force in 1997 and which subsequently exploited the post-9/11 difficulties of incumbent network carriers, put them among the first to react to a changing world with business models more suited to the future than the past. They now dominate the European LFA sector, and it is difficult to see new entrants – of which there will doubtless continue to be many – challenging their dominance for some time to come on anything other than a local basis.

Whilst significant barriers to entry certainly stand in the way of 'me-too' ventures, deregulated markets are nonetheless sufficiently dynamic that new opportunities will emerge from time to time for start-ups that are quick to respond with fresh business models. In the United States, for example, the maturing of Southwest and the attendant upward pressure on its non-fuel costs might well be creating an opportunity for lower-cost competitors. At the time of writing it remains to be seen whether Virgin America does indeed have a potentially profitable new perspective on the market; Skybus appeared to, but evidently did not.

ENVIRONMENTAL PRESSURES

Thirty years ago drink-driving and smoking in public places were a lot more socially acceptable than they are today. If parts of the European press are to be believed, air travel could be about to join them in the 'sin bin'. Irrespective of how accurate or timely the apocalyptic media stories turn out to be, there is now no question that the air transport industry is under threat of having its growth constrained by environmental pressures.

The threat is by some considerable margin greater in Europe than elsewhere. However, it is spreading rapidly in North America; by the end of 2007 the issue had accelerated from close to a standing start a year earlier to a point where five states, the District of Columbia, and the city of New York had jointly petitioned the Environmental Protection Agency to regulate aircraft emissions and the Senate was debating a proposal to start emissions trading by 2012. There is recognition of a problem in fast-developing parts of Asia, but no imminent prospect of environmental concerns overwhelming the imperative for rapid economic growth.

This section of the chapter will summarise the sources of aviation's environmental footprint, outline possible policy responses, and comment on the way ahead.

Aviation's Environmental Footprint

The primary sources of concern are: noise; emissions; and depletion of non-renewable resources. Other issues specific to the industry, which will not be discussed, include the disposal of effluent from deicing and MRO activities and the dismantling of retired aircraft. Many of the topics considered here are explained in more detail by Williams (2007).

Noise   Noise is certainly on the global environmental agenda, but relative to climate change it is in practical terms very much a local issue in the vicinity of each particular airport. The most significant contributor to airport noise is aircraft landing, taxiing, and – particularly – taking off. The main sources of aircraft noise are powerplants (nacelles, fans, internal moving parts, and exhaust gases) and airframes (especially high-lift devices and undercarriages).

Significant strides have been made by the industry over the last several decades:

* ICAO's Model for Assessing the Global Exposure to the Noise of Transport Aircraft (MAGENTA) has recorded a decline in the number of people worldwide affected by noise at DNL55, a commonly used definition of 'nuisance' derived from the Day–Night Sound Level scale, from 30 million in 1998 to 20 million 5 years later;
* current generation aircraft are around 75 per cent (20 EPNdB) quieter at take-off and landing than jets entering service in the 1960s.

The problem is that the industry's rate of output growth is outpacing its ability to reduce noise per aircraft movement, so that in aggregate it is getting noisier.

ICAO's preferred solution, advanced by its Committee on Aviation Environmental Protection (CAEP) in 2001, is what it calls a 'balanced approach' to locally identified and documented problems. This has four parts, the first of which is in fact a global initiative whilst the others are to be locally tailored:

1. Reduce noise at source by progressively tightening aircraft certification standards as technology advances. This has been going on since the 1970s. (Ben-Yosef [2005, Chapter 5] provides a comprehensive account of the economics and politics behind evolving noise regulations.) In 2001 it was agreed that although Chapter 3/Stage III aircraft were not to be phased out globally, from 2006 new designs had to be certified in accordance with the tighter ICAO Chapter 4 requirements.

2. Improve land-use planning to prevent the encroachment of noise-sensitive uses close to airport boundaries.
3. Introduce noise abatement procedures, such as: restrictions on take-off thrust settings, the use of high-lift devices, and reverse-thrust; noise-preferential runways and routings; and displaced thresholds.
4. Restrict operations. Some airports either cap or ban night-flights, some have a noise-weighted quota (e.g., London Heathrow's QC2), some charge higher fees for noisier aircraft (notably the older Chapter 3/stage III types), and some impose an annual movement cap (e.g., Paris Orly, at a figure of 250,000 agreed with local communities). Restrictions can be particularly onerous for cargo operations, which tend on the whole to fly older aircraft than many passenger airlines and, in some markets, serve customers who require shipments to move overnight; in order to protect the interests of US-owned integrators, the United States in May 2008 announced that it would be raising European airport night flight restrictions to the status of a bilateral issue in second stage open skies negotiations with the EU beginning that month.

GAO (2007d) reviews efforts underway in the United States to reduce the impact of aircraft noise on local communities, and how these mesh with development of the NextGen ATM system.

Airframe aerodynamics have been greatly improved over the last 30 years, whilst higher bypass ratios and acoustically designed nacelles have contributed to lower engine noise. Although emissions currently generate more headlines, efforts to reduce noise are continuing; the EU, for example, has targeted a 10dB reduction between 2000 and 2020, and co-funds research alongside industry. Problems nonetheless remain: first, noise can be an important local issue which is both real to affected residents and susceptible to use by outside campaigners with a wider environmental agenda; second, whilst higher engine bypass ratios lead to quieter powerplants, they raise emissions of nitrogen oxides (NOx).

Emissions   This is a topic which poses several questions. Answering them is beyond the scope of the present book, but references have been provided to enable readers so inclined to delve deeper.

1. What is climate change and what are its consequences? IATA (2004a, p. 26) has this to say:

    Climate change can be defined as the perturbation of the earth's energy balance through natural or man-made emissions of water vapour (H_2O), methane, nitrogen oxides (NOx) and halocarbons. According to experts, consequences of climate change could include changes in global average surface temperatures (commonly referred to as 'global warming'), local changes in average precipitation or the frequency and intensity of heat-waves.

    A widely used measure of climate change is 'radiative forcing'.
2. Is climate change happening? There is now a broad consensus that it is (Stern 2006; IPCC 2007). Opinions do, nonetheless, still differ. Whereas the climate change theme does not necessarily play well in parts of Texas, to deny it in Europe is now akin to heresy – which is why it needs to be factored into any discussion of potential constraints on air transport output.

3. If the climate is indeed changing, how quickly is it happening? Apparently quite fast (ibid.).
4. What is the impact of human activity through the burning of fossil fuels? This is still a matter of dispute, but the consensus referred to above rates it as increasingly fundamental (ibid.).
5. What is the contribution of aviation? Aircraft certainly emit gases and particles which alter the concentration of greenhouse gases in the atmosphere, and they are unique in doing this at altitude as well as on or close to the ground; they also produce contrails which trigger cirrus cloud formation. Whilst the effects of some types of emission are reasonably well understood (e.g., CO_2), this is not the case for others (e.g., NOx). As a whole, aircraft are believed to contribute around 3.0 per cent of the total radiative forcing attributable to human activities (IPCC 2007). References on this topic include IPCC (1999, 2007), JPDO (2006), BALPA (2007), ICAO (2007b) and the http://www.enviro.aero website – the latter a cross-industry initiative launched under the umbrella of the Air Transport Action Group (ATAG). Box 4.3 provides a primer.

Box 4.3: Aircraft Emissions

Two sources of aircraft emissions have a well-established direct effect on climate change: carbon dioxide (CO_2) and water vapour.

1. Burning a kilo of kerosene produces 3.16 kilos of CO_2, which is believed to remain in the atmosphere for around a century, during which time it traps solar energy and depletes the ozone layer. CO_2 accounts for around 70 per cent of aircraft emissions (ICAO 2007b). There are two 'positive' arguments the industry can make: first, because CO_2 emissions are closely linked to fuel-burn it has a strong cost incentive to reduce them – an incentive reflected in the gains achieved in fuel efficiency (i.e., fuel burn per seat and, with the help of higher load factors and longer average stage-lengths, per RPK) since the dawn of the jet age; second, aviation, which supports eight per cent of global GDP, is responsible for no more than two per cent of global manmade CO_2 emissions (IPCC 1999). In other words, around 97 per cent of CO_2 emissions are natural, and aviation produces just one-fiftieth of the remaining three per cent. Unfortunately the Achilles' heel in the industry's position is that output is projected to grow by so much, and the time taken to develop new technologies and introduce them into the fleet to a point where they can have a material impact is so long, that by 2050 aviation will be responsible for three per cent of man-made CO_2 emissions. Together with its visibility, the undeniable growth in air transport emissions at a time when other sectors are being expected to reduce theirs is what makes the industry such an appealing target for environmental activists.
2. Water vapour, which accounts for just under 30 per cent of aircraft emissions, combines with emitted particulate matter to form contrails which then, to an extent not yet fully understood, contribute to formation of cirrus clouds.

Despite what the popular media might imply (and, sometimes, erroneously state), there is far less proven science available to determine the impact of other aircraft emissions such as nitrogen oxides (NOx), volatile organic compounds, and sulphur dioxide (the latter attributable to the sulphur content of oil and therefore of kerosene); neither is the effect of their interaction at altitude known with certainty. Although accounting for less than 1 per cent of aircraft emissions, NOx gains the most publicity: the case against is that it contributes (along with sulphur dioxide) to acid rain, contributes to production of the greenhouse gas ozone in the troposphere, and also combines with volatile organic compounds at low altitude to affect air quality and contribute to smog formation; on the other hand, it is known to destroy the greenhouse gas methane at altitude, and the formation of ozone helps protect against surface exposure to ultraviolet radiation. Since 1986, ICAO (in Annex 16, Volume II) has established and progressively tightened engine certification requirements in respect of NOx (and several other emissions, but not CO_2); its most recent NOx standards took effect in January 2008 and applied a 12 per cent tightening, which brought the aggregate since 1986 to 40 per cent. Unfortunately, the higher engine bypass ratios used to reduce noise, fuel consumption, and CO_2 emissions also raise NOx emissions.

A clear example of the potential impact on industry output that limitations on aircraft emissions may have in future comes from London Heathrow, where one source of the delay in going ahead with construction of a third runway has been concern that it would lead to breach of EU air quality legislation (Williams 2007).

Depletion of non-renewable resources   Peak oil theory argues that a combination of finite supply and technical barriers to increased rates of production will inevitably lead to global oil output peaking and thereafter irreversibly declining. The key questions are when this will happen and how steep the decline will be.

1. *When?* Some observers believe that we are now more or less at the peak (e.g., oilman turned hedge fund manager T. Boone Pickens), whereas a review of academic studies conducted by the GAO (2007a) identified predicted peaks ranging for the most part out to 2040 (only one outlier putting back the peak into the next century). Uncertainty regarding the timing arises from differing estimates of: the amount of oil still in the ground; how much of that oil is accessible given different technological, environmental, cost, and geopolitical scenarios; and the rate at which the demand for oil will grow. If 2040 sounds a long way off, consider how many kerosene-burning B777s, B787s, A350s, A380s, and B737 and A320 replacements will still be in the fleet as the wells begin to run dry.
2. *How steep?* This depends on the answer to the previous question because the more distant the peak, the more time there is available to develop alternative fuels and more efficient ways of using the oil that must still be used – which in turn implies that the decline would be less steep.

The industry already has strong incentives related to both cost and emissions for continuing its longstanding and successful efforts to improve aircraft fuel efficiency: thus, a B737-800 burns 45 per cent less fuel per seat than a B737-200, and the fuel-burn per passenger-mile of the B787 and A350 rival that of a small car. Once again, however, a problem lies in the fact that the industry's projected output growth is outpacing the rate at which it is able to deliver fuel-efficiency improvements. Its demand for fuel is therefore continuing to grow at a time when, according to peak oil theory, supply will soon begin to tighten. Given this background and the development lead-times involved, the need to consider alternatives to kerosene is pressing.

Multi-stakeholder initiatives to identify and develop viable alternative fuels are under way in the United States (e.g., the Commercial Aviation Alternative Fuels Initiative), Europe, and under the auspices of IATA. There are several alternatives.

- *Synthetic fuels*, which are manufactured from coal, gas or biomass using updates of the 80-year-old Fischer–Tropsch process and are now usually referred to as coal-to-liquid (CTL), gas-to-liquid (GTL) or biomass-to-liquid (BTL) fuels, probably present the most immediate solution. South African Airways has for many years sourced 'top-up' CTL fuel at Johannesburg from Sasol; 50/50 blends of CTL and Jet-A1 have been used there since the late 1990s, and a 100 per cent CTL fuel was approved for use in April 2008. Qatar will have a commercial GTL processing plant online by 2011 – which is one reason why Qatar Airways partnered with Shell and Airbus in early GTL flight tests. By 2008 the US Air Force had already certified B52s and C-17s for fuelling with 50/50 JP-8 and synthetics as part of its Assured Fuels Initiative, and aimed to certify its entire fleet by 2011 in order to meet a target of cutting kerosene use in half by 2016; several of the engines involved, notably the CFM56 and PW2000, are in widespread commercial use. In early 2008, Airbus flew an A380 with one of its Trent 900s running on a blend of 40 per cent GTL and 60 per cent Jet-A1; the target is apparently 100 per cent GTL by 2013.

Synthetics have the advantage that they can be used as 'drop-ins' – that is, they do not require any changes to aircraft design or ground infrastructure. On the other hand, Fischer–Tropsch plants are expensive to build and the nature of their processes results in the life-cycle CO_2 output from GTL and CTL being equal to or worse than that of Jet-A1 (GTL compensating somewhat by eliminating sulphur and reducing particulate emissions); the attractions of GTL and CTL therefore lie more in the direction of energy security or possibly cost savings, assuming the price of crude continues trending upwards, rather than reducing greenhouse gas emissions. BTL offers better, but more distant, prospects of reducing greenhouse gas emissions.

- *Biofuels*, the name given to fuels produced from renewable and sustainable biomass irrespective of the process used, can be an answer not just to diminishing and increasingly expensive oil stocks but also to issues associated with climate change. Much depends upon the carbon life-cycles of the particular feedstock used. Although they absorb CO_2 whilst growing, some feedstocks do not absorb sufficient to outweigh emissions created during cultivation, fuel production, and use. Biofuels have anyway been considered problematic until recently because:
  - many tend to coagulate or freeze at temperatures well above those encountered by aircraft at cruising altitude;
  - some potential feedstocks such as corn, soybeans, and rapeseed need a great deal of land in order to be produced in industrially meaningful quantities, and compete with food production.

However, during the course of 2007 solutions to both problems appeared closer than had previously been the case, with algae becoming the front-runner amongst several promising feedstocks being used in proof-of-concept research – partly because it yields as much as 30 times more fuel per acre than alternatives. Virgin Atlantic, in cooperation with Boeing and GE, flew a B747-400 in non-commercial service in early 2008 with one engine running on a blend incorporating 20 per cent BTL (derived from nut oil), and Air New Zealand is cooperating with Boeing and Rolls Royce on a similar initiative using algae. Airbus, jetBlue, IAE, and Honeywell are partnering on research into algae and other second generation biofuels, as are Continental, Boeing, and GE. Nonetheless, whilst synthetic fuels are already in commercial use, biofuels are at best a medium-term prospect; sourcing sufficient feedstock without directly or indirectly harming the environment or impacting the production and price of food is likely to be as challenging as any purely technical problems. Airbus has 'pencilled-in' 2030 for their widespread use.

- *Hydrogen* might have long-term potential, but in the shorter term is problematic because it would require aircraft design and ground infrastructure to be radically changed. Fuel cells to provide inflight electrical power are a shorter-term, but nonetheless probably still distant, prospect.

As already noted in respect of emissions, the industry's problem is not so much its present contribution to the issue of non-renewability as the rate and visibility of its growth. It presently accounts for just 2–3 per cent of global fossil fuel use and 13 per cent of what is used by all modes of transportation – well behind road transport's 75 per cent. However, the amount of investment tied up in a fleet set to double in size over the next 20 years and in existing fuel storage and delivery infrastructures, together with the time and money that will be required to effect radical change, mean that unless a new fuel capable of use in today's engines and infrastructure becomes widely available within that timeframe the availability (as well as the cost) of oil is likely to be an issue well within the career-spans of those starting out in the industry today.

Possible Policy Responses

Several public policy responses might be available. For example:

1. *Internalise the external costs* Economists define as an external cost any negative by-product from an activity which the party responsible does not directly pay for – examples being noise and emissions harmful to the environment. One response is to make the polluter internalise the cost, by imposing a tax or some other financial penalty. We will touch on the possible cost implications of this response in the next chapter. (For a comprehensive discussion of external costs in the context of transport economics, see Button [1993, Chapters 5 and 7].)
2. *Subject output growth to an administrative cap* There are voices in Europe advocating this. For example, the UK Parliament's Select Committee on Environmental Audit has expressed willingness to cap the growth of air transport output to a rate no greater than measurable improvements in fuel efficiency, and the European Parliament – most of whose members regularly use airlines to commute to and from Strasbourg – rarely misses an opportunity to assault the air transport industry on the basis of factually inaccurate and poorly argued 'research'.

Notably in the UK but also to an extent in some other European countries, there have been over the last ten years or so several instances of the public becoming stirred into a state approaching mass hysteria. This happened in late 2006, when politicians dusted off their previously hidden green credentials and normally responsible newspapers published front page collages of easyJet aircraft alongside Hummers. A YouGov poll conducted for the British Air Transport Association in August that year found that although 56 per cent of respondents expressed concern about the effect of air transport on the environment, only 13 per cent had changed their travel behaviour: there is nonetheless latent danger in that second figure. The industry needs to be proactive in confronting the threat. What this means will be considered next.

The Way Ahead

The position taken here is that: climate change is almost certainly happening; man is most probably contributing to it or to its rate; the role of air transport emissions is small and still not fully understood; the growth and visibility of the industry nonetheless make it a target for politicians and lobbyists with a green agenda; and there is a nascent possibility in some parts of the world, notably Europe but before long possibly also the United States, that public perceptions may turn against the industry's continued rapid output growth. The threat is impossible to quantify and difficult to time, but it is real. Action is required, and there need to be two strands:

1. *Action by individual airlines* There are four:
    *   Formulate and implement an environmental management programme across the entire business (including fleet planning, and ground and flight operations): not only can this be argued to be an ethical duty, but many corporate travel buyers – particularly in Europe – are now taking seriously the environmental commitment of their suppliers. Some investors also look for evidence of corporate social responsibility (or, to use its latest label, 'environmental and social governance'). Several airlines have had such programmes for years, but have perhaps not publicised them as widely to customers as they should now be doing.
    *   Issue regular environmental reports: a number of those airlines that have been publicising their efforts have done so through the medium of regular reports – Lufthansa (2006) providing a good example. A battle of perceptions is underway in Europe: each airline's brand image versus the increasingly negative image of the industry.
    *   Offer customers the opportunity to participate in carbon offset schemes: their efficacy is as yet uncertain and take-up is often small after an initial flurry (although Jetstar is apparently averaging better than 15 per cent). A growing number of customers in Europe and North America are beginning to expect to have the option – and a growing number of airlines are providing it.
    *   Take proactive steps to counter the misleading propaganda put forward by some environmental lobby groups, journalists, and competitors (e.g., those European rail companies not above massaging facts in their advertising to raise their own environmental 'credentials' above those of airlines). Air France, for example, has had to argue its case against rail operators' claims, whilst easyJet has been notably active in putting the industry's case to the public at large (e.g., through a national newspaper campaign).
2. *Action by the industry as a whole* First, the industry needs to accept the possibility that a decade or two from now, well within the service life of an aircraft ordered today, multiple weekend breaks each year and excessive business travel *could* be as socially unacceptable in some parts of the world as drink-driving (always assuming that high oil prices and resulting high airfares have not already made them unaffordable to many). Second, the industry needs to accept that although it has a strong record in environmental matters (e.g., regarding engine technologies) and a genuine complaint that some of its environmental footprint is imposed upon it by outside forces (e.g., inefficient airspace design and antiquated ATC technology), it has spent too much time preaching this message to the converted within its own ranks or quietly lobbying politicians who at the end of the day are more likely to be influenced by voters and

the media and whose most profound interest in the industry lies in raising taxes from it. Third, a corollary of the last point is that until recently insufficient effort has been made to reach the public at large. What is needed is a consistent and open-ended communications campaign, involving both advertising and public relations and managed by communications professionals with global reach, to get the message out. What is that message?

- First, the industry contributes far more than most casual observers probably realise to the economic, social, and cultural fabric of the planet. (See the opening pages of Chapter 1 for figures and references.) Given that the only scientifically reliable assessment puts at just 3.0 per cent air transport's share of the total man-made contribution to climate change (IPCC 2007), any significant constraint placed on its growth would do serious economic and social harm without producing commensurate environmental benefits.

- Second, there is still only limited understanding of the true environmental impact of aviation. The exception to this is carbon dioxide emissions, which the industry is already heavily incentivised (by the price of fuel) to reduce and has been successful in reducing on a per unit of output basis.

- Third, the industry has been taking its environmental responsibilities seriously for several decades – in fact, much longer than many if not most other industries. ICAO has been doing this through CAEP and the noise and emissions certification standards imposed pursuant to Annex 16 of the Chicago Convention; IATA has been acting through its Environment Committee (ENCOM) and its predecessor. Others active in the field include the Air Transport Action Group (ATAG), Airports Council International (ACI), the Civil Air Navigation Services Organization (CANSO), the International Coordinating Council of Aerospace Industries Associations, and a large number of government agencies engaged together with universities in various research initiatives (e.g., in the United States, Europe, and Japan). In April 2008 the CEOs of 13 leading industry associations, ANSPs, and manufacturers signed a declaration which in effect adopted IATA's four-pillar commitment to work towards carbon-neutral growth by: investing in technology; improving operational practices; improving use of industry infrastructure; and supporting the use of positive economic incentives (the latter being thinly disguised code for 'rationally implemented global emissions trading – in due course and in preference to yet more taxes or a melange of regional trading schemes').

   Industry is paying half the €1.6 billion budget for the 7-year Clean Sky Joint Technology Initiative launched in early 2008 by 16 European countries and 86 companies and research organizations to find ways of achieving a set of ambitious CO_2 and NOx reduction goals established by the Advisory Council for Aeronautics Research in Europe (ACARE). These goals target reductions between 2000 and 2020 of 50 per cent in aircraft perceived noise, 50 per cent in CO_2, and 80 per cent in NOx. In 2007 the EC and the FAA established the Atlantic Interoperability Initiative to Reduce Emissions (AIRE), for the purpose of investigating and implementing procedures and practices capable of lowering emissions; in 2008 Airservices Australia, Airways New Zealand, and the FAA launched the Asia and South Pacific Initiative to Reduce Emissions (ASPIRE) with similar objectives. IATA is promoting a zero-emissions aircraft by mid-century. How attainable such targets are is unknowable, but at the very least they are evidence of positive intent to continue building on the palpable advances already made. Few other global industries can make such a claim.

- Fourth, the practical results of having taken environmental responsibilities seriously are evident in the fact that each new generation of transport aircraft is so much cleaner, quieter, and fuel-efficient than its predecessors. Fuel consumption across the global fleet measured in litres per 100 passenger-kilometres fell 37 per cent between 1987 and 2007, whilst perceived noise from current-generation aircraft is 75 per cent lower than from first-generation jets (Airbus 2008); a full A380 emits less CO_2 per passenger-kilometre than the current (2008) EU target for cars and burns only three litres of fuel per 100 passenger-kilometres. In 2007, IATA's Fuel Efficiency Gap Analysis programme identified opportunities to save \$1.33 billion in fuel expenditures and 6.7 million tonnes of CO_2 emissions, and the Association's work with ANSPs led to 395 route improvements estimated to have the potential to save 3.8 million tonnes of CO_2 per annum.
- Fifth, in some parts of the world politicians and other vested interests are standing in the way of further improvement in the industry's performance. Eurocontrol's Performance Review Commission reports each year on ATM efficiency in Europe. In 2006 it held fragmented airspace responsible for indirect routings and a high proportion of flight delays; the following year it estimated that horizontal routing inefficiencies alone were responsible for generating 4.7 million tonnes of otherwise unnecessary CO_2 (Eurocontrol 2007). Globally, and despite IATA's continuing success in negotiating shorter air routes, inefficient ATM generates as much as 73 million tonnes of unnecessary CO_2 each year (Bisignani 2007); in total, inefficient infrastructure is responsible for the annual production of 100 million tonnes of unnecessary CO_2 (IATA 2007d). (For comparison, ICAO [2007b] estimates that civil aviation was responsible for 600 million tonnes of CO_2 emissions in 2005.)
- Sixth, cattle generate twice as much greenhouse gas each year as do aircraft.

IATA has taken an important step by launching its Environmental Campaign to promote public awareness of what aviation is achieving, and working to achieve, in respect of the environment. In particular, it has established the four pillars for CO_2 reduction mentioned above. In similar vein, the www.enviro.aero website also mentioned above is a source not only of factual information but also communications resources. ICAO's CAEP has for many years been active and highly effective at a technical level, and in 2007 a new Group on International Aviation and Climate Change was authorised and the first triennial Environmental Report (ICAO 2007b) was published; these important contributions do not always get sufficiently widespread publicity outside the industry – something which the organization's Environmental Unit is addressing. Unless the air transport industry as a whole deploys twenty-first century media management techniques to present a coherent and coordinated message to external stakeholders, the fact that it is actively and successfully confronting its environmental responsibilities will be overwhelmed by better organized special interest groups, the battle for the hearts and minds of those who matter most to the media and to decision-making politicians (i.e., voters) will be lost, and output will at some point be constrained below what it might otherwise have been. The fact that in February 2008 UK fund manager Standard Life Investment announced that after consulting with members it had decided to exclude airline stocks from its ethical funds *could* be taken as an inconsequential gesture of no great importance to the \$500 billion airline industry; it *should* be taken as another straw in an increasingly ominous wind.

PILOT SHORTAGES

Unless a very significant economic reversal derails the industry's optimistic 20-year growth projections, we are at the beginning of a period in which some carriers will find output constrained by pilot shortages. There are two reasons:

1. Rapid fleet expansion. Airbus (2008), for example, projects a growth in the fleet from 13,284 in 2006 to 28,534 in 2026 – and these figures exclude freighters and aircraft with fewer than 100 seats. (Embraer [2008] sees the number of 61–120 seat aircraft rising from 2,460 to 7,320 over the same period.)
2. Lack of foresight. Flight operations departments at major airlines have for many years been well aware of the declining flow of ex-military pilots. They have also had access both to publicly available manufacturers' fleet forecasts and to internal fleet plans. But many have been quick to furlough or to cut pay and benefits in downturns, so damaging the relative appeal of a flying career, and some have terminated long-running pilot cadet schemes; others have retained schemes but been slow to ramp up throughput. There is also a problem of basic economics: pilots are expensive, especially in the context of an industry in which cost management is now so critical, yet it is difficult to put downward pressure on the price paid for a 'commodity' that is in short supply – particularly when that commodity is increasingly traded in a global market – and still expect to acquire more of it.

IATA estimates that 325,000 pilots will have to be recruited between 2007 and 2025 (*Airlines International*, June 2007, p. 40). ICAO's increase in the recommended pilot retirement age to 65 was in part a response to impending shortages. Belated expansion of flight-training schools around the world may ultimately be sufficient to meet demand. In the meantime, some airlines will face shortages that could limit output. These shortages may affect some types of carrier more than others. Regionals, which feed pilots as well as passengers to the majors, will be particularly affected; in Australia, for example, Regional Express began cancelling services then routes in 2007 because of pilot shortages. Cargo carriers may also feel pressure; Lufthansa's Chinese affiliate Jade Cargo Airlines was in early 2008 unable to give a starting date for North American services already almost a year behind schedule because of having insufficient pilots. The largest, highest-paying network carriers will probably be the least affected, but even in this group periodic problems delivering the schedule can be expected over the next few years.

VI. Capacity Management: The Supply Side

In the short term, it is generally more expensive to adjust supply than to manage demand in order to balance output produced (ASMs etc.) and output sold (RPMs etc.). There are nonetheless various short-term supply-side capacity management options:

1. *Fleet management* There can be merit in having a fleet of owned aircraft supplemented by leased units with a rolling spread of return options – although the relatively high rentals associated with short-term operating leases need to be carefully considered. Maintenance should be conducted off-peak whenever possible.
2. *Flight scheduling* Because an airline is not a geographically fixed operation serving just one market, it can schedule its available capacity to produce output and meet

demand in different markets at different times. Having a balanced portfolio of routes that peak at different times can, assuming the right fleet composition, allow capacity to be shifted in order to offset demand variations.

3. *Scheduling other resources* Staff, at call centres and on check-in desks for example, can be scheduled in response to predicted demand on a shift-by-shift basis. Some categories of staff can be cross-trained/multiskilled, subject to union agreements where applicable; productivity can be raised by having front-line staff do back-office jobs when demand is low, and back-office staff move into the front office when demand is peaking. The use of part-time staff, particularly in customer service positions, is now widespread within the industry; a key issue in respect of part-time customer-contact staff is whether they can be effectively acculturated – because corporate culture, through the impact it has on the style and tone of service delivery, is a critical variable in any high-contact service business. Again, the maintenance of equipment, facilities, and staff (i.e., vacations and training) should be scheduled for off-peak periods.

4. *Outsourcing* Some inhouse functions and processes can be supplemented during peak periods by the use of external service providers (i.e., tapered integration).

5. *Increasing customer participation* Internet bookings and automated check-ins are just two examples of how airlines are taking pressure off supply bottlenecks within their service delivery systems by increasing customer participation in certain activities.

6. *Making customers wait* Whether or not they are physically in line, any customer waiting for service is in effect queuing. A queue is equivalent to an inventory of physical items insofar as it performs the same function: it is a buffer. Queues mediate between the rate at which customers present themselves for service and the rate at which the service delivery system is able to accommodate them. Delay at various points in customers' activity cycles (Holloway 1998b), extending from reservations through service delivery, results from there being inadequate capacity to accommodate current demand; what is acceptable will depend upon customers' expectations – a consideration that should be reflected in the effectiveness/efficiency trade-off built into design of each service package and the system established to deliver it (Holloway 2002). Some customers (e.g., those on charter flights) are more likely to tolerate check-in or boarding queues and slow onboard service attributable to low flight attendant ratios, for example, than others (e.g., those travelling first or business class on a long-haul scheduled carrier). Also, substantial queues in check-in and/or security processes that significantly lengthen the total journey time on a short-haul flight might detract from the competitiveness of air transport in markets where surface modes represent viable substitutes.

An outline of available approaches to demand management was provided at the end of Chapter 2. Together, the management of demand and of supply are the essence of capacity management.

VII. Conclusion

Output can be controlled on the following levels:

1. By deciding upon the competitive (i.e., product and geographic) scope of the operation: this was discussed in Chapter 1. It will be touched upon again in Chapter 6 when we look at network design.

2. By securing and managing (in particular, scheduling) the capacity to produce output – notably the fleet, the facilities, and the human resources needed: scheduling and fleet management are the subjects of Chapters 7 and 8 respectively.
3. By managing the pricing and release of seats from the inventory created by committing to a schedule: pricing was discussed in Chapter 3, and revenue management is the subject of Chapter 9.

Before continuing the discussion of capacity management in Part 3 of the book (Chapters 6 to 9), we will look at the remaining supply-side element in the operating performance model around which Part 2 has been structured: unit cost.

5

Unit Cost

The problem lies in reconciling my gross habits with my net income.

Errol Flynn

The unit cost of output is the last of four elements in the operating performance model around which Part 2 of the book has been structured.

TRAFFIC × YIELD > < OUTPUT × UNIT COST
= OPERATING PERFORMANCE (i.e., PROFIT or LOSS)

Unit cost is total operating cost divided by output, and is therefore expressed as cost per ASM (ASK) or ATM (ATK). This chapter will look first at different definitions of cost and approaches to the accounting treatment of costs, and will then briefly review significant airline cost drivers. Broad approaches to cost management within the industry will be discussed. Three critical points to take from the chapter are that:

- most costs are open to a variety of definitions and interpretations;
- passengers do not care about airline costs, but most do care about fares;
- the purpose of incurring any cost is to generate revenue. It is possible in some markets to make money with a high-cost/high-yield product as well as with a low-cost/low-yield product. From a financial perspective, what matters is how productive each dollar of expenditure is in generating revenue. From a competitive perspective, what matters is how an airline's costs compare with those of competitors targeting the same customers – because a carrier with lower costs can in principle use its advantage to earn higher margins and/or to price aggressively and gain market share.

I. Cost Defined

Cost data is an important input into most decision-making processes. The problem is that there is often no single number that can be identified as *the* cost of something. Take an aircraft: if it was bought several years ago for $40 million, this is its *historic cost* – something accountants will want to reduce on the balance sheet by taking an annual depreciation charge, but economists will regard as partly *sunk* and therefore to that extent not relevant to future decisions; if it could be sold now (either outright or as part of a sale-and-leaseback) for $25 million, that part of the $40 million historic cost is not yet sunk and any incremental income that could be earned by reinvesting the $25 million more profitably elsewhere represents the *opportunity cost* of not doing so; if a replacement today would cost $55 million, this is its *replacement cost*. Which of these costs is relevant depends on the nature of the decision being taken.

TOTAL OPERATING COST

In the airline industry, it is usual to distinguish between operating and nonoperating costs; the former are incurred conducting air transport operations, whilst the latter are attributable to activities other than air transport as well as to decisions in respect of how to finance the business. Our concern in this book is with total *operating* cost (TOC). One approach to analysing TOC is to look at cost behaviour.

Cost Behaviour: Fixed And Variable Elements Of Total Operating Cost

'Cost behaviour' refers to the manner in which costs vary in response to managerial action. The action with which we are particularly concerned here is decisions taken in respect of output volume.

- *Fixed costs* do not vary in response to changes in output within the capacity range of existing production facilities, notably the fleet. (Fixed costs should not be confused with sunk costs: a sunk cost is a past expenditure that cannot be recovered, whereas a fixed cost is a current or future expenditure that is unconnected to output level.)
- *Variable costs* are costs which do vary with the level of an airline's output. Examples include fuel, landing fees, navigation charges, and flight-hour and cycle-driven maintenance costs. Variable costs move in the same direction as output, but the two do not necessarily change in direct proportion – which is why average cost per unit of output produced tends to be different at different levels of output. The variable costs incurred producing one million ASMs or ATMs will not be twice those incurred producing 500,000, for example; much will hinge upon the operating economics of the network and aircraft involved. The behaviour of variable – and therefore total – costs within a particular operating system will also depend in the short run upon factor productivity and the impact of the law of diminishing returns, and in the long run upon economies of scale and scope; these concepts will be explained later in the chapter.

A decision to outsource ground-handling, catering, or maintenance can be driven by a number of motivations, including a desire both to reduce costs and to make them more transparent. Another critical motivation might be to transform fixed into variable costs. As air transport markets have been deregulated or liberalised they have become more volatile. Airlines accordingly need the flexibility to react to changes in the volume and/or nature of demand more quickly than the heavily integrated, high-overhead architectures of long-established carriers have typically permitted.

The importance of time horizons   In time, every fixed cost will ultimately become variable. Economists use the following concepts:

- *The short run* is any period during which the cost of at least one input is fixed.
- *The long run* begins at any point in the future when all costs become variable – in other words, the point at which the firm will be able to free itself from current commitments and entirely reconfigure its operating system. Total cost and total variable cost become the same by definition, because there are no longer any costs that are fixed.

For most firms that are 'going concerns', the long run is an analytical concept rather than an actual point in time – although for small, flexibly configured firms in certain types of (generally non-capital-intensive) industry this need not necessarily be so. From our perspective considering the airline business, there are three important points to stress:

1.   The closer in we come along a timeline, the higher the proportion of an airline's costs that is fixed. Whilst output can be curtailed relatively swiftly, as in the aftermath of 9/11, fixed costs associated with the production infrastructure and corporate overhead take time to adjust; it is not necessarily a simple matter to sell aircraft or return them to lessors, lay off or furlough staff, or terminate gate and other facility leases. A high proportion of airline costs is fixed in the short run and difficult to avoid. This is why the rate of cash-burn is so high when an airline's revenue is cut by strike action or other significant system disruptions. Conversely, it makes attractive the heavy discounting of already-scheduled seats that would otherwise fly empty in order to generate at least some revenue contribution rather than none. In the short run, perhaps as much as 80 per cent of a scheduled carrier's costs can considered fixed (Flint 2001).
2.   As the timeline is stretched, a higher proportion of costs becomes variable and more readily escapable – that is, a carrier's management has more discretion to reconfigure its operating system and cost structure. For instance, fixed costs associated with owning a fleet of aircraft remain fixed only until such time as the airline is able to adjust the size and/or composition of that fleet. The time required to vary these 'fixed' costs will reflect a number of considerations. If it is intended to add aircraft, a feasible timeframe for achieving this will depend upon the carrier's financial status and the availability of appropriate units from manufacturers, operating lessors, and the secondary market. On the other hand, if the intention is to dispose of aircraft, the timeframe will depend upon the state of the secondary market, manufacturers' willingness to accept trade-ins against future deliveries, and/or the flexibility allowed by lease documentation with regard to early return.
3.   There is clearly merit in having flexibility to reconfigure production processes as rapidly as possible in response to changing levels of input prices and factor productivity, and also to fluctuations in demand. However, the larger and more complex an airline's operating system, the longer the 'long run' is going to be relative to, say, a small, non-unionised start-up that outsources many of its non-flying activities.

Over-focusing on short-term network and fleet analysis can lead to an almost unconscious acceptance of most costs as fixed. The shorter the time-horizon adopted, the more true this is. Conversely, by lengthening an analysis we can unearth more potential flexibility (Frainey 1999).

Operating leverage   One reason why in aggregate the industry performs so badly during recessions and benefits strongly during upturns is that the effects of demand cyclicality are magnified by the high financial and operating leverage from which many airlines suffer. Financial leverage is high when debt and equivalent obligations fund a large proportion of total assets relative to the proportion funded by stockholders; whereas dividends can be reduced or eliminated, debt interest (a nonoperating expense) has to be paid whatever is happening on the revenue side. Operating leverage, which is what we are concerned with here, is high when a large proportion of an airline's short-run TOC is fixed; again, fixed costs have to be met regardless of what is happening to revenue. When revenue grows off an unchanged debt and fixed asset base, profits are *leveraged* up; when revenue shrinks, and pending reduction in debt and fixed assets, profits are *leveraged* down.

Most airlines find it difficult to rapidly adjust their fixed costs downward when output begins to run ahead of demand. This can happen where too many new aircraft are delivered relative to prevailing requirements, or when demand growth falls below expectations – two circumstances that frequently coincide. Any downturn in traffic and/or yields could rapidly take an airline's revenue below the level required to meet fixed costs – something that happened to a lot of carriers in 1991 and, more dramatically, in 2001/2002. At this point, every dollar of additional revenue loss comes straight off the bottom line.

In practice, how high an airline's operating leverage really is depends in part on the time horizon applied, in part on assumptions about the prevailing state of the secondary market for tradable assets (notably aircraft), and in large measure upon the scale of the operations concerned. A small airline that has outsourced extensively and flies aircraft which are either on short-term leases or are owned but could readily be sold into a currently buoyant secondary market might be shrunk or closed down fairly quickly; the same cannot be said for a large network carrier. The industry's high operating leverage is therefore a generalisation which, whilst broadly true, needs to be put into a specific context.

Because financial statements tend not to provide a breakdown between fixed and variable costs as such, external analysts generally have to estimate operating leverage by categorising different expenditure line items as either fixed or variable. An alternative is to calculate the 'degree of operating leverage', which is the percentage change in operating profit between two periods divided by the percentage change in sales.

PRODUCTION FUNCTIONS, COST FUNCTIONS, AND THE IMPACT OF OUTPUT DECISIONS ON COSTS

Any airline's TOC reflects the operating characteristics of the industry, the design of that particular carrier's operating system, the prices paid for input resources, and the efficiency with which resources are used; another critical variable will clearly be its level of output. These variables are encapsulated in each firm's production function and cost function, the importance of which is explained in Box 5.1.

Each individual airline's cost structure – the relative sizes of different line items and the proportion of fixed and variable costs – will affect the cost impact of output decisions.

Box 5.1: Production Functions and Cost Functions

An airline's operating system is in economic terms a production process in which inputs – factors of production – are combined to produce output. The quantity that can be produced is a function of the factors of production used and the efficiency with which they are combined; so is the quality of output produced – although, as we saw in Chapter 4, much of microeconomic theory treats output as homogeneous. A production function is a quantitative statement of the relationship between factor inputs used and the volume of output produced – of the alternative input combinations that can produce a given level of output or, conversely, of the output that can be produced by a given set of factor inputs. The technology available within an industry is the fundamental driver of any production function, but managerial discretion with regard to choice of inputs and how they are deployed is clearly important.

If a production function is combined with a schedule of input prices, the result is a cost function. A total cost function relates TOC to output levels, and so helps provide insight into the impact of output changes on costs. One approach is to graph cost on the vertical axis against output on the horizontal and use least-squares regression on historical data to fit a curve that will help describe likely cost movements in response to output changes. Cost functions can also be developed algebraically. Since the mid-1990s, major airlines have been using increasingly sophisticated models to explore both the cost implications of different output decisions and areas where operational efficiency could be improved. (Various generic cost models are also available from industry associations and the principal airframe manufacturers. Although these models are undoubtedly useful, particularly when comparing the operating costs of alternative aircraft types, individual carriers have such different cost structures – attributable to their unique fleets, networks, schedules, labour forces, and operating strategies, for example – that only customised models should be used for profit planning purposes.)

In addition to TOC, there are two other important cost concepts to be aware of: average cost and marginal cost.

1. *Average (or 'unit') cost* is, as we saw earlier in the Chapter, TOC at a given level of output divided by the number of units of output produced (i.e., ASMs or ATMs, etc.). Average costs are rarely the same at different levels of output.
    *   In the short run, average cost is comprised of average fixed cost and average variable cost. The presence of fixed costs means that short-run total cost can be averaged down by increasing output within the available capacity range. In other words, by fully utilising currently available capacity more output can be produced over which to spread the fixed costs associated with that capacity. What this means in practical terms is that provided additional output generates revenue in excess of variable costs, the addition of output within the existing capacity range can improve the profit potential of all services – both existing and new.
        Average cost is, however, unlikely to change uniformly. Because TOC seldom varies in direct proportion to output, average cost is not a constant; the short-run average cost (SRAC) curve is often found to have a 'U' shape when average cost on the vertical axis is graphed against output on the horizontal. The law of diminishing returns in fact tells us that the marginal productivity of variable factor inputs added to a fixed production facility will increase rapidly at first – leading to a marked decline in average cost as TOC rises less than proportionately with output – and then flatten off and reverse, causing an eventual upturn in average cost.
    *   In the long run, the question is whether average cost can be reduced further by adding incremental capacity and generating yet more output over which to average (existing and incremental) fixed costs. The answer will depend upon the shape of the long-run average cost curve (LRAC), which in turn is heavily dependent upon what can theoretically be achieved given the nature of the particular industry's

production process. Where average costs fall in response to increases in output beyond the existing capacity range economies of scale are present, and where they rise diseconomies kick-in as capacity grows further. Minimum efficient scale (MES) is achieved where LRACs are at a minimum – that is, at the bottom of the LRAC curve; beyond MES the LRAC curve will be flat or will rise, depending upon the industry concerned.

The greater the size of MES relative to total industry output, the smaller is the number of competitors that can simultaneously produce at MES and the higher the industry's concentration ratio is likely to be. For example, if MES is equivalent to 25 per cent of industry output, there is in principle room for only four competitors producing at minimum LRAC – and the implication of this is that any other competitor in the industry will suffer a cost disadvantage. In practice, other considerations, not the least of which in many industries is the speed of technological change, complicate this simplification. It is nonetheless true that the more significant economies of scale are, the larger an industry's dominant firms are likely to be. In particular, industries requiring heavy investment in facilities and equipment carrying high fixed costs tend to benefit more from economies of scale than labour-intensive industries. The presence of economies of scale in the airline business is a hotly debated topic that will be looked at later in this chapter.

To summarise, in the short run firms inherit production process configurations which are likely to be suboptimal for given conditions, with the result that SRACs are inevitably above LRACs. As the time horizon stretches out, it becomes possible to vary progressively more factor inputs. What the firm is faced with, therefore, is a series of SRAC curves – each above the LRAC curve, but touching it at their lowest points. Economies of scale are present where a firm can reduce unit cost by increasing capacity and output; a key issue, of course, is whether the incremental output can be sold at a profit.

2.   *Marginal cost* is, as explained in Chapter 3, the change in TOC resulting from a one-unit change in output. When changes in airline output are discussed we are clearly not interested in movements of plus or minus one ASM or ATM at a time; nonetheless, the expression 'marginal cost' is widely used in this context, and will be used here. As long as marginal cost is below average cost, each additional unit of output will reduce average cost; as soon as marginal cost exceeds average cost, each additional unit of output will raise average cost. Of course, whether this matters will depend upon what is happening to marginal revenue (i.e., the revenue earned from each marginal unit of output); in general, there is merit in producing additional output if the revenue it earns exceeds the cost of producing it – an observation that is consistent with the argument of neoclassical microeconomics that profit is maximised at a level of output where marginal cost and marginal revenue are equal.

The Cost Impact Of Output Changes

Subject to a particular airline's cost structure, some general comments can be made about the impact of short-run output changes on total, average, and marginal costs.

Total cost   At zero output, TOC and total fixed costs will be the same; there will be no variable costs because there is no output to generate them. At any level of output above zero but within the range of existing capacity, an increase in output will increase TOC by the amount of variable cost incurred in producing that output; fixed costs remain unchanged. As output rises, so does TOC – unless efficiency can be improved by changing the operating system in a way that alters the relationship between output and cost. One objective of the corporate restructurings undertaken by a number of airlines in recent years has been to break their established output/total cost relationships by becoming more efficient. Technology has historically played the major role in improving this relationship (e.g., more efficient airframes and powerplants, online distribution, and e-ticketing); since the late 1990s, reorganization of the value chain and of working practices within it have made a growing contribution.

Once existing capacity is fully utilised, further increases in output bring with them additional fixed costs which create a marked step-up in TOC. Particularly in capital-intensive businesses such as airlines, capacity increases tend to come in indivisible 'lumps', creating marked steps in the cost function. For example, assume a single-aircraft 'fleet'. This aircraft bears fixed costs whether it is flying or not. Further assume that it is currently operated on one rotation a day over a single short-haul route. If the aircraft is capable of operating, say, four rotations a day on this route and the schedule is in fact increased to four departures in each direction, two things will happen:

- in absolute dollar terms, fixed costs remain the same, variable costs (e.g., fuel, airport and ATS charges) rise, and TOC therefore increases;
- fixed cost per unit of output will decline, because unchanged fixed costs are being spread over four times as many ASMs or ATMs (given four rotations are now operated rather than one). Whether TOC per unit of output (i.e., average or unit cost) also falls will depend upon whether the averaging down of fixed costs is sufficient to outweigh the increase in variable costs; in many cases it will be.

Now assume that demand is starting to be spilled. To meet market needs the requirement is to add a fifth frequency rather than operate a larger aircraft; because the original aircraft is able to operate no more than four daily rotations, the fifth frequency requires a second aircraft.

1. Although demand comes forward in units of one or more passengers at a time, capacity is added, and output is produced, by significantly larger units – that is, by aircraft. These represent what are called 'indivisibilities', because a chosen type cannot be divided into smaller units of capacity to better match output to demand. Indivisibilities occur throughout an operating system, wherever capacity (e.g., stations, gates, simulators, maintenance bays) must be added in larger 'lumps' than demand comes forward to fully utilise. Supply and demand are fundamentally difficult to match in industries where significant indivisibilities are present. At the level of the individual route there are indivisibilities stemming from: aircraft size; slot and gate allocations; staffing; and infrastructural resources. Potential output is constrained by the most limiting of these indivisibilities, and any increase in output beyond that limit will require additional capacity – perhaps a larger aircraft or more gates, for example. Such step-ups in capacity carry with them significant incremental fixed costs.
2. An expanding airline's TOC therefore rises in clearly defined steps associated with the addition of fixed costs attributable to each new aircraft (as well as to the addition of other 'lumpy' assets). Clearly, much will depend upon the size of the carrier concerned. Adding an aircraft or a station to the operating system of a small, recently established airline will produce a much more dramatic impact on that carrier's TOC than would adding an aircraft or a station to, say, American's system.

In summary, an airline's current capacity generates certain fixed costs. That capacity will support a range of output from zero to whatever can in theory be produced at full utilisation. Output beyond capacity at full utilisation requires the addition of further capacity, which brings with it additional fixed costs. Because aircraft and some other elements of an airline's operating system are indivisible below certain levels, the additional fixed costs they bring with them are sufficiently significant to cause a marked step-up in aggregate fixed costs and therefore in TOC. If the new capacity is not at first fully utilised, additional fixed costs per unit of output (i.e., per ASM or ATM, etc.) will be high; as utilisation of the new capacity increases, variable costs associated with ramping up output will rise but fixed costs will be spread over a growing volume of output and so will be averaged down on a per unit basis. This process repeats itself every time existing capacity (e.g., the current fleet) reaches full utilisation and further capacity is added. One possible implication of all this is outlined in Box 5.2.

Average cost and marginal cost   When output is increased within the range of existing capacity, (short-run) marginal cost is equivalent to the variable costs of this increased output. (This is not necessarily the same as saying that it is equivalent to the average variable cost of all output – which might be higher or lower than the marginal cost of new output, depending upon how cost-effectively that new output is produced.) If on the other hand production of the marginal output requires extra capacity, fixed costs attributable to that new capacity must be absorbed into marginal cost. For instance, returning to the earlier example of one aircraft flying four rotations on a single route:

- The marginal cost of putting the next passenger into the last available seat on the fourth departure is equivalent to the variable cost of carrying that passenger (e.g., distribution cost, revenue accounting, ground-handling, catering, and fuel-burn). This is essentially a traffic cost.
- On the other hand, the marginal cost of putting the first passenger onto the fifth flight, operated by a newly acquired aircraft, would be the sum of variable and fixed costs associated with acquiring and operating that extra aircraft. This would represent both a traffic and a capacity cost. (In early 1982 Pan Am was achieving high seat factors on its daily non-stop from New York JFK to Tokyo Narita and so decided to schedule a second service on certain days of the week; shortly after that decision was taken, the author was among just 18 passengers on a B747 operating one of those second services.)

Simplistic though this example is when set against today's scheduling, fleet assignment, and revenue management tools, its purpose is to underline the point that different decisions regarding how to respond to market requirements by scheduling output on a route – that is, how to strike a balance between aircraft size and frequency of service – can carry very different cost implications. It also draws out two other points that were met in Chapter 3 when marginal cost pricing was discussed:

1. *Looking to the past: the need to recover the full costs of existing capacity* Because of the high fixed costs involved in operating a sizeable scheduled airline, average cost per unit of output (encompassing average fixed as well as average variable costs) will usually be well above short-run marginal cost – which, as we have seen, can closely approximate the increase in variable cost attributable to adding output. Product perishability and a widespread perception of low marginal costs exert severe pressures on airlines' pricing discipline, particularly in periods of recession and overcapacity, by tempting them to apply short-run marginal cost pricing and ignore the need to at least cover average total cost if break-even is to be sustained and bettered.

Box 5.2: Production Indivisibilities and the 'Empty Core'

Production indivisibilities are central to a concept that was mentioned earlier in the book and has been widely discussed over the last few years, at least in academic circles, in respect of the airline industry. The idea of the 'empty core' is that because of production indivisibilities an industry might not be able to sustain an optimal level of supply, but instead has to subject itself to destabilising bouts of undersupply or oversupply – with financial instability the consequence (Telser 1978).

In simple terms it might be, for example, that one flight is insufficient to meet demand on a route and leads to high fares whilst two flights generate excess output and lead to unsustainably low fares (i.e., below average cost). At a wider industry level, periodic oversupply as aircraft ordered at a cyclical peak are delivered into the next downturn is another source of instability. The outcome in an unregulated market could be constant swings from profit to loss as entrants come and go – perhaps in the extreme leading to withdrawal of service altogether (Hanlon 2007). Proponents of US deregulation argued that the airline industry should not be subject to such bouts of 'destructive competition' because it has low fixed and sunk costs relative to total costs and, in the absence of economies of scale, is naturally competitive; competitive equilibrium should be attainable. Evidence from the early 1990s and 2000s suggests the latter view is too sanguine (Ben-Yosef 2005).

---

2. *Looking to the future: the need to pay for future capacity expansion* Variable cost and marginal cost should not be confused. Although average variable cost in particular is frequently treated as analogous to marginal cost, there is no reason why the cost of the next unit of output produced should equate to average variable cost (or, indeed, to average total cost). The common expression 'marginal cost pricing' should therefore be used with care. Pricing output at or near the variable cost of producing it might very well approximate *short-run* marginal cost pricing if it is produced using only existing capacity; but if demand pressures suggest that in due course investment in additional capacity will be required in order to accommodate future demand, pricing at or near today's variable cost takes no account of the long run need to pay for that new capacity.

    For example, a 1992 study of the US domestic system by consulting firm Avitas calculated marginal costs to be approximately 23–28 per cent of TOC at load factors between 55 and 70 per cent, rising as high as 40 per cent when load factors reach 90 per cent. Any operating system burdened by high fixed costs can have short-run marginal costs well below average cost over a wide range of output, but once pressure to add capacity results in the system incurring more fixed costs, then marginal cost can become substantial. This is why the marginal cost involved in adding traffic to a system experiencing low load factors is lower than when high load factors imply that many flights are already facing an overdemand situation.

II. Airline Cost Classification

OPERATING, NONOPERATING, DIRECT, AND INDIRECT COSTS

Figure 5.1 illustrates a common approach to airline cost classification using functional categories. *Nonoperating costs*, which are not directly related to the transportation of

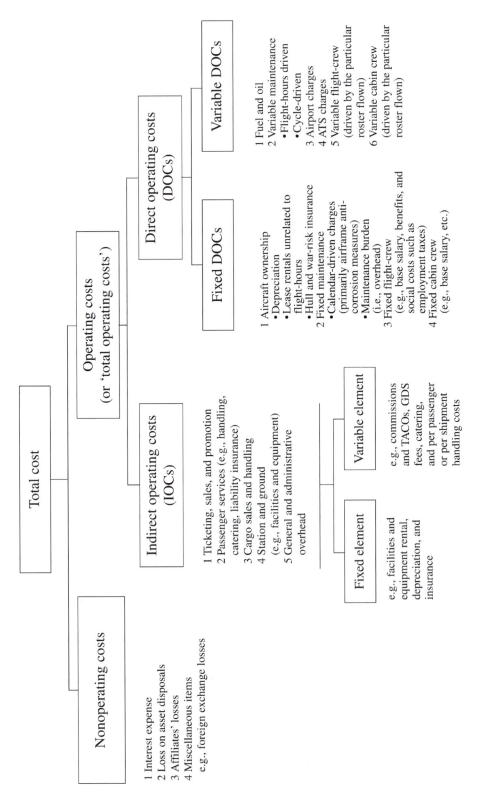

Figure 5.1   A possible airline cost classification

passengers or cargo, can vary so widely between airlines as a result of different corporate activities and financial structures that inter-airline comparisons are often of limited use. *Operating costs* arise from the production and sale of air transport output (i.e., ASMs, etc.), and can be 'indirect' or 'direct'. *Indirect operating costs* (IOCs) are costs related to the sale and delivery of passenger or cargo services that are independent of the composition or usage of an airline's fleet. *Direct operating costs* (DOCs) are largely dependent upon the types of aircraft in the fleet and how they are operated – that is, flight operations – and so would change if the fleet were changed or operated differently. DOCs can be calculated on a periodic system-wide basis, or they can be calculated per flight-hour for each aircraft type as an input into fleet and network management decisions. DOCs have both variable and fixed elements. For analytical purposes it is common for cash operating costs to be broken out of DOCs; the most significant DOC that does not qualify as a cash operating cost is depreciation (a non-cash charge).

The most comprehensive publicly available data on airline costs can be found in the US DOT's Form 41. Several consultancies prepare subscription-based analyses of what is a complex array of statistical schedules, but the Air Transport Association does provide a useful (and free) quarterly 'snapshot' on its website in the form of a Passenger Airline Cost Index for US carriers.

A distinction that we have already met is sometimes drawn between the following types of DOC:

1. *Capacity costs* These include:
   - aircraft-related fixed costs such as insurance, depreciation, calendar-driven maintenance costs, and lease rentals;
   - leg- (or flight-) specific costs without payload, such as airport and airway charges, variable (i.e., hourly or per cycle) maintenance, basic fuel, and fixed handling charges.
2. *Traffic costs* These are payload-specific costs such as incremental fuel-burn, catering, variable passenger- and cargo-handling charges, and cargo documentation. Travel agencies' commissions and overrides and GDS fees in respect of passengers carried should also be included where relevant.

Capacity costs (i.e., the costs of providing capacity and producing output) are by far the most significant element in any airline's cost structure. Nonetheless, unit costs are to some extent driven by traffic volumes as well: if an airline's load factor were to rise significantly whilst system capacity and output remained largely unchanged, higher traffic costs would drive up unit cost in the absence of efficiency gains.

There are four important points to take from this discussion:

1. Different types of airline have different cost structures, and within any category of airline individual carriers will also vary somewhat in their split between DOCs and IOCs. Very broadly, DOCs might account for as much as 80 per cent of a charter airline's TOC because of minimal sales, distribution, and promotional expenses; for scheduled carriers, the range is more likely to be 50–70 per cent – although much depends on fuel prices at the time, on average stage-lengths, and on labour costs. We will look at the significance of these factors later in the chapter.
2. Whilst Figure 5.1 is a representative example, there is no universal agreement on how to allocate costs between direct and indirect categories. Debate does, however, tend

to focus on just a few line items. For example, 'cabin crew' and 'airport and en route' are sometimes classified as IOCs, coming under 'passenger services' and 'station and ground' respectively. (In fact, wherever specific airport and en route charges relate to the weight of the aircraft concerned there is a strong case for treating them as DOCs; similarly, cabin crew numbers are arguably better treated as DOCs because they are driven to a significant extent by aircraft type.) Catering is sometimes categorised as a DOC; maintenance burden is frequently classified as an IOC.

3. Many operating costs have both a fixed and a variable element. The shorter the time horizon, the greater the proportion of costs that is fixed. In the very short term, a scheduled carrier that has committed to a timetable is essentially a fixed cost operation. Cost escapability is discussed in Box 5.3.

4. Airline costs are driven to a far greater extent by the cost of producing ASMs and ATMs than by the costs of carrying traffic.

Box 5.3: Cost Escapability

Costs are the outcome of resource acquisition and allocation decisions. In the airline business we can think in terms of four levels of decision-making:

1. *Industry entry decisions* A decision to enter the airline industry will entail establishment of a corporate infrastructure which generates general and administrative overheads.
2. *Network design, scheduling, and other product decisions* These generate fixed fleet, crew, maintenance, and station costs, as well as a marketing and service delivery infrastructure carrying its own overhead burden.
3. *Flight-related decisions* Any decision to operate a flight, whether in accordance with a schedule or not, leads to expenditures which are usually classified as variable DOCs. Notable amongst them are fuel, ATS, airport, handling (passenger and ramp), and variable crew and maintenance costs.
4. *Passenger-related decisions* Acceptance of each individual passenger onto a flight with seats available will give rise to costs such as travel agency commission, GDS fees, food, and marginal fuel-burn.

Very approximate numbers can be attached to these four levels for a given airline by allocating relevant accounting categories to each. Most IOCs and fixed DOCs will go into levels 1 and 2, whilst flight variable DOCs and passenger variable DOCs will go into 3 and 4 respectively.

Costs are 'escapable' at each level to the extent that they can be avoided by taking an alternative decision: not to form an airline; not to fly the chosen network or schedule; not to operate a particular flight; and not to carry an individual passenger. However, we saw earlier in the chapter that a high proportion of an airline's costs will inevitably be fixed in the short run. Just how escapable costs are in any particular case will depend upon the timeframe under consideration and the cost structure of the airline concerned – specifically, the proportion of TOC that can be considered fixed over the timeframe in question. For example, when Continental announced a 20 per cent cut in schedule immediately after 9/11, its CEO admitted that TOC would only drop by ten per cent as a result. Furthermore, when a flight or a route is cut, variable costs will be saved immediately but fixed costs that cannot also be cut right away have to be spread over less output – and this can put upward pressure on unit costs until such time as fixed costs can also be pared. Network carriers offering a wide range of products from complex hubs and sustaining significant corporate infrastructures will inevitably have a smaller percentage of TOC that can realistically be considered escapable in the short run than will a small competitor offering a simple product over a point-to-point network and outsourcing many of its activities.

For external consumption, airlines generally use a simplified version of the operating/ nonoperating cost breakdown in their income statements. Internally, a more analytical approach to cost analysis is required.

ALTERNATIVE APPROACHES TO COST ANALYSIS

By Department

Carriers tend to have different departmental structures, and they can also differ in their choices regarding how to allocate given types of expenditure to different departmental (or, indeed, functional) categories. This hinders comparison. It is anyway arguable that aggregating a number of separate activities having different economic characteristics and cost drivers into, say, a marketing department is not very helpful.

By Product

The idea here is that each product should be charged not only with the direct costs that went into producing and delivering it, but also with an allocation of the indirect costs. This approach is referred to as 'absorption costing', because indirect costs are 'absorbed' into product costs.

Airlines produce ASMs (ASKs) and ATMs (ATKs); they measure the part of this output that has been sold as RPMs (RPKs) and RTMs (RTKs). Customers, on the other hand, buy seats or cargo space between many different origins and destinations. Linking costs incurred producing ASMs and ATMs to the cost of carrying a particular passenger or shipment in an O&D city-pair is inevitably going to be difficult. Airlines wanting to cost individual products therefore face two problems: identifying the product and allocating costs.

Identifying the product   There are several different ways to define 'the product' – by geographical region (e.g., regional, domestic, short-haul international, long-haul international), by cabin (e.g., first, business or economy class), and/or by fare type (e.g., full fare, APEX, etc.). Every departure has schedule and routing attributes that make it a product in its own right, in addition to which there may be separate cabins onboard and there will almost certainly be people in each cabin travelling on different fares that carry different restrictions (and so could be characterised as different products); in a hub-based network, there will also be people in each cabin who are travelling in different O&D markets. In the case of cargo, there are other issues – such as whether a shipment is time-definite (and if so whether overnight, two-day, and so on), and whether it requires special handling and/or documentation.

Allocating costs   Having identified separate products, the next challenge is to allocate costs to each. One of the unusual features of the airline industry is that so many different air transportation products are produced by essentially the same operating system within any given carrier. This gives rise to a significant number of costs that are not readily separable for allocation to specific types of output. It is worth defining three concepts at this point:

1. *Joint products* Joint products arise as an inseparable consequence of a single production process. This might be:

- inevitable: for example, the availability of belly-hold space for cargo is often an inevitable by-product of the provision of passenger services;
- planned: for example, the production of passenger and cargo output on the main deck of a combi can be varied, so one is not an inevitable by-product of the other. Similarly, a single flight into or out of a hub might produce joint products in several different O&D markets, but this is a function of scheduling rather than the production of inevitable by-products.

2. *Joint cost* A joint cost is the cost of producing two or more products arising from the same inputs. The trip cost of a flight can be considered the joint cost of producing several sets of joint products. For example: passenger output in each of the onboard cabins; passenger and cargo output on the single flight-leg concerned; shares of passenger and cargo output in all the O&D markets served by the flight.

3. *Common cost* A common cost is the cost of any one input used simultaneously in the production of several products. Flight crew are an obvious example; the costs of operating a hub or, indeed, any station are another.

These definitions are widely accepted; see, for example, Rutherford (1992). However, there are others. Button (1993) defines a joint cost as an input which *inevitably* gives rise to the output of two or more products in fixed proportions, and a common cost as an input which gives rise to one or more products but subject to neither inevitability nor fixed proportions. Thus, fuel cost for a flight would be a joint cost where a flight inevitably produces fixed amounts of passenger and (belly-hold) cargo output; the costs of operating a hub on the other hand are 'common' to each of the flights serving that hub, but are not 'joint' because there is nothing inevitable about which routes will be linked into the hub or which aircraft types will be assigned to fly them.

In this book, the definitions used in points 1–3 above have been adopted, as much for the sake of simplicity as for any other reason. The task is therefore to:

- identify each separable cost and allocate it to the individual product to which it gave rise;
- identify each common cost and devise a method for allocating it amongst each of the joint products to which it gave rise.

The guiding principle when allocating costs is to identify those that are *avoidable* should the decision be taken to discontinue the product concerned. Common costs can only be escaped jointly, so any allocation to different products must therefore be arbitrary. Flight-crew costs, for example, can only be allocated arbitrarily between the costs of carrying passengers and those of carrying cargo, or between the costs of producing different passenger products on the same flight. (In Chapter 3 we saw that some airlines treat their output of cargo space as a by-product of passenger operations and require prices only to cover variable costs, whilst others cost output on a fully allocated basis – albeit using allocations that are arbitrary.) Similarly, catering supplies and flight attendants' salaries can readily be allocated to passenger as opposed to cargo products – but how should they be allocated between the different O&D markets served by a flight into or out of a hub?

In summary, costs might be common across: onboard products, such as passengers and cargo or first and business class; output in different O&D markets, as happens when passengers travelling between different origins and destinations are carried on the same aircraft into or out of a hub; or routes and departures, because the same ground personnel and equipment may service many of both. Costs incurred by a single-class LFA operating an out-and-back route structure will on the whole be more easily separable, and so more readily allocated to different services, than costs incurred by a multi-product network carrier.

It would indeed be helpful for airline managers to be able to walk down an airplane knowing with reasonable certainty what it cost to put each passenger into their seat and serve them whilst they are there. Unfortunately, this becomes increasingly difficult as the number of products that an airline produces within a single operating system increases, the proportion of total costs that could be considered common increases, or the ratios of fixed to variable and indirect to direct costs increases. As noted in Chapter 3, the further any analysis moves away from consideration of TOC, the deeper it is venturing into the realm of opinion.

By Route

Route cost calculations require aggregation of the following for each flight-leg operated on the route: variable DOCs (e.g., fuel, airport and airway charges); variable IOCs – notably variable traffic costs such as agency commissions and overrides, GDS fees, catering, and traffic-handling (passenger and cargo); and allocated shares of fixed IOCs and DOCs. The allocation drivers for fixed IOCs are usually route ASMs or ATMs (or perhaps RPMs or RTMs) as a proportion of the system-wide total. Allocation-drivers for fixed DOCs are very often block-times; for example, aircraft ownership costs can be calculated by dividing into each ownership line item (e.g., depreciation, rentals, hull and war-risk insurance, etc.) the annual fleet or subfleet utilisation (in hours) for the type(s) operating the route and arriving at an hourly charge that can then be applied to operations on that route.

Figure 5.2 illustrates how DOCs might be allocated to a particular flight. Box 5.4 summarises the build-up of different flight-leg cost metrics.

Box 5.4: Flight-leg Costs

Several different cost figures can be derived in respect of a flight-leg:

- Trip cost = variable DOCs + variable IOCs (e.g., agency commissions, catering) + an allocation of fixed DOCs + an allocation of fixed IOCs. (Note that depending upon the purpose of analysis, fixed and variable IOCs might be excluded; for example, whilst allocated IOCs should be included in an internal analysis of route profitability, they would most likely be excluded if the economics of two alternative aircraft types were being compared as part of a fleet planning exercise.)
- Hourly cost = trip cost ÷ block-time in hours.
  ('Block-time' is the elapsed time from off-block to on-block, sometimes referred to as gate-to-gate or chock-to-chock.)
- Aircraft-mile cost = hourly cost ÷ block-speed in mph.
  ('Block-speed' is distance flown ÷ block time.)
- Seat-mile (or 'unit') cost = aircraft-mile cost ÷ available seats or, alternatively, trip cost ÷ ASMs produced.
  (As will be seen in Chapter 10, this should be compared with unit revenue – that is, revenue per ASM or 'RASM'.)
- Revenue-mile cost = aircraft-mile cost ÷ seats sold or, alternatively, trip cost ÷ RPMs.
  (This should be compared with yield – that is, revenue per RPM.)

Generally, trip (and therefore aircraft-mile) costs increase as aircraft size increases – although a modern aircraft might have better economics than a smaller but older type as a result of technological improvements. Conversely, unit cost tends to fall as aircraft size increases because the fixed portion of aircraft-mile and trip costs does not generally grow proportionately with output; again, technological improvements can break this general relationship such that a relatively new type (e.g., the B777) might on certain stage-lengths have better unit costs than an older, larger type (e.g., the B747-400).

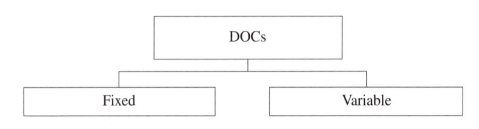

Fixed

Hourly allocation Depreciation, rentals, hull and war risks insurance, fixed flight-crew and cabin crew salaries and benefits, maintenance overhead, calendar-driven maintenance charges.

*****

Alternatively, fixed DOCs can be allocated on the basis of ASMs or ATMs produced by a flight; this calculation requires aggregating fixed DOCs, dividing the sum by system ASMs or ATMs to arrive at a cost per ASM or ATM, and multiplying this by the output of the flight concerned. (Fixed IOCs can also be allocated in this way.)

Variable

Hourly allocation Variable crew salaries; flight-hour driven maintenance charges.

Cyclic allocation Cycle-driven maintenance charges; passenger and cargo handling.

Load-driven Catering; passenger liability insurance.

Actual expenditure Fuel; ATS charges; airport charges; crew expenses.

Figure 5.2   An approach to the allocation of direct operating costs to a flight

The cost of operating in an O&D market served other than by a non-stop route can in principle be calculated by aggregating the costs of operating the connecting routes that serve it. In a hub-and-spoke network, of course, any route into or out of a hub might serve multiple behind/beyond markets; the cost of serving a connecting market must therefore be calculated by allocating a proportional share of route costs. In other words, some of the costs of serving the Phoenix–Boston market over Dallas are borne by other markets that are also served by the Phoenix–Dallas and Dallas–Boston routes (e.g., Phoenix–Miami and Albuquerque–Boston markets). Where an O&D market is served over a hub, it is not unusual for the carrier to add a per passenger 'connection cost' for the purpose of internal analysis so that the market bears at least some of the expense of maintaining the hub.

By Fleet And Sub-Fleet

Most airlines analyse costs by fleet and subfleet. This approach can be particularly useful when comparisons between types are being drawn for fleet planning purposes. It is also important to the fleet assignment process; where different types could be assigned to a route, the choice should in principle be the type or variant that maximises the gap between operating revenue and operating cost given the particular schedule.

By Activity

There are profound cost implications inherent in how, as well as which, activities are undertaken to deliver a service. Chapter 1 touched upon the strategic importance of this. Isolation of individual activities within, perhaps, cross-functional processes allows costs to be classified and managed by reference to the activities that consume them. Activity-based costing (ABC) requires investigation of:

- the resources consumed – man-hours, flight-hours, computer time or materials, for example;
- the activities in which these resources are used – that is, the work they do, such as reservations, check-in, transportation, delivering inflight service, etc;
- the cost drivers underlying each activity.

ABC systems collect costs by activity and then allocate shares of each activity's aggregate cost to products, markets, departures, stations, fleets, individual aircraft, cycles, entire schedules, and other 'cost objects' on the basis of the amount of each activity the cost object consumes. The purpose is not simply to control raw expenditures, but to assist airline managers in making cost-effective decisions by identifying costs with activities and isolating non-value-adding activities. Whereas the traditional approach of allocating costs to departures, products, routes, and fleets can answer the question 'What is happening?', ABC systems dig deeper to answer the question 'Why is this happening?'

British Airways began looking at ABC approaches in the late 1980s, but relatively few carriers have followed. Many do not have management accounting systems aligned with activities. To realign them from their existing, predominantly departmental, focus towards processes that flow through the organization and across functional boundaries is expensive and can be politically sensitive. Furthermore, ABC relies heavily on surveys and estimates, and ABC systems can be expensive to operate (Max 2007).

By Contribution

Any excess of revenue over variable costs is a 'contribution' made by the product, route, department or other profit centre concerned towards coverage of the airline's fixed costs. Figure 5.3 illustrates one possible approach to graphing the contribution margin of a route or an individual departure – that is, the percentage by which it is covering or failing to cover variable costs. By graphing contribution margin against seat factor, yield can be brought into the analysis insofar as it is fairly clear that a high seat factor/negative contribution margin service is suffering from unsustainably low yields; on the other hand,

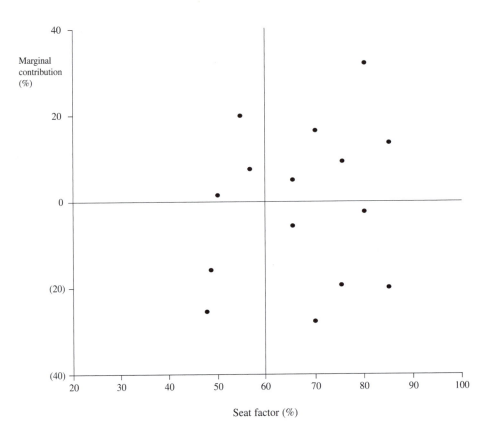

(Note: Each dot might represent the performance of a route over a period of
time or, alternatively, a specific departure by time of day and day of week.)

Figure 5.3   Contribution margin plotted against seat factor
Source: Adapted from Ingold and Huyton (1997)

a low seat factor/negative contribution margin service may have a volume problem as
well as (or instead of) a yield problem. Either might benefit from a reduction in output
– perhaps a smaller aircraft or fewer frequencies.

Accountants sometimes argue that even a flight that is more than covering its variable
operating costs and so making a contribution to fixed costs is ripe for axing if it is not
profitable on a fully allocated basis. This begs several questions:

- What else might be done with the aircraft? If given the existing schedule it would
  be idle when it could otherwise be operating the service under consideration there
  might well be a case for keeping it in the air, because as long as variable costs
  – specifically, cash operating costs – are more than covered (in both directions),
  a positive contribution is made to ownership and other fixed costs that would
  still be accruing were it on the ground. Not to do so would leave the fixed cost
  burden on existing services unnecessarily high on a unit output basis. Using this
  argument, for example, America West in the mid-1990s launched an extremely

low-yield night operation out of Las Vegas. If, on the other hand, there are more profitable uses for the aircraft than having it operate the service in question, these opportunity costs need to be considered.

- What impact will dropping the service have on the airline's presence in the affected market(s)? Bearing in mind the S-curve effect mentioned in the last chapter, for example, will reduction in output have a disproportionate effect on sales volume and revenue? Will there be any spillage of high lifetime-value customers who prefer a particular service and use it regularly?
- What will be the impact on network revenue and profit attributable to losing any feed the flight generates?
- Is one of the reasons for its poor contribution margin the fact that the service carries an unusually high share of non-revenue FFP redemptions, and if so what impact might its elimination have on the attractiveness of the FFP? Would allocating a proxy revenue figure to the service be preferable from a system perspective (Baldanza 1999)?
- If a service that is barely breaking-even on a fully allocated basis were to be withdrawn, the share of overhead allocated to it would instead have to be allocated to the balance of the network. What impact would that have on the profitability of those newly burdened routes?

In the short term, when we can think of aircraft ownership costs as fixed, the answer will probably be that any contribution made by a service to those costs should be accepted unless there are clear opportunity costs involved in not redeploying the aircraft. Furthermore, the contribution method of cost analysis can allow new routes some breathing space in which to establish themselves; new routes (if well chosen) generally make a positive contribution quite quickly, but take longer to build sufficient revenue to withstand a full allocation of fixed costs.

At some point, however, an expectation needs to be imposed on all flights that they must cover their fully allocated costs – unless there is some very sound competitive or network justification for cross-subsidising them from flights that are in fact profitable on a fully allocated basis. One justification, for example, might be that the internal revenue prorate used does not do justice to the value of, say, a short-haul route which makes a significant contribution to the network as a whole. Some network carriers tackle this problem by calculating each flight's 'beyond contribution'; this involves netting an assumed cost, perhaps in the 25–30 per cent range, off the price of a multi-leg ticket and ascribing the balance to *each* leg as revenue. The rationale is that if either leg had not been flown, the overall itinerary could not have been sold and so the beyond contribution would have been lost. The danger lies in losing sight of the fact that revenue is being double-counted; at the extreme, every flight in a network can be made to appear profitable even while the network as a whole is losing money.

Their high operating leverage makes airlines very volume-dependent – under constant pressure to generate revenue in order at least to make a contribution to high fixed costs. Airlines with expensive infrastructures in place to serve the requirements of high-yield passengers can suffer particularly badly whenever traffic growth drops off and/or yields weaken, leaving soft revenues pressing down on a high fixed cost base. The danger in maintaining unprofitable services in the long term simply because they are making a positive contribution is that if several competitors adopt a similar approach it will result in sustained overcapacity, excess output, and – in all likelihood – weaker yields than would otherwise be the case. This is something that has happened during most economic downturns with the notable exception of late 2001, when many carriers moved with historically unprecedented speed to reduce output.

III. Cost Drivers and Their Management: Introduction

In 2002, airlines as a whole were struggling to break even with oil prices around $20 per barrel. Five years later oil prices had quintupled, yet most carriers were profitable; indeed, not until prices moved above the $110–120 range in early 2008 did talk turn to the unsustainability of the industry as presently structured. A strong revenue environment after 2004 made a significant contribution to the turnaround, but its underlying driver was the transformation of network airlines' cost structures. Sources of this transformation were for most carriers a combination of: network redesign to eliminate unprofitable flying; fleet rationalisation to reduce the number of types and 'right-size' aircraft to markets; more efficient use of fuel; reduction in the number of employees and, in many cases, pared pay and benefits for those who remained; depeaking of hubs and fine-tuning of schedules to improve utilisation of aircraft and station resources; outsourcing of non-core processes and functions; shift to direct distribution; renegotiation of GDS contracts; and in some cases reductions in service levels. Several US majors achieved their transformation under the protection of Chapter 11 bankruptcy laws; Northwest, for example, achieved annual cost savings of $2.4 billion whilst in bankruptcy, well over half of which were extracted from labour.

There are two fundamental aspects to cost management:

1. An airline ought not to be incurring any costs other than those that are essential to the delivery of services, as designed, to the markets and segment(s) being targeted.
2. Underlying forces which drive the costs necessarily incurred must be understood and, as far as possible, actively managed. What 'actively managed' means is attending to:
   - the absolute cost of each input, such as the unit cost of labour (i.e., labour cost per ASM);
   - the productivity of each input, such as ASMs per employee or per dollar of employment expenditure.

   A carrier's unit cost (CASM) is influenced both by the absolute level of input costs and by the productivity of inputs used. If productivity is rising, it is quite possible for unit costs to decline irrespective of changes in absolute input costs. High productivity can go some way towards countering the adverse impact of high input costs, but the ideal is clearly to combine as far as possible both high productivity and low input costs. With the industry's real yields continuing a secular decline in response to increasing competition, the ability to manage input costs and ensure that the resources they buy are used as productively as possible is a critical management discipline.

The essence of cost management is therefore to ensure that customers get what they expect and are prepared to pay for, and that airlines spend as little as possible delivering it to them at a level *consistent with specified quality standards*. Considered in this way, cost management can be a formidable competitive weapon. It is no easy task, however. In order to remove just a cent from a 2006 unit cost of 11.98 cents, Alaska Airlines would have needed to reduce its $2.8 billion TOC figure by $233 million; whilst 'only' an 8.3 per cent reduction, this amount is equivalent to that year's maintenance expenditure for the entire Group (i.e., both Alaska and Horizon) and comfortably exceeds consolidated expenditures on both aircraft rentals and landing fees.

Fleet, network, and schedule choices are any airline's fundamental cost drivers. However, the next three sections of the chapter will drill-down deeper by using the widely recognised 'value chain' metaphor to look in turn at: upstream costs; the internal operating system; and distribution. There will inevitably be some overlap.

IV. Cost Drivers and Their Management: Upstream Costs

Unlike many other capital-intensive global industries (e.g., oil), the airline industry is not on the whole vertically integrated. Whilst this is consistent with contemporary management thinking which favours outsourcing any activity that does not contribute to a company's core competences, what is unusual about the commercial air transport industry value chain is that its key constituents (i.e., airlines) have as a group performed extremely poorly in financial terms relative to constituents downstream and, particularly, upstream (e.g., airports).

This section of the chapter will look upstream. It begins with a brief comment on supply chains. It will then consider two of the most significant upstream costs: fuel, and airport and air traffic charges.

SUPPLY CHAINS AND THEIR MANAGEMENT

The vertical scope decision was discussed in Chapter 1. Start-ups generally rely on external suppliers for a high proportion of inputs. Established carriers have also in many cases been outsourcing a growing range of activities. The purpose of supply chain management at any type of airline is to orchestrate suppliers, and perhaps also their suppliers, to deliver cost-effectively whatever the airline requires in order to meet customers' expectations.

The nature of relationships between airlines and suppliers has changed in recent years. Purchasing has been evolving from a reactive, transactional, administrative procurement function to an activity involving the proactive *management* of a network of suppliers within an integrated supply chain. Current trends in the management of supplier relationships include the following:

1. Centralisation of procurement to concentrate bargaining power, together with the increased use of consortium purchasing by affiliated carriers and alliance partners. Consortium purchasing might extend beyond alliances, and may also extend outside the airline industry in respect of non-aviation supplies. Joint procurement by alliance partners is not always as easy to orchestrate as press releases might suggest, however; sometimes there is a quality issue, and sometimes there is a question of longstanding relationships between member airlines and different suppliers.
2. The exertion of constant pressure on suppliers to stabilise or reduce costs. Costs of individual purchased items are no longer the sole criterion; more important is total cost within the entire supply chain – including administration, transportation, insurance, and inventory costs.
3. A growing willingness to use innovative approaches such as spares leasing, flight-hour maintenance agreements or membership of business services swap organizations.
4. Closer attention to suppliers' quality, innovation, customer orientation, and delivery reliability, and a willingness to benchmark supplier performance.

5.   Efforts to reduce each carrier's total number of suppliers. There are two issues here, however. On the one hand, global airlines want global suppliers, and in some supplier industries (e.g., flight catering) that is what to a still highly circumscribed extent they are beginning to get. On the other hand, large carriers have so many 'production sites' that they are often compelled by circumstances to retain a greater number of vendors than they would ideally want.

6.   Willingness to consider long-term, single-source contracts based on relationships with suppliers which – whether correctly or not – are popularly characterised as being driven more by the dynamics of partnership than by traditional vendor–customer relationships. From the airlines' perspectives, cost transparency and predictability are important motivations alongside cost reduction. These arrangements require a new set of management skills which are strategic in nature rather than purely transactional.

7.   The growth of electronic commerce, the primary attractions of which are accelerated transaction speeds and the stripping out of both inventory and manual processing costs.

FUEL

Fuel has historically accounted for 10–15 per cent of the industry's TOCs but now accounts for 20–40 per cent (with LFAs and all-cargo operators tending towards the top of this range). By early 2008, approximately 30 per cent of IATA carriers' TOCs were attributable to fuel, having risen from 13 per cent in 2001. In Asia-Pacific the figure is generally well above 30 per cent because of the region's low labour costs (and correspondingly higher ratio of fuel costs to TOCs) relative to Europe and North America. Given consumption patterns in the first half of 2008, each dollar on the price of a barrel of oil added $1.6 billion to the industry's costs; to take a specific example, the additional cost to British Airways at that time was £16 million per dollar a barrel increase. Taking the US industry consumption rate at 20 billion gallons a year, each additional cent paid per gallon costs $200 million.

It is not just the absolute amount of expenditure which bears thinking about – $136 billion in 2007 and, according to IATA estimates, perhaps as much as $200 billion in 2008 – but the speed with which it has increased since the turn of the century. In early May 2008, IATA's website (www.iata.org/whatwedo/economics/fuel) quoted from Platts a jet fuel price index of 391.4, based on 100 in the year 2000; the year-on-year rise had been 69 per cent. ATA figures show that average jet fuel prices rose 216.6 per cent from 2000 to the first quarter of 2008 (whilst the average passenger fare fell 0.5 per cent over the same period). Despite efficiency improvements, by mid-2008 it was costing US carriers over 4 cents in fuel expenditure to generate one ASM, compared with 0.97 cents just seven years earlier. In 2005 a combination of rising oil prices and downward pressure on unit labour costs resulted in fuel CASM exceeding labour CASM at US majors for the first time.

Fuel Cost Drivers

The most significant fuel cost drivers are:

1.   *The age and fuel efficiency of a particular carrier's fleet* We will look at fleet structure shortly.

2. *The market price for jet fuel* This is determined by both the price per barrel of crude oil and the 'crack spread' (or 'refinery margin'); the latter is a margin above crude that in North America fluctuated fairly narrowly in the $3–5 per barrel range throughout the 1990s, averaged $18.59 from 2002 to 2007, hit $30 in early 2008, and by May that year stood at $40. Jet fuel prices therefore actually rose faster than prices for crude during the latter's surge in (northern) spring 2008. (To understand what this means to an airline in practical terms, consider that Air New Zealand – a relatively small carrier – burns around 9 million barrels a year.) The crack spread is expected to decline as more capacity to refine Jet-A comes on-stream from 2009/2010.

3. *Regional market price pressures* There are seasonal pressures on fuel prices in certain parts of the world, notably North America and to a considerably lesser extent northern Europe. Partly this reflects the fact that jet fuel is similar in specification to other middle distillates such as diesel and heating oil. The demand and spot price for heating oil rise in response to severe winter weather, which in extreme cases can lead to the diversion of refining capacity in affected regions away from the production of jet fuel; similarly, capacity can be diverted to gasoline production when there is particularly heavy demand during the North American summer driving season. Therefore Singapore jet fuel, for instance, often trades fractionally below US benchmarks (i.e., New York Harbor, Gulf Coast, and Los Angeles/West Coast).

4. *Network design* Fuel costs contribute an increasing proportion of total trip costs as stage-length rises. Separately, operations in and out of congested hubs generally consume more fuel than when less congested airports are used, particularly where waves of hub arrivals and departures are tightly scheduled.

5. *Local factors at airports on a carrier's network* These can include: the expense of physically supplying fuel to particular airports; whether or not there is competition amongst suppliers driving down the costs of both fuel and into-plane services (e.g., hook-up fees); and the impact of any government taxes or duties (applied, pursuant to the Chicago Convention, only in respect of fuel for domestic flights). Of particular importance are the costs at a carrier's hub(s) or main base(s) because of the significant proportion of its operations these account for.

6. *Exchange rates* Because the market price of oil is quoted in US dollars, a carrier whose revenues are denominated primarily in other currencies will benefit when the dollar depreciates against those currencies. The share of TOC attributable to fuel will also tend to be lower than it otherwise would be whenever the majority of an airline's labour costs are paid in a currency that is strengthening against the dollar.

Fuel Cost Management

Industry mythology has long held that the cost of fuel is not 'controllable'. The general *price* of fuel is certainly not controllable, but any single airline's *expenditure* on fuel (and therefore the fuel cost line item for that specific carrier) is manageable at the margins; given the recent price escalation even marginal improvements may be very significant. Steps that can be taken to manage expenditure on fuel include: hedging; purchasing practices; operational practices; and fleet modernisation.

Hedging Air France-KLM saved approximately €600 million in 2006 as a result of fuel hedges, and Southwest saved $2.2 billion in the four years beginning Q1 2003. For an airline not to hedge or to hedge its fuel requirements only partially is in fact to run a speculative short position in a highly volatile input. Nonetheless, not every airline chooses to hedge; as jet fuel prices surged in April 2008, for example, United was only 16 per cent hedged for the year (compared with Southwest's 70 per cent). Even those that do hedge can face challenges: first, the absence of exchange-traded jet fuel contracts means that it is often closely correlated proxies such as gasoil or heating oil rather than jet fuel that are hedged, and this creates a spread risk – albeit one that can be mitigated by over-the-counter basis options and swaps; second, less creditworthy airlines might have trouble locating a counterparty for long-term hedges, and any airline will have to cash-collateralise a hedging programme – something that can be a problem for a carrier with poor liquidity; third, an airline that fully hedges (something which in practice is very rare) and then subsequently reduces output to well below projections will have to close-out surplus positions – perhaps at unfavourable prices. Also, if the spot price and available contract prices subsequently fall below the prices at which hedges were established, the airline will end up paying more than it would otherwise have done – something which happened to several carriers in 2006 (e.g., Delta). However, hedging should be seen as an insurance against unforeseeable rises in the price of a volatile input rather than as a profit centre, and if this philosophy is unpalatable it is always possible for a hedged carrier willing to pay the premium to purchase put options to protect itself against falling prices (which Qantas, amongst others, has done); alternatively, a carrier could hedge itself not by buying forward contracts but instead by buying call options. In the final analysis, hedging in a market undergoing what seems to be a secular upward shift is at best a short-term palliative – as was seen when some of Southwest's highly successful hedges introduced from 2003 onwards began rolling off in 2006/2007. (Whether hedging enhances enterprise value at all is a matter of debate in the corporate finance literature. A study of the US airline industry by Carter *et al.* [2006] concludes that it does.)

Purchasing   Some carriers band together to increase their bargaining power by making consortium fuel purchases, although not necessarily within the structure of the broader global alliances.

Operational practices   There is a long list of potential fuel-saving measures available, which includes:

- reducing aircraft empty weight by cleaning, being attentive to the weight of cabin fittings, and perhaps also implementing explicit weight reduction programmes during heavy checks;
- eliminating unnecessary passenger service items, and sampling periodically to ensure that passenger and carry-on baggage weights assumed using approved standards do not overestimate actuals and therefore aircraft gross weight;
- optimising aircraft centre-of-gravity in the mid to aft range of the envelope to minimise induced drag attributable to forward positioning;
- ensuring that flight controls are properly rigged to avoid even minor misalignments;
- checking the accuracy of instruments (because an under-reading mach-meter will lead to an aircraft being flown faster, and therefore consuming more fuel in the cruise, than intended);
- repairing dents, damaged seals, panel misalignments and other surface irregularities that can increase airframe drag;

- regularly washing engines between shop visits to maintain the aerodynamic efficiency of compressor blades;
- planning flights carefully to: optimise horizontal and vertical profiles consistent with day-of-operation weather; optimise the aircraft's Cost Index; select suitable alternates to minimise carriage of reserve fuel; and where appropriate use en route redispatch via an intermediate point on long-haul flights to reduce fuel reserves relative to those required for pre-flight dispatch direct to the final destination (a technique that is sometimes used to increase payload at the extremes of the payload-range envelope rather than to reduce fuel weight);
- using economic tankering programmes to provide flight-crew with real-time guidance in respect of optimum purchase locations on short-haul rotations;
- subject to overriding safety considerations and local conditions, stipulating and monitoring procedures for: taxiing (e.g., single-engine on a twin or two-engine on a quad – but there are implications in respect of brake wear, loading on the remaining engines, tight-turn capabilities, and warm-up/cool-down requirements for the unused engines); take-off (e.g., derated thrust – but this will only save fuel in the longer term, through reductions in engine wear); initial climb (e.g., clean-up as soon as possible – but leaving high-lift devices deployed can make sense to accelerate time and minimise ground-distance to a turning point if the turn is onto a heading more than 90 degrees off the departure runway heading); step-climb and cruise (e.g., using RNAV to fly user-preferred direct routings where onboard equipment permits, and keeping as close as possible to the aircraft's optimum altitude at different stages of the flight given its reducing weight and prevailing weather conditions – subject in congested airspace to flight level availability); descent (e.g., using RNP procedures to fly power-idle continuous descent approaches – something which is not yet widely feasible at the most congested airports); landing (e.g., limiting use of reverse thrust); and turnaround (e.g., using ground power units and other sources of airport-supplied power rather than auxiliary power units [APUs] where possible and whenever a turnaround is sufficiently long to justify the cost implications of cycling the APU through a shut-down and restart);
- monitoring actual fuel-over-destination (FOD) levels to minimise systematic carriage of unnecessary reserves that add weight and, on long-haul legs, might displace cargo; and
- monitoring fleet performance to identify individual tail-numbers recording above-average fuel-burn (e.g., implementing a cruise performance monitoring programme and comparing different aircraft on the same or similar routes).

The rescheduling of their hubs by some US network carriers to reduce congestion has also helped; we will look at 'continuous' and 'rolling' hubs in the next two chapters.

Fleet modernisation and modification   In the longer term the industry will benefit from the growing proportion of its fleet comprised of fuel-efficient new models such as the B787, A350, and – much further ahead in time – replacements for the B737 and A320 series. New types bring aerodynamic refinements, lighter weights attributable to greater usage of carbon-fibre and electronics, more efficient systems, and significant improvements in engine technology. In the meantime, exterior and interior modifications can help reduce fuel-burn. For example, Delta believes that a programme initiated in mid-decade to retrofit blended winglets on B737NGs, B757-200s, and B767-300ERs will result in 3.5 per cent fuel-burn improvements. Engine OEMs are also constantly working on refinements to their existing products to improve fuel-burn and reduce maintenance costs; an example is IAE's SelectOne build standard for the V2500, certified in 2008 and expected to reduce fuel-burn and CO_2 emissions by 1 per cent and improve onwing time by 20 per cent. CFM had the previous year introduced its own new Tech56 standard for the competing CFM56. Interior modifications can also help: for example, Frontier's 2007 investment in lightweight seats for its Airbus fleet was expected to save $5–6 million per annum at then-current fuel prices and aircraft utilisation levels, offering a 3–4 year payback.

Conclusion   Airlines can certainly manage their fuel consumption and costs, but in the final analysis they are always exposed to an unforeseen and sustained run-up in market prices. When this happens the best form of protection is to have one or both of a strong and liquid balance sheet and sufficient pricing power to pass incremental costs on to customers; few airlines have both, except perhaps fleetingly at the top of an economic cycle, and many have neither. Hence the importance of an unremitting focus on non-fuel costs as well.

AIRPORT AND AIR TRAFFIC SERVICES COSTS

Airlines are estimated to have paid close to $44 billion in airport and ATS charges in 2007. In addition to airport and ATS charges, other key cost drivers in this category include ground-handling and delays. Readers interested in further exploring the subject of airport and ATS charges should refer in the first instance to ICAO (2004, 2006).

Airport Charges

These break down broadly into aircraft- and passenger-related charges, and can include *inter alia* levies in respect of: landing (and/or take-off), parking, security, turnaround (e.g., jetway/airbridge and baggage systems), passenger numbers, cargo throughput, lighting, after-hours movements, and perhaps also noise surcharges (e.g., Zurich and Sydney), emission surcharges (e.g., certain airports in Switzerland, Sweden, France, Germany, and the UK), and charges for use of lounges, offices, airside facilities, and other space made available to a particular carrier (or group of carriers) by the airport operator. Aircraft charges might be flat, weight-related or both, and certain of them – commonly airbridge and other airside facilities, less commonly landing charges – might be priced differently at peak and off-peak times.

Airports are amongst the most profitable participants in the air transport industry value chain. Many benefit from high operating margins, strong cash-flows, and a pricing environment that substantially protects them from risk – which is why several have attracted private equity investment.

Issues associated with airport charges   Airport charges have three key drivers: airport operating costs; the recovery of capital expenditures; and the objective of the airport operator to earn a return on its capital. These drivers give rise to a number of issues, some of which have been aired publicly and at quite high volume in recent years, with individual airlines and IATA on one side of the debate and individual airports and the Airports Council International on the other.

1. *Efficiency and quality of service* It is a widespread contention amongst airlines that because many if not most airports are natural monopolies, they are not subject to the intense competitive pressures that have affected the airline business over the last few years and so are under little pressure to improve either the efficiency or the effectiveness of their service delivery. A counterargument is that in a world of global networks built around competing hubs and of footloose LFAs willing to quickly drop unprofitable operations, airports as a whole are neither natural monopolies nor sheltered from competition. The truth lies somewhere in the middle ground. First, hubs certainly do compete for flow traffic, and in North America when they compete ineffectively they can be closed; but no matter how strongly it is argued that London Heathrow, Paris CDG, Amsterdam Schipol, and Frankfurt Main compete against each other for flow traffic, the operators of these airports can be certain that British Airways, Air France-KLM, and Lufthansa are not going to vacate the premises any time soon. Whilst passengers can choose to fly over an alternative hub in an instant, airlines cannot readily abandon the investment in markets and infrastructure sunk into their main bases. Second, regional and secondary metropolitan airports, particularly in North America and Europe, are certainly in competition with each other to attract, retain, and expand LFA service – but this is little consolation to users of other airports such as Auckland International or Sydney Kingsford Smith, both of which are clearly monopolies and need to be regulated as such.

2. *Recovery of capital expenditure* There are two issues here. The first is whether a proposed capital investment is justified by projected traffic growth and the needs of users – both airlines and their customers; in recent years we have seen two ends of the spectrum, with some airport operators accused by airlines of 'gold-plating' (i.e., over-investing) – as at Dublin and London Stansted – but others showing themselves willing to offer basic low-fare terminals, shorn of costly accoutrements such as lounges and airbridges (e.g., Changi – where handling charges for the Budget Terminal are upwards of 50 per cent lower than for existing facilities). Gold-plating investments can be a problem for airlines even where airport pricing is regulated; for example, if a regulator price-caps on the basis of an acceptable rate of return on the airport's regulated asset base but fails adequately to control either new investment or the valuation of existing facilities, the airport might in effect benefit from a protected return on investment irrespective of whether its capital expenditures are efficiently implemented and actually meet users' needs. (In fairness it has to be noted that airport planning horizons are exceptionally long and have to take into account not only what today's airlines *say* that they want but also what these carriers and others might *actually* want perhaps a decade or more in the future.)

    The second issue is whether investments should be pre-financed by increasing the charges of current users during the construction phase, or recovered from future users subsequent to commissioning. Airports and to some extent economics argue in favour of pre-financing – the economic argument being that those who are putting pressure on today's facilities should pay an economic price for the investment in future capacity required to meet their growing demand; airlines on the whole argue that as a matter of principle they should pay only for what they are currently using (IATA 2006b), and express concern that pre-financing gives airports carte blanche to embark on what for them are risk-free investments which may be poorly justified and will be paid for by airlines who may never use them. For example, one reason why Quito Mariscal Sucre is currently the most expensive airport in Latin America is that charges have been raised to finance the new airport being built at Tababela; similarly, egregious above-inflation price rises were authorised by the regulator (i.e., the CAA) for London Heathrow and Gatwick in March 2008 to pay for developments at the two airports which the operator was unlikely to be able to finance for itself because of high gearing. In early 2008 the US DOT proposed potentially far-reaching changes to a 1996 policy on airport charges, one element of which was that airlines operating at congested airports could be subject to charges related to the cost of building new facilities. Around the same time the European Parliament also endorsed the principle of pre-financing. ICAO (2004) does in fact accept that pre-financing might be justifiable, but only under very limited circumstances.

3. *Charging basis* In principle, an airport's costs and revenues each have one of two sources: 'aeronautical activities' connected with airline operations, and 'non-aeronautical activities' connected with retail concessions, parking, and other businesses not directly linked to the movement of aircraft or their payloads. The issue is whether these different categories of costs and revenues should be lumped together into a 'single till' or separated out into 'dual tills'. Historically, the approach has been to adopt a single till (referred to in the United States as the 'residual approach'): all categories of cost are lumped together and non-aeronautical revenues are then subtracted from the total before arriving at a residual sum (comprising net cost and an allowance for profit) which would have to be covered through aeronautical charges; airlines generally prefer this approach, primarily because they view all forms of commercial activity at an airport as dependent on the passenger and visitor streams which they alone create but also because it avoids the knotty problem of allocating costs and revenues to different 'tills'. Airports, on the other hand, increasingly argue for a dual till (referred to in the United States as the 'compensatory approach') on the basis that their retail expertise is primarily responsible for the generation of non-aeronautical revenues – which should therefore be ring-fenced rather than used to subsidise aeronautical charges. In early 2008 the European Parliament accepted the dual-till approach as a legitimate alternative.

4. *The need for regulation* Since the UK government privatised the former British Airports Authority over two decades ago a growing number of airports around the world have either been sold outright to the private sector or been opened to private investment and/or management by way of long-term concessions. Whilst it would take a true iconoclast (or somebody who has recently had the opportunity to compare London Heathrow and Singapore Changi) to argue that privatisation is bad, it is a trend which has nonetheless posed two problems for airlines. First, governments have not been above raising charges to 'fatten' a state-owned airport operator for full or partial privatisation, as happened at Paris CDG ahead of the initial public offering by Aéroports de Paris (ADP); other techniques with a similar purpose include revaluing an airport's asset base upwards to provide a higher charging basis for cost recovery, inflating the airport's projected cost of capital, and moving to a dual till approach. Second, the private sector monopolies granted to certain airports (e.g., Auckland) and groups (e.g., BAA in south-east England and central Scotland) require the oversight of strong regulators, but too often what has happened is that a passive regulatory regime has imposed few constraints (e.g., New Zealand, until

changes were introduced in 2007) or an active regime has been distorted by regulatory capture – an example, as airlines see it, being the 'capture' of the UK's CAA by BAA. Several Latin American airports, notably in Argentina and Mexico, have been handed to the private sector under poorly structured concession agreements which leave unregulated concessionaires free to earn monopoly profits.

On the other hand, unnecessary regulation can create its own burdens. At the time of writing the European Commission is considering submissions in respect of a draft directive on airport charges which would, if implemented in its present form, impose a regulatory structure – of as yet unclear efficacy – on airports processing more than 5 million passengers per annum or 15 per cent of their country's national traffic. Some of the airports that would be ensnared are regional and secondary facilities which compete actively against each other for LFA services and do not need regulation – unlike monopoly hubs and systems such as ADP and BAA. In addition to being too broad in scope, the proposal as it stands is likely to be ineffective insofar as it calls for transparency and EU-wide consistency in calculating charges, but imposes neither price regulation nor a requirement to justify prices.

Whilst many airlines at first welcomed airport privatisation as a further step towards a fully liberalised and privatised air transport industry, most would now say that what matters is not who owns the airports they serve but whether those airports are: efficient and effective in delivering services that customers need; transparent with their cost and revenue data; willing to consult openly about future infrastructure requirements; non-discriminatory as between users; and – where a surrogate for competition is required by local circumstances – effectively supervised by a truly independent regulator who is willing to eliminate monopoly pricing and, by avoiding a simple cost-plus pricing regime, to incentivise the airport operator to improve its cost-effectiveness and justify investments.

The following additional points are also important to a discussion of airport charges:

- On the whole it is fair to say that landing charges bear little relation to the true cost of each operation; the norm is some variant of average cost pricing, with aircraft weight the usual charging unit. Certainly, few airports practice peak-hour pricing to reflect the greater burden placed on infrastructure by airlines using them at such times and so contributing to congestion. Airports in around a dozen countries do use congestion (or peak) pricing, however; in the United States, Boston Logan has had a scheme for many years, but its implementation has been successfully challenged in the courts. The early 2008 DOT proposal mentioned above moved in the direction of congestion pricing by suggesting that charges per aircraft movement could be levied in addition to existing weight-based charges, and that charging within multi-airport systems could legitimately be designed to move demand away from congested facilities towards others that are less constrained. Clearly an attempt to get airlines to shift schedules from peak periods at congested airports and to use larger aircraft for peak departures, the proposal was greeted unenthusiastically by both ATA and IATA – not least because of its potentially negative implications for hub-and-spoke operations.

  The problem with congestion pricing from a network carrier's point of view is that the nature of hubbing makes it impossible to shift a significant share of output to off-peak periods in response to the economic signal being delivered;

in short-haul point-to-point business markets where demand is driven in large part by the rhythm of the business day, peak pricing is unlikely to have an impact unless the penalty is very large and is fully passed through to customers – and even then the scale of the impact is unlikely to be significant set against the scale of peak congestion at the airports concerned. More likely, any pass-through of costs from airlines to customers will not be market-specific – so the effect of congestion pricing may be to transfer money from airline customers generally to congested airports, but not to influence demand at those facilities. The fact that airlines stand as a buffer between the party levying the congestion charge (i.e., the airport) and the party making the purchase decision (i.e., the traveller) makes congestion pricing a less effective model for airports than for other facilities where these two parties come into direct contact – such as toll roads and cinemas (two examples frequently cited by proponents of airport congestion charging).

- Airport fees represent a higher proportion of costs on a short-haul than a long-haul flight.
- Major carriers in the United States own or hold long-term leases on a considerable amount of the gate and terminal space they use, particularly at their hubs and focus cities. Airport charges there accordingly relate to a greater extent to the use of runways and taxiways than is the case elsewhere in the world, where charges for the use of terminals and gates can be significant. On the other hand, US majors intent on owning terminals have to raise substantial sums to finance this capital expenditure (often in conjunction with revenue bonds issued by the airport authority). Another side-effect of this structure is that through majority-in-interest clauses in their lease agreements US majors sometimes have a significant influence on whether and on what terms potential competitors can gain access to existing infrastructure and on whether or not airports can expand to accommodate potential competitors.
- Outside the United States and Europe, explicit service-level guarantees are seldom part of an airport–airline relationship. Airlines generally have little control over the quality of service they and their passengers receive from airport operators, particularly where there is a monopoly ground-handling company.

The management of airport charges   Exercising some degree of management control over airport charges can range from frustratingly difficult to downright impossible, notably where a network carrier comes up against a single facility or group monopolising access to a major destination. Several LFAs gain at least some of their cost advantage over network carriers by flying, wherever possible, to secondary airports that charge lower fees and are in many cases sufficiently keen to attract business that they offer competitive long-term deals. Indeed, at a number of previously underserved secondary and regional airports the relationship between airline and airport has been fundamentally reversed by the advent and attitudes of LFAs: rather than the airport being a supplier of infrastructure to an airline which is a captive customer, the airline has become a supplier of revenue-generating passengers to the airport. Airports in this position are in effect bidding against each other for a share in the capacity of LFAs' fleets. (These airports also have fewer congestion problems than major hubs, contributing to lower taxi and holding delays and to faster turnaround times.)

More generally, IATA has been proactive in confronting the most onerous airport charging regimes. (Its views on the need for economic regulation of airports and ANSPs and the shape that regulation should take can be found in the briefing paper *Economic Regulation*, available at http://www.iata.org/economics.)

Ground-Handling

The landside and airside handling of passengers, baggage, and cargo and the handling of aircraft on the ramp are labour-intensive processes which many airlines now outsource at stations away from their main base(s). Despite the trend towards outsourcing and also a certain amount of consolidation around suppliers such as Swissport, Servisair, and Menzies, this nonetheless remains a fragmented industry at a global level.

In respect of both airside and landside operations, airlines face broadly two situations:

1. *No choice* At many airports outside North America and the EU ground-handling has historically been a monopoly in the hands of the airport authority, its sole concessionaire or the national carrier. This situation, which is still widespread, is sometimes associated with opaque linkages between pricing and costs, the inability of airlines to select which services in a bundle they wish to purchase, and perhaps with inferior quality. It is difficult for a carrier to control the quality of its ground product under these circumstances, and this may affect either or both operational performance (e.g., baggage reclaim time below specifications) or brand image (e.g., poor attitudes on the part of the agent's customer service personnel).
2. *Choice* Where a choice exists, the outsourcing menu might include independent handlers and also airlines (perhaps including the national airline or other locally dominant carrier) whose scale of operations at the airport concerned is enough to justify an in-house handling operation with capacity for third-party sales. If instead a carrier wants to self-handle, it will need sufficient scale and also access to facilities. Many airports that allow competitive ground-handling nonetheless limit the number of providers, particularly airside, for practical reasons; Article 6 of EU Directive 96/97, for example, allows provision of specified services to be limited to two providers under defined circumstances. Finally, choice might exist in respect of some activities (e.g., line maintenance or catering) but not others (e.g., fuel supply or customer services).

A final point in this category is that ground-damage to aircraft costs airlines around $4 billion each year. Much of this is eventually recovered from insurers, but the cost inevitably feeds through into premiums. The IATA Safety Audit for Ground Operations (ISAGO), an initiative modelled on the IATA Operational Safety Audit (IOSA) introduced for airlines in 2003, was established in 2007 with a mandate that includes looking into ways of reducing ground damage.

ATS Charges

Air traffic management (ATM) involves three primary tasks:

1. Airspace design and management: this encompasses the structuring of airspace blocks, the design of route networks, and the management of traffic flows within the structure. The primary cost impact is felt through inefficient routings and flight delays, which will be considered below.
2. Infrastructure development: an important issue is, again, whether investments should be pre-financed by incorporating their costs into current charges.

3.   Air traffic services: these comprise both advisory services and ATC services en route, in terminal areas, and in the immediate proximity of airports (charges for the latter sometimes being incorporated into airport landing fees). They rely on ground and airborne infrastructures to support CNS capabilities. Air traffic services (ATS) are the subject of this subsection.

The following generalisations apply:

* With the major exception of the United States, ATS charges are generally recovered through user fees. Because the US National Airspace System is funded by various excise taxes, carriers there feel the impact of ATS charges on the revenue side of their income statements – in the form of reduced revenues to the extent that taxes are absorbed, or reduced demand to the extent that they are passed through into prices. In Europe and elsewhere user charges show up as DOCs and so contribute to some of the higher operating costs typical of many European airlines.
* Those countries that do charge fees, which include the vast majority of states, generally use distance flown, aircraft maximum take-off weight (MTOW) or a formula including the two – although a few apply uniform fees instead. Some grant discounts in respect of domestic flights and also flights that originate or terminate in the country.
* In the absence of consultation, airlines can find themselves confronted with charges keyed-off an ATS cost base over which they have no say. Put crudely, monopoly ANSPs can decide what to spend and then set about recovering costs from the airlines. This was brought home when traffic in 2002 fell below projections and led several European ANSPs to impose stiff (i.e., 20 per cent or more) fee increases on remaining movements in order to achieve their cost recovery objectives. Similarly, there is little incentive for traditionally structured (i.e., government-operated) ANSPs to improve efficiency if the costs of inefficiency can simply be passed on to customers; participants in SESAR have estimated that systemic inefficiencies in Europe cost as much as €3.4 billion per annum.
* ICAO has in the past rejected LRMC pricing as a basis for ATS (and airport) charges. Its policy is that costs should be established by dividing estimated charging units (i.e., aircraft transits, adjusted for MTOW, distance covered, services used, etc.) into the cost base – therefore charging on the basis of average cost rather than costs actually imposed by particular users (notably peak-period users). Policy recommendations have since become more flexible, with 'economic pricing principles' (i.e., LRMC) acceptable subject to cost transparency and consultation with users (ICAO 2000).
* Regional airlines in Europe are disproportionately affected by price increases because of the greater share of ATS charges on a short flight relative to a medium- or long-haul sector. The threat they face was evident in the Eurocontrol proposal put forward in 2000 to move from a weight- and distance-based charging mechanism to a flat-rate fee structure – something that would not only have increased absolute costs for small aircraft by up to 80 per cent, but would have left them paying very much higher per-seat charges than larger aircraft.
* There is growth, albeit slow, in the number of ANSPs which are no longer government departments but have instead been corporatised within the public sector

or privatised. In principle this trend should reinforce a transition to commercial costing and pricing. Experiences in those few countries where the delivery of air traffic services has been commercialised have indeed been positive for airlines in the sense that fees have often been reduced and service quality has improved (mbs 2006).

- There are areas of the world where little correlation exists between fees charged and the quality of service. In some states, for example, high fees accompany a poor air navigation infrastructure. Even where the quality of the infrastructure is high, as in Western Europe, service actually received by airlines is impaired by widespread peak delays.

Delays

Close to a quarter of flights in Europe and a third in the United States are delayed (Airbus 2008). Delays and suboptimal flight profiles add several billion dollars to airline operating costs each year as a result of: non-productive fuel consumption; non-productive labour costs; non-productive flight-hour-based maintenance costs; and the handling, accommodating, and reaccommodating of affected passengers. Irregular operations caused by serious delays have a knock-on effect which undermines productivity as aircraft, gates, equipment, people, and other resources have to be reassigned from what, presumably, was a near-optimal schedule. Also, some of a fleet's apparently high utilisation figure might represent wasted time that could have been used on additional productive revenue service; in the worst case, service delays can mean that an airline needs more aircraft to perform a given schedule than would otherwise be the case.

In 2005 Lufthansa's passenger fleet spent the equivalent of 420 days flying holding patterns, burning enough fuel to take 300,000 passengers from Frankfurt to Mallorca and back. The ATA estimates that delays cost US airlines $8.1 billion in 2007, whilst the Joint Economic Committee of Congress put the figure at $19 billion; the latter source has estimated the wider cost of delays to the US economy at $41 billion. In Europe, the continent's now environmentally conscious politicians are presiding over an airspace structure which causes 12 million tonnes of wasted CO_2 to be emitted each year at a cost to airlines of some €3.3 billion. Solutions lie in:

- exploiting CNS technology advances to move away from rigid ground-based systems and procedures to flexible, user-driven satellite-based systems;
- restructuring airspace;
- increasing airport capacity.

The first of these is doable but expensive and raises unresolved funding issues (e.g., the US NextGen programme). The second is easier in some parts of the world than others but is never entirely straightforward; in the United States the New York/New Jersey/Philadelphia Metropolitan Area Airspace Redesign project has faced a certain amount of local resistance, whilst in Europe opposition related both to sovereignty and job protection stands in the way of progress; in China, airspace is still largely under military control. The third has long been beset by environmental objections in North America and Europe – objections which can only be expected to intensify.

Nonetheless, the story is not one of unremitting gloom. IATA has been working successfully with a number of ANSPs to optimise long-haul routes and the FAA is actively supporting introduction of RNAV SIDs and RNP approaches; Delta is saving around $30 million each year by using RNAV tracks out of Atlanta, whilst American's saving at DFW has been closer to $50 million. Vertical separation minima have been successfully reduced in several regions. Airspace capacity may well be finite, but technology exists or is on the horizon which can assist in using what is available much more intensively than many of today's half-century-old procedures and systems permit; what is needed is sufficient political will to fund, develop, and deploy it – and more airport capacity so that an increasingly efficient airspace system does not just become a quicker way of getting to a stack. (Cook [2007a] provides rigorous coverage of delay and its costs.)

V. Cost Drivers and Their Management: The Internal Operating System

The design of an airline's operating system should be driven by two factors:

1. *Strategic position* Whatever strategic description of itself an airline has chosen – as an independent regional, a franchised regional, a low-fare carrier, a point-to-point premium operator, a network carrier, a charter airline, an all-cargo airline serving line-haul markets, or an all-cargo carrier offering value-added services, for example – this position should drive design of the operating system.
2. *Market position* Whether an airline has a single service concept (e.g., Southwest) or a multi-service portfolio (e.g., American), the operating system must be configured to deliver each type of service to targeted customers in a manner consistent with the desired positioning of that service relative to competitors in customers' perceptions. This must be done as efficiently as possible given what it takes to be effective in targeted markets (i.e., to at least match customers' expectations).

This section of the chapter will look at the cost implications of: service design; process design; labour; the fleet; maintenance; productivity; and finally scale.

SERVICE DESIGN

The services offered by a carrier reflect its choice of strategic and market position and are a critical driver of unit costs. In other words, an airline's unit costs are strongly influenced by the characteristics of the demand it chooses to serve. This is a broad field that is fully covered in Holloway (2002). For the purpose of the present chapter, the following important variables can be highlighted: network and schedule; scope; seating density; service level; and the balance between load factors and seat accessibility.

Network And Schedule

Because capacity costs have such a significant impact on TOC, network design and the schedule flown are absolutely top-tier cost drivers. In deregulated or liberalised environments both need to respond to the requirements of the markets and market segments being targeted. The following paragraphs consider cost implications of: hub-and-spoke networks; stage-lengths; traffic density; frequency; and aircraft size.

Hub-and-spoke networks   Whilst these are efficient systems for gathering traffic from multiple origins and distributing them to multiple destinations, they can bring heavy fixed costs associated with the facilities, equipment, and staff required to handle the artificial peaks created by each wave of incoming and outgoing flights. The larger the number of daily waves a hub can serve, the more output is produced over which to spread these fixed costs and the lower will be the cost per ASM and enplaned passenger imposed by hub infrastructure. (Chapter 6 will look in greater detail at the costs and benefits associated with hub-and-spoke systems.)

Stage-lengths   The further a given type is flown, the higher will be its trip cost because fuel, airway, and possibly crew costs will increase. On the other hand, unit cost (i.e., cost per ASM or ATM) will be lower because more output is being generated over which to spread fixed costs (such as depreciation, insurance, and lease rentals), and because the high variable costs associated with take-off fuel, airport charges, and cycle-driven maintenance are also being spread over that larger output of ASMs. Other things being equal it costs less to produce ASMs or ATMs with a given type as average stage-length increases. There are, however, two caveats:

1. Most aircraft have an optimal range at which unit cost will be minimised.
2. At some point along its payload-range envelope every aircraft has to begin shedding payload in order to boost range – with potentially negative revenue implications.

Nonetheless, it is broadly fair to generalise that longer average stage-lengths are usually associated with higher aircraft and crew utilisation, lower fuel-burn per block-hour, and lower (cycle-driven) maintenance costs (Williams 2002). A corollary of this is that an airline's unit cost is just an average: a US network carrier's system CASM reflects its very different domestic, Atlantic, Pacific, and Latin America subsystem CASMs, for example. Each subsystem CASM is in turn the result of averaging costs across the subfleets used to serve the region concerned, as well as some perhaps arbitrary cost allocations between regions. In fact, each subfleet, fleet, and airline has a *cost curve*: with CASM plotted on the vertical axis and stage-length on the horizontal, a cost curve falls from left to right – sharply at first, then flattening. It falls because, as just noted, fixed costs can be spread over a greater output of ASMs as stage-length increases. Unit cost comparisons between carriers should therefore be approached with caution where they have not been adjusted for the different average stage-lengths (and fleet compositions) of the airlines concerned.

Traffic density   This refers to the volume of traffic carried on a route or a network over a given time period. Economies of density are present when unit cost falls as the volume of traffic carried within an unchanged network rises (Graham and Kaplan 1982; Caves *et al.* 1984; Bailey *et al.* 1985). Density can increase on a route for one or more reasons:

1. It might grow naturally over time in response to economic and/or demographic developments in the markets served by the route.
2. It can be generated by airlines exploiting price-elasticity by offering low fares and stimulating both new customers and additional sales to existing customers.

3. It can be affected by airlines' network design decisions. In particular, by channelling traffic from a spoke city onto a single route into a hub irrespective of ultimate onward destination an airline ensures that the route is much more dense than any non-stop routes from the spoke city to each of those destinations would have been. This allows the carrier to operate larger aircraft with lower unit costs than the spoke city could otherwise have supported (and/or offer more frequencies down the spoke). In multi-hub systems serving double-connect markets, higher traffic densities on inter-hub routes can also support larger aircraft than would otherwise be the case. Where hub-and-spoke network designs are used to reroute traffic flows, economies of density can be traced to unit cost reductions that arise from carrying unchanged traffic volumes over a more geographically constrained network which nonetheless serves the same number of points as before.

As density increases on a route, airlines have broadly four choices:

- *Accept higher load factors* Fine in the short run because it leads to a lower cost per passenger, as unchanged aircraft-mile and trip costs are spread over more passengers, ultimately this will lead to unacceptable levels of demand spill. Although capacity costs are unchanged, traffic costs will rise so there might be upward pressure on unit costs – hopefully more than offset by higher revenue.
- *Add more seats to existing aircraft* This lowers cost per passenger and also unit cost, because each flight is now generating more RPMs and ASMs off substantially the same trip cost. It does, however, degrade the inflight product.
- *Use a larger aircraft on some or all departures* This should reduce unit costs but will probably increase trip costs, and must always be subject to the caveat that average loads achieved on existing aircraft must be above the break-even load for the larger aircraft given yields on the route concerned.
- *Add frequencies* This generates incremental trip costs but improves the quality of service from the perspective of certain segments of the market, notably business travellers, and so might lead to firmer yields. Ultimately, the S-curve effect described in Chapter 4 could result in higher market share such that both the existing and additional departures can be operated by larger aircraft; in this case not only will marketing benefits accrue, but the unit cost declines associated with economies of density will also have been exploited.

Economies of density can be an important competitive weapon where it is less expensive for an incumbent to add traffic to an existing route than it is for a new entrant to carry traffic on the same route – say, because the challenger has a less established market profile and so must operate a smaller aircraft (with higher unit costs).

The primary source of economies of density is aircraft size. Large aircraft generally have lower seat-mile costs than smaller types of a similar technological generation; major improvements in airframe design and powerplant efficiency from one generation to the next can, however, break this relationship. Unit costs fall as aircraft get larger because increases in trip costs and aircraft size tend not to bear a linear relationship – the result being that trip costs increase more slowly than the output of ASMs when a larger aircraft is assigned to a given route. There are several reasons for this: large aircraft do not necessarily burn more fuel per seat-mile than smaller aircraft; they do not require additional pilots; neither, given a specific number of engines and systems, do they demand proportionately more maintenance; and up to a point, they can also be both structurally and aerodynamically more efficient.

Economies of density should not be confused with economies of network size. Whereas economies of density exist when unit cost declines can be attributed to increased volumes of traffic being carried within an unchanged network (i.e., with points served held constant), economies of network size exist where unit cost declines as the number of points served increases (i.e., as the network expands geographically). Several academic studies have cast doubt on the existence of economies of network size (e.g., Brueckner and Spiller 1994), whilst others suggest that returns to network size may be fairly constant depending on network design (Button and Stough 2000). In a study of Canadian airline data, however, Basso and Jara-Diaz (2005) identified substantial returns to spatial scope and suggested that these economies might be of particular benefit when expanding smaller networks. Beyond doubt is that returns to increasing *density* are often considerable.

Frequency   Deciding how to serve a route requires an airline to make choices with respect to aircraft capacity and frequency – notably whether to offer a small number of flights with a larger aircraft or greater frequency with a smaller aircraft: as we have seen, the larger aircraft will probably have higher trip costs but lower unit costs, because fixed costs are being spread over the larger volume of ASMs its size allows it to produce on any given flight-leg; the smaller aircraft will probably have lower trip costs but higher unit costs. (This assumes the aircraft are from the same technological generation.) High frequencies are therefore generally more expensive to produce than low frequencies, all other things being equal. If it is assumed that a route can support four daily rotations with a 90-seater or two with a 180-seater, the former will be more expensive to schedule. Four rotations may appeal to the business segment, of course, so the firmer yields they provide could more than compensate for the higher unit costs of this option – something seen on many routes in North America and Europe, where average aircraft size trended downwards in the years immediately following deregulation.

In principle, the market should make the decision. In practice, the presence or absence of competition and the composition of a particular airline's fleet will also be influential – as may the terms of relevant bilateral ASAs if the route concerned is international and still subject to commercial regulation.

Aircraft size   Two observations can be made in respect of the deployment of large aircraft. First, they can only be used efficiently when the combination of traffic density and product-driven frequency decisions supports their assignment. Second, it is sometimes the case that the larger an aircraft the fewer the routes in a given network on which it can be deployed, and this might harm utilisation; should this happen, hourly charges for fixed ownership costs (e.g., depreciation, insurance, etc.) will be higher than might otherwise have been the case, with the result that any unit cost advantage these aircraft may have over smaller but better utilised alternatives on the routes they do fly will be eroded. Third, the generally higher trip costs of larger aircraft raise the commercial risk of deploying them; their lower seat-mile costs are irrelevant unless enough of those seats can be sold to get above break-even load factor given yields available in the markets concerned.

Scope

Looking at internal operations, we are in the process of considering the cost implications of service design; alongside network and schedule, another consideration under this heading is competitive scope – a topic first introduced in Chapter 1. Economies of competitive scope are attributable to one or more shared inputs making joint production of different types of output by a single carrier cheaper than the production of each by separate carriers. They can arise from the sharing of production costs (as when passengers and cargo are carried on the same aircraft) or the sharing of marketing costs (as when general corporate advertising stimulates demand in multiple markets); they can be captured within an organization (as when a carrier extends its network using its own fleet and other resources) or through a market transaction (such as franchising or code-sharing).

Economists in fact argue about the existence of economies of scope. Some consider them to be nothing more than a facet of intra-organizational linkages (e.g., Porter 1985, p. 328). Others believe them to be the very reason why multi-product firms exist, arguing that if single-product firms were more efficient producers there would not be any multi-product firms (Panzar and Willig 1981); indeed, they lie at the heart of Prahalad and Hamel's (1990) popular concept of 'core competencies'. Spitz (1998, p. 492) notes that many research studies point to economies of scope, along with economies of density, as the principal forces driving adoption of hub-and-spoke networks.

Competitive or horizontal (as opposed to vertical) scope can be divided into two elements, as we saw in Chapter 1.

1. *Geographic scope* Economies of scope may be evident when unit costs decline as the number of markets (but not necessarily the number of points) being served by an airline increases. For example, by adding a new point-to-point service between two stations already served on other routes, or by fine-tuning a schedule to facilitate an increase in saleable connections over a hub, it might be possible for a carrier to add new markets and new traffic without necessarily increasing fixed station and ground costs. Even if a route is added by introducing a new station to the network, it will usually be cheaper in unit cost terms for a carrier already serving one end of the route – particularly a hub – to introduce service than for a greenfield start-up. The fixed costs of operating a hub are spread across all the markets served over that hub – so the more markets it supports within its existing capacity range, the lower will be the unit costs of output channelled through it.

    To take a broader example, an airline flying only a single route between Tucson and Cincinnati would be constrained by the limited amount of local traffic: it would at best be able to offer only a low-frequency service using relatively small aircraft. Its unit costs would also be adversely affected by the fact that fixed station expenses at Tucson and Cincinnati would be spread over just the relatively small volume of output required to support local traffic. If, however, the route were operated by an airline that hubs at Cincinnati, the Tucson spoke would attract not only local traffic but passengers travelling beyond Cincinnati to other domestic and international points on that carrier's network. This additional traffic would support some combination of larger aircraft and higher frequencies than local traffic alone could justify. The hubbing airline therefore has access to unit cost advantages attributable both to economies of density (gained by operating larger aircraft) and economies of scope (gained by producing on each Tucson–Cincinnati flight output that can be sold as seats in many different markets connecting Tucson with points beyond Cincinnati). Fixed station costs at Tucson and Cincinnati would also be spread across a higher volume of output over a wider range of markets than the single-route operator has available to it.

2. *Product scope* Economies of scope can arise when it is cheaper to produce different types of output on a single aircraft than to produce each type in different aircraft. Most obviously, output produced in first, business, and economy/coach class cabins on the same departure can share fixed costs – and, incidentally, benefit from the economies of density derived from operating a larger aircraft than would be required to serve just one type of traffic on a given route. The same argument might also be applied to different 'fare products' in the same cabin – that is, passengers in the same cabin travelling on different fares and subject to different booking and travel restrictions. However, whilst it may be cheaper in unit cost terms to offer separate products within the same operating system than to offer each separately, this is not inevitably the case; some, although not all, low-fare and charter airlines sell a single cabin and a limited range of fare-products. Similarly, airlines offering single-aircraft premium-only services have decided that yields will be sufficient to compensate for economies of scope (and density) forgone by offering just one product per departure. Much depends on the choice of strategic position and the particular type of value an airline wants to offer to its customers.

Economies of scope can also be identified in respect of marketing (especially marketing communications, promotions, and distribution) and in various operational support functions such as scheduling (Fitzroy *et al.* 1998). The advantage might be reinforced by the strength a large network and product range add to loyalty programmes (e.g., FFPs, corporate rebates, and overrides). However, there remains an unresolved debate about whether we are dealing in some of these areas with economies of scope (evident when unit costs fall as a result of different types of output being jointly produced) or economies of scale (evident when unit costs fall as a result of aggregate output increasing) – a debate that perhaps excites economists more than practitioners.

As with economies of density, a critical point to keep in mind is that economies of scope favour incumbents over new entrants and other small challengers: in essence, this is because the larger an airline's product range and network the greater are its opportunities to benefit from the fact that aggregating separable costs attributable to multiple products with the common costs attributable to producing them together can sometimes lead to a lower unit cost than would be the case were each output produced separately.

Other Aspects Of Service Design

Network and schedule (together with associated choice of aircraft) are, as already noted, the critical cost drivers flowing from service design. There are other important drivers, however. Simply put, premium products cost more to produce than basic economy/coach products; clearly, it must be the intention that the revenue per ASM (i.e., unit revenue or RASM) earned from these products will more than compensate for their higher unit costs.

Seating density The more seats there are on a given aircraft flying a given leg, the more ASMs will be produced over which to spread fixed costs – and so the lower unit costs will be. The most obvious example of high seating density/low seat-pitch being used to drive down unit costs can be found amongst charter carriers and LFAs. For example, the fact that a B757-200 operated in high-density charter configuration might have 230 seats against 180 in two-class scheduled service immediately reduces the seat-mile costs of the charter carrier by over one-fifth compared to a scheduled operator (assuming constant trip costs); this is an extreme comparison between alternatives likely in practice to be pitched at different market segments, but it exemplifies the point. Taking another somewhat extreme example, Thai International had to withdraw ultra-long-haul A340-500 non-stops between Bangkok and the United States in 2006 because it was unable to generate sufficient traffic willing to pay the non-stop premium necessary to operate economically what is a heavy aircraft relative to the chosen low-density seating configuration. Box 5.5 takes a closer look at seating density.

Seating density is in fact part of a multifaceted service design decision encompassing: how many onboard classes of service to offer; what the appropriate seat pitch and aisle width is for each class given market conditions; galley requirements (number, size, and functionality) – driven by the catering to be provided, the extent to which catering supplies have to be carried outbound for return flights, and the style of service (which could, for example, affect the number of trolleys required); lavatory numbers – driven by the desired passenger/lavatory ratio; and storage requirements – driven by the need to provide closets

---

Box 5.5: Seating Density

Seating density is a critical economic variable.

- Increasing it: reduces passenger comfort and may adversely affect yields if high-yield passengers are lost; takes pressure off load factors (perhaps temporarily); reduces demand spill (perhaps temporarily); raises aircraft seat-mile productivity; and reduces unit cost.
- Reducing it: improves passenger comfort and so may boost yield (although this was apparently not American's experience when it last removed seats from coach); puts upward pressure on load factors if demand is already strong (and so is best done in conjunction with either cyclically weak demand or a fare increase keyed off a product upgrade sufficient to sustain a price premium); could increase spill; reduces aircraft seat-mile productivity; and raises unit cost.

In both cases, the net revenue impact will depend upon how changes in unit revenue (RASM) and unit cost (CASM) balance out under the particular circumstances. We can nonetheless generalise that a carrier positioning itself as an LFA needs high seating density, and if seats are removed by any airline higher yields will be needed from the remaining seats to cover forgone revenue (unless load factors are currently so weak that the lost output has little impact on demand spill). For example, removing a single row of 10-across seats from a B747-400 to give remaining coach/economy passengers no more than an inch of extra pitch may jeopardise several million dollars in revenue: the exact figure will vary, but if it is assumed that an average economy/coach load factor of 80 per cent would put eight of these seats into the air with passengers in them for, say, 5000 hours a year (i.e., around 250 return trips between the US West Coast and Europe) it can be seen how the figures mount.

Scheduled airlines in particular face difficult compromises between product specification and production cost when deciding on cabin configuration. This is an area that lies at the interface between cost and revenue streams; it has to be driven by the airline's service concept, set within the context of prevailing economic and competitive conditions. Thus, a typical two-class A330-300 would have around 330–335 seats, whilst long-haul LFA AirAsia X has configured for 396; a 396-seat aircraft generates 20 per cent more ASMs per trip than a 330-seat aircraft – and 16.6 per cent lower unit costs (assuming the same trip costs, which is unlikely given the different business models involved).

in premium cabins. Within upper limits established by type certification and lower limits imposed by aircraft economics in the context of yields in the market(s) to be served, it is for airline product planners to decide how to allocate available cabin floorspace; their decisions will certainly have unit cost implications and will probably also affect yields.

Service level   The key cost driver in this category is cabin crew ratios. Again, product planners have to establish a level between the legal minimum number of crew required per aircraft type and the economically viable maximum. Most LFAs stick to the legal minimum number. Some carriers use variable staffing formulas to determine the number of flight attendants required for each flight, with an extra crew member being scheduled once passenger numbers rise above a particular threshold. Fine in principle, this can cause service quality problems – particularly on mainline narrowbodies which anyway have relatively small crews. First, passengers travelling on a flight carrying a load just below the threshold may experience markedly poorer inflight service than others travelling on the same type carrying a load just above the threshold. Second, a flight booked at just below the threshold close to departure which has more go-shows than no-shows may well depart with one fewer flight attendants than passenger numbers actually require (given the airline's service specification). Finally, a variable staffing formula will always be difficult to implement when crews are working complex integrations for a large network carrier.

Other service attributes   Number of check-in desks and their staffing levels, number of gate staff, lounge access, catering, IFE availability and content, and the entire range of other attributes that might be made available as part of a particular service package all influence output costs. What is appropriate depends upon a finely balanced assessment of market requirements, costs, and the revenues that can be earned. Immediately before the post-9/11 cutbacks, American's market positioning and broad product scope led it to spend an average $8.57 per passenger on catering as against most other US network majors in the $4–5 range; Southwest, consistent with its strategic positioning as a low-fare carrier, was spending just 25 cents per passenger.

IFE is a particularly interesting source of costs insofar as not only does the hardware and software have to be maintained and the content purchased, but with weights of several thousand pounds the systems now available for long-haul widebodies carry a considerable life-cycle fuel-burn penalty. Flat-bed seats in long-haul premium cabins are also heavier than their more simple predecessors, largely because of the weight of electric motors. So heavy are the customised premium cabin interiors on some airlines' A340-600s that in 2007 operators were advised to consider limiting cargo payloads in forward holds to counter aerodynamic performance penalties arising from a suboptimal nose-down cruise attitude. Service decisions affecting the economics of an operation in fact go down to details such as how often aircraft are deep-cleaned, how frequently seat cushions are changed, and whether window shades should be removed (as by Ryanair).

Load factor/seat accessibility   Seat accessibility is a measure of the probability that a booking can be made in the desired class on the desired flight at any given point in time before departure. The higher the average load factor on a flight, the lower its seat accessibility is likely to be – certainly close to departure; this important service attribute will be met again in Chapter 9 when revenue management is discussed. Although a significant aspect of service design, seat accessibility is fundamentally a revenue-side issue insofar as it is primarily late-booking, high-yield business travellers who benefit from high levels of seat accessibility. There is, however, a cost impact: low load factors generate lower traffic costs than higher loads on the same aircraft type (something that will probably be of little consolation unless the traffic that *is* being carried is generating high yields to compensate).

Conclusion In Respect Of Service Design

The purpose of service design and development is to create an offer able to satisfy the expectations of targeted customers. The more demanding these customers are, the more expensive delivering service up to their expectations becomes. When one airline has a higher CASM than another this is not *necessarily* because of relative inefficiency: offering high-cost services can be perfectly rational if customers are willing to pay a premium for them. If customers are not in fact willing to pay, then there is indeed a problem – as US network carriers discovered after 9/11. When recession causes corporate clients to trade-down to economy/coach and reduce overall travel activity, carriers whose strategic position leads them to concentrate heavily on this segment may face the challenge of having high product costs to spread over a weak traffic base – with the result that cost per passenger might rise at the very time when yields are already softening.

PROCESS DESIGN

Having looked at service design, this review of the impact internal operations can have on airline costs will next consider process design.

National safety regulations have had a significant impact on the organizational structures of airlines, particularly in respect of flight operations and maintenance activities; US Federal Aviation Regulations, for example, mandate the existence of certain functions and job titles. It is nonetheless generally fair to say that airlines as a whole have been slow to move towards more process-oriented structures, choosing in many cases to retain a traditional pattern of functional 'silos' (Garvin 2000).

The manner in which processes are designed will clearly have an impact on costs. Two important variables in process design are complexity and divergence.

1. *Complexity* is a function of the number of activities involved in a given process. The fewer sequences and activities there are, the lower the complexity of a process.
2. *Divergence* reflects the degree of latitude allowed for the varying of an activity or the reordering of a sequence. The less latitude permitted, the lower the divergence in a process and the greater the level of standardisation (of activities, policies, and procedures, for example).

Airlines need as far as possible to ensure that the complexity and divergence designed into their processes reflect the chosen strategic position and operating strategy. Both should be as low as possible for an LFA; an airline offering premium services might instead want to introduce a higher level of divergence into its front-office (i.e., customer-contact) processes, although both economic feasibility and possible threats to service consistency may act as constraints. However, if we move away from the meta-level of process design and consider what is needed within the context of individual processes, it is clear that *flexibility* – always important – is becoming increasingly critical. The reason for this is that, as noted in Chapter 1, business models are not only now more varied and multifaceted but are subject to almost constant reassessment.

Being constrained by legacy architectures, whether these reflect organizational design or IT infrastructure, is a significant disadvantage. To take just one example, many airlines are in the process of considering or implementing transformational changes in what is perhaps their most critical system: reservations. Legacy systems are expensive to maintain, unsuited to the contemporary online sales environment, ill-equipped to accommodate ancillary selling, and unable to respond rapidly to a marketplace in which service offers might be bundled or unbundled and can change frequently. Middleware grafted onto legacy systems can be an interim solution, but in due course all airlines will have to move to more modern reservations platforms – examples of which include Amadeus' Altea, Unisys' Aircore, and – particularly for LFAs and smaller point-to-point operators – Navitaire's New Skies. The transition will be neither quick nor inexpensive, however, as illustrated by the several years it has taken British Airways to switch to Altea from its legacy in-house system. Neither will it necessarily be trouble-free, as illustrated by WestJet's abortive switch to the Aires system which ended in a substantial write-down in 2007.

Broadly, it is fair to generalise that complexity tends to be expensive wherever it appears; this is not necessarily a problem provided it contributes to desired customer value and is reflected in the revenue stream. It is nevertheless the case that process simplification – that is, the eradication of unjustifiable complexity – has become central to airline cost reduction and management; Box 5.6 looks at IATA's approach.

Box 5.6: Simplifying The Business (STP)

'We are challenging ourselves as an industry to find cost reduction opportunities in our industry's complex processes. While today's consumers expect convenience, they are not willing to pay for the complexity that makes it possible. The answer is in simplifying processes and making the most effective use of technology.' This statement introduces one of IATA's most important current initiatives: Simplifying the Business (http://www.iata.org/whatwedo/simplibiz). The initiative focuses on five core projects in an effort to strip an estimated $6.5 billion of costs out of the international system:

1. E-ticketing: mandatory since 31 May 2008, and saving airlines several hundred million dollars per annum compared with the costs of producing, storing, issuing, and processing paper tickets. (IATA has estimated a $3 billion annual saving based on $9 per ticket, but other estimates are significantly lower.)
2. Common-use self-service (CUSS) kiosks: to reduce the number of manual desk check-ins and also avoid the costs of introducing inefficiently small numbers of single-airline proprietary kiosks away from a particular carrier's main hub(s). IATA estimates that savings of $1 billion per annum could be realised were just 40 per cent of check-ins to migrate to CUSS kiosks (IATA 2007c). By the end of 2007, 85 airports had CUSS kiosks installed.
3. Bar-coded boarding passes (BCBPs): to replace magnetic strips and first generation BCBPs with standardised second generation BCBPs by 2011, thereby allowing passengers to print their own passes and move through airport facilities without staff contact. Around 100 airlines are now doing this. (Some carriers, All Nippon being one, are already going further by sending boarding passes in electronic format to customers' mobile devices.)

4.   Radio frequency identification (RFID) for baggage: to replace bar-coded labels, thereby improving read-rates and so reducing costly manual intervention and lowering the current 1 per cent global mishandling rate.

5.   E-freight: to strip as much paper as possible out of airfreight shipment processes, accelerate customs clearance and handling, and improve the accuracy of messages passed between forwarders and airlines. Pilot programmes were launched in late 2007, involving 6 forwarders and 7 carriers serving 20 routes between Canada, Hong Kong, the Netherlands, Singapore, Sweden, and the United Kingdom; over the next few years these will be deepened (in terms of the percentage of trade covered on each route and the number of document types covered by agreed digital standards) and broadened (in terms of the number of countries and participants involved). IATA believes savings could amount to $1.2 billion per annum were e-freight implemented industry-wide.

In 2008 IATA announced a second-stage STB programme focusing on check-in, baggage acceptance, disrupted operations, boarding, and post-flight processes. Pilot projects in respect of each are intended to develop industry-wide standards.

'Simplification' does not necessarily require the stripping out of all complexity. It is often the case that complexity supports customer choice and brand differentiation. In this case, simplification might involve not the elimination of process complexity, but the use of IT to hide it from customers and service providers – as well as, ideally, minimising its cost.

Each activity in every process has its own particular cost drivers – input prices, productivity, scale, and/or scope (i.e., the ability to share costs with other activities), for example. These need to be identified and managed. Always bearing in mind that costs should be considered not just in an absolute sense but in the context of their contribution to customer value and to revenues, there are four broad approaches that can be taken to paring activity costs (Turney 1991): activity reduction; activity elimination (either absolutely or through outsourcing); activity redesign; and activity sharing (with alliance partners, for example).

One final point: no matter what type of business model is adopted, how well processes are designed, or how efficiently resources are scheduled, things will go wrong. 'Things' in most cases encompass one or more of: maintenance, ground-handling (of passengers and aircraft), weather, airport or airspace congestion, or staffing issues (e.g., sickness or strikes) – all of which lead to passengers, aircraft, crews, and other resources being somewhere they are not scheduled to be or doing something they are not scheduled to be doing. How often an airline is faced with 'irregular operations' (IROPS), how effectively it formulates plans to deal with them, and how efficiently it implements those plans are all important cost drivers.

LABOUR COST

Labour Cost Drivers

There are several variables driving labour costs: staff numbers; salaries and benefits; social costs; the terms of labour contracts; seniority; training policies; and the extent of outsourcing.

Staff numbers   Staff are traditionally looked upon as an airline's most significant 'controllable' cost and are therefore in the firing line when times are hard – as in the early 1990s and, more dramatically, in 2001/2002.

Salaries and benefits   On the whole, airline staff are highly paid in comparison with other workers in their local economies, and pilots in particular account for upwards of 30 per cent of labour costs at some carriers. There are, of course, exceptions to this generalisation – as first officers at some US regionals can attest. It is likely that high levels of demand for pilots and other skilled staff, notably mechanics/engineers, to accommodate substantial growth in the fleet and in employee retirements over the next 20 years will place upward pressure on unit labour costs (i.e., labour cost per ASM or ATM).

Social costs   Employment taxes and/or compulsory employer payments into state social security and pension programmes represent a substantial proportion of total labour costs in some countries, particularly in western Europe. LFAs operating multiple aircraft and crew bases across the continent face particular administrative complexity and in some cases, notably those of Ryanair and easyJet, higher costs than they would face in their home countries. Arguments that subjecting them to local social costs undermines the free flow of capital and labour guaranteed by various EU treaties have been rejected by France's highest court and appear at the time of writing to be likely to be put to rest by EU legislation.

Labour contracts   Most long-established airlines are unionised across all major 'craft' groups. The terms of labour contracts can be critical to airline costs not just in respect of the salaries and benefits they confer, but also in respect of restrictions that they might contain in the following areas:

1. *Work practices* Start-ups and also unionised carriers with broadly cooperative labour groups (e.g., Southwest) often benefit from more job flexibility (i.e., less tightly drawn demarcation of task responsibilities) and fewer restrictive work practices than some of their competitors have to contend with. This feeds through to relatively high productivity levels per dollar of human resource expenditure. For example, having flight attendants prepared to undertake light cabin cleaning or dispatchers prepared to help load baggage can contribute to faster turnarounds and, across a large system over a significant span of time, help boost aircraft utilisation.

2. *Scope clauses* The expression 'scope clause' can be applied to any union contract that restricts or prohibits the contracting-out of union-controlled work (Jenks 2001). However, it is an expression most commonly used in respect of pilots' contracts. To protect highly paid jobs, mainline pilots' contracts at most US majors and some European network carriers impose a variety of limits on the number, size, and/or output of regional aircraft operated under codeshares by these carriers' regional partners or subsidiaries. Some clauses restrict either the ASMs or the block-hours that can be flown by regionals under the major's code to a fixed percentage of the ASM or block-hour figures generated by the major, or the major and its regionals combined, over a defined period of time.

    The problem from a major's perspective is that the seat-mile economics of regional aircraft can often support only the relatively low flight-crew salaries paid by regional carriers, and not the higher salaries of mainline pilots. This may leave a major with an unpalatable choice between accepting the limit on regional fleet expansion imposed by a scope clause or staffing any expansion with expensive mainline pilots.

Scope clauses have had a profound effect on network and fleet management in the United States, and have affected the design of regional jets sized around the 70–75 seat range where many scope limitations kick in. Scope clauses have also restricted Lufthansa's deployment of aircraft having more than 70 seats for operation under the carrier's brand by regional affiliates. (The terms of its agreement with pilots' union Vereinigung Cockpit appear also to have pushed the carrier towards joint ventures, either as an alternative or a supplement to Lufthansa-crewed mainline operations, in certain cargo and leisure markets.) However, US network restructuring in the aftermath of 9/11 – specifically, the passing of thin mainline routes to regional operators – put pressure on the sustainability of scope clauses in their established form. Most US majors have been successful in negotiating relaxations, and it seems likely that scope clauses will eventually disappear – perhaps in the depths of the next recession.

Seniority   Long-established carriers often have more senior and more highly paid workforces than younger competitors – a problem that particularly afflicted TWA, for example. More generally, one of the side-effects of lay-offs and furloughs is that to the extent that it is junior staff who are affected first, *average* labour cost per head can actually rise; this has to be offset by productivity growth amongst those who remain. On the other hand, early retirements can lower *average* labour costs. What happens to *unit* labour cost as a result of changes to staff numbers will clearly depend upon the relationship between the number of employees affected, the seniority of those employees, the salary levels of retained employees, and the output produced at the revised staffing level.

As their workforces age and gain seniority, low-fare start-ups can find it difficult to sustain low pay levels beyond the initial phase of operations without adversely affecting staff morale; in the long term, a low-fare business model demands high staff productivity more than it requires substandard pay. Failure to take account of this truism lay at the root of many of America West's problems before its 'merger' with US Airways.

Training   An airline's approach to non-mandatory training – its accessibility, scope, content and frequency, for example – will in part be determined by the nature of its service concept(s). A carrier offering differentiated service, particularly one with a high-quality brand image, will spend more per head on customer service training than a low-fare carrier.

Extent of outsourcing   An airline which outsources functions such as MRO, ground-handling or catering in effect transfers the labour costs into a different accounting line item. This complicates labour cost comparisons with more vertically integrated carriers.

Other considerations   The share of labour cost in TOC varies not only in response to the factors listed above, however, but also in response to the sizes of other expenditure line items – notably fuel. Also, lower airport and airway costs in the United States than elsewhere tend to boost the share of labour costs in US airline TOCs. Finally, the strength of a non-US airline's home currency (in which most labour expenses are met) relative to the US dollar (in which fuel, lease rentals, and sometimes airport charges are denominated) can also distort relativities, as Japanese and eurozone carriers have found during periods of yen and euro strength against the dollar.

Labour Cost Management

Often cited, somewhat simplistically, as any airline's largest 'controllable cost' – overlooking the impact of unionisation in many countries, the importance to customer service of strong staff morale, and the fact that it is frequently the youngest, cheapest staff who get laid-off – labour costs are nonetheless usually the first line item to come under scrutiny when times are tough. This is inevitable given that they constitute such high proportions of most airlines' TOCs. Scrutiny in this context means one or more of:

- reducing employee numbers;
- negotiating reductions in pay and benefits;
- changing work rules (e.g., hours worked or tasks to be undertaken) to improve productivity (e.g., ASMs per employee or per dollar of employment cost);
- outsourcing activities to suppliers with lower labour costs.

According to statistics from the Air Transport Association of America (http://www.airlines.org), the average number of full-time equivalent employees at US airlines peaked in 2000 at 546,655, before falling back to 432,002 in 2005. Labour cost peaked at $37.5 billion in 2001, then fell to $31.6 billion in 2005 – still a billion dollars above the 1999 figure. Partly as a result of drops in employee numbers and average remuneration, but also because of the change in relativities brought about by rapidly rising fuel prices, the percentage of operating costs accounted for by labour declined from a 2002 peak of 37.3 per cent to 25.5 per cent in 2005; in the third quarter of 2007, it stood at 23.4 per cent. Network carriers bore the brunt of the adjustment which these figures describe. They have also been responsible for much of the consequent reduction in unit labour cost, and have therefore narrowed their labour cost disadvantage relative to LFAs: network carriers reduced unit labour costs from 4.4 cents in 2000 to 2.5 cents five years later, whilst the LFAs managed just a 0.5 cent reduction over the same period to 2.0 cents.

Issues complicating the management of labour costs   There are several:

1. *Unionisation* During economic downturns staff reductions and salary freezes or give-backs are widespread, but during upturns the pendulum swings strongly in favour of labour; the recovery in US airline finances during 2007 quickly brought forward arguments from labour that having borne most of the pain arising from the post-9/11 restructuring, they should share in the ensuing gain. A related problem is pattern bargaining, under which any gains negotiated by a union at one airline become embedded as the union's baseline negotiating position when contracts with similar employees at the next airline become amendable.
2. *Service* Airlines are service businesses. There is a stream of research in the services management literature that draws explicit linkages between employee satisfaction on the one hand and both customer satisfaction and corporate profits on the other (Heskett *et al.* 1997; see also Holloway 2002). Whilst some carriers have a culture and management style that seem to enable them to keep employee satisfaction high and unit costs under firm control (the connection between the two often being high productivity – as in the case of Southwest), many others have a history of combative labour-management relations that inevitably feed through into employee and customer dissatisfaction. In either case, simultaneously reducing labour costs and

maintaining employee and customer satisfaction is exceedingly difficult. It is perhaps therefore not surprising that after half a decade of turmoil, the US airline industry famously found itself ranked below the Internal Revenue Service in the University of Michigan's 2007 American Consumer Satisfaction Index.

Aside from any impact that staff cuts might have on morale, there are operational challenges to bear in mind as well when 'lean' systems and/or self-service technology are introduced to enable a static or shrinking labour force to deal with a rapidly growing number of customers. British Airways (with its baggage problems at Heathrow in 2006/2007) and jetBlue (with its weather-related meltdown in February 2007) provide two of the most noteworthy – but certainly not the only – examples of what can go wrong when understaffed and/or inordinately lean operating systems with insufficient slack built-in are stretched beyond breaking point by irregular operations. Whilst giving customers control of bookings (over the Internet) and check-in (online and at airport kiosks) is increasingly accepted as good business practice and indeed an essential part of some carriers' business models, there is as yet no fully automated system able to cope reliably and effectively with the reaccommodation demands stemming from a major disruption to operations.

3. *Equity* There is an argument that senior executives have over the last two decades come to capture for themselves too much of the value created by public corporations generally; in parts of the airline industry, this phenomenon has been made more stark by the fact that so many of its constituents destroy rather than create value. Recent circumstances raise at least two questions. First, does the financial performance of the companies that populate this industry justify the magnitude of the rewards accruing to senior executives? In some cases an affirmative response can be argued, but in many it cannot. Second, is it in the long term interests of a high-contact service business to let the most senior executives profit richly from a financial turnaround built on the financial and professional sacrifices of the workforce? Nothing in either simple logic or services management research supports a positive response.

    It is instructive to compare the reactions of the respective labour forces at Delta and Northwest when these two exited Chapter 11 within weeks of each other in 2007. Delta's executive suite was perceived (rightly or wrongly) to have shared in the sacrifices of reorganization and the general attitude of the workforce going forward was positive, whereas at Northwest the vast payouts awarded to a few top managers created clearly articulated resentment amongst some groups of workers. Among carriers that stayed out of bankruptcy after 9/11 but required financial sacrifices from employees, Continental's senior management chose to forgo over $20 million in performance-related benefits in 2006 whereas the top echelons of American and its parent AMR Corporation split close to $200 million the following year – having earlier avoided bankruptcy largely by extracting multi-billion dollar wage and benefit concessions from staff. On the other side of the Atlantic, British Airways spent the better part of a decade under-funding its main staff pension scheme and then trying to negotiate concessions from members – but only after the company's directors had first created a new scheme for themselves.

The importance of culture Given declining real yields, there is no question that effective management of labour costs and productivity is critical to the long-term survival of most airlines. How this is achieved owes much to culture. Some airlines are institutionally confrontational (e.g., Ryanair), some have had senior officers who at times appear to give high priority to their own personal interests irrespective of how these might be interpreted by employees (e.g., American), whilst others focus more on the impact that labour management practices have on corporate culture and – through that medium – service quality and customer satisfaction. Few observers looking at the remuneration of senior executives, particularly the departure packages granted to the company's Chairman and President in 2007, would reckon Southwest ungenerous to those at the top. Yet this has to be set against the fact that this highly unionised airline of over 33,000 employees, who now rank amongst the US industry's best-paid, has never furloughed staff or cut their packages. It was throughout most of its history able to manage average labour cost per employee by expanding rapidly and recruiting more, less senior, staff to offset the growing seniority of the existing workforce; when growth began to slow and unit labour costs relative both to network carriers emerging from Chapter 11 and to lower-cost LFAs began to be an issue in recent years, it offered generous voluntary buyouts to senior staff. At the time of writing Southwest's unit labour cost is third-highest amongst the majors, exceeded only by American and Alaska, so how long this benign policy can continue if lower output growth becomes the norm remains to be seen. Nonetheless, Southwest's experience to date underlines the fact that management of labour costs is not simply a matter of sharp pencils; it has a cultural context and an implication for service which, ultimately, can affect the revenue side of the income statement as well.

THE FLEET

This section will consider the impact of fleet structure and aircraft ownership on costs. Maintenance costs will be considered in the next section.

Fleet Structure

As noted above in the context of network design and scheduling, the critical issue with regard to a fleet is its appropriateness to the various payload-range missions expected of it. Subject to this, key cost drivers are as follows:

1. *Fleet size and composition* Large fleets of a type can benefit from economies of scale – although what is meant by 'large' is a matter of opinion; certainly, a 40-aircraft fleet will benefit from economies unavailable to a 2-aircraft fleet, but it is doubtful that operating 150 of a type generates significantly more economies than operating 100. Flight-crew and spares commonality amongst families of the same type (e.g., the B737NG series and the A320 series) can extend these economies across a range of different aircraft sizes. Conversely, Irrgang (2000, p. 175) lists the following areas in respect of which inefficiencies arise from operating too many types: maintenance activities; maintenance inventory; ground equipment; number of pilots required; pilot training and qualification costs; average aircraft utilisation; and reduced flexibility in recovering from schedule disruptions.
2. *Aircraft age* Older airframes and powerplants may impose higher DOCs than newer types having a similar mission profile because their higher maintenance costs and fuel consumption outweigh lower ownership costs – although much will depend upon just how old an aircraft is (as this affects maintenance costs), the extent to

which it has already been depreciated, the prevailing level of fuel prices, how readily manufacturers are prepared to offer discounts off the list prices of new aircraft, and levels of utilisation. In the case of long-haul aircraft, older types may require intermediate stops that newer models are capable of overflying without a payload penalty.

3. *Aircraft size* We have already seen that larger aircraft are generally cheaper to operate in unit cost (although not trip cost) terms than smaller aircraft of the same technological generation having a similar mission capability. This advantage is sometimes referred to as 'aircraft economies of scale' (Bailey and Panzar 1981, Graham *et al.* 1983, Caves *et al.* 1984), although the term has fallen from use.

4. *Aircraft speed* Because output expressed in either ASMs or ATMs is a function of seats or payload available and distance flown, a faster aircraft will produce more output in a given time than a slower aircraft having the same capacity, allowing fixed ownership costs to be more widely spread and therefore lower on a per unit basis. There might of course be a price paid for this in terms of higher variable costs if the additional speed is reflected in increased fuel-burn. Therefore the comparison that matters is between the most economical cruise speeds of different types rather than their maximum speeds.

5. *Cabin configurations* Multiple cabin configurations within a fleet or subfleet can generate additional expenses which might be unnecessary unless each configuration is specifically designed in response to the demand characteristics of different markets. An example of configuration tailored to demand is the operation of a type fitted with both first and business class cabins in addition to economy/coach on routes where there is strong demand from premium passengers, and just business and economy on other routes where first class traffic is thin. Emirates, for instance, has specified its A380s in three configurations: three-class, 489-passenger long-haul configuration with crew rest accommodation; three-class, 514-passenger medium-haul configuration without crew rest accommodation; and two-class, 644-seat high-density configuration. The same carrier uses a two-cabin configuration on some routes served by its B777s and A330s, and three cabins on others, and several US majors have different configurations for domestic and international services operated by B767s and B777s.

In addition to the question of whether or not to tailor the number of cabins on a type to demand on different routes there is the related question of whether to configure a given cabin on a particular type (e.g., the business class cabin) differently for different routes. Clearly, some degree of aircraft assignment flexibility might be lost in either case, even in large subfleets – because, in effect, the subfleet is being further subdivided; for example, the decision taken by American in 2002 to reduce the number of different configurations on its international B777s was estimated to have led to scheduling efficiencies equivalent to adding two aircraft to the subfleet.

Ownership Costs

Airlines are not only labour-intensive service businesses, they are also capital-intensive. Capital-intensity shows up in equipment rental and asset depreciation figures.

Categories of ownership cost It is generally true that how an airline chooses (or is constrained) to finance its fleet will impact upon operating costs. Although detailed practices with regard to accounting for leases and owned aircraft vary depending upon generally accepted accounting principles (GAAP) in each airline's home jurisdiction, and will also in many cases be influenced by tax considerations, the following generalisations can be made:

1. *Operating lease rentals* When an airline takes an aircraft on a true operating lease it has use of that aircraft for a relatively small proportion of its economic life, and therefore does not have an economic interest in it beyond current operational use. Operating lease rentals are charged in full as an operating cost on an airline's income statement. (They are in fact fixed DOCs.) The value of the aircraft does not appear on the airline's balance sheet, so depreciation is *not* chargeable (although it is notionally embedded in the rental figure). Definitions of what constitutes an operating lease can vary depending upon a given country's GAAP.

2. *Costs of economic ownership* When an airline owns an aircraft, or is deemed to have an economic interest in it equivalent in effect to bearing the risks and rewards of ownership, the ownership cost breaks down as follows:
   - Depreciation is charged as an operating expense (again, a fixed DOC). Within the parameters established by applicable GAAP, an airline can influence depreciation charges by: choice of method (e.g., straight line, declining balance, etc.); choice of depreciation period – with a shorter period front-loading the charges and perhaps reducing near-term taxable income, and so having beneficial cash-flow effects by deferring the payment of tax; and by adjusting assumed residual value – with a smaller residual value increasing depreciation charges over any given number of years. Generally, new narrowbodies are written down to approximately 10 per cent over 10 or more years, whereas widebodies are commonly depreciated to 10–15 per cent over 15 years or longer; however, policies vary between carriers, depending upon tax issues and the extent to which it is thought desirable to build up equity in owned aircraft by depreciating them for accounting purposes more rapidly than their cash secondary market value is falling.
   - Interest, whether attributable to debt from general corporate borrowing or from a specific aircraft-related transaction, is not an operating expense but is charged as a nonoperating item.

   As noted above, operating leases reduce operating income but in most countries do not appear on an airline's balance sheet. Owned aircraft on the other hand reduce operating and nonoperating income, through depreciation and interest respectively, and do appear (net of depreciation) on the balance sheet; because it is a non-cash item, adding back the annual depreciation charge to operating income can be a significant 'source' of cash flow in a capital-intensive business such as an airline. However, the industry as a whole has historically been able to finance little more than half its capital investment from internal cash-flows, and many airlines achieve far less than half; this in part accounts for high levels of debt and growing reliance on operating lessors.

   One final point: some airframe–engine combinations are less popular in the secondary market than others, and so can be more expensive to finance.

3. *Insurance costs* The principal types of coverage related to aircraft are hull, liability (third party and passenger, baggage, cargo, and mail), and war risks and allied perils. Unsurprisingly, the availability of war risks and allied perils coverage was withdrawn subject to the standard 7-day notice period in the immediate aftermath of 9/11, and

the costs of all forms of cover spiralled; industry premiums of around $1.25 billion in 2001 more than tripled the following year. (Subsidies from the US government to its airlines after 9/11 included war risk cover; although the war risk market had long since stabilised, the government was still providing subsidised cover in 2008.)

The cost of hull cover for most carriers had eased by mid-decade, helped by significant improvements in the loss-rate – down to a record low of 0.75 per million departures in 2007 (0.68 for IATA members) – and by the entry of more underwriters into the market. Whilst there is inevitably an element of randomness in any one year's figures, efforts to improve safety and move towards greater inter-regional consistency have benefited considerably from programmes such as IATA's IOSA and ICAO's Universal Safety Audit. Aviation insurance is not a market in which the 'law of large numbers' applies, however, so a relatively small run of events could readily wipe out the premium pool and cause underwriting capacity to leave the market once again. In 2007, for example, estimated losses of around $1.8 billion (up from $400 million in 2006) exceeded premiums amounting to approximately $1.5 billion. Whilst 2007's result did not immediately drive capacity from the market, with the number of flights per annum rising it will be critical to keep the loss rate falling if confidence is to be retained.

A small number of airlines, notably including Continental and Lufthansa, bundle aircraft and related insurances into an integrated enterprise risk management (ERM) system. The purposes of an ERM system are to understand (i.e., identify and quantify) and manage (i.e., prioritise and mitigate) risks across departments and processes, and to reinforce an organization-wide safety culture. (Note that the initials ERM are perhaps more commonly associated with enterprise *resource* management systems.)

Strategic implications of ownership cost   Newer aircraft generally impose higher ownership costs than older types with a similar mission profile. Historically, low-fare start-ups have tended to favour older aircraft with low ownership costs; beginning with jetBlue's well-capitalised appearance in 2000, however, most now choose where possible to launch with new or relatively young models because their fuel efficiency, reliability, and low maintenance costs are considered more important than low ownership costs – particularly when they are to be intensively utilised. Allegiant, which has a network and schedule generating relatively low utilisation, was an exception. (Ben-Yosef [2005] argues that the trend of LFA start-ups launching with new aircraft during the post-9/11 downturn was attributable to particularly aggressive pricing of narrowbodies for this sector by Airbus and Boeing.)

MAINTENANCE COSTS

As well as being an important source of airline costs, aircraft maintenance is significant in the contribution it makes to safety, dispatch reliability, flight completion rates, and schedule integrity, and to the preservation of aircraft residual values. Maintenance is therefore a question of branding and asset management as well as regulatory compliance. The maintenance management objective must be to make the fleet available in an appropriate condition (internally and externally) when and where required to support performance of the schedule, and to do this as cost-effectively as possible.

The MRO market, sometimes referred to as M&E (maintenance and engineering), was worth approximately $41 billion in 2007. Around 40 per cent of it is in North America and 25 per cent in Europe, but the fastest growth rates are in India and the Asia-Pacific region (which together currently account for less than 20 per cent). Over 30 per cent of the market is attributable to engine work, just under 25 per cent each to line and component maintenance, 15 per cent to airframe heavy maintenance, and the balance to modifications. The primary maintenance costs are labour, materials, burden/overhead, and payments to outside contractors (i.e., for outsourcing). The share of maintenance in DOCs has historically fallen within a few percentage points either side of 10 per cent, but with the recent rise in fuel costs it has dropped well into single digits for most carriers. The unit cost metric of interest is MRO cost per ASM or ATM; as with any metric involving ASMs, the figure will depend in part on aircraft utilisation and seating densities as well as the efficiency of maintenance activities. An alternative calculation is MRO cost per block-hour.

Two final points: first, it is important to remember that reported MRO costs encompass just the outgoings, ignoring revenue forgone during out-of-service time – something which should be factored into assessment of MRO performance, whether in-house or outsourced; second, airlines leasing aircraft are normally required to make payments into one or more maintenance reserve accounts in order to provide for future maintenance expenditures – which this enforced cash provisioning in effect brings forward.

Maintenance Cost Drivers

The following subsections look at the more important maintenance cost drivers. Most apply whether or not maintenance work is outsourced, although some (notably economies of scale) may vary as between the two options depending upon fleet size.

Fleet age   There are two aspects to 'age' in the present context:

1. *The age (or generation) of an aircraft type* Whereas a B747-400 D-check (i.e., the most thorough form of heavy maintenance) might require as many as 60,000 man-hours, a B777-300 should require closer to 8000. Each new generation brings with it improvements in design, reliability (driven by improved prognostics and diagnostics), and maintainability. Occasionally there is a major step-change; for example, with the introduction of composite fuselage barrels on the B787, airframe maintenance man-hour costs on this and future generations of aircraft will fall well below those associated with aluminium airframes. Similarly, each new generation of engines brings with it improved onwing times and easier, modular maintainability. The result is that MRO costs for older types can be two or three times the equivalent of more modern types designed for similar missions.
2. *The age of particular aircraft in an airline's fleet* Ageing aircraft cost more to maintain than new models. Factors which affect airframe condition over time include: the number of flight-hours and cycles recorded; whether or not the aircraft has spent significant time on the ground in humid, maritime or desert environments; runway and overnight parking conditions on the network; and maintenance standards (both in general and with particular regard to galleys, lavatories, and cargo holds exposed to spillages of potentially corrosive liquids). The principal threats are corrosion and fatigue, either

independently or in conjunction. Powerplant and component maintenance costs also rise with age, particularly in respect of engine rotating parts and hot sections. Another consideration is that a greater proportion of a young fleet is likely still to be under warranty and several years away from heavy checks – an advantage for LFAs with rapidly expanding fleets, but one which dissipates over time as growth begins to slow. Finally, a separate but related variable is how early in a type's production run particular aircraft came off the manufacturer's line. The first couple of dozen or more of a type to be produced may not benefit from fixes to early manufacturing or operational problems. Sometimes more than just a couple of dozen aircraft are involved; for example, A380s built between 2007 and 2012 are likely to turn out to be several tonnes heavier than the build standard applicable from 2012 onwards (although still within guarantees).

Fleet composition   Having more types in a fleet and more configurations in a subfleet increases complexity and therefore maintenance cost. The obvious response is to simplify the fleet by operating the fewest possible types and standardising configurations. A more subtle approach is to consider whether the incremental costs of complexity are exceeded by the incremental revenues to which it gives rise; it is this type of analysis that has led some LFAs to diverge from the basic single-type business model by adding a second type to their fleets (e.g., Virgin Blue and jetBlue), and some airlines to operate given types with multiple configurations targeted at different markets (e.g., Emirates and Cathay Pacific).

Network design   There are several maintenance cost drivers under this heading:

1. *Average stage-lengths*   Long-haul aircraft can have significantly lower flight-hour maintenance costs than short-haul types (Clark 2001). They usually have fewer cycle-related costs, including fewer transit and turnaround checks, in addition to which they benefit from higher utilisation over which to spread maintenance burden. They also spend more of their time aloft in dry and relatively stable air.
2. *ETOPS/LROPS*   Rules applied to 'extended-range twin-engine operations' and increasingly to long-range operations (LROPS) generally, irrespective of the number of engines, impose a need to increase spares provision to support more demanding minimum equipment list (MEL) requirements on flight-legs without ready access to en route diversionary airfields.
3. *Proximity to maintenance facilities*   As far as in-house maintenance is concerned, costs will be influenced by the number and location of maintenance facilities on the network and how readily they can be accessed (particularly overnight in respect of short-haul aircraft) given aircraft assignments flowing from the carrier's schedule. Airlines located in remote parts of the world suffer additional costs arising from the distance aircraft and components have to travel for outsourced maintenance, and also possibly from the need to hold a larger spares buffer to compensate for being on the end of long supply lines – although OEMs are increasingly placing key inventory in strategically located warehouses worldwide.

Aircraft utilisation   High daily utilisation accelerates both scheduled and unscheduled maintenance – particularly in the case of short-haul aircraft operating a lot of cycles. This is, of course, a price worth paying insofar as aircraft do not earn revenue unless they are flying and the more time they spend in the air the greater the amount of output they are generating over which to spread fixed costs (including maintenance burden). A related point is that the more intensively a short-haul aircraft is utilised the more daily turns it is likely to make, and this will place upward pressure on line maintenance costs.

Operational practices   Some airlines carefully monitor flight-crew engine handling, particularly during take-off and climb phases, to ensure that operating temperatures are neither higher than they need be nor high for longer than they need be.

Maintenance philosophy   Some carriers are much less inclined to delay implementation of service bulletins (SBs) and deferrable airworthiness directives (ADs) than others. The acceptability of non-MEL defects also varies between airlines; some carriers like to fix defects as soon as is practical, whereas others are more prepared to defer items. (If aircraft are leased, of course, lessors will have a voice in whether and when ADs and SBs are terminated.) Finally, some airlines have more of a predilection for customising maintenance programmes and undertaking extensive engineering work or modifications on their aircraft than others; British Airways used to be a prime example, but has over the last decade made a concerted effort to move back towards standard maintenance planning documents (MPDs) for each type. The advantage of customisation is that it can tailor MRO activities more closely than the manufacturer's MPDs to the specific network and operations of the airline concerned; the disadvantages are that it adds complexity and also increases the costs associated with transitioning aircraft to another carrier after sale or lease expiry.

Maintenance programme design   The manner in which required tasks are packaged into maintenance programmes for airframes and engines will affect costs through the impact that design has on the frequency and complexity of each activity. A complicating factor can sometimes be the presence in a fleet of different aircraft of the same type subject to different maintenance programmes because they are owned by different lessors – although if an aircraft is on a medium- or long-term lease it will most probably be integrated into the lessee's maintenance programme. Also, the efficiency of maintenance programmes can sometimes be compromised when new aircraft are added to an existing fleet of the same type subject to the same certification requirements as the older models, but with no account being taken of subsequent advances in design, materials, or manufacturing technology since the original models came off the production line. On the other hand, it is common for check intervals to be extended across an entire type, with the agreement of appropriate airworthiness authorities, after experience with that type has been gained; for example, the A-check interval for an A340 was 400 hours on entry into service in 1993, but by the end of 2007 had been extended to 800 hours.

Maintenance planning   Effective maintenance planning balances two considerations:

1. *The need to maximise time between checks*   It is essential to ensure that as little scheduled maintenance as possible is undertaken before it needs to be – in other words, that all allowable calendar time, flight-hours, and cycles are fully used and none is wasted by premature checks and early disposal of life-limited parts.
2. *The need to balance throughput and maximise utilisation at in-house maintenance facilities*   The challenge of scheduling shop visits when aircraft, engines and components need them, yet also ensuring that maintenance capacity is fully utilised is complicated by the industry's demand peaking – which means that at certain times of the day, week, and/ or year every airline will want as many of its aircraft as possible available for service.

A key challenge in the management of maintenance planning is establishing a critical path for each check given that routine activities will inevitably uncover the need for unscheduled maintenance – some of which might be allowed for in the project plan, some of which might be deferrable and scheduled for subsequent action, but some of which may have to be dealt with immediately and could put pressure on the return-to-service date.

Maintenance input costs   There are three primary categories:

1. *Labour costs* Line maintenance costs are practically all accounted for by labour, whilst approximately two-thirds of airframe intermediate and heavy maintenance costs are driven by man-hour rates (Lam 1995). Only around 10–15 per cent of engine maintenance costs are attributable to direct labour.

     Maintenance man-hour rates vary not only between carriers, but also between different areas of the world. North American hourly rates are generally lower than those in Europe – which means that in order to be competitive, MRO operations such as Lufthansa Technik and Air France Industries need to offer fast, reliable maintenance turnaround/cycle times, meaningful economies of scale, and high quality. Man-hour rates in parts of Asia are lower still, but are subject to sustained upward pressure.

2. *Material costs* These account for over half of engine and component maintenance costs, but much less in respect of airframes (ibid.). The rapidly rising cost of OEM engine parts (i.e., parts manufactured by the original equipment manufacturer, such as GE or CFM International) has been of particular concern to airlines over the last decade.

3. *Overhead/burden* What is true for the fleet is true for other airline assets, including maintenance facilities: utilisation (of hangars, bays, repair shops, and of maintenance planning, administration, record-keeping, and quality control resources) needs to be as high as possible to generate maximum output over which to spread fixed costs. (Utilisation in this case is a measure of man-hours and facility time that is booked relative to what is available.) Whereas labour rates are a key airframe maintenance cost driver, the capital costs of facilities are a significant driver in respect of powerplant and avionics maintenance (accounting for over a third of total engine maintenance costs). The fact that materials and overhead account for such a high proportion of engine maintenance costs helps keep the role of independent third-party shops much lower in respect of engine overhaul than airframe maintenance: given that engine OEMs have a substantial measure of control over the prices of proprietary materials and benefit from significant economies of scale in the allocation of overhead, independents have only their man-hour rates to compete with – something that OEMs can counter by shifting labour cost disadvantages into mark-ups on their materials.

The high costs of tooling, technical training, and test facilities together with the increasing reliability of equipment (i.e., lower shop visit rates) imply the need for large fleets over which to spread fixed maintenance costs. Even some airlines that have sizeable fleets are now finding it more cost-effective to enter into long-term maintenance agreements with OEMs and third-party providers.

Productivity   Assuming the availability of required facilities, there are three potential influences on maintenance productivity:

1. *The effectiveness of maintenance programme design and maintenance planning* We touched on both of these above.
2. *Labour productivity* This is usually driven by the time taken to perform given tasks relative to established standards. It is likely to be a function of training, work practices, and experience. With regard to the latter, there are maintenance cost learning curves to be exploited as familiarity grows with an aircraft type or a manufacturer's products generally; one advantage of outsourcing – aside from the saving in capital costs associated with investment in hangars, bays, shops, and tooling – is that a smaller airline can benefit from the contractor's experience.
3. *Inventory productivity* Inventory bears potentially heavy carrying costs whether used or not. The question of inventory productivity is therefore closely linked to the scale of operations it is intended to support.

Scale   Economies of scale are present when unit costs decline as a function of increasing output. Estimates vary, but there is little argument that economies of scale are present in the maintenance business. Possible sources include:

1. *Man-hours available* The scale of a maintenance facility is generally measured in terms of the bookable man-hours available in a year. The unit cost advantage of a 3 million man-hour heavy maintenance shop over one with half this capacity can be as high as 20 per cent.
2. *Inventory size* Inventory can be categorised as: spare engines; rotables; repairables; expendables (i.e., items discarded after use); and consumables (e.g., oil). Spare engines and rotables are together by far the most significant items in value terms – although an 'aircraft on the ground' (AOG) situation can as easily develop from a stock-out affecting a cheap expendable. As fleet size and therefore output of ASMs or ATMs increases, the value – and therefore the inventory cost (i.e., finance, depreciation, warehousing, and insurance) – of spares needed to support each aircraft (at a given level of confidence, often 95 per cent, with regard to the availability of spares when required) will fall. This is particularly true of rotables, which when held in inventory can support several aircraft as readily as just one; broadly, a sixfold increase in fleet size might require a doubling of the rotables inventory. Overall, there is little doubt that the unit costs of supporting a larger fleet are lower than those of supporting a small fleet. There is a rule of thumb that a single-aircraft 'fleet' requires inventory worth as much as 50 per cent of that aircraft's value, dropping to 25 per cent when the fleet grows to ten units, and to ten per cent when it reaches a hundred units. (For mathematical precision in preference to rules of thumb, readers are referred to queuing theory.)
   Introduction of a new type can generate a significant initial provisioning (IP) expense, the size of which will depend upon an airline's bargaining strength and the extent to which it outsources using fixed-cost maintenance contracts. If the powerplant used on the aircraft is already in operation with the airline, this will reduce IP expenses quite considerably. Any fleet build-up after purchase of the first few aircraft dramatically decreases the spares-to-aircraft ratio and the value of inventory as a percentage of total investment in the fleet. A somewhat smaller cost reduction then

occurs in later years as the airline uses up any excess parts inventory left over from IP and better manages its purchases of replacement parts, concentrating on those that have demonstrated a relatively high failure rate. Introduction of a mature type usually results in lower initial costs because the airline is able to benefit from the maintenance experience of other carriers.

One way for a relatively small carrier to overcome these problems is to outsource in order to exploit economies of scale available to larger airlines, OEMs, or sizeable independent shops.

Aircraft characteristics   Very broadly, absolute maintenance costs for aircraft of a similar technology level increase with maximum take-off weight and with engine thrust. With regard to individual aircraft, many carriers closely monitor the fuel consumption and maintenance costs of each 'tail number' to uncover particularly expensive problems as they develop. Another technique sometimes used is to target the known cost drivers on each airframe and engine to bring them under better control.

Market positioning   Requirements in respect of cabin and exterior airframe cleanliness will affect deep cleaning frequency and also standards with regard to the acceptability of cabin defects – each of which should be driven by an appreciation of what type of value the airline is trying to deliver to its customers. They will have a direct bearing on maintenance costs.

Concluding point   Finally, it is worth noting the following distinction in respect of maintenance cost calculations. Block-time is the time from engine start-up at origin to shut-down at the end of the flight-leg; flight-time, on the other hand, is the time from unstick to touch-down (and therefore excludes taxi-out and taxi-in times). Whereas hourly DOCs as a whole are normally calculated per block-hour, it is not unusual for hourly maintenance costs to be expressed per flight-hour. In this case a conversion factor, perhaps based on the experience of the carrier concerned with regard to taxi-times at the particular airports it serves, may need to be applied in order to integrate hourly maintenance cost figures into aggregate hourly DOC figures.

Maintenance Cost Management

MRO unit costs are trending downward in part because of the greater reliability and maintainability designed into each new generation of aircraft, but also as a result of several airline cost-containment strategies. This section will briefly consider: maintenance outsourcing; inventory management; lean methods; use of engine diagnostic tools; maintenance programme design; and PMA parts.

Outsourcing   MRO activities can be undertaken in-house or they can be outsourced; depending upon its labour rates, existing infrastructure, and strategic ambitions a carrier might choose to outsource some MRO activities whilst retaining others in-house. Where outsourcing is chosen either single or multiple providers can be used, and transactions can either be ad hoc (charged on a time and materials basis) or wrapped into comprehensive long-term flight-hour-driven or total support contracts.

Although practice has been far from uniform across the industry, there has been a discernible trend over the last 30 years or so: initially, airlines other than the smallest carriers tended to perform the majority of MRO activities in-house; during the 1980s came the beginnings of a movement towards outsourcing some activities, but almost invariably on a transactional basis; the 1990s saw a growing number of carriers entering into long-term contracts under which OEMs, other airlines, or independent providers agree to deliver total support either for specific systems or processes (e.g., airframe, engines, components or materials management) or for entire fleets (i.e., total fleet management solutions). Under the latter, which can last from a few years to the entire life of the asset, financial and operational risk related to MRO activities is substantially transferred to the provider.

Between 2002 and 2007, the six largest US majors moved MRO outside the airline to the point where over 50 per cent is now outsourced. The principal exception to this trend has been American. Globally, it is thought as much as 60 per cent of MRO business is now outsourced, and this percentage is expected to continue growing. Engine repair and overhaul work is the most widely outsourced activity, with approximately 70 per cent being undertaken by outside contractors; the reason for this is the high cost of tooling, which requires greater volume of throughput over which to spread fixed costs than most airlines can generate – especially given the reliability and impressive onwing times achieved by modern powerplants. The next most outsourced activities are airframe heavy maintenance and modification, which have lower barriers to entry; the driver in these cases is the competitive labour costs that independent shops in North America and airline or joint venture facilities in Asia (notably for widebodies) and central America (for narrowbodies) are able to offer. However, high fuel costs to ferry empty aircraft to distant MRO providers may outweigh this advantage. The least-outsourced activity is line maintenance; although this is also a heavily labour-intensive activity, less than 20 per cent is outsourced because many airlines still consider it too critical to schedule integrity, customers' perceptions of reliability, and therefore brand image to put in the hands of others.

There is no single answer to the question of whether or not to outsource the MRO function, and both an airline's history and the influence of stakeholders such as unions and politicians can be as strong as any assessment based on transaction cost economics or shareholder value analysis. Long-term power-by-the-hour and life-cycle product support agreements allow stable maintenance cost projections and remove the burden associated with investing in shop facilities and inventory; they turn potentially volatile variable costs into more predictable fixed costs and they can be cost-competitive with in-house alternatives – to the extent the provider passes through the benefits of lower labour rates and economies of scale. Nonetheless, that maintenance outsourcing is not a necessary prerequisite for low costs is borne out by the fact that several large and long-established north European charter carriers have extensive in-house facilities (e.g., Monarch), and LFAs such as Gol and Virgin Blue have been expanding their in-house MRO capabilities in recent years.

Clearly, the best decision is the one that keeps as much of an airline's fleet in the air as long as possible and as cheaply as possible, subject to the constraints of safety, regulatory compliance, and required reliability levels. Equally clearly, even an airline which outsources all or a substantial part of its MRO activities needs to have strong in-house technical management capabilities, both to discharge its legal responsibilities and to ensure that arrangements remain commercially as well as technically cost-effective.

Inventory management   There is reckoned to be spares inventory worth approximately $44 billion in the global supply chain (*AeroStrategy Comment* 2006). Around 61 per cent is estimated to be held by airlines at maintenance bases and line stations, 20 per cent by MRO service providers, 16 per cent by manufacturers, and 3 per cent by distributors and redistributors; rotables and consumables account for 42 and 24 per cent respectively, spare engines 11 per cent, and airframe structural parts 6 per cent, whilst the balance is comprised of 'piece-parts' such as turbine blades, circuit boards, etc. (ibid.). If the annual cost of financing and holding this material is assumed to be around 15–20 per cent of value, the scope for savings is obvious: every $1 million of inventory per aircraft that can be shed will generate a saving of $150–200,000 per annum. Although a conscious trade-off between dispatch reliability and investment in spares (both in an absolute sense and in terms of the stations to which they are distributed) will be an important influence on inventory levels and therefore inventory costs, it has for some time been recognised that there are too many spares in the pipeline and most airlines have been addressing the problem.

Some steps taken have acted more to push responsibility for inventory back up the supply chain than to reduce it. These include: sale of surplus inventory; sale of either entire inventories or just slow-moving parts to distributors subject to a long-term inventory management and supply contract; taking inventory either on consignment (i.e., where the supplier retains ownership until use) or on a just-in-time basis from dispersed supplier inventory hubs; engine and rotables leasing; and flight-hour-driven maintenance and/or materials management agreements.

Other steps have been taken that in the long run should strip inventory out of the system. These include the reduction of OEM catalogue lead times, and the shortening of repair and overhaul times to put repairables and rotables back into live inventory more quickly; the benefit in the latter case is that items in live inventory can support the fleet whereas items in a repair shop cannot, so the less time they spend in a shop the fewer of them will be required overall to provide the desired level of support. Some large carriers are allowing other airlines to access their inventories in return for a fixed fee per calendar period or per flight-hour. Finally, a longstanding technique used throughout the industry is spares pooling; the International Airline Technical Pool (IATP) has been in existence since 1949, and more recently individual groupings of airlines have come together to form inventory pools at outstations. (In return for a monthly fee, IATP allows its 100-plus members to access parts locally in response to an AOG situation, rather than having to make spot deals or ship inventory from one of their bases.) That these efforts are succeeding is borne out by the fact that the value of inventory in the supply chain has been more or less stable over the last decade despite a substantial increase in the global fleet.

Lean methods   There has been some success importing lean and six-sigma techniques from manufacturing industries into the maintenance hangar and repair shop. This involves not the reorganization of tasks mandated by an agreed maintenance programme, but reorganization of how tasks are prepared, supported, and performed. The objective is to improve the productivity of labour and materials by eliminating waste (i.e., zero-value input) – whether of employee time or work-in-progress inventory; the desired outcome is lower cycle time using fewer resources.

Redesign of workspaces is one element of 'lean' models. Processes are also redesigned to ensure that the right materials and tools are available at the right place at the right time to avoid mechanics having to hunt down what they need once a task has been started. Technology is playing a significant role. Examples include the following:

- digitisation and online provision of maintenance manuals, technical publications, service bulletins, engineering drawings, parts catalogues, and other OEM-provided resources is gradually eliminating time spent by staff updating paper libraries and is also accelerating look-up times and ordering processes;
- hardened laptops and wearable computers hold out the prospect of bringing higher productivity to the shop-floor and the ramp;
- RFID is beginning to contribute to more efficient management of parts and their service histories;
- real-time return-to-service updates are helping integrate maintenance operations more closely with other functional areas, most notably aircraft assignment and operations control.

A new generation of enterprise resource planning (ERP) systems customised for the MRO environment has also enabled more accurate maintenance planning and a more integrated approach to forecasting, purchasing, transportation, and warehousing; the result should be elimination of 'just-in-case' inventory.

Significant achievements have been reported – such as a reduction from 3500 to 2500 in shop-hours required for an engine overhaul (*Aviation Week & Space Technology*, September 4, 2006, p. 49). However, there are limits to the process analogies that can be drawn between manufacturing and MRO; notably, much MRO work has to be undertaken in space-constrained areas (e.g., the flight-deck) in respect of which access time can itself be considered a constrained resource.

Increasing use of engine diagnostic tools   An important development over the last decade has been the impact that engine health monitoring (EHM) or engine condition trend monitoring (ECTM) systems have had on reliability and operating costs. In the past, data has commonly been downloaded periodically using a quick access recorder, but increasingly it is being fed real-time for almost instant automated analysis by airline maintenance centres, OEMs, and/or MRO providers. The purpose is not just to 'fix things before they break', but also to help plan and schedule future maintenance.

Maintenance programme design   Two trends that have been running for a number of years are: the gradual shift, based on experience, away from time- and cycle-based overhaul towards on-condition maintenance of non-life-limited parts; and the reduction of aircraft out-of-service time by breaking heavy checks into smaller parcels and combining them with other regular checks – referred to as 'phased' or 'equalised' maintenance programmes.

PMA parts   Rapid inflation in the price of OEM-supplied parts has made cheaper PMA (parts manufacturing approval) spares supplied by non-OEM manufacturers an increasingly attractive alternative. This is still a small market with a primarily North American footprint, but the entry of parts manufacturers such as Pratt & Whitney (targeting CFM engine parts), a Chromalloy and Delta TechOps collaboration, and Lufthansa affiliate Heico has contributed to growing awareness and market acceptance. The unwillingness of some leasing companies to accept PMA parts, together with conservative attitudes amongst airline managers in other areas of the world, are also changing (although specialised engine lessors do still tend to insist on use of OEM parts at all times throughout a lease). British Airways, for example, has been a user of PMA parts for several years and has recently expanded coverage in cooperation with Heico.

OTHER COSTS AND POTENTIAL COSTS

Amongst the many considerations in this catch-all category, just four will be highlighted: security, environment, passengers' rights, and administration.

Security

IATA estimates that security is costing its members in the region of $5.9 billion each year; the ATA estimate is $4.5 billion ($3 billion in the form of taxes and charges payable to the Department of Homeland Security). There are several issues:

1. Perhaps the most significant issue is who should pay. The airlines' perspective is that whilst they are certainly responsible for the basic security of their customers, the threat of terrorism now faced is a threat levelled not at them or even at the air transport system generally but at individual states and the international order. Accordingly, it is states that they should shoulder the burden of defending themselves, their residents, and their visitors. The picture is far from uniform; in the EU, for example, countries are free either to absorb security costs or to pass them on to airlines or passengers. On the whole, it is nonetheless fair to generalise that airlines are faced with costs in respect of security that are not imposed on other forms of transport, and too many governments launch unfunded – and sometimes poorly reasoned – security initiatives which airlines are left to implement and then either pay for or charge to customers. Even where an airline is able to pass security costs through to passengers, there could well be an effect on demand – depending upon the price-elasticity of the markets concerned.

2. A second issue is the lack of international uniformity in procedures and data requirements. IATA is promoting a uniform approach through its Security Management System, which has been incorporated into IOSA, but many states have been slow to accept the need for consistency. One example is the requirement for advance passenger information to be transmitted to destination countries – sometimes, as in the particularly noteworthy case of the United States, to multiple agencies in the same country; because each has its own set of priorities, there is no standardised electronic submission format with common data fields. This adds cost. On a more positive note, the EU in early 2008 introduced measures intended to standardise screening and airside access control.

3. With regard to cargo, legislators in some countries seem on occasion to overestimate the availability and capabilities of security technology or to be unfamiliar with the practical realities of the international air cargo business (e.g., time-sensitivity and reliance on passenger aircraft for close to half the world's cargo output). The result is that they sometimes focus on screening at the airport to the detriment of further developing a multilayered approach to security throughout the entire supply chain. In summer 2007, legislation was enacted giving the US Department of Homeland Security 3 years to achieve 100 per cent screening of cargo carried on passenger aircraft. Forwarders and airlines are the initial focus of the Transportation Security

Administration's Certified Cargo Screening Program, rolled out at LAX in March 2008; at the time of writing it is not known whether screening by truckers or by known shippers using 'certified methods' referred to in the legislation will also be acceptable. The question of who will ultimately pay for required equipment is presently open.

At some North American and European airports in particular a balance has yet to be struck between the need to reassure passengers and as far as possible secure the system, and the need to provide paying customers with a tolerable service experience. Giving potential customers a good reason not to fly cannot be sound business practice.

Costs Associated With Climate Change And The Environment

Noise and emissions generated by aircraft impose a cost on affected individuals and on society as a whole. Because such 'external' costs are rarely borne by the producer, noise surcharges on landing fees providing an obvious exception, they are not incorporated into the price of output and therefore users – passengers and cargo shippers – do not pay the full cost of the products they purchase. If they did, prices would be higher and demand growth less pronounced. Ironically, because of its contribution to the cost of the infrastructure it uses the air transport industry can make a sound case that it internalises costs to a greater extent than subsidised alternatives such as roads and railways; because of its exceptional safety record it also imposes lower social costs per passenger-kilometre than more accident-prone modes, notably road transport, and this should also be weighed into the balance. Nonetheless, the political momentum in favour of getting the airline industry to internalise costs associated with its impact on the environment has grown rapidly in Europe over the last few years and is showing signs of accelerating in North America. Two approaches are favoured: taxes and charges; and emissions trading.

Taxes and charges The mathematics underlying calculation of any external cost are rarely straightforward or indisputable. It is even more rare for there to be a direct linkage between government-imposed environmental taxes and 'real' environmental costs. More often such taxes are a cynical revenue-grab dressed in green; the current UK government is a master of such devices, and in early 2008 the Dutch government used environmental concerns as justification for a plan to impose further taxes on departing passengers. Neither government ring-fences proceeds for the benefit of the environment, and the exclusion of transfer passengers and cargo from the Dutch scheme suggests that its designers wanted to mitigate the impact on KLM's sixth-freedom business as much as they wanted to protect the environment.

Although some governments have for many years taxed fuel used on domestic flights and applied the funds either to aviation-specific purposes (e.g., the United States – in principle) or general revenue (e.g., India), fuel used for international flights is largely untaxed. Pursuant to provisions of the Chicago Convention and ICAO recommendations, around 97 per cent of bilateral ASAs prevent signatories from taxing fuel used by the other party's carriers for international service. The fear amongst airlines is that some governments might be inclined to break this 60-year practice to boost their environmental credentials. There is therefore an emerging consensus in the industry that, given the inevitability of change, a market mechanism such as emissions trading would be preferable to yet more 'green' taxes.

Emissions trading   The purpose of an emissions trading scheme (ETS) is to reduce emissions of CO_2 by imposing caps and requiring emitters to acquire permits (through grant, auction, or purchase) for each tonne emitted; if CO_2 abatement measures cost less than the market price of any permits required were a firm's emission level to remain unchanged, there is an economic incentive to take those measures. Where an ETS is 'open', the market for carbon encompasses firms in different industries; where a market is closed, firms may only buy and sell permits within their own industry – a problem for aviation because there would likely be few sellers given high traffic growth forecasts and limited scope to quickly lower emissions. The EU intends bringing air transport into its existing open ETS. The details have yet to be finalised and the co-decision process involving the European Parliament and culminating in approval by the Council of Ministers will not be concluded before publication of this book. The situation at the time of writing is as follows:

- In December 2006 the European Commission (EC) proposed that:
    - air transport should be brought into the EU's existing ETS in two stages, from January 2011 for intra-EU flights and 12 months later for flights between EU and non-EU airports;
    - each airline would, like other enterprises in the ETS, have to surrender every year one EU emissions allowance (EUA) for each tonne of CO_2 emitted that year;
    - EUAs should be sourced from an annual allocation, which in the case of the airline industry would be capped at the equivalent of 100 per cent of its average annual carbon emissions in the years 2004–2006. Ninety-seven per cent of each year's allocation should be distributed free to individual airlines on the basis of their share of industry RTKs, and the balance should be auctioned;
    - airlines subsequently emitting more CO_2 in any year than their EUAs entitle them to emit would have to purchase additional units, at the prevailing open market price, from enterprises emitting less than their own allowances of EUAs. Alternatively, carbon credits could be purchased from enterprises which have implemented emissions reduction projects (i.e., Emission Reduction Units (ERUs) or Certified Emission Reduction (CER) units – definitions of which can be found on links at http://unfccc.int/kyoto_protocol/mechanisms/emissions_trading/items/2731.php). Firms exceeding their allowance and unable to buy additional permits would be fined a fixed amount per tonne of exceedance.
    The stated objective is to get producers who do not cut their emissions to pay, and thereby incentivise, others who do – although the flaw in this argument is that industries which have in the past worked less hard than airlines to reduce carbon emissions are now to be rewarded for their late start.
- In November 2007 the European Parliament, without even attempting an impact assessment, voted on amendments to the EC proposal suggesting that:
    - air transport in its entirety be brought into the ETS in 2011;
    - the initial allowance should be an amount of EUAs equivalent to 90 per cent, rather than 100 per cent, of the 2004–2006 baseline;
    - 25 per cent of the initial allowance should be auctioned, rather than the 3 per cent or less under the EC's proposal;

- the cost of each carbon purchase should be doubled to take NOx into account;
- airlines should eventually participate in their own closed ETS rather than the multi-sector EU ETS.

The latter proposal would be particularly damaging to aviation. Because airlines would have no access to benefits from other industries' excess allowances or carbon reduction projects, they would end up paying 'fines' for a growing proportion of their emissions as output rises and caps are reduced; in effect, they would be paying economically inefficient carbon levies set, doubtless at punitively high levels, not by the market but by regulators.

- In December 2007 the Council of Ministers, representing individual member states, came to an agreement largely supporting the EC's proposal:
  - air transport in its entirety should be brought into the ETS in 2012;
  - the initial allowance should be set at 100 per cent of the 2004–2006 baseline, with 10 per cent auctioned;
  - operators on thin routes to/from and within the EU should be entitled to opt out of the ETS;
  - three per cent of the sector's carbon credits should be reserved for new entrants and fast-growing airlines.

There remains some politicking and some fine-tuning of definitions to be done. To add further uncertainty to an already murky situation, however, the EC in January 2008 unveiled proposals to amend the existing EU ETS in its third stage (2013–2020) in a way that could lead to 100 per cent of EUAs being auctioned. Quite where this initiative is headed is as yet uncertain. Also, the EC is currently (i.e., 2008) consulting on separate proposals to address NOx emissions; there is concern that despite uncertain science regarding its effect at altitude, NOx will also be subjected to an economic penalty – perhaps by incorporating it into the CO_2 capping regime, as already proposed by the European Parliament.

Whilst a growing number of airlines now accept that some form of ETS is likely to be imposed on them in due course, there are undoubtedly problems with the European approach:

1. Consider the following facts: the commercial life of an aircraft is likely to exceed 30 years, so even as fuel-efficient new airframes and engines enter service the proportion of the fleet that they represent rises only gradually; traffic growth over the next two decades has been projected to exceed 5 per cent per annum (subject to whatever damping effect high oil prices, and therefore perhaps significantly higher than anticipated fares, might have on demand growth), whereas incremental fuel-burn improvements from in-service aircraft are unlikely to be better than 1 or 2 per cent; the fleet will be burning fossil fuels well into mid-century – unless a biofuel alternative can be quickly commercialised. Despite significant past and forecast improvements in the fuel-efficiency, and therefore the environmental performance, of its fleet the air transport industry is almost inevitably going to be a net purchaser of carbon credits. Even if IATA's challenge to create a carbon-neutral industry by 2050 proves to be an achievable long-term goal, there appear to be clear structural reasons why air transport cannot simultaneously both grow and reduce its carbon footprint over the next two or three decades. The ETS therefore imposes very real costs on airlines, and on those who benefit from the now pivotal role the industry plays in the global economy.

Attaching a cost to emissions trading is impossible at present. An impact assessment of the EU ETS conducted by Ernst & Young and York Aviation (Ernst & Young 2007) estimated a cost range of €9.8 billion to €45.3 billion over the period 2011–2022, based on 5 per cent traffic growth and depending upon the assumed price per tonne of CO_2; higher figures would apply were a larger percentage of initial allowances to be auctioned than originally proposed by the EC. The study took issue with the EU's assumption that low price-elasticity will enable airlines to pass through most of these costs without substantial loss of traffic, and argued that no more than a third would in fact be passed through. KLM has been quoted (*Aviation Week & Space Technology*, September 17 2007, p. 71) as foreseeing 2.3–7.2 per cent of its connecting traffic being diverted to hubs outside the EU, and margin reductions in the 2–4 per cent range. These figures are still speculative.

2.   Whether initial proposals to set aside 3 per cent of total sector carbon credits for new entrants will prove adequate in such a dynamic industry is open to question.

3.   The legality of the plan under the Chicago Convention, which prohibits levies on international flights other than for navigation and landing, will not go unchallenged by non-EU airlines and their governments. Europe's failed attempt several years ago to ban hush-kitted aircraft only marginally compliant with Chapter III noise regulations, which was successfully challenged by the United States, suggests that the confidence of EU lawyers with regard to the scope of the Union's international obligations is not invariably well-founded.

4.   Many argue that what is needed is not fragmented national or regional schemes but a uniform global ETS, and that ICAO is the proper forum within which to develop it. Whilst aviation emissions were excluded from the Kyoto Protocol, the instrument (in Article 2, paragraph 2) does place responsibility for bringing about their reduction in the hands of named industrialised countries *working through ICAO*. ICAO's Assembly authorised the organization's Council in 2001 to work with member states on development of market-based methods for mitigating the impact of aviation on climate change. However, with regard to a potential global ETS the sixth meeting of the Council's Committee on Aviation Environmental Protection (CAEP) concluded in 2004 that a *closed* ETS for aviation alone would be economically unattractive; the organization clearly does not have a mandate to design and implement the single *open* global ETS that some, particularly outside Europe, believe is the best way forward. Moreover, the EU, dissatisfied with what it perceives as a lack of progress within ICAO, has proposed that the UN Framework Convention on Climate Change (UNFCCC) would be a better medium through which to develop a global emissions trading regime for aviation. ICAO has nonetheless taken the practical step of drafting guidance material for the participation of aviation in national and regional trading schemes within the context of UNFCCC (Doc 9885).

5.   If Europe's politicians are as enthusiastic about limiting emissions as their promotion of the ETS implies, they would do well to address themselves first to the ATM inefficiencies which lead to the wasting of 21 million minutes and 12 million tonnes of CO_2 each year in the continent's airspace.

This is not just a European challenge, of course. By mid-2008 several bills addressing issues related to emissions were making their way through the US Congress, including one (the Lieberman–Warner Climate Security Act) which sought to impose a cap-and-trade scheme on transport (along with power producers and manufacturing companies) by 2012; the Air Transport Association estimated the annual cost to airlines of the ETS as proposed would start at around $5 billion and rise steadily thereafter. Whilst there were always doubts that legislation would be enacted in the final months of the Bush administration, it is clear that this is not a challenge to the industry that will go away; further evidence of growing pressure for change could be found in the mid-2008 request for public comments made by the Environmental Protection Agency, seeking input on whether, and if so how, it should regulate aircraft greenhouse gas emissions.

Passengers' Rights

This is a broad and somewhat amorphous subject, in respect of which comments will be restricted to current issues in the EU and the United States. (The discussion does not refer to legal duties in respect of passengers who are disabled or have reduced mobility.)

European Union   Regulation 261/2004 established rules regarding compensation and assistance due to passengers in the event of involuntary denied boarding, delay, and cancellation where a flight originates in, or is operated into, the EU. Its implementation has not been without difficulty and misunderstanding, with the result that further consultations with stakeholders were initiated by the EC in 2007. There are in fact objections to the entire underlying principle of the legislation: first, airlines are made accountable for disruptions outside their control (e.g., weather, strikes, infrastructural congestion), subject only to a limited 'extraordinary circumstances' exclusion; second, the fact that compensation is paid at a flat rate rather than pro rata to the fare means that the burden falls disproportionately on LFAs, to the extent that payments due can sometimes be a multiple of the fare; third, competing modes of transport are not subject to the same compensation regime. The cost to airlines of Regulation 261/2004 is uncertain and highly variable, but has been estimated by IATA to be around $700 million per annum.

United States   Irrespective of its achievement moving over three-quarters of a billion passengers safely each year under increasingly difficult circumstances, the airline industry has an image problem in the United States. Both the National Airspace System and the operating systems of many individual carriers are stretched, and the result of insufficient slack can be seen in statistics for delays, cancellations, mishandled baggage, and customer complaints – as well as in adverse press coverage. Against this background there also occur from time to time very rare but very newsworthy customer service failures such as those of Northwest at Detroit in 1999, American in the Dallas area in winter 2006, and jetBlue at JFK in February 2007; all involved poor operational responses to unusually difficult weather conditions, leading to passengers being marooned on grounded aircraft for many hours. These failures have led to calls from politicians and passengers' rights groups for a passengers' bill of rights. To date the airlines' powerful Washington lobby has prevented such a development at federal level, the 'cost' being limited to a 12-point Customer Service Commitment. How long this rearguard action can survive continuing deterioration in customer service, and whether activists will have greater success at state than at federal level, remains to be seen. The New York legislature enacted a rights bill into law in 2007 and this has provoked interest in several other state legislatures; however, at the time of writing it seems likely to be overturned on constitutional grounds.

The United States has legislation governing compensation for involuntary denied boarding which dates back to 1962 and was most recently updated in 2008, but none in respect of delays, cancellations, or assistance to affected passengers. If strong demand growth continues to run up against capacity discipline within the context of an under-resourced infrastructure for many more years, the grass roots pressure to remedy this situation is likely to grow.

Administration Costs

With their lean, flexible, non-bureaucratic structures, both established LFAs and start-ups can be expected to have lower unit administration costs (i.e., lower administration cost per ASM or ATM) than airlines with long histories behind them. The latter are often weighed down by inherited overhead, as well as by the complexity of their operations.

PRODUCTIVITY

Some Definitions

This subsection will define utilisation, productivity, and then efficiency and effectiveness.

Utilisation   Utilisation is a measure of the extent to which a resource is being used; it can be expressed either in absolute terms (e.g., aircraft utilisation in average block-hours per day or per year), or as a percentage of what is possible (e.g., cabin floorspace utilisation as a percentage seat factor). All resources – staff, ground equipment, airport terminals and gates, simulators, information systems, and distribution channels, for example – should be utilised as fully as possible; of course, the most significant resource to be concerned with is aircraft. An airline's production capacity expressed in terms of aircraft seats or cargo space is fixed, but output in terms of ASMs and ATMs can often be increased by raising fleet utilisation. For example, Boeing's 2007 20-year fleet forecast was little changed from the previous year despite higher forecast growth in output and traffic because it was anticipated that improved aircraft utilisation over the period would enable carriers to generate output equivalent to a year's growth without adding to the fleet (Boeing 2007).

Aircraft utilisation has a profound impact on unit costs. This is because increasing utilisation allows more output to be generated without a commensurate increase in fixed costs (such as annual depreciation and insurance charges). However, high utilisation is an objective that carries with it some interesting complexities.

1. We have already seen that production capacity bears certain fixed costs that do not vary with output. If output is low relative to what existing capacity is capable of producing, fixed costs per unit of output (i.e., per ASM) will be high; as output rises within the range of existing capacity, fixed capacity costs are being spread across that greater output and so should be falling on a per unit basis. On the other hand, the same utilisation improvement that puts downward pressure on unit costs by spreading fixed costs over more output also boosts total cost by the amount of the incremental variable costs associated with that additional output; for example, any improvement

in utilisation based on higher en route speed would be earned at the cost of increased fuel-burn. A key question is therefore whether additional output can be sold – and sold at prices sufficient to generate incremental revenue in excess of the increase in TOC.

2. From this last point can be drawn a significant but often overlooked conclusion: higher utilisation does not *control* costs, but it can reduce their wastage. A production process with a given capacity bears a certain level of fixed costs, attributable to the resources used to create and sustain it. Increasing output within the predetermined capacity does not affect that resource expenditure, it simply results in less of it being wasted on overcapacity. Although it is often viewed as a cost-control mechanism because of its effect on unit cost, the fact is that capacity utilisation is as much a matter of revenue generation as it is of cost control. (Increased utilisation leading to lower average cost might permit lower prices, for example; if demand is sufficiently elastic, lower prices could stimulate sales and – provided incremental costs are at least covered – increase operating profits.) Any consideration of revenue generation in this context inevitably leads back to the topics of product costing and pricing.

3. Not only are we faced with deciding whether incremental output generated by boosting aircraft utilisation can be sold profitably, we are again confronted with the issue of what is meant by 'profitably'. Accountants may expect each departure to generate a profit after all costs, including fixed as well as variable costs, have been fully allocated. Others might argue that because the manner in which costs should best be allocated across products, markets or routes is open to debate, there is no sound basis here on which to make scheduling decisions. They might go on to say that what matters is whether sufficient output on an additional flight can be sold to cover its variable costs and make a contribution to fixed costs. If a flight can make such a contribution, it is usually better to have an aircraft in the air producing output and generating revenue than sitting on the ground – notwithstanding that accountants could characterise the flight as unprofitable on a fully allocated basis.

Maximising resource utilisation is now a critical element in the operating strategies of all well-managed airlines. It has profound strategic implications:

- *Low-fare carriers* LFAs depend upon high cabin floorspace utilisation (i.e., high seating densities/low seat pitches) and high aircraft utilisation to keep their unit costs competitively low. The key to high aircraft utilisation is fast turnarounds facilitated by: avoiding congested hubs (unless, as in the case of easyJet at London Gatwick, access to price-sensitive but nonetheless relatively high-yield business traffic justifies an exception to the rule); minimal provision of catering (which reduces re-supply times between flight-legs – as well as saving weight and freeing-up galley space for extra seating); quick passenger embarkation procedures (often helped by the absence of seat allocation); not carrying belly-hold cargo in narrowbodies; refusing to interline; forgoing online connecting traffic; and having a single-type fleet. Although there are variations in the formula as noted in Chapter 1, a critical part of most LFA strategies is a single-type, single-cabin, simple-product operating system with high levels of utilisation. The importance of Southwest's legendary fast turnarounds, for example, is reflected in the fact that were they on average just 5 minutes longer the airline would have needed 18 additional aircraft to support its winter 2006 schedule (Finney 2006). (That schedule, incidentally, required 2773 daily turns from a fleet of 461 B737s.)

- *Charter carriers* Charter airlines serving European vacation markets also rely on high-density cabin configurations and high aircraft utilisation.
- *Network carriers* The broad geographic scope of most network carriers impacts on aircraft utilisation in two ways:
  - *Short-haul operations* Network carriers' aircraft utilisation is generally lower than figures achieved by LFAs and charter airlines for comparable types. A given type operated on a point-to-point network should be able to achieve higher utilisation than the same type operated in a hub-and-spoke network because hubs are often congested, causing delays in the air and lengthening taxi times, and because hub scheduling has to allow time for passengers and baggage to make connections from incoming flights before each aircraft can depart again. Where a hub is capable of generating a revenue premium from the connectivity benefit it offers passengers originating at outstations this might compensate for utilisation disadvantages, but when either alternative hubs or hub-bypass services are available such premia come under pressure.
  - *Long-haul operations* The longer the average stage-length operated by a particular type, the higher should be its annual average utilisation because it will spend less of its time on the ground. This is one reason why the unit cost of long-haul operations is generally lower than the unit cost of short-haul operations. (Although true at the extremes of intercontinental against short-haul, how true this is in the middle ground will depend very much upon network design and scheduling – topics covered in Chapters 6 and 7.)

    Many network carriers have taken one or all of several steps to improve aircraft utilisation: depeaking hubs to raise resource utilisation generally and to reduce (or stem the worsening of) congestion, improving turnaround times by reengineering airside operations, and flying more point-to-point hub-bypass routes. The ultimate objective of measures such as these is to reduce unit cost (CASM) by spreading fixed costs over a larger output of ASMs produced from an unchanged resource base (and, of course, to sell the incremental output at a profit).
- *Cargo carriers* Integrated carriers such as FedEx tend to operate hub-and-spoke systems dependent on overnight short- and medium-haul feed using aircraft that can generate only low levels of utilisation. Accordingly, the high fixed costs of new aircraft are difficult to justify and there is widespread reliance on older models that have lower ownership costs to spread across their relatively low output of ATMs. On the other hand, expensive newer aircraft such as FedEx's A300-600Fs or UPS' B747-400s require the high levels of utilisation that can be generated by flying longer routes between hubs and major gateways.

Productivity   Productivity is the ratio of outputs to inputs – either all inputs aggregated or just a single category, such as labour. Dresner (2002) distinguishes between several different types of measure commonly used to assess airline productivity:

1. *Partial productivity metrics* These include:
    - Labour productivity (e.g., ASMs, ATMs, RPMs, or RTMs per employee or per labour-hour).
    - Flight equipment productivity (e.g., ASMs or RPMs produced per flight-hour, day or year).

- Other partial productivity measures (e.g., output per gallon of fuel).

   Although simple to calculate and widely used, partial productivity measures suffer from the fact that they make no allowance for economically rational trade-offs that might be made between different types of input – such as using more labour and less automation (i.e., capital) in a low labour cost but capital-constrained environment. (Vass (1996) provides an example of a somewhat more technical study of comparative labour productivity, illustrating that although partial productivity measures *can* be calculated using just simple ratios this does not have to be the case.)

2. *Measures of total productivity* These include:
   - *Total (or multi-) factor productivity* uses indices of total input and total output to measure output produced per unit of input. (Morrell [2002a] provides an illustration of how total factor productivity can be calculated, and a recent paper from Vasigh and Fleming [2005] describes a study using the technique.)
   - *Data envelopment analysis*, a linear programming technique, was originally developed as an efficiency metric. (Schefczyk [1993] has used the method to analyse airline operational performance.)

3. *Statistical decomposition approach* This attempts to control for carriers' different characteristics – generally by regressing gross productivity scores on variables such as average stage-length, traffic density, various measures of corporate scale, and so on (Morrell op. cit.). Its disadvantage lies in computational complexity relative to partial productivity measures.

Dresner (op. cit.) concludes that although gross measures and statistical approaches are more comprehensive in their assessment of productivity, and the latter in particular should be preferred for inter-firm comparisons, their complexity makes it likely that simpler partial productivity measures will continue in widespread use. He therefore draws attention to studies by Windle and Dresner (1992, 1995) which suggest that RTK and RPK per employee are the partial productivity measures most highly correlated with total factor productivity.

Efficiency and effectiveness Efficiency is maximised when a given level of inputs is generating as much output as possible or when a given level of output is being generated by the minimum level of inputs possible. Effectiveness is maximised when a targeted standard of performance is attained. The economic appeal of an operating system that is delivering output both effectively (i.e., in conformity with customers' expectations) and efficiently (given the nature of the output concerned – whether long-haul first class or short-haul low-fare ASMs, for example) is that fixed costs are being spread over as much output as the system can produce given available inputs and also quality requirements.

Managing Productivity

The importance of getting as much output as possible from airline resources has already been stressed. Steps taken to increase the productivity of *aircraft* have been mentioned – steps such as accelerating turnaround times and designing both networks and schedules to be efficient as well as effective. Efforts to improve *staff* productivity include: outsourcing labour-intensive processes; greater automation, especially of back-office processes such as routine purchasing and spares inventory handling, for example; wider use of part-time and seasonal employees; more flexible work-rules and staff multi-skilling, where allowed by union contracts; wider use of scheduling models to help assign staff in response to actual requirements (e.g., assignment of check-in staff on the basis of queuing models combining service level requirements and day-of-operation flight loadings, assignment of cabin crews in response to bookings, assignment of baggage handlers in response to projected volumes of loose-loaded baggage on incoming narrowbodies); and having customers participate more actively in service delivery (e.g., Internet booking, self-service check-ins, smart-card airport facilitation). Some carriers targeting high-yield segments have also invested in improved staff training, the intention being that consistently high service standards will reduce time spent on service recovery and so raise productivity.

It is important to remember that whilst high resource productivity is critical to every airline, there are nonetheless some points to beware of:

1. Productivity figures can be deceptive. They are often arrived at by dividing into revenue or output a numerical measure of workforce or asset base (although there are many other ways to calculate productivity). Clearly, productivity can rise if the numerator increases more rapidly than the denominator. It can also rise if the numerator edges up only sluggishly or even remains static, whilst at the same time the denominator shrinks; shrinkage could reflect greater efficiency, but it might instead result from inadequate investment. A key question is therefore whether productivity improvements built on a shrinking resource base represent a trimming of 'fat' or a seepage of fundamental resources and skills needed to sustain long-term profitability. Bear in mind that:
    *   Productivity growth and market share decline can go hand in hand.
    *   Productivity growth and profits can move in different directions. An airline could for example increase productivity by raising seat density whilst leaving staff numbers and fleet size unchanged, but if this product deterioration causes high-yield customers to defect and so erodes revenue it is possible that profits will suffer. Conversely, in 2006–07 jetBlue removed six seats from its A320s to bring capacity down to 150, thereby allowing it legally to reduce the number of flight attendants from 4 to 3 (i.e., one for each 50 seats or fraction thereof); clearly, whilst productivity in terms of ASMs per remaining flight attendant will rise as a result of a decision such as this, the real question is whether absolute labour costs saved exceed revenue forgone from the missing seats.
    The moral is that increasing output through higher resource productivity is only half the battle; the other half is selling incremental output – and selling it at an adequate yield.
2. The institutional context, the structure of the operating system (i.e., network, fleet, and processes), and the nature of output (i.e., design of the product) have a profound impact on just what is possible. For example, labour productivity largely depends upon:
    *   Hours worked per annum, which might be affected by regulation and/or union agreements.
    *   The structure of each particular airline's operations. Some productivity measures – notably the widely favoured metrics ASM or ATM per employee – respond positively to larger aircraft, longer stage-lengths, and scheduling for high frequencies. Large aircraft do not require proportionately more staff to schedule, dispatch, operate, and maintain than smaller aircraft; long stage-lengths

operated by large aircraft generate more ASMs and ATMs per dispatch than short flight-legs operated by small aircraft; high frequencies in principle provide better opportunities to optimise aircraft, crew, and station personnel than low-frequency operations (Doganis 2001). With regard to productivity expressed in ATMs (as opposed to ASMs) per employee, carriers generating significant freight revenues tend to benefit from the fact that selling space and handling ULDs are less labour-intensive than similar activities on the passenger side (ibid.).

- The efficiency of work processes and their level of automation.
- The extent of outsourcing. Retaining functions such as catering, maintenance, IT, and ground-handling in-house has little or no bearing on airline output, but does have a significant impact on staff numbers and therefore staff productivity.
- Whether the airline offers premium products requiring high staff to customer ratios. Passengers are buying a range of experiences when they purchase an air trip. The value they perceive themselves to be getting from their purchase, and its relationship to expectations, should provide a context for productivity improvements; highly productive staff do not inevitably equate to highly satisfied, loyal or profitable customers. For example, cutting cabin crew in business class will raise the productivity of those who remain (expressed in ASMs per employee), but what impact will it have on the perceived experiences of passengers, on their loyalty, and on the carrier's share of the lifetime revenue potentially available from frequent, high-yield travellers?

3. Local productivity can be affected by wider corporate decisions. For example, the productivity of resources at an outstation – reflected in cost per enplaned passenger and the unit cost of station operations – will be affected by a wide variety of factors, some of which will not necessarily have been decided locally:
   - *Network design* If a station is served by, say, two routes and one of these is dropped because it is unprofitable, there are two possible side-effects to bear in mind:
     - Pending any reduction in personnel (which might be rapid) and station overhead (which will be slower), and assuming frequencies are not added to the remaining route, station costs per departure will rise – because there are now fewer departures over which to spread fixed costs – and the productivity of station resources will fall.
     - As it is now having to bear station costs in their entirety rather than sharing them, it is possible that the apparent profitability of the remaining route will deteriorate. This underlines the interconnectedness of network decisions – and might, incidentally, argue for spreading station costs over all routes that benefit from traffic flows originating from each station.
   - *Operational decisions* The profitability of a station might, for example, hinge on decisions taken with regard to: the aircraft type(s) assigned to serve it, bearing in mind that different types have different operating economics; whether line maintenance is to be outsourced or handled internally; and the extent to which spares inventory (of line replaceable units, consumables, and expendables) will be held locally to support in-house line maintenance.

Conclusion Whilst productivity certainly matters, and there is a place for metrics such as ASMs produced per employee or per dollar of employment expenditure, what matters more is how much of the output generated by an airline's resources or expenditures has been sold and at what price. This points to the importance of metrics which connect costs to the revenue side rather than to another metric (i.e., ASMs or ATMs) on the output side; examples of such metrics include revenue per employee, revenue per dollar of employment cost, revenue per flight-hour (by type), and operating revenue per dollar of operating cost – the last being particularly valuable because it takes into account the effects of outsourcing and code-sharing on employee numbers and flight-hours respectively.

Productivity Comparisons

Particularly where directly competing airlines pay broadly the same for their inputs (i.e., labour, fuel, insurance, aircraft, ATS, etc.), any sustainable competitive advantage held by one carrier in respect of unit costs is likely to be attributable to higher productivity. Important potential sources of higher productivity include labour flexibility (with roots in labour agreements and/or corporate culture) and efficient design of the operating system (i.e., fleet and network structures, resource assignments, processes and activities).

However, productivity comparisons between any two airlines or groups of airlines have their dangers. The root of the problem is that airline output is not homogeneous (Oum and Yu 1998). First, different service concepts carry with them very different staffing and resource commitments – as is most notably underlined by the productivity differences that can be anticipated between staff serving long-haul premium passengers and those working in a short-haul, low-fare environment. Second, decisions whether to outsource or retain in-house key ancillary functions such as maintenance and engineering – and, if retained in-house, whether to bid for significant volumes of third party work – can have a profound impact on staffing and resource levels. Third, different network structures, particularly in respect of average length of haul, also affect certain types of productivity comparison, as do aircraft size, national salary levels, and currency rates of exchange. For example, Boeing (2007, p. 11) compares a B747-400 carrying 420 passengers on one 9500-kilometre flight with a B737-800 carrying 148 passengers on each of eight 640-kilometre flights during a similar time span: the former generates just short of 4 million RPKs against the latter's 757,000, but the B737 transports nearly three times as many passengers. Which is more productive?

SCALE

This section starts by addressing the question of growth, and then goes on to define economies of scale and to comment on their role in the industry.

Growth

Despite periodic cyclical downturns and the more serious recessions beginning in 1991 and 2001, the airline industry has since the Second World War been a growth industry insofar as both its revenues and traffic have regularly risen by multiples of the growth in global GDP.

The attraction of growth   Putting aside what economists refer to as 'agency problems' that arise when airline managers (i.e., 'agents') pursue their own interests at the expense of stockholders (i.e., their 'principals') by pursuing empire-building strategies that fail to create shareholder value, it has been widely assumed in the industry that growth offers advantages on both sides of the income statement.

1. *The revenue/demand side* The benefits here derive from market presence:
    *   new routes or additional frequencies can stimulate demand;
    *   passengers prefer non-stop, through-plane, and connecting single-carrier service in that order and prefer same-airline routings, so an extensive network will have broader appeal than a geographically limited route system – an appeal enhanced by FFPs;
    *   incremental output can be used to discourage or eliminate competitors on a route (although egregious capacity dumping might come under the scrutiny of antitrust/competition authorities in some jurisdictions);
    *   size can bring powerful benefits at a fortress hub and, more generally, a large carrier is often in a strong position to exercise price leadership in at least some of its markets;
    *   size should be accompanied by wider brand recognition.
2. *The cost/output side* Economies of scale are present when unit cost falls in response to growing output. This will happen when incremental output is added at a cost lower than the current unit cost – as when labour is added at the bottom of the seniority list and pay-scale, for example, or a growing airline's bargaining strength vis-à-vis suppliers leads to lower input costs. Resource productivity might also rise as output grows; in 2000, for example, TAP Portugal implemented a strategy of growing output off an unchanged labour force (which could not easily be reduced). However, there are two cautionary points:
    *   Output expansion that is not paced by demand growth will place downward pressure on yield and/or load factor.
    *   New capacity comes with fixed costs attached, as we have already seen, so the output it generates not only has to be sold but sold at prices sufficient to more than cover those incremental costs. Having unit production costs that are low relative to those of competitors is only half the battle; the other half is having production costs that are also low relative to the prices at which output can be sold.
    Many observers in fact doubt the existence of economies of scale in the airline industry.

Economies Of Scale In The Airline Industry

The presence or absence of economies of scale in the industry has been a hotly debated issue. Early empirical evidence, for example Caves (1962) in respect of a regulated market and Levine (1965) in respect of a deregulated market, surfaced doubts about their existence, and this argument was used by the pro-deregulation lobby in the United States to dispel fears regarding the likelihood of consolidation in pursuit of greater efficiency derived from scale. Early post-deregulation studies by Caves *et al.* (1984) and Gillen *et al.* (1985) tended to confirm the absence of economies of scale in the US industry insofar as long-run average costs do not necessarily fall as output of ASMs and ATMs is expanded. However, subsequent studies (e.g., Creel and Farrell 2001) have found contrary evidence.

The notion that it is possible to grow out of cost difficulties by averaging down unit costs had a compelling hold on parts of the industry during the 1980s in particular – notably amongst the US 'Big Three'. However, the structural problems facing most US majors were never more than temporarily suppressed by growth, and after 9/11 economic survival in most cases involved significant shrinkage of output; indeed, the financial turnaround beginning in mid-decade was largely predicated on capacity discipline in domestic markets.

Regarding whether size really does matter in the airline industry, two general observations seem fairly well-supported by observable facts.

- On the one hand, there are activities in respect of which economies of scale appear to be present, some of which have already been noted: maintenance, catering, ground-handling, etc. Another benefit of size is bargaining strength vis-à-vis external suppliers. There can also be economies of scale in flight operations insofar as operating just a handful of a type is usually more expensive in terms of maintenance provisioning and crew training and utilisation than having a more significant fleet. However, it is not always clear whether available economies are economies of scale, scope, or general market presence. (Bear in mind that economies of scale are present when unit costs decline as output of a given product increases, whereas economies of scope are present when unit costs decline as the range of products being produced is increased. Given that there is considerable debate surrounding how to characterise the airline 'product' – by departure, by cabin, or by fare class, for example – it can be seen that drawing a definitional line between economies of scale and scope is difficult as well as, perhaps, somewhat artificial.)
- On the other hand, there seems to be no direct correlation between ASMs or ATMs produced and average cost; if there were, United would have lower costs than Southwest. Consider also that if the world's airlines are taken as a whole, neither the lowest unit costs, the largest operating profits nor the best operating margin correlate to size as measured by the output of ASMs or ATMs.

Several issues in fact arise when trying to relate different airlines' unit costs to volume of output in order to identify economies of scale:

1. Different fleet and network structures inevitably mean that one airline's cost of producing an ASM is seldom precisely the same as another's, and if it is we are dealing with coincidence given the fundamentally different economics of operating different aircraft (e.g., different types, capacities, and ages) over different networks (e.g., different stage-lengths and traffic densities) pursuant to different schedules. A figure of, say, 150,000 ASMs could be generated by flying 150 seats for 1000 miles, 250 seats for 600 miles, 400 seats for 375 miles, and so on; similarly, 150 seats flown 1000 miles could be carried on one 150-seat aircraft, two 75-seat aircraft, or three 50-seat aircraft. The economics of generating 150,000 ASMs of output will be very different in each case and will clearly produce very different costs. Decisions will be driven by marketing as well as cost considerations.

2. Just as production processes are not homogeneous, neither is output. One source of heterogeneity was touched upon above: service frequency. As we saw in Chapter 4, there are others. Airlines produce different types and/or mixes of output. At the

extremes, services designed to satisfy the expectations of short-haul business travellers are clearly going to be more expensive to produce than medium- or long-haul charter services targeted at the leisure segment. ASMs produced by Southwest or Ryanair are not the same as ASMs produced in American's first class Flagship Suite – and neither, evidently, are their production costs.

3. Airlines face different input costs (particularly fuel, airport and ATS charges) depending upon the scope of their network and, particularly, costs at their hubs and other principal centres of operations.

4. Airlines also differ markedly in their levels of productivity. Some carriers make every unit of expenditure work harder than others, therefore needing less expenditure to pay for a given level of output. (Different regulatory environments can also affect productivity, notably with regard to flight-crew duty-times.)

5. International comparisons are inevitably complicated by currency volatility. When the dollar is strong, exchange rates can impact heavily on carriers whose networks give them no or limited sources of dollar revenue with which to meet fuel bills and operating lease rentals – which are fundamentally dollar-denominated.

Conclusion   As far as flight operations are concerned, economies of scale are still widely believed to be negligible. However:

• To the extent that it is rarely twice as expensive to operate two flights as it is to operate one, they do exist.
• Recent empirical research has found that economies of network scale may exist where adding points to a network permits aircraft utilisation to be increased (Brueckner and Zhang 2001; Ng and Seabright 2001).

Larger economies nonetheless seem to be derived less from the operation of aircraft themselves than from activities elsewhere in the operating system. Airlines are also widely believed to benefit from marketing economies of scale, although there is a semantic question about whether unit cost advantages derived from this source are not in fact economies of scope or perhaps even more general effects of size and market presence. Economies derived from the purchasing power of large enterprises might also be attributed to either scale or scope.

Learning

We have seen that economies of scale relate to unit cost declines associated with rising output. A similar but quite distinct phenomenon is 'learning', which is evident when unit cost declines are associated not with single-period increases in output but with cumulative output over time. (Some writers distinguish between 'learning curves', which result from improved human task efficiency, and 'experience curves' that are derived from improved machine efficiency; others use 'experience curves' as the generic umbrella for unit cost declines attributable to both human learning and machine efficiency.)

Although any form of human activity should benefit from learning over time, the unit cost advantage of the phenomenon is perhaps more strongly evident in mass production manufacturing industries than in service businesses; indeed, the importance of learning underpinned pursuit of market share and use of tools such as the Boston Box in many manufacturing industries from the late 1960s through the 1980s. That said, there are undoubtedly learning advantages available in areas such as maintenance (Kline 1999), scheduling, and operations control – although outsourcing can allow relatively new carriers to benefit from the experience of long-established suppliers. It is on the demand side rather than in respect of output that learning may have its most profound effect, however; incumbents with a long market presence should have access to both a broader and a deeper understanding of customers' expectations (Button and Stough 2000). Customer insight is not always accessed and leveraged, of course.

VI. Cost Drivers and Their Management: Distribution

Over the last two sections we have been using the value chain metaphor to look at costs. Upstream costs – the supply chain, fuel, and airport charges – were considered in section iv. Section v. discussed costs associated with the internal operating system, in particular: service design; process design; labour costs; the fleet; maintenance costs; costs associated with security, the environment, passengers' rights, and administration; productivity; and scale. This section will complete the review by looking at distribution costs and their management.

THE DISTRIBUTION FUNCTION

Distribution has three purposes:

- selling – that is, acting as a channel to market;
- adding value for the customer in the form of:
  - convenience (e.g., time and place utilities when making a purchase);
  - information (e.g., destination-related advice for leisure travellers, and back-office functionality for business accounts);
- building relationships with customers – something that is difficult to achieve when a channel intermediary, such as a travel agent or a freight forwarder, is involved.

This section of the chapter will look first at the different aspects of distribution strategy, then at distribution costs, and finally at cargo distribution. Actions taken by carriers to manage distribution costs will then be considered.

Distribution Strategy

'Distribution' is a word used generically to describe the process of delivering products to customers. In the case of airlines, the product in this narrow context is a ticket (now generally electronic rather than paper) or a cargo air waybill (still normally paper). More specifically, what is being distributed is information about price and availability, followed – although not in all cases – by confirmation that a seat or cargo space has been reserved, and then by evidence of a contract of carriage. Airlines have available several different 'distribution channels' through which to sell and deliver products, and their choice of which channels to use and how to use them is a 'distribution strategy'.

Distribution channels   A fundamental distinction can be drawn between direct and indirect channels.

1. *Direct channels*   These could include one or more of an airline's own proprietary website (or different websites for different market segments, such as frequent flyers or corporate clients), call centres, airport counters and kiosks, remote kiosks (in hotels or retail outlets, for example), and city offices (an expensive and therefore rapidly disappearing channel). (Web channels, incidentally, might offer access just through PCs and laptops, or they might also support distribution through web-enabled mobile devices.) The common aspect of these channels is that there is no intermediary standing between the travel purchaser and the airline: contact is direct.
2. *Indirect channels* Intermediaries in passenger markets come in a variety of forms, with some more common than others depending upon the market concerned:
    *   *Travel agencies*   These can be distinguished on two dimensions. First, a distinction can be drawn between 'traditional' agencies and online agencies. The former have physical sales offices as well as, in the case of larger companies, call centres and highly functional websites. The latter include not only the numerous leisure- or business-oriented brands associated with owners of sites such as Travelocity, Expedia, and Orbitz, but also more focused auction sites (arguably a convenient outlet for distressed inventory) pioneered by Priceline and Hotwire, and meta-search engines (also called 'travel aggregators') such as Kayak, SideStep, and Bezurk. Second, a distinction can be drawn between agencies specialising in business travel, now commonly referred to as travel management companies or TMCs, and agencies more oriented towards general leisure travel or niche activities and destinations. This distinction mirrors a separate but related distinction between:
        –   'managed travel programmes', usually established for mid- to large-sized companies which require services in respect of one or more of travel policy compliance, billing, accounting, reporting, tracking, security, and provision of emergency support (which TMCs, together with GDSs, are able to provide but most airline websites cannot);
        –   unmanaged travel (which is the field of individual, and some business, travellers).
    *   *Wholesalers and consolidators*   These are large agencies which buy products in volume on a net fare basis and onsell to the public or to smaller retail agencies at a margin. They are more active in some markets than others, being notably prevalent in parts of Europe and Asia. The words are often used interchangeably, but where 'consolidators' deal exclusively with airline tickets they are in effect a subset of a wider group of 'wholesalers', some of whom also purchase and onsell products from other travel suppliers (such as hotels and car rental companies).
    *   *Packagers*   These intermediaries assemble various travel products from different suppliers at wholesale prices and package them for retailing to the public. The most common are tour operators, which have been a force in the European leisure industry for over half a century; more recently, cruise lines have grown rapidly and become important wholesale purchasers of airline products in a small number of markets which feed their operations. (Clearly, the distinction between wholesalers and packagers is not always clear-cut. Another complication is that some airlines operate their own inbound and outbound tour packagers, to which space is made available at wholesale prices – albeit on a direct rather than intermediated basis.)

- *Alliance partners* The release of space on an airline's flights that has been marketed by a code-share partner also represents a form of intermediated sale. We will return to this below and in Chapter 6.

Standing between traditional agencies and the airlines have for many years been several global distribution systems (GDSs). The largest are Galileo/Apollo and Worldspan (all owned by Travelport), together with Sabre and Amadeus; in addition, there are others oriented more to particular regions – most notably Asia (e.g., Abacus, Axess, Infini – all partnered by Sabre – Topas, and Travelsky). Their original role was to distribute airline schedule, seat availability, and fare information to subscribing agencies, and to provide those agencies with the functionality to book space and manage bookings. In response to increasingly onerous fees imposed by GDSs on airlines from the mid-1990s onwards, which we will return to shortly, two new channels emerged: first, larger agencies and wholesalers in some markets opened 'direct connect' channels to particular airlines bypassing the GDSs; second, a small number of alternative GDSs appeared – known at first as GNEs (GDS new entrants or 'genies') and more recently as ACPs (alternative content providers). The most significant ACPs to date have been G2 Switchworks, ITA, and Farelogix; whilst undoubtedly successful in related fields (e.g., ITA's development of a new reservation system designed to accommodate Air Canada's innovative approach to bundled and branded fares), there is a consensus that their early promise as alternatives to legacy GDSs is unlikely to be fulfilled.

Distribution strategy   Given the availability of so many potential distribution channels, each airline has to decide which ones to use and how to use them in order to gain access to particular segments of targeted markets. This is the essence of a *distribution strategy*. The choice is driven by a requirement to balance cost against the needs and preferences of targeted purchasers. Needs and preferences will depend upon variables such as:

- the level of access customers have to different types of channel (e.g., relying almost entirely on the Web, as Ryanair now does, will not work for AirAsia because the latter serves a region where Internet penetration and credit card possession are lower than in Europe);
- the complexity of itineraries (e.g., business travellers are likely to have more complex itineraries and a need for more frequent changes than can yet be accommodated on many airline websites);
- the local importance of agencies in the sales process (e.g., in many parts of Asia there is a complex, tiered structure of agencies and corporate travel purchasers underpinned by personal relationships which might not readily open themselves to analysis on the basis of economics alone).

The archetypal LFA business model eschews agency and GDS channels in favour of direct distribution. Many LFAs in fact do follow this model (e.g., Ryanair), but there are two reasons why many do not:

- In some parts of the world Internet penetration and credit card ownership are still sufficiently low that other means of reaching customers and receiving payment are necessary. Agencies are an obvious channel, particularly where they can be encouraged to bypass GDSs by booking direct through the airline's website;

another approach is to use telephone call centres to take reservations and to have arrangements with local retail outlets – such as post offices and banks – to accept payment. Air Arabia takes the latter approach.

- Elsewhere, notably in North America and Europe, LFAs in search of additional revenue and higher yields have increasingly turned towards the corporate sector, making necessary some level of involvement with agencies and GDSs – certainly if coverage of the larger corporate accounts is targeted. (In fact, some of the larger LFAs which offer high-frequency service connecting business centres – easyJet, for example – are sufficiently popular with corporate clients that TMCs have for years been using 'work-arounds' to access web fares in the absence of GDS availability; when in 2007 easyJet did start distributing through Amadeus and Galileo, the per segment fees it passed on for each booking were so high that many TMCs ignored the new channels and continued using established work-arounds.)

LFAs that do choose to cut themselves off from agencies, which are capable of 'pushing' sales, may have to devote greater effort to generating 'pull' through PR and advertising – a challenge to which Ryanair has notably risen, for example.

Network carriers generally offer such a wide range of different products to so many market segments that they are more likely to opt for a multichannel strategy. Conversely, charter airlines benefit from being able to sell much of their output in bulk to a relatively small number of (often affiliated) tour organizers, and so do not bear either the fixed costs of a large sales and distribution organization or the variable costs attributable to agency commissions and GDS fees; the growing proportion of their output accounted for by seat-only sales is generally distributed through direct, rather than intermediated, channels.

Technology has been a critical driver of both the move to direct distribution of their product by airlines over the Internet, and the growth of alternative intermediated channels. Technology in this sense refers not just to the increases in speed and decreases in cost associated with data transmission and storage, but also to the burgeoning functionality of *distribution media*. In particular, the growing use of XML-based interfaces under the auspices of the Open Travel Alliance (OTA) has enabled information to be presented and acted upon in many more ways than is permitted by legacy systems, and has facilitated online fare-shopping by enabling much greater interfacing between what would previously have been isolated supplier systems: feed on schedules, availability, fare rules, and pricing can be drawn together for presentation to intermediaries and customers, and can now be customised for presentation to a specific channel, point of sale, or purchaser.

Distribution strategy is a large and complex topic about which it is only possible here to make some broad generalisations:

1. A carrier which makes a strategic choice not to use a particular channel is potentially isolating itself from any segment of demand served by that channel; the airline therefore needs to have alternative access to the demand, or to have reached the conclusion that it is either insignificant or too expensive to serve.
2. A distribution strategy should be driven not by considerations of channel cost alone, but channel profitability. In addition to cost, the following have to be considered:
   - accessibility: in person, online, via mobile phone or PDA;
   - information transmission: schedule, availability, price, conditions;
   - functionality: booking and payment, changes, ancillary sales (e.g., seating, catering, food, insurance).

3. An airline following a multichannel strategy will increasingly want the ability to manage the release and pricing of inventory by point of sale.
4. An airline wanting to offer bundled and branded fares, as pioneered by Air Canada, will need the ability to upsell – something which GDS legacy architecture has not in the past facilitated but which the GDSs, led in this context by Amadeus, are now addressing.

Distribution Costs

An airline's 'total distribution cost' (TDC) can be difficult for an external analyst to disaggregate: rather than sitting in one or a small number of distinct departments, it encompasses a broad range of labour costs (e.g., the sales force, distribution planners, reservations agents, and support staff), marketing costs, IT and communication costs (e.g., to support websites, kiosks, call centres, and reservations systems), click-through payments to Google and other search engines, rent for downtown and airport space, agency-related costs (e.g., commissions, overrides, non-volume low season 'spot incentives', and print material), GDS costs, credit card fees, and fraud. (In the United States even the DOT's exceptionally comprehensive Form 41 report does not break out GDS booking fees, for example.)

Another complication is that whereas agency compensation has historically taken the form of commission and overrides, both of which are discussed below, it is now common in some markets for airlines to wholesale net fares and leave the intermediary to make its income from a mark-up to retail customers; whereas commissions and overrides are bookable expenses, net fares generate a reduction in revenue rather than an explicit expense. The discounts embedded in net fares and similar price breaks negotiated with corporate clients are also in effect distribution costs which, again, under many countries' accounting practices are subsumed into the revenue side of the income statement rather than broken out as expenses. All this makes comparisons between airlines, and sometimes even between different time periods for the same carrier where its distribution strategy has changed, somewhat challenging.

Common measures of distribution cost include:

1. *Sales and distribution cost as a percentage of transport revenue* This peaked for US carriers at over 20 per cent in 1995 (Delta) in response to rising use of agencies by consumers and increasing base commissions in the years following deregulation, but it has since fallen in most cases to below 10 per cent.
2. *Sales and distribution cost per RPM* Whilst same-carrier comparisons from year to year are valid provided cost definitions and allocation methods remain unchanged, comparisons between different airlines should be approached cautiously because different network structures can affect their validity. Specifically:
    *   length of haul: the figure for a long-haul carrier should be lower than for a short-haul carrier operating out of the same home market because fixed transaction costs associated with each sale are being spread over a larger number of RPMs;
    *   channel structures and remuneration practices in the markets served: for example, whereas sales in short-haul European and North American markets are increasingly made direct or – if intermediated – commission free, long-haul sales out of Asia are likely to involve commissionable agency sales.

3. *Sales and distribution cost per originating passenger* This can be a useful metric, particularly in conjunction with the figure for a carrier's average fare (i.e., average transport revenue per originating passenger). Note that the denominator is originating rather than enplaned passengers, in order to eliminate the double-counting of connections.

Aside from staffing and other costs that might fall under the heading of a variety of line items (e.g. 'sales and reservations', 'gate and counter'), there are five aspects of airline distribution costs that bear particular consideration: agency incentives, other agency-related expenses, GDS fees, credit card fees, and interline ticketing costs.

Agency incentives   There are four principal incentives:

1. *Commissions* In 1977 just prior to deregulation, 55 per cent of US airline sales were made through travel agencies; by the mid-1990s, consumer uncertainty in the face of constantly changing schedules and prices had driven this figure above 80 per cent. By 2006, high Internet penetration together with the airlines' enthusiasm for direct sales had forced the agency share back down to a little over half, and the expectation is that it will continue to decline. Globally, base commissions traditionally ran as high as 10 per cent of a sold fare, but their level now varies enormously depending upon where the sale has been made (e.g., whether or not it is the airline's home market – in which case sales might generate no or low commissions), the extent of reliance on agency sales in the market concerned, and the nature of the journey (e.g., long-haul sales might be commissionable whereas short-haul/domestic sales are not). Practice still varies widely; for example, in the same week in May 2008 that Northwest announced it would no longer pay commissions to agents selling its services out of Japan, Italian carrier Air One offered US agents 11 per cent to sell seats on its new transatlantic flights from Chicago and Boston to Milan.
2. *Commission overrides* Overrides, which can be paid both by airlines having a weak position in particular markets and by strong carriers wanting to consolidate market share, are payments made by airlines to selected agencies that reach agreed sales targets. Even carriers which refuse to pay commissions, either at all or on certain categories of fare, commonly enter into override agreements where they continue to use agency channels. However, most are now much more focused in their use of overrides than in the past, and programmes are increasingly being assessed by relating their cost to the margin gained from incremental traffic rather than by reference to market share alone.
3. *Net fares* A distinction can be drawn between two sales models. First, the agency model: an agent is paid a commission keyed-off the price of the ticket sold (i.e., the fare is commissionable). Second, the merchant model: an agency pays wholesale prices for tickets, and retails them at a mark-up (i.e., the fare is net); as noted above, the forgone mark-up is as much a distribution cost to the airline concerned as a commission would have been, but it is reflected in the carrier's accounts as an unreported reduction in revenue rather than a reported expense.
4. *Payments to online agencies* Some airlines pay commissions to online agencies and some, whether or not sales are considered commissionable, make payments to bias display or tie-break algorithms in their favour. On the other hand, many carriers will not pay commission and several that have strong Web brands try as far as possible to block online agencies from accessing their sites at all (e.g., Southwest); they argue

that any loss of revenue from preventing online agencies screen-scraping fares onto their own sites is mitigated by the fact that the airline cannot make ancillary sales to customers booking through those sites.

Other agency-related expenses   Commissions and overrides are just two aspects of the costs involved in distributing through agents. There are others. First, major airlines generally have sales forces tasked with telephoning and visiting key agencies. Second, money paid by customers to agencies finds its way to airlines through billing and settlement plans established in each country and takes longer to reach the airline than cash from direct sales. (The equivalent in the United States is the Area Settlement Plan operated by the Airlines Reporting Corporation.) Third, it has not been uncommon to incentivise individual agents with mileage awards and prizes, both on an ongoing basis and as part of a fixed duration, locally targeted sales campaign.

GDS booking fees   When a travel agent uses a GDS to access airline content and make a booking, the GDS levies a booking fee per segment. Because each flight under a different flight-number is a separate segment, even a simple return itinerary connecting over a hub is likely to generate four segments chargeable at several dollars each. Given that, unlike travel agency commissions and credit card fees, GDS booking fees are flat amounts, they take a disproportionately large bite out of cheaply priced fare classes and short-haul revenues generally. We will look later in the chapter at how airlines have tackled GDS booking fees; Box 5.7 considers the broad range of issues which have arisen between GDSs and airlines in recent years.

Box 5.7: Airlines' Issues with GDSs

1. *The absolute cost of booking fees* By the early years of the current decade US airlines were paying in excess of $2 billion per annum in GDS fees, and these fees had been increasing at an annual rate of 7 per cent – much faster than passenger enplanements. The rate of increase was particularly troubling given the dramatic decline in telecommunications and computing costs (although the GDSs would argue that the explosion in fare-comparison shopping, and the worsening look-to-book ratio, meant that more messages were having to be sent per confirmed booking than in the past).

2. *The method of calculating booking fees* Originally charged on the basis of net bookings (i.e., gross bookings less cancellations), GDS pricing structures (particularly in the US domestic market) became predominantly transaction-based – applying fees to amendments and cancellations as well as bookings. This not only contributed to rapidly rising fees, it also left airlines paying for transactions that generated no boarded passengers and therefore no flown revenue. The problem was exacerbated by GDSs incentivising agency transaction activity by lowering or eliminating equipment lease charges in return for high transaction volumes – irrespective of whether the transactions concerned produced revenue for the airlines. This led to a number of questionable practices intended to boost agency income by 'churning' reservations:

    *   *Passive bookings* These arise when an agency builds the passenger name record (PNR) required to track bookings and facilitate ticket issuance through a GDS. Legitimate uses include the taking over by an agency of bookings made directly with an airline. Passive bookings are nonetheless open to abuse; although they are relatively easy to isolate by use of billing information data tape (BIDT) audit software, getting GDS vendors to acknowledge abuse and refund fees can be difficult – which is why some US carriers have chosen to hold agencies accountable for invalid bookings.

- *Multiple bookings* These are reservations made on more than one flight for a single passenger, perhaps as a fall-back in case a meeting overruns.
- *Duplicate bookings* These are additional reservations for the same passenger on a single flight, perhaps made in error by an agency. Sometimes two or more agencies will reserve space for a single passenger on the same flight(s) when that passenger has asked for competing price quotes but in the end only accepts one of them. Whilst airlines can and increasingly do use revenue integrity software to pick these up in their own reservations systems, multiple and duplicate bookings made through GDSs represent a source of unproductive fees.
- *Speculative bookings* Some agencies book space on high-demand flights out of their local hub just in case valued clients have a late need for seats on these departures.

3. *Bias* 'Screen bias' was a major concern when most GDSs were owned by airlines inclined to incorporate algorithms which favoured their own services over those of competitors; regulators addressed this threat in both the EU and the United States during the 1980s. 'Architectural bias' arises where a carrier both owns a GDS and hosts its in-house reservations system within it, thereby accelerating the speed of communication between the two systems compared with what can be achieved by other airlines' externally hosted systems. The fact that amongst the four largest GDSs only Amadeus now has any airline ownership has allayed many concerns related to bias. Airline ownership of regional GDSs remains widespread in Asia, however.

4. *Market power* In the absence of direct connections, a given GDS might be an airline's only channel to the agencies subscribing to that GDS (given that most agencies subscribe to only one system). A GDS will, under these circumstances, be a monopoly supplier of access to the agencies concerned.

5. *Inflexible legacy architecture* GDSs have traditionally been hallmarked by private networks, specialised hardware, cryptic languages, and limited search capabilities – particularly in the absence of human intervention. Being legacy systems they have had difficulty integrating with other data sources, and insufficient flexibility to accommodate the à la carte product and pricing offers being made by an increasing number of airlines adopting a broader range of business models than seen in the past. The GDSs are having to respond to this challenge by moving towards open systems and web-based services.

6. *Release of commercially sensitive information on MIDTs* Some airlines are wary of GDS participation because their detailed sales, pricing, and agency transaction data will be available to any competitor purchasing an MIDT. (With direct sales growing as a proportion of total sales the share of market data available to GDSs – and therefore accessible to competitors through MIDTs – is in fact declining, but such data nonetheless remains hugely important to larger airlines' network and distribution planning efforts and to their understanding of market dynamics.)

Despite this litany of issues, it needs to be borne in mind that GDSs are important to TMCs, so any airline wanting comprehensive access to TMC client bases cannot ignore them.

Credit card fees With the growth of direct sales on the Internet, the share of airline TDCs accounted for by credit card fees has risen sharply over the last ten years. By 2006 IATA members were paying over $3 billion per annum, accounting for close to a quarter of TDCs. Credit card fraud is also a growing, albeit still relatively small, concern.

Although not a cost, an issue of some importance arising from relationships between airlines and credit card processors was thrown into sharp relief in April 2008 when Frontier attributed entry into Chapter 11 bankruptcy protection to the unilateral decision of its principal processor to increase the standard 'hold back'. It is normal practice for processors to retain a small percentage of each transaction to cover themselves against flight cancellation or airline illiquidity, but in light of pressures on the airline industry at that time Frontier's processor instituted a significant increase which the carrier was unable to absorb.

Interline ticketing costs   There are two aspects to this issue:

1. We saw in Chapter 3 that prorate dilution can be looked upon as a cost insofar as it is likely to reduce the revenue of any carrier interlining passengers with other airlines. The incidence of non-alliance interlining is now much smaller than it used to be, and an increasing proportion of interlining involves code-sharing on allied carriers – one of which (the operating carrier) operates the flight and one of which (the marketing carrier) sells the seat to an interlining passenger. Code-sharing is a form of distribution, and as such its costs – usually in practice opaque to outsiders because each deal is privately negotiated – are in principle distribution costs.
2. Prorate payments due (re international itineraries) are netted through the IATA Clearing House. Whilst the system functions efficiently, an airline can nonetheless wait some time to receive revenues in respect of passengers already carried when another airline issued their tickets and received payment for the whole journey from them (perhaps because that carrier was the first to be used on a multi-airline itinerary). This can have negative cash flow implications. Prorate billings and receipts also need to be checked for accuracy, and this is not a cost-free activity.

LFAs in many cases avoid prorate dilution, cash-flow delays, and revenue accounting complications by refusing to interline. This will usually be reflected in their much lower collection times, and correspondingly higher debtor turn rates, than network airlines.

Cargo Distribution

The problem that many cargo carriers and combination airline cargo divisions face is that they have little direct contact with end consumers of their services – that is, shippers and consignees. The customer in most cases is a forwarder or consolidator which has an interest in shopping around for the cheapest rates it can negotiate; shippers and consignees have little incentive to specify a particular airline, and cargo space is very often commoditised as a result of carriers' invisibility in the airfreight marketing system.

Many airlines simply accept the traditional situation, offering a simple airport-to-airport line-haul service. Others have taken a two-pronged approach that has as much to do with the revenue side as the cost side of operating strategy:

1. Building direct relationships with selected high-volume shippers (perhaps on an industry-specific basis), offering value-added services, and generally strengthening their brands. This is not a popular approach within the forwarder community.
2. Partnering with key forwarders in an attempt to offer a more coherently priced, integrated, and branded time-definite door-to-door service than the traditional airfreight product has provided, and in doing this counter the inroads increasingly being made by integrated carriers such as FedEx and DHL in international markets. On the whole, it has to be said that this development is still not widespread and that some airline–forwarder relationships remain ambivalent at best and adversarial at worst.

MANAGING DISTRIBUTION COSTS

Particularly since the mid-1990s, airlines have successfully used a broad menu of approaches to bring spiralling distribution costs under control: reducing travel agency commissions; disintermediation; increasing use of single-carrier fares; controlling GDS expenses; and controlling credit card expenses.

Reducing Travel Agency Commissions

The traditional agency commission system is fundamentally flawed inasmuch as it is driven by airfares rather than by the amount of work associated with each transaction. Commissions payable to bricks-and-mortar agencies began to come under sustained attack in 1994 when Delta first capped them. In 2002, Delta led a further assault on distribution expenses by eliminating base commissions on tickets sold in the United States and Canada. Remuneration would henceforth be driven by incentive agreements negotiated with each agency; in other words, incentives that had previously been treated as commission *overrides* were to replace commissions themselves at the heart of sales remuneration.

Commission capping and reduction have since spread beyond the United States, and both caps and commission rates have been ratcheted down; indeed, zero is now the standard in some markets. Commissions payable to Internet agencies have also come under pressure, with some airlines now refusing to pay – although others do still pay a service fee on bookings. There continues to be inexorable downward pressure on travel agency commissions, but the road towards a zero-commission model is uneven and depends upon conditions in individual markets. Some broad generalisations are nonetheless possible:

1. In the *United States*, most airlines no longer pay base commissions on domestic fares, and commissions payable on international fares have been significantly reduced – although network carriers do still pay privately negotiated overrides. This has had several consequences:
    *   According to ATA figures: absolute commission costs peaked in 1993 at $7.7 billion, but by 2005 had declined to $1.5 billion; as a percentage of passenger revenue they peaked at 12.8 per cent in 1992, but dropped to 1.7 per cent in 2005; their share of operating costs peaked at 10.7 per cent in 1991 and 1992, but had fallen to 1.2 per cent by 2005; and commission cost per ASM peaked in 1993 at 1.01 cents, before dropping to 0.15 cents in 2005. (Note that the fact commissions amounted to 1.7 per cent of passenger revenue does not mean that this was the average level of commission paid; an airline's average percentage commission paid is a function not only of what is handed to agencies, but also what share of total sales is intermediated rather than direct.)
    *   There has been a significant consolidation in the US agency business, with the number of full-service and ticket printer locations dropping from 46,765 in 1995 to 21,754 in 2006. The result has been the elimination of many smaller agencies and the consolidation of survivors into powerful groups, some regionally focused and others global in coverage (notably Amex, Carlson Wagonlit, HRG, and BCD).
    *   The surviving agencies' business model has been changed from one under which suppliers, in this context the airlines, pay commissions for the writing of tickets to one under which end-purchasers pay fees for consultancy and

travel management services; in other words, they are now the consumers' rather than the suppliers' agents, and they must add value to justify their fees (something that has required increased expenditure on staff training and technology – which again favours larger agencies). Because leisure travellers with straightforward itineraries are disinclined to pay fees when they can book for themselves on the Internet, agencies have had to focus either on business accounts – the domain of TMCs – or leisure niches oriented towards particular regions or activities.

- By virtue of the volumes of business they transact, larger TMCs have gained a greater share of airline override payments and increased negotiating leverage with the GDSs (e.g., no or lower payments for equipment).

2. In *Europe*, the move to reduce and then eliminate base commissions, at least on domestic and short-haul fares, was led by British Airways and quickly followed by other network carriers. Practice does, however, vary between countries. In some markets (e.g., the United Kingdom) there is a significant number of consolidators selling long-haul fares in particular on a merchant (i.e., net fare) basis.

3. In *Asia*, Singapore Airlines eliminated base commissions on published fares sold in its home market as long ago as 1999, and in both Singapore and Malaysia there has been a trend towards charging fees to customers and away from reliance on commissions. Air New Zealand has reduced the base commission on domestic and trans-Tasman fares to zero and on long-haul fares to 4 per cent, whilst Qantas is moving in a similar direction. In other countries the pace of change has been slower, in part due to the existence of complex layers of consolidators, agents, and subagents bound together by longstanding business and personal relationships. Indeed, across Asia as a whole the number of agencies is actually still growing.

4. Despite the pressure airlines have been placing on agency-driven costs, it should not be forgotten that agencies remain an important part of many airlines' distribution strategies. An airline might benefit from sufficient brand awareness in its home market that it need not rely on agencies or pay their commissions, but when it enters a new and unfamiliar market there can be considerable value gained from the existence of an established infrastructure of agencies (and perhaps the use of one in particular as a general sales agent). Although their revenues are under pressure and this is leading to consolidation within the industry in some countries, travel agencies will remain important distribution channels for many categories of scheduled airline – notably network carriers. However, as alluded to above, their role is changing in three important respects:

- Survivors are having to deliver value-added services to their clients such as corporate travel management services or assembly of leisure travel packages, for example. The trend away from a commission-based remuneration structure to a fee-based, transaction-driven model will continue.
- Some airlines are building 'preferred supplier' relationships with agencies in key markets, developing joint promotional programmes and making special deals available only through these partners.
- More generally, compensation will be driven by an assessment of the benefits an airline gains from each relationship rather than by the shotgun approach of the traditional commission structure. Rewards might, for example, be varied as between different markets, flight numbers, and seasons.

Disintermediation

When no intermediary is involved and payment for a booking is made at or shortly after the time of reservation the airline concerned not only avoids paying commission, it also gains a cash-flow benefit compared with using the agency system. Disintermediation has three strands:

1. Encouraging use of airline websites, so eliminating agency commissions and GDS booking fees, and reducing call centre workload. In their annual Airline IT Trends Survey for 2007 (*Airline Business*, July), SITA and *Airline Business* reported that a sample of 100 airlines – which included some of the world's largest – revealed 35 per cent of ticket sales to have been made on their websites and 13 per cent through call centres; the former percentage was growing year on year, whilst the latter was declining.
2. In the case of network carriers, using FFPs, direct marketing, and affinity credit cards to enhance brand loyalty and, over time, develop a direct relationship with their customers – thereby prising control of customer relationships and brand presentation away from intermediaries. There is doubt regarding how successful these types of initiative have been; in particular, the commoditisation of frequent flyer miles in some markets (e.g., their award by credit card companies for expenditures unrelated to air travel) appears to have seriously undermined any customer loyalty that FFPs might once have engendered towards particular carriers (itself a debatable issue). On the other hand, Southwest appears to have been successful with its 'Ding!' desktop tool for alerting customers to special offers in their chosen markets that cannot be accessed through other channels.
3. Again in the case of network carriers, making net fares – that is, fares net of agency commissions and GDS fees – available to preferred corporate customers who book direct.

Encouraging direct access to their websites has been a key part of most airlines' distribution strategies for the last decade; close to two-thirds of sales are now online in North America, although the level in Europe is less than half that and Asia is even further behind. Whilst disintermediation has had a positive impact on distribution costs, there are issues involved which are sometimes overlooked:

- The price transparency of the Web has added to downward pressure on yields or, to put it another way, has compelled airlines to share savings with customers; carriers generally find that fares sold over the Web are on average well below fares sold through the agency/GDS channel, in part because agencies still have access to large corporate accounts but also because online buyers tend on the whole to be proactive in searching out alternative service–price offers (the emphasis in this channel often being on price).
- The cost differential between online and agency sales is usually favourable, but the gap is not as wide as folklore suggests once the costs of supporting the website and paying external service providers are taken into consideration.
- Ready access to fare information by price comparison sites has in some cases raised the look-to-book ratio from 30 or 40 to 1 up to several hundred to 1. Not only can this put yet further pressure on yields, it can also place heavy processing

loads onto CRSs. There are two widely used methods for dealing with this if it is deemed a problem by an affected airline (which is not inevitable):

- fare information can be cached to keep price enquiries away from back-end transaction processing. Where management of a CRS is outsourced, the airline should pay a reduced transaction fee for enquiries to the cache which do not proceed to the back-end;
- site-scraping robots can be blocked, either generally or according to their specific origin.

• Customers are not drawn to airline sites through brand-power alone, and where a carrier decides to distribute actively through search engines (primarily Google) there will be marketing costs associated with sponsored key-words, advertising, and click-throughs.

Increasing Use Of Single-carrier Fares

One of the most significant features of deregulated markets has been a rapid rise in the cost of full fares and the correspondingly high proportion of passengers travelling on discounted fares. Most discounted fares are not good for carriage on another airline, so eliminating prorate dilution. (Of course, joint fares offered by alliance partners are increasingly weighing in the other direction.)

Controlling GDS Booking Fees

A number of the issues that have arisen between airlines and GDSs were outlined above. In order to understand how airlines have set about reducing GDS fee payments, it is necessary to be aware of a little more background.

1. Fundamentally, agencies want access to the inventory of as many airlines as possible in order to be able to provide the widest range of travel alternatives to their clients, whilst airlines – or at least those willing to do business through intermediaries – want access to as many agencies as possible in order to penetrate the market segments each serves. The role of the GDSs is to act as a hub between thousands of agencies and hundreds of airline reservations systems, thereby avoiding the uneconomic alternative of establishing perhaps millions of direct connections. What is being hubbed is messages passing between agencies and airlines about space availability, prices, fare rules, bookings, amendments, and passengers' special requirements. The scope of the messages depends upon the level of functionality at which an airline chooses to participate in a particular GDS – schedule-level, booking-level, or full participation, for example.

2. Because of training and equipment costs, and at one time also for contractual reasons, most agencies subscribe to only one GDS. Traditionally they have paid a subscription fee and perhaps also equipment rental charges, but larger agencies have been able to negotiate compensatory signing bonuses. Controversially from the airlines' perspective, it was also normal for agents to be incentivised by fee rebates to maximise transaction volume across the GDSs so that GDS fees chargeable to airlines would correspondingly increase.

3. Airlines have historically paid segment-based transaction fees to the GDSs for each agency booking made through them. This gave rise to two problems: first, fees per segment rose rapidly throughout the 1990s and early 2000s, and reached unacceptably high absolute levels; second, the fact that agents were being incentivised by GDSs to generate high transaction volumes irrespective of whether a given transaction led to receipt of flown revenue by the airline(s) booked meant that a proportion of fee expenditure was anyway unproductive.

4. Concerned by the prospect that the large airlines which at the time owned each of the GDSs would bias the systems against other carriers, the US DOT introduced 'CRS Rules' in 1984 and in Europe the EC broadly followed suit in 1989 with a 'CRS Code of Conduct'. Two particular aspects of these regulations fell foul of the 'law of unintended consequences' by actually cementing the market power of the GDS oligopoly:

    *   *mandatory participation* rules required 'parent carriers' (i.e., airlines which owned a GDS) to maintain at least the level of participation in other GDSs that each maintained in their own system – which prevented those carriers from negotiating down the fees charged by other GDSs because the airlines concerned could not plausibly threaten either partial or total withdrawal of content (although under the US Rules it was permissible for a carrier to withhold Web fares from any GDS);
    *   similarly, *non-discrimination requirements* prevented a GDS from negotiating better fees for one carrier than for any other having a similar level of functionality – which, again, stifled market forces in an unforeseen way despite a noble motive (i.e., the banning of favourable deals between a GDS and its airline owner).

In the United States, the competitive landscape has changed in the airlines' favour. First, only Amadeus – which is a relatively small player in North America – amongst the leading GDSs now has airline shareholders, and even these are in a minority position. Second, technology is making it more economic, and consolidation is making it more commercially feasible, for airlines to offer 'direct connect' solutions (i.e., application programme interfaces) to large TMCs and major corporate travel buyers, allowing them to bypass the GDSs; most online agencies already bypass GDSs – although this has some negative implications which are mentioned below. Third, deregulation of GDSs following sunset of the CRS Rules in 2004 has empowered airlines to negotiate a new business model, the core elements of which are: a reduction in booking fees in return for making all fares, even the lowest, available to a GDS; significant reduction of incentive payments by GDSs to agencies; and payment of 'opt-in' fees by agencies in return for access to the carriers' full inventory content (fees which are lower if a GDS with which the carrier has negotiated a preferential agreement is used, and which may or may not be passed on to travel purchasers). The fulcrum of this new dynamic has been the TMCs' perceived need for access to carriers' full content of seats and fares, a need which is open to question, and the airlines' freedom to discriminate with regard to how they each distribute their content.

In Europe, the CRS Code of Conduct was reviewed in 2007 and in November that year the EC proposed several amendments, which at the time of writing had yet to be voted on by the European Parliament. In a significant departure, airlines were to be free to negotiate content and fee structures individually with each GDS; however, because Amadeus was explicitly stated no longer to have airline 'parents' despite 46.8 ownership by Air France/KLM, Iberia, and Lufthansa, this may allow these carriers to seek further dominance of their respective home markets by entering into perfectly legal deals to give Amadeus favoured access to their fares and seat inventories for distribution to agents in those markets. Having said that, in early 2008 Lufthansa apparently took Amadeus and the other GDSs by surprise when it introduced 'Preferred Fares' for sale in Germany, Switzerland, and Austria; the fares are available to agencies that sign up for the programme, but if they choose to access them through a GDS rather than direct on the airline's agency site they will be surcharged – albeit at a lower rate than agencies which have not signed up and do not even get access to the fares. Amadeus did not respond immediately, but Sabre – which has a much smaller share of the markets concerned – negotiated a waiver of the surcharge on its subscribing agencies in return for lower fees to Lufthansa.

By taking this approach Lufthansa was following several others (e.g., British Airways and KLM) acting to reduce GDS costs in home markets where their brands are strong enough to impose favourable terms on the agency/GDS channel. The GDSs, paced by Amadeus in 2004 and followed by Travelport in 2006, have in fact been edging towards a 'home and away' price structure, setting lower fees for bookings made in a carrier's home market where agencies arguably add less value.

In Asia, airlines still rely heavily on GDSs – which process as much as 90 per cent of the region's bookings, compared to something closer to 50 per cent in North America. Incentive payments to agents from GDSs – particularly GDSs with relatively low market shares – are also more prevalent than is now the case in Europe and North America.

In both North America and Europe, GDSs are playing an increasing role in LFA distribution strategies. Some LFAs have used the channel since they started (e.g., WestJet), some have had an 'on-again-off-again' relationship with it for many years (e.g., Southwest and jetBlue – both now more on than off), and some resolutely refuse to use it (e.g., Ryanair). Nonetheless, close to half the world's LFAs are believed to have some level of participation in at least one GDS, and there is growing recognition that access to higher-yield corporate accounts – an increasingly important source of revenue growth for LFAs, alongside ancillary sales – necessitates trying to strike a favourable deal with one or more GDSs. Technology is now an enabler rather than a barrier to this happening; the newer LFAs have IT systems based on XML that are unable to talk to GDS legacy systems, but after years of – arguably rather slow – progress the GDSs have begun to embrace XML.

Controlling Credit Card Fees

The rise in fees payable by airlines to credit card companies, which has been a corollary of the growth of direct sales over the Internet, has prompted carriers to take a number of steps.

1. Negotiation of lower charges, either across the board or with a preferred partner – perhaps incentivising customers to use the partner's card, especially if co-branded with the airline concerned.
2. Promoting alternative payment mechanisms such as PayPal or UATP (the Universal Air Travel Plan – a long-established airline-owned card plan which offers lower costs than other card networks).
3. Surcharging customers who pay by credit card – a practice more widely accepted in Europe than in some other parts of the world.

VII. Cost Management in Practice

This section opens with general observations regarding cost management strategies. To provide a practical context the template LFA cost model is then summarised, followed by comments on the efforts made by network carriers to restructure their costs.

COST MANAGEMENT STRATEGIES

Conventional wisdom holds that labour is the only significant controllable cost in an airline – equipment costs, fuel, airport and ATS charges in particular being largely uncontrollable. This is too simplistic. Most costs have a core that is substantially uncontrollable – at least in the short run – and a margin which, if cost drivers are well-understood and properly addressed, can be managed. The real issue is therefore not whether a cost is controllable, but how large the margin of control actually is. For example, to say that labour costs are controllable but fuel costs largely are not misses the point. People and fuel are both necessary to run an airline; the costs of both are manageable at the margin, albeit to different extents, and it is management's responsibility to grasp control and also to optimise the productivity of each unit of expenditure.

The following generalisations can be made about cost management strategies. (Note that this discussion applies in respect of 'normal' market circumstances, rather than extraordinary conditions such as the aftermath of 9/11 when airlines might be more concerned with short-term survival.)

1. A cost management strategy treats costs not so much as absolute numbers that must inevitably be minimised, but as revenue-generators that need to be proactively *managed* within the context of the particular type of value embedded in each airline's service concept(s). Taking costs in aggregate, by function, and/or by category, a cost management strategy should concern itself not just with their size but with their productivity – that is, the revenue earned per unit of expenditure.
2. Cost management efforts – whether aimed at lowering absolute input costs or raising input productivity – require a framework, and that framework is provided by the customer value being offered to each targeted segment. Cost management cannot be a strategy in itself; it is a fundamental management discipline which becomes a strategy only when linked to a defined revenue generation strategy within the context of a chosen competitive strategy that embodies the airline's strategic position – as an LFA, an all-premium niche carrier, or a network carrier, for example. Cost structures should not have a life of their own. Their sole purpose is to make possible the delivery of a particular type of customer value. The idea of customer value can therefore be used to help determine which costs should be reduced, which eliminated, and which justifiably increased. It can be useful to think about this in terms of activities:
    *   *Value-adding activities* These contribute directly to why customers make the purchase decisions they do. Consider what the impact on purchase behaviour would be were an activity to be eliminated or performed to a different standard.
    *   *Enabling activities* These contribute to the maintenance of the business and enable it to serve customers. An example is payroll administration. Many could in principle be outsourced (as, of course, could some value-adding activities).

- *Value-destroying activities* These contribute nothing to customer value and nothing to business maintenance. Acquiring and holding excess parts inventory is an example.

  In respect of both value-adding and enabling activities, opportunities might exist to improve efficiency; value-destroying activities need to be eliminated.

3. As well as analysing *which* activities are undertaken and whether they are consistent with the carrier's service concept(s), consideration should also be given to *how* they are undertaken. Airlines each combine inputs differently. An individual airline's cost structure can change dramatically in response not only to changes in the cost behaviour of activities, but also as a result of changes to the way in which activities are configured within the various processes comprising its value chain – that is, as a result of changes to operating strategy.

4. It follows that although cost *management* frequently involves cost *cutting*, the two are not necessarily synonymous. Cost management implies cutting costs wherever possible but with a purpose, rather than slashing them across the board; sometimes it might even mean increasing them if incremental revenues more than compensate for incremental costs. In other words, the supply side (i.e., production costs) should not be considered in isolation from the demand side (i.e., revenue generation). Short-term cost minimisation and long-term profit maximisation do not inevitably equate, particularly when serving premium segments.

There are two parts to an income statement: there is a revenue side as well as a cost side. Low costs are a route to profitability, not an end in themselves. The fundamental challenge confronting any business is to get costs into line with prices that customers are prepared to pay for the services being offered – that is to efficiently produce output that is effective in delivering the type of value targeted customers expect. This is easier to write about than to achieve; as Dwight D. Eisenhower said, 'Farming is easy when your plow is a pencil and you're a thousand miles from the corn field.' What is certain is that to have any hope of achieving it in today's market environment it is necessary to approach airlines as systems of activities that need to be managed with strategic consistency (i.e., in accord with a single strategic theme) and as an integrated whole. This takes us back to the brief discussion of strategy in Chapter 1.

THE LFA MODEL

Many of the topics covered in the present chapter can be tied together by summarising the baseline (or hard-core/bare-bones) LFA business model, first introduced in Chapter 1.

1. *Service design*
   - High-frequency service on a predominantly short-haul point-to-point network.
   - Use of secondary airports in preference to major hubs.
   - High-density, single-class cabin configuration.
   - No assigned seating.
   - No catering, or limited provision on a pay-as-you-go basis.
   - Few onboard amenities, and limited airport customer service.
   - A limited range of 'fare products' (i.e., a simple, segment-based tariff structure).
   - No FFP.
   - No belly-hold cargo.

2. *Process design*
    - Emphasis on direct sales, preferably over the Internet.
    - No interlining.
    - No hubbing (in the sense that passengers are not sold guaranteed online connections, and baggage is not transferred between flights).
    - Lean administrative processes.
    - Outsourcing of noncore processes.
3. *Productivity*
    - Maximisation of resource utilisation, especially staff and aircraft (the former reflected in high staff-to-passenger ratios, the latter facilitated by rapid turnarounds).
    - High cabin planning factors (i.e., targeted load factors).
4. *Fleet structure* Standardisation on a single aircraft type, usually in the 150–170 seat capacity range in high-density configuration.
5. *Other common themes* These include efforts to produce a simple but reliable product that is recognised as sound value for money, to be number one or two in market share on each route flown, and to grow ancillary revenues aggressively.

The virtuous circle linking sustainably low costs to a strategic position based on price leadership is:

- relentless focus on cost (rather than just periodic programmes in response to a crisis), leading to...
- a sustainable ability to offer competitively low fares, leading to...
- volume growth stimulated by price elasticity, leading to...
- economies of density and scale, reinforcing the...
- relentless focus on cost.

Any break in the circle, as when costs rise or markets become saturated and the stimulatory effect of low fares weakens, can pose a potential problem.

Much of the strategic behaviour of incumbents in response to liberalisation and deregulation during the 1980s and 1990s was directed towards creating multi-product networks centred on regionally dominant hubs, complex price structures, and captive distribution channels. The result was that fixed and sunk costs together with economies of scale, scope, and density played a far greater role in shaping industry structure than proponents of deregulation had envisaged, raising barriers to entry and doing serious damage to the argument that air transport markets as a whole are readily contestable. What the LFAs eventually did in response was to use new market freedoms to innovate around these barriers by developing low-cost business models based on point-to-point route structures, simple prices, and direct distribution.

The LFA model is of course not uniformly applied, and as explained in Chapter 1 the number of alternative business models built on top of the basic low-cost/high-productivity platform has grown rapidly in recent years. However, every deviation from the 'bare-bones' LFA template carries with it cost implications. The question then becomes whether the additional costs are necessary either to protect existing revenue from encroaching competition or to earn incremental revenue from customers willing to pay more for additional service.

NETWORK CARRIER RESTRUCTURING

As markets have been progressively deregulated or liberalised since the late 1970s and increasingly opened to competition, network carriers have responded in a variety of ways. In most cases the response has involved one or more of:

1. *Organizational restructuring* Programmes have focused on organizational form, the purpose usually being to de-layer hierarchies and in some cases to create strategic business units out of what were previously internal cost centres. The objectives are generally to accelerate decision-making, clarify accountability, relocate decisions closer to the customer, and promote an entrepreneurial and customer-focused mindset.
2. *Process reengineering* Making a large airline smaller in output terms in order to bring down costs does not necessarily change its structure or cost base; business processes may have to be re-engineered as well.
3. *Network redesign* Surprisingly, several major airlines in the United States left it until the 1990s to start paying close attention to the profitability of individual routes. The result when it came was in some cases network retrenchment (e.g., Northwest), and in others the running down of secondary hubs (e.g., American and Continental). Majors in both North America and Europe have for over a decade been outsourcing to regional partners thin short-haul routes unsuited to mainline fleet and cost structures. As the 1990s progressed, the arrival of large numbers of regional jets led to expansion of hub catchment areas and the growth of regional airline hubs (e.g., Comair at Cincinnati). The process of handing over marginal mainline routes accelerated rapidly in the United States after 9/11 and ran in parallel with a reduction of mainline capacity by most network majors, accompanied from mid-decade by a strong shift in the focus of expansion towards international markets. In response to the 2007/2008 surge in oil prices, however, many carriers were compelled to cut both mainline and regional routes as part of wider efforts to reduce output.
4. *Low-cost operations* The continuing steady expansion of Southwest and AirTran in the United States and the more rapid growth of European LFAs such as easyJet and Ryanair has provoked a variety of responses from established network carriers. Some US majors, paced abortively by Continental and USAir and followed by United and Delta (and then USAir again, in its later incarnation as US Airways), established low-cost 'airlines within airlines'; Air Canada did the same. Alitalia, bmi, British Airways, Iberia, LOT, Lufthansa, KLM, and SAS are amongst those that have tried similar approaches in Europe, although they have generally chosen to establish subsidiaries or jointly owned affiliates rather than separate internal divisions on the US model. In Asia, the Korean and Japanese 'majors', together with Singapore Airlines, have followed broadly similar paths to the European carriers. With regard to the strategy as a whole, the jury remains out. The US initiatives have failed (Morrell 2005), although United's Ted lingered on until 2008. Conversely, Qantas appears to have found success with Jetstar, which is being used not just to combat domestic low-fare competition and take over the parent's low-yield international routes, but to act as a vehicle through which to enter new long-haul markets.

    The intended sources of savings relative to mainline operations have been: process improvements (e.g., faster turnarounds of a single-type fleet, leading to higher

aircraft utilisation than the parent can achieve); lower wage costs and higher staff productivity; and no-frills onboard and ground products. Potential dangers include:
- failure to create a clear sub-brand identity, leading to unfulfilled customer expectations based on the parent's brand positioning;
- failure to offer a distinct value proposition, instead selling merely a detuned version of the full-service product;
- the risk of cannibalising the mainline client base;
- in the case of 'airlines within airlines' as opposed to separately incorporated and externally staffed subsidiaries, difficulties re-acculturating staff transferred from the parent.

5. *Alliances* Alliances can be strategic, involving membership of oneworld, SkyTeam, or Star, or they might be tactical and involve cooperation in respect of individual routes or organizational functions. Alliances have been widely successful in increasing traffic densities on existing routes and extending network scope without requiring the investment that would be necessary to grow internally – assuming, in the case of international markets, that internal growth would have been a permissible option. Although the primary effect of the three global alliances was initially felt on the revenue side through network restructuring and code-sharing there have in addition been input cost benefits (e.g., joint purchasing and the combining of ticket offices and sales forces) and productivity benefits (e.g., through higher utilisation of both operating and marketing resources arising from joint activities such as ground-handling and marketing communications). Costs have been saved on a number of international routes by replacing tag-end sectors with code-shared connections. In other words, alliances can have a beneficial impact on costs through the economies of scale, scope, and density they promote. Oum *et al.* (2000) have also found clear productivity improvements attributable to entry into an alliance. (Iatrou and Oretti [2007] provide a thorough review of the history, costs, benefits, and likely future development of alliances.)

6. *Outsourcing* Outsourcing involves moving into the external supply chain a process or activity formerly performed in-house. We have already covered this topic extensively in the present chapter, as well as in Chapter 1. Established carriers have been increasingly prepared to use outsourcing to reduce costs where this is feasible and, sometimes more significantly, to transform into variable costs the fixed costs associated with infrastructure supporting what are now considered by some to be non-core activities such as maintenance, catering, cargo, ground handling, certain accounting functions, training, reservations, IS/IT provision, FFPs, and non-airline functions (e.g., property management). For example, in 2000 Northwest performed line maintenance and most heavy maintenance in-house, whereas 7 years later heavy maintenance had gone and line maintenance was in-house only at the carrier's Detroit and Minneapolis hubs.

7. *Offshore relocation* There have been two, relatively small-scale, developments under this heading:
- *Facility relocation* Airlines based in high-cost locations have in a few cases relocated internal back-office functions and activities such as mainframe computer centres, software development, and revenue accounting to cheaper offshore locations. Carriers that outsource airframe maintenance sometimes also use MRO shops in low man-hour cost environments – notably parts of the Asia-Pacific region and Central America. Facilitated by cheaper and better telecommunications, this is a development that mirrors the migration of many manufacturing industries to low-cost locations.

- *Offshore staffing* Japanese carriers have been particularly noteworthy for their use of foreign flight- and cabin crews based overseas to reduce costs. Some of the largest US and European long-haul carriers (e.g., United and Lufthansa) have also tapped relatively low-cost foreign-based cabin attendants; inevitably, there has been union opposition to any further significant growth of this phenomenon.

Nonetheless, just how fragile several years' hard-won gains can potentially be in this industry was made clear in the first half of 2008: Continental and Northwest, two of several possible examples, found themselves facing prospective fuel bills for the year respectively $1.5 billion and $1.7 billion higher than budgeted just a few months earlier. With revenue under threat from a weakening economy and little 'fat' left to cut on the expenditure side of the income statement, the domestic business models of US network carriers were again coming under intense pressure.

CONCLUSION

That cost management is now one of the principal strategic battlegrounds being fought over by competing airlines is beyond doubt. But accountants with sharp pencils, or indeed axes, are insufficient. What is necessary is to ingrain cost management into corporate culture. For continuous cost improvement to be ingrained into a corporate culture – something that is far more effective strategically than periodic, often crisis-driven, 'slash-and-burn' cost-cutting exercises – several prerequisites have to be met:

1. *Training* Cost management is learned. Educating people about the strategic and competitive importance of cost management is a worthwhile investment. Strategy needs to be widely understood.
2. *Participation* People closest to the action are often in the best position to identify cost management opportunities. They need to be consulted and to be involved in decision-making that affects what they do and how they do it.
3. *Reinforcement* Changed behaviour needs reinforcing. If the same things are measured and the same performance metrics are used as in the past, new behaviour – specifically, a more thoughtful and proactive approach to cost management – cannot be sustained.

Costs are easy to add in a booming market when traffic and revenue are growing strongly, but they can be difficult and painful to shed when revenue growth slows or turns negative. Furthermore, the high short-run operating leverage faced by most airlines means that even though output can be reduced relatively quickly, costs – particularly fixed costs – are more sticky. A key discipline is therefore never to add unnecessary costs, whatever the market is doing.

VIII. Summary

This chapter has identified different types of cost, looked at how airline costs might be classified and analysed, identified key cost drivers, and considered some of the more important cost management initiatives undertaken by the industry. It has been noted in several different contexts that capacity costs are amongst the most significant element in an airline's cost structure. Capacity management is the subject of the next four chapters.

PART 3

Capacity Management

Practical men, who believe themselves to be quite exempt from any intellectual influences, are usually the slaves of some defunct economist.

John Maynard Keynes

The fundamental objectives of capacity management are straightforward:

1. To minimise revenue loss from spillage (i.e., production of insufficient output to meet potentially profitable demand).
2. To minimise excess output (i.e., production of ASMs in excess of what can profitably be sold).
3. To minimise spoilage (i.e., production of unsold ASMs which could have been profitably sold but for no-shows, misconnections, etc.).
4. To maximise resource productivity (consistent with the airline's chosen strategic and market positions, and with the type of value it is offering its customers).

Capacity management is a broad and multidisciplinary topic, encompassing: market and route evaluation; schedule development; fleet planning; manpower and facilities planning; pricing (i.e., deciding what fares and conditions should be applied to each product offered in each market); revenue management (i.e., deciding how many seats at each type of fare should be available on each departure); and the assignment of aircraft and manpower. Pricing was discussed in Chapter 3; the other topics are discussed in the next four chapters. Chapter 6 examines network design, Chapter 7 considers scheduling, Chapter 8 looks at fleet management, and Chapter 9 provides an introduction to revenue management.

6

Network Management: Design

I've been to almost as many places as my luggage.

Bob Hope

CHAPTER OVERVIEW

The terms 'network structure' and 'route structure' are not strictly synonymous. A network structure is an assemblage of routes which gain strength from interconnectedness; its fundamental purpose is to optimise connectivity and passenger flows, with the result that optimising flows of aircraft and crews within it can be challenging. A route structure, on the other hand, is not primarily designed to integrate passenger flows and can more readily accommodate aircraft and crew optimisation. This might seem pedantic, but in fact it goes to the heart of recent changes within the industry: *network structures* designed to flow passengers around them on an integrated basis carry cost disadvantages relative to *route structures* which can be designed to flow aircraft and so maximise their utilisation. We will look at this below. Unless a distinction needs to be drawn, however, the present chapter will use the word 'network' to encompass both structural forms.

Network management has two elements: design and scheduling.

- Network design implements the geographical scope decision discussed in Chapter 1. It addresses two fundamental questions: which markets do we want to serve – in other words, which markets should we be adding or deleting? And, in the case of a hub-based carrier, what are the financial implications of the network structure used to serve our markets – in other words, what would be the implications of adding or deleting specific routes, and (for multi-hub carriers) of channelling O&D flows in a different way?
- Schedule planning addresses several fundamental questions with regard to individual routes: if a route is to be added, how many flights should be scheduled and when? If an additional frequency is to be added, when should it be scheduled to depart? What will be the financial implications of these decisions, or of any other adjustment to the existing schedule? What are the financial implications of changing the size of aircraft operating particular departures?

The three main sections in this chapter will look at network design, network strategies and tactics, and network outsourcing. Chapter 7 considers scheduling, as well as the interface between network and fleet management. Clearly, answers to the questions above are closely tied to decisions taken in other areas of capacity management – notably fleet management and revenue management. These are the subjects of Chapters 8 and 9 respectively.

I. Network Design

An airline's network is an overt manifestation of strategic behaviour. It is:

- a key source of brand identity, because its network helps define what type of carrier it is;
- a revenue driver, because network design and scheduling are core service attributes offered to customers;
- a cost driver, because network design and scheduling are critical elements in any airline's cost structure;
- a source of competitive strength or weakness, because a network is something that competitors have to choose whether to confront or avoid;
- a potential hedge against economic cycles that affect some markets but not others and, if international in scope, against currency fluctuations.

This section of the chapter will review alternative network designs. The first part provides definitions of terms that will be used in both the present discussion and also in the discussion of revenue management in Chapter 9, and it also briefly outlines the key variables affecting network economics.

MARKETS AND ROUTES

Revenues are earned in O&D 'markets', whereas aircraft operating costs are generated flying 'routes'. The words 'market' and 'route' can be synonymous, but often they are not. An O&D *market* exists between a passenger's points of origin and destination. O&D markets can take one of several forms from a network design perspective:

1. Point-to-point markets can exist between:
   - two hubs or gateways (e.g., Dallas and Miami, or New York and London);
   - a hub and a secondary or tertiary point (e.g., Dallas and Tucson);
   - two secondary or tertiary points (e.g., Tucson and Albuquerque).
2. Single-hub behind/beyond markets can take one of several forms:
   - secondary or tertiary point to another secondary or tertiary point over a hub (e.g., Tucson–Chicago O'Hare–Hartford);
   - secondary or tertiary point to a hub over another hub (e.g., Tucson–Dallas–Miami);
   - hub to a secondary or tertiary point over another hub (e.g., Dallas–London–Edinburgh).
   (Note that in the second and third of these configurations two hubs are involved in the journey, but hubbing only takes place at the intermediate hub whilst the other is either an origin or destination.)
3. Double-hub behind/beyond markets (i.e., 'double-connect' or 'cross-feed' markets) usually involve an origin in a secondary city (e.g., New Orleans or Leipzig) or a tertiary city (e.g., Burlington or Erfurt), transfers at two hubs, and a final destination in another secondary or tertiary city. Most examples are found in multi-hub international alliance structures (e.g., Milwaukee–Detroit–Amsterdam–Stuttgart), although some thinner transcontinental markets in the United States are also served over two hubs.

A *route*, on the other hand, links two points using the same aircraft under the same flight number. It can be operated as either of the following:

1. A non-stop service: this is one flight-leg (or 'sector') between start and end-point (e.g., London–Edinburgh).
2. A through- or direct service: in this case there are two or more consecutive flight-legs because intermediate stops are made (e.g., Tucson–Cincinnati–New York JFK operated as a through-service by a single aircraft under the same flight number). A special case is the triangular route, where the same aircraft flies consecutive flight-legs under different flight numbers. An example of this is the Hong Kong–Cairns–Brisbane–Hong Kong rotation flown (in both directions) by Cathay Pacific: the Cairns–Brisbane flight-leg carries Hong Kong–Brisbane O&D passengers ticketed on CX102 (a Hong Kong–Brisbane route with an intermediate stop in Cairns) as well as Cairns–Hong Kong passengers ticketed on CX103 (a Cairns–Hong Kong route with an intermediate stop, well off-track, in Brisbane).

If the same flight number is used but a change of aircraft is required at an intermediate point, this is functionally equivalent to two connecting routes being used to serve the market. It might happen, for example, where a single flight number is used for Portland (Oregon)–Cincinnati–JFK service but passengers have to change planes in Cincinnati and board an aircraft that originated in Tucson and is operating onwards from Cincinnati to JFK under multiple flight numbers. Flights across US domestic hubs in particular have in many cases been through-numbered to improve their GDS display positions; in the above example, the Cincinnati–JFK leg might operate under several flight numbers corresponding to a range of different origins behind Cincinnati, but all except the Tucson-originating same-plane service would require a connection at Cincinnati and so do not in fact offer direct service. (The term 'duplicate leg' is sometimes used to describe an arrangement under which, for technical or commercial reasons, a single leg carries more than one flight number; the same expression can also be used to describe a code-shared flight operated under more than one airline's flight number.)

Any given market might therefore be served in one or more of several ways:

1. *Non-stop route* (e.g., Hong Kong–Los Angeles) Route and market are synonymous for passengers originating in Hong Kong and destined for Los Angeles.
2. *Direct, multi-stop or through-plane route* (e.g., Hong Kong–Tokyo–Los Angeles on the same aircraft operating under the same flight number) Depending upon traffic rights, this route might serve Hong Kong–Tokyo and Tokyo–Los Angeles markets as well as Hong Kong–Los Angeles. (Using terminology we will meet in Chapter 9 in the context of revenue management, we can say that the Tokyo–Los Angeles *flight-leg* may carry passengers travelling on Hong Kong–Los Angeles and Tokyo–Los Angeles *segments*.)
3. *Connecting routes* There are several possibilities:
    *   *Online (or 'intraline') connections* These involve an en route change of planes but use a single airline's aircraft. Flight numbers might or might not change:
        –   different flight numbers: a change of aircraft at a hub often, although not invariably, involves a change in flight number;
        –   same flight number: a single flight-number might be used on two connecting routes. As noted above, this has historically happened in US domestic

markets to improve GDS display positions. 'Funnel flights' involving a
change of gauge are sometimes used at hubs and international gateways
such that an incoming long-haul flight might connect with a short-haul leg
operated by a smaller aircraft but under the same flight number.

- *Code-share connections* These use an airline's designator code on connecting
services actually operated by the aircraft of another carrier. (We will discuss
code-sharing later in the chapter.)
- *Interline connections* Increasingly rare, these involve connections between the (non-
code-shared) services of two or more different airlines. Passengers might benefit
from joint fares negotiated between the carriers for specific markets, and will
almost certainly benefit from through-ticketing (although not necessarily through
boarding passes issued at the first point of check-in) and from baggage interlining.
Most LFAs refuse to interline because of the costs and prorate dilution it involves.

Clearly, whilst any one route can serve one or several markets, any one market might
be served by several alternative routes. Each of the different options open to a particular
airline for serving the markets available to it carries separate marketing mix implications,
because each offers customers a different set of benefits and nonmonetary costs (e.g.,
the shorter elapsed journey times of non-stop flights, the seamless service of intraline
connections, the disadvantages of any change of planes or intermediate stop); it also
carries its own different set of operating costs. Box 6.1 looks at one of the implications for
competition arising out of the distinction between routes and markets.

Box 6.1: Market Competition in the Absence of Route Overlay

Airlines can compete in a market without any route overlay at all. For example, Singapore
Airlines serves the London–Sydney market by connecting London–Singapore and
Singapore–Sydney routes; Star Alliance partner Thai International serves the same market by
connecting London–Bangkok and Bangkok–Sydney routes. Delta might serve the Buffalo–LA
market over Cincinnati, whilst Continental serves it over Cleveland. This is one reason why
the immediate competitive impact of a proposed alliance or merger should be considered in
terms of market duplication as well as route duplication; mergers and alliances can materially
reduce competition in O&D markets even where there is little or no route overlay.

NETWORK ECONOMICS

In principle, we could visualise a network of 'demand linkages' – that is, lines connecting
every city-pair within an airline's accessible service area that generates O&D demand.
From an individual customer's point of view, it might be preferable if this hypothetical
network of demand linkages were duplicated by actual airline service – in other words,
by an airline operating a network of non-stops which precisely corresponds to O&D
demand. Because the industry's operating economics preclude this, what happens
instead is that every carrier has to make network design choices that lead to some O&D
markets being served non-stop (in which case demand and network links are indeed
congruent), others being served by multi-stop (i.e., direct) or connecting service, and
some not being served at all (at least by a single carrier). These choices are in fact the
essence of network design.

Within the context established by a particular carrier's strategic description of itself – as a regional, a low-fare point-to-point operator, or a network major, for example – and by the characteristics of the demand being served, and also subject to whatever service obligations or route licensing formalities are imposed by governments, airline managements have more freedom than in the past with regard to how they choose to structure their networks. These choices involve balancing the requirements of different market segments (e.g., for high-frequency non-stop service) against the economics of aircraft operation (which can make high-frequency non-stop service, for example, more expensive to deliver than lower frequencies using larger aircraft).

Network costs are driven in particular by the economies of scope and density, the stage-lengths, and the resource utilisation levels inherent in the design of a network and its accompanying schedule. Revenues reflect in part the quality of service embedded in these same network design and scheduling decisions.

Costs

The most significant network cost drivers were highlighted in Chapter 5. All are impacted by fleet composition.

1. *Economies of scope* These are in evidence when it is cheaper, in terms of average cost, to produce two products together than to produce each separately. In the context of network design, economies of scope arise when passengers travelling in many different O&D markets are combined for at least part of their journeys on a single aircraft – in other words, when the output produced by a single aircraft flying from point A to point B is sold to passengers originating behind A and/or destined beyond B as well as to passengers in the A–B city-pair market. Economies of scope are accessed by channelling traffic over one or more hubs; they are a significant motivation for building both single-airline and alliance hub-and-spoke systems.

2. *Economies of density* We saw in Chapter 5 that these are in evidence when unit cost declines as a result of an increased volume of traffic being carried between points already served. The primary source of economies of density is aircraft size: because increases in trip cost and in aircraft size do not have a linear relationship, larger aircraft generally return lower seat-mile costs (although higher trip costs) than smaller types of a similar technological generation flown on a given flight-leg. One way of exploiting economies of density is to design a network such that traffic flows are channelled onto routes that would otherwise support only smaller aircraft with higher seat-mile costs. Because of the bar-bell double-hub network structure KLM and Northwest designed, for example, behind/beyond traffic flows channelled between hubs at Amsterdam and Detroit support high-frequency service with low seat-mile cost widebodies that the O&D market between these two cities could never support by itself. (There has been some academic debate in respect of the presence and significance of economies of density; Windle [1991], Kumbhakar [1990], Keeler and Formby [1994], and Romero-Hernandez and Salgado [2005] have all reported their presence.)

3. *Average stage-length* One of any airline's fundamental cost drivers is its average stage-length. This can be calculated in two ways:
    *   Average stage-length = total aircraft miles or kilometres flown per annum ÷ annual system-wide revenue departures.

- Weighted average stage-length = (length of each sector × flights per annum on the sector) ÷ annual system-wide revenue departures.

Other things being equal, unit costs of producing output on long-haul routes are generally lower than is the case on short-haul routes. Conversely, it will cost more to produce a given output of ASMs as average stage-length decreases. Box 6.2 explores this phenomenon.

Network design and scheduling decisions affect the availability of economies of scope and density and drive average stage-length; they also affect the utilisation of aircraft and

---

Box 6.2: The Cost Impact of Average Stage-Length

The tapering of unit costs as length of haul increases is a fundamental fact of airline economics, and one that can have a particularly influential effect on operating margins because costs generally taper more rapidly than fares.

Longer stage-lengths contribute to lower unit costs for the following reasons:

- The time an aircraft spends on the ground for turnarounds or transit stops declines relative to airborne time as average stage-lengths increase. This facilitates higher aircraft and crew utilisation, and hence higher productivity.
- Similarly, average block-speed is higher than on shorter sectors, raising hourly aircraft productivity and so generating more units of output over which to spread fixed operating costs.
- Fuel-burn per mile flown declines the longer an aircraft remains at its optimal, fuel-efficient cruising speed and altitude(s), with the result that fuel costs for a given aircraft with a given payload rise less than proportionately as the length of haul increases.
- Terminal costs decline as a proportion of route costs when stage-lengths increase. The same is true of traffic costs, such as reservations, and ground-handling. For example, an airline selling 5000 RPMs will incur lower reservations, ticketing and handling costs if the sale is generated by carrying one passenger 5000 miles than if five passengers are each carried on 1000-mile journeys.
- Cycle-related maintenance costs (e.g., in respect of undercarriage assemblies) do not accumulate as rapidly in respect of long-haul aircraft as they do when shorter flight-legs are being operated.

In summary, the unit cost of operating a given aircraft with a given payload falls as stage-length increases because the fixed costs associated with each flight are spread over a larger output, and also because the variable costs do not increase proportionately with distance. For example, the cost per ASM for a B747-400 configured with 380 seats falls by around half as stage-length increases from 600 to 6000 miles. Unit cost improvements are most dramatic as stage-lengths rise from short- to medium-haul. However, the relationship is not constant, and as the length of haul becomes extreme, relationships between unit costs and stage-lengths tend towards being linear.

Airlines operating shorter stage-lengths are not necessarily at a disadvantage provided they are able to recover their higher unit costs by earning relatively higher unit revenues (i.e., revenue per ASM) than their long-haul counterparts, or compensate with some combination of low input costs and/or high factor productivity. (Bear in mind when looking at the system unit costs of a carrier operating a mixture of short-, medium-, and long-haul stage-lengths – say, United – that these costs have been 'averaged' down by the beneficial impact of operating the long-haul flight-legs; its short-haul unit costs will be higher than the system-wide average, and therefore probably even more uncompetitive against an LFA than might at first glance appear to be the case.)

of station resources. At the most fundamental level, costs associated with network design hinge upon two decisions taken with regard to how each market should be served:

1. *Non-stop or connecting service* Flying non-stop eliminates the incremental fuel-burn required for take-off and climb-out from the intermediate hub, and may eliminate any route deviation required to reach it; landing at the hub increases maintenance costs because of the additional cycle it involves – something of particular importance in respect of engine and landing-gear maintenance; and stopping will also involve additional airport and handling charges. Furthermore, an increase in non-stop flying can raise aircraft utilisation.

   On the other hand, if connecting flights into and out of a hub are operated by larger aircraft than the non-stop market could support by itself, these aircraft may have lower seat-mile costs. Furthermore, ultra-long-haul non-stop flights involve cost penalties attributable to hauling exceptionally large fuel loads into the air and taking longer to reach optimal cruising altitudes.

2. *Capacity versus frequency* There are two variables to consider:
   - High-frequency services between two points using relatively small aircraft are generally more expensive to produce in terms of CASM than lower-frequency services using larger aircraft. The key question (assuming adequate availability of aircraft and, if relevant, traffic rights) is what the market is demanding in respect of frequencies (e.g., double-daily or better long-haul, day-return possibilities short-haul, or connections into multiple waves throughout the day at a nearby hub), and the extent to which high-yield segments are present in the market and willing to cover the costs of mounting high frequencies. Conversely, smaller aircraft will generally have lower trip costs – assuming they are of the same technological generation as larger aircraft with which they are being compared; this might, depending upon pricing in the market concerned, make their use commercially less risky insofar as fewer passengers are needed in order to break even.
   - As noted above, by channelling over a single hub all the passengers outbound from a spoke city to multiple final destinations it is possible to mount higher frequencies (and/or to use larger aircraft) down the spoke to the hub than would be possible were non-stop services used to link the same origin to each of those same final destinations.

   The last two decades show that airlines will, as a rule, opt for frequency over capacity. Evidence of this has been the declining average size of aircraft in many markets. Despite rising congestion, the FAA (2008) is projecting a continued decline in US domestic mainline aircraft size (calculated as ASMs ÷ miles flown) from 150.6 seats in 2007 to 147.7 seats in 2025; the size of regional aircraft, on the other hand, will rise from 49.6 seats to 63 seats over the same period. Taking the mainline and regional fleets together, the average size of aircraft in US domestic service is expected to fall from 120.3 seats in 2007 to 118.6 seats in 2025 (ibid.). Some observers nonetheless see the global market as a whole trending towards larger aircraft (Airbus 2008). Finally, it should be noted that the traditional relationship between aircraft size and costs is not necessarily going to hold in the future. Generally, the smaller the aircraft the lower will be its trip (and aircraft-mile) costs but the higher will be its unit (i.e., seat-mile) costs; the B787 and A350 have broken this relationship by offering lower seat-mile costs than significantly larger aircraft – even relatively modern types.

Revenue: The Network Product

Passengers prefer, in order, non-stop, direct, online connecting, and lastly interline routings (Carlton *et al.* 1980). Preference for flying non-stop can sometimes be reflected in firmer yields – at least in business and first classes. Against the benefit of non-stops will need to be balanced the fact that operating over a hub and so combining different O & D passengers onto each departure from the origin should allow higher outbound frequencies and access to a wider range of markets from that city than non-stop service would permit. Also, many markets do not have the density or mix of traffic to support non-stop service – or at least not the high-frequency non-stop service demanded by the business segment. Airlines nonetheless have to bear customers' preferences in mind when designing their networks – as well as bearing in mind what competitors are doing. The result of this is that the world's larger network carriers, alone or with alliance partners, are now more focused than ever on their customers' complete journeys – wanting to design networks capable of carrying as many customers as possible all the way, to achieve this seamlessly, and to capture the entire revenue stream from customer itineraries.

In the low-fare sector of the industry, network and schedule can sometimes be key discriminants between apparently similar business models. For example, whereas Ryanair has tended to concentrate on rapid network expansion, largely to secondary and tertiary airports, easyJet's early years were marked by more attention to network density – that is, to building high frequencies on a relatively tight network (largely serving primary airports). This contrast to some extent reflects the distinction between easyJet's targeting of price-sensitive business travellers (who appreciate high frequencies) in addition to leisure and VFR traffic, on the one hand, and Ryanair's targeting of ultra-price-sensitive segments on the other (Lawton 2002). In the United States, jetBlue's early 'skimming' strategy of entering but taking a relatively small share of already dense markets contrasts with Southwest's strategy of stimulating markets through a combination of low fares and high frequencies (Ben-Yosef 2005).

TYPES OF NETWORK

Networks can be categorised from both the customers' point of view and from an operational perspective.

Customers' Perspective

There are basically two types of network design from a customer's standpoint: connecting and same-plane.

Connecting/hub-and-spoke   The majority of connecting traffic is channelled over hubs on single-carrier connections, although a significant and growing proportion connects between alliance partners (often on code-shared flights). Interline connections account for a declining share of connecting traffic.

Same-plane/point-to-point service   Same-plane/point-to-point service, which as we have seen can be either direct (i.e., with an intermediate stop but no change of planes or flight number) or non-stop, may arise in a variety of different circumstances:

1. Most LFAs offer primarily point-to-point service, as do a significant number of small- and medium-sized long-haul carriers (e.g., Virgin Atlantic and LanChile).
2. The increased availability of new-generation regional jets, mainline narrowbodies, and ultra-long-haul widebodies having long ranges relative to their predecessors has allowed network carriers and their affiliates to introduce non-stop hub-bypass services.
3. Even within a hubbed network it is likely that up to half and sometimes significantly more than half of traffic will be travelling in local O&D markets originating in or destined for the hub.

Operational Perspective

The spatial form of airline networks can be categorised in a wide variety of different ways; Bazargan (2004) and Burghouwt (2007) provide comprehensive and well-referenced summaries of the theory underlying alternative forms. From an airline's operational perspective, four structures in particular merit comment: linear, grid, radial, and hub-and-spoke.

Linear   The pre-deregulation route structures of several US trunk carriers were largely linear, although there was some hubbing by Delta and Eastern in Atlanta. Geography imposes a linear structure on the systems of some long-haul international carriers. Linear service is often associated with one-stop or multi-stop routeings. Although widely considered commercially unappealing, the cost and revenue implications of these are not always clear-cut; for example, a route from A to B and on to C, combining A–B, A–C, and B–C flows, might attract sufficient traffic to support a larger aircraft with better seat-mile costs than could be supported on separate A–B, A–C, and B–C routes. The downside of the A–B–C route is that because passengers from A to C are being offered a poorer quality service, yield might suffer.

Grid   These networks generally encompass short- and medium-haul routes focused on a small number of major cities, linking these cities both to each other and to locations in between using a combination of non-stops and multi-stops. Schedules may or may not be coordinated over the main cities, but often they are not. The pre-deregulation route structures of several US carriers exhibited grid patterns. Another example is the Indian domestic networks focused on Mumbai, Delhi, Kolkatta, and Chennai. The networks of some European LFAs are also evolving into loose grid patterns; as noted above, integrated scheduling in these cases is normally optimised to flow aircraft and crews around the system rather than passengers.

Although sometimes cited as an example of a linear structure, Southwest's network has grid characteristics; there is evidence of these in its high levels of station activity – averaging in the 45–50 departures per day range (but with several stations having over 100) – underlining the fact that wherever possible each station is connected to a number of others on the network. When Southwest adds a new station, it quickly builds service to/from several existing online stations and adds sufficient frequencies to allow it to dominate each market; operations are scheduled throughout the day to maximise gate-turns as well as staff and equipment utilisation. Linking two stations already served from other points (i.e., 'connecting the dots') is cheaper, in both operational and marketing terms, than introducing a new route where the carrier has no established market presence at one end. Advantages include the improvement in station resource utilisation, and also in general market presence (reflected in top-of-mind brand recall) that arise from offering high frequencies to a broad range of different destinations.

A more unusual feature of Southwest's network is that out of several of its stations (e.g., Chicago Midway) non-stop service in some markets is supplemented by one- and two-stop service. Indeed, a combination of non-stops, multi-stop direct services, and connections that are enabled less by integrated scheduling than by high frequencies throughout the day at certain cities makes the Southwest network more integrated from a customers' perspective than folklore, or a casual glance at its route map, would suggest.

Radial   These are broadly out-and-back operations radiating from a single base ('single-radial') or multiple bases ('multi-radial'). Bases do not act as hubs over which transfer traffic is channelled. Depending on stage-lengths and demand characteristics, routes may be either non-stop or multistop. Several European LFAs have multi-radial networks, operated non-stop. Allegiant and Ryanair (linked by a Ryan family shareholding in the former) operate archetypal out-and-back radial structures from their US focus cities and European bases respectively, with crews and aircraft returning home throughout the day and overnight.

Hub-and-spoke   Hubs add a temporal dimension to the radial form, insofar as they exist not just by virtue of network design but also as a result of scheduling decisions. They can develop in one or more of three ways:

1. *By design*   Since deregulation in the United States, the network majors have consciously developed hubs that interchange traffic between integrated banks of arrivals and departures. Internationally, KLM and Singapore Airlines have been operating sixth-freedom hubs for several decades, Emirates successfully set out to do the same in the late 1980s, and many other European and Asian majors now try as far as geography and traffic rights permit to schedule hub arrivals and departures into well-integrated waves.
2. *By frequency growth*   Some carriers operate with such high frequencies into and out of one or more key stations that the ready availability of convenient connections in effect simulates a continuous hub operation. This is the case for Southwest at Chicago Midway, Phoenix, Las Vegas, and (since spring 2008) at Denver, for example, and is also the case for Ryanair and easyJet at several of their bases. (What distinguishes this type of LFA station from a classic network hub is that incoming and outgoing flights are not explicitly scheduled to connect, that scheduling gives precedence to minimising aircraft turnaround times rather than maximising available passenger connections, and that passengers who do choose to connect typically have to collect and recheck their baggage – although the latter is not necessarily true of all LFAs.)
3. *By default*   In this case, still exemplified by a number of small- and medium-sized 'flag carriers', traffic might well be fed over the airline's home base but little effort is made to design and schedule a tightly integrated network. (Interline connections may

or may not be significant.) This type of network, which was also common amongst European majors until the late-1980s, might be characterised as a 'random hub' insofar as connections tend to arise randomly rather than through intent.

Non-stop hub-bypass services, both long- and short-haul, have steadily become more numerous as network carriers seek competitive advantage by fragmenting network flows both to improve service and pre-empt competitive attacks on spoke cities. Technological developments, such as regional jets, variants of mainline narrowbodies with transcontinental range, and ultra-long-haul widebodies, have facilitated the trend. Carriers doing this are offering customers the benefit of a shorter journey time and avoidance of hub congestion. The trade-off for the airline is that, on the one hand, it is gaining better market access but, on the other, it has to forgo economies of scope and density associated with indirect routings over a hub. In many cases, hub-bypass services are interwoven with connecting services to maintain competitive O&D market frequencies.

It is possible to draw a distinction between two types of hub-bypass route:

1. *Secondary city to secondary city* Bypassing hubs altogether, this has been most common in regional markets in both North America and Europe; as LFA competition has gathered momentum it is also being seen in US and European mainline markets. When city-pairs at the periphery of a hub-and-spoke network warrant point-to-point service it might be worthwhile for a hubbing airline to pre-empt competition by offering some non-stop flights, so attracting sufficient traffic to discourage competition (unless the competitor has a sustainable price or service advantage), whilst still retaining most of the flow across its hub. Launch costs would be relatively low because both stations are already online from the hub, and the market concerned is already being served.
2. *Hub to secondary city* Bypassing a second hub or gateway, this type of route has become particularly common in long-haul international markets. An example would be Dubai–Newcastle non-stop, bypassing hubs in, say, London or Amsterdam.

Conclusion Linear, grid, and radial structures are these days often rolled into the single descriptor 'point-to-point'. The contrast between point-to-point and hub-and-spoke business models is fundamental to the modern industry because it marks a critical distinction between how different airlines perceive their core product and build the operational infrastructure necessary to deliver it. For a point-to-point airline, the product sold is segment-based: each flight offers passengers a single-segment product and routes are largely independent of each other in the sense that the operating system is designed to optimise the flow of aircraft rather than passengers. For a network airline, on the other hand, the product sold is journey-based: passengers are offered a journey from their origin to their destination, encompassing more than one segment if a connection is required, and routes are integrated so that passengers can flow optimally around the system. The distinction also underpins different approaches to pricing and revenue management: a network carrier must have the capability to offer several million different fares and to accommodate perhaps dozens of booking classes offered over thousands of different segment combinations, including segments flown by interline partners; a point-to-point carrier which does not interline, on the other hand, can price on a segment basis and need not concern itself with the opportunity cost of releasing space to connecting passengers rather than local traffic on any given segment. We will revisit this in Chapter 9.

A CLOSER LOOK AT HUB-AND-SPOKE NETWORKS

Formed by routes radiating from a hub, the heartbeat of these networks is a schedule which maximises the number of feasible connections for incoming passengers whilst keeping their connecting times within some defined and acceptable limit. The following terminology is important:

1. *Banks, waves, and complexes* These words describe groups of aircraft/flights that are scheduled to arrive at a hub and then depart again within a given window of time, so allowing passengers to make any of a large number of connections. However, their definitions are not settled. Some authors refer to separate 'complexes' of incoming and departing aircraft, and define two connecting complexes as a 'bank' or 'wave' (e.g., Berdy 2002, p. 121). Some refer to an incoming wave and an outgoing wave comprising a complex (e.g., Hanlon 2007, p. 139). Others refer to an incoming 'bank' and an outgoing 'bank' being linked together in a 'wave' or connection 'complex' (Dennis 1994, p. 131). This book takes the latter approach – so distinguishing between banks on the one hand and waves or complexes, each comprised of two connecting banks, on the other. (Readers with a particular taste for semantics might want to know that the word 'complex' is sometimes used to encompass not just a wave, but also the gates, aircraft, equipment, and personnel used to service it.)
2. *Windows* A 'window' is the period from the first arrival in an inbound bank to the last departure in the next outbound bank that schedule planners give themselves to balance schedule connectivity and saleability. The longer a window, the greater will be the number of feasible connections because more flight-pairs (i.e., pairs of arriving and departing flights) are likely to exceed the minimum connecting time (MCT) allowable at the airport concerned to transfer between flights; conversely the shorter a window, the tighter connections will be – and the more saleable the schedule to time-sensitive customers.

Defining A Hub

The word 'hub' is open to several definitions:

1. The FAA defines as a 'hub' any US airport generating 0.05 per cent or more of national enplanements, but it does not load the term with any scheduling or other operational implications. Specifically, 0.05–0.249 per cent of enplanements qualifies an airport as a small hub, 0.25–0.999 per cent as a medium hub', and one per cent or over as a large hub. (Any airport generating less than 0.05 of enplanements is a non-hub.)
2. Colloquial, especially journalistic, usage often refers to airports that handle large volumes of traffic and/or are the home bases for particular airlines as being hubs, even when inbound and outbound schedules are not coordinated.
3. Airlines (including integrators such as FedEx and UPS) generally define a hub as an airport where inbound flights are scheduled to arrive from outlying origins within a short period of time, disembarking passengers (and/or unloading freight) for transfer to onward flights scheduled to leave shortly afterwards for a wide range of destinations. (To be precise, a 'hub' in its commercial sense is actually the physical infrastructure and operational capability of the airline concerned and its code-share

partners that enables this to happen, rather than the airport itself; thus, there are two hubs at Chicago O'Hare – American's and United's.) Hubs of this type – often referred to as complex hubs – act as switching centres, intermediating flows between multiple origins and multiple destinations, as well as contributing O&D traffic of their own. (It was noted above that at some of their bases or 'focus cities', the larger LFAs have sufficiently high frequencies on a sufficiently wide range of routes that passengers can create their own connecting itineraries. This is not hubbing, however, if the LFA schedules to optimise aircraft and crew utilisation not passenger connections, prices per segment rather than offering through-fares to passengers who choose to connect, and leaves responsibility for missed connections firmly in the hands of customers.)

Complex hubs can be analysed in a variety of ways. For the purpose of the discussion here, it is helpful to think in terms of following variables:

- *Stage-length* Hubs can connect one or a combination of:
  - short-haul to short-haul;
  - short-haul to long-haul and vice versa;
  - long-haul to long-haul.
  Many hubs combine all three, but with different degrees of emphasis on each. US hubs such as Charlotte, Cleveland, Salt Lake City, and Denver primarily serve short-haul to short-haul transfers whereas Singapore and Dubai are oriented towards long-haul to long-haul. European hubs tend to be more balanced, but with the larger ones such as Paris CDG and Frankfurt quite strongly oriented towards long-haul connectivity compared with smaller hubs such as Vienna and Munich – in part because of the volume and nature of local O&D demand available to the larger hubs.
- *Directionality* Flows might be:
  - unidirectional, moving traffic predominantly from one side of the hub to another in successive waves (e.g., Delta at Cincinnati, operating east–west and vice versa);
  - omnidirectional, moving traffic from and to all points of the compass within a single complex (e.g., Northwest at Memphis).
  Most flows of traffic through a hub are directional insofar as they pass from one side of the hub to the other. Some short-haul feed might, however, be non-directional – such as a flight taken westwards to connect with a medium- or long-haul flight to the east; Dennis (1994) refers to hubs with significant flows of this type as 'hinterland hubs'.
- *Number of waves* From a standing start in the mid-1990s, Air France transformed Paris CDG into a six-wave hub within less than a decade. As noted below, the larger US hubs have tended to move away from wave intensities of this magnitude in favour of 'rolling' operations.
- *Scale and scope of operations* The literature is beset with terms which draw often ill-defined distinctions between hubs, mini-hubs, mega-hubs, and focus cities. Each conveys a workable impression of the scale and nature of operations at an airport, but no precision. A leading industry publication (*Unisys R2A Scorecard*, November 2004, p. 23) has defined a hub as an airline operation at a given airport which offers at least 35 daily departures, serves at least 12 non-stop destinations, provides at least 35 non-circuitous city-pair connections, and enplanes at least one

million passengers annually of which at least 20 per cent are online connecting passengers. The corresponding figures for a mega-hub are 200 or more daily departures to 50 or more non-stop destinations, enplaning six million or more passengers annually of which 50 per cent or more are making online connections. These figures are arbitrary, but in the absence of any generally accepted definitions they offer workable guidelines of what the terms hub and mega-hub mean when used in a commercial context (as opposed to the FAA's purely statistical approach).

Staying with complex hubs, we can distinguish two types of system:

1. *Single-hub systems* Most non-US airlines with hub-and-spoke networks are constrained by the size of their domestic markets and/or by aeropolitical regulations to operate single-hub systems (e.g., Emirates and Singapore Airlines).
2. *Multi-hub systems* These exist in three forms:
   • The largest US majors have developed multi-hub systems, some of which include several primary and secondary hubs. By connecting spoke cities (e.g., Portland, Oregon) to more than one hub (e.g., Denver and Chicago O'Hare), it is possible to offer higher frequencies and/or wider timing choices in behind/ beyond markets (e.g., Portland–New York JFK) than a single hub might permit; alternatively, where one hub has no spare capacity available to add an extra spoke, it may be possible to connect that spoke to another, less congested hub. The relatively long ranges of regional jets and new-generation mainline narrowbodies are allowing hub catchment areas to be extended far more widely than was feasible until the late-1990s, therefore permitting more multi-hub spoke connections from outlying stations (as well, incidentally, as increasing hub-bypass operations). Integrated carriers FedEx, DHL, and UPS have also developed multi-hub systems in North America, Europe, and Asia.
   • Some non-US majors have developed limited multi-hub strategies, but with mixed success. Infrastructure constraints at single-runway London Gatwick contributed to British Airways' decision to de-hub its operations there and concentrate flow-traffic on Heathrow – which is also constrained, but does at least offer far more connections even if it is not a true hub in the US sense. Alitalia failed in its attempt to build Milan Malpensa into a second hub alongside Rome Fiumicino. On the other hand, Lufthansa has been supplementing its Frankfurt hub by building Munich and, through subsidiary Swiss International, Zurich; Air France-KLM is developing a multi-hub strategy at Paris CDG and Amsterdam, with Lyons as a small secondary hub and Rome to be added if a takeover of Alitalia is ultimately consummated. The Cathay Pacific–Air China relationship appears to be evolving a multi-hub system incorporating Beijing, Shanghai, and Hong Kong, but at the time of writing this is very much in its early days and the outcome is far from certain; China Southern is also attempting a double-hub strategy encompassing Beijing along with its principal base in Guangzhou. On the whole, however, there is little single-airline secondary hubbing outside the United States.
   • Global alliances have been actively developing multi-hub systems linking partners' hubs on different continents. Particularly significant have been the North Atlantic bar-bell systems which draw traffic (e.g., from Luxembourg)

into a hub on one side of the Atlantic (e.g., Paris CDG), and channel it to a partner's hub on the other side (e.g., Cincinnati) for onward distribution to a final destination (e.g., Omaha). Because of the multi-hub domestic systems operated by their US partners, transatlantic alliances often benefit from multiple bar-bell structures – allowing origins behind Amsterdam to be connected to US secondary points beyond one or more of Detroit, Memphis, and/or Minneapolis, to take the KLM/Northwest network as an example.

In any type of multi-hub system, three tasks arise which do not affect single-hub systems: the assignment of spokes to one or more of the alternative hubs; determination of inter-hub linkages (i.e., frequencies and capacities); and the routing of O&D flows through the network (when there are commercially viable alternative paths).

Hub Quality

The strategic quality of a hub depends on several factors:

Geographic centrality   A hub that is geographically central within its defined catchment area (e.g., Denver) can benefit from a balanced spread of primary, secondary, and perhaps also tertiary destinations in opposite quadrants. Similarly, a hub which sits astride a significant linear traffic flow (e.g., Singapore) can offer connections subject to minimal deviation. Deviation can be expensive in terms of additional operating costs and, if O&D journey times are increased to the detriment of GDS display positions, perhaps also in terms of softer yields and forgone revenues.

1. *US hubs* Although some large US hubs clearly channel significant volumes of long-haul international traffic (e.g., Miami and Newark) and others are building international volumes as network carriers continue to shift capacity into overseas markets, most remain primarily driven by short- and medium-haul domestic flows. Geographic centrality is therefore largely a question of location relative to the flows being targeted (e.g., Northeast–Florida, Midwest–Deep South, southern transcontinental, and northern transcontinental).

2. *European hubs* Most major North European hubs rely heavily on feeding long-haul routes. In part this is because of the historical significance of intercontinental routes to carriers such as Air France, British Airways, KLM, and Lufthansa. It also reflects the fact that a higher proportion of short-haul traffic in Europe than in the United States is carried on routes that are:
    *   sufficiently dense to accommodate relatively high-frequency non-stop service;
    *   sufficiently short to make:
        –   intermediate hubbing an unattractive option;
        –   surface modes a viable alternative.
    Another factor is the structure of the European leisure market: first, a significant proportion of intra-European vacationers are carried on point-to-point charter and LFA services rather than by network carriers; second, the growing short-break market is largely focused on centres that can support non-stop service from most major origins. However, flows between secondary European cities are not insignificant, and carriers such as Lufthansa and Swiss International which have centrally located hubs

relative to both north–south and east–west intra-European flows are better positioned to benefit than peripherally based carriers such as British Airways, Iberia, and SAS. Airport congestion attributable to a mix of high demand and a smaller number of independent runways than is available at the largest US hubs nonetheless makes it unlikely that Europe will ever develop a system of hubs to rival the United States. If European LFAs continue their current growth trajectories, something which has to be open to doubt, they can be expected to make deeper inroads into network carriers' local traffic; the rapidly expanding, and in most cases heavily subsidised, high-speed rail network – which already carries nearly as many intra-European passengers per annum as the network carriers and LFAs combined – can also be expected to erode more of the local traffic moving in and out of hubs.

3. *Asian hubs* Singapore Airlines, Cathay Pacific and, to a lesser extent Malaysia Airlines and Thai, have exploited their geographic positions astride traffic flows between Europe and Australasia to build sixth-freedom hubs at their home bases. Japanese and Korean carriers have more recently, on a smaller but now rapidly expanding scale, begun exploiting the location of Tokyo and Seoul to gain access to flows between North America and secondary Chinese destinations unable to support non-stop transpacific service. Since its acquisition of Dragonair, Cathay has also become a more significant competitor in long-haul flows to and from Chinese cities.

4. *Middle Eastern hubs* The centrality of Dubai in a global sense is being exploited by Emirates to tap flows between the Americas, Europe, and Africa on the one hand and Asia on the other. Etihad and Qatar Airways seem keen to duplicate this strategy.

5. *Latin American hubs* COPA has used the centrality of Panama City to develop a hub which exploits flows in thin markets, connecting cities to the south and north using a mixed fleet of narrowbodies.

Particularly in US domestic multi-hub systems it is important to avoid hub clutter – something that in the past troubled US Airways' hubs at Pittsburgh, Baltimore (since de-hubbed), Philadelphia, and (in respect of some north–south flows) Charlotte. The proximity of Singapore and Bangkok in the context of sixth-freedom flows between Europe, the Middle East and Australasia was seen by some observers as a problem when Singapore Airlines joined the Star Alliance – of which Thai International was a founding member. In Europe, some degree of directional or market specialism is necessary to make sense of proximate hubs such as Frankfurt, Munich, and Zurich in the case of Lufthansa, and Paris and Amsterdam in the case of Air France-KLM.

Strength of feed The economics of hub-and-spoke operations are based largely on the economies of scope and density available to a large, integrated hub-based network and on the fundamental fact that any type of network grows stronger (in the sense that its service offer and therefore its revenue potential improve) with each connection that is added to it. We can think in terms of several types of traffic feed:

1. *Regional feed* Perhaps the archetypal example of traffic feed, highly developed in North America and increasingly so in Europe, is provided to major airlines by regional carriers that have fleets and cost structures better suited to short-haul routes linking secondary and tertiary points to a hub. Regionals can offer three particular sources of strategic value: first, traffic feed is valuable to the major if an excess of revenues over costs arises in respect of those passengers who would not otherwise have flown

on the major but for the regional connection; second, once feed into a hub has been locked up, the lack of readily accessible feed for competing services can represent a formidable barrier to entry; third, even if a hub is not dominated, control (ownership or contractual) over a locally important regional might be used to ensure that as far as possible feed is not timed to coordinate with a competitor's schedule.

There is in particular a view that hubs fed by numerous thin spokes can be more resistant to attack from point-to-point, especially low-fare point-to-point, competition than a hub primarily fed by dense routes. The development of 'fortress hubs' in the United States after deregulation was predicated on dominating traffic into and out of a metropolitan airport, and swamping markets within 500 miles of it with high-frequency services to ensure unchallenged regional feed. The range capabilities and passenger appeal of regional jets have undercut this dominance strategy, however, by making even spoke cities close to a hub potentially accessible to another carrier's more distant hub. The strategy was further undercut by surging oil prices in late 2007 and early 2008, which led several majors to initiate extensive cuts in regional flying. Box 6.3 further considers the topic of regional feed.

Box 6.3: The Structure of Regional Feed Arrangements

This is a complex strategic issue which will be simplified here into two related questions.

1. Should regional feed be owned or contracted? There is no right or wrong answer, and different strategies have been implemented even by the same carriers at different times. During the 1990s there was a tendency for majors in both the United States and Europe to develop their feed largely in-house, either through organic growth or acquisition. In recent years the landscape has become more varied. In the United States, several large regional airline holding companies have developed, notably Mesa Air Group and Republic Airways Holdings, which each own several carriers operating – often under separate certificates – for different majors. Alongside these are independents and in-house regionals (e.g., Northwest's Compass and Mesaba, and US Airways' Piedmont and PSA Airlines). In late 2007 American's parent AMR Corporation announced that American Eagle was for sale, and Delta was at the same time giving active consideration to selling Comair. In Canada, by early 2008 Air Canada's parent ACE Aviation Holdings had sold its stake in Jazz. In Europe, whilst British Airways has 'sold' its regional operations to Flybe – operations which, because of congestion at Heathrow, never really functioned as a true source of regional feed – both Lufthansa and Air France-KLM retain a mix of in-house and partially owned subsidiaries. TAP Portugal acquired Portugalia in order to secure feed for a reorganised three-wave hub at Lisbon. The pros and cons can be summarised as follows:
    *   Network carriers need to secure regional feed to reinforce hub dominance (i.e., to achieve 'horizontal foreclosure' by excluding competitors from access to flow traffic across the hub), but purely contractual code-sharing and franchise arrangements might not prove permanent if a regional's ownership changes hands (e.g., Delta's experience when Business Express changed ownership in 1999 and began instead to feed American). Conversely, in a market downturn it might be simpler – although not necessarily cheaper – to remove capacity provided by in-house regionals than to renegotiate contracts with unaffiliated regionals.
    *   Furthermore, in-house regional operations can make valuable contributions to the corporate bottom line. (The counter-argument, of course, is that balance sheets might benefit from the proceeds of selling-off profitable regional affiliates. This was a major justification for regional spin-offs by Continental and others beginning in 2002.)

•   Against ownership of regionals is the likelihood that over time any regional controlled by a major will experience upward cost pressures.
•   In addition, having a portfolio of ownership and contractual relationships with a spread of different code-share partners, perhaps feeding the same hubs down different spokes, in preference to ownership alone can limit the sort of damage done to Delta by the Comair strike at what at the time was a single-feeder hub at Cincinnati.

2.   How should contractual arrangements be structured? Until 2001, US majors and non-owned regionals tended to cooperate under prorate agreements, which left regionals bearing some of the commercial risk as well as the operating responsibility. Since the majors began down-gauging their domestic networks in 2001–2002 by handing routes over to regionals, common practice has been to enter into capacity purchase agreements (CPAs) under which regionals are paid on either a cost-plus, a fee-per-departure, or a fee-per-ASM basis. Terms vary, but it is usual for the major to take on all commercial functions and accept revenue, fuel price, and insurance risk while the regional's responsibility extends to the costs of ground and flight operations. The advantage for a regional is that earnings risk is eliminated (something that in the past has helped many of them finance large RJ orders); the advantage for a major is that capacity is guaranteed without in most cases having to invest in aircraft, and control over scheduling and pricing leaves it free to revenue-manage regional output. Target operating margins in the 10–15 per cent range established in the early round of CPAs at the beginning of the 2000s helped account for strong earnings performance in the US regional airline sector. More recently, majors have exerted downward pressure on these targets by putting contracts out to competitive tender and generally taking a tougher negotiating stance. In its 2007 agreement with Pinnacle, for example, Northwest limited the regional to an 8–10 per cent operating margin and took a share in any excess.

Herein lies a challenge for the future, however: under some CPAs in respect of 70-seat regional jets (e.g., Northwest/Pinnacle) the major supplies aircraft and fuel as well as all the marketing functions, leaving the regional to do little more than provide crews, line maintenance, and certain other ground support until five or so years later it has to bid again. Quite irrespective of uncertainties arising from proposed and actual consolidation amongst the majors, this is not a stable business model for a regional. Even where – as is still predominantly the case – aircraft are supplied by the regional, from a major's perspective regionals are no longer partners but commodity suppliers of output which periodically bid against each other largely on price; in effect, they are close to being (wet-) leasing companies.

On the other hand, whilst US regionals certainly came under pressure during contract re-bidding in 2006–2007 and in many cases had to give up the comfort of high guaranteed margins, the counterpoint is that they won greater freedom to fly for more than a single major – thereby diversifying geographic and commercial risk. In pursuit of diversification, SkyWest has bought Atlantic Southeast and bid for ExpressJet, whilst Pinnacle has bought Colgan. At the time of writing, the Republic Airways Group (Republic, Chautauqua, and Shuttle America) flies for American, Continental, Delta, United, and US Airways – and was therefore relatively unaffected by cancellation of its contracted flying for Frontier in early 2008. In a difficult market, however, even diversification may be insufficient: despite also flying for United and US Airways and pursuing ventures in Hawaii and China, the potential cancellation of a contract to fly for Delta was enough in mid-2008 to raise doubts about the financial future of Mesa Air Group.

In the final analysis, how much the freedom to diversify is really worth will depend upon the impact of higher fuel costs on the economics of RJ operations, and the willingness of majors to pay for continued access to this type of output. Contractual arrangements commonly provide the majors with an option to reduce block-hours or ASMs purchased, subject to some stated minimum; this was an option widely exercised in 2008 as rising fuel costs and softening domestic demand made the operation of 50-seat (and smaller) RJs uneconomic on many routes. Beyond that, even some quite long-term contracts stretching many years into the future allow for cancellation subject to notice; this was also an option which, because of both deteriorating economics and the prospect of consolidation and network rationalisation amongst the majors, looked set to be increasingly exercised.

The predominant model in Europe is for regionals to be fully functioning airlines rather than pure capacity providers. Many are subsidiaries of the network carriers whose brands they fly. Air France, for example, wholly owns Brit Air, CityJet, VLM, and Régional and has direct and indirect minority stakes in CCM and Airlinair respectively. (What is interesting about the Air France 'family' is that even the wholly-owned subsidiaries use the brand under franchise agreements structured similarly to arm's-length agreements between unconnected parties.) There are also independents which fly primarily for majors, and others which operate largely self-sufficient systems (e.g., Flybe).

One final point: although the focus here has been on regionals as providers of hub feed, many – particularly in Europe – also operate significant point-to-point hub-bypass schedules which can benefit a network carrier by generating brand loyalty through market presence. Around half of Air France's regional flying, for example, does not touch its Paris or Lyon hubs.

2. *Feed for long-haul international services* Significant international hubs generally rely on either or both regional and short-/medium-haul mainline feed. This is particularly true of European and Asian hubs, as well as a small number of US hubs (e.g., Miami and San Francisco). The presence or absence of feed can have a profound influence on network design at the individual route level. For example, Emirates' extensive feed from the Indian subcontinent into its Dubai hub allows it to operate a daily non-stop Dubai–Birmingham (UK) service tapping ethnic O&D markets; British Airways, on the other hand – confronted by negligible feed behind its small Birmingham operation, thin local Birmingham–Dubai traffic, and no network beyond Dubai – cannot justify operating on the route itself.

In fact, the last example is at the core of the challenge posed by Emirates in respect of flows between Europe on the one hand and Asia and Australasia on the other. By drawing traffic into its Dubai hub from an increasing number of secondary European cities such as Newcastle and Venice then flowing it onwards, Emirates is able to offer one-stop service in thin markets that cannot support direct flights by third- or fourth-freedom carriers. Whilst European airlines will continue to have a competitive advantage in the thicker O&D markets able to support daily or more frequent non-stop service (e.g., Frankfurt–Shanghai), Emirates poses a very real long-term threat to their own hubs' intra-European feed (e.g., Birmingham–Frankfurt–Shanghai).

3. *Alliance feed* As many as 40 per cent of US passengers flying overseas originate behind international gateways; foreign carriers lacking an alliance with a strong US partner face an uphill battle accessing this flow traffic. More generally, a key purpose underlying alliance formation is the exchange of traffic between networks. Given the tens of thousands of city-pair markets that multi-hub international alliances can serve 'online', joint network planning and scheduling that allows them to pick-up just a few passengers a day in each can translate into significant revenue gains over a year.

It is therefore critical that as far as possible a carrier's schedule is timed to exchange traffic with partners' services. For example, airlines will want their international services to arrive at a partner's hub in time to maximise onward connections to a conveniently timed outbound bank, and they will want their return long-haul services to depart after receiving feed from an incoming bank; achieving this given the constraints imposed by time zones, airport curfews, and the need to minimise the turnaround times of long-haul aircraft at partners' hubs is not always easy.

4.   *Intermodal feed* For passengers, modal interchanges between air transport and railways have been common in Europe for several decades, and are being both extended and upgraded with the widening of high-speed train services; aside from straightforward feed through airport railway stations, there is some code-sharing between airlines and train companies (e.g., Air France/SNCF and Lufthansa/Deutsche Bahn) and an integrated AIRail product feeds Lufthansa's Frankfurt hub from Cologne. Some regional and short-haul mainline flights into hubs that compete against high-speed rail services will undoubtedly lose local traffic to the point that they are no longer viable even as feeders for long-haul routes, especially if high fuel prices continue to adversely affect the operating economics of 50-seat RJs. There is therefore the prospect that, particularly in western Europe, both intermodal feed and straight O&D competition from trains will help release slots at those hubs that are well-connected to the rail network. Interestingly, Air France has expressed a desire to start its own high-speed rail feeder system when EU rail competition is opened up next decade; time will tell.

Given the distances some US domestic passengers are prepared to drive in order to access Southwest's low fares, there is an argument that these customers are providing their own intermodal feed. Although this point might sound somewhat semantic, its practical impact is that at a given station Southwest may have a larger surface catchment area than would a full-service carrier charging significantly higher fares. Its traffic volumes at these stations may therefore suffer less from the absence of short-haul regional feed than might otherwise be the case.

In both Europe and North America, airlines make extensive use of trucks to feed freight onto medium- and long-haul flights. Also on the freight side, several airports around the world (e.g., Seattle-Tacoma, Dubai, and Sharjah) have developed as sea–air transfer points.

Local traffic The amount, mix, yield, and growth potential of the local traffic it can generate to supplement flow traffic is also an important measure of a hub's quality, as is the balance between originating and terminating local traffic (which can affect the directionality of support that day-return passengers travelling to or from the hub provide to the first and last banks each day). Figures quoted for local traffic as an ideal minimum of total hub traffic range from 25 to 40 per cent. In the US domestic market, Continental's Newark hub relies on local traffic for just under 70 per cent of its volume, whilst US Airways' Charlotte hub is only around 20 per cent local. Insufficient local traffic was one of the arguments behind withdrawal from some of their secondary hubs by US majors in the 1990s. The potential importance of local traffic to hub profitability is a principal reason why the 'wayport' concept advanced in the 1990s – the idea of relocating hubs from congested metropolitan airports to newly developed facilities at geographically convenient but lightly populated locations – was stillborn on the passenger side of the industry. (Some authors apply a less restrictive definition of wayport, under which a hub such as Charlotte which has low volumes of local traffic rather than none at all would qualify; see, for example, Ivy [1993]).

Most majors like to rely to whatever extent is possible on captive, and therefore often reasonably high-yield, local traffic out of hubs which – with one or two notable exceptions such as Chicago O'Hare – they successfully dominate. Absence of strong, high-yield local traffic may leave a hub overdependent on flow traffic which can in some cases be relatively low-yield if other airlines are competing to attract it over alternative hubs. One of the reasons for KLM's relatively low yield at various times despite the reasonably high quality of its product is that its small local market leaves it more reliant on connecting traffic than, for example, British Airways and Lufthansa – both of which are based in major traffic-generating countries.

Hub dominance   The scale of a carrier's presence at a hub can be measured in terms of its percentage of aircraft and/or seat departures and – where relevant – its control over slots, gates, and terminal space. A dominant carrier may benefit from the S-curve effect, economies of scope and density, high station resource utilisation, premium yields from local traffic, local marketing strength, and – at slot-constrained airports – protection behind a significant structural barrier to entry. There is little doubt that hub-and-spoke systems have been an important force behind consolidation in the US domestic market, and are set to play a similar role in the global market.

Expansion potential   Whilst capacity constraints do impose a barrier to entry and so protect incumbents, the lack of terminal space and/or runway slots can also be a significant strategic constraint. This is clearly observable in the comparison between British Airways' problems at London Heathrow, where the scheduling of large and integrated waves has been impossible, and Air France's expansion potential at Paris CDG.

Attractiveness to passengers   Hubs are fundamentally attractive because of the range and timing of connections they offer, but where there is little to choose between two competing hubs in this respect it could be that physical factors such as the availability of lounges and other facilities and the design of public spaces might influence choice of airline. A testament to the attractions of connectivity is Heathrow's ability to retain its position as the world's largest international airport, in terms of passenger throughput, despite the deplorable service experiences imposed on many of its customers.

Hub efficiency   Particularly when a customer's choice of airline is driven by minimum elapsed journey time, a carrier wanting to attract that passenger to a service which involves connecting over its hub needs to ensure that MCT at the hub is competitive with MCTs at competing hubs. Tight MCTs require airline, suppliers of outsourced services (e.g., passenger- and baggage-handling, etc.), and airport authority to work together in order to sustain an acceptable service level (Nichols and Sala 2000). This is not only a revenue-side issue; long MCTs at a hub can feed through into less efficient resource utilisation. Important factors can be the opportunity to use proximate gates to facilitate passenger and baggage transfers over high-volume connections, and the opportunity to use the same gates for each significant high-frequency market throughout the day (Berdy 1998). The ideal situation is where an airline can effect all its online and alliance transfers under one roof. This should reduce MCTs compared with multi-terminal operations, and it is something the three global alliances are working to achieve at each of their largest hubs.

Conclusion   When evaluating a hub, the most critical considerations are geographical location relative to intermediated traffic flows, the economic potential of the catchment area, the availability of uncongested infrastructure or the ability to develop it, the prevailing pattern of service in respect of quality and price, the volume and yield available from local traffic, the cooperativeness of the airport authority, and the costs of operating a station. In the final analysis, what an airline makes of a hub's various qualities will depend to some extent on the effectiveness of scheduling; we will look at scheduling in Chapter 7.

Hub-And-spoke Networks: Pros And Cons

We will consider these from both airlines' and passengers' perspectives.

Airline perspectives: positive factors   There are several:

1. *Connectivity* Hub-and-spoke systems provide better network connectivity, and so wider market coverage, than linear networks. Any given number of points can be linked over a hub with fewer departures than non-stop or direct services would require. Furthermore, once a hub has been established each additional spoke magnifies the linkage benefits – that is, substantially broadens the range of markets served. Ten spokes could theoretically provide direct service between ten outstations and the hub as well as connecting service between 45 different pairs of outstations, for example; were the number of spokes to be increased 50 per cent to 15 the number of direct services would also increase 50 per cent to 15, but connecting services would increase 133 per cent to 105. (The formula for this calculation is $n(n-1)/2$, where n is the number of spokes radiating from a hub.) Good connectivity can underpin greater revenue capture from a given area and, assuming feed is online rather than interline, can help reduce prorate dilution compared with what can happen when journeys are interlined.

2. *Load factors* It is generally true that the larger an incoming bank of arrivals, the easier it is to support outgoing flights. A 150-seat aircraft leaving a hub after the arrival of a bank from 25 points, for instance, would need on average to pick up only 4 passengers from each incoming flight to achieve a 66.6 per cent load factor (ignoring local traffic); if the bank brought flights from only ten points, ten connecting passengers would be needed from each to achieve the same result. (Of course, what really matters is revenue rather than raw load factors, and this will depend upon the yield earned from each passenger, which may be lower for connecting services than for non-stop routes between the same origin and destination.)

    In this context mention needs to be made of the A380. Depending on respective configurations, these aircraft will carry well over 100 more seats than a B747-400. Where an A380 is being operated out of a slot-constrained hub on a route reliant to a significant extent on feed, there will inevitably be upward pressure on the average size of regional (and mainline narrowbody) aircraft required to feed it.

3. *Costs* By channelling passengers from multiple origins to multiple destinations a hub-and-spoke network can address to some extent the production indivisibilities that arise from having to split an airline's output of seat-miles amongst different city-pair markets; hub-and-spoke networks allow more city-pair markets to be served for a given level of output (i.e., ASMs, etc.) than other forms of network. Alternatively, fewer legs need be flown to serve a given number of O&D markets.

    • We have already noted that *economies of scope* are generated when it costs less to combine onto one departure down a spoke to a hub passengers wanting to travel beyond that hub to several destinations than it would to provide non-stop or direct services to each of these destinations using smaller aircraft operated at lower frequencies (something which, in thinner markets, might anyway not be feasible).

    • *Economies of density* arise when the combination of traffic onto a spoke allows larger aircraft with lower seat-mile costs to be used than could otherwise be supported at acceptable load factors – although these economies might be traded-off against higher frequencies using smaller aircraft, depending on the market segments being targeted and the airline's market positioning. Economies of density are essentially 'aircraft economies of scale', with minimum efficient scale dependent upon the stage-length concerned relative to the operating economics of available aircraft.

- *Marketing economies of scale*, particularly information economies, can be exploited when a carrier is able to identify itself strongly with a hub and its hinterland, especially if local distribution channels can be dominated as well. The widespread brand awareness that often attaches to a large carrier can have the effect of curtailing information search by potential customers who simply assume that airline's presence in the market in which they want to travel without further investigating alternatives; challengers have to spend heavily on marketing communications in order to overcome this disadvantage – particularly when it is reinforced by FFP membership and corporate deals.

4. *GDS display priority* Assume a carrier has three services coming from origins O_1, O_2, and O_3. Each uses a separate aircraft to hub H and then a single aircraft (perhaps one of the original three, or perhaps another) from H to destination D. Further assume that the airline markets services from O_1, O_2, and O_3 to D under three different flight numbers. A local passenger enquiring about travel between H and D around the time of the airline's departure on this leg will find the agent's GDS screen displaying three different flight numbers even though the carrier is operating just one aircraft. This use of funnel flights for 'screen padding', which has in the past been restricted by codes of conduct in some jurisdictions, can have the effect of pushing competitors' services to the bottom of the important first page of the GDS display from which many agency bookings originate – particularly if the enquiry is schedule- rather than price-driven. (Even when online agencies or meta-search engines are used, screen padding as a result of funnel flights or, in a different context, code-sharing can relegate competitive price quotes to a second or lower page.)

5. *Revenue* A number of academic studies were cited in Chapter 4 as evidence supporting the view that some US network carriers are able to earn premia from local traffic into and out of a dominated hub – although there is a question regarding the extent to which these are attributable to a business-oriented traffic mix rather than market power alone (Lee and Luengo-Prado 2005). The evidence from elsewhere in the world is less definitive.

6. *Strategy* Also significant for the few carriers with aspirations to play leading roles in one of the three global alliances is the widespread view that such roles are closed to airlines that do not possess a major hub in one of the world's principal traffic-generating regions.

Airline perspectives: negative factors   Circumstances vary, but negative factors might include the following:

1. Average stage-lengths could be reduced by a hub stopover, depending upon network geography; unit production costs generally rise as stage-lengths fall.
2. Hub-and-spoke networks require each passenger to be flown a greater distance between origin and destination, and journeys entail the extra costs of landing, ground-handling (of aircraft as well as passengers), and take-off at the hub. We have also seen that passenger flows across hubs create costly complications in respect of pricing and revenue management which are largely absent from point-to-point operations.

Furthermore, airlines incur additional costs when passengers and/or their baggage fail to make connections. The presumption has been that all these different operating costs are lower than the costs of providing low-frequency direct or non-stop service in multiple city-pair markets, and are outweighed by the benefits derived from channelling traffic flows over a hub. As demand grows in thin markets and aircraft capabilities improve, this argument can weaken, leading to market fragmentation and the development of hub-bypass routes.

3. Hubs are expensive to build and operate. They require investment in infrastructure to support the transfer of passengers and baggage which in turn creates a heavy structural cost burden; that infrastructure is in essence a production capability offering throughput capacity, and like all forms of capacity it needs to be fully utilised in order to spread fixed costs over the maximum possible amount of output (in this case, flights). Furthermore, the capacity to accommodate transfer passengers and their baggage is not needed by local passengers originating or terminating at the hub, yet – depending upon fare structures in the local and transfer markets concerned – they might well be burdened with a share of its cost; in fact, this can be an important source of an LFA's cost advantage when it competes head-to-head against a network carrier in local markets in and out of a hub city.

Perhaps the most significant problem associated with hubbing is that its essence is to concentrate traffic into banks of arrivals followed closely by banks of departures. Such self-inflicted peaking, as with all peaking phenomena, comes at a cost: first, resources may be inadequately utilised between waves; second, because resources are heavily utilised during each wave, slack resources and time buffers need to be built into the system to accommodate the random variances from planned flows (of aircraft, passengers, and crew) that inevitably arise. The cutting of slack 'to the bone' by US majors in pursuit of cost savings between 2001 and 2004 was a significant contributor to customer service problems when traffic growth accelerated during the cyclical upturn that followed.

Traffic has risen at a handful of the largest hubs to the point that no sooner has the last flight in an outbound bank departed than the first of the next inbound bank is arriving. By the 1990s, for example, incoming banks were as little as 1–1½ hours apart at American's Dallas-Fort Worth hub. At this point, and notwithstanding that many observers do not draw the distinction, it is worth distinguishing between two similar but different types of non-peaked hub (Burghouwt 2007):

•   *Continuous hubs* These arise where demand in local O&D markets with the hub at one end is sufficiently strong to support high-frequency services, and the frequency of these services creates the opportunity for passengers with destinations beyond the hub to transfer there. An example is British Airways' hub at London Heathrow. This type of operation is also sometimes referred to as a 'random hub', although there is an implication in that expression of a less dense schedule and perhaps longer transfer times than a continuous hub can offer. (See Berdy [1998] for a discussion of continuous flow networks.) Southwest operates what are continuous hubs in all but name at several airports (e.g., Baltimore-Washington, Chicago Midway, Phoenix, and Denver). On the other hand some LFAs operate what on the surface appear to be continuous hubs, but in many cases they will not sell through tickets because their strategy is based around single-segment revenue and cost models (e.g., Ryanair at Stansted); these operations, where passengers who transfer have to buy two tickets and check-in separately for each sector, are not hubs in the sense of the term used in this book. Because continuous hubs offer lower connectivity (i.e., fewer marketable connections in a given period of time) than a wave is likely to offer, there will be some loss of flow traffic; they are therefore best implemented at hubs supported by strong local traffic.

- *Rolling hubs* These are similar to continuous hubs, but arise less from the natural growth of demand in local markets in and out of the hub than from a conscious decision on the part of airline network planners to de-peak the pre-existing wave structure of a hub which has grown to the point where congestion costs have become unacceptably high. For example, in the course of a network-wide capacity reduction programme announced in 2002, American began 'de-peaking' DFW and O'Hare – spreading operations more evenly across the day and accepting longer connecting times. Delta has done the same in Atlanta. There are two factors behind a decision to de-peak: first, the need to put downward pressure on unit costs by raising utilisation of aircraft and hub resources; second, recognition that for many segments of the market price (as delivered directly to consumers by the Internet) is more important than longer connecting times (which previously had to be minimised to ensure high display positions in GDSs used by travel agents). The downside, of course, is that high-yield segments tend to be time-sensitive.

Continuous and rolling hubs both reduce the disadvantages of self-inflicted peaking by spreading resource utilisation more evenly. An alternative to introducing a rolling hub which might be suboptimal but nonetheless help overcome infrastructure constraints could be to schedule flights from some spoke cities to alternate inbound banks; there would be a revenue impact, however, if loss of frequency into and out of the affected spoke cities degrades service to the point of driving demand to competitors.

4.   Aircraft may have to spend too long waiting on the ground during each hub turn because passengers need time to connect off arriving flights, and sometimes also because of ground and terminal area congestion; gate utilisation may also be low as a result. Dwell-time at a hub will depend in part on efficiency in allocating aircraft arriving early in an inbound bank to early departures in the connecting outbound bank – something that will in turn depend upon whether the particular type(s) or variant(s) operating early inbound flights are sized correctly to serve early outbound flights.

Dwell-time is likely to increase as flights are added to a bank. Assume 30 arrivals at an average rate of one every 40 seconds, connecting time between last arrival and first departure of 30 minutes (although in reality this is a pairing that might be designed to carry minimal traffic in the O&D market concerned and so be sacrificed to increase efficiency), and an average departure rate of one per minute: the window for the complex is 20 + 30 + 30 = 80 minutes. Assuming we add one incoming and one outgoing flight and maintain the same MCT of 30 minutes, the dwell-time of at least some of the existing aircraft will be increased – albeit by just a few seconds; add more than one flight and magnify the effect across a year's schedule at the hub, and the impact on aircraft utilisation becomes more pronounced.

Another potential source of aircraft utilisation problems is that the need for flights to arrive at and depart from a hub within a fairly narrow time window will mean, in the absence of creative network design and scheduling, that aircraft serving spokes with the shortest flight-times will spend longer periods on the ground at outstations before returning to the hub than will those serving distant points. This clearly imposes lower utilisation and, therefore, unit cost penalties. (We will return to the topic in Chapter 7.)

Having said all this, it is worth pointing out that the aircraft utilisation penalties just described are at their worst where short-haul aircraft are involved in a wave. Long-haul to long-haul connections impose a lesser burden because long-haul widebodies are anyway expected to spend longer on the ground during turnarounds than efficiently utilised short-haul aircraft require. In this sense, the inefficiencies involved in operating Emirates' four-wave hub at Dubai are of a lower order than those arising at the largest US domestic hubs.

5. Taxiway and terminal area congestion increase unproductive fuel-burn.

6. Difficult choices might be faced with regard to the location of light maintenance activities when aircraft are 'stabled' overnight at outstations in order to offer early departures to the hub – something which most LFAs do not do. This can particularly affect short-haul aircraft which might otherwise undergo phased checks at night were they at the home base or some other maintenance facility. (A phased check involves the breaking down of intermediate checks into work packages that can be spread over a number of lighter checks performed overnight were the aircraft stabled at a hub with a maintenance facility, but not if it is stabled at an outstation.)

7. Yields from flow traffic in respect of which there might be more competition than local traffic attracts at a dominated hub can sometimes be low. Against this, of course, flow traffic may help exploit economies of density by allowing the use of larger aircraft than could otherwise be supported by local traffic alone. The balance will vary from case to case, but dissatisfaction with low yields from main cabin flow traffic was one reason behind British Airways' downsizing strategy launched in 1999.

8. On-time performance is vital to the integrity of a hub-and-spoke system, but can be hostage to technical faults, traffic congestion, operational inefficiency, and the weather. A widespread schedule disruption at a hub tends to propagate around a hub-and-spoke system more readily than across a simple, linear system. In a worst-case scenario, enforced holding or diversion of an incoming bank could, if different aircraft are involved, lead to subsequent waves backing up on the first – bearing in mind that the last arrivals of an incoming bank and the first arrivals of the next incoming bank might be less than two hours apart at a four-wave hub. Irrgang (1995a) provides a thorough explanation of the problem. This was one reason why American chose in 2001 to isolate the Chicago O'Hare hub from the rest of its system; Lufthansa also manages its Frankfurt and Munich hubs as separate operational entities.

9. Balancing local and flow traffic to maximise revenue can be difficult. Generally, an airline will earn more revenue from carrying two separate local passengers into and out of a hub than one connecting passenger in the same booking class on the same flights; this is because fares taper with distance, so the two local passengers are each likely to pay more per mile or kilometre than the connecting passenger. Furthermore, it is often – although not invariably – the case that a carrier has more market power over local traffic into and out of its hub than it does over connecting traffic, because connecting traffic might (depending on market geography) have a wide choice of alternative networks available. However, there are two complicating factors:

    •   First, many carriers unable to sell a high proportion of their seats to local traffic, particularly during off-peak periods, need fill-up flow traffic. (The alternative is to operate smaller aircraft sized more appropriately to the local market and less reliant on flow traffic; if these smaller aircraft have higher seat-mile costs, the product offered must in principle be good enough to sustain the firmer yields now required.)

- Second, it will not always be the case that selling seats to local passengers travelling in a low-yield booking class (e.g., deeply discounted economy/coach) will be optimal from a network revenue standpoint if these seats are no longer available to a higher-yield connecting passenger (e.g., a late-booking, full-fare economy/coach passenger). Certainly, the through-fare in a given booking class will almost invariably be lower than the sum-of-sectors level (i.e., the aggregate of fares in the same booking class sold separately on the two connecting flights); on the other hand, several different booking classes will be sold within any given cabin on each of the two segments, so the revenue impact of carrying through- as opposed to local traffic will depend upon the effectiveness of the carrier's RMS. We will explore this point in Chapter 9.

Weighing up the pros and cons of hubbing presents no general rule as to its merits relative to more traditional network designs. Hub-and-spoke networks are effective traffic gatherers and distributors, but they are not necessarily efficient in terms of resource utilisation; as O&D markets become more dense and demand for hub-bypass service grows, neither are these networks necessarily effective in terms of delivering customer satisfaction. Many LFAs (e.g., easyJet in CAA 2003) contend, often with the backing of high operating margins, that the 'economies of simplicity' inherent in a point-to-point operation outweigh any economies of scope or density gained from a hub-based network; put another way, what is being argued is that any reduction in costs attributable to economies of scope and density is overwhelmed by the structural costs embedded in a sizeable hub. On the other hand, LFAs airberlin and AirTran have built significant parts of their network strategies around hubs. Perhaps the safest conclusion that can be drawn at present is that the economics of a hub depend upon points served, traffic mix in local markets with the hub at one end, traffic flows that can be created by channelling O&D demand over the hub, yields available, and how efficiently hub operations are managed.

To the extent that structural costs are high in a hub-and-spoke network relative to a point-to-point alternative, that network needs to deliver connectivity benefits sufficient to generate a revenue premium. In other words, if a network carrier cannot get its CASM down to the level of competing LFAs, it needs to have something in its offer to customers which enables it to generate a correspondingly larger RASM; in premium classes in some markets the quality of the ground and inflight product should help in this regard, but other than this it will fall on the strength (i.e., connectivity) of the network to generate that premium. As LFAs continue to expand their geographical scope, this is not a challenge that is going to become any easier for European, North American, and Asian network carriers to meet in their short-haul markets (out to 5 hours). A good example of the current pace of that expansion can be seen in Ryanair's October 2007 announcement that it would in the following schedule season add 70 new routes to the 550 already being operated.

Passengers' perspectives   These vary widely, depending to a large extent upon the impact of network structure on the availability and price of service in those markets in which individual passengers want to travel. Two concerns are commonly expressed:

1. *Spoke cities*   The concern here is that as hub-and-spoke systems are developed, spoke cities frequently lose non-stop service to destinations other than hubs and their

quality of service suffers as a result. Although this can be true, there are several counterpoints:

- First, the channelling of flow traffic over hubs often gives passengers originating in spoke cities access to a wide range of O&D city-pairs, many of which could not support non-stop service from those cities.
- Second, it is likely that they will benefit from higher frequencies to the hub and onwards to other destinations than non-stop services in individual O&D markets could sustain.
- Third, as traffic density increases in an O&D market served over a hub, it is possible that direct or non-stop hub-bypass services will anyway be introduced – perhaps to supplement, rather than replace, connecting service.
- Fourth, passengers travelling from a spoke city connected to different airlines' separate hubs could benefit from competitive fares to a destination beyond those hubs. This is most likely to be the case in medium- and long-haul markets. For example, the GAO (2006) notes that a passenger travelling from Harrisburg, Pennsylvania to Seattle has a choice of six connecting hubs, whereas a journey to Rochester, New York offers only two alternatives. (This is consistent with the study's finding that US domestic city-pairs more than 1500 miles apart have benefited from an increase in the average number of competitors from 2.3 in 1980 to 4.2 in 2005, whereas markets shorter than 250 miles have seen a decrease from 1.6 to 1.4.)

In the final analysis, as soon as demand in an O&D market is judged sufficient to support non-stop service with 150- to 180-seat aircraft at a reasonable frequency, the chances are that in Europe or North America an LFA will now step in to offer hub-bypass service. This has happened widely in Europe, for example, where LFAs now link hundreds of secondary city-pairs previously linked only over network carrier's hubs.

2. *Hub cities* The primary concern in respect of 'fortress hub' O&D markets is that passengers might have to pay a premium because of pricing power exercised by the dominant carrier (a topic discussed in Chapter 3). Sources of pricing power could include co-option of airport facilities, influence over local agency channels, the attractions of the carrier's FFP to passengers based near the hub and so having easy access from there to multiple destinations around its network, and information economies of scale.

On the other hand, passengers living close to the hub benefit from having higher frequencies on offer to more destinations than would otherwise be the case, which leads to several possible advantages: less time is wasted waiting for low-frequency departures or changing planes at another hub, scope exists for day-return trips to a wider range of destinations, and greater opportunities arise to 'earn and burn' FFP awards. Furthermore, hub dominance is sometimes not as overwhelming as cursory analysis might make it appear: dominance of a hub airport is not necessarily the same as dominance of local traffic into and out of the city served by that airport (e.g., Southwest and easyJet both use secondary airports to compete with network carriers' nearby hubs in the same metropolitan areas or regions); second, a hub airline's dominance of local enplanements might not be as great as its dominance of aggregate local and connecting enplanements (e.g., British Airways has a much less dominant share of local traffic to and from London Heathrow than of aggregate local and flow traffic); third, dense routes out of a hub might support point-to-point competition, particularly during voids between the hubbing carrier's complexes, so depriving that carrier of some of its monopoly power.

More generally, hubs are becoming increasingly unpopular, especially with business travellers, because of congestion and delays. Post-9/11 security procedures sometimes add to the problem and threaten MCTs.

II. Network Strategies and Tactics

It can be useful to distinguish between network strategies and network tactics.

1. *Network strategy* This defines the number and nature of points served (i.e., the mix of primary, secondary, and tertiary points and of city-break, longer vacation, business, and VFR destinations), routes used to serve them, and output (i.e., frequencies and capacities) offered. It is the service proposition on which everything else in an airline should be built insofar as it links directly through to an airline's strategic description of itself – as a full-service global network carrier, as a low-fare point-to-point operator, as a regional, and so on. What represents a strong network will depend upon the competitive strategy and product positioning of the airline concerned. In designing its route structure Ryanair, for example, looks to points that:
   - can be served at relatively low cost (i.e., secondary or tertiary airports);
   - will support reasonable frequencies using B737s (although not necessarily daily);
   - contain in their catchment areas significant or potentially significant segments of price-sensitive demand – whether from VFR passengers (e.g., UK–Ireland, UK–Italy, UK–Poland), leisure (including city-break) passengers, or (where frequencies are sufficiently high and airports not unduly remote) business travellers.

2. *Network tactics* In liberalised and deregulated competitive environments, networks are both less proprietary and more dynamic than they were when tightly regulated. Rapidly changing competitive environments demand tactical responses – increases or reductions in frequencies, the rerouting of services in particular city-pair markets, and the introduction and elimination of routes.

NETWORK STRATEGIES

The principal parameters within which network strategies unfold are:

- competitive strategy and product positioning;
- commercial regulation affecting both access to markets and permissible output (i.e., frequencies and capacity) – a constraint that is diminishing in many national and international markets but nonetheless remains an important consideration in others;
- national ownership requirements – which, other than within the EU, Australasia, and a few Latin American countries, preclude foreign control of airlines;
- infrastructure constraints.

Some carriers are by design point-to-point operators; this is particularly true of LFAs, charter carriers and national airlines whose home bases provide limited hubbing opportunities. Nonetheless, if we look at two apparently similar airlines, it is often possible to identify significantly different network strategies: whereas Ryanair generally targets secondary airports (e.g., Frankfurt Hahn), easyJet is willing to serve major airports (e.g., Nice and Paris Orly) where it believes higher costs can be covered by firmer yields. Furthermore, as noted in Chapter 1, some LFAs do serve connecting flows. US LFAs fall into three distinct groups in this regard: Spirit and jetBlue connect less than 5 per cent, Southwest connects around the mid-teens, whilst AirTran connects approximately 30 per cent.

Network carriers, and the regionals and/or other affiliates that feed them, by definition operate hub-and-spoke networks. In addition, many also operate tag-end flights, 'free flights' (i.e., legs scheduled for otherwise unutilised aircraft downtime and unconnected to a hub complex), and point-to-point or hub-bypass routes in markets strong enough to support non-stop service. However, whilst flow traffic is clearly at the heart of a network carrier's operation, only in the case of Northwest and Delta amongst the US majors does it approximate half the total; figures for the others range from Continental in the high 30 per cent range to United in the mid-40s.

Within the context of the fundamental dichotomy between point-to-point and hub-and-spoke strategies, three distinct but related phenomena are currently observable:

1. *Market fragmentation*   When non-stop service becomes viable in an O&D market currently served only by connecting segments over a hub, market fragmentation occurs. Viability might be due to one or both of:
   • demand growth – attributable to demographic growth, economic growth, and/or price stimulation – transforming a thin market into one capable of sustaining regular non-stop service;
   • improving aircraft performance, such that smaller aircraft with capacities better suited to thin markets now have sufficient range to fly non-stop sectors that could previously be flown only by aircraft too large for the market concerned.
   Market fragmentation has occurred in all types of circumstance: long-range regional jets have opened non-stop service on routes too small to support mainline narrowbodies; mainline narrowbodies with transcontinental, and in some cases intercontinental, range have opened non-stop service on routes too small to support widebodies; and medium-size widebody twins – initially the B767 and A310, now the B777, B787, and A330 – have opened non-stop service on long-haul routes too small to support B747s at similar frequencies. Market fragmentation involving secondary city to secondary city hub bypass routes has been particularly common in regional and short-haul mainline markets; because long-haul markets with a secondary city at one end usually require hub feed at the other, market fragmentation in this case has generally involved a new non-stop spoke from a hub replacing double-connect service over a second hub (e.g., Savannah–Atlanta–Budapest rather than Savannah–Atlanta–Paris–Budapest).
   Boeing has been a strong proponent of the view that growing demand for air travel is met primarily by increasing frequencies on existing routes and then eventually offering non-stop service in O&D markets previously unable to support it. The argument is that passengers prefer higher frequencies and more non-stops rather than larger aircraft, and the evidence has been that whilst numbers of frequencies and non-stops have grown over the last several decades, the average size of aircraft in the global fleet (i.e., ASKs ÷ aircraft kilometres flown) has declined. Aeropolitical liberalisation – allowing carriers more freedom to choose which international routes they fly, how often, and with what equipment – provides a key support for further market fragmentation.

2. *Market consolidation* Not so much an alternative network strategy as an alternative view on how markets will develop, the argument here is that although there will undoubtedly be significant market fragmentation the bulk of traffic growth will come in non-stop inter-hub O&D markets that are already dense and support multiple daily frequencies. The outcome, particularly given worsening congestion at these airports, will be an increase in average aircraft size. Despite forecasting similar air traffic growth rates to Boeing, Airbus foresees average aircraft size in the global fleet rising 20 per cent from 2006 to reach 215 seats by 2025.

3. *Market polarisation* Airlines are relatively unusual businesses insofar as most have traditionally delivered all their products within the same operating system. Market polarisation implies that in future customers wanting premium service will be offered premium-only aircraft, whereas more price-sensitive travellers will opt for single-class LFAs. Polarisation is not new: European charter carriers have been highly focused operations since their inception over 50 years ago, Pacific Southwest pioneered one-class service within California around the same time, and Laker's Skytrain concept dates back to the 1970s. What has brought the strategy into greater relief over the last few years has been the global proliferation of LFAs, both short- and long-haul, and the emergence of all-premium routes and airlines. On the other hand, it was noted in Chapter 1 that several LFAs have moved away from single-class products, and the likelihood that all-premium operations will break out of their niche is not high – at least in the short term.

Liberalisation and technology, both aircraft and information technologies, are together enabling a multitude of different business models to evolve. Some will fail because they are unsound, some will fail because they are poorly implemented, but many will succeed. Proponents of fragmentation, consolidation, and polarisation will all be able to find examples to back their arguments. The traditional business model, rather than just its accompanying network structures, is in the process of fragmenting into a plurality of offers.

Network Strategies In Different Markets

The US domestic market In the rapidly changing landscape of the last few years, three strategic phenomena stand out:

1. *Hub de-peaking* We touched upon this earlier. Its essence is that in order to improve resource utilisation and productivity at a hub, one of two steps is taken:
    *   The number of waves is increased to the extent that across the day there is relatively little slack time between the last bank of departures and the next bank of arrivals. This is possible only at mega-hubs capable of supporting six or more waves a day.
    *   The activity level is maintained as before, but instead of being concentrated into a small number of peaks is spread more evenly throughout the day. The number of saleable connections might fall and/or connecting times in some markets might rise, but any revenue hit is compensated by higher resource productivity.

        Some airlines, notably American, have made more progress than others with smoothing peaks. A study by Lott (2006) found that at American's DFW hub no 30-minute period had more than five departures above the daily average number of departures per half-hour; the figure two years earlier had been eight periods. At Chicago O'Hare, American's figure of two stood in marked contrast to United's 13.

2. *Hub bypass* Non-hub point-to-point flying by network carriers and their regional partners has grown strongly since 2002. Demand growth in many short- and medium-haul O&D markets that have to date been able to justify only connecting service over a hub has been such that non-stop or direct flights have been introduced either to supplement or to replace hub connections. The payload–range capabilities of new generation regional jets and mainline narrowbodies are helping accelerate this market fragmentation. The preference of most passengers for avoiding the delays and misconnects increasingly associated with large hubs has added impetus to the trend. The FAA calculates the ratio of domestic passenger enplanements to O&D passengers each year; the closer the ratio is to one, the greater the proportion of passengers that is flying point-to-point and not connecting. After hovering around 1.37 or 1.38 enplanements per O&D passenger between 1995 and 2003, the ratio had declined to 1.3 by 2007 (FAA 2008); interestingly, whilst network carriers mirrored (in fact, drove) the national trend, the ratio for LFAs actually rose between 2004 and 2007 (ibid.).

3. *Increased international flying* In response to growing LFA competition in domestic markets and the availability of higher yields overseas, most of the US network majors (with the notable exception of Continental) have been shifting capacity away from domestic markets. Close to half of Continental's revenues are already international, and Delta is targeting something similar. Whilst the opening of routes to China flown by B777s has gained a lot of attention, another development has been redeployment of B757s and B767s away from domestic routes onto relatively thin North Atlantic routes to midsize European and Middle Eastern cities. Northwest and, particularly, Continental have been building B757 services from their US hubs to secondary cities in Western Europe (e.g., Glasgow, Edinburgh, and Bristol), whilst Delta has by virtue of having a large B767 fleet at its disposal been able to penetrate further into central and Eastern Europe (e.g., Bucharest).

However, the de-peaking and bypassing of hubs is not a precursor to dismantling them. Despite the growth of their international services as a proportion of total output, the hubs of US network airlines remain primarily domestic in focus and a great deal of domestic O&D traffic arises in markets too small to support direct service (Lott 2004; Meehan 2006); even in dense markets between New York and Los Angeles and New York and San Francisco, as much as 15 per cent of traffic currently connects over an intermediate hub – because of brand loyalty, price-consciousness, or perhaps inability to obtain a non-stop seat. Notwithstanding the consistent increase in non-hub domestic flying, hubs are a necessary response to the geography of air transport demand in the United States. It is likely that despite ongoing growth in hub-bypass services, hubs will continue to process a significant proportion of domestic traffic into the foreseeable future; they create value for travellers to and from small and midsize communities by offering connectivity and frequency (i.e., schedule convenience). In addition, their hubs are critical to the viability of many of the new international services inaugurated by network majors over the last few years. Whilst hubs are alive and well, however, the concept of the fortress hub is on much shakier ground in a world where well-capitalised LFAs have sustainably low costs and the Internet makes product information instantly available and prices totally transparent.

The intra-European market Within Europe, hubs cannot be expected to intermediate traffic flows between primary centres because distances are generally too short and traffic densities are sufficient to support high-frequency non-stop services. Infrastructure constraints, the high costs per seat of operating small regional aircraft at some airports, a growing high-speed rail network, and the still significant role of charter carriers in leisure markets also limit the prospects for intra-European hubbing. Indeed, infrastructure constraints have been one reason behind the spread of hub-bypass services in Europe.

Given these factors and also the sustained growth of LFAs in markets supporting service with 150-seaters, it seems likely that European network carriers' short-haul mainline operations will focus on feeding their medium- and long-haul networks and serving dense markets that have sufficient relatively price-insensitive high-yield traffic to support these airlines' high cost bases. Whilst intra-European hubbing between pairs of secondary and tertiary centres will continue to grow at relatively uncongested primary hubs such as Paris CDG and at secondary hubs such as Munich, there will be particularly strong growth in nonhub flying by regionals.

LFAs are continuing to expand point-to-point links between previously unserved or underserved regional and secondary metropolitan airports, and between these airports and established destinations traditionally served by either the network carriers or charter airlines. Whilst talk of market saturation is often heard there is at the time of writing no apparent slow-down in the rate of route development and fleet augmentation. How long this can continue, and what impact a slowing in the rate of growth would have on LFA unit costs, is an open question.

The impact of LFAs has been well-documented: they have forced network carriers to offer lower fares and less complex tariff structures wherever there is head to head competition (e.g., between London and Zurich); they have more or less eliminated network carrier competition at several airports (e.g., Cologne); they have brought affordable air travel to previously underserved regions throughout the continent; and they have compelled charter carriers to enter the scheduled business and/or focus more of their traditional charter flying further afield (e.g., thin seasonal routes to the eastern Mediterranean and long-haul).

Long-haul international markets With one or two exceptions, most long-haul international networks tended until the 1980s to be linear in design and heavily oriented towards one or a small number of primary gateways in each country. In most countries these gateways were the capital city and/or significant commercial centres. Since the 1980s several have become hubs; in the United States they have been supplemented by the growth of newer inland hubs, such as Houston and Detroit, supported by domestic feed. While this process was unfolding, traffic on the North Atlantic was being fragmented by the growth of flows from gateways or primary hubs at one end (e.g., New York or Washington DC) to secondary cities (e.g., Nice or Düsseldorf). The same is now happening in Asia.

Several types of long-haul international hub can be identified:

1. *Third- and fourth-freedom domestic–international hubs* This is the traditional model under which, say, United feeds domestic traffic onto its own long-haul services out of Washington Dulles and American does the same out of Miami. Conversely, inbound international flows channelled over Dulles and Miami are distributed across their respective domestic networks.
2. *Fifth-freedom hubs* These are relatively rare. They exist where an airline registered in Country 1 and operating one or more routes to Country 2 and beyond to several

other countries has traffic rights to carry local traffic between Country 2 and those other countries. Northwest and United hold extensive fifth-freedom rights beyond Tokyo, for example, and both have developed Narita as an interchange point for traffic from various US origins travelling on to multiple destinations in Asia; flows in the reverse direction are also hubbed over Narita. The availability of long-range twins and the opening of transpolar air corridors to serve non-stop hub-bypass routes to South and South East Asia from North America are together reducing the significance of Narita as a fifth-freedom hub for transpacific traffic, but rights beyond Tokyo nonetheless continue to provide valuable access to intra-Asian routes for the US carriers that hold them.

Delta inherited from Pan Am a substantial fifth freedom hub at Frankfurt in the early 1990s, but subsequently dismantled it. Iberia used Miami as a change-of-gauge fifth-freedom hub, but abandoned the operation in the face of post-9/11 security restrictions. Qantas has implemented the strategy at Singapore for many years – feeding traffic from points such as Darwin, Brisbane, Cairns, Adelaide and Perth to connect with Singapore–Europe services flown by B747-400s originating in Melbourne or Sydney; it is likely that Jetstar will mount a similar operation across a South East Asian hub when services to Europe are inaugurated.

On the cargo side, Lufthansa has a number of fifth-freedom hubs around the world, and on a much larger scale FedEx, UPS and DHL all have fifth-freedom hubs in Asia and Europe. The US–EU open skies agreement effective since March 2008 in principle gives carriers from both sides of the Atlantic the opportunity to offer international 'beyond service' into any third country which will grant them fifth-freedom rights, and therefore to build fifth-freedom hubs; in practice, such services will be offered in most cases by alliance partners (see below).

3. *Sixth-freedom hubs* Sixth-freedom hubs exist where a carrier combines fourth and third freedoms to pick up traffic in one foreign country (e.g., Australia) destined for another (e.g., France) and channel it over a hub in its own country (e.g., Dubai). Cathay Pacific, KLM, and to a lesser extent Swissair were operating reasonably well-integrated sixth-freedom hubs several decades ago, and in the 1970s Singapore Airlines was amongst the first of a new wave of Asian carriers to develop the strategy further. Emirates followed in the 1980s, and more recently Etihad and Qatar Airways have begun to lay the foundations of what are intended to grow over time into significant sixth freedom operations. The capabilities of ultra-long-haul aircraft now place any suitably equipped airport anywhere on the globe within non-stop reach of the 24-hour hubs at Dubai, Abu Dhabi, or Doha, and therefore hold out the prospect of one-stop connections between any two large or midsize cities on the planet. The particular challenge to European and Asian network carriers in their long-haul markets posed by rapidly expanding Middle Eastern airlines, most notably Emirates, should not be underestimated. Over 70 per cent of Emirates' traffic out of the UK connects in Dubai, and by connecting Dubai to secondary European cities such as Manchester, Newcastle, and Hamburg it is creating viable alternatives to established hubs such as London and Frankfurt. By early in the next decade, Emirates will be the world's largest long-haul carrier measured by seats offered.

One of the most notable points about Singapore Airlines and the Gulf carriers is that by successfully tapping into sixth freedom flows they have been able to grow larger and faster than would have been the case had they to rely only on O&D traffic in and out of their relatively small home economies. These days, few international carriers of any size fail to make some effort to coordinate flows over their 'hubs', but not many others are making a real living out of it. This is nonetheless a phenomenon that is continuing to grow and which, in some long-haul O&D markets, is adding a fair amount of spice to price competition.

4. *Interline and alliance hubs* The smooth transfer of passengers between carriers at points where networks meet – facilitated by interline agreements and well-developed IATA procedures – has been a necessary consequence of the post-war Chicago regulatory regime, and has transformed a collection of hundreds of route systems into what is from a passenger's perspective a 'virtual network' of global proportions. Out of this 'interline hubbing', much of which has historically been random rather than tightly coordinated, has more recently evolved 'alliance hubbing'. The difference is that either in specific individual markets, across a route-group, or globally, two or more airlines enter into closer marketing ties than those consistent with traditional interline agreements, using one or more of coordinated scheduling, code-sharing, joint fares, joint inventory and revenue management, joint promotional activities, mutual recognition of high-value passengers, and shared FFPs to keep passengers 'online'. Alliance hubbing almost invariably takes place at one of the partner's hubs, but an interesting new example of an alliance hub – or perhaps more accurately, interchange point – is the use of London Heathrow by SkyTeam. This development has been facilitated by the EU–USA open skies agreement and the partners' freedom to co-locate in Terminal 4 subsequent to British Airways' move to Terminal 5 – both effective March 2008; inevitably, though, slot constraints will prove a barrier to the growth of a fully functioning multi-wave hub. Box 6.4 takes a closer look at alliance hubbing.

Box 6.4: Alliance Hubbing

A scheduled airline's core product is the schedule of departures within its network. If that network can be broadened and/or the schedule can be deepened by incorporating the departures of an alliance partner, the airline has more to offer its customers. For instance, American makes up for having a weaker presence in Asia than Northwest or United by code-sharing with Japan Airlines over Narita. A fundamental objective of the three global alliances is therefore to design networks that not only tap O&D traffic in major non-stop markets, but also maximise access to flow traffic in connecting markets unable to support high-frequency non-stop service. They do this by:

- creating multi-hub systems able both to dominate inter-hub markets and to capture flows of traffic originating at secondary or tertiary points behind one hub and destined for secondary and tertiary points beyond another. On inter-hub routes, a relatively high proportion of traffic, over 40 per cent in the case of KLM and Northwest, might be accounted for by double-connecting cross-feed;
- using code-sharing and, in regional markets, franchising to extend network reach and, together with highly integrated scheduling, maximise city-pair connectivity with the objective of capturing and retaining online a high proportion of end-to-end journeys made in targeted market segments.

No individual airline has, or is likely to develop, a truly global network. Alliances might be a carrier's only way into some markets for aeropolitical reasons (e.g., the airline has no traffic rights and is precluded from controlling a foreign carrier that does), for economic reasons (e.g., its fleet and/or cost structure are unsuitable for the markets concerned or those markets will not support competing services), for infrastructural reasons (e.g., slots are unavailable at a desired destination), or for financial reasons (e.g., the airline has insufficient resources to develop new markets on its own).

The economic and marketing motivations behind international alliances are not dissimilar to those that drive any type of hubbing, with the one difference that they are a vehicle for 'market share gain without balance sheet pain'. In what may however turn out to be a zero-sum game in the end, alliances endeavour to win market share by offering higher frequencies and shorter journey times to more destinations than their competitors. They are also a means of coming to terms with the prevailing international aeropolitical regime while politicians ponder just how much of that regime is going to survive. The three alliances (Star, oneworld, and SkyTeam) now incorporate carriers which in aggregate carry more than half the world's scheduled traffic.

An open question is the role that LFAs might play in alliances. There are two aspects:

1. *LFAs and the big three alliances* Jetstar, GOL, and Virgin Blue have shown themselves the most ready to interline with network carriers, and there has been talk of WestJet establishing a relationship with oneworld. On the other hand, after Aer Lingus transformed itself into an LFA it chose to leave oneworld. Whilst the likes of Ryanair are unlikely ever to form business relationships with network carriers, there are clearly some short-haul LFAs – particularly those with a less bare-bones brand proposition – for which the ability to exchange passengers with long-haul carriers makes commercial sense; both WestJet and Virgin Blue, for example, need access to international carriers if they are to compete against Air Canada and Qantas for domestic passengers transferring to overseas flight. Lufthansa's 2007 purchase of a significant minority stake in jetBlue may lead eventually to a commercial relationship based on cross-feeding transatlantic traffic – although whether this would necessarily bring jetBlue closer to Star has to be doubted.

    What stands in the way of closer integration is in many cases not so much the contrasting business models as gaps in technology: most LFAs have reservations systems designed to support simple point-to-point route structures that will not interface with systems used by much larger network airlines, and neither do they have the capability to integrate into a global FFP. Technology providers will in due course clear this hurdle. A more enduring challenge is likely to be the added, and difficult to calculate, costs of interlining – not least the cost of reaccommodating outbound long-haul passengers who because of a missed connection become the responsibility of an LFA which is earning only a very small prorate for carrying them in the first place. Neither are the back-office costs of managing and accounting for an interline agreement insubstantial. Further bilateral links between unaffiliated LFAs and long-haul network carriers are likely where the former have a strong domestic route structure and a reasonable product and the latter have no alternative local partner within their own alliances, but most LFAs will stay out of the three global groupings.

2. *LFAs allying with each other* Germanwings has loose cooperation agreements with both bmi's bmibaby and Clickair (to be merged with Vueling), as well as an arrangement with airberlin. In 2008, Southwest and WestJet announced plans to code-share. Air Asia has raised the idea of website cross-selling with both easyJet and Ryanair, albeit without immediate success, and in early 2008 began exploring an Australian joint venture with Virgin Blue. However, whilst further code-shares and the development of website cross-selling of the Aer Lingus/jetBlue type are both likely, these and similar arrangements cannot be compared to the global alliances. Indeed, the Aer Lingus/jetBlue arrangement involved neither code-sharing nor interlining. What the two carriers agreed was to allow customers to combine fares, therefore creating sum-of-sectors prices rather than joint fares which would need prorating; baggage transfers at JFK were also part of the deal.

Just as in the US domestic market geography supports the continued existence of hubs to serve markets that cannot support non-stop service, the same is true on the global stage. Aside from London, and to a much lesser extent New York and Paris, there are very few cities that can support large numbers of high-frequency, non-stop long-haul international routes on the basis of local traffic alone. Most routes of this nature require feed at one or both ends. Indeed, lost in the debate between Airbus and Boeing with regard to the extent of market fragmentation to be expected over the next few decades is the fact that many of the relatively thin new non-stops made economically viable by B787s and A350s will have a hub at one end. These aircraft might slow the development of double-hubbing – as Tokyo is overflown en route from North America to secondary points in Asia, for example – but they are certainly not hub killers.

Cargo Networks

The overwhelming majority of airlines fly cargo in the belly-holds of passenger aircraft, and therefore do not operate separate passenger and cargo networks; scheduling and capacity conflicts can sometimes arise between passengers and cargo, and passenger requirements generally prevail. All-cargo airlines and combination carriers that operate owned and/or wet-leased freighters have more network design and scheduling flexibility; basic network design options remain the same, however. With regard to hub-and-spoke systems, it is noteworthy that there is more concentration on the cargo side than on the passenger side of the industry: the top ten cargo hubs account for around two-thirds of cargo movements, whereas the top ten passenger hubs account for only one-third of passenger movements (Taneja 2002). At Gulf hubs, as much as 80–90 per cent of the cargo brought in by carriers such as Emirates, Etihad, and Qatar Airways is in transit. The growth of focused cargo alliances is likely to add further momentum to this pattern of concentration.

Alliances in fact raise issues of some interest on the cargo side. From a positive perspective, it is the case that provided freight arrives on time, in good condition, and properly documented, neither shippers nor consignees are generally concerned about which alliance partner's aircraft are used or what routing is followed; code-sharing raises fewer service delivery issues than on the passenger side, provided standards of service at customer interfaces are compatible and consistent. Less positively, some alliance members are arguably not as committed to freight as their partners, and this has led in several cases to 'alliances within alliances' such as WOW – the now largely inactive cargo link-up initiated in April 2000 by Star members Lufthansa, SAS, and Singapore Airlines, and subsequently joined from outside Star by Japan Airlines. SkyTeam is in principle both a cargo and passenger alliance – although, again, Air France and Korean Air appear on the surface to have a much deeper corporate commitment to the cargo business than do several of their partners.

If airfreight growth outstrips growth in passenger traffic over the next two decades by as significant a margin as forecasts suggest, it is likely that we will see further separation of passenger and freighter operations and therefore the growth of more freight-only networks. Particularly in noise-sensitive areas such as Europe which also face severe congestion at major hubs, it is possible that cargo networks will increasingly encompass regional airports with good surface access specialising primarily or entirely in handling freight movements. Leipzig, a DHL hub and home of the carrier's AeroLogic joint venture with Lufthansa, is just one example.

NETWORK TACTICS

There are two sets of constraints when a route is being evaluated:

1. *Practical constraints* These include: the type(s) of aircraft available in the fleet on whatever timeline is being applied – specifically, their payload and performance capabilities relative to the routes and airports under consideration; the availability of traffic rights and airport slots, if relevant; other operational considerations such as aircraft and crew rotation issues; and availability of other required resources.
2. *Economic constraints* The issue here is whether a new route can generate a profit after taking into account revenues, operating costs, and the opportunity cost (if any) of not deploying aircraft on an alternative route. Considerations include: passenger and cargo demand forecasts for local traffic on the route and O&D traffic in other markets which might flow over the route; forecasts of airline market share in the market(s) and segments concerned; pricing and revenue forecasts; the operating costs of aircraft to be used (which will in part be a function of the capacity–frequency trade-off inherent in scheduling decisions); and route start-up costs (which might be lower than otherwise where both end points are already served by the carrier concerned). Models now widely used to evaluate route profitability incorporate most of these considerations, but some have difficulty integrating competitive effects to accurately estimate market shares.

This section of the chapter will touch on just two specific tactical contexts within which route entry or exit decisions might need to be framed: attacking a hub; and responding to a challenger. The section will end with some general comments.

Attacking A Hub

There is little doubt that hubs can be a source of significant competitive advantage – notwithstanding concerns about their costs, the downsizing and closure of some secondary hubs in the United States, and the success of point-to-point carriers. The purpose of hub-and-spoke systems is to enlarge the scope of network coverage, and in doing this they can create both operational and marketing barriers to entry. One of their strengths is the ability to consolidate feed down relatively thin spokes onto denser routes between hubs and other major centres. Network flows such as this are arguably more defensible against low-fare entrants than dense linear route patterns; relatively few city-pair markets are sufficiently large to support multiple competitors operating non-stop or direct at commercially viable frequencies and acceptable load factors, and an established hub-based carrier adding one more route to an already substantial network is more likely to be able to sustain service in a thin market than a significantly smaller entrant.

A wide network served with high frequencies over one or more integrated hubs can therefore offer a differentiated product which is difficult and expensive to compete against. An additional barrier to entry exists when ownership, franchising, or tight contractual code-sharing agreements lock up most or all of the regional carriers available to feed a hub, leaving any challenger with insufficient flows to support competitive frequencies at adequate load factors. Once a well-resourced and well-managed airline has established a properly integrated hub-and-spoke network, competitors face an uphill battle breaking into the system. Many choose to avoid head-to-head confrontation. Those that relish a fight can try one or more of the following:

1. Direct entry into dense or potentially dense point-to-point hub markets requiring little or no network feed in order to be viable. Several different approaches have been used:
    *   *Full-service* Virgin Atlantic and British Midland in the 1980s and 1990s targeted, respectively, the densest long- and short-haul point-to-point markets out of London in order to compete against British Airways without bearing the full force of its integrated network. This approach will only work where local traffic is sufficiently dense. At the other extreme, one reason why Delta remains unchallenged on transatlantic routes into and out of Cincinnati is that competitors cannot match its feed there, whilst local traffic to and from overseas centres is not sufficiently dense to support point-to-point competition by itself. (Whether Cincinnati is an economically viable hub in the longer term is another matter.)
        Flying a thin terminating service into another carrier's hub can be challenging even for the strongest competitor. In October 2006 Emirates launched Hamburg–JFK as an extension of its Dubai–Hamburg service; the schedule was halted in March 2008, in part because non-stop A380 services were to be launched between Dubai and JFK the following schedule season but no doubt also because of the advantage Continental's competing Hamburg–New York service gained from flying in and out of its Newark hub.
    *   *Low fares* Low-fare challengers can generate significant new traffic in price-elastic segments, as Southwest and Ryanair have proven, and they can take market share from incumbents (e.g., easyJet in the London–Nice market). Some LFAs have chosen to tackle hubs head-on; AirTran has done this successfully at Atlanta, and Frontier much less successfully at Denver. Others tackle hubs using nearby secondary metropolitan airports; Southwest has done this at Dallas Love Field, Chicago Midway, and Baltimore, whilst easyJet and Ryanair have done the same in the London area.
2. Introduction of a multi-stop service across the hub being attacked, allowing traffic flows in more than one market to support each other (e.g., Frontier's 2007 introduction of a Denver–Memphis–Orlando operation across Northwest's Memphis hub – although this arguably had more to do with adding service out of Denver than mounting a serious attack on Memphis).
3. Draining traffic from one or more spokes by offering:
    *   an alternative routing over the challenger's hub;
    *   non-stop hub-bypass service (which will provide shorter journey times than the incumbent's connecting service but, depending on the aircraft used, will almost certainly support a lower frequency – unless low fares can be used to stimulate traffic).
4. Linking the challenger's hub, assuming it has one, to the targeted hub so that the competing networks either side of those respective hubs provide a counterweight to each other (e.g., Northwest flying into O'Hare from Minneapolis).
5. Interlining traffic with the hub carrier. This has long been the traditional technique for augmenting an airline network without widening route entry. Some large carriers have tried to reduce their interlining and the interchangeability of unrestricted tickets

in order to raise barriers to the entry of actual or potential competitors. Lufthansa, Air France, Aer Lingus and others adopted this tactic in the 1980s and early 1990s against Air Europe, Dan Air, and British Midland. The European Commission has ruled such behaviour an abuse of dominant market position rather than purely a matter of commercial choice. Nonetheless, the multilateral interline system that grew up after the second world war to create a worldwide 'virtual network' for any carrier irrespective of the scope of its own system, is gradually being narrowed by: intraline hubbing and passengers' preference for single-carrier connections where connections are necessary; the attractions of FFPs; the spread of code-sharing and of preferential marketing agreements; and the single-carrier condition attached to the discounted tickets on which a high proportion of passengers now travel.

Responding To A Challenger

Barkin *et al.* (1995) have suggested the following broad approach for established network carriers responding to a challenge:

1. Understand the challenger's strengths: does it have specific cost or differentiation advantages and, if so, how sustainable are they?
2. Assess the threat to the incumbent's core business(es): for example, will the challenger significantly affect hub traffic flow?
3. Develop specific tactics tailored to the circumstances in each individual market. These will depend upon the incumbent's resources and capabilities, the importance of the particular market concerned in terms of traffic and profits, and the likelihood that the challenger might continue to grow and eventually create difficulties elsewhere in the incumbent's network. We will look briefly at five possible responses to an actual or potential challenge:
   - *Block entry* This could involve one or more of several actions: make entry impossible through, for example, spatial pre-emption of slots, terminal space or route licenses; make entry too expensive by, for instance, reinforcing the loyalty of the existing customer base, making it more costly to penetrate; make the rewards of entry unattractive or, at best, uncertain by signalling a willingness to lower fares and/or add capacity in response to entry.
   - *Withdraw* This could be acceptable if the route concerned is unprofitable, generating little premium or connecting traffic, if the incumbent has other opportunities to deploy its resources profitably, and if there is no substantial danger that withdrawal would strengthen the challenger for a future assault on another part of the network. On the other hand, many routes operated by network carriers do indeed contribute valuable feed and so, quite frequently, make a positive contribution to network profitability even if not themselves profitable on a fully allocated basis. In extreme cases, ceding such routes might undermine hub economics to the point that a vicious circle of spoke-cutting is initiated to re-establish network profitability – perhaps ultimately threatening viability of the hub itself. The operational characteristics of a large hub-and-spoke network make downsizing in response to stagnant or declining revenues, whether resulting from competition or a recession, very difficult to effect without causing a disproportionate further loss of traffic. Less dramatic, although also

potentially damaging, is the loss of FFP members compelled to rely on other carriers in the vacated market(s).

• *Compete* When a start-up is attacked early and forcefully enough, it might find profitability difficult to establish and therefore access to additional tranches of capital with which to fund expansion less readily available – unless it has the resources of a wealthy corporate or individual shareholder behind it. Whether or not the challenger is a start-up, wherever it enters with low prices then fare matching – ideally on a capacity-controlled basis – is the most simple and widespread response. If a fare war is the outcome, as often happens, it can be important for the incumbent to have enough capacity available to put into the market and ensure that the challenger does not walk away with a disproportionate share of any incremental traffic stimulated by the competition. This can be an expensive exercise; a high-cost incumbent might find unit revenue falling below unit cost, and if restrictions on the new low fares have to be lax to compete with the challenger the incumbent may suffer revenue dilution as high-yield passengers trade-down.

Non-price responses might include increasing FFP awards, boosting agency incentives (in markets where agencies remain important), fine-tuning schedules, and launching advertising or promotional campaigns. At their most aggressive, responses could include capacity-dumping, predatory scheduling, and route overlay – the latter involving a major responding to a small low-fare challenger's entry onto one or two of its routes by duplicating most or all of the challenger's network (something Northwest is alleged to have done to Reno Air in the early 1990s). What an incumbent can get away with in terms of competitive response could depend upon the nature of competition law in the jurisdiction concerned, the attitude of the authorities responsible for enforcing it, and the speed of due process.

Swamping the market with capacity, matching fares, and fashioning creative non-price responses worked well for US majors having to deal with the early waves of start-ups in the 1980s and 1990s, but it has not been effective in dealing with the critical mass achieved by Southwest or by the well-capitalised start-up LFAs launched since 2000; neither have these approaches worked for European network carriers faced with growing LFA competition in short-haul markets. In order to compete, incumbents have therefore had to take more fundamental steps by restructuring (in effect simplifying) their revenue and cost models and, in a few cases but with mixed results, by establishing their own LFAs. Perhaps the most noteworthy example has been Aer Lingus, which chose to benchmark itself not against its traditional network competitors but against hometown rival Ryanair, in the process reinventing itself as a 'value-added' (as opposed to bare-bones) LFA.

• *Coexist* This response might, for example, lead a network incumbent to cede most of the price-sensitive segments of local traffic to a low-fare challenger whilst continuing to serve both connecting passengers and higher yielding, predominantly business passengers in the local market. The incumbent may also retain a small slice of the most price-sensitive segment by offering capacity-controlled fill-up fares. Such a response is fine as long as there are sufficient volumes of traffic in each segment to keep both carriers content, and provided business traffic – particularly local rather than connecting business traffic – values the incumbent's service differentiation more highly than the challenger's lower fares.

- *Join forces* A network incumbent might decide to forgo bruising fare wars by withdrawing from a market in which it is challenged, whilst at the same time protecting its FFP membership base in that market and also its network coverage by entering into a marketing agreement with the challenger. For this to work: service levels offered by the airlines concerned should not be too far apart, which means that the challenger must in most cases be offering something more than rock-bottom service at rock-bottom prices; and both schedule integration and some degree of operational alignment must be feasible. As with any route withdrawal, the incumbent might later face a renewed challenge elsewhere in its network if the beneficiary continues to grow on the basis of what has been ceded to it, and at some point decides that the potential gains from a more aggressive posture outweigh the advantages of continued cooperation (Holloway 1998b).

Sometimes the source of a threat is not just one carrier's activities, but instead a more general strategic change in circumstances. Having built a short-haul domestic and European network and an inventory of slots at London Heathrow second only to British Airways, bmi decided that given the growth of LFAs in point-to-point markets to and from London its own future growth should be oriented more towards medium- and long-haul markets. This was a principal motivation behind its acquisition of British Mediterranean in 2007.

Concluding Comments

Traditionally, route planning has been a relatively slow process, particularly where regulatory authority to operate a route had to be obtained, and once inaugurated a route was often given several years to show profits; some never did, of course. Today, it is common for an airline to have core routes in its network or route structure which together define its strategic approach and market positioning, and to implement a more fluid approach to others – entering, adjusting, and exiting more dynamically than in the past.

Some LFAs in particular are prepared to enter routes almost speculatively, give them as little as three or four months to prove themselves, and depart if expectations are not met. They can do this because their ground product requirements are often minimal and they tend to target unconstrained airports which, in some cases, offer incentives to start new services; there are relatively few sunk costs at the route level. Where a new route links two stations already served, the risks are commensurately lower. There is an important philosophical point here: whereas the traditional industry approach has been to think first of potential markets and then how best to serve them, the archetypal LFA approach is to think first about aircraft and crew utilisation and then about which markets can justify the deployment of capacity.

Despite all the talk of hub de-peaking, point-to-point service, and hub-bypassing, the hub is alive and well and network carriers are still prepared to protect it. In early 2007 Frontier announced that it would add service to Northwest's Memphis hub from its own hub at Denver as well as from Las Vegas and Orlando; the following day AirTran announced service to Memphis from its focus city operation at Orlando. Northwest's immediate response was not only to match the new offers by beginning service from Memphis to each of Denver, Las Vegas, and Orlando, but also to attack Frontier's own Denver hub by inaugurating service there from Indianapolis. Some habits die hard.

III. Network Outsourcing

The network design process involves not just deciding upon the pattern of routes to be operated but also who will operate them. In the case of LFAs this is generally a non-issue. For network carriers the choice lies between using their own aircraft or outsourcing capacity provision. Many airlines are now extending their marketable networks by entering into code-share, block-space, and/or franchise arrangements; by the end of 2007, there were more than 600 such agreements in place.

CODE-SHARING

Code-sharing involves an airline placing its two-letter designator code (e.g., AA, UA, BA) on a flight operated by another carrier; it is a bilateral arrangement between the carriers concerned, and whilst code-share partners might well be members of the same global alliance this is not necessarily the case. When the operating carrier is a regional, its own code might not be applied to the flight – which is therefore marketed only under the code-sharing major's designator code. Where two mainline carriers code-share, it would be usual for the operating carrier's designator to be applied alongside that of the code-sharing partner; the flight numbers following each designator may be identical or different. There will usually be at least some degree of schedule alignment between partners, and in many cases this alignment is close. Code-sharing can involve passenger and/or cargo sales on a given flight. The airline whose aircraft operate the flight is generally known as the 'operating carrier', whilst others which simply apply their designators are 'code-sharing carriers'. Although the overwhelming majority of code-shares involve just two airlines, intensifying cooperation within the global alliances is leading to more multi-partner code-shares than have been seen in the past.

Code-shares can be either tactical, route-specific arrangements or part of a wider strategic relationship which in its most developed form might offer a common service (e.g., KLM and Northwest's World Business Class). These are sometimes referred to as 'naked code-sharing' and 'common product code-sharing' respectively; the latter is still rare.

Code-sharing agreements contain many standard elements, but each is nonetheless unique. Where the balance of benefits lies will depend in large measure upon the partners' relative strengths and negotiating skills. Something that often needs particular attention is projection of the code-sharing partner's corporate identity. This might require the presence of that partner's staff and/or signage at different points in the operating partner's service delivery system and be reflected in the phrasing, possibly also the language, of terminal and inflight announcements. Code-sharing partners sometimes place one or two cabin staff onto flights either to establish a visible presence in the aircraft generally, or to identify and serve their own premium passengers in particular. This latter practice raises the following issues:

- *Labour relations* Duty-times, inflight rest procedures on long-haul flights, and whether staff should fly in addition to or instead of the operating partner's cabin attendants will have to be agreed.
- *Service standards* Service levels and procedures are likely to differ between partners until such time as they have a common product to offer consumers.
- *Costs* Additional training is required for the code-sharing partner's staff in respect of service and safety procedures on the operating partner's aircraft.

Types Of Code-Sharing

The following is just one of several possible typologies.

Franchised code-sharing   In this case the operator is a franchisee of another carrier, operating under that other airline's brand identity and not using its own designator code. It has primarily been a domestic phenomenon within the United States and parts of the EU single market, although British Airways has franchised UK carriers specialising in thin medium-haul markets as well as airlines in Africa. Where a franchised regional is acquired by its franchisor, it is no longer technically a franchisee or code-share partner but is in fact just a separate subsidiary or division of the mainline parent (e.g., Delta's acquisition of Comair). We will look at franchising shortly.

Connection (or complementary) code-sharing   What distinguishes this from code-shared connections between franchisor and franchisee is the fact that the operating partner retains its own designator on the flights concerned alongside that of the code-sharing partner, and retains its own brand identity. Two types of connection code-sharing can be identified:

1. *Non-reciprocal/single-sector code-sharing* It is sometimes the case that where a short-haul flight connects with a medium- or long-haul flight, the former carries the code of both the operating partner and the code-sharing partner whilst the latter carries just its operator's code. This might happen where a non-affiliated regional feeds a long-haul major with flights that bear both its own code (reflecting presence in its own short-haul markets) and the major's code (to simulate an online connection for the major's long-haul passengers), but sees no benefit in putting its own code on the major's long-haul flights because it has no presence in medium- or long-haul O&D markets – where its designator code therefore has little marketing value.
       Non-reciprocal code-sharing can also arise where an alliance is balanced in favour of one of the partners. During much of the period of their relationship in the mid-1990s, for example, the 'BA' code appeared on a large number of USAir domestic flights whilst the 'US' code did not appear on British Airways' flights.
2. *Reciprocal/through code-sharing* In this case alliance partners place their respective codes on services connecting beyond each other's hubs. For example, transatlantic United flights into Frankfurt connect onto Lufthansa flights bearing both the UA and LH codes, and Lufthansa flights into Chicago O'Hare connect onto United flights bearing both the LH and UA codes.

Connection or complementary code-sharing extends the networks of one or both partners. It can cover international–domestic connections or vice versa, international–international connections, or domestic–domestic connections.

Parallel code-sharing   There are two principal types:

1. *Sole service* The parties consolidate their services on a route, with only one of them operating flights. This often happens on thin routes unable to support more than one operator at frequencies satisfactory to business travellers (e.g., Qantas and Japan Airlines between Tokyo and Brisbane).

2. *Dual service* Both partners operate their own flights on a route, but each code-shares on the other's services. The objective here might be to increase the number of frequencies each has available to offer for sale without physically increasing the number of flights (e.g., Qantas and British Airways on routes from London to Sydney and Melbourne).

Conclusion A passenger's itinerary could take in each of these different types of code-sharing. From the passenger's perspective the typology is fairly meaningless; from an airline's point of view, however, it can be analytically useful. From the point of view of competition authorities the distinctions drawn may be critical, as we will see shortly.

Pros And Cons Of Code-Sharing From An Airline Perspective

The primary motivations for code-sharing are as follows:

1. *To broaden network reach* By putting its code on another airline's services, a carrier can gain access to particular markets despite:
    *   not having the required traffic rights to operate its own services;
    *   not having the fleet or cost structure necessary to serve the market(s) concerned;
    *   not having sufficient market presence to mount a sustainable service (perhaps because one end of the market is another carrier's hub and there is insufficient local traffic to support service without the benefit of feed);
    *   being unable to obtain the slots required to offer sufficient frequencies or appropriate departure times.
    Conversely, the absence of a code-share at the far end of a long-haul route can be fatal. VRG Linhas Aereas, the successor to Varig now wholly owned by Gol, was unable to sustain services to London, Rome or Frankfurt in the absence of code-shares or interline agreements with economically viable prorates; all three routes were discontinued in March 2008 after just a single schedule season in operation. (Later in 2008 a combination of high fuel prices and a relatively old fleet forced VRG to drop all services outside South America.)
2. *To deepen network coverage* Code-sharing might allow a carrier to increase the number of saleable frequencies offered on a route it already serves by placing its code on another airline's services. This could be beneficial where traffic on the route would not support an increase in actual flights, where the code-sharing partner has insufficient aircraft to operate more of its own services, or where airport congestion or lack of traffic rights create barriers to additional frequencies.
3. *To improve the GDS display positions of connecting services* Where GDSs are still important to distribution, there are two issues:
    *   *Online preference* Most connecting passengers have a preference for remaining online, and this is reflected in the priority given by GDS display algorithms to online connections over interline connections in some jurisdictions (e.g., the United States, but not the EU). By taking an existing interline connection and entering into a code-sharing agreement with the other airline, a carrier can turn that connection into a 'virtual online' service and improve its GDS display position. Even where GDS screen position is not affected, the appearance of online service as far as customers are concerned can provide sufficient revenue-side benefits to justify a code-sharing agreement.

- *Screen padding* Code-sharing can also lead to the dual (in the EU) or multiple listing of the same flight under different designator codes and flight numbers, resulting in competitors being pushed further from the top of the first page of screen displays. The same applies in respect of displays presented by some online agencies and meta-search sites.

4. *To develop alliance strategy* Extending point 3 above, code-sharing is a critical element in the competition between alliances to attract flow traffic (alongside service attributes such as through-check-in, shared terminals and lounges, cross-recognition of high-value customers, and access to wider FFP benefits).

5. *To contain costs*   As well as marketing benefits, code-sharing also has cost-side attractions insofar as it allows carriers to exploit economies of scope and density without increasing output or having to bear the fixed costs associated with internal/organic growth – thereby holding down production costs and helping support load factors. It can also allow inefficient tag-end sectors to be eliminated.

6. *To safeguard traffic rights* Strong international carriers are sometimes compelled to code-share with a weaker national airline which either does not want, or is unable, to participate in a particular third/fourth freedom market.

There are potential downsides, however. It is possible for carriers – particularly those operating short-haul routes – to have their yields put under pressure both by prorate deals crafted in favour of the partner competing in lower-yielding (but perhaps more profitable) long-haul markets, and by the periodic fare wars that tend to erupt between larger airlines in competitive markets; on the other hand, independent US regionals selling output to majors on a fee-per-departure or fee-per-ASM basis are protected from both these problems.

There are, in addition, several broader issues in respect of code-sharing. We will look at these next.

Code-Sharing: Some Issues

Competition issues From the competition and consumer welfare angle there are arguments for and against code-sharing. We need to take two perspectives:

1. *Network competition* Code-sharing that allows two carriers to link in order to compete more effectively for flow traffic against another airline or alliance with a larger network or better coverage of certain O&D markets can be pro-competitive. On the negative side, the only serious competitive threat faced by the emerging global alliance networks is from the small number of other global alliances; although further shuffling of partners is probable, it is unlikely that the number of global alliances will exceed three – implying that from a network perspective the global market is going to be consolidated into an oligopoly.

2. *Market competition*   What concerns customers, of course, is the level and type of competition in the city-pair markets in which they want to travel. Once the alliances have settled down into relative permanence, their impact on competition will depend very much on the dynamics of whatever particular market is being considered and upon the watchfulness of competition authorities.
   - Assuming the absence of collusion, arguably something of a stretch given the industry's history, behind/beyond markets should benefit from competition

between the different alliance networks trying to attract flow traffic over their respective hubs. Competition will probably be most intense in respect of discretionary traffic moving on discounted fares.

- The prospects for local inter-hub traffic are not encouraging. This is particularly true in respect of time-sensitive (primarily business) travellers, who might not look upon a service that involves changing planes at a competing airline's hub (e.g., London) as a viable alternative to a non-stop route (e.g., Frankfurt–Washington).
- It can also sometimes happen that a small carrier flying into a large airline's fortress hub and in need of both onward connections to offer arriving passengers and feed to boost outbound traffic has little practical alternative other than to code-share with the dominant carrier – which is the only one able to offer the required range of connections over that hub. Several Latin American carriers serving Miami, for example, have been obliged to come to terms with American Airlines' dominance there by code-sharing with what would otherwise have been their primary competitor on international sectors in and out of the gateway.

Where carriers code-share simply to reduce the number of operators on a route, the outcome might be anti-competitive. Franchised and complementary/connection code-sharing could be anti-competitive if partners able to compete by extending their own networks choose instead to code-share. The threat in parallel code-sharing is that it might remove some or all of an existing competitor's services from a route.

In a study of four North Atlantic alliances during the mid-1990s, Oum et al. (2000) found that output and consumer surplus were more likely to increase after alliance formation if the partners' networks are complementary and have limited overlap than where routes are congruent or parallel. Where networks are complementary, even inter-hub services are likely to be boosted in order to exploit that complementarity by increasing the double-connect possibilities for cross-feed traffic.

In any international market, much might depend upon the terms of the bilateral ASA in force between the countries concerned. A liberal or open-skies bilateral permitting new competitors to enter a market against two former competitors which decide to code-share raises less of a prima facie competition issue than would be the case were the two code-sharers each the sole carrier designated by their respective governments under a highly restrictive, protectionist bilateral. In reality of course, the fact that a market is contestable from a regulatory perspective might not make it economically contestable if one end is slot-constrained (e.g., Frankfurt) or if the origin and destination are hubs dominated by the code-sharers, with both carriers having sufficient network strength at each to make market entry a sporty prospect for competitors (e.g., Paris and Atlanta).

Competition laws are used by the authorities in some countries to ensure that code-share partners continue to compete across those dimensions of the marketing mix that still remain open to competition, but the beneficial impact of such measures is in many cases open to debate:

- Service design competition in respect of attributes such as safety, routing, schedule, frequency, and the inflight product is removed by definition on any given code-shared flight.
- Whilst competition in pricing and marketing communications should still be present unless antitrust immunity has been granted, cynics might question the

extent to which airlines that have entered into agreements specifically casting each other as 'partners' will – other than in exceptional circumstances – compete aggressively to unload seats on a shared airplane.

- Competition laws are either non-existent or weakly enforced in many countries, and even where they do exist it is still not uncommon for airlines to be specifically exempted. Several transatlantic alliances have been granted antitrust immunity by US authorities on the grounds that open skies agreements allow competitors to launch or expand service against the cooperating partners, and any route (e.g., inter-hub) or market segment (e.g., time-sensitive business travellers) not freely contestable can be carved out of the immunity grant. The practical effect of immunity is that partners are able to cooperate closely on capacity, scheduling, marketing communications, pricing, and revenue management decisions, and to consult with regard to commission levels, net fares, and FFP policies, for example; in other words, they are able to sell jointly out of a shared inventory and, if they wish, share costs and apportion profits. One advantage of antitrust immunity as far as pricing is concerned is that joint fares can be introduced quickly in response to market changes, rather than having to be formally negotiated case-by-case as arms-length prorate agreements.

  Some 'carve-outs' have indeed been imposed by the US DOT in respect of time-sensitive – that is, full-fare – local traffic in transatlantic inter-hub markets; the result of this is that in those particular market segments the partners have to compete on pricing and promotion, and run their own individual risk of profit and loss. Similarly, in approving the Air France takeover of KLM and Lufthansa's cooperation with SAS, Swiss International, and Austrian the European Commission required the carriers to surrender slots to challengers wanting access to inter-hub routes; to date, several years later, no challengers have come forward.

Notwithstanding its potentially negative effects, code-sharing can have a positive impact on competition and consumer welfare. It may add competition to a market in which otherwise only a traditional interline agreement would be competing against one or more established non-stop, direct or online connecting services. It can also permit flights to be operated, or frequencies to be increased, on routes which otherwise would not support the same level of service; indeed, the additional supply of output might even stimulate traffic and, perhaps, lead to the eventual entry of new competitors. It may improve other aspects of service quality by facilitating or encouraging, for example:

- integrated scheduling, ideally leading to more connections and/or reduced layovers;
- through check-in and baggage interlining;
- connections to proximate gates within the same terminal buildings at hubs or traffic interchange points;
- shared lounges;
- joint tour products;
- reciprocity between FFPs;
- lower joint fares resulting from competition between alliances to serve individual city-pair markets over alternative hubs.

Of course, most of the benefits just listed are, or could be, made available through commercial arrangements without the inclusion of code-sharing (CAA 1994).

Deception of customers   In addition to competition issues, there is also a question of whether or not code-shares deceive customers. In 1984, one leading airline had this to say: 'British Airways believes that it is intrinsically deceptive for two carriers to share a designator code' (Comment on NPRM Docket 4219, 1984). Not a lot has changed since – apart from airlines' attitudes, of course.

A designator code on a flight tells a customer what to expect in terms of service quality. Leading airlines spend hundreds of millions of dollars each year designing, branding, and promoting their services to ensure that this is the case. A customer who buys service based on that designator but is instead exposed to a different standard offered by another carrier without being made aware this would happen, has been deceived. Problems most frequently arise when the operating carrier offers standards below those marketed by the code-sharing carrier. But even where this is not the case, there is still an important matter of principle at stake. An additional source of problems is confusion that can arise when passengers holding tickets bearing the designator of a code-sharing partner do not appreciate that they should be checking-in at the terminal and desks used by the operating partner. Finally, there is scope for confusion in respect of which carrier is liable to consumers should there be an accident or some lesser incident.

Airlines in general argue that code-sharing seems not to be an issue that greatly troubles consumers and, if it were, the marketplace would impose its own sanctions on carriers choosing to enter partnerships with airlines that are significantly weaker in terms of service or safety. They might also argue by analogy that somebody buying, say, Coca Cola in different countries receives essentially the same product irrespective of the fact that each is produced and bottled locally. This analogy could be defensible in the case of common product code-sharing, but such arrangements remain a small minority of total code-sharing deals. Air transport consumers have a right to be concerned with the not inconsiderable chance in many other cases of finding 'tap-water' in the bottle. The particular nature of what is an image-sensitive industry makes this promiscuity with their reputations potentially dangerous for airlines.

The heart of the matter is information, and regulations have been introduced in some jurisdictions (e.g., the EU) mandating that passengers be informed at the time they make their purchases which airlines will operate the services they have booked. It is unclear how effective such regulations are.

International regulatory issues   When considering international regulatory issues, it can be helpful to distinguish between bilateral code-sharing and third-country code-sharing. For example, Delta putting its DL code on an Air France transatlantic flight to Paris is 'bilateral code-sharing' (because only two countries are involved); on the other hand, putting the DL code onto an Air France international flight beyond Paris (e.g., to Africa or the Middle East) is 'third-country code-sharing'. In the latter case, the third country concerned might adopt any position ranging from 'no objection' to an outright ban – a position that will depend in general on its aeropolitical policy stance, and in particular on the terms of its bilaterals with the United States and France.

Whilst some governments take a relatively relaxed view on airlines' freedom to enter into code-share agreements, most insist that code-sharing partners must either have existing traffic rights in markets where their codes are displayed for sale or obtain explicit authorisation. The United States takes the latter position (although this is a non-issue for carriers incorporated in countries with which open skies ASAs have been concluded). The EU has yet to adopt a formal stance on intra-EU code-sharing, but it does have the power to review agreements within the context of competition law.

Elsewhere in the world the regulatory position remains variable and ill-defined. What is generally true, however, is that having initially been considered primarily a marketing device, code-sharing has in recent years moved onto the agendas of bilateral negotiations. A minority of governments now see code-sharing as a quasi-traffic right, arguing that it can provide to designated carriers access in excess of agreed bilateral limitations and to undesignated carriers access into markets which they have no current right to enter. Future bargaining positions could be eroded, according to this view, were foreign carriers to obtain market access through code-sharing without their governments first having to come to the negotiating table and offer something in return. The counter-argument is that the only flights physically operated are those which have been bilaterally agreed by the origin and destination states, and all code-sharing does is channel traffic onto certain of those flights. What matters in practice, however, is less the merit of either argument than the reality that potential bargaining chips are difficult to resist.

Conclusions On Code-Sharing

Based on their own original research and a partial review of others' findings, Oum *et al.* (2000) have concluded that code-sharing is likely to have beneficial effects on competition, service quality (notably frequencies), and pricing when it involves linkages between two or more complementary networks serving behind-gateway/hub to beyond-gateway/hub markets; they are less sanguine about parallel code-sharing on overlapping routes, particularly those serving inter-hub markets. More generally, we can argue that the competitive impact of code-sharing will depend upon who would have been in the market without it, who is left there because of it, and how intensely any remaining competitors set about competing.

There is as yet no proven general case that global network alliances using extensive code-sharing between their members to compete in open skies environments will inevitably be conducive to consumers' interests. The effect of each of these alliances needs to be considered not within the generalised context usually presented by their proponents, who picture competitive battles being waged between networks across some imprecisely defined global marketplace, but in the context of specific individual markets – assessed in terms of their size, whether real opportunities exist for other network airlines or niche carriers to enter, and the availability of viable alternative routings. In approving the overwhelming majority of applications for code-sharing between US and foreign carriers, the US DOT has found the arrangements to be in the interests of consumers. However questionable some of these judgements might have been in individual cases, consumers' interests were at least ostensibly a major point of reference in the evaluation. Some other governments, in contrast, appear to be more concerned about code-sharing partners posing as holders of traffic rights they have not been awarded than about them posing as the providers of services they do not in fact provide.

As far as the potential for consumer deception is concerned, the case is much clearer. Consumers are exposed to deception unless the partners to a code-share arrangement have essentially merged their products. Point-of-sale disclosure is clearly the answer, but anecdotal evidence suggests that this remains inconsistent. In fairness, the problem appears more often to lie with distributors than with airlines themselves. Disclosure might anyway not always disclose very much – as in the United States, where some reservations media list independently owned regionals code-sharing with majors not as separately identifiable airlines but under the generic network name of their associated major (e.g., United Express).

Code-sharing is not inevitably to a consumer's disadvantage; few people booking on Delta and finding themselves travelling on Air France should feel mightily aggrieved by differential service levels. The issue here is whether somebody buying 'Coke' from an airline has a right to find 'Coke' in the bottle – irrespective of how good the '7-Up' actually in it might be. In the case of some other alliance relationships, consumers could have much more specific cause for complaint.

BLOCK-SPACING AND JOINT SERVICES

Blocked-Space Agreements

Code-sharing is often effected on a 'free-sale' basis, under which the code-sharing partner pays a price for each seat taken from the operating partner's inventory – a price that will vary depending upon the negotiated rate for the cabin concerned; any difference between the two carriers' use of booking classes can be resolved by 'class mapping', using equivalence tables (Iatrou and Oretti 2007). There would be no commitment to take a specific number of seats on each flight. An important point whenever revenue management remains the sole responsibility of the operating partner is agreement on the overbooking policy, mismanagement of which could have negative consequences for the code-sharing partner's reputation.

Alternatively, code-sharing agreements – on passenger and/or cargo services – might involve blocked-space. In a blocked-space arrangement, which need not necessarily involve code-sharing but often does, the code-sharing partner buys seats on the operating partner's flights (at a price below free-sale) and sells them under its own designator from a separate inventory. Arrangements might cover every available class on the flight to provide the purchaser with its required traffic mix, or they might be more limited. There are two types of blocked-space agreement:

1. *Hard blocked-space agreements* The operating airline sells a pre-specified number of seats to the non-operating/code-sharing airline. The purchaser might also be allowed to sell back unused seats prior to an agreed cut-off or return date – a 'modified blocked-space' agreement.
2. *Soft blocked-space agreements* The nonoperating/code-sharing carrier purchases an unspecified, but capped, number of seats in response to demand as it materialises. (The only difference between this and a free-sale agreement is the fact that the number of seats available is capped, and the expressions 'free-sale' and 'soft-block' are in fact often treated as synonymous. Both structures involve a 'sell and report' arrangement which differs from the firm allocation of a 'hard-block' agreement, under which the purchasing carrier manages its allocation autonomously from the operating carrier.)

(A further variation is the 'seat exchange agreement', under which one airline provides capacity on its services in exchange for capacity on the other airline's services on the same route.)

The advantage of hard blocked-space agreements to the seller is that a proportion of its output is underwritten by guaranteed sales to the partner; this might be sufficient to justify an increase in frequency, which could in turn lead ultimately to a larger market share. Against this is the fact that the sale will be at 'wholesale' prices, which implies that the seller may lose revenue if any of its own 'retail' traffic is spilled or gets displaced into the partner's block. The latter could occur where the partners continue to compete on price and promotion, and also because their respective networks behind the origin and beyond the destination of the code-shared flight might offer different benefits to customers. It can therefore sometimes be the case that there are fewer potential sources of conflict between the partners in a free-sale agreement than in a blocked-space deal.

Blocked-space agreements are a relatively common feature of code-sharing, and can be particularly useful when partners do not have the necessary immunity from competition laws (where applicable) to allow them to manage their seat inventories jointly. Block-spacing can also arise outside the context of alliance arrangements and code-sharing. For example, a European airline with a service terminating in Singapore might want to secure space for its interline passengers travelling to and from Australia on another carrier's heavily booked flights by entering into blocked-space agreements with that carrier between Singapore and points in Australia and vice versa.

Joint Services

Whereas under a blocked-space agreement each carrier independently manages its own allocated space, revenue management for a joint service is undertaken by one carrier acting for both or by both acting together. Inventories on joint services can be jointly priced and promoted, in which case the partners are not competing against each other. Joint services generally require either a revenue-sharing agreement, based on some level of assumed costs attributed to the operating partner, or a cost- and revenue-sharing agreement.

Some states consider joint services to be essentially the same as code-sharing agreements, whereas others maintain a distinction founded on the fact that partners do not separately bear their own commercial risks. In the latter case they might be frowned upon by competition laws. This is one reason why antitrust immunity has had to be sought for several of the transatlantic alliances; wide-ranging immunised joint ventures now lie at the heart of these airlines' North Atlantic operations, a notable exception to date being the British Airways/American Airlines relationship (because the partners refused to release the large number of Heathrow slots that regulators demanded in return for immunisation when it was applied for in the 1990s).

FRANCHISING

Franchising involves a substantial carrier with a strong brand (the franchisor) licensing to a franchisee (usually for a period of 5 to 10 years) the use of brand identity (e.g., aircraft livery, cabin design, crew uniforms, signage, logos, and brand names), the associated service concept, and aspects of the service delivery system. The franchisor's designator code is applied to franchised services (and the franchisee's usually is not). The franchisee will be a separate corporate entity, with its own air operator's certificate (AOC) or local equivalent, in which the franchisor may or may not hold an equity interest. Freedom with regard to network design and scheduling varies, but the franchisor is likely to want meaningful input if not total control. (Note that this discussion of franchising excludes consideration of operations that are wholly-owned subsidiaries or in-house divisions of a larger carrier.)

The franchisee typically pays a front-end licensing fee and an ongoing royalty for use of the brand, the sizes of which will to some extent depend on the balance of benefits each party anticipates from the relationship. Franchisees might also either choose or be obliged to use various services provided by the franchisor for which they make separate payments – including possibly brand advertising, training, traffic handling, reservations, sales, inventory control, revenue management, revenue accounting, and management services.

The use of reservations and revenue accounting support is frequently compulsory. These and other services are sometimes provided at a level of sophistication in excess of what is needed by a regional airline and, despite usually being sold 'at cost' and perhaps benefiting from economies of scale, the price could be well above what it would cost the franchisee were the same work to be undertaken in-house. Distribution costs will also tend to be relatively high because most major airlines (i.e., franchisors) require a presence in all the largest GDSs at the highest levels of functionality available. Finally, it is quite likely that the major will have product standards that impose additional service delivery costs on the franchisee.

Most commonly to date it is corporate brand identities that have been franchised into sub-brands – such as Delta Air Lines into Delta Connection. Franchising does not always involve creation of a sub-brand, however; former British Airways franchisees GB Airways and British Mediterranean operated under the corporate master-brand because they offered the same levels of service (i.e., the Club Europe and Euro Traveller sub-brands) as the mainline operation on short- and medium-haul flights, and Frontier let Republic fly E-170s under the mainline brand for much the same reason (until cancellation of the deal in early 2008). In contrast, regional carriers doing business as Delta Connection do not mirror Delta's mainline service offers, and so are separately identified using the 'Connection' sub-brand.

Franchising has until recently been essentially a cost-driven US domestic and intra-EU phenomenon – the principal exceptions being British Airways' agreements with two carriers in Africa. Since mid-decade, however, LFAs Tiger Airways, AirAsia, Lion, and Jetstar have been using franchising to extend their brands throughout east and South East Asia and Australia; much has been made of parallels with fast-food franchising and other retail-oriented non-traditional approaches to airline expansion, but in reality this pattern has developed in large part because of difficulties obtaining sufficient traffic rights to some Asian countries and because of restrictions on foreign ownership (other than in Australia). A similar motivation lay behind the establishment by LAN and TACA of branded affiliates in neighbouring Latin American countries. Equity investment and strong influence, if not full control, over franchisees' operations – rather than just commercial activities – have been a distinctive feature of these more recent arrangements. However, some countries will not permit franchising where:

- the franchisor is a foreign carrier, because a franchisor could be deemed to have commercial control over a domestic franchisee and most countries' laws forbid foreign control of their airlines;
- the franchisor does not have underlying traffic rights for the route(s) being operated, particularly where only the franchisor's code would be used on the flight(s) concerned.

Cross-border franchising, outside the EU single market and a handful of other countries, therefore potentially falls foul of the restrictions on foreign ownership and control of airlines found in most domestic legal systems and bilateral ASAs (Denton and Dennis 2000). Labour groups in the United States see cross-border franchising as an end-run around ownership and control laws, and their opposition to the concept was made clear in the course of US–EU open skies negotiations and the tortuous approval of Virgin America's start-up.

Benefits And Risks For Franchisors

From a franchisor's perspective, franchising can be looked upon as one or all of:

- a channel to market (i.e., to markets the franchisor would not otherwise be able to access, either at all or as cost-effectively);
- a brand extension;
- capacity outsourcing.

Franchising is an alliance strategy which can be pursued in conjunction with a franchisor's own operations and those of its subsidiaries, as well as in tandem with non-franchise code-sharing agreements. There can be several potential benefits from franchising:

1. In return for little or no additional up-front investment, a franchisor can generate revenue from the licensing of its brand. Terms vary, but the franchisor might benefit from both an initial lump-sum payment and annual licensing fees.
2. Depending upon the extent of network complementarity, the franchisor might gain incremental revenue from traffic feed. Any increase in traffic that contributes to higher load factors rather than capacity increases will have a positive impact on RASM.
3. Franchisors are able to extend and maintain awareness of their brands in regions where they have no traffic rights or, more usually to date, no ability to offer service given their labour costs and/or fleet structures relative to the demand characteristics of the markets concerned (i.e., price-sensitivity or lack of density); this is typically the case with franchised feeder services, for example, but it can also apply to relatively dense but low-yield leisure routes. Awareness of a major brand stimulated by a franchised regional in an area where the major is not strongly represented might translate into brand loyalty when customers from that regional airline's catchment area face a choice between the major and a competitor on medium- or long-haul journeys. This is particularly likely if, as is probable, the franchised regional and the major share an FFP. Franchisors can in this way leverage their system-wide resources and skills to create revenue-generating intangible assets. Nonetheless, brands should in general only be franchised into regions where there is at least a basic pre-existing level of brand equity, and franchising should always be part of a coherent regional strategy.
4. It is possible that franchising on a significant scale could generate sufficient incremental business for some of the franchisor's functional units that their retention in house can be justified as an alternative to outsourcing – assuming that outsourcing is under consideration.

In practice, the balance of franchisor benefits between traffic feed (i.e., using a franchisee to operate what would otherwise be uneconomic or inaccessible routes), simple fee generation, and other potential contributions will vary from situation to situation. Much depends on network synergies.

There are relatively few risks for franchisors:

1. The most obvious is poor franchisee service quality. This can in principle be addressed by carefully crafted service level agreements covering variables such as flight completion rate, on-time performance, and customer satisfaction and complaint levels. Some US franchise agreements based on fee-per-departure or per ASM payments from a major to a regional in fact impose hold-backs from due payments, released once performance criteria are established as having been met.

2. Another risk is the implication for the major's reputation were a franchisee to collapse financially – particularly where a collapse is sudden and leaves passengers stranded.

3. As we saw earlier, a major might also be exposed to a decision by an independently owned franchisee to realign with a competitor, and so perhaps deprive the franchisor of traffic feed and market presence. (This concern was one of the reasons why several US and European majors began in the late 1990s to acquire full control over some or all of their regional franchisees. Another reason was pursuit of the economies of scale and better integration that could, in principle, be achieved by centralising management of regional operations – a justification which became less compelling when the imperative of simplicity rose to the fore during subsequent restructurings.)

4. Less dramatic but still potentially damaging is the possibility that franchisors might face labour relations problems were franchisees to be perceived by unions as a form of low-cost flight operations outsourcing – which, of course, is what they are. This is seen most clearly in the scope clauses incorporated into pilots' contracts at many US majors.

5. Franchisors rely on franchisees being responsive to any significant shift in fundamental marketing strategy, particularly a shift affecting brand identity.

6. Finally, wherever a franchisee represents a corporate master-brand but offers a diluted product, as opposed to a product separately positioned as a distinct sub-brand, the risk of failing to meet consumers' expectations with regard to brand consistency is very real.

Conclusion   The US network majors, Air France-KLM, and Lufthansa continue to use a mixture of subsidiaries and independent franchisees to feed their hubs. British Airways, an early enthusiast for extending the model beyond its origins in regional feed, pulled back significantly as franchise agreements ended in 2007 and 2008. The carrier lost its presence on several routes when franchises involving GB Airways (which was sold by its owners to easyJet), British Mediterranean Airways (which was sold by its owners to bmi), and Loganair (which entered into a new franchise agreement with Flybe) were terminated; many of the routes involved were thin or low-yield and so not particularly attractive to British Airways, which itself entered those on which it wanted to maintain market presence – but the move nonetheless represented a noteworthy withdrawal by what is a global brand. An unexpected growth area for the model has been its use by South East Asian LFAs to attempt an 'end run' around the Chicago system.

Benefits And Risks For Franchisees

Benefits   Against a background of growing industry concentration, cynics might argue that the outstanding benefit of a franchise from the franchisee's perspective is likely to be survival. However, even carriers whose survival is not in doubt can benefit from association with a strong, well-managed brand.

1. *Revenue-side benefits*   Franchisees expect to gain incremental revenue as a result of the marketing communications, sales, and distribution power of their partner, from network synergies (reflected in higher traffic figures and load factors), from a strengthened image (reflected in firmer yields), and from customer loyalty built on strong branding and participation in an attractive FFP. Network growth is also frequently associated with franchise agreements. Franchisees get to provide what is in principle (if not always in practice) a respected, usually high-quality product that boosts their market presence with both customers and travel agents – and often they get to charge accordingly. Although they sometimes have to pay richly for the privilege, franchisees might also benefit from knowledge transfer in respect of product design, marketing communications, distribution, and revenue management.
2. *Cost side benefits*   Cost savings could be available through joint purchasing and from certain economies of scale in respect of services acquired from the major. Technical assistance can also be valuable. We have seen already that it has become the norm for regionals franchised by US majors to be remunerated under long-term capacity purchase agreements; the advantage to a regional of moving from a revenue-sharing model to a capacity-purchase model akin to wet-leasing is that subject only to whatever control the major might have over capacity, scheduling (i.e., the number of departures), and inventory management, cash flow is reasonably secure throughout the duration of the agreement and both marketing expenses and marketing risks are avoided.

Risks   Against the undoubted benefits and aside from any financial costs attributable to fees, services, and management reporting requirements, franchisees – particularly when they are existing carriers rather than start-ups – must weigh several potential disadvantages.

1. The loss of an independent identity in their markets, which might be irrecoverable were the franchise agreement to be terminated. This problem could in principle be circumvented by a carrier operating only some of its routes as a franchisee, retaining its own brand identity in other markets; there are few examples of this. In the United States, the problem has been ameliorated somewhat by the growth of holding companies which provide franchised regional feed to different majors using separate subsidiaries, thereby spreading risk for the corporation as a whole.
2. The loss of traffic feed from carriers other than the franchisor. This is not an issue in the United States, either for the above-mentioned holding companies and their subsidiaries or for independents; many of the latter interchange as much as 70 or 80 per cent of their traffic with the major airlines whose brands they license. In Europe and elsewhere, franchisees sometimes depend on a more balanced mix of local traffic, code-share connections with the franchisor, and interline connections – and it is the latter that can be threatened.

3. Yields from local traffic will almost certainly be higher than from transfer traffic – but the key question in this respect, of course, is whether or not the regional can actually survive on local traffic alone in the absence of flow traffic exchanged with the franchisor.

4. There might be times when a franchisee wants to adjust fares but is constrained from doing so.

5. Because franchisors are generally large airlines with slower decision-making processes than are customary at smaller franchisees, gaining approval for initiatives that bear on the product (including network planning) or the brand identity can sometimes be frustrating for a franchisee.

6. There is always a danger that the franchisor might move mainline equipment into markets developed by an independent regional franchisee. United gained a reputation for this type of behaviour in the late 1980s and early 1990s, for example. (Conversely, some franchisors use franchisees' smaller aircraft to provide off-peak service on mainline routes those franchisees could not otherwise serve, and after 9/11 US majors in particular engaged in extensive route transfers to franchisees as well as in-house regionals.)

7. Franchisees might eventually be pressed by their staff for pay and benefits closer to those available from the franchisor, which could undermine the cost advantages offered by smaller airlines in the thin markets they are usually franchised to serve.

8. Finally, a franchisee can suffer if the franchisor's brand runs into difficulties (e.g., a high-profile strike or accident).

Benefits And Risks For Consumers

When a franchisor franchises and carefully monitors the use of a strong brand, franchising has the potential to offer consumers standards close to those delivered by the franchisor in its own operations – subject always to limitations imposed by equipment type. By offering a well-branded and quality-controlled product, franchising is likely to be better able to meet consumer expectations than is naked code-sharing. Of course, when the quality of service associated with the franchised brand deteriorates, this point loses validity.

Sometimes, though, the consumer pays handsomely for benefits offered by high-cost/high-fare branded products, especially in uncontested point-to-point markets (see Denton and Dennis 2000, p. 186). Particularly on thin regional routes, the danger that small independent carriers will be overwhelmed by the network strengths of franchised competitors is a very real threat to competition. There has, however, been little outward sign of concern from regulators.

The counter-argument might be that such markets would anyway support no more than one operator or, alternatively, that without network synergies available as a result of the franchise relationship no service at all would be economically feasible. This is particularly true of services linking a secondary or tertiary point to a major's hub: the major itself might not be equipped to provide service, whilst a competitor may not be inclined to enter a low-density route into a powerful, non-affiliated hub – leaving a choice between franchised service or no service.

IV. Summary

This chapter opened by drawing a distinction between markets and routes, before going on to discuss network economics and different types of network – the latter seen from both customers' and carriers' perspectives. Hub-and-spoke networks received particular attention – again, from the perspectives of both passengers and airlines. The second section of the chapter looked at network strategies and tactics, whilst the third discussed different approaches to network outsourcing.

At the beginning of the chapter the point was made that network management involves both network design and scheduling. Having covered design in the present chapter, we will move on to look at scheduling in the next. The two chapters after that will focus in turn on fleet management and revenue management.

7

Network Management: Scheduling

Lose an hour in the morning and you'll be all day hunting for it.

Proverb

CHAPTER OVERVIEW

Scheduling choices determine frequencies, departure timings, crew rosters, passenger and aircraft routings and, particularly over hub-based networks, the extent of connections between points served. An airline's schedule is its core service attribute and revenue driver insofar as safe, reliable delivery of a schedule is what satisfies customers' most basic air travel need: the need to be somewhere else by a certain time. Because of its impact on aircraft choice and on the utilisation of equipment, staff, and other resources, a schedule is also – along with network design – a critical cost driver. Scheduling therefore lies at the interface between the revenue and cost sides of an airline's income statement.

This chapter will look at scheduling as a response to demand, to the economics of supply, and to external constraints. It will then consider hub-and-spoke scheduling, and scheduling tactics. The final section will draw together Chapters 6 and 7 to consider the interface between network management and fleet management. Fleet management is the subject of Chapter 8. We will begin by considering a typical schedule development process.

I. The Schedule Development Process

Although practices vary, scheduling is in essence an iterative process encompassing the following steps:

1. Decide which markets to serve based on demand forecasts, corporate strategy, and (where relevant) the availability of route licenses or other required forms of designation. This should have been done as part of a wider marketing planning exercise and will have been the key input into network design.
2. Take the demand forecast for each targeted market and assume a market share.
3. Decide on the frequencies to be offered, with specific regard to any trade-off between marketing and cost considerations inherent in choices of aircraft size and frequency of operation. This will involve assumptions regarding product quality, market share, price (with yield or average fare as a proxy), and load factors. (The relationship

between price and load factor assumptions is important; other things being equal, planned load factor for a given departure operated by a given aircraft type should be set at the level which maximises revenue (expected number of passengers × average fare). Targeting a higher load factor might not maximise revenue if achieving that target requires the average fare to be reduced; it may also raise spill costs. Both points will be revisited in Chapter 10.) Operational considerations also need to be factored in, notably:

- the payload–range capabilities of potentially suitable aircraft types given sector length and frequency requirement;
- the capabilities of the airports concerned to accept different types both from a flight operations perspective (e.g., runway length and obstacle clearance) and passenger-handling perspective (e.g., terminal, including counter and gate, capacity).

4. Narrow down the chosen raw number of frequencies to specific timings and routings on the basis of market preferences, network connectivity criteria (including intraline, alliance, and possibly also interline connections), and airport slot availability (where relevant).
5. Establish block-times for each flight-leg.
6. Establish minimum ground (turn or transit) times.
7. Assign to each departure an aircraft type (given the fleet available as a result of fleet planning decisions – the subject of Chapter 8).
8. Calculate hours per annum expected of each aircraft type and factor-in maintenance requirements.
9. Assign to each departure a specific aircraft (i.e., 'tail number') of the type identified in step 7, to create aircraft rotations (routings) which:
   - integrate the schedule using as few aircraft as possible given block- and minimum ground-times;
   - incorporate the maintenance requirements for each aircraft and the maintenance capabilities at airports it will visit.
   The flip-side of ensuring that each departure has a tail number assigned to it is that every aircraft is given a routing cycle. The period of time over which a routing cycle extends will depend upon airline practice, the type of network (e.g., point-to-point out-and-back from a base or complex multi-hub), and the lengths of haul involved.
10. Consider availability of human and other resources. This will require, in particular, a crew schedule that gets as much flying out of pilots as is possible and incurs the lowest feasible expenses in respect of layovers (i.e., allowances and accommodation charges). What is possible will be a function of schedule planning, the location of crew bases, and the terms of duty-time regulations and union contracts.
11. Predict competitors' strategies and reactions.
12. Iterate from 2 to 11.

(Bazargan [2004] takes a more technical look at many of the above steps, describing basic optimisation models used to solve the problems each presents.)

Clearly, the scheduling/schedule planning function must work closely with the commercial/marketing function, regional sales offices, maintenance planners, flight operations, and station managers. Aside from its cross-functional dimensions, what makes airline scheduling a complicated undertaking is that it involves optimising the allocation of resources to meet demand across a network rather than on a single route.

Particularly in a multi-hub network, demand can be served by flowing traffic along a number of alternative paths; the more liberal the regulatory environment, the wider the choices are likely to be.

Advance schedules out to two years ahead look at markets on a very general level, expressing demand in terms of RPMs and fleet capacity in terms of ASMs. Other than in the case of a start-up, scheduling begins not with a blank sheet of paper but with the current schedule as a foundation and both market and fleet developments as critical new inputs. Many carriers operate a core schedule comprising standard departure times and flight numbers, overlaid by seasonal adjustments; these adjustments might include changes to the size of aircraft operating some of the core services, changes in flight frequencies, and/or the seasonal introduction and deletion of routes.

The closer in we come towards an operational schedule, preparation of which might begin, say, 12 months ahead of introduction, the more influential current schedules become and the more we need to be thinking in terms of specific routings, passenger numbers, marketing communication programmes, fare changes, and equipment types. Scheduling at many carriers is a semi-annual process, with new schedules appearing in spring and autumn; US domestic operations are an exception insofar as some majors introduce new schedules as often as every other month.

An entire timetable cannot be fully optimised because there are simply too many possible outcomes. However, computational complexity can be overcome to some extent by the use of heuristics (i.e., techniques capable of producing good if not perfect solutions), and powerful simulations are available to facilitate rapid 'what if' analyses. There is no shortage of highly capable software to support decision-making with regard to each individual step in the process: market size and share models; fleet assignment and rotation optimisers; spill models;.maintenance planning models; passenger routing models; GDS display simulators (to generate market share estimates for inputting into schedule profitability models); and schedule dependability models, which simulate a schedule to detect particular reliability problems (Smith *et al*. 1998). Each enables solution of different fleet planning, aircraft assignment, routing, and scheduling problems subject to a range of possible constraints. The point to bear in mind is that within the context established by those constraints (e.g., to maximise profits or passenger-miles, to minimise fleet size or operating costs, etc.) they all have broadly the same purpose: to relate output to forecasted demand. What differs is simply the timescale being applied.

Once flight schedules have been established, optimisation models are available to assist with resource scheduling – the allocation of flight crews, ramp personnel and equipment, and check-in, gate, and other customer service staff, for example.

Figure 7.1 illustrates some of the variables that must be considered as part of a schedule development process. Figure 7.2 integrates these variables into a timeline.

II. Scheduling: A Response to Demand

Although this section considers scheduling as a *response* to demand, it needs to be kept in mind that routing and scheduling decisions are attributes of the service an airline offers into each of its markets, and as such will themselves have an *impact on* demand. How significant they are relative to other independent variables, most notably price, will depend upon the characteristics of the demand being served in a particular market (a proxy for which would be its traffic mix).

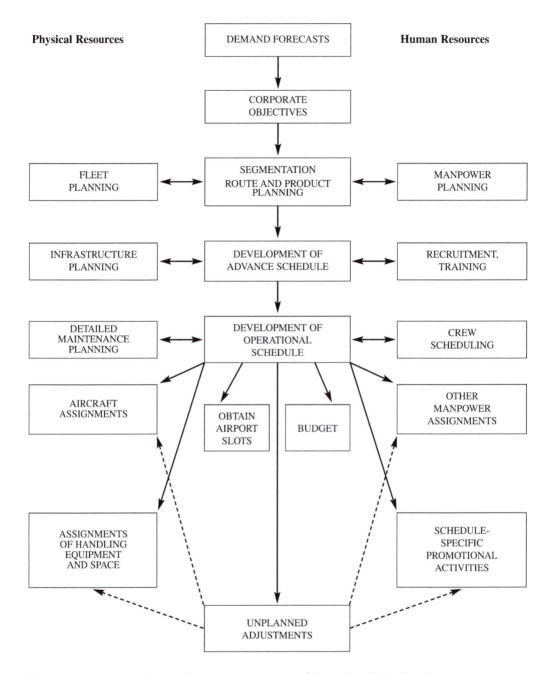

Figure 7.1   A schematic representation of the schedule development process

Source: Holloway, S., *Aircraft Acquisition Finance*, Pitman, 1992.

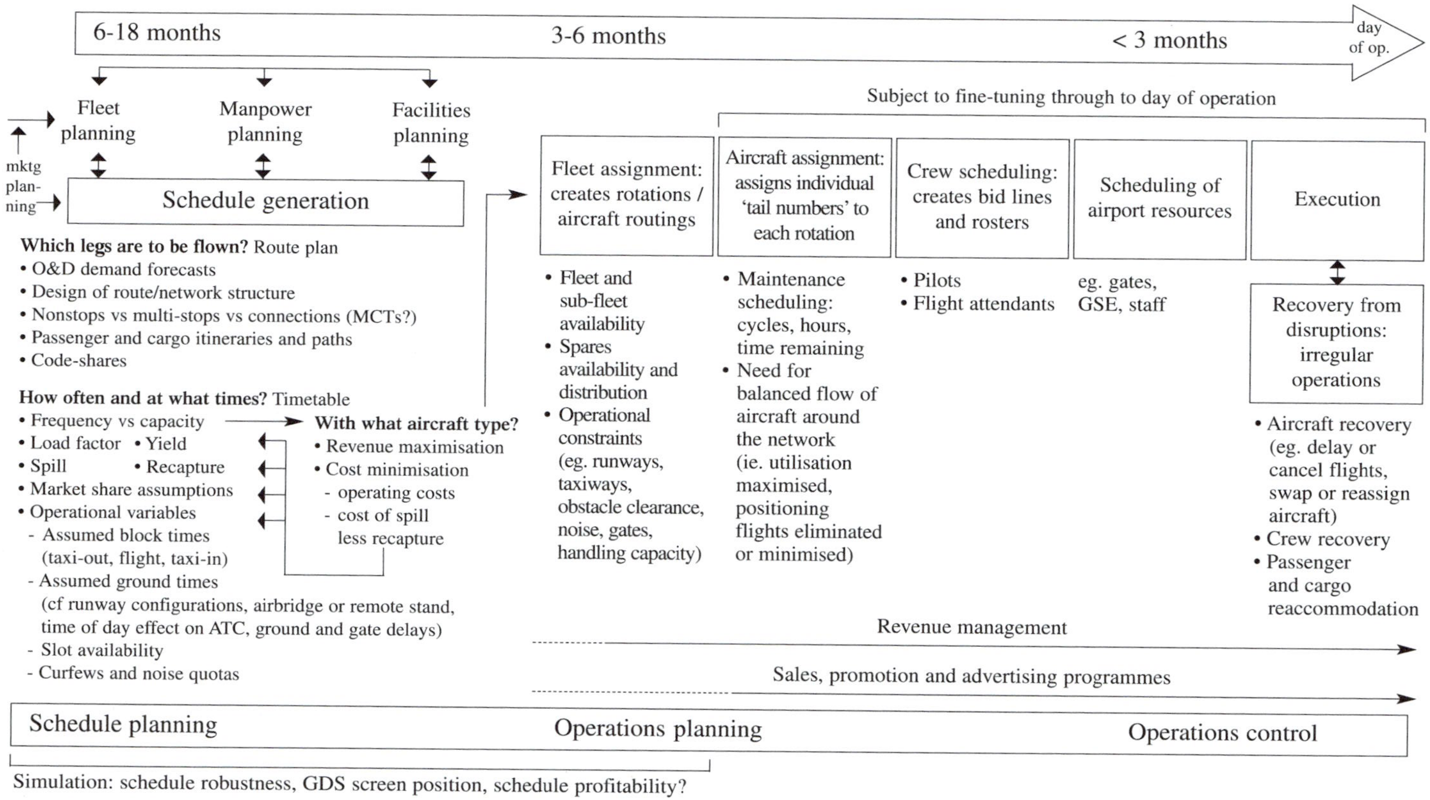

6-18 months   **3-6 months**   **< 3 months**

mktg plan-ning

Fleet planning   Manpower planning   Facilities planning

Schedule generation

Which legs are to be flown? Route plan
• O&D demand forecasts
• Design of route/network structure
• Nonstops vs multi-stops vs connections (MCTs?)
• Passenger and cargo itineraries and paths
• Code-shares

How often and at what times? Timetable   **With what aircraft type?**
• Frequency vs capacity   • Revenue maximisation
• Load factor   • Yield   • Cost minimisation
• Spill   • Recapture   - operating costs
• Market share assumptions   - cost of spill
• Operational variables   less recapture
 - Assumed block times
 (taxi-out, flight, taxi-in)
 - Assumed ground times
 (cf runway configurations, airbridge or remote stand,
 time of day effect on ATC, ground and gate delays)
 - Slot availability
 - Curfews and noise quotas

Subject to fine-tuning through to day of operation

Fleet assignment: creates rotations / aircraft routings
• Fleet and sub-fleet availability
• Spares availability and distribution
• Operational constraints (eg. runways, taxiways, obstacle clearance, noise, gates, handling capacity)

Aircraft assignment: assigns individual 'tail numbers' to each rotation
• Maintenance scheduling: cycles, hours, time remaining
• Need for balanced flow of aircraft around the network (ie. utilisation maximised, positioning flights eliminated or minimised)

Crew scheduling: creates bid lines and rosters
• Pilots
• Flight attendants

Scheduling of airport resources
eg. gates, GSE, staff

Execution

Recovery from disruptions: irregular operations
• Aircraft recovery (eg. delay or cancel flights, swap or reassign aircraft)
• Crew recovery
• Passenger and cargo reaccommodation

day of op.

Revenue management

Sales, promotion and advertising programmes

Schedule planning   Operations planning   Operations control

Simulation: schedule robustness, GDS screen position, schedule profitability?

Figure 7.2   A scheduling timeline

THE THEORY

An airline's timetable is both a production schedule and the specification of a core service attribute. Because demand is in effect a continuous variable, passengers in each market will have preferred departure times throughout the day. On the other hand, supply is a discrete variable driven by the capacities of specific aircraft departing at specific points in time. A passenger having to take a flight at a time other than when they would prefer to depart will suffer an amount of disutility which depends on just how far apart the actual and preferred departure times are; if this 'schedule delay' (Douglas and Miller 1974a) is sufficiently severe and alternatives exist, that passenger might be spilled to a competitor offering a better-timed departure.

But passengers care about when they will arrive as well as when they can depart. As far as markets served by non-stop routes are concerned, these two variables are linked almost by definition; when a market is served by two routes connected over a hub, however, schedule delay becomes a function not just of departure frequency from the origin, but also of scheduled transfer times and departure frequency from the hub.

An airline able to design and deliver a timetable that minimises schedule delay is offering a valuable product feature for which members of those segments of demand that value their time particularly highly, in most cases business travellers, will sometimes be prepared to pay a premium. In addition to routing, which was considered in the last chapter, there are three considerations here: frequency, departure timings, and reliability.

Frequency

The more frequencies an airline offers in a given market, the greater the likelihood that the timing of one of its departures will be close to when a potential passenger wants to travel. We saw in Chapter 4 that there is a widely recognised S-curve relationship between frequency and market share, such that a carrier offering more than half the frequencies in a market is likely to have a market share higher than its share of frequencies (Fruhan 1972). Furthermore, an airline operating at greater frequency in a market than its competitor(s) is providing customers who have fully flexible tickets a wider range of rebooking options. Offering more frequencies than competitors may also lead to a better presence high on the first page of GDS displays – which remain important in agency channels.

Market preference for higher frequencies was one reason why an historical uptrend in the average size of aircraft in the global fleet came to a halt in the early 1980s, as the effects of deregulation began to take hold in the United States and carriers started competing for market share by operating smaller aircraft at higher frequencies than previously. Deregulation, liberalisation, and the evolution of hub-and-spoke systems have contributed to a tendency to meet growing demand first by raising frequencies, and only as demand thickens further by increasing aircraft size (Boeing 1997). Availability of new airport capacity can have a similar effect; for example, the opening of a fourth runway at Tokyo Haneda, adding 40 per cent to the airport's available slots, is expected to lead to sharply higher frequencies in many current markets and a fall (from 313) in the average number of seats per departure.

In short-haul markets, particularly those with heavy business traffic, frequency can be a critical service differentiator and on some routes hourly departures are justifiable. In long-haul markets, on the other hand, the situation is different for two reasons: first, whilst many passengers will have preferred departure times, these preferences tend not to be as finely grained to the nearest hour or so as they are in short-haul markets; second, interplay between time zones, block-times, and airport curfews limits scope for multiple daily frequencies on many long-haul routes – particularly east–west and vice versa. It is also arguable that other than on the relatively small number of long-haul routes serving dense point-to-point markets (e.g., LHR–JFK) or a multi-wave hub (e.g., Dubai), the high costs of mounting more than two or three daily services begin to outweigh passenger benefits, and the operation of larger aircraft should be considered a better way to meet long-haul demand growth.

Departure Timings

Having decided upon frequencies and their general timings, attention also has to be paid to precise timings. In some competitive markets, particularly short-haul, adjusting a departure time by just a few minutes can lead to meaningful traffic gains and losses – most notably when fine-tuning in a market dominated by business traffic has a significant impact on GDS display screen positioning relative to competitors. Assume, for example, that a schedule change affecting a particular daily departure results in the loss of just one passenger and, say, a $400 sale each day: the annual revenue loss would be $146,000. Depending upon the assumed variable costs of carrying those passengers and whether or not commissions would have been payable on sales, the forgone contribution to fixed costs could represent a significant proportion of that figure. Multiplying this across several hundred daily departures, it is clear that the stakes are potentially very high and it is easy to understand why airlines in competitive markets devote so much time to the fine-tuning of departures. On the other hand, the shift towards more transparent price-oriented Internet channels has made leisure and VFR segments somewhat less schedule-sensitive.

Another point to bear in mind about departure timings is that in a hub-and-spoke network the scheduling of departures into and out of a hub will have an impact on the number and saleability of connections. Minimum connecting times (MCTs) may be important in this regard; they are driven not simply by structural issues such as the capacity of baggage-handling and passenger facilitation infrastructure, but also by whether aircraft are predominantly parked at contact gates or remote stands, whether inter-terminal transfers are required (including whether alliance partners operating code-shares are co-located in the same terminal), and whether high-volume connecting flights can be guaranteed proximate gates. We will look at hub scheduling later in the chapter.

Reliability

Having a well-designed schedule with competitive departure timings is only half the battle: the other half is delivering it. Weather and congestion take schedule reliability outside the complete control of any airline, although investment (e.g., in head-up displays or RNP capabilities) may be able to reduce weather delays. In Europe, many large airports have slot controls and hourly limits which mean that other than in extreme cases weather conditions have relatively little impact on runway throughput. At most US hubs, in contrast, there are no slot controls to spread demand with the result that peak throughput can be very much lower in poor weather than under favourable conditions. Other factors affecting reliability include the efficiency of passenger-handling and aircraft turnaround procedures, line maintenance capacity, policies in respect of the holding of line replaceable spares at outstations, and the potentially disruptive unscheduled maintenance requirements often associated with ageing aircraft.

Ontime performance is a key metric on both sides of the income statement: first, it is an important product attribute, and a potential loyalty driver for business travellers in particular; second, significant deviations from a planned schedule, whether attributable to a single event or an accumulation of minor disruptions, cost money. Different airlines have different metrics for dispatch, en route, and overall schedule reliability. For example, some monitor dispatch reliability to the minute whereas others record as ontime any departure up to 15 minutes after the scheduled time. Several carriers place greater emphasis on ontime arrivals, arguing that this is what really matters to customers; there is of course likely to be a close relationship between dispatch reliability and ontime arrivals, but just how close this relationship is will depend upon both en route time-keeping and whether scheduled block-times are tight or instead build-in a buffer to absorb delays.

Given sufficient resources (e.g., functioning equipment, properly trained and motivated people, adequate spares, and enough time to accomplish required processes), many controllable delays can be eliminated. Some airlines strive to achieve the highest level of reliability they can despite the costs involved, addressing in particular the root causes of persistent delays to particular departures. Others are more prepared to tolerate delays to a certain percentage of flights as an inevitable by-product of the efficiency/effectiveness trade-off lying at the heart of operations management. The latter approach is not without risk in competitive, business-oriented markets.

There is now no shortage of software available to model the robustness of alternative schedule plans; its output is not one dominant solution, but a frontier of alternatives suggesting how changes to a planned schedule might impact upon the particular performance metrics being analysed. The approach taken is generally to assess each line of flying in a proposed schedule against historical flight performance distributions and/or 'what if' scenarios to assess probable reliability and identify potential vulnerabilities. Key qualities of a robust schedule are that it:

- meets the business rules and constraints imposed for regular operations (e.g., regarding commercial requirements and aircraft and other resource availability);
- permits disruptions to be dealt with locally as far as possible (e.g., local aircraft or crew swaps, limiting propagation throughout the rest of the system);
- minimises the time taken, cost expended, or profit forgone to recover from irregular to regular operations;
- delivers operating performance metrics to the required standard.

Two important considerations driving the robustness of a planned schedule and therefore the reliability with which it can be expected to be executed are block-times and turnaround/transit times.

Scheduled block-times   These can vary seasonally on long-haul routes (to take account of winds) and by time of day on short-haul routes (to take account of departures or arrivals occurring at times of particular congestion at the airports concerned). Another issue can be airport configuration; moving from Terminal 4 on the periphery of London

Heathrow to Terminal 5 located between the two runways was expected to reduce British Airways' taxi-times by an amount equivalent to the utilisation of one long-haul aircraft per annum.

One approach to the establishment of block-times is to develop a histogram of actual times for a given flight over a scheduling season, then in the next corresponding season schedule a block-time somewhat longer than the achieved mean. This technique builds in, on average, a small buffer within which to absorb delays. Some airlines go further by publishing deliberately more conservative block-times; as well as keeping passengers satisfied with time-keeping on individual flights, this can also help PR in those few countries where individual carriers' punctuality rates are in the public domain. Padding block-times is not without its problems, however:

1.   The shorter a flight, the less opportunity there is to recover time lost to a departure delay, yet any meaningful buffer inserted into the schedule to deal with potential delays will represent a more significant percentage of actual block-time than is likely to be the case in respect of a long-haul flight.
2.   Too much buffer time can make a flight appear uncompetitive on GDS displays; it might also reduce connection possibilities where MCTs are breached by pushing out the scheduled arrival time.
3.   Too much buffer time might also lead to ground delays if consistently early arrivals have to wait for assigned gates to become free.
4.   Costs rise where crews are hourly-paid.

Scheduled turnaround/transit times   'Turn-times' are determined in the first instance by how long it takes to turn around an aircraft of the type likely to be operating each leg at the airports in question, modified by any requirement to allow time for connecting passengers to make transfers and perhaps to await specific high-volume inbound connections before departure. Ground times could also need a contingency buffer where the airport from which an inbound flight departs is prone to delays at the time of day the flight leaves, unless potential delays have been factored into the block-time allowed. Finally, a crew change during aircraft turnaround might also lengthen ground time.

By scheduling aggressive turn-times an airline can raise aircraft utilisation, but it has less of a ground-buffer in which to absorb delays – either to the flight concerned (which can have knock-on effects as the aircraft continues its rotation behind schedule) or to inbound connections (which might have less time to link with that aircraft). Having previously taken a considerable amount of ground-time out of its domestic schedule, American responded to a summer of heavy delays and missed connections in 2007 by reconsidering the tactic. There are three sub-issues here:

1.   Any airline operating a high-activity hub-and-spoke system can face congestion (e.g., on taxiways and aprons) as well as heavy resource loading during peaks of activity at the hub, and yet its product to a large extent stands or falls on achieving high levels of schedule reliability. Hub-and-spoke systems generally require longer turn-times than point-to-point operations in order both to provide a buffer that can help prevent delays propagating across subsequent waves, and to contribute to the optimisation of connectivity between incoming and outgoing banks. Minimum turn-time for a given type arriving at a hub as part of an inbound bank might therefore be considerably longer than for the same type at an outstation.

2.   A number of structural features contribute to the ability of LFAs to build the economics
     of their operations on fast turn-times and the high aircraft utilisation to which these
     contribute.
     - First, LFAs have no need to consider the requirements of connecting passengers
       because most operate point-to-point services; those that do carry significant
       volumes of flow traffic (such as Southwest at some of its highest-frequency
       stations) do not schedule connections as such, but rely instead on high
       frequencies to simulate a continuous hub.
     - Second, the complexity of ramp operations is minimised in many cases by
       having a single-type fleet, limited catering, and no need to interline or intraline
       baggage.
     - Third, these carriers commonly operate into secondary airports unburdened by
       congestion.
     - Fourth, a relatively continuous spread of frequencies throughout the day even
       at high-volume stations avoids the self-inflicted peaking, and the need to allow
       for the resource bottlenecks to which it sometimes leads, that hub-and-spoke
       carriers have to accommodate.
       Low-fare carriers are nonetheless not immune to delays. A common Ryanair
     operating pattern therefore schedules aircraft onto 4 morning flight-legs with 25-
     minute turnarounds, separated by a 1-hour midday 'firebreak' from 4 afternoon legs
     also operated with 25-minute turnarounds.
3.   Whilst reducing aircraft turn-times can allow a carrier to generate more block-hours
     and therefore a higher output of ASMs from an unchanged fleet, the question arises
     whether this incremental output can be sold at prices in excess of variable costs (so
     making a contribution to fixed costs that would not have been made had utilisation
     been lower).

(Wu and Caves [2000] outline a mathematical model that can be used to optimise the
trade-off between aircraft utilisation and turn-time.)

Conclusion on schedule reliability   Aggressive timetabled block-times and tight
turnarounds increase aircraft utilisation but, unless carefully managed, can threaten both
punctuality and schedule integrity. There is a trade-off to be arrived at between reliability,
revenue, and cost. In fact, since the mid-1990s US majors as a whole have been steadily
stretching scheduled domestic flight-times to mask the true scale of delays. In mid-2007,
for example, United's 1800 departure from Philadelphia to San Francisco was scheduled
to take 33 minutes more than had been the case a decade earlier, and scheduled block-
times on many flights between New York and Washington area airports are closing in on
twice the times published in the mid-1990s. By incorporating anticipated delays (often,
in practice, the mean of anticipated delays for each separate flight number) into their
schedules, airlines are better able to achieve the DOT's ontime target of being within 15
minutes of scheduled arrival time – although padding alone cannot cope with weather- and
congestion-related peak summer delays. Conversely, some airlines persist (presumably
for commercial reasons) in scheduling arrival times they have good reason to believe have
a low probability of being met – something which provoked a DOT investigation in 2007
and is exemplified by US Airways' Flight 154 from Philadelphia to San Francisco, which
was more than 15 minutes late on every occasion in February that year and 'achieved' an
average delay of 61 minutes (Bailey 2007).

THE MARKETING IMPLICATIONS OF A SCHEDULE

Every feasible schedule is a separate product, with its own saleability. (See Clampett [1998] for a description of how software relates different schedule choices to different yields.)

Passenger Markets

A network airline endeavouring to forecast its probable share of traffic in an O&D market will run through several steps: first, it will estimate market demand; second, it will identify alternative paths (i.e., flights or combinations of flights) that passengers might feasibly use to travel from the origin to their destination; third, it will apply a model of customer decision-making to weight path preferences; finally, share can be allocated to available paths (Boeing 1993). (A *path* describes the route(s) passengers could take from a particular origin to a particular destination, whereas an *itinerary* describes the actual flight-numbers booked by an individual passenger.) Scheduling plays a significant role in the modelling of path preferences: this is because, as was noted in Chapter 2 and reiterated earlier in this chapter, each customer's travel choice is in principle bounded by a 'decision window' framed between the earliest departure and latest arrival times considered acceptable given the context of the journey. To be acceptable, an itinerary must allow departure from the origin and arrival at the destination within that window, and preference is likely to rest with a choice which comes closest to matching a customer's ideal departure and arrival times (hence the importance of frequency) whilst minimising total journey time (hence the importance of non-stop flights).

Of course, depending upon the purpose of a journey and who is paying these time preferences may be weakened by price considerations. They may also be weakened by loyalty programmes and, particularly on long-haul journeys, perceptions of service quality differences between competing airlines. The following comments outline a few of the scheduling issues that affect different segments of passenger markets.

Business segments   A schedule targeted at business travellers will be more expensive to produce than one targeting primarily leisure or VFR segments, but higher costs should in principle be compensated by firmer yields. To be attractive to business travellers, a schedule needs the following:

1. *Frequent departures*   The greater the frequency an airline is able to offer, the better will be its chances of attracting passengers whose requirement is the next available flight and of retaining the loyalty of regular travellers. The economic rationale for this is that business travellers value their time more highly than travellers in other segments, and therefore bear higher costs if forced to wait beyond their preferred departure times; in other words, they have a lower 'schedule tolerance' (ibid.) than leisure travellers. It was noted above that a pronounced relationship generally links frequency share and market share. This is especially true in short-haul markets, where in respect of flights up to 2–2½ hours in duration frequency has been found to have a very strong influence on demand from business travellers (particularly where multiple FFP memberships are the norm). However, there is a 'saturation frequency' in every market; what this means is that up to a certain point the addition of an extra frequency might attract incremental demand to the extent that it falls within the

decision windows of as-yet unserved customers or adds convenience generally, but beyond that point the addition of further frequencies offers little new to the market and the time may have come to increase aircraft size instead in order to accommodate future demand growth; British Airways is at or close to saturation frequency between LHR and JFK, for example.

2. *Consistent and convenient timings*   Efforts should be made to maintain consistency with regard to departure timings (e.g., 16:00 daily – rather than 15:35 one day, 16:10 the next and so on). Although as already noted airlines do fine-tune their timings, there is merit in consistency insofar as regular departures will become familiar to frequent travellers and to agency staff. What represents a convenient timing will vary from market to market, and will also depend upon whether connections are required that lengthen journey times. With regard to short-haul business travel, particularly in potential day-return markets, we can make the following generalisations: at stations where originating traffic predominates, offering the first outbound and last inbound services can be competitively advantageous; at stations where traffic originating elsewhere predominates, offering the first inbound and last outbound services might be preferable.

3. *Coordinated timings*   As far as possible, an airline operating a hub-and-spoke system must ensure the coordination of its schedules to minimise waiting time for online transfer traffic and reduce the temptation for passengers to connect onto another (non-allied) carrier.

4. *Competitive total journey times*   As noted in Chapter 2, demand for air transport is subject to a time-elasticity such that all else being equal an increase in trip time will cause a decrease in demand. The demand for business travel is on the whole more time-elastic than the demand for leisure travel – although short-break leisure markets will be more time-elastic than markets for trips of longer duration; the marketing implication of this generalisation is that demand for business travel can be stimulated by reducing total journey time (whereas on the whole it is price which has a more stimulatory effect in leisure markets).

Leisure and VFR segments   A scheduled airline intending to penetrate a leisure or VFR market will benefit from travellers generally being less demanding in their schedule requirements. On the other hand, the fact that leisure and VFR travellers tend to be price-sensitive means that they generate softer yields, so airlines serving them need to develop schedules that are relatively cheap to produce – implying high aircraft utilisation, perhaps larger aircraft operating at lower frequencies than business travellers would require, and high seat factors. Note that a complicating factor in Europe has been the important role of charter airlines operating high-frequency, round-the-clock summer services to Mediterranean leisure destinations; their higher costs keep most network carriers out of all but the densest of these markets, but LFAs targeting owners of second homes and vacationers who now prefer to use the Internet to make their own arrangements rather than buy packaged holidays have been making significant inroads into year-round – as opposed to highly seasonal – markets.

Conclusions regarding distinctions between segments   Whilst some markets are clearly business-oriented (e.g., into London City), some are clearly leisure-oriented (e.g., into Las Vegas), and some are predominantly VFR (e.g., UK–Ireland), the fact is that most scheduled airlines carry a mix of traffic on all but a few of their routes. Scheduling will target the requirements of the predominant segment on a given route.

Cargo Markets

Scheduling is also one of the factors which define an airline's cargo product. Shippers and forwarders often prefer freight to travel at night, particularly in the express segment. This permits late acceptance of outbound shipments; depending upon the time zones being crossed and the urgency of the shipment, it may also facilitate early delivery the next day. Whereas these requirements can be met when all-cargo aircraft are being operated, freight capacity on combis and in the belly-holds of passenger aircraft is usually scheduled to fit the requirements of travellers rather than shippers. Furthermore, where carriers choose to operate short- and medium-haul passenger routes at high frequencies using narrowbodied aircraft into which freight must be loose-loaded, rather than widebodies capable of accommodating ULDs, they will find it very difficult to offer a freight product competitive with surface modes – assuming these to be well-developed in the markets concerned. (Yan and Chen [2008] provide a brief illustration of network flow models used to schedule cargo airlines, particularly when operating within an alliance.)

SUMMARY

Having designed a network of non-stop, direct, and/or connecting routes with which to serve the geographical markets they want to serve, an airline's managers need next to decide how often and at what times each route will be flown. Despite being treated separately here for convenience, network design and scheduling decisions cannot in practice be dealt with in isolation from each other or from the aircraft selection and fleet management decisions we will be touching upon in the next chapter; each is an integral part of the capacity management challenge.

For economists, a high level of service quality has typically been associated with high frequencies and consistent departure times. What is meant by high frequency will depend in large measure upon the length of haul involved. Frequency can be a vital competitive factor in short-haul markets generally, and in particular where business travellers represent a significant segment of demand and/or viable competition exists from surface transport.

Because markets are dynamic and supply side constraints are inevitable, no schedule is ever likely to be optimal – which means that the process of fine-tuning, and on occasion fundamentally reworking, the schedule is ongoing. Even were optimisation feasible, unless it were to provide sufficient slack to accommodate inevitable day of operation disruptions, what might appear to be optimal at the planning stage would very likely prove suboptimal in execution.

III. Scheduling: A Response to the Economics of Supply

At the heart of operating strategy is the task of balancing efficiency (minimum cost) against effectiveness (maximum customer satisfaction). Scheduling is an important part of the trade-off because as well as being its core product, a schedule is an airline's 'production plan'; the efficiency with which the plan is implemented drives both costs and, through the impact of reliability on customer satisfaction and repeat business, revenues.

A schedule will directly affect unit revenue, yield, and load factor on the revenue side of the income statement, and unit cost on the other side. We will break down this complexity by looking first at the costs and benefits of using high frequencies – rather than larger aircraft operated at lower frequency – to deliver a given level of output, and then at the effect of scheduling on resource utilisation.

THE COSTS AND BENEFITS OF USING HIGH FREQUENCIES TO SUPPLY OUTPUT

We have already seen that an airline's schedule should ideally be driven by the time-preferences of targeted customers. Where high frequencies are required by a given market or segment, there are both costs and benefits to consider.

Costs

High frequencies are expensive to produce relative to lower frequencies with larger aircraft (of the same technological generation). There are three issues here:

1. If acceptable load factors are to be achieved, high frequencies on any route generally require the operation of smaller aircraft than could be sustained were frequencies lower. Although their individual trip costs might be lower, the seat-mile costs of smaller aircraft are generally higher than the seat-mile costs of larger aircraft of a similar technological generation – as we saw in Chapter 5. In other words, the unit cost of supplying 400,000 non-stop ASMs a day between two points 1000 miles apart will be higher if output is generated by flying 400 seats in four 100-seat departures rather than two 200-seat departures; the question therefore arises whether unit revenue earned from producing output over four flights rather than two are sufficient to cover those higher costs and earn a profit.
2. Departure cost per enplaned passenger will most probably rise as passengers are split into an increasing number of departures, because the fixed handling and dispatch costs associated with each flight are being spread over a smaller number of passengers per flight.
3. Slot productivity, in terms of passengers enplaned or RPMs produced, is lower when a departure at a slot-constrained airport is flown by a smaller aircraft than would be used were the service concerned to be operated by a larger aircraft at a lower frequency.

Against these costs can be balanced a number of potential benefits.

Benefits

We have seen that the more frequently an airline serves a given route, the more likely it is that it will be able to match a greater proportion of customers' preferred departure times, or at least reduce the implicit time-costs of not matching them. This can provide one or both of two benefits:

1. Because business travellers generally value their time more highly than most leisure travellers, the demand for business travel has historically been sufficiently price-inelastic to permit airlines to build into their tariffs a charge to compensate for the

high seat-mile costs that high frequencies imply on all but the most dense routes. Routes with a substantial business travel segment are therefore likely to be able to support the costs of a high-frequency operation – although almost by definition a high-frequency schedule will include several off-peak departures (e.g., away from the morning and afternoon/early evening peaks in short-haul business markets), and these might suffer from yield softness.

2. As we have already noted several times in different contexts, the S-curve theory holds that the carrier with most frequencies on a route (assuming a given aircraft size) will attract a higher percentage market share and revenue share than the proportion of total frequencies contributed by its services. The S-curve is commonly derived from a plot of market share (the dependent variable) on the vertical axis against frequency share on the horizontal, although other formulations – such as revenue share against share of non-stop seats – are also widely used. Although not universally accepted, there are reasons why this dominance theory might be borne out in practice:

- Assuming a reasonable spread of departure timings (i.e., effective time-of-day coverage), the carrier with most frequencies – the dominant carrier – could very plausibly come closest to meeting the time-preferences of a greater proportion of total passengers on a route than its frequencies represent as a proportion of total frequencies; this could hold until so many frequencies are offered that customers attribute little or no further value to time savings brought about by another frequency – as in the British Airways LHR–JFK example mentioned above.

- Offering more frequencies than competitors is likely to lead to a position for the airline's services at or close to the top of the first page of GDS displays more often than would be achieved by lower-frequency competitors – assuming the enquiry is schedule- rather than price-driven.

- If an airline offers, say, three return flights on a route each day it is providing nine return products insofar as a passenger departing on any of the three outbound services can return on any of the three inbound services. (These are not necessarily all day-return products, of course.) On the other hand, a competitor offering two return flights has only four products available; by offering just one extra rotation, the first carrier is therefore able to provide nine of the thirteen single-carrier products on offer. This accounts for the tendency of strong competitors in a market not dominated by any one of them to want to at least match frequencies.

High frequencies have generally been held to yield a revenue premium insofar as they attract schedule-sensitive business travellers who value the flexibility to book and rebook at short notice, and who accordingly tend to purchase relatively high late-booked or walk-up fares. Thus, offering 300 seats a day in a market by scheduling double-daily 150-seaters is likely, in many markets, to generate more revenue than a single 300-seat departure. The question therefore is whether those incremental revenues outstrip the incremental costs of offering two flights rather than one. This question becomes even more potent when a carrier adds a new type in order to build frequencies in business markets during off-peak times of day – part of Virgin Blue's strategy in buying Embraer 170s and 190s to supplement its B737-700/800s.

There is a caveat, however: where a route out of a network carrier's hub relies heavily on feed, the ability to add further frequencies outside existing waves might be constrained – unless, perhaps, a smaller aircraft is available and can be filled above break-even load factor by local O&D traffic. In other words, a hub carrier's frequency per destination might well be constrained by the number of waves it operates at the hub.

Particularly – but not only – in business segments, frequency is one of the most important forms of non-price competition open to airlines in liberalised or deregulated markets. Pursuit of both network reach and schedule dominance have together been a key motivator behind hub-and-spoke carriers building service at their hubs; in other words, a network carrier able to establish broad market coverage out of a hub and frequency dominance in most or all of those markets is very likely to dominate market share. That this is not an immutable law, however, is evidenced by the elimination of several US Airways hubs by Southwest. Indeed, many point-to-point operators also strive to build frequency dominance as soon as possible after entering a market. Whilst there will always be exceptions, there is often a strong argument for growing a network or route structure in the following order of priority: build frequencies on existing routes; add links between stations already served; add links to new stations.

Conclusion

The smaller an aircraft serving a route, the sooner demand growth is likely to lead to spill. Models have been developed, notably by airframe manufacturers, to help arrive at frequency/capacity trade-offs given demand conditions in both directions on a route. The fact that demand in both directions has to be considered is clearly important.

At what point should a move to a larger aircraft be made? The answer depends on two primary considerations:

1. The capacity/frequency trade-off required by demand, competition, and product design requirements in the market(s) concerned.
2. Average load factor and yield on the existing departures.
    *   Load factor: in principle, we might shift to a larger aircraft if we do not want to add frequencies and the load factor achieved on the current aircraft exceeds break-even load factor on the larger aircraft (given known route operating costs and assumed pricing).
    *   Yield: rather than adding output, pressure could be taken off load factors on the existing aircraft by firming yield (i.e., raising prices and/or allocating less space to low-yield fares).

(See Schipper [2001] Chapter 7 for an introduction to the economic modelling of frequency choice in air transport markets.)

RESOURCE UTILISATION

The more that resources are used, the more output they should be able to produce. The more output they produce, the greater is the amount of output over which the fixed costs associated with acquiring and operating each resource can be spread and the lower is the average fixed cost of each unit of output produced. Assuming that incremental output can be sold at a price in excess of the variable costs incurred in producing it, resources need to be utilised as much as possible. Scheduling can help or hinder this effort.

Aircraft Utilisation

A schedule will determine the number of block-hours and cycles flown, and this – in concert with fleet size and structure – will be the most significant of any airline's cost drivers. The task is to keep aircraft in the air as much as possible, and to deploy each type in markets where its profit-earning potential can be maximised. Market liberalisation or deregulation can assist in two ways:

1. Airline managers are in principle freed to manage networks and schedules to arrive at their own preferred balance between the exigencies of market demand and aircraft utilisation.
2. Pricing freedom allows them to make a range of discounted fare offers in order to achieve acceptable load factors on flights operated by types that would be too large for a route were less pricing flexibility available. (This assumes that the discounted fares are profitable, of course; if they are not, then a smaller type needs to be deployed.)

However, even airlines which share broadly similar business models and operating strategies do not necessarily adopt the same approach to aircraft assignment. For example, Europe's two largest LFAs, easyJet and Ryanair, base often small numbers of aircraft in multiple cities across the continent and operate a complex structure of overlapping point-to-point services, whereas Southwest flows its entire fleet around the whole network.

We have already seen that two linked scheduling decisions in particular can have a profound impact on aircraft utilisation: transit/turnaround times and scheduled block-times. An even more profound issue is the nature of the markets being served. Short-haul markets generally support lower aircraft utilisation than medium- and (particularly) long-haul markets for two reasons: first, short-haul aircraft spend more time on the ground because their flight-legs are by definition shorter; and second, short-haul passengers are often unwilling to fly at night whereas passengers travelling in one or both directions on many long-haul routes have no alternative. There are some caveats here, however:

- The effect of turn-times can narrow the gap somewhat insofar as transit times for long-haul aircraft are usually an hour or more and turnaround times are longer than that, whilst low-fare short-haul carriers in particular are able to turn aircraft around in 20–30 minutes. The utilisation gap between the two types of operation nonetheless remains significant.
- Carriers able to overnight short-haul aircraft at a maintenance facility can use downtime for phased checks and/or deep cleaning.
- Some short-haul markets do tolerate overnight scheduling if fares are sufficiently low. Most obviously, North European charter carriers operate 24-hour schedules to the Mediterranean and back throughout the peak summer season. In the mid-1990s America West began 'Nite Flite' services at Las Vegas. In the late 1990s Cathay Pacific started offering low-fare intra-Asian passenger services at night on flights being operated primarily to move belly-hold freight under contract for DHL.

The fundamental issue with regard to aircraft utilisation is the way in which an airline manages its output in response to the characteristics of demand in markets being served. Additional frequencies boost aircraft utilisation, but whether or not they are feasible will depend on traffic density and mix: density has to be sufficient to support higher frequencies, and the traffic mix has to generate yields sufficient to support the cost of operating them. (Density and mix are of course linked variables intermediated by the price-elasticity of demand.) In general, higher frequencies provide airlines with more flexibility in aircraft and crew scheduling – the latter subject to regulatory and also often contractual duty-time restrictions – and so facilitate higher utilisation.

Network geography can also be significant. Relative proximity to South America enables TAP Portugal to devote just one aircraft to most South Atlantic routes whereas carriers based in northern Europe cannot schedule a 24-hour return rotation. Finnair, based astride the great circle route between north-west Europe and points in east Asia, has a similar advantage over many of its west European competitors.

Demand peaking complicates the scheduling task. There might not be enough of the right aircraft available to generate output at peak times, but there will likely be more than enough in off-peak periods. We have seen that the answer to the latter problem could be to boost off-peak utilisation by deploying aircraft onto non-core routes or by adding capacity in existing markets. Whether or not this can be done profitably depends upon how the word 'profitable' is defined, which in turn is in part a function of cost allocation.

Efficient scheduling can have a profound impact on aircraft utilisation – effectively augmenting the fleet without acquiring additional aircraft; incremental output produced by the higher utilisation of existing resources generally comes very much cheaper than that produced by new assets, because the latter bring with them an extra set of fixed costs. On the other hand, over-aggressive scheduling affects reported ontime performance and this, as already noted, has led some US carriers in particular to stretch their block-times – the benefit being improved perceptions amongst customers.

Utilisation Of Resources Other Than Aircraft

An airline's flight schedule drives the scheduling of other resources. Fortunately, there are large numbers of software products now on the market to help even small carriers without their own operations research functions optimise the deployment of human and other resources. The following represent just a sample of the areas covered (Baldanza and Lipkus 2000).

Flight-crew scheduling   The scheduling of pilots is amongst the most challenging of resource scheduling/productivity optimisation problems because they are subject to legal and contractual duty-time limits as well as recurrent training requirements, because their scheduling must also generally reflect intangible quality-of-life requirements, and because pilot schedules have to be integrated with layover accommodation (the securing of which can also be automated). Pilot scheduling is a particularly critical exercise because this employee group represents such an expensive resource. It is also computationally intensive, and for this reason is typically broken down into two stages: crew pairing and crew rostering (Bazargan 2004).

Pilot scheduling has been increasingly integrated with aircraft routing in some short-haul networks (e.g., American and Delta) because the ability to keep a crew and an aircraft together through a sequence of short-haul rotations can reduce crew turn-times. For example, if an aircraft can be turned in 30 minutes whilst a crew connection requires 45 minutes, it might under certain assumed integration patterns be possible to raise aircraft utilisation by keeping one crew with the aircraft for as long as is legally and contractually permissible; this also reduces the possibility that an aircraft ready to depart from a hub on schedule will be delayed by the late arrival of its crew on another aircraft. However, the fact that aircraft utilisation each day generally exceeds legally permissible crew duty times means that crew scheduling and aircraft routing have to be treated as distinct problems (ibid.).

Although some airlines do still use heuristic or even manual techniques, optimisation models are now commonly deployed to solve flight-crew scheduling problems. Butchers *et al.* (2001), Christou *et al.* (1999), and Yu *et al.* (2004) describe solutions developed for Air New Zealand, Delta, and Continental respectively to address three fundamental crew management tasks:

- The formulation of hiring and training plans.
- The generation of legally and contractually allowable generic pairings, each beginning and ending at a crew base and lasting several days.
- The *rostering* of crew members to monthly bid lines (lines of work) which incorporate sequences of *pairings* interspersed with rest days. This is done either by assignment to pre-constructed lines or, more commonly, by bidding on the basis of seniority.

The objective is normally to cover the schedule at minimum total cost – pay, allowances, hotel and meal, ground transport, and deadheading – subject to legal, contractual, quality of life, and other specified constraints such as minimum times to change aircraft. (See Dillon and Kontogiorgis (1999) for a discussion of these tasks in the context of scheduling reserve flight-crews at US Airways. For a recent study on how to integrate the crew scheduling and aircraft assignment problems with each other and with day of operation crew recovery, see Medard and Sawhney (2007).)

The scheduling of flight attendants is not dissimilar in principle, but with one significant distinction where an airline operates multiple aircraft types: whereas pilots generally have current ratings on only one type, or a closely related family of types, cabin crew can very often be rostered across different sub-fleets.

Ground staff scheduling Rostering models are available to help optimise staff assignments subject to shift patterns and labour contract constraints (ibid., Broggio *et al.* 2000). Again, there is an effectiveness/efficiency trade-off to be arrived at within the context of a particular airline's service concept. Because time spent waiting for service is an important input into customers' perceptions of an airline's overall service package, it is critical that carriers assign resources – specifically, human resources – to processes such as check-in, baggage acceptance, and boarding in quantities sufficient to deliver the timeliness of service that targeted customers expect given the product concerned. Due to pressure on costs in recent years this is not an imperative that has been universally adhered to, especially by some US and European majors; also, LFAs tend, as a matter of strategy, to be sparing in their assignment of check-in and gate staff.

Scheduling station resources The higher the number of departures per station, the more output there is over which to spread fixed costs associated with ramp, terminal, and other station resources. On the other hand, those resources themselves – counters, gates, ground equipment, catering facilities, line maintenance capacity, and baggage handling systems for example – also need scheduling to ensure sufficient availability during peak periods. (Whether each of these is the responsibility of the airline, the airport authority, or a third-party service provider will of course vary from station to station.) Peaking is a problem insofar as a given investment in station resources might be adequate to support a certain number of turnarounds spread relatively evenly throughout the day, but not the same number of turnarounds clustered into a small number of waves – hence the appeal of rolling hubs.

In summary, the higher the number and more even the spread of daily departures, the higher station resource utilisation is likely to be; the lower the number and more peaked the pattern of departures, the lower it is likely to be. (Bear in mind that where ground support equipment [GSE] is type-specific, its utilisation is driven not by raw departure figures but by departures of the aircraft type concerned.)

IV. Scheduling: A Response to External Constraints

Deployment of capacity is constrained by more than a need to balance the characteristics of demand with the costs of supply at an acceptable price. It is also constrained by external considerations such as time zones and their impact on the commercial viability of arrival and departure times (especially in respect of long-haul flights), curfews and noise quotas, the terms of bilateral ASAs governing international flights, the availability of take-off and landing slots (discussed in Chapter 4), airport MCTs, gate space and counters at congested airports, and also by competitors' activities. Deregulation removes a significant constraint. In Europe, for example, LFAs have been able to respond to the removal of artificial constraints on routes, aircraft size, and frequency by creating a dense web of routes operated at frequencies tailored to suit both market demand and operational requirements. Gulf LFAs Air Arabia and Jazeera, on the other hand, are constrained by the terms of bilateral ASAs to operate some routes less than daily.

Curfews   Curfews are a constraint in some markets, particularly long-haul. For example, the fact that neither Singapore nor Hong Kong has a night curfew makes it feasible for westbound departures to be timed for the late evening, which allows them both to pick up incoming daytime feed and then arrive in Europe in the early morning after the end of any local curfews and in time to make onward connections. Conversely, the fact that Tokyo Narita has a 2300–0600 curfew makes westbound evening departures non-viable because they would have to leave mid-evening and so arrive in Europe in the middle of the night – which means that most westbound flights from Narita to Europe depart in the morning and arrive in the afternoon. (Tokyo's problem in this context could be solved after the opening in 2010 of a fourth runway at Haneda, which does not have a curfew; late-evening departures to Europe, arriving in the early morning would be feasible – were the government to permit the airport to be used for long-haul services such as these.)

Time zones   On many long-haul routes (especially North Atlantic, North Pacific, and Europe–Asia) the effects of time zones tend to frame relatively narrow windows within which competitors must cluster if they are to schedule feasible and/or desirable arrival times – with feasibility and desirability determined by passenger preferences, airport curfews and noise quotas, and the availability of onward connections.

Eastbound departures from the US east coast to Europe generally leave in the late afternoon or early evening because any earlier and they would arrive in the middle of the night whilst any later and they would miss the outbound bank of southbound and eastbound medium- and long-haul connections that leave major European hubs in the morning. Westbound flights to Europe from East and Southeast Asia tend to leave late in the evening in order to avoid curfews at European airports and to catch outbound morning banks for short-haul intra-European connections. These intercontinental timings feed through to the timings of return legs insofar as airlines generally want to boost aircraft utilisation by turning their aircraft around as quickly as possible; where time zones preclude this (e.g., Qantas at London Heathrow), downtime during the day can be used for phased maintenance work. As demand has grown in some dense international markets such as New York–London, Singapore–London, and Hong Kong–London, it has become increasingly feasible to schedule earlier departures carrying predominantly local traffic that prefers a daylight flight and is not concerned about poor availability of onward connections off an evening arrival.

Seasonal time changes to and from daylight saving can also pose a challenge whenever they require a choice between maintaining year-round consistency of timings either at the point of departure or, alternatively, at the destination. The challenge is exacerbated where convenience relative to connecting services at one or both ends of the route is important to the maintenance of flow traffic (Vomhof 2007).

V. Scheduling a Hub-and-Spoke Network

Scheduling over one or more integrated hubs clearly poses challenges more complicated than those faced in traditional, out-and-back networks. Many can be attributed to the fact that, more so than point-to-point operators, hub-and-spoke carriers design and schedule *routes* but serve *markets*; the schedule established for each route has to take account of the requirements of customers in the various different markets served by that route.

The marketing objective of any hub is to maximise connectivity between points of origin and final destinations, subject to a commercially and operationally acceptable layover between each pair of incoming and outgoing flights. This section will start by looking at the impact of network design and scheduling on the density of traffic on individual routes, and then consider a selection of other hub scheduling issues.

THE IMPACT OF NETWORK DESIGN AND SCHEDULING ON TRAFFIC DENSITY

It was stressed at the beginning of the last chapter that 'route' and 'market' are not necessarily synonymous; passengers travelling on a particular route (e.g., Dallas–Miami) could have connected from behind (e.g., Albuquerque) and/or be connecting beyond (e.g., to St. Thomas) – and therefore may be travelling in a different O&D city-pair market (e.g., Albuquerque–St. Thomas) to the non-stop market served by the route concerned. The way in which a network is designed and scheduled will affect the routing of these flows, and in doing this impact upon traffic densities – and therefore the optimum choice of aircraft – on individual routes. The carrier in the above example might, for instance, also offer an inter-hub route from Dallas to San Juan, together with connections providing a schedule that some Albuquerque–St. Thomas travellers prefer to the routing via Miami.

Hub-and-spoke networks have been developed to manage traffic flows by using hubs to accumulate and distribute passengers (and freight) from and to outlying points. They can affect traffic densities and equipment choice on individual routes in one or all of three ways:

1.   We noted above that because flights down a spoke to a hub carry passengers proceeding on to multiple destinations, they have higher densities and can in principle be operated by larger aircraft than point-to-point flights serving each individual market out of the spoke city could support – thereby reducing unit (i.e., seat-mile) costs.
2.   Hubs in either single-airline or alliance multi-hub networks can be connected by relatively large aircraft and/or relatively high frequencies to exploit the increased traffic generated by channelling flows between them. Traffic densities between Detroit and Minneapolis and between Detroit and Amsterdam are both very much higher than they would be were these cities not hubs between which double-connect flow traffic is being channelled. Indeed, one of the most important marketing benefits of a multi-hub alliance is that integration of the separate networks often supports higher inter-hub frequencies than would otherwise be the case, making available a greater range of alternative connections between origins behind one hub and destinations beyond the other.
3.   By offering alternative paths and (depending upon scheduling decisions) perhaps more connection opportunities, a multi-hub network may provide a higher level of service than a single hub. On the other hand, it might actually reduce densities on some routes; taking the example above, availability of a Dallas–San Juan inter-hub connection will divert some Albuquerque–St. Thomas traffic off the Dallas–Miami and Miami–St. Thomas routes and onto the Dallas–San Juan and San Juan–St. Thomas routes. (Whilst Albuquerque–St. Thomas traffic is fairly thin, if we think of traffic flowing between hundreds of origins and hundreds of destinations in thousands of city-pair markets – no matter how thin each might be in itself – the potential impact of route and scheduling decisions on traffic density, aircraft selection, and therefore the economics of individual routes is clearly significant.)

Of course, all that such networks are doing is reorienting traffic flows. The basic decision regarding how to allocate capacity still has to be made within this reoriented framework: higher frequencies with smaller aircraft offering lower individual trip costs and perhaps higher seat-mile costs, or fewer frequencies with larger aircraft whose seat-mile costs will probably be lower and whose individual trip costs will be higher – but whose aggregate trip costs may or may not exceed aggregate trip costs associated with higher-frequency/lower-capacity options.

Schedule saleability can be affected by even minor changes in departure times, and the financial effects of this are leveraged through load factors. For example, if a schedule change results in an increase of just five or ten extra connecting passengers, much of the additional revenue earned should go straight through to the bottom line because of the low marginal costs of carrying them. On the other hand, the same operating leverage effect means that diversion of just a few passengers can turn a series of flights from profit into loss – perhaps because the revised schedule is less attractive than a competitor's schedule, because its GDS display screen position has been compromised, or because it dislocates linkages between flights. Tretheway (1998, pp. 652–653) exemplifies the point:

> Consider the example of a new service from Boston to Vancouver. If the flight is off-peak, perhaps at 3P.M., the carrier must cover the cost solely through origin and destination traffic. But if the flight

can arrive during the noon 'Asian flight bank,' the carrier may be able to win an extra fifty connecting passengers per day. These incremental connects not only generate incremental Boston–Vancouver revenues but also contribute traffic to other flights such as Vancouver–Nagoya, Vancouver–Tokyo, Vancouver–Beijing, Vancouver–Hong Kong, Vancouver–Kuala Lumpur, and so forth. Supposing that the average airfare is $2,000 for a Boston–Asia passenger, then the airline's ability to grow on the peak is worth an additional $100,000 *per day* in incremental system revenue. On an annual basis, this comes to $36 million. A carrier building a hub could find similar incremental peak-period revenues on a range of potential routes. Growth off-peak is expensive (or, more precisely, uneconomic).

Generally speaking, only if there is very strong local traffic, a need to match a competitor's frequencies, and/or a profitable opportunity to raise aircraft utilisation is it justifiable for a hub-and-spoke carrier to operate flights into a hub that are unconnected to a wave – or, at a de-peaked hub, to a reasonable number of marketable connections.

SOME OTHER IMPORTANT HUB SCHEDULING ISSUES

Hub scheduling also gives rise to several other issues, the most important of which we will look at in the next few subsections.

Infrastructure Congestion

There are three levels on which congestion might make itself felt:

1. *Schedule adjustment* If runway, gate, and/or terminal capacity is constrained at a hub, an airline might have relatively little flexibility to reschedule a particular arrival or departure. (Of course, a dominant carrier at a slot-constrained hub should in principle be able to reallocate its slot portfolio more readily than minor players with smaller portfolios.) When a route serves two slot-constrained hubs, the adjustment challenge is even greater.
2. *Outstation connectivity* It is possible that decisions might have to be taken to exclude certain spoke cities from connection to a capacity-constrained wave, giving them connections instead into alternate waves. (In fact, depending upon the nature of points served on a network it could be that not every spoke will anyway merit a connection to every complex. A leisure destination might not need connecting to the early and late waves that are so important to business markets and which generate intense peaks, but could well suffice with being connected just to lower volume waves in the middle of the day. However, this might not apply to destinations serving short-break leisure traffic that needs late-Friday outbound and late-Sunday inbound services.)
3. *Hub development* At its most extreme, an infrastructure constraint might prevent a carrier from developing a fully effective hub at all. The facts that London Heathrow has only two runways and that until completion of Terminal 5 its long- and short-haul passengers were largely segregated into separate terminals on different parts of the airport have prevented British Airways from developing a fully functioning hub; the single runway at London Gatwick remains a constraint on large-scale hubbing. Both situations compare unfavourably with those at some other European hubs, most notably Paris CDG and Amsterdam Schipol, and at the principal US hubs. (Whereas around 60 per cent of Air France traffic at CDG connects, the figure for British Airways at Heathrow peaked in the mid-1990s at approximately 40 per cent and has since declined.)

Hub Sequencing

A hub generally serves spokes of different lengths which, depending on the equipment used as well as the stage-lengths involved, dictate different block-times. This can be seen at its most extreme in combined domestic/international hubs, and it raises the question of how most efficiently and effectively to sequence flights in incoming and outgoing banks.

Taking the hypothetical example of a domestic hub, assume that the flight-time from hub H to spoke city A is 70 minutes and from H to spoke city B is 90 minutes. Further assume that both aircraft leave H at approximately the same time and will need to have completed their rotations and be ready to depart H again 4 hours later as part of a 240-minute hub-repeat cycle. (A hub-repeat cycle is defined by the time between the same points in consecutive complexes [Dennis 1994] – such as first or last arrival, or first or last departure.) The aircraft serving B will spend 60 minutes (i.e., 240–90–90) on the ground during the 4-hour cycle, whilst the aircraft serving A will spend 100 minutes (i.e., 240–70–70) on the ground; both have too much slack time, but the problem at spoke city A is particularly egregious. ('Slack time' is time spent on the ground in excess of what is required to turn an aircraft around.) This simple example points to several issues:

1. *Aircraft utilisation* Short spokes in particular can threaten aircraft utilisation. Answers might include:
   - multi-stop or triangular routings, although these have to be balanced against the product degradation they entail for some passengers;
   - scheduling short spokes out last and back first to minimise slack time at the outstation, and allocating the incoming aircraft to an early departure in the next outbound bank so that it does not simply spend a long period on the ground at the hub rather than at the outstation.

   Choosing instead to bring the aircraft back off a short spoke significantly ahead of the next inbound bank might be an option as well, but the risk arises that if the spoke city is also connected to another carrier's hub then passengers may choose that carrier should it offer a better aggregate O&D journey time. Even where this is not the case and passengers have no alternative other than to travel via the hub in question, if competing carriers also serve that hub and schedule convenient connections the spoke might simply be feeding those competitors – something that any schedule-planning department should in practice be keen to avoid.

   The problem is less acute when a short spoke feeds into a rolling or continuous hub. The traffic flows at a sizeable multidirectional rolling hub such as Chicago O'Hare are likely to be sufficient to allow an aircraft turning quickly at a nearby spoke city to return to the hub and feed a significant number of points outbound, even though the lack of a tightly defined wave leaves it unable to feed every potentially feasible destination on the other side of the hub within a commercially acceptable connecting time.

2. *Pacing spokes* The most distant outstation served by a hub (i.e., the one with the longest block-time) is often referred to as a 'pacing spoke'. The longer a pacing spoke, the more scope there is to encounter en route delays and, more significantly, the more it eats into the hub turnaround time between successive inbound and outbound banks. Flights serving the longest spokes therefore tend to be amongst the first to leave in a departing bank and are often amongst the last to arrive in an inbound bank. This could present connectivity issues, depending upon the precise relationship between

out-and-back block-times on the one hand and the length of the hub-repeat cycle on the other. Another option, or in some cases a necessity, might be to connect the longest spoke(s) to alternate inbound banks rather than to every one. In a multi-hub system the best way forward could be to connect a distant spoke city to alternate inbound banks at more than one hub in order to maintain behind/beyond O&D frequencies.

Looking at hub-sequencing on a more general level, there are several other issues:

- *Last-in first-out* Some observers argue that the last aircraft on an inbound bank and the first on the connecting outbound bank should be a through-numbered same-plane service that supports good local traffic on both inbound and outbound legs and, importantly, a strong through-flow – the latter to minimise waiting times for a significant number of passengers (Berdy 1998). There is a counter-argument that placing high-volume arrivals late on an inbound bank and high-volume departures early on an outbound bank can disrupt an unnecessarily large number of connections in the event of inbound delays – particularly delays affecting the high-volume arrival.
- *Widebodies* As far as possible, widebodies should be scheduled to arrive early and depart late in connecting banks to allow time for their slower turnarounds and, especially in the case of international flights, longer passenger facilitation processes.
- *Regional aircraft* Particularly where they are parked on remote stands and passengers have to be bussed (as well, perhaps, as making inter-terminal transfers), there can be merit in scheduling regional aircraft to arrive early and depart late in connecting banks.

Misconnections

Because in a large network not all points that might merit connections can necessarily be linked in a single wave, due to capacity constraints at the hub for example, decisions often have to be taken in respect of which points are in fact to be connected in each wave; furthermore, some thin spokes anyway might not support flights connecting into and out of every wave. This type of timetable asymmetry could affect the opportunity to make day-return trips in short-haul markets, and/or same-day connections in medium- or long-haul markets. One way around the problem might be to pair two thin and reasonably adjacent spokes into a triangular routing (e.g., H–A–B–H for wave 1 outbound and wave 2 inbound, followed by H–B–A–H for wave 2 outbound and wave 3 inbound). On a separate but related point, it is unlikely that medium- and long-haul routes into and out of a mixed domestic/international hub will connect with every wave; some might sustain only daily or double-daily widebody services, and most will face some sort of time zone constraint on scheduling flexibility.

Even once a decision has been taken to feed a particular spoke into an arriving bank, it might not be feasible to schedule that arrival to connect with every departure on the other side of the wave; the overlapping of inbound and outbound banks (i.e., the scheduling of the first departure for a time that is less than the MCT from the last arrival) might be necessary to overcome infrastructural constraints or to sustain acceptable aircraft utilisation levels. If in order to meet hub efficiency and schedule saleability targets it is inevitable that some flights on an inbound bank cannot deliver the MCT required to connect with some flights on the corresponding outbound bank, these misconnections should only be scheduled in respect of markets with relatively small and/or low-yield O&D traffic flows.

Where To Overnight Short-Haul Aircraft

Much depends upon whether a particular short-haul spoke city is predominantly an origin or a destination – or, alternatively, whether there is reasonable balance.

Spoke city as origin   Where a spoke city is a strong outbound traffic generator, carriers will in many cases want to overnight an aircraft there to provide a competitive early departure that is able to feed the first outbound bank from their hub and – in some short-haul markets – to offer day-return possibilities in the local market between the outstation and the hub; this is a common operating pattern within both Europe and North America, because many secondary and tertiary points on short- and medium-haul networks are more significant originators of outbound traffic than magnets for inbound traffic. However:

- the assumption here is that the block-time concerned allows a departure that is both marketable (i.e., not before 06:00) and yet early enough to fit into the hub's first inbound bank, but in fact some longer short-haul spokes might cause a problem in this regard;
- time zones can also have an influence: westbound first-out departures which cross time zones can benefit from time 'saved', whilst early eastbound departures might be penalised to the point where they arrive at the hub too late to connect with the first outbound bank.

Against the marketing benefits offered by overnighting down a spoke have to be weighed the costs of crew accommodation and allowances, and the fact that aircraft stabled away from a maintenance base are not available for phased checks or deep cleaning. These problems can be avoided if there is a partner based at the spoke city which could operate the first outbound service as a code-share.

Spoke city as destination   Some spokes are less likely to originate early-morning traffic than to attract it, either from the hub itself or from origins behind the hub. The fundamental question is where the bulk of this inbound traffic originates. If it largely flows from behind the hub, there might be a strong case for stabling aircraft overnight at originating cities. If it originates primarily at the hub, there could be a case for serving the spoke destination ahead of the first inbound bank (because feed from that bank is not being relied upon), using aircraft stabled overnight at the hub. Another consideration is whether the airline in question has incoming overnight long-haul traffic to feed early-morning short-haul departures from the hub and compensate for a lack of short-haul feed at that hour – something that is often the case at major European hubs, for example.

By choosing to overnight short-haul aircraft at a hub rather than at outstations a carrier is in effect breaking a wave – leaving an 'orphan' late-night inbound bank without onward connections, and an 'orphan' early-morning outbound bank without short-haul feed. There need to be sound commercial and/or operational reasons for doing this.

Delay Propagation

A delay can easily propagate around a highly integrated and tightly scheduled hub-and-spoke network. One approach to dealing with this is building more buffer time into the schedule. For example, in 2001 Northwest put back by 15 minutes the third and fourth waves at its Memphis hub to allow aircraft more time on the ground at spoke cities between waves two and three and by doing this provide an opportunity to catch-up with any earlier delays. It is critical that the first departures of the day in a short-haul network keep to schedule to avoid as far as possible the risk that early morning problems will propagate throughout the day.

Scheduling Multi-Hub Networks

To maximise the connectivity of multi-hub alliance networks it is desirable to schedule partners' networks as a single entity – as Air France and Delta are now doing. (This is only permissible for US and European airlines when antitrust immunity and European Commission approval respectively have been granted.) There are two key variables with regard to both single-airline and alliance multi-hub network scheduling: spoke connections and inter-hub connections.

Spoke connections   Fundamental decisions include the selection of the hub(s) to which each spoke city is to be connected and, in the case of connections to more than one hub, the choice of how many waves at each to connect into. (Note that scheduling simultaneous departures to different hubs could induce a peaking problem at the spoke city, leading to resource utilisation penalties.)

Inter-hub connections   There are two types:

1. *Non-stop* Common in both international alliance hubbing and US domestic multi-hub systems, inter-hub non-stops are used both for local traffic and – more particularly in the case of international networks – to channel double-connecting flow traffic between secondary or tertiary points behind one hub and beyond the other. It is important as far as possible to ensure that a departing flight coincides with an outbound bank at the first hub (to ensure it receives good feed from the earlier inbound bank) and arrives during an inbound bank at the second hub (to ensure good onward connections on the other side of the wave). Time zones often complicate this challenge in respect of long-haul flights; a related scheduling difficulty arises on some long-haul inter-hub routes where one or both of the hubs operate only a small number of daily waves, so limiting cross-connect possibilities.
2. *Multi-stop* Particularly in US domestic systems, it is not uncommon for an aircraft to leave one hub on a one- or two-stop journey to another hub. By doing this it is serving the intermediate point(s) as part of an outbound bank from the first hub, and an inbound bank to the second hub. This type of aircraft scheduling can help to get around some of the spoke-city slack time (i.e., low aircraft utilisation) problems discussed above, but the potential downside is that it may also contribute to the propagation of delays between hubs – which is why some carriers have chosen to isolate particularly troublesome hubs from the rest of their system when assigning

aircraft (e.g., United at Chicago O'Hare). Operating patterns such as this are still relatively uncommon amongst European majors, most of which have just a single significant hub, but with consolidation gaining momentum more possibilities to integrate aircraft flows around joint short-haul systems will arise.

Generally, the more hubs in a network that are accessible to each origin and destination and the higher the inter-hub frequencies, the more competitive the airline or alliance will be – in terms of frequency and journey time – in double-connect markets. (See Dennis [2000], for example.)

Weekend Schedules

Some short-haul operations have weekend schedules significantly different from their weekday schedules to accommodate different patterns of demand, different volumes of traffic, and perhaps also the need to release aircraft for charters or maintenance. Together, these considerations might require different routing patterns (e.g., replacing non-stops with connecting service), different frequencies and the assignment of different aircraft types. Short-haul weekend operations can also present a fleet assignment challenge, with the need to link aircraft location on a Friday night into the weekend schedule, and on a Sunday night into the weekday schedule. (See Kontogiorgis and Acharya [1999] for an approach to the solution of this problem.)

The Impact Of Network Design And Hub Scheduling On Fleet Mix

If we assume that the number of daily waves at a particular hub is given and that as far as possible it is desirable to have most spokes connected into every one, then clearly the frequency of service to and from each outstation is also given. If we further assume that a carrier operates, say, four waves a day at a particular hub, it is fairly unlikely that traffic on each spoke will support four return trips using a single aircraft type; some might support four B757 rotations, some four A320 rotations, some four CRJ200s, and some will require a mix of different types at different times of the day and week. Hub scheduling strategy will therefore superimpose itself on the specific requirements of individual routes to determine an optimal fleet mix – a mix which, incidentally, can benefit greatly from the availability of different-sized variants within families such as the B737, A320, CRJ, and Embraer series. We will return to this last point in Chapter 8.

The Future For Hubs

Notably in the United States, the period after 9/11 saw hubs come under intense scrutiny because the high costs of operating them – relative to offering point-to-point services – were no longer being underwritten by high-yield business travellers in the new, profoundly weakened revenue environment. Some observers have questioned the continued viability of hub-and-spoke systems generally, and in particular the scheduling of arrival and departure banks into tight time windows. It is too early to perform 'last rites' on hub systems, however.

Hubs will survive   There are two principal reasons:

- First, despite the ongoing growth of hub-bypass operations there will continue to be many relatively thin markets connecting secondary and tertiary points which can only be served by hubbing, because non-stop service at a marketable frequency is uneconomic.
- Second, too much has been invested by majors in their hubs to walk away from them. Less emotionally and more pertinently, because the network majors as a whole will have difficulty getting their short-haul unit costs down to the levels achieved by low-fare competitors they need sources of differentiation in order to generate the higher RASMs that their higher CASMs make essential. Hubs offer a connectivity benefit for which some market segments are prepared to pay.

Hubs will have to continue becoming more efficient   We have seen that one of the primary sources of cost in a hub operation is the adverse impact that self-induced peaking has on resource utilisation. We have also seen that some majors have addressed this problem by de-peaking their busiest hubs (e.g., American at Chicago O'Hare, Dallas-Fort Worth, and Miami). De-peaking gives precedence to the maximisation of aircraft and hub resource utilisation over the minimisation of mean and median passenger connection times. Instead of arrivals and departures being bunched into a number of waves operating within tightly constrained time windows, they are spread more evenly throughout the day: if a day's departures are broken down into 30-minute blocks, a peaked hub will have several blocks in which the number greatly exceeds average whilst a rolling hub will have fewer and smaller deviations. The benefits to the airline of a 'rolling hub' are higher resource utilisation and lower airside and landside congestion, whereas the cost to the passenger is generally longer connection times. The position can be summarised as follows:

- De-peaking was *necessitated* at several US hubs after 9/11 by a precipitous decline in the high-yield traffic relied upon under the post-deregulation network carrier business model to support the high cost of hub operations.
- De-peaking was *facilitated* by the increased willingness of consumers – particularly in US domestic markets – to accept longer elapsed journey times, attributable largely to longer hub transits, in return for the lower fares now being demanded. It has also been facilitated by the growing significance of Internet distribution relative to traditional agency channels: whereas GDS screen position, in part reflecting elapsed journey times, can be an important driver of consumer purchase behaviour when agencies are used, Internet channels tend to be more price-oriented. (This is not to say that journey times are now unimportant – just that their weighting relative to price has become weaker in the post-9/11 US revenue environment.)

De-peaking is not the answer at every hub. First, it is easier to de-peak a mega-hub than a secondary hub; de-peaking a relatively small hub with just a few daily waves can risk depriving it of critical mass in terms of marketable connections. Of course, this might be less an argument *against* de-peaking a secondary hub than an argument *for* closing it. Second, several international hubs outside the United States were not undermined by soft revenues to quite the same extent as was the case in respect of US domestic hubs after

9/11. Even where de-peaking is either infeasible or unwarranted, however, the majority of hub-and-spoke carriers have put a great deal of effort into raising hub efficiency – and scheduling is clearly central to such initiatives.

VI. Scheduling Tactics

What a carrier needs to achieve tactically with its scheduling will depend upon both overall strategy (e.g., whether predominantly hub-based or point-to-point) and the local competitive situation in O&D markets served. A network carrier, for example, will want to ensure that its schedule contributes to hub strength in terms of destinations served, share of departures, and share of slots and/or gates (where relevant), thereby helping create a significant barrier to entry at the hub as well as achieving high levels of network connectivity. For many carriers, frequency domination is a key scheduling objective and we will look at this first. We will also consider the importance of code-sharing and GDS displays in a scheduling context.

An important point to be borne in mind is that whether to improve its own schedule saleability or respond to a competitor's tactics, a carrier operating a tightly integrated multi-hub system (as in the US domestic market) may find it difficult to effect what might on the surface appear to be relatively minor schedule adjustments. A schedule change can, for example, have knock-on effects on the allocation of crews, station resources, maintenance capacity, and perhaps therefore other aircraft, and also on network connectivity.

FREQUENCY DOMINATION

We have already noted that deregulation, liberalisation, and the consequent emergence of hub-and-spoke networks have shaped decisions to serve growing demand, first, by increasing frequencies, and only as demand builds further (or infrastructural congestion requires) by then using larger aircraft. This approach is supported by the S-curve theory, which argues a carrier dominating frequencies on a route will benefit from a disproportionately high market share. Conversely, it has also sometimes been a reason for reluctance to cut output when conditions on a route call for retrenchment – the fear being a disproportionate loss of revenue.

The classic Southwest scheduling tactic adopted by several LFAs elsewhere in the world is to enter an underserved or badly served, dense or potentially dense, price-elastic point-to-point market with reasonably high initial frequencies, then build rapidly and dominate output whilst at the same time stimulating demand with sustainably low fares. There are actually two types of route to consider in respect of this tactic:

1. *Routes with no alternative intermediate hub* In this case, a competitor cannot engage in frequency competition by combining O&D traffic in the market concerned with traffic in other O&D markets and channelling it over the hub; there is no alternative to competing head-on in the point-to-point non-stop market. With most US majors having substantially higher short-haul operating costs than Southwest, this is unattractive insofar as their mainline operations are concerned – which is one reason why some decided to launch low-cost operations, before eventually 'biting the bullet' and tackling mainline cost structures after 9/11.
2. *Routes with an alternative intermediate hub* Where they have an intermediate hub available, the power of their hub-and-spoke networks does in principle allow

the other US majors to compete with Southwest on frequency. One of the reasons behind Southwest's success, however, is that it only enters routes that other carriers could or do serve over their hubs when these routes will support the addition of high-frequency non-stop or through-plane B737 services so that it need never be outcompeted on frequency; Southwest generally uses low fares and the price-elasticity of unserved or underserved market segments to build traffic to the density required to achieve this.

CHALLENGING AN INCUMBENT ON SHORT-HAUL POINT-TO-POINT ROUTES

A new entrant onto a route already served by frequent departures will not be offering potential customers a substantial reduction in schedule delay. Nonetheless, entry onto short-haul point-to-point routes serving a significant O&D business segment is likely to be effective only if the entrant comes close to matching the incumbent's frequencies. Even where this is economically and physically possible, it raises potential problems:

- In the short term, while demand is catching up, route entry might lead to excess output and a drop in yields.
- If it is operating aircraft having broadly the same capacity as the incumbent, the entrant will – because of the incumbent's stronger initial market presence – achieve lower load factors. If on the other hand it tries to balance market share and share of capacity offered in order to keep load factors in line with those of incumbents, whilst maintaining approximate parity in frequencies, the entrant will have to operate smaller aircraft; these may have seat-mile cost disadvantages that will need to be outweighed by lower absolute costs and/or higher productivity elsewhere in the operating system.

This is why it is clearly advantageous to target underserved price-elastic markets that have sufficient growth potential to absorb a high proportion of the incremental output brought online by a challenger, and why it is also advantageous for the challenger to have lower costs than the incumbent so that it can profitably sustain the low-fare stimulus and maintain acceptable load factors.

There are few circumstances under which a low-frequency challenge can be sustained against a high-frequency short-haul operation. Two possibilities are:

1. Where a hub carrier enters a route primarily to feed one or two of its waves rather than to tap local O&D traffic.
2. Where a low-frequency entrant offers a distinct benefit not offered by the high-frequency incumbent. Most often this will be a price benefit, and the challenger will position itself – at least publicly – as representing no threat to the incumbent's core business, either because it has no ambition to grow or it is not targeting potential flow traffic or high-yield local traffic. Having watched Delta fall for this 'puppy dog ploy' when ValuJet started operations out of Atlanta in the early 1990s, it is unlikely that any incumbent would now be sanguine.

INCUMBENTS' RESPONSES

Incumbents can use scheduling to fight off market entrants. One approach is to overschedule – that is, oversupply the market and, in all likelihood, weaken yields to the extent that the entrant cannot meet its revenue or profit projections. As we saw in Chapter 4, entrants can be attacked either by swamping them with new services, matching their frequencies head-to-head, by bracketing or sandwiching them, or by scheduling away from them to avoid the possibility of incoming passengers making a convenient offline connection. The sustainability of overscheduling will depend upon the extent to which the incumbent is able and willing to cross-subsidise the route in question, and also whether or not the challenger is financially able to sustain low yields.

There is a question as to whether this type of response is in fact commercial or predatory, and care might be needed in some jurisdictions that have actively enforced competition laws – although, as also noted in Chapter 4, predation is notoriously difficult to prove.

GDS AND SEARCH ENGINE DISPLAYS

So far in the discussion we have looked at the tactical scheduling of 'real' flights. In the battle to ensure marketplace visibility for their offers, some carriers have been using what could be characterised as aggressive techniques to make their schedules appear more competitive than in fact they are. The battleground as far as the business segment is concerned is usually page one of TMCs' GDS displays. A technique used in North America has been to allocate to each service from an outstation to a hub not only its own 'local' flight number, but also several additional flight numbers each tied into an onward flight connecting out of the hub; in this way the single service to the hub receives multiple listings that can push competitors' flights further down the screen – or off the first page altogether. Code-sharing offers similar opportunities where, for example, a single flight is listed separately under each partner's designator codes. (Ghosting and screen-padding are not permissible in some jurisdictions.)

It might be thought that such techniques will not work with regard to price-, rather than schedule-, sensitive leisure travellers who search the Web for fares. However, it is not uncommon for the same flight to get multiple listings in response to a search, thereby forcing other flights which might be only marginally more expensive but considerably more convenient onto the second or subsequent pages. On the whole, it is nonetheless true to say that the advent of the Internet – with presentations now more often ordered by price rather than schedule – has made minor variations in departure and total travel time less significant in this segment of the market than when retail agencies had greater control over information and relied on GDS displays to effect their role as 'gate-keeper'.

CONCLUSION

The essence of network management at a growing number of large airlines is to:

* *Rationalise current networks*, focusing on the profitability of individual routes and schedules. If part of a network requires a small sub-fleet which because of its size

is expensive to operate and maintain, for example, there could be an argument for dropping the routes concerned – perhaps instead code-sharing with a carrier that has a fleet and/or cost structure better-suited to serving them.

- *Extend the network and expand the schedule* – that is, add output – whilst taking on as few as possible of the incremental capacity costs that would be required to achieve this through organic growth. Code-sharing has become an important tactical weapon for use in schedule building, as well as a vehicle through which to pursue wider strategic ambitions.

VII. Interfacing Network and Fleet Management

Although the presence or absence of aircraft with particular payload–range capabilities in an airline's existing fleet does in practice have a profound impact on network management decisions, if we start with a blank sheet of paper it is network management that should drive fleet management.

- *Network design* The design of a network – which markets to serve and which routes to serve them with – reflects a balance between marketing and operational considerations, with the former predominant whenever possible, set within the context of a particular airline's strategic description of itself – as a network carrier, a regional, a point-to-point operator, or a leisure-oriented charter airline, for example. Network design establishes the broad parameters for fleet selection and management.
- *Scheduling* Having designed a network in response to actual and forecasted demand in O&D markets, scheduling is an attempt to allocate across a range of possible frequencies and timings the output required if the anticipated shares of targeted markets are to be captured. This demand allocation exercise, first discussed in Chapter 2, drives requirements for different types and variants of aircraft.

Consider the hypothetical example of an airline serving an O&D market between two non-hub points in which an average 400 passengers want to depart the origin each day (given certain assumptions about prices and other demand-determining independent variables). For the airline, the cheapest option – other things, such as aircraft utilisation issues, being equal – would be to operate a single high-density widebody with low seat-mile costs. For prospective passengers, this would pose two problems: first, many will not want to travel at or near the departure time of this single service; second, quite a few will be unwilling to endure a high-density seating configuration.

If the market has a significant segment comprised of business travellers, we might find that on average, say, 160 want to depart between 06:30 and 09:00, 160 want to depart between 16:00 and 19:00, and the remaining 80 want to leave at various other times throughout the day. The airline has several alternative options for meeting this demand:

- It could schedule non-stops – perhaps a single 180-seater or two smaller aircraft during each of the peak periods, and either a single 100-seater or two 50-seat RJs during the day. This would of course be an expensive schedule to mount in terms of both seat-mile and aggregate trip costs, so yields would need to be sufficiently firm to support the costs involved.

- Bearing passengers' time-preferences in mind, another approach open to a network carrier might, depending upon the geography of the market, be to route some services over a hub in order to thicken departing traffic volumes by combining traffic headed for other destinations onto the aircraft and perhaps in doing this raise frequencies above the number of non-stops that could be supported by a 400-passenger per day market.

The presence of a reliable LFA in the market, offering perhaps three daily B737 non-stops, could of course undermine either strategy by softening yields and offering competitive journey times. This simple example nonetheless underlines the complexity of combined network and fleet management. Let us consider another. Assume competitive pressures set a given fare for a journey from Hartford to San Francisco. Further assume that there are three feasible routings open to a particular carrier:

1. Regional feed to JFK, connecting with a transcontinental widebody.
2. Mainline narrowbody service to Chicago O'Hare, connecting with another mainline narrowbody.
3. Non-stop hub-bypass service using a mainline narrowbody.

An airline might, for the sake of argument, design its network to incorporate one or more of these options. Because each involves different production costs for the output being sold and for competitive reasons these costs cannot be reflected in the fare, ignoring the possibility that a premium *might* be earned on the non-stop route, profits will differ between routing alternatives. Further complicating the issue, as we will see in Chapter 9, is the fact that carrying passengers on two-leg itineraries over New York and Chicago involves opportunity costs insofar as they occupy seats that could instead have been sold to passengers – perhaps higher-revenue passengers – travelling either in the local markets or in other Hartford O&D markets (e.g., Hartford–Omaha via either New York or Chicago).

Whilst the exigencies of network management should be highly influential on fleet management decisions it is, as noted above, inevitable that at least in the short run the composition of a particular carrier's fleet will have a strong influence on network design and scheduling.

VIII. Summary

After first looking at a typical schedule development process, we discussed scheduling as a response to several influences: demand, the economics of supply, and various external constraints – such as time zones, airport curfews, slot availability, and so on. We then considered issues associated with scheduling a hub-and-spoke network, before next looking at alternative scheduling tactics. The chapter ended by exploring the interface between network management (design and scheduling) on the one hand, and fleet management on the other. Fleet management is the subject of the next chapter.

8

Fleet Management

There are three routes to disaster: gambling is the quickest, sex is the most enjoyable and technology the most certain.

Georges Pompidou

CHAPTER OVERVIEW

Having considered network management over the last two chapters, we turn next to a second topic central to managing capacity: fleet management. Traditionally, fleet *planning* has focused on aircraft acquisition. Many large airlines now take a broader view, with fleet *management* encompassing:

- aircraft acquisition and financing;
- tactical fleet management;
- asset value maintenance; and
- trading.

This chapter will concentrate on the first two subjects.

I. Aircraft Acquisition and Financing

An airline is in principle a portfolio of resources – some tangible, many intangible – brought together to pursue a corporate mission or purpose. In the same vein, a fleet is a portfolio assembled to fulfil a number of payload-range missions – although the word 'assembled' perhaps understates what is in many cases a huge capital investment decision spread over a long time horizon. The primary objective of fleet planning is to equate production capacity – more specifically, the output that capacity is able to produce if efficiently utilised – with forecast demand, given certain price and other marketing assumptions. In the past, there was a fairly close relationship between range and payload: the longer the range, the larger the aircraft – which gave rise to particular challenges when trying to develop long, thin routes. This relationship no longer holds, and a wide choice of payload-range mission capabilities is now available.

There are two fundamental reasons for acquiring aircraft:

1. *Replacement of existing capacity* It might be necessary to replace part of the current fleet because of high operating costs, unacceptable noise or emissions, limited remaining structural life, inadequate passenger appeal, type rationalisation, or an ongoing fleet

457

rollover policy intended to maintain a low average fleet age. The task generally is to find an aircraft capable of performing a largely unchanged mission more effectively and/or efficiently than the aircraft to be replaced. Recently, however, some carriers have been imposing greater capacity discipline on themselves by replacing older aircraft with types that are not just more operationally efficient, but smaller; Japan Airlines is a good example, gradually running down what was the world's largest B747 fleet and instead buying B777-300ERs configured with around 30 fewer seats but compensating for the loss of revenue by burning considerably less fuel and generating significantly lower trip costs. (The loss of revenue itself has been relatively small because load factors on the B747s were low enough to allow much of their traffic to be absorbed, at a higher load factor, by the B777s.)

2. *Capacity growth* Because the demand for air transport services is on the whole continuing to grow, the need to replace ageing aircraft that are becoming expensive to operate or environmentally unsound is often interlaced with the need to increase capacity. Incremental capacity might be needed for one or both of two purposes:

- *Growth within the existing network* Aircraft acquisition could be necessary to accommodate traffic growth arising from either or both an expanding market or improved market share. Growing demand can in principle be met by using larger aircraft and maintaining frequencies, by operating more of the same aircraft at higher frequencies, or by some combination of the two. (It can also be met by raising utilisation, increasing seating densities, and/or accepting higher load factors.)

- *New missions* Capacity might be needed to satisfy new mission requirements beyond the capability of the existing fleet, such as the introduction of ultra-long-haul services.

An 'absorption ratio' can be calculated for an individual airline or, indeed, for a group of airlines (e.g., US majors) or the industry as a whole. This is the ratio of outstanding orders (aircraft units or number of seats) to the existing fleet, net of planned disposals or retirements. When projected absorption runs well ahead of forecast demand growth, questions need to be asked. For example, assuming annual passenger demand growth of 5 per cent and fleet retirements equivalent to 3 per cent of current capacity, we might expect fleet augmentation of around 8 per cent per annum. If this percentage or its equivalent 'orders-to-fleet' ratio is substantially exceeded, there might be an overcapacity situation developing. (On the other hand, it should be borne in mind that at a macro-level demand growth is usually measured in RPMs – which can be produced by aircraft of many different sizes, and therefore numbers, flying many different alternative stage-lengths – whilst purchases and retirements are measured in discrete aircraft or, less usually, seat numbers. So, for example, a single-airline or industry-wide shift to higher frequencies using aircraft similar in size or smaller than aircraft already operated might raise aircraft acquisition numbers without necessarily threatening overcapacity.)

There are two reasons why fleet planning should be treated not as a separate, isolated or occasional exercise, but as an ongoing process intimately linked to strategic and marketing planning:

1. *Changes in the marketplace* A fleet can only ever be optimised to serve one particular set of markets at one particular point in time; as existing markets change in size and/ or structure and as markets are added or deleted, the fleet will become suboptimal. Fleet planning is therefore a continuous process of reassessment.

2. *Changes in corporate priorities* Fleets and networks are managed within the wider context provided by decisions about which markets and segments to serve, and how to serve them. If, for example, an airline decides to change its market position by offering higher frequencies and/or an improved inflight product this could well have an impact on its optimum fleet. Similarly, when British Airways decided in the late 1990s to de-emphasise low-yield flow traffic and concentrate on premium traffic, particularly in point-to-point markets, this had an immediate impact on its projected fleet mix – with future requirements shifting from B747-400s to B777s, and from B757s to the A320 series.

AIRCRAFT EVALUATION: PASSENGER AIRCRAFT

The intention here is to highlight some of the principal issues that arise in the course of comparative aircraft evaluations. Readers interested in a more detailed explanation of fleet planning should refer to Clark (2007).

The People Involved

In any airline, various people will want to have their say in fleet planning decisions. Ideally, functional influences should be balanced. On occasion, however, discussion might be oriented towards the interests of operations personnel concerned primarily about aircraft performance and maintainability, marketing personnel preoccupied with product design, or finance people focused on operating costs and the appeal of the different types to financiers (or alternatively the willingness of respective manufacturers, and possibly their export credit agencies, to provide finance or credit support). Political factors sometimes come into play, and government interference in the decision-making processes of national carriers is not uncommon.

Collation Of Airline-Specific Data

The type of data required will include the following:

- *Network data* Markets to be served and the route patterns and frequencies flown to serve them. This data flags payload requirements.
- *Route data* Flight-legs to be operated and alternate airports for each destination; stage-lengths; reserve fuel requirements; en route meteorological assumptions; and turnaround times. This data flags likely speed and range requirements.
- *Airport data* Runway lengths, slopes, and construction; obstacle clearance; elevation; average and extreme meteorological conditions; taxiway and apron widths and load-bearing capabilities; dimensions of parking spaces on the ramp and at gates; and terminal infrastructure and handling capacities. This data flags the need for specific capability requirements, such as good hot-and-high performance.
- *Current fleet* When considering new types an airline will often benchmark its analysis against types with similar mission capabilities that it currently operates.

- *Product requirements* There are several variables:
    - Through their impact on frequencies and seat accessibility targets, product requirements will affect the capacities of aircraft needed to operate a given route network.
    - Onboard passenger service requirements by class are derived from marketing decisions in respect of service attributes such as seat pitch and width, aisle width, bin sizes, entertainment and communication systems, and provision and location of galleys and lavatories. Cabin cross-section can affect passengers' overall perceptions of spaciousness, the feasible seating configuration across each row (which itself affects both passenger perceptions and, on widebodies, the efficiency of meal service in the main cabin), and the scope for different galley, lavatory, storage, and crew rest-area options. (The ability to operate ultra-long-haul flight-legs depends upon the provision of crew rest-areas which, if located below the main deck rather than in a cabin ceiling void, may displace revenue payload.)
    - In some regional markets passengers are unwilling to accept turboprop service when jet alternatives are available.
    - Carriers with significant freight businesses will in addition have specific freight-related requirements in respect of belly-hold capacities and cross-sections, and container compatibility with other types in the current fleet that will be retained into the foreseeable future.

Clearly, the network is the key consideration. The more varied it is in terms of market density, frequency requirement, and stage-length the more complex an airline's fleet is going to be if it tries to tailor that fleet precisely to route variables. This has been a particular challenge for network carriers, whose business model requires feed for their hubs across a broad spectrum of stage-lengths and route densities. The question is whether the costs of complexity are adequately compensated; in the strong US revenue environment of the 1990s they were, whereas after 9/11 broadly they were not. As noted elsewhere in the book, point-to-point carriers are under less pressure to tailor their fleets to their routes – instead choosing routes where their fleets can most profitably be deployed.

Marketing Analysis

Airlines must make their strategic fleet acquisition decisions on the basis of forecasts that run many years into the future. Three types of forecast in particular have to be used:

- *Demand forecasts* Unconstrained demand is the number of passengers willing and able to fly, based on specified price and service-level assumptions and independent of output available for sale. It can be forecast by region, by O&D market, and by market segment. A common approach is to forecast aggregate growth, then focus down onto individual markets and segments – but, as we saw in Chapter 2, it is also possible to build upwards from the market level.
- *Traffic forecasts* 'Traffic' is the share of demand that is actually met. A particular airline forecasts its traffic on the basis of assumed market share – again, a function of certain price and service level, particularly frequency, assumptions.
- *Revenue forecasts* Revenue models link traffic forecasts to variables such as fare structures, freight rates, discounting, prorate dilution, and agency commissions.

It was noted in Chapter 2 that there are two complementary approaches to the building of forecasts: macro and micro.

1. *Macro- or top-down approach* A fleet must be able to produce the number of ASMs required to accommodate forecast RPMs at the planned load factor. In the case of a large airline, this exercise might be broken down into a number of subnetworks each containing different traffic densities and stage-lengths (e.g., short-haul mainline, medium-haul, intercontinental, and regional); even a small airline might be broken down into subnetworks if one or two of its routes have particularly strong characteristics that distinguish them from others in the network.

    A forecasted requirement for output growth on a network or identified subnetworks could, if relatively small, be met by improving utilisation of current capacity – through revised scheduling or increased seating density, for example. Alternatively, it might point to a capacity gap and consequent need for additional aircraft – particularly if some of the existing fleet will have to be retired for operational or marketing reasons.

2. *Micro- or bottom-up approach* Using this approach, a demand allocation model is calibrated to explain the link between consumer behaviour variables and traffic on specific flight-legs and segments in the current network, and then used to forecast future traffic on a flight-leg and segment-specific basis. It is first assumed that traffic will continue to flow on existing flights over existing routes unconstrained by load factor considerations (i.e., irrespective of available capacity); the next step would then be to arrive at a required number of seats by adjusting for acceptable load factors; finally, consideration of frequency, routing, seat accessibility, and network development issues would lead – via 'what if' analysis – from a raw seat number to several different potential aircraft sizes. Clark (ibid.) points out that despite their undoubted appeal, most notably the output of detailed aircraft assignments and route performance statistics, demand allocation models have several drawbacks in the context of strategic fleet planning:

    *   beyond a relatively short time horizon (say, 3 years), the causal relationships in historical data upon which they are calibrated can be upset by market changes attributable to demand volatility and/or competitive action;
    *   although flight- and segment-specific data is widely available, most carriers do not have the O&D demand data that models really need (although it can be accessed through MIDTs bought from the GDSs);
    *   the data acquisition and processing required place a heavy burden on the resources of small airlines, yet if their quality is not good the output of these models will be suspect.

For fleet planning out to ten years or more, top-down approaches are preferable. Beyond the relatively short term, bottom-up analysis of individual markets becomes hostage to stochastic vagaries and to structural market changes – not the least of which is the effect of strategic behaviour by competitors who cannot yet be identified. The bottom-up approach is considerably more appropriate to the fleet assignment challenge than to longer-term fleet planning.

Consideration of airline-specific data and marketing data together should lead the fleet planning team to a broad, preliminary conclusion with regard to candidate aircraft and the approximate numbers likely to be required. The more varied a carrier's network in terms of traffic densities and stage-lengths, the more likely it is that the theoretically optimal fleet composition will contain more types than is going to be desirable once operating cost considerations are brought into the analysis; compromises and trade-offs are inevitable. Figure 8.1 summarises the analysis.

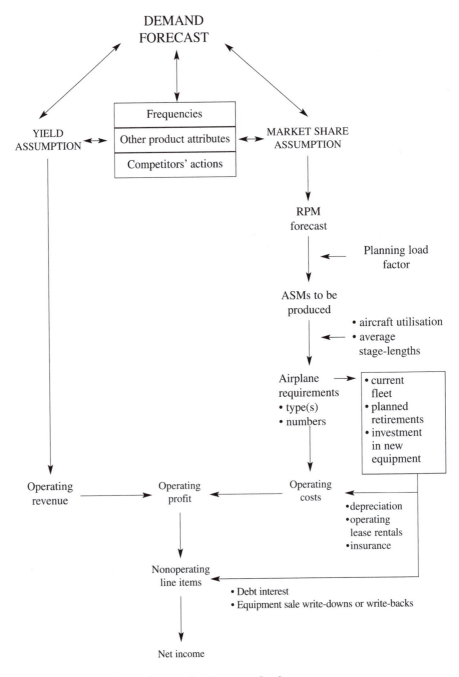

Figure 8.1   Overview of a marketing analysis

As noted in the last chapter, a particularly important trade-off revolves around how to produce output on each route – the trade-off between aircraft capacity and frequency. A route might have sufficient traffic to support relatively large aircraft, but the marketing requirement to offer high frequencies in order to feed other routes or to provide higher quality service to business travellers could argue in favour of smaller aircraft with less attractive seat-mile costs. (Of course, it is no longer axiomatic that smaller aircraft will have higher unit costs than larger aircraft flying the same leg – something particularly evident in the case of the B787 and A350.)

Aircraft size, together with chosen seating configuration, inevitably has a strong impact on earnings. *Spill models* can be used to estimate, under different assumed demand conditions, the number of passengers likely to be spilled off the smaller of any two aircraft under consideration. The value of lost revenue must at the very least be offset by lower acquisition and/or operating costs in the case of the smaller aircraft. However, not all spillage will necessarily be lost to the carrier because of the recapture effect, whereby a passenger unable to be accommodated on one flight might be booked instead on another service operated by the same airline. This recapture effect is strongest where the carrier has a high frequency on the route concerned and/or can rely on brand loyalty, possibly attributable to an FFP. Conversely, in an integrated network oriented towards online connections over a hub, spill on one leg of a passenger's multi-leg itinerary might lose the carrier that entire itinerary, even if there is space available on the other legs.

There are also *profit profiling models* available which relate monetary profits to route density (passengers per week, say) so that the profit impact of choosing aircraft of significantly different sizes can be evaluated over a range of traffic forecasts. As a general rule, a larger aircraft should *never* be put onto a service until the average passenger load achieved on the aircraft it is replacing exceeds the load required for that larger aircraft to break even on the route concerned (assuming unchanged revenue).

Conclusion   Demand growth tends over time to thicken traffic on most routes. Aside from accepting higher load factors and/or raising seating densities, it can be met in one or more of three primary ways: adding larger aircraft; adding frequencies; and/or fragmenting the markets served by a particular route – that is, by replacing a direct/multi-stop or connecting service with a non-stop service which diverts traffic from the existing route(s). Decisions about how demand is to be served and traffic allocated are therefore as important to fleet planning as forecasts of demand itself.

Technical Analysis

Technical analysis, which generally follows the ATA 100 coding formulated by the Air Transport Association in the United States to facilitate description of aircraft components and systems, will consider:

- structures and flight controls;
- mechanical systems;
- avionics and instrumentation systems;
- propulsion systems.

The systems of different aircraft are compared by ranking them in respect of attributes describing their design objectives, overall safety, reliability, redundancy, maintainability, simplicity, use of proven technology, and effects on the airline's existing equipment and personnel infrastructure. Fleet planners will also want answers to a variety of questions related to aerodynamics, stability and control, interior noise, exterior noise and emissions, and certification criteria. The *structural efficiency* of an aircraft (i.e., payload relative to weight) is an important cost-related issue which is increasingly being addressed by using composite materials to replace aluminium in the airframe. In this respect the B787 and A350 mark a significant shift in structural, as well as systems, technologies; the result is dramatically lower seat-mile costs than can be achieved by significantly larger types.

Performance Analysis

'Performance' refers to the capabilities and limitations of an airplane in different phases of flight. It is outlined in each aircraft's performance manual and can be illustrated by expressing graphically a number of relationships – the most widely recognised of which is perhaps the payload-range diagram. Performance analysis involves looking at maximum take-off weight (MTOW) and its various components, payload capabilities at different ranges, and range capabilities with different payloads to gain a sense of the aircraft's performance and economics in the context of the airline's present and likely future networks. A carrier might be looking for a type optimised for a specific group of its routes having particular stage-lengths and payload requirements, or it might be more interested in the flexibility to operate an aircraft profitably across a number of different mission profiles. Finally, an issue of critical importance is now the environmental performance of competing airframe/engine combinations – specifically, noise and emissions in different phases of flight.

In addition to more general analyses, performance will often also be evaluated, using the airline's standard procedures, at a limiting airport and on a limiting route within the network that are subject to abnormally demanding operational requirements. Separately, some short-haul operators wanting to maximise aircraft utilisation by keeping turnaround and transit times to a minimum will be interested in the ability of a type to operate multiple sectors without refuelling – so much so that an aircraft's 'range' in this sense can be an important input into evaluation exercises even though the routes served might each fall well within its performance capabilities. (Clark [2007] looks in detail at performance evaluation and is an excellent source of information on the subject.)

Cost Analysis

This subsection distinguishes between capital and operating costs. In fact, capital cost feeds through into fixed DOCs through 'cost of ownership' line items such as depreciation and/ or lease rentals. Furthermore, what really matters is the cost of acquiring and operating an aircraft across its entire life cycle, and it is therefore life-cycle costs as a whole that need to be the focus of analysis. At a growing number of airlines, shareholder value is the framework used for this analysis: the acquisition and operation of an aircraft must be seen to add value through its impact on either or both revenues and costs.

The most important point to bear in mind is that whilst an aircraft's capital and operating costs are critical, they are – like any costs incurred – relatively meaningless figures outside the context of revenue generated. The revenue competing aircraft types can generate, and therefore their service design implications in respect of variables such as the onboard product and also frequency/capacity trade-offs on the airline's network, needs to be weighed against life-cycle costs. We will return to this in the section of the chapter on pricing and economic analysis.

Capital costs   Different manufacturers break down their prices in different ways, but most will include the following elements:

> Aircraft list price at standard specification for each available airframe–engine combination
> + options (which might include standard options, customised options, seller-furnished equipment (SFE), and buyer-furnished equipment (BFE) and could, if not already certified for the type, entail additional certification costs)
> − negotiated discount (a function of order size, importance of customer, existing order backlog, current market conditions, and the stage of its product life cycle the aircraft has reached)
> = Aircraft contract price
> + price escalation per agreed inflation formula (something many large airlines will no longer accept – a few now even being able to negotiate a clause entitling them to a price reduction if another buyer obtains a better price from the manufacturer during a defined period after contract signing)
> − the value of credit notes from the OEM(s) already held by the airline and/or any fleet integration assistance (i.e., financial support from a manufacturer to smooth the integration of its aircraft into the fleet of an airline currently operating a competitor's products, and perhaps provided in preference to offering a larger discount which might then serve as a benchmark in future price negotiations with the same airline or with other carriers)
> + change orders initiated by the airline after contract signing
> = Flyaway price
> + product support (i.e., training of engineers/mechanics and aircrew, initial provisioning with spares, and the cost of any type-specific ground support equipment)
> = Total investment
> ÷ number of seats on the type in the airline's configuration
> = Total investment per seat

Price per seat (list price/maximum number of seats or average number of seats in airline use) has historically trended upwards with each successive generation of aircraft technology that has been introduced. The reasons have been general price inflation in the global economy and the constantly improving levels of technology and performance incorporated into new types (Trevett 1999). However, airlines – particularly carriers with strong bargaining positions – are no longer willing to accept ever-increasing capital costs for new generations of aircraft performing essentially the same missions as those they replace unless they offer substantially lower DOCs.

Direct operating costs   We saw in Chapter 5 that DOCs are operating costs that are dependent upon the type of aircraft being flown. They have two elements:

- variable costs calculated per flight-hour (e.g., fuel cost per flight-hour and flight-hour-related maintenance costs);
- fixed costs calculated per annum (e.g., insurance, depreciation, and maintenance overhead).

The first and perhaps most fundamental calculation is therefore to arrive at a total operating cost per flight-hour for each type under review, which will be the sum of:

Variable DOCs per flight-hour + (annual fixed operating costs ÷ estimated annual flight-hours)

Certain variable DOCs, notably fuel-burn, crew costs, and en route charges, are sensitive to the stage-length chosen for a DOC analysis. Standard formulae have been developed by aircraft manufacturers and airline trade associations to assist with DOC forecasting. However, care has to be taken to ensure their underlying assumptions are compatible with a particular airline's network, fleet size, and operating environment.

DOCs incurred by alternative aircraft flying a given stage-length, selected for the evaluation because it is either representative or particularly challenging within the context of the carrier's network, can be examined using different criteria. The following are perhaps most critical:

1. *Trip cost* This generally rises as aircraft capacity increases within the same technological generation. (*Aircraft-mile costs* can be calculated by dividing stage-length into trip cost.)
2. *Seat-mile (or unit) cost* This generally declines as aircraft capacity increases within the same technological generation. (Airlines with substantial freight businesses will want to look at the cost per ATM as well as per ASM.)

Because aircraft-mile and seat-mile costs vary depending upon stage-length selected and larger airlines operate any one type over many different stage-lengths, it is normal to use cost per block-hour as another basis for comparison.

Carriers commonly benchmark cost analyses against types in their present fleet already used for the mission under consideration. Figure 8.2 provides a simple illustration of what the results of this exercise might look like. Relative to the base model, aircraft A offers savings on both ASM and trip costs, whilst aircraft B offers substantial ASM savings but a higher trip cost. The reason for this could be that aircraft B is larger than both aircraft A and the base model – raising questions about whether or not the additional output it generates can be sold profitably given projected demand on the routes it will fly. This analysis can be undertaken for each route, for a typical route, or for a number of core routes – depending on the size of the airline involved.

Box 8.1 looks at the elements of seat-mile cost.

Both seat-mile costs on the one hand and trip costs on the other are important considerations in any cost analysis, and they have to be traded-off very cautiously. It is not axiomatic that airlines should always choose aircraft with the lowest seat-mile costs.

- In some short-haul and/or business markets frequency is such an important consideration that it largely drives choice of aircraft; in cases such as this, trip costs can be a more powerful factor than seat-mile costs.

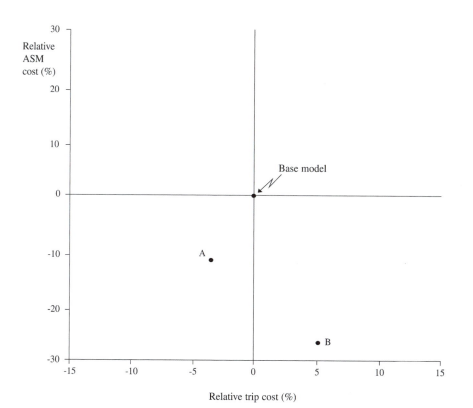

Figure 8.2 **A format for presenting the direct operating costs of different aircraft types over a given stage-length**

Box 8.1: Seat-Mile Costs

Cost per seat-mile (or seat-kilometre) is attributable to absolute input costs and aircraft productivity. Aircraft productivity is here defined as ASMs per hour or other period of time. Two key drivers of aircraft productivity are capacity and block-speed.

- *Capacity* The larger an aircraft, the more output (ASMs or ATMs) it will produce per hour of flight at any given speed (because it is carrying more seats and cargo capacity over the same distance as a smaller aircraft – assuming comparable block-speeds).
- *Block-speed* The faster an aircraft, the more output it will produce per hour of flight assuming a given capacity (because it is carrying the same number of seats and amount of cargo capacity over a longer distance than a slower aircraft).

Productivity feeds through to unit costs because the more output an aircraft produces each hour, the more output there is over which to spread fixed DOCs. Unit cost curves vary between types, but they are generally U-shaped when cost per ASM (on the vertical axis) is graphed against range (on the horizontal). This reflects a unit cost decline as stage-length and hourly productivity increase until the point is reached where payload must be sacrificed to obtain further range, and productivity suffers. (This point is equivalent to 'range at maximum payload' in a payload–range diagram.) An aircraft can be said to be optimised for the point at which its unit cost curve bottoms-out; an interesting question is how steep the sides of the 'U' are – because this gives some idea of the flexibility the aircraft offers for serving suboptimal stage-lengths.

- Second, depending upon a particular airline's network structure, it is possible that smaller aircraft will provide greater assignment flexibility – in which case their lower hourly productivity might be more than compensated by the higher utilisation they are able to achieve than larger aircraft suited to only a handful of routes.

The ideal objective, therefore, is to select a fleet of aircraft that is not only sized to suit the network it has to serve, but also combines the right mix of seat-mile and trip cost characteristics to serve it economically. Small carriers might be able to undertake the required analysis on a route-specific basis, but larger airlines will have to aggregate routes into subnetworks differentiated by stage-lengths and demand characteristics.

Powerplant Analysis

Particularly where there is a choice of engine suppliers for an airframe and therefore heightened price competition between powerplant manufacturers, the percentage of an initial investment in airframe and engines combined that is accounted for by the engines can be as low as 20 per cent (Golaszewski and Klein 1998). On the other hand, fuel and engine maintenance are such significant elements in DOCs that the percentage of typical life-cycle costs accounted for by powerplants can exceed 50 per cent (ibid.). Whether this pricing model will change as PMA parts eat into engine OEMs' high-margin aftermarket businesses and reduce their willingness to 'give away the razor in order to sell blades' remains to be seen.

Engine evaluation involves consideration of technical issues, analysis of any differences in aircraft performance attributable to alternative engines on a given airframe, and an economic analysis of individual airframe/engine combinations. There are many different technical metrics that engineers use to assess powerplants, amongst the most significant of which in respect of turbofans are thrust, specific fuel consumption (i.e., the quantity of fuel required to provide one pound of thrust for one hour under stated conditions), fuel-burn given an assumed payload-range mission, exhaust gas temperature margin (i.e., the amount by which an engine's maximum turbine temperature exceeds its operating temperature), and the thrust-to-weight ratio. An aircraft's fuel-efficiency is a function of aerodynamic efficiency (i.e., lift-to-drag ratio), propulsive efficiency (i.e., fuel-burn) and structural efficiency (i.e., structural weight as a percentage of MTOW). Each carrier will want to be certain that an engine has sufficient thrust to accommodate the most challenging take-off conditions that the type concerned will confront in its system. Noise and emissions levels are also now critical evaluation parameters.

At a very general level of analysis, two important issues are fuel-burn and maintenance variables.

1. *Fuel-burn* Long the most critical element in an engine evaluation, the importance of fuel-efficiency has become paramount with the recent increase in oil prices and growing concern about CO_2 emissions. An airline will want in particular to investigate the commercial productivity of alternative engines – how many ASMs or ATMs each airframe/engine combination will deliver per gallon, pound or kilo of fuel consumed on routes that it will typically serve and assuming a seating configuration, load factor, and cargo load appropriate to marketing requirements. Stage-lengths can be plotted (on the vertical axis) against ASMs or ATMs generated per unit of fuel consumption. This is arguably a more useful metric than block fuel consumption.

2. *Maintenance variables* Maintenance cost is a significant element in any engine's life-cycle cost, but it will vary between operators depending upon network structure (i.e., engine usage) and institutional factors (i.e., whether maintenance is outsourced or undertaken in house). Powerplant families built around common cores have come into vogue since Rolls-Royce launched the concept 20 years ago with the shared three-shaft, eight-stage intermediate-pressure compressor, and six-stage high-pressure compressor design that underpins Trent series commonality. As in the airframe manufacturing business, a great deal of development now comes from derivatives rather than brand new models. Engine families reduce spares and maintenance training costs when a carrier operates several derivatives of the same type – perhaps used on different airframes (e.g., the CFM56 on A320s and A340-200/300s). In principle, as airlines increasingly outsource powerplant maintenance and supply chain management under power-by-the hour and similar types of agreement they should become less concerned about commonality. British Airways has mixed GE and Rolls-Royce engines on its B777s; on the other hand, Air France-KLM – which has one of the largest airline MRO operations – tried hard throughout 2007 and 2008 to get the GEnx onto the A350 programme as an alternative to Rolls-Royce in order to ensure some degree of commonality with the carrier's GE-powered B777s.

Noise and fuel-burn were the key parameters for powerplant evaluation in the 1980s, after which reliability came into sharper focus. These days, airlines are requiring low fuel-burn, noise, and emissions along with high reliability – the latter reflected in better technical dispatch reliability, reduced maintenance requirements, and lower shop-visit rates (and therefore longer onwing times); improvements in maintainability and onwing replacement of modules are also expected. There is an argument that on short-range aircraft engines should be optimised for maintenance, whilst for longer-ranges they should be optimised for fuel-burn. Because take-off is the point of maximum stress for engine parts, particularly in the hot section and the high-pressure turbine, maintenance cost will be a key driver of life-cycle cost for engines on short-haul aircraft. (See Pickett [2002] for a comprehensive review of the powerplant selection process.)

One final point worthy of comment is the question of market share amongst engine suppliers and, in particular, the availability of choice to airlines. General Electric and its joint venture affiliate CFM International powered 75 per cent of all Airbus and Boeing aircraft delivered in 2007; they achieved this by virtue of their dominant single-source position on many Boeing programmes, notably the B737 and long-range variants of the B777, and their better than half share on Airbus' fastest-selling type – the A320. Their 97 per cent share of Boeing deliveries that year probably represents a high-water mark given that deliveries of B787s, on which there is a choice of engines, are ramping up. Nonetheless, the dominant role of GE as an engine supplier, reinforced by GECAS' strong position in the operating lease market and unwillingness to purchase aircraft without GE powerplants, is something airlines wanting healthy competition amongst OEMs would do well to keep an eye on – particularly as the race to power next-generation narrowbodies intensifies over the next decade.

Avionics

Some avionics systems (e.g., flight management, display, autopilot, and engine control and monitoring systems) have traditionally come 'bundled' with the aircraft as 'seller-furnished equipment' (SFE), whereas others – notably CNS and data management systems – have been buyer-furnished; buyer-furnished avionics might either be essential (e.g., to meet current and perhaps anticipated future minimum CNS equipment requirements in airspace to be used) or discretionary (e.g., head-up displays – HUDs). However, Boeing in particular has been moving away from this model and towards provision of relatively few flight-deck avionics options; most systems on the B747-8, for example, come as standard – something intended both to reduce integration and certification costs, and to add support to aircraft residual values.

A significant development in respect of SFE since the early 1990s has been that whereas in the past multiple avionics manufacturers chosen for their particular areas of expertise built 'boxes' to specified levels of functionality which were then handed over to the airframe OEMs for integration with other 'boxes', now a small number of prime (tier-1) contractors are responsible for delivering tested and fully integrated systems; Rockwell Collins' role as B747-8 flight-deck systems integrator is an example, as are the similar roles awarded to Thales in respect of the Bombardier Dash 8-400, ATR42/72-600 series, and Sukhoi Superjet 100. This ties with a trend towards greater equipment integration in order to save space, weight, and maintenance cost (the latter reflecting fewer parts and LRUs); an example is Honeywell's Aircraft Environment Surveillance System (AESS) for the A380, which brings together several surveillance capabilities in one unit: E-GPWS, mode S transponder, TCAS, and weather radar.

As with other technologies, airlines have become increasingly value-conscious in their assessment of buyer-furnished avionics applications. Life-cycle costs – rather than capital or operating costs alone – are again the key issue; flight-hour maintenance cost agreements entered into with avionics OEMs are providing airlines with added certainty in this respect. The key issue is whether the cost of equipment is outweighed by improved safety, higher revenues (e.g., resulting from a reputation amongst high-yield travellers for good on-time performance in low-visibility winter conditions), or reduced operating costs. (Kanellis [1999] analyses a HUD investment decision, and Nickum [2002] outlines an economic model for evaluating avionics purchases.)

One advantage that avionics suppliers have over other OEMs is that whereas developments in materials sciences and propulsion technologies are not always cheap or easy to apply to older airframes, new avionics able to justify themselves financially can often be retrofitted. If a decision is made to forgo a factory-fitted avionics option, there might still be a possibility of retrofitting an upgraded version at some later time. (Options pricing theory now allows this type of flexibility to be priced as a 'real option' – although there is little evidence that many airlines yet do this.) On the other hand, the growing functional integration of each successive generation's airframes, flight control systems, and avionics – together with the increasing integration of avionics packages themselves – may limit future avionics choices insofar as a greater range of applications will become standard equipment rather than an option.

Options And Customisation

Although more complex typologies can be used, the basic breakdown is as follows:

- *Standard specification* This is the base aircraft, or perhaps a high gross weight version subject to additional certification and purchase costs. There will be some latitude for customisation to a particular airline's requirements in minor respects.

- *Seller-furnished equipment (SFE)* These are 'catalogue options' supplied by the manufacturer. Some represent equipment or subsystems that have to be bought from one supplier or another (e.g., lavatories and overhead stowage) and which might therefore come ready-certified, whilst others might not have to be bought at all (e.g., non-essential avionics). The B747-400, for example, had 126 lavatory options.
- *Buyer-furnished equipment (BFE)* Major items in this category have traditionally included seats, galleys, entertainment systems, and CNS equipment. On some freighters (e.g., the A330-200F), cargo-loading equipment is BFE. Choice of BFE can make several thousand pounds' difference to the weight of a long-haul type operated by one carrier compared to the weight of the same type operated by another carrier – with obvious life-cycle fuel-burn implications.

Options add to the cost of new aircraft not simply because of the manufacturing inefficiencies and costs to which they give rise, but also because everything going onto an aircraft requires certification; certifying multiple options is more expensive than certifying a single standard item. There has been intermittent pressure from airlines to cut the scope of customisation and option availability in order to reduce aircraft purchase prices, benefit from economies of scale in respect of pooled spares, and remove a complication from secondary market trading. Manufacturers have to an extent responded. Boeing, for example, has moved from full customisation to a set of predefined interior configurations (referred to as 'standard selection interiors'); whilst a wide range of standard options is still available to choose from on the B787, for example, freedom to select non-standard BFE has been limited largely to first and business class seating. Both Airbus and Boeing have come closer to flight-deck standardisation on the A380, A350, and B787. Boeing has also designed a standard engine pylon on the B787 to facilitate swapping between the type's Rolls-Royce and GE engines – although how much use will be made of this capability in practice is open to question.

One hurdle in the way of standardisation is that several airlines serving long-haul business passengers with what they consider to be market-leading products feel the need to customise wherever possible in order to distinguish their brand identities. That said, the argument in favour of standardising equipment that passengers do not see – on the flight-deck, for example – is compelling insofar as standardisation can contribute significant cost reductions. Alliances should in principle advance this process and, with their claims of seamless service, extend it into visible areas of the cabin that can be used to establish a common brand platform. Clearly, the case for standardisation of freighters is overwhelming. There has been some, but relatively little, progress towards standardised buys within alliances.

The growing significance of a small number of major operating lessors is a source of additional pressure towards standardisation. In particular, highly customised widebodies can entail significant transition costs when moved from one lessee to another. Yet even here if an airline is prepared to commit ahead of ordering to a long enough lease, customisation is likely to be on the table.

Customer Support Analysis

Initial provisioning   Initial provisioning (IP) with spares, including spare engines, and ground support equipment must be programmed to correspond with the rate of aircraft deliveries. Typical questions are: what has to be acquired to optimise inventory costs against target dispatch reliability and what expenditures will this require? Can spares be taken on consignment rather than purchased outright? What are the assumed hours/cycles upon which IP estimates are based, and are they realistic? What has been the price history of spares in recent years, and how readily are they available from legitimate sources other than OEMs? What sort of reputations do the manufacturer and its suppliers have for responsiveness to urgent requirements? Is credit available? Must foreign currency be paid out before orders are shipped (a particularly important issue for airlines in some developing countries)?

Airlines are now analysing IP requirements – and, indeed, inventory policies in general – more carefully than at any time in the past. Whilst dispatch reliability and service levels have to be maintained, efforts are being made to exploit both new opportunities for closer working relationships with suppliers and the reliability of express delivery services to cut inventory costs. Much depends on an airline's operating profile, notably forecast hours and cycles, and the location of its network relative to suppliers' distribution centres. Many airlines in fact now prefer to keep as much inventory as possible in the supply chain rather than hold it themselves, and materials management programmes offered by OEMs and MROs are becoming increasingly popular. Even more comprehensive than materials management, total support packages with defined service-level commitments from OEMs (e.g., GoldCare for the B787) or from MROs such as Lufthansa Technik provide an alternative encompassing all aspects of maintenance and supply chain management.

Training and technical support   The *training package* will cover aircrew (initial conversion training) and engineers. *Technical support* should cover the following:

- *Technical publications* to ATA 100 specification standards, supplied in negotiable quantities.
- *Field service*, which may involve secondment of technical representatives to an airline operating a substantial fleet of a particular type.
- *Operations support*, which may run to the provision of line training captains and route-proving assistance, and should certainly encompass updates of technical data, airworthiness directives, and service bulletins.

Whereas large airlines will often have airframe and engine manufacturers' representatives attached to their engineering departments, small carriers risk finding themselves less well provided for. They should therefore ensure that in the *Product Support Agreement* OEMs undertake to dispatch qualified support personnel several times each year to discuss any problems that have arisen. In the final analysis, airlines should enquire with other, similar, operators regarding their product support experiences. Also, it is too easy to focus on the airframe or powerplants and lose sight of the fact that there is much more to an aircraft; support will be required from component manufacturers as well, raising questions about the nature of contractual relationships with this type of OEM and their regional support infrastructures.

In practice, OEMs are now in most cases strongly committed to keeping their customers satisfied. Airbus has over 250 customer support representatives in close to 150 cities, as well as support centres (Toulouse, Washington DC, and Beijing), round-the-clock AOG support, a global MRO network, spares stores (Hamburg, Frankfurt, Singapore, and Washington DC), a customisable online documentation and support environment, training centres (Toulouse, Hamburg, Miami, and Beijing), and a programme for analysing and building on operators' product experiences. Boeing's Commercial Air Services unit offers a range of support services through MyBoeingFleet.com. One of the challenges facing Russian and Chinese manufacturers endeavouring to enter international markets is convincing prospective customers that support will meet international standards.

Warranties and guarantees   These will be given by the airframe manufacturer, engine manufacturer, and other equipment vendors. They should cover, inter alia, design, materials, workmanship, service life, component reliability, repair turnaround, dispatch reliability, maintenance cost, maximum parts cost, spares buyback, shop visit rate, cost per brake landing, fuel-burn deterioration, etc. Aircraft weight and performance undertakings, particularly for launch orders, should comprise inter alia:

- weight-related guarantees: manufacturer's empty weight; operating weight empty; payload;
- field performance guarantees: take-off distance; landing distance; take-off weight and landing weight achievable at given airports under pre-specified operating conditions;
- en route performance guarantees: all-engine and engine-out rates of climb; single-engine ceiling (for twins); cruise-specific air range; mission payload; payload-range performance.

Some of these guarantees might come with an allowable fixed or percentage margin of exceedance, but others (e.g., field performance) often will not. Compliance with margin allowances could be tested by reference to an approved document or by a field test under approved conditions. How shortfalls in fuel-efficiency are to be handled needs particularly careful consideration, given that in practice it can sometimes be difficult to attribute small exceedances with certainty to either engines or airframe (Robertson 2008). Settlement of disputes, after any contractual 'time to cure', could be by rejection of the aircraft (normally short-term, with late delivery compensation payable), lump-sum compensation, measured compensation based on an identifiable economic impact during a stated performance shortfall period (e.g., restricted payload on given routes), or product improvement at the manufacturer's expense.

The Fleet Commonality Issue

Airlines have to balance two sometimes conflicting pressures when structuring their fleets:

1. *The need to minimise the number of types in the fleet*   The imperative behind this is of course to save money; cutting back on the number of types in a fleet saves pilot and mechanic training, line servicing, ground equipment, and inventory management costs. Several US network carriers in particular have since 9/11 been reducing the number of types and variants they operate (as well as the number of aircraft in total); Delta, for example, simplified its fleet from 13 to 7 types and variants in the 5 years to the end of 2006 – although, by way of comparison, United and Continental dropped only one each (the B767-200 and MD-80 respectively). With regard to LFAs, as noted elsewhere in the book, the 'template' business model stipulates a one-type fleet (but see 2 below).

2. *The need to tailor the fleet to the route structure* There are two points here:
    - *Network carriers* By definition, the network carrier business model requires that hubs be fed down spokes which vary enormously in payload and range requirements. The more varied the network structure the more diversified the fleet required to serve it – unless the carrier decides assigning aircraft that are suboptimal for a route or route-group is preferable to adding another type. The key is this: complexity almost always adds cost, but provided it generates revenues meaningfully in excess of those costs (with the word 'meaningfully' being used here to imply a buffer against risk and uncertainty in commercial performance) then complexity might be justifiable. Lufthansa, for example, chooses to have a diversified fleet graded quite closely to each of its route-groups – hence the decision to buy a substantial number of B747-8Is to fill a capacity gap between its A340-600s and A380s.

        An example of added complexity is provided by ultra-long-haul services, which tend to be operated by small subfleets because there are at the moment relatively few commercially sustainable routes longer than 16,000 kilometres. These routes can be expensive to operate because of the cost of hauling vast quantities of fuel into the air on take-off, additional crew costs, low seating densities, and diseconomies associated with small subfleets of aircraft such as the A340-500 and B777-200LR. Revenue premiums must therefore be obtainable to justify these higher costs; Thai found that between Bangkok and New York they were not, whereas Singapore Airlines has had more success on its non-stop routes to New York and Los Angeles because it is able to generate greater high-yield business traffic. In practice, the cost implications of niche fleets need to be considered on a case by case basis. First, some are simply variants within a much larger fleet; Emirates, for example, currently operates a relatively small number of B777-200LRs within a large B777 subfleet comprising several variants. Second, niche or not, ultra-long-haul operations are important to the network strategies of several carriers – notably in the Middle East and India but also elsewhere.

        A different type of example is provided by Copa. Having built a successful flow network over its Panama City hub using just B737s to connect south and central American cities unable to sustain non-stop service at marketable frequencies, it chose to add the Embraer 170/190 families in order to gain access at lower trip costs to thinner traffic flows too small to justify B737 service.
    - *LFAs* As noted elsewhere, some LFAs – notably Virgin Blue and jetBlue – have also added Embraers in order to add off-peak frequencies on routes still primarily served by mainline narrowbodies, to connect smaller communities to their hubs, and/or to supplement or replace connecting service with new hub-bypass routes. (In fact, any category of airline with a single-type fleet may lack the flexibility to add frequencies if the type it operates is too large for off-peak loads.)

OEMs have promoted the concept of fleet commonality to help airlines overcome the conflicting requirements to, on the one hand, grade aircraft to demand profiles on each of their routes and, on the other, minimise fleet complexity. 'Commonality' refers to the presence in an airline's fleet of a family of airframe derivatives (e.g., the B737-600/700/800/900 series or the A318/319/320/321 series) and/or engine derivatives (e.g., the Rolls-Royce Trent series).

Airframe families The 'family' concept extends not just to variants of the same type such as the B737 and A320 series and the various regional jet families, but also to different but closely related types such as the A330/340 and the B757/767. It offers several potential advantages.

1. *Aircraft assignment flexibility* Traditionally, airlines have adjusted their deployment of different types and variants at the beginning of each timetable period or season (although some carriers have insufficient flexibility within their fleets to adjust even to seasonal fluctuations in demand, other than by changing frequencies and concentrating heavy maintenance during slack periods). In principle, having two or more variants of a single family available within the subfleet of a particular type can provide flexibility to adjust capacity to demand right up to the day of operation. In practice, it is not clear how widely this flexibility is used other than when timetables are changed. As much as anything else, a large network carrier with a complex flight schedule and aircraft routing pattern may find it difficult to make unforced late changes to aircraft assignments without this having a knock-on effect on the rest of the day's flight programme and perhaps also on maintenance schedules; carriers operating less complex out-and-back assignment patterns have more opportunity to exploit fleet flexibility. We will look at aircraft assignment below.

2. *Aircrew training and rostering flexibility* These have two aspects:
   - *Common type ratings* A significant advantage of the family concept is that all aircraft in, for example, the B737NG series share a common type-rating and so can be flown on a single license endorsement. Common type rating allows the aircraft assignment flexibility provided by having variants with different payload–range capabilities in a single sub-fleet of a type to be complemented by the flexibility to roster pilots to fly any of these variants.
   - *Cross-crew qualification (CCQ)* Airbus has developed CCQ, which leverages common design concepts, handling characteristics, and cockpit configurations between types to reduce the transition from the A320 series to the A330/340 series from a 25-day conversion course to a few days of 'differences training'. As a result of CCQ, Airbus has been able to offer the prospect of 'Mixed Fleet Flying' (MFF), where pilots who have cross-qualified maintain currency on both series and so can be scheduled to fly any aircraft in either subfleet. (It should be noted that even where CCQ and MFF are not applied, having different aircraft types produced by the same manufacturer in a fleet can reduce training costs. For example, pilots transitioning from the A320 or A330/A340 families onto the A380 can do so in 13 working days – approximately half the time taken by pilots moving from other types; Boeing expects similar benefits for pilots transitioning from the B777 to the B787 series.)

   The benefits of this flexibility are argued to come from lower training costs than would otherwise be incurred by pilots converting between aircraft with different payload–range capabilities, and cost savings from reduced pilot numbers – the latter attributable to having a single pool of pilots from which to draw for routine rostering and to cover late crew and aircraft changes, rather than a larger number of smaller, less flexible pools supporting a broader range of types. How significant these benefits are will depend upon the size of an airline's fleet and the nature of its route network; airlines with large subfleets of a single variant will tend to gain less benefit than others.

3. *Spares inventory and type-specific ground support equipment (GSE)* Families benefiting from extensive spares and GSE commonality can offer lower investment and inventory carrying costs than the alternative of having to support several types, each with fewer aircraft in the subfleet. This is true at maintenance bases, but particularly so at outstations performing just line maintenance.

    *   *Capital expenditures* One advantage of fleet standardisation is that the capital expenditure required for each aircraft added to a fleet of the same type diminishes (ignoring inflation) because expenditure on parts inventory, spare engines, type-specific GSE, and training pursuant to the acquisition is lower than would be the case were a new type to be introduced. (This is one reason why manufacturers sometimes have to price aggressively or offer generous fleet integration finance in order to get airlines to switch allegiance.) The family concept extends these benefits.

    *   *Operating costs* Inventory costs include insurance, handling, storage, and depreciation. If having a family of aircraft in a subfleet increases the number of aircraft in that subfleet to the point that a particular item of inventory is able to support more aircraft than it otherwise would, this will contribute to lower inventory costs compared to the alternative of having more types and smaller subfleets in the overall fleet.

    The Embraer 170/190 series provide a good example: there is 95 per cent commonality between the 170 and 175 and between the 190 and 195, whilst commonality between the 170/175 and the 190/195 runs close to 90 per cent.

4. *Training and rostering of maintenance personnel* At a general level, because maintenance personnel become familiar over time with the design concepts and maintenance procedures associated with a particular manufacturer's aircraft there will inevitably be a learning curve to climb if a new manufacturer's products are introduced into a fleet. Extending the argument, personnel familiar with a particular type are likely to be more efficient dealing with variants of that type than switching periodically to different types. Aside from any efficiency gains that might arise, commonality is argued to offer training and scheduling benefits in respect of maintenance personnel that are similar to those offered in respect of pilots.

Commonality within a family can raise the productivity of aircraft, crews, and maintenance inventories whilst also allowing the airline to fine-tune supply to demand on a departure-by-departure basis. It allows airlines to balance the need for fleet rationalisation (i.e., the minimum number of types) against the need for fleet flexibility (i.e., the maximum network-relevant payload–range capability spread). That said, how significant the benefits of commonality are will vary from airline to airline. In particular, whilst small carriers can benefit from economies of scale associated with being able to build a reasonably sized fleet out of relatively small numbers of different variants, the largest carriers – particularly the US and European majors – generally have numbers of aircraft, pilots, and maintenance personnel so large and schedule integrations so complex that the benefits of commonality are perhaps fewer than a small operator might experience. Another potential problem is that shrinking a type in order to complete the lower-capacity end of a family might sometimes impose weight penalties as a result of design having been optimised for the larger base model; this can lead to higher operating costs that may erode some of the benefits of commonality. The A318 comes to mind.

Powerplant families   Not only is essentially the same engine used across airframe families such as the A320 or B737 series, but it is now usual for derivatives of a common core to be found on entirely different types – such as the Rolls-Royce Trent 900 on the A380 and 1000 on the B787, and the GEnx-1B on the B787 and -2B on the B747-8; indeed, it is difficult for an engine to be commercially successful unless derivatives are available on alternative airframes. As with airframe commonality, there are inventory, maintenance infrastructure, and personnel training and scheduling benefits to be gained from powerplant commonality. On the other hand, power-by-the-hour and life-cycle maintenance cost agreements can be used to shift the burden of a mixed engine inventory onto OEMs or third-party MRO shops which have enough volume in each engine type to pass through to the airline some of the benefits arising from economies of scale. Commonality might still offer cost savings in respect of line maintenance if this continues to be handled inhouse.

Conclusion   In an ideal world, it might be arguable that a network carrier should operate just three families of aircraft – regional, narrowbody mainline, and widebody mainline. Similarly, a point-to-point LFA should stick to just one type. The substantial investment in existing fleets, the emergence of diverse new business models, and the desire of some carriers to keep OEMs' 'pencils sharp' for follow-on orders by purchasing from each will continue to ensure that the world is, in this respect, far more complex than ideal.

Other Considerations

Amongst the additional considerations likely to enter into a fleet planning exercise are:

1. The timing of a manufacturer's available delivery positions relative to need and/or planned phase-out of current aircraft.
2. The availability of offset deals.
3. The availability of vendor financing or financial support (possibly including trade-ins against current aircraft, integration funding to support the inevitably higher costs of introducing a new type into the fleet, and/or concessions on prepayments prior to delivery).
4. Cargo container compatibility.
5. The ease with which loose-loaded baggage can be loaded and offloaded to facilitate efficient narrowbody turnarounds. More generally, turnaround times can be a significant consideration in respect of aircraft operated on high-frequency short-haul networks. The Embraer 170/190 series come with a guaranteed 20-minute turnaround time attributable in large measure to a 2 × 2 seating configuration and, in particular, to the related fact that these are long aircraft for their capacity and so can accommodate the simultaneous positioning of all required GSE.
6. Whether a carrier has a single-type or single-manufacturer fleet policy. One of Southwest's many sources of cost advantage over other US majors has been its single-type fleet of B737s (albeit mixed between classics and NG series). Several other US majors have made long-term commitments to Boeing. On the other hand, some carriers prefer not to be over-reliant on a single supplier. A key issue is whether on a life-cycle basis DOC savings derived from commonality are outweighed by capital cost savings attributable to price competition between manufacturers; easyJet decided that they were when in 2002 it ordered deeply discounted A319s for its previously all-Boeing fleet.

7. The growth potential of the type (i.e., scope for weight increases and development of derivatives).

8. Projected residual values (RVs). Some airframe–engine combinations have better RVs than competing models designed for similar missions, and this can affect financiers' appetite to take on their asset risk, as well as the long-term preservation of the airline's capital (if the aircraft are to be owned rather than leased). Key factors affecting RV aside from the operating characteristics of an airframe–engine combination are the number of units in the global fleet and both the number and regional spread of operators; the more popular a type and the wider it is spread across different markets around the world, the easier it should in principle be to remarket and the less RV risk it should pose for financiers. Given the nature of these criteria, it will be interesting to see how RV estimates develop for the A380.

    Another variable affecting RV is how early in a type's production run the aircraft concerned will have left the factory. Because later aircraft benefit from weight reductions and various other enhancements, it is often the case that they maintain RVs better than aircraft produced significantly earlier in the production run.

9. Confidence in the manufacturer to abide by its undertakings. The question of confidence in the future of the manufacturer is something brought sharply into focus by the demise of Fokker, the takeover of McDonnell Douglas, and the withdrawal of Saab and BAE Systems from commercial airframe assembly. When a manufacturer leaves its markets, long-term product support may or may not be thrown into question; experience to date in this regard has not been particularly bad, although periodic parts shortages were reportedly one reason behind American's decision taken in 2002 to begin retiring its F100 fleet. More problematic for affected operators are the impacts on both the secondary market value of the current fleet and on future fleet development plans – problems faced by British European (now Flybe), which was in the process of re-fleeting around the RJX when BAE cancelled the programme in 2001. Even where its long-term survival is not in doubt, any manufacturer new to the global market inevitably faces a significant challenge establishing credibility as a reliable supplier given that significant fleet decisions cannot be taken lightly or reversed inexpensively.

10. Whether the carrier concerned is prepared to be a launch customer. The benefits of being a launch customer are price, marketing profile, and early access to lower operating costs. The disadvantage is exposure to service entry problems and possession of the first few aircraft off the line – before weight reduction or manufacturing improvement programmes have kicked in. Cathay Pacific, having had some difficult experiences with new types in the early 1990s, prefers at present not to launch new models, for example.

11. Political pressures. The fact that Israeli and Japanese airlines operate few Airbuses undoubtedly owes as much to politics as to aircraft economics. However, globally this is not the issue it was several decades ago.

Pricing And Economic Analysis

Every aircraft acquired should be capable of contributing positively to shareholder value. The fundamental variables that determine whether or not this can be achieved are capital cost, projected operating revenues and costs, and RV.

Price Few airlines pay the 'sticker price'. Launch orders, bulk buys, and orders from strategically important customers in particular attract sometimes substantial discounts. When alternative engines are available on an airframe, heavy discounts off engine list price are also likely to be available, and this can clearly have a profound impact on total aircraft price. Another consideration is product substitutability: although competing manufacturers produce closely matched types and variants for most payload–range missions, one manufacturer's product might sometimes be better suited to a particular airline's network and demand characteristics. If this is not the case and competing products are essentially substitutes for each other, pricing is likely to be finer. All of this needs to be set against general market conditions. When backlogs are low, there are 'white tails' in storage, and demand is weak, manufacturers are clearly going to be more accommodating with regard to price than in a tight market. Some carriers (e.g., easyJet, Ryanair, and Qantas) have proven particularly adept at benefiting from soft prices in a buyers' market.

On the whole, it is fair to say that pricing has more to do with what purchasers will bear than with manufacturing cost. What a purchaser will bear has to be capped below the economic value of a particular aircraft operated on its specific route network. There is no deterministic reason why the amount an airline is prepared to pay for an aircraft, established after analysing future cash flows based on what it considers to be realistic assumptions, should have any relationship to the manufacturer's cost of building that aircraft and allocating overheads to each unit produced. Of course, manufacturers hope that it does – otherwise they have got their costing wrong. From an airline's perspective, the driver in price negotiations must be the economic value of the airplane to that particular carrier and not some target discount off the sticker price.

Economic analysis Any aircraft's *output* productivity (i.e., ASMs, ATMs) is primarily a function of its payload capacity, speed, and utilisation; consideration of *economic* productivity requires further assumptions to be made regarding load factor and yield. A choice of aircraft will be driven by many different considerations, but in principle the chosen type should generate more cash than it will absorb over the study period and yield a positive net present value (NPV) and acceptable internal rate of return (IRR). In simple terms, cash flows are projected and then discounted back to present value:

Present value (PV) of cash operating revenues over the assumed ownership period
Less   PV of cash operating expenses over the same period
Plus   PV of residual value of the aircraft (and remaining spares and equipment) at the end of the period
Less   Initial investment (in the airframe and engines, spares, ground equipment, maintenance tooling, training, and fleet integration)
=   Net present value (at the assumed discount rate)

(Discounted cash flow techniques are in fact not without their shortcomings; Stonier [2001] reviews some of these and discusses the potential for use of real options in fleet planning decisions.)

Clearly, the purpose of any economic analysis should not be just to compare alternative acquisitions; another important comparison to be made is between these alternatives and the current (baseline) case – the alternative of retaining the existing fleet, possibly after some form of cabin, flight-deck, and/or powerplant upgrade. If an aircraft is being bought to replace an existing aircraft rather than to accommodate demand growth, the analysis should take into account any resale proceeds attributable to selling the existing aircraft and should focus in particular on the NPV of incremental changes to operating revenues and costs attributable to the replacement decision.

Outcomes will of course be sensitive to forecasts in respect of revenue drivers (e.g., demand, market share, load factors, and yields) and cost drivers (e.g., fuel, maintenance, training, and labour costs), and also to the assumed discount rate. Forecasts and assumptions will therefore have to be varied as part of a sensitivity analysis to establish how robust the conclusions are under different operating and interest rate scenarios. One approach is to use Monte Carlo simulation to accommodate a range of different probability distributions in respect of key variables on both the cost and revenue sides of the analysis. Manufacturers frequently assist by providing route suitability and comparative cost studies, but these are sales documents and as such need to be treated cautiously.

Finally, it should be borne in mind that whilst all airlines face constraints on the availability of investment funds, carriers in some countries have to do their budgeting not only under a capital rationing constraint but also under a foreign currency rationing constraint; they must therefore analyse foreign currency cash flows as well as total cash flows. Whilst this problem is often at its most serious for carriers in developing countries, most non-US airlines face a natural short-dollar position attributable to dollar-denominated expenditures on aircraft acquisition and on fuel purchases (set against revenues that tend to be heavily weighted towards their home currencies); hedging can help, but the life of most hedging instruments and techniques is short compared to the life of a new-build aircraft.

Contracting

Once a purchase has been finalised in principle, the next step will be signature of a letter of intent that briefly outlines the airline's agreement with the manufacturer but makes the signing of a firm contract conditional on production of an acceptable customised specification, price, and delivery schedule, together with other required documentation, within an agreed time period.

Deposits will usually be payable on signature of the letter of intent or memorandum of understanding, but these may be quite small – depending upon the prevailing market situation, whether discounts off sticker price are applied as a reduction to all advance payments or are front-loaded to eliminate early payments, and on whether the airline is holding any credit notes from the airframe or engine manufacturer. Further payments will usually be due on signing a contract, and in instalments thereafter with the balance due on delivery. The PV of an aircraft's purchase cost can be materially affected by variations in the amount and timing of progress payments.

Aircraft acceptance criteria will be specified in the contract. Large carriers frequently have engineers resident at the manufacturer's facility, at least for the duration of a delivery programme, to monitor construction and accept delivery.

AIRCRAFT EVALUATION: CARGO CAPABILITIES

Passenger Aircraft

Despite continued growth in the freighter fleet, which numbers just over 2000 at the time of writing and is expected to grow to 3980 by 2026 (Boeing 2007), just under half of the approximately 40 million tonnes per annum of international airfreight still moves in the belly-holds of passenger aircraft. An airframe design, particularly a widebody, might be optimised for passengers or specifically for a passenger/cargo mix. This can be an important consideration for a carrier earning a substantial proportion of its revenues from cargo. Aircraft belly-hold volumes and overall payload capacities need to be considered, and a determination arrived at as to which is most significant from the point of view of the particular airline's network.

Freighters and Combis

The forecast trend is for a gradually increasing proportion of airfreight to be carried in freighters, and US security restrictions imposed on belly-hold cargo shipments aboard passenger aircraft may over time accelerate this trend; Boeing (2007) forecasts that 55 per cent of capacity will be offered by freighters in 2026. There are several additional considerations to be borne in mind with regard to all-cargo and combi aircraft (the latter being defined here as aircraft that carry both passengers and cargo on their main deck).

- *Design density* As noted in Chapter 4, freighters are limited in respect of volumetric capacity as well as payload (i.e., weight). Design density is that density which combines the full use of volumetric capacity with the highest payload feasible. (The 'density' of cargo is weight ÷ volume, expressed in pounds per cubic foot. The B747-8F and B777F have a design density around 10 lb/ft^3, for example; the A380F, on the other hand, was offered to the market with a lower design density by virtue of its much larger volume – something which made it more attractive in principle to integrators than to general freight-haulers.) It is important that on any individual route an aircraft does not 'cube (or 'bulk') out' too far ahead of the payload at which it would 'weight out'. If the density of freight actually carried is below the design density for the aircraft concerned, payload capacity will be left unutilised; this can be a particular problem for some narrowbodied freighters. Manufacturers might base their economic studies on average freight densities closer to the design density (i.e., higher) than many airlines will actually come across in practice, because this obviously raises the payload output of their aircraft.
- *Access door dimensions* These affect the ease with which containers, pallets, and outsize shipments of different dimensions can be loaded.
- *Fuselage cross-section* This governs the size of containers which can be accommodated and the volume of space above standard containers, once loaded, available for payload make-up.
- *Weights* Cargo doors, strengthened floors, and onboard handling equipment carry significant weight penalties.

The cargo traffic mix on a particular airline's network can be a critical criterion when considering the relative importance of an aircraft's volumetric and weight capacities. More generally, whilst a small package carrier would in most cases be more concerned about volume considerations than payload, for a line-haul carrier specialising in heavy freight it is tonnage over different flight-legs on its particular network that is likely to be more significant.

Although Boeing and Airbus offer factory-built freighter versions of several of their models, over three-quarters of the freighters currently in operation are converted passenger aircraft whose value had dropped sufficiently to make conversion a sound economic prospect. Under normal market conditions, the value of a passenger aircraft might be expected to drop into the range where cargo conversion becomes economic once it is 12–15 years old; during deep recessions, as in 2001/2002, the number of parked or under-utilised aircraft can put such downward pressure on values that conversion of younger aircraft (with more attractive operating costs) becomes economic – at least for those with faith in a rapid cargo market upturn. Rising fuel prices can also increase pressure on the operating economics of older types and variants, accelerating their retirement from passenger service. Conversely, when passenger demand is buoyant and lift is in short supply, there might be insufficient aircraft available for conversion.

The conversion market is shared between OEMs and third-party holders of supplemental type certificates, such as Israel Aerospace Industries. OEM strategies differ, with Boeing preferring to work through partners (e.g., Taikoo Aircraft Engineering's B747-400BCF programme in China) and Airbus more willing to participate directly (e.g., the A320/321 conversion joint venture between Airbus affiliate EFW and Russia's United Aircraft Company).

Close to 75 per cent of the additions to the global freighter fleet over the next 20 years or so are likely to come from passenger conversions (Boeing 2007), largely because the generally lower utilisation of cargo aircraft than similar types in passenger operation makes the economics of conversion more compelling than the purchase of a new freighter for all but a relatively small number of cargo networks. Unless the DOCs for a new-build are sufficiently below those of a converted older aircraft, the high ownership cost of a production freighter will very often overwhelm the acquisition plus conversion costs of an older aircraft. Sometimes, however, the greater payload–range capabilities, lower fuel and maintenance costs, and greater dispatch reliability of factory-built freighters offer a compelling advantage over conversions, particularly to airlines offering premium, time-sensitive products in long-haul markets. This can particularly be the case when, as at the time of writing, secondary market prices for 15–20-year old passenger aircraft fit for conversion are historically high and availability is low.

AIRCRAFT EVALUATION: USED AIRCRAFT

Much the same economic analysis needs to be applied whether a proposed aircraft purchase involves new or used units. There are several arguments advanced in favour of new aircraft.

1. *Costs* Although used aircraft are cheaper in terms of capital costs (e.g., lower depreciation and interest payments), their cash DOCs (i.e., excluding ownership costs) tend to be higher than those of newer aircraft designed for similar missions.

There are several reasons for this.
- Aircraft performance declines as the airframe ages because surface deterioration increases drag.
- Weight gradually rises over time as a result of engineering modifications, the accumulation of moisture, the accretion of dirt in places not readily washed, and (at least between heavy checks) the addition of paint layers. Furthermore, later line numbers of an aircraft type are sometimes lighter than aircraft produced earlier in the production run as experience allows initially conservative design margins to be relaxed.
- The specific fuel consumption of engines tends to increase as they age. This can be mitigated to some extent by regular internal washing and sound maintenance, but modern engines are anyway designed for improved consumption compared with their predecessors. A steeply rising fuel price can be the single most important factor weighing against the purchase, or retention, of older aircraft.
- Maintenance costs, particularly in respect of unscheduled maintenance, rise as airframes and engines age; a B737-300 can cost in excess of $1 million a year more to maintain than a new -700, for example. (If unscheduled maintenance adversely affects dispatch reliability, as is likely, this could have a negative impact on yield to the extent that business travellers are discouraged from booking. One of MAXjet's several problems was reliability issues with its relatively old B767-200s.) Neither do older aircraft benefit from manufacturers' warranties. Ultimately, as aircraft get close to the end of their economic lives it can in fact be the impending approach of the next heavy check which sends them for parting-out and scrapping.

2. *Passenger preference* Although if asked most passengers would probably opt for new aircraft over old, the reality is that relatively few have any accurate idea how old an aircraft is and arrive at judgements based on standards of external and interior appearance. Several airlines nonetheless perceive a virtuous circle linking assumed passenger preference to fleet management strategy: a premium brand image leads to a sound base of high-yield traffic, leading in turn to strong cash flow that is enhanced by the favourable operating economics of newer aircraft, by the stronger secondary market values of young models traded out of the fleet on a regular rollover cycle, and by the tax shelter available from a policy of depreciating new purchases rapidly over a brief period of ownership and therefore deferring cash outflows to tax authorities. Singapore Airlines is the most widely quoted practitioner in this regard, although its rollover period is not as short as it once was. Of course, the virtuous circle can be broken by a prolonged cyclical downturn in aircraft secondary market values.

3. *Finance* Depending upon an airline's particular circumstances and also prevailing market conditions, it can on occasion be easier to arrange financing for new aircraft than for a secondary market purchase. Manufacturers become more generous with pricing and financing during a downturn, for example – although where order backlogs are large going into the dip their largesse might be less forthcoming.

Older aircraft therefore become increasingly unattractive to operate as fuel and maintenance costs rise; added to this are growing environmental pressures. Amongst start-ups there is now a tendency to launch with new aircraft (e.g., Virgin America) or at least launch with older aircraft but replace them as soon as possible (e.g., AirAsia). Several long-haul start-ups, however, have been exceptions to this trend – notably MAXjet, Eos, Silverjet, VivaMacao, and Oasis Hong Kong. Furthermore, if high utilisation is difficult to generate because a carrier serves relatively few markets at relatively low frequencies, it might well make sense to accept the higher operating costs of older aircraft in order to reduce the burden of high ownership costs. Allegiant Air took this approach, for example, choosing a fleet of MD-80s to operate its low-yield, low-frequency routes in thin leisure markets to/from Las Vegas and Florida. Any airline flying new aircraft will need to maximise utilisation in order to spread high ownership costs, such as depreciation or operating lease rentals, across as many hours flying and as much output of ASMs and ATMs as possible and keep downward pressure on unit costs.

With regard to freighters, the secular decline in real freight yields makes high ownership costs associated with the sticker prices of new aircraft a serious burden which all but a few airlines seem unwilling to bear. Whilst several Asian and European airlines and some of the integrated carriers have the demand base and network structures to accept high ownership costs in order to benefit from the operating cost and range advantages of new models, many others are content to rely on converted passenger aircraft.

AIRCRAFT FINANCE

Aircraft can be financed from an airline's internal funds or a mix of internal funds and debt; alternatively, they can be acquired using one of a wide range of available lease structures – a key defining feature of which is the percentage of its economic life over which the airline has use of the aircraft. Export credit financing and support from manufacturers can also play a role. This is what is generally referred to as 'the financing decision'. It is typical in both corporate finance textbooks and the practice of many airlines to separate the investment decision (which aircraft should be acquired and at what cost?) from the financing decision (how should the acquisition be financed?). Unfortunately, different financing alternatives available in respect of competing aircraft can sometimes have a profound impact on the NPVs of cash flows arising from different choices. (See Stonier [1998] for an explanation of the various methods available to model interactions between investment and financing decisions.)

Investment and financing decisions are influenced by three cycles, each of which is distinct but all of which interact with each other:

1. *The airline industry demand cycle* As noted in Chapter 2, air transport is a cyclical industry. Despite the barely restrained euphoria of 2005–2007, there is as yet no evidence that the world has changed in this respect. Linked to the demand cycle is what might be called an aircraft 'pricing cycle': when the air transport market turns down there is a tendency for airlines to order fewer aircraft, and manufacturers' prices will soften. Several airlines have been adept at exploiting this cycle by placing large orders at very favourable prices during cyclical downturns.
2. *The financial cycle* Financial markets cycle from periods when credit is easily available and interest rates are low, to periods when conditions are tighter.
3. *The equipment cycle* Each type and variant has a life cycle. Unless a design is a runaway success from the outset as the B787 has been, there are risks in ordering aircraft – particularly niche aircraft – early in their life cycles; examples of aircraft slow out of the blocks include the B717, B777-200LR, and B747-8I. Conversely, aircraft coming off a production line late in the type or variant's life cycle and with a more efficient successor in sight can suffer heavy economic depreciation while still quite young unless bought at a substantial discount.

Aircraft are resources that are expensive to acquire and introduce into service, long-lived, and subject to cycles in secondary market values that are neither predictable as to onset nor as to depth or duration. This makes them a particularly risky class of asset. Fleet acquisition is an investment decision which, like all other investment decisions, depends for its efficacy on assumptions made with regard to future revenues and costs. Considerable effort might go into making these assumptions as robust as possible, and 'sophisticated' discounting techniques can be used to evaluate cash flows. However, in the final analysis airlines are investing perhaps billions of dollars based on forecasts of demand, and assumptions about input costs, utilisation, yields, and seating densities, as far into the future as 10 to 15 years. Many cannot forecast these variables with sufficient accuracy over periods considerably shorter than this.

Such uncertainty argues for the use of a two-pronged approach to fleet acquisition and financing: a core fleet of owned aircraft, and the balance on flexible leases permitting either their retention for a secondary period or their return to lessors on short notice and with minimal exposure to asset value risk. Air New Zealand has used this financing strategy for a number of years. Continental provides another good example of strategic flexibility. At one point in 2007 it had a fleet of 368 aircraft. Assuming all leases were renewed (but no new leases were signed), all purchase options were exercised (but no new purchases were made), and no owned aircraft were retired, the maximum fleet in 2011 would have been 467; on the other hand, if no leases were renewed, no options exercised, and the owned B737-300/500 subfleet were retired the fleet would have been 371.

When capacity is needed only on an interim basis, wet leasing might be a viable – albeit perhaps expensive – alternative. Box 8.2 looks at the topic.

Box 8.2: Wet-Leasing

There has traditionally been a distinction between 'dry leasing' of aircraft only, which is the core business of major operating lessors such as ILFC, and 'wet leasing' of aircraft and flight-crews. The wet-leasing of foreign-registered aircraft and crews often requires approval from the lessee's regulatory authorities; approval might be time-limited, and conditional on domestic aircraft being unavailable. Some countries have an outright ban on inbound cross-border wet-leasing.

A form of wet-leasing that has gained prominence over the last decade is the ACMI contract. Under an ACMI lease a carrier provides additional lift to scheduled airlines on an aircraft, crew, maintenance, and insurance basis – leaving lessees to supply the traffic rights and the loads, and to meet DOCs such as fuel, airport and ATS fees, and handling charges. Aircraft are generally contracted on a multi-year basis at a guaranteed minimum monthly utilisation, which the lessee might be permitted to vary by a few percentage points if required, and subject to a fixed cost per block-hour.

The ACMI lessor is insulated from short-term market risk (because it gets paid throughout the contract period irrespective of load factor), fuel price risk (because this is the lessee's problem), and currency risk (because it can negotiate contracts in the same currency in which most of its costs are denominated – often US dollars). Advantages from the lessee's point of view vary from case to case:

- A lessee might be able to contract for cargo lift at rates below the costs it would incur were it to operate its own freighters. This is most likely to be the case where the lessee can support only a small inhouse freighter fleet; once it grows to the point where a reasonably sized fleet can be justified, ACMI arrangements might either be unnecessary, or useful only to provide temporary supplemental lift – during peak periods or to test a new market, for example.

- ACMI leases might allow a carrier to tailor output to the needs of an individual route which cannot be efficiently served by its current fleet.
- ACMI leases can allow a carrier to expand, either according to a long-term growth plan or in response to a fixed-term contract with a particular shipper or forwarder, without taking on the ownership risk inherent in further building its own fleet.
- ACMI leases can also be used to cover capacity gaps when aircraft are withdrawn for heavy maintenance – particularly when they are withdrawn from relatively small fleets with little scope to cover capacity shortfalls.

ACMI leases are most common in respect of freighters, but passenger aircraft are also leased on this basis. Atlas Air became the major cargo ACMI lessor in the 1990s. Examples on the passenger side include Qantas' long-standing contract with National Jet Systems on thin domestic routes, and the use of ACMI leases (as well as the lessors' AOCs) by several start-ups during their early years of operation (e.g., easyJet). As noted in Chapter 1, Lufthansa and Swiss International have wet-leased small numbers of B737s and A320s from PrivatAir for long-haul all-premium services. Although the lessee usually has more direct operational control than would be the case under a naked code-share agreement, branding issues can still arise in passenger operations unless aircraft are painted in the lessee's livery and both cabin design and configuration are consistent with the desired brand image – something that is very unlikely when the lease is short. Finally, it is arguable that some capacity purchase agreements between US majors and regionals are in essence wet leases with added ground services.

Buying-in capacity on the strength of demand which fails to materialise to the extent anticipated can be very expensive, and the risk argues strongly in favour of an airline expanding its core fleet gradually, leasing at the margins, timing lease expiries to coincide with new deliveries into the core fleet, and negotiating leases with both extension and early termination rights. This type of flexibility carries its own costs – but rarely are these as punishing as overinvestment in an inappropriately sized or structured fleet, locked in place by inflexible funding arrangements. Inevitably, though, it tends to be creditworthy airlines that can negotiate the most flexible arrangements with financiers.

II. Tactical Fleet Management

This section of the chapter will look at tactical fleet management from two perspectives: aircraft assignment and routing, and cabin floorspace flexibility.

AIRCRAFT ASSIGNMENT AND ROUTING

An airline with a fleet of given size, composition, and maintenance requirements and with an established schedule to be met faces what are referred to in the literature as 'the aircraft assignment problem' and 'the aircraft routing problem'. We touched on these in Chapter 7 as well as earlier in the present chapter, and saw that fleet assignment modelling is in many respects an operational extension of the longer term and more strategic modelling of future fleet requirements: scheduling, fleet planning, and aircraft assignment are closely related elements of the wider capacity management challenge.

Once a baseline schedule has been established and evaluated by a schedule profitability model, the next step is to assign available aircraft types to the scheduled flights. The objective of a fleet assignment model is to maximise the contribution of the given schedule by maximising the gap between revenue capture (based on demand and yield forecasts) and DOCs (based on known data) – subject to operational constraints. The most important constraints are: *cover* – each flight must be assigned to exactly one type; *capability* – the assigned type must be operationally capable of performing the flight; *balance* – the number of aircraft of a given type arriving at a station must equal the number departing; and *count* – the total number of each type assigned cannot exceed the number in the fleet. With regard to revenue, one immediately apparent issue in a hub-and-spoke network with a high proportion of flow traffic is that whilst DOCs arise per flight-leg, revenues are generated by itineraries – many of which are multi-leg, and some of which could be completed by following alternative paths through the network (most notably in a multi-hub system). An element of subjectivity is therefore clearly present amidst the science of optimisation.

Fleet assignment models are commonly based on spill models that estimate how much demand will be turned away given the use of a particular aircraft on a particular departure – the objective in this case being to minimise the sum of DOCs and spill costs net of recapture (Belobaba and Farkas 1999). Quite aside from the fundamental problem that demand is volatile on a departure-by-departure basis, a point we will return to in a moment, some of these models have had structural shortcomings. For example:

- While most will net-off estimates of no-shows from forecasts of unconstrained demand, few make allowance for the impact of revenue management policies in respect of overbooking and with regard to the effect on spill of different booking limits imposed on different booking classes. A related point is that the use of RMSs results in different passengers in the same booking class on a single flight into or out of a hub having different revenue values depending upon their respective itineraries. (These concepts will be discussed in Chapter 9.)
- There can also be a broader problem with regard to flow traffic across a hub. Some fleet assignment models are leg-based, designed to respond to traffic and revenue forecasts for each leg and assuming passenger demand to be independent of demand on other legs. This approach ignores leg-interdependence and network effects – the fact that limiting output on one flight-leg could reduce traffic on connecting flight-legs (ibid.; Jacobs *et al.* 2001).

At the moment fleet assignment and routing, maintenance routing, and crew assignment problems are still largely solved sequentially – which means that the optimal solution for one becomes the initial input for the next, and that the ultimate outcome is likely to be suboptimal. The ultimate goal is to integrate scheduling, fleet assignment, aircraft routing, maintenance planning (i.e., maintenance routing), and crew assignment into a single model capable of producing one optimal solution. However, as noted in the last chapter, optimising a schedule is – given the near infinite number of variables and possible permutations – a far tougher task than optimising aircraft and crew assignment separately.

Aircraft assignment is therefore still part of a time-line of different activities.

1. Some months in advance (perhaps 3–6 in domestic markets, but closer to 12 in many international markets) a schedule is fixed (subject perhaps to possible late adjustments), flights are advertised in distribution channels, and early – usually low-yield – bookings begin to load.

Once a schedule has been built and published, weekly rotations of generic aircraft are created to match aircraft types (subfleets) to scheduled flight-legs and through-services in a minimum-cost *assignment* that is feasible given the number of aircraft in the subfleets of each type operated by the airline; the turn-times of different types at each station have to be allowed for, and the availability of adequate pilot duty-time in aggregate per type also needs to be considered. 'Minimum-cost' in this sense refers both to aircraft operating costs and to the opportunity costs of spilled passengers attributable to offering insufficient output relative to demand.

One additional issue often encountered is the need to balance directionality on a route at specific times of day. An aircraft large enough to accommodate a high proportion of demand going into a major business centre during the morning peak might very well be too large for demand on the return leg. One answer could be to use a smaller aircraft and accept spill; another could be to allocate very few seats to low-yield (or FFP redemption) booking classes inbound, and far more on the outbound leg.

3. The next step is to design sequences of flights ('lines of flying') to be flown by specific aircraft, taking account of the maintenance requirements of each. This is the *aircraft routing problem*.

4. By this stage, crew scheduling will also need to be addressed by creating pairings and individual rosters.

5. Actual demand in respect of any particular departure will inevitably fluctuate around the mean, sometimes quite widely. Throughout the booking cycle an RMS should monitor demand and release space on the assigned aircraft at different fares – a process that will be discussed in Chapter 9. Marketing communications and promotional initiatives might also be used to help fine-tune demand.

6. Most carriers rework initial fleet assignment and routing solutions in response to changing commercial and operational circumstances right up to the day of operations (see Jarrah *et al.* 2000). If close to the departure date (which could mean a few hours to a few days, depending on fleet and network circumstances) it is apparent that the assigned aircraft is either too large or too small for demand coming forward at the prices being asked, an aircraft swap might be considered. The objective of aircraft reassignment and the tailoring of output to actual demand is to provide support to load factors and/or yields, and also to either reduce trip costs if the aircraft originally assigned was too large or boost revenues if it was too small. Two forms of swap are possible:

- *Between different types* Aircraft types vary with regard to their mission flexibility. The greater the spread of payload–range mission profiles a type can operate economically, the more flexible it is.

- *Between different variants* Carriers operating only one or two types as well as airlines with a broader fleet mix can benefit from having families of related models such as the A320 or B737 series. As discussed earlier in the chapter, these benefits extend beyond the capacity management flexibility being discussed here; other advantages include elimination of additional line maintenance and equipment costs often attributable to operating multiple types into any one outstation.

The ability to swap aircraft with different capacities on or close to the day of operation is referred to as dynamic fleet management (DFM) or demand-driven dispatch (D^3).

Dynamic Fleet Management

Whilst the capacity of an assigned aircraft is fixed, demand on any departure varies around the mean for that flight with the result that sometimes there will be excess output, spoilage or both (i.e., seats fly empty) and sometimes there will be spill (i.e., demand is unsatisfied because the aircraft is too small). Hence the appeal of DFM. The scope an airline has to practice it depends on two variables (Berge and Hopperstad 1993; Clark 2000, 2001):

1. *Network structure*   A short-haul out-and-back assignment pattern which rotates aircraft regularly through a hub or main operating base is more conducive to late reassignments than either a long-haul linear or a grid structure that commits each aircraft to a particular pattern as soon as it departs the first airport. Not only do short-haul out-and-back routings assist in efforts to match output to demand, they can also help isolate schedule disruptions at a single hub or base – whereas assignments that route aircraft out of one hub and via outlying stations to another can propagate delays across an entire multi-hub system; SAS has adopted out-and-back routings on its intra-Scandinavian operations from Copenhagen, Oslo, and Stockholm in order to boost aircraft utilisation and assignment flexibility, and also to limit delay propagation between the three.
2. *Fleet structure*   Aircraft swaps presuppose a fleet of different-sized aircraft – ideally including aircraft from families which share operational characteristics that allow aircraft to be substituted close to departure with minimal impact on crew and other resource scheduling.

Even when an airline has a sufficiently varied fleet, there are nonetheless several potential obstacles to late reassignment:

1. *Replacing an assigned aircraft with a smaller aircraft*   This raises a number of issues:
    *   Passengers might perceive a smaller aircraft (e.g., a narrowbody substituted for a widebody, or a regional aircraft substituted for a mainline narrowbody) as a less attractive service environment.
    *   Some of the cabin crew originally scheduled for the larger aircraft might be left unutilised.
    *   Cargo may have to be offloaded.
    *   Depending upon the nature of its network, an airline might find the larger aircraft that is being replaced difficult to reassign profitably. Carriers with a small number of aircraft that are significantly larger than the rest of their fleet and which have few routes sufficiently dense to support these aircraft can sometimes, for this reason, find it difficult to maintain satisfactory utilisation levels.
2. *Replacing an assigned aircraft with a larger aircraft*   This may also pose problems:
    *   The destination airport clearly has to be able to accommodate the larger aircraft – in terms of runway length and loading, and terminal capacity, for example.
    *   Additional cabin crew may need to be available.
3. *Replacing any type with another*   Whenever aircraft are reassigned, the maintenance requirements of the tail numbers involved need to be considered, as do the downline implications of having them out of position. Other issues also arise, one of which is that changes in available seat inventories will have to be communicated to the

reservations system, RMS, and external distribution channels (notably GDSs). When the swap is between different types rather than within a single-type family, the following factors need to be kept in mind:

- Pilot rosters will be affected: pilots must be legally and contractually available to fly the swapped-in aircraft on the routing concerned, and the downline effect of their use on this routing should not harm crew utilisation.
- The availability of line replaceable spares and suitably qualified line maintenance engineers at the destination airport might be a consideration if the substitute type is seldom operated on the route concerned and not supported by another operator at that airport.
- Reassignment might be constrained where the types involved have markedly different block-speeds on the flight-leg if this is sufficient to materially threaten schedule integrity (including the sequencing of flights in and out of a hub).
- Flexibility can also be constrained on some routes where the range of the substitute aircraft is inadequate given the payload it is being assigned to carry. (This applies within families of a type as well as between types.)
- The capacity of the swapped-in aircraft must be suitably sized not only for the flight under consideration, but also for booked loads on return or onward flight-legs.

The attraction of DFM stems from something first noted in Chapter 2: the random fluctuations in demand that can be experienced, particularly in high-yield segments, not only on a time of day, day of week, or week of year basis, but also from departure to departure of the same flight. The primary tool for dealing with short-term demand uncertainties is price, but where an airline has a variety of different hull-sizes in its fleet each capable of flying a given mission economically, aircraft swapping can also be a useful tool on or close to the day of operation. DFM comes into its own in particular when the swapping-in of a larger aircraft (or variant) than originally scheduled enables a carrier to accommodate an unanticipated late surge in high-yield, time-sensitive bookings. In practice, however, swapping aircraft within a sizeable and tightly integrated schedule is never going to be straightforward, if only because of its downline implications.

FLOORSPACE FLEXIBILITY

Capacity management is concerned not only with the number and types of aircraft in a fleet, but also with how their floorspace is configured. Floorspace within each unit is the real production capacity derived from operating aircraft, and how it is configured can have a significant impact both on output and yield. We will look at just three examples.

1. Rapid cabin reconfiguration has been practised for a number of years on short-haul aircraft in Europe, such that by moving a curtain or lightweight rigid partition the size of a narrowbody business class cabin can be increased or reduced. Seat pitch remains the same as in the economy cabin. Such flexibility is valuable, both because it allows the accommodation of peak early morning and late afternoon business class demand on any given route, and because it also facilitates deployment of aircraft on a range of sectors with entirely different traffic mixes.

   Where partitions are moveable in this way, convertible (also referred to as 'variable geometry') seats are often used to reduce the number of passengers across each row in business class. These are generally heavier than standard economy class seats. Perhaps more importantly, they suffer from marketing disadvantages when competitors offer fixed and less dense business class seating configurations. For example, the flexibility to reconfigure a row from 3 × 3 economy to 2 × 3 or even 2 × 2 business class seating is a valuable capacity management tool, but if the competition is offering a fixed 2 × 2 business class layout – possibly with greater seat pitch and recline as well – there is a clear trade-off in product quality. Convertible seats nonetheless remain in widespread use in Europe; in Asia, All Nippon has installed them on B737-700s, permitting near-instantaneous switching between a 136-seat single-class layout for domestic service and a 118-seat two-class layout for short-haul international service.

2. The far higher standard of seating comfort and access to other amenities required in business class on long-haul flights has generally precluded short-run floor-plan flexibility. One particular problem, increasingly met as well on the short-haul aircraft of some carriers, is that seats are now very frequently wired to entertainment and communications systems. Another problem is the difficulty of relocating galleys and lavatories on long-haul aircraft. Boeing has addressed the latter challenge with the 'flex zone' concept; pioneered on the B777, these zones allow galleys and lavatories to be relocated to pre-engineered areas in the cabin as part of a relatively short reconfiguration process. There is a weight penalty, of course, but the marketing flexibility in respect of seasonal demand fluctuations on a given route or reassignment of an aircraft to a different type of route with a different traffic mix can be significant.

3. One obvious way to adjust the output of ASMs produced by any given amount of flying is to change seating density. This is a relatively cheap and easy way to adjust output, but it is not without its engineering costs and neither should it be done without first giving consideration to the impact it has on the inflight product, customer satisfaction, and future revenues. Reservations and revenue management systems will also have to be updated.

    • *Raising densities* Most commonly this involves reducing seat pitch, although it could be done by replacing some galley or storage space with seats. Each aircraft is certified for a maximum number of seats; full-service scheduled carriers will very rarely approach this maximum, other than on some high-density Japanese domestic services, but single-class charter and low-fare operators come much closer. The addition of seats may require more cabin crew.

    • *Reducing densities* There have been two service design developments that have led to lower densities in some long-haul markets. First, a number of carriers have been extending the seat pitches available to their long-haul business class passengers; an early example was British Airways' introduction of flat-bed seats in 2000/2001, and this approach has now become relatively widespread amongst carriers with serious aspirations to access high-yield business. Second, a growing number of airlines have introduced premium economy cabins, a significant feature of which is seat pitches longer than in economy. Separately, US carriers have from time to time experimented with taking seat rows out of some or all of their domestic aircraft to give additional seat pitch either to every coach seat (e.g., American) or to high-yield passengers and high-value frequent flyers provided with an intermediate product in the front rows of coach (e.g., United); however, this is an approach better-suited to a down-market when yields are soft and load factors are under pressure so it is not surprising that American, for example, reversed its 2001/2002 initiative when the market started to recover in mid-decade.

The common thread running through each of the past few paragraphs has been that greater flexibility in the use of cabin floorspace and the reduction of set-up times can be an important capacity management tool. Aside from the special case of intra-European business classes with convertible seats and easily movable partitions or curtains separating them from the economy cabin, floorspace flexibility is not a flight-by-flight option.

Before leaving this section, Box 8.3 looks at the flexibility offered by mixed passenger/cargo operations using convertible, quick-change (QC), and combi aircraft.

Box 8.3: Convertible, Quick-Change, and Combi Aircraft

Convertibles Aircraft convertible between passenger and all-cargo configurations can be useful for smaller airlines serving passenger markets that experience extreme peaking (e.g., transatlantic leisure markets during the northern summer) and wanting to deploy at least part of their fleets into cargo markets that peak at different times (e.g., pre-Christmas). Martinair used this approach successfully for many years. A particular type of convertible narrowbody sometimes encountered is the quick-change (QC) model.

QCs Aircraft designed for rapid conversion between passenger and freight operations first appeared in the 1960s, but subsequently fell from favour. In France, Aeropostale (succeeded by Europe Airpost) continued to operate a largely QC B737 fleet, allowing its core night postal operations to be supplemented by daytime passenger services flown on behalf of Air France; Italian carrier Mistral Air, a subsidiary of Gruppo Poste Italiano, also operates B737-300QCs. In both cases the changeover process was designed to effect installation or removal of palletised passenger seats in under an hour. (The same timeframe applies to the B737-700QC, whereas the -700 convertible requires around 5 hours to remove or install passenger seats.) Relatively few aircraft have QC capability, and all are inevitably short-haul narrow-bodies. Their inherent problems are that: change-over is labour-intensive; palletised passenger seats weigh more than regular seats; and configuration for passenger service may require galleys and storage space that are redundant in cargo usage. Damage to wall-panels is not uncommon.

Combis These aircraft carry both passengers and cargo on their main decks. (Some observers still refer to any widebody passenger aircraft as 'combis' because they have substantial underfloor cargo capacity; that is not the usage adopted here.) Combis are inherently flexible insofar as they can be used to develop new routes or to offer higher frequencies on existing routes than would be sustainable by an aircraft of similar size having broadly the same DOCs but relying just on passenger traffic (perhaps supplemented by belly-hold cargo). One approach might be to enter a new route with combis where there is freight demand sufficient to deliver revenues fairly rapidly whilst the passenger market is being developed. For combis to be useful, either adequate freight demand has to be present on the route concerned or that route must be part of a network within which cargo flows can be redirected towards it; if neither is the case, a smaller (passenger) aircraft is the better alternative.

Combis have fallen from favour somewhat in recent years, primarily for the following reasons:

- Stringent cargo compartment fire regulations introduced following an accident in the mid-1980s have imposed an additional weight and therefore cost penalty.
- The schedule requirements of passengers and shippers are sometimes difficult to reconcile. (This is, of course, a problem also confronted in respect of freight carried in the belly-holds of passenger aircraft; how serious it is will depend upon the mix, and therefore service requirements, of freight traffic on individual routes.)
- The emphasis airframe manufacturers have placed on the development of derivatives

since the 1980s has meant that airlines now have a wide range of mission capabilities from which to choose in respect of available passenger aircraft, and so have less need for combis to develop new passenger routes or niches.

Combis nonetheless remain important to some carriers' long-haul fleets (e.g., EVA Air and KLM), and even have a niche in a very small number of short-haul fleets (e.g., Alaska Airlines' B737-400 combis). Recent developments have focused on cutting down the time taken to adjust main-deck configurations to different mixes of passengers and freight.

Although convertibles, QCs, and combis all offer capacity management flexibility, this comes with a cost: there is a weight penalty attributable to strengthened floors, access doors, additional onboard equipment necessary for handling freight, and (in combis) fire suppression capabilities. An airline must be confident that it has sufficient freight traffic at adequate yields to justify the higher than necessary DOCs these aircraft will be generating whenever they are only (or, in combis, also) carrying passengers; by-product costing and marginal-cost pricing of freight are, or at least should be, out of the question.

CONCLUSION

The aircraft available for assignment within a network have a profound effect on profitability because the seat-mile and trip costs, as well as the marketing implications, of types in different size categories vary considerably. What airlines with more than one type or variant in their fleet need to be doing is matching aircraft to flight-legs with a view not to optimising individual flight assignments, but to maximising network profitability. Tactical fleet management is a key ingredient of cost-conscious, market-oriented capacity management.

V. Summary

This chapter has shown how fleet management meshes tightly with network design and scheduling. The next chapter will look at the final aspect of capacity management being covered in this part of the book: revenue management.

9
Revenue Management

Managing is like holding a dove in your hand. Squeeze too tight, you'll kill it. Open your hand too much, you let it go.

Tommy Lasorda

CHAPTER OVERVIEW

Revenue management (RM) can enhance total revenue by 4–5 per cent (Talluri and van Ryzin 2004), the precise figure depending upon the type of network operated, the airline's starting point in the discipline, and the sophistication of competitors' systems. RM does this by attempting to maximise revenue earned from a schedule of departures; the challenge lies in the fact that the largest network carriers can operate several thousand departures each day, serving tens of thousands of O&D markets with several million fares – many of which change daily yet are sold up to a year in advance. Such complexity can create a universe of several million fare products from which revenue has to be maximised. This chapter will:

- define RM and identify its objectives;
- outline the circumstances that favour deployment of a revenue management system (RMS);
- describe quantity-based and price-based approaches to RM;
- describe the essential differences between leg- and segment-based RM on the one hand and origin and destination (O&D) itinerary management on the other;
- identify the critical components of an RMS; and
- highlight differences between the revenue management of passenger and freight traffic.

I. Introduction

REVENUE MANAGEMENT DEFINED

Revenue management is the practice of maximising revenue generated from a fixed seat inventory which is perishable at the time of departure. It does this by controlling the release of seats for sale at different fares – in other words, by optimising the passenger mix. The RM problem can therefore be characterised as a decision whether or not to accept a booking request; the answer to this problem depends upon whether or not revenue earned by accepting the request exceeds revenue that could be earned by denying it and retaining the seat(s) for later sale at a higher price. Specifically, RM is the art and science of balancing:

- spoilage cost – a potential loss of revenue keyed off the probability that if a request for space is denied now, that seat will be empty at departure;
- displacement cost – a potential loss of revenue keyed off the probability that if a request for space is accepted now, higher revenue that could have been earned by delaying its release will be forgone;
- diversion cost – a potential loss (or in this case dilution) of revenue keyed off the probability that a customer allowed to purchase a fare at a given price would in fact have been willing to buy up to a higher-priced fare.

Pricing and seat inventory control are often now much more closely integrated than in the past – some airlines even integrating them fully. No longer is pricing necessarily accepted as a given which precedes and stands separately from seat inventory control. Figure 9.1 illustrates how revenue management and pricing relate to each other within the context of revenue and profit planning.

A CLOSER LOOK AT THE OBJECTIVE OF REVENUE MANAGEMENT

We saw in Part 2 of the book that an airline's operating performance is the result not of one factor alone, but of a complex series of interactions between output decisions (ASMs and ATMs produced), the unit cost arising from those decisions (cost per ASM or ATM), the volume of output that is actually sold (RPMs and RTMs), and the yield earned from output sold (revenue per RPM or RTM). The fact that the fixed costs involved in operating a schedule, largely capacity-driven rather than traffic-driven, represent such a high proportion of total costs defines the core RM task: having scheduled a given level of output on each flight-leg, accepted the fixed costs associated with producing that output, and – however temporarily – settled on tariff structures for the one or more markets served by each flight-leg, the challenge is to maximise revenue earned from the output produced. (The fact that output is delivered by *flight-legs* whilst prices and revenue relate to *markets* is an anomaly that will be looked at later in the chapter when O&D revenue management is discussed.)

The objective of passenger RM is therefore to maximise the revenue earned from each departure given the constraints imposed by cabin capacity and the applicable fare structure. This implies maximisation of revenue per ASM or ATM *produced*, rather than maximisation of yield (i.e., revenue per RPM or RTM, which in effect means per ASM or ATM *sold*); neither is maximisation of load factor in itself the objective – although it might in fact be a by-product of effective RM.

1. *Yield maximisation* The goal of RMSs is to maximise the revenue earned from each seat flown and therefore from each flight. To achieve this it is necessary to sell as many seats as possible and at the same time maximise the yield from each seat sold; this is not the same as maximising the yield from a flight (or, indeed, from an entire system). Assume for example that a carrier has two seats remaining on a 3000-mile flight just about to depart, one in business class for sale at $1000 and one deeply discounted at $300. Yield from the former would be 33.3 cents per RPM (i.e., $1000/(1 passenger × 3,000 miles)), whilst yield

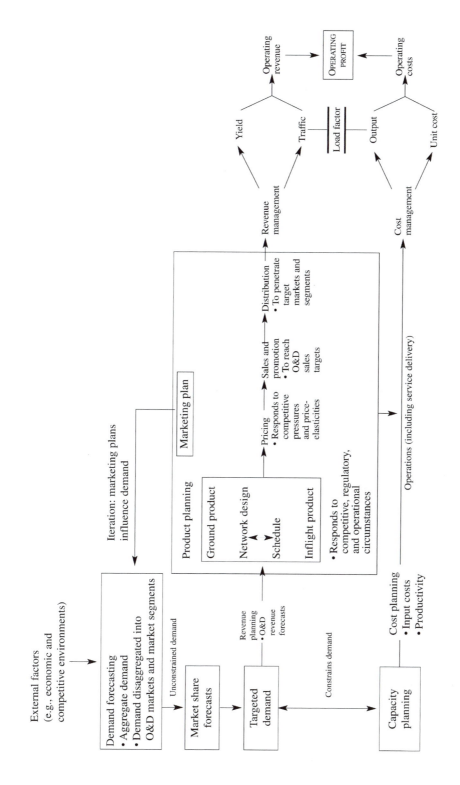

Figure 9.1   Revenue management in the context of revenue and cost planning

from the latter would be 10 cents. Assuming that average yield from passengers already booked for the flight is less than 33.3 cents but above 10 cents, acceptance of the business class passenger would increase yield from the flight; clearly, accepting the passenger paying a deeply discounted fare would reduce average yield even though it would increase revenue from the flight as a whole. A (flight) yield maximisation objective would therefore suggest denying space to the extra coach/economy passenger even though the seat would then fly empty and the airline would forgo $300 revenue – something that is obviously unsound. The objective should be to maximise yield not by departure, but in the sense that every seat actually sold is sold for the highest yield that can be earned from it; if that yield is only a few cents, then this is better than having the seat fly empty even if these few cents have the effect of lowering average yield for the flight as a whole. The important point to remember is that airlines bank revenue, not yield.

2. *Load factor maximisation* Maximisation of revenue and maximisation of load factor may well amount to the same thing on a low-demand flight; on a high-demand flight, however, high load factor is a given and the challenge becomes one of ensuring that space is released to the highest-yield demand that is 'bidding' for it. Maximising load factor is therefore an objective of RMSs, but not in isolation. Load factors can generally be maximised by selling inventory early in a flight's booking cycle at rock-bottom prices, but this will not maximise the revenue that flight could earn – it will simply build market share at the cost of revenue dilution; what an RMS tries to do is ensure that each seat is occupied by a passenger willing to pay as much as or more than anybody else in order to occupy it.

The fundamental objective of an RMS is therefore not necessarily to maximise yield or load factor, although an airline will certainly want to monitor yield in the context of its product positioning and desired traffic mix and to keep load factors high in order to minimise spoilage of unsold seats for which there is demand.

3. *Revenue maximisation* The objective of RM is to maximise unit revenue from a given schedule – that is, to maximise revenue per ASM or ATM produced (i.e., RASM or RATM). This is done by balancing average price and capacity utilisation (Weatherford and Bodily 1992). On a low-demand flight it can be achieved by maximising load factor; on a high-demand flight it can be achieved only by ensuring as far as possible that space is released to the highest-yield demand coming forward – that is, by ensuring that each seat is sold to the person willing to pay most to sit in it. What airlines really want to maximise of course is profit or shareholder value, but because their short-run capacity costs are fixed and the variable (traffic) costs associated with each additional passenger are relatively small we can take revenue maximisation as a good short-run proxy for profit maximisation – or, indeed, for the maximisation of contribution.

Finally, note that yield and average fare are related but distinct metrics. Average fare is: operating revenue ÷ originating revenue passengers. It is a metric often used by LFAs. Yield, on the other hand, is distance-weighted, being revenue per RPM rather than revenue per passenger. Using an RMS to maximise revenue is likely to lead to an average fare (and a yield) higher than would be the case were maximising load factor the objective and lower than were yield maximisation being targeted. What matters, however, is not average fare in isolation but average fare × load.

CONDITIONS APPROPRIATE FOR REVENUE MANAGEMENT

Revenue management is a useful tool for airlines because it works best under circumstances widely found in the industry (Kimes 1997; Herrmann *et al.* 1998):

- *Fixed capacity carrying high fixed costs* In the short run, an airline's capacity is fixed by the potential output of its fleet at full utilisation, and the output it actually produces from this capacity is broadly fixed by published schedules. The high short-run fixed costs associated with a scheduled airline's infrastructure impose pressure to maximise output over which to spread those costs, and to sell that output rather than allow space to fly empty.
- *Perishable output* The inability to inventory output after production means that any seats or cargo space unsold at departure will be lost.
- *Heterogeneous customers* Customers vary widely in terms of the value they place on different product attributes, their patterns of usage, and their purchase behaviours. The demand for airline services can be segmented in many different ways, but for revenue management purposes the two most important segmentation variables are willingness to pay (i.e., price-elasticity) and willingness to pay to be on one flight rather than another (i.e., time-preference).
- *Demand variability* The fact that air transport demand is variable by time of day, day of week, and/or season allows airlines to use price to redirect less time-sensitive/more price-elastic demand to off-peak and other low-demand flights, and to allocate a greater proportion of space on peak or high-demand flights to time-sensitive/less price-elastic segments willing to pay the most to travel on those flights.
- *A production system that is inflexible in the short term* Airlines cannot easily respond to short-term demand variability by varying supply.
- *Low marginal production and sales costs and high marginal revenue* We saw in Chapter 5 that short-run marginal costs are generally considered to be low in the airline business (although in reality they are not always as low as they might appear). Their low marginal costs and high marginal revenues, together with the ability to segment markets by willingness to pay, provide airlines with the opportunity to offer a tiered pricing structure capable of maximising revenue from price-inelastic segments whilst also stimulating demand from more price-elastic segments.
- *Reservations system* Revenue management works most effectively when output is sold in advance by a reservations system able to discriminate between purchasers.
- *Data availability* The most sophisticated approaches to revenue management require an ability to forecast demand by market segment and by departure. This calls for a great deal of historical sales data against which to calibrate forecasting and decision-support models.

The fact that demand can be segmented takes us back to the discussion in Chapter 3 with regard to uniform, discriminatory, and differential pricing. The following subsections briefly revisit that discussion.

Uniform Pricing

The simplest pricing strategy is to apply a single fare; there is then no need for revenue management. The flaws in this approach were discussed in Chapter 3: depending upon the level at which the single price is pitched, some consumers will travel on fares well below the maximum they would have been prepared to pay (and so retain significant amounts of consumer surplus – revenue that is lost to the airline), whilst more price-elastic consumers might be excluded by a price that is higher than they are willing to pay.

Figure 9.2 illustrates uniform pricing under two extreme scenarios. In both cases, area 1 represents revenue lost to consumers who would have been prepared to pay higher fares (i.e., consumer surplus), whilst area 2 represents revenue lost because some potential consumers are unwilling to pay the single fare; areas 1 and 2 together represent unaddressed revenue that an RMS can tap into.

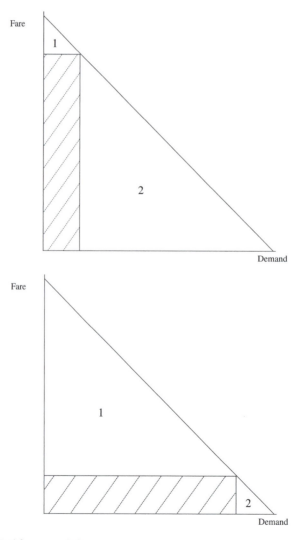

Figure 9.2   Uniform pricing

Discriminatory Pricing

It was explained in Chapter 3 that to maximise revenue by tapping into the consumer surplus left untouched by uniform pricing, an airline ideally needs to know how much each passenger would be prepared to pay in order to travel on a particular flight. For the purpose of illustration, Figure 9.3 assumes the idealised model of first degree price discrimination: each potential consumer divulges the maximum (or reservation) price that they are willing to pay.

Suppose the service package is sold at a single price of $600. Consumers A to D will buy, and will each benefit from a consumer surplus; consumer A will benefit from a surplus of $800 (i.e., $1400 – 600), B from one of $600, and so on. Consumer E will buy, but will not benefit from any consumer surplus; consumers F and G will not buy, because they do not value the service at $600 – a figure that is above their reservation prices. If the airline were to eat into the consumer surplus (the area above the $600 price line and below the demand curve) by raising the price, it would drive E, then D, then C out of the market – losing their revenue despite them being willing to buy *at a price*. Alternatively, by lowering the single price in order to target F and G, the airline will cede consumer surplus (i.e., potential revenue) to the others (and perhaps create an overdemand situation). Obviously, it is preferable for consumer surplus to be accessed by having every potential buyer pay a price as close as possible to their reservation price, and this is illustrated by the vertical boxes in Figure 9.3.

Each flight departure offers finite capacity, of course. Assume we are flying only a 6-seater so there is insufficient space for all seven of our potential consumers. Further assume that we know each consumer's reservation price and are able to sell to each at

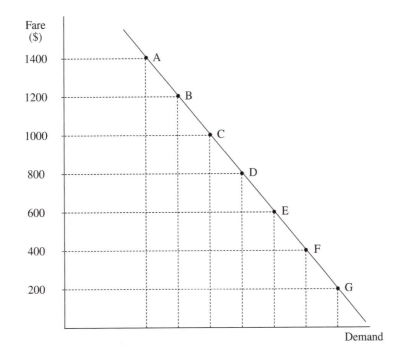

Figure 9.3   Discriminatory pricing under a single demand curve

these respective prices. Clearly, we do not want to sell space to G until we are reasonably confident that the same space cannot be sold to one of the others at a higher price. If only six including G eventually want to travel, then selling space to G is better than having an empty seat; but selling space to G, then to B, C, D, E, and F only to find that the day before departure A wants to travel but cannot get a seat is suboptimal from a revenue maximisation standpoint. Revenue management systems should help prevent this happening; specifically, they should protect space for late-booking, high-yield passengers on high-demand flights – a capability that translates into the service attribute called 'seat accessibility'. This is evidently easier to achieve in a larger aircraft than a 6-seater, insofar as sales can be made well in advance of departure to a number of low-yield purchasers such as G whilst still protecting seats for those willing to pay more and coming forward at a later time.

Taking another simplified example, an airline operating a 170-seat flight could, for the sake of argument, fill it well in advance by offering $125 fares. This would generate up to $21,250 in revenue, but it would also remove seats from the inventory for which later-booking passengers would have been prepared to pay more. If, instead, the airline offers five fares – with varying restrictions attached to keep segments of demand apart – such that 15 seats are available at $350, 25 seats at $275, 40 seats at $250, 50 seats at $175, and only 40 seats at $125, then (ignoring any connecting or interline traffic) its potential revenue rises to $35,875.

Differential And Discriminatory Pricing Revisited

As a practical matter, an airline cannot know every potential customer's reservation price. What therefore often happens is that the pricing department segments the market by willingness to pay, creates a fare basis for each segment, and then ring-fences all but the full, on-demand fare with conditions designed to restrict revenue dilution (i.e., high-yield, price-inelastic customers buying lower fares designed to exploit the elasticities of more price-elastic segments). In principle, every fare should be designed to exploit the targeted segment's price-elasticity with a view to generating just the amount of demand required to achieve high load factors, maximum revenue and a traffic mix consistent with the carrier's market positioning; in practice, life is rarely as precise as this.

When a market is segmented, the question arises as to whether segments should be served by significantly different service packages. In Chapter 3, it was noted that there has been some debate about whether customers travelling in the same cabin on different tariffs (i.e., combinations of fare and conditions) are the subjects of discriminatory or differential pricing. This distinction matters because discriminatory pricing assumes a single demand function and demand curve, whilst differential pricing models assume multiple demand functions and demand curves – one for each fare product: optimal capacity and revenue management decisions cannot be made if we are working on incorrect demand curve assumptions.

In Chapter 2 it was noted that in a dynamic marketplace, demand curves will frequently shift as a result of changes in non-price determinants of demand. Thus:

1. A change in an independent variable that leads to a rightward shift in the demand curve (e.g., a successful advertising campaign, a favourably received inflight product upgrade, an increase in consumers' incomes, a decrease in the prices of complementary

products such as destination hotels, or increases in competitors' fares) can enable a carrier:
- either to sell higher volumes at the same price – in which case capacity might have to be added, bringing with it incremental costs that need to be considered;
- or to sell the same volume at a higher average price – which might simply involve reallocating inventory away from low-yield fare classes and expanding allocations for high-yield fare classes.

2. If we reverse any of the examples above and assume a leftward shift in the demand curve, the response might be to down-gauge the aircraft used in the market concerned (if this is an option given fleet composition) or reallocate inventory in favour of low-yield fare classes.

Clearly, managing or responding to changes in determinants of demand is complicated by uncertainty over how many demand curves we are actually dealing with. Belobaba and Farkas (1999, p. 220) note that, 'The use of a single demand density to represent total demand for a single departure does not account for the different fare class demands or their corresponding fare values. Yet, it is a fundamental assumption of [yield management] systems that different demand densities exist for each fare class offered.' In other words, RM models should assume that we are dealing with differential pricing – that each fare, fenced by rules and restrictions from other fares, is a different product with its own demand curve. Nonetheless, some RM models do assume just a single demand curve.

If it is accepted that each fare class has its own demand curve, another question arises: is demand for fares in one booking class on a given departure statistically independent of demand for fares in other booking classes? For example, if demand for space in one fare class is denied, to what if any extent will that demand move to another, higher fare class? Most early RM models assumed statistical independence. However, there is now a widely-held view supporting the interdependence of demand (Hopperstad 1994). We will return to this issue below when dynamic pricing is discussed.

II. Approaches to Revenue Management

An important distinction can be drawn between two broad approaches to RM:

1. *Traditional approach* From the 1970s onwards, airline pricing departments began offering what ultimately became multitudes of different fare products – essentially price offers fenced-in behind a ring of conditions on purchase and restrictions on usage which a consumer had to be able to satisfy. These fare products were based on increasingly fine-grained market segmentation which assumed insight into consumers' willingness to balance price against an ever-more arcane and complex array of rules and conditions; the purpose of the rules was primarily to prevent revenue dilution arising from the purchase of discounted fares by travellers whose willingness to pay is high. The assumption of insight was not always well-founded (Dunleavy and Westermann 2005).
2. *LFA approach* Many LFAs do not segment their markets on the basis of willingness to abide by complex rules and restrictions, but instead offer at any one time a single price for a single fare product on each departure – that price generally increasing as the day of operation draws closer. Because fares are priced one-way, restrictions such as minimum, maximum or mandatory Saturday night stays cannot be applied; on the other hand, fares

will usually be non-refundable and changes will either be forbidden or made subject to a fee plus payment of any additional fare. Allocation of space is therefore not an issue because instead of there being multiple fare products for sale, there is in fact only one bucket open at any one time: the issue is when to close offers at the current price and open offers at the next higher price – something which requires much closer integration of the pricing and RM functions than has traditionally been the case. Several network carriers have chosen to adopt this simplified approach in short-haul markets where they compete with LFAs, although – as will be noted again below – most do still have more than one fare available per cabin at any given time. (Some LFAs also utilise multiple buckets; Southwest, for example, currently operates with more than a dozen.)

Two leading writers in the field of RM (Talluri and van Ryzin 2004) characterise these approaches respectively as 'quantity-based revenue management' and 'price-based revenue management'. What this means is as follows: with the traditional approach multiple fare products are created, their prices are fixed, and the heart of the RM task is to maximise revenue through capacity control – that is, by optimising capacity *allocation* between products; with the LFA approach there is one, undifferentiated, largely restriction-free product on sale at any one time, and the heart of the RM task is to maximise revenue through *dynamic pricing* – that is, by adjusting the price point currently on sale (the 'active price') as unconstrained demand evolves. (The word 'unconstrained' refers in this context to the absence of the artificial constraints on demand imposed by the existence of separate fare products with what are assumed to be their own independent demand distributions. An ultimate constraint – aircraft capacity – still exists, of course.) Quantity-based RM is considered first, then the price-driven approach will be summarised.

QUANTITY-BASED APPROACH: CAPACITY ALLOCATION

Revenue management as still widely practised is an allocation-based system. It is part of a sequential demand management process which begins with schedule planning and pricing. It should in principle be integrated or, at the very least, closely coordinated with those functions.

1. First, a schedule is established taking into account the volume and nature of demand in the markets served.
2. Second, demand for each flight is forecast.
3. Third, a fare structure is created which segments demand on each flight with a view to maximising revenue earned from the departure. This structure should in principle be consistent with the airline's market positioning – that is, consistent with the targeted traffic mix – and responsive to characteristics of demand such as willingness to pay (i.e., price-elasticity) and willingness to pay for space on a particular departure (i.e., time-preference). There are two elements to a fare structure, which are further explained in Box 9.1 and exemplified in Table 9.1:
   • fare bases – essentially tariffs, or combinations of price point and conditions;
   • booking classes (26 of which have been established by IATA for distribution through the GDSs) – essentially 'buckets', each comprising a small number of similarly priced and conditioned fare bases. (The number 26, incidentally, is attributable to capacity limitations in early computer systems which could handle only a single-letter designator per class.)

Box 9.1: Fare Bases, Booking Classes, and Cabins

Figure 9.4 illustrates the relationship between fare basis, booking class, and cabin.

Cabins To the extent that aircraft are operated with fixed cabin partitions (i.e., partitions are not easily moveable and seating configurations are markedly different in each cabin), revenue management must in the short run be applied to each cabin separately. The more floorspace flexibility available, as on certain intra-European flights with movable curtains or partitions separating business and economy classes, the more flexibly an RMS can operate (Pak et al. 2003).

Booking (or fare) classes These are the units into which a flight's seat inventory is divided in an allocation-based RMS. They are the fare products referred to above and they are represented for the most part by letter designators such as Y, H, M, Q, or V which vary between carriers and markets. In most markets today each cabin of an aircraft – first, business, premium economy, and/or economy/coach – will be divided into booking classes; these divisions are virtual rather than physical. Taking a long-haul economy cabin as an example, Y class might be an unrestricted one-way fare, whilst other letters might refer respectively to a discounted one-way fare, and 7-, 14-, and 21-day advance purchase round-trip excursion fares – the round-trips perhaps subject to minimum and/or maximum stay restrictions; each fare other than Y is likely to be subject to some form of condition – either a prohibition or a fee – applied to changes and cancellation. The purpose of rules, restrictions, and conditions is to act as a 'fence', preventing the diversion of potentially high-yield customers towards lower fares. The scope of conditions has narrowed in markets subject to LFA penetration.

Fare bases Some, although not all, of the booking classes sold by an airline might be further differentiated. For example, a 21-day excursion fare in V class might be unavailable at certain times of year, or it might be sold at different prices in defined low, shoulder, and peak seasons; discounts might also be available in this class for children, military or government personnel. Each of the fares available within V class, perhaps at different times of year or subject to different conditions, is a separate fare basis represented by its own alphanumeric code. Each fare basis is grouped into one of a smaller number of booking classes in order to simplify the management of seat inventories within CRSs. The fare bases in each booking class should have broadly similar values and booking restrictions; ideally, the variances between fare-bases within a booking class should be minimised and the differences between booking classes should be maximised. Table 9.1 provides a hypothetical illustration of a possible outcome once fare bases have been incorporated into booking classes.

Summary Booking classes, any one of which may or may not be comprised of underlying fare bases, are tariffs which combine a price and, in the case of restricted fares, a set of purchase and/or usage conditions. They each represent an offer being made at a particular time to different segments of demand in the market concerned, with segments defined by cabin preference, price-sensitivity, time-preference, and willingness or ability to accept various conditions. It is the job of an RM department to allocate available capacity between booking classes with a view to maximising revenue. It is these booking classes that are each characterised as a fare product for the purposes of RM.

---

4. Fourth, seats available on each flight are *allocated* into different available booking classes, booking limits are applied to low-yield classes in order to protect the seat inventory in higher classes, and the inventory as a whole is then managed until departure by revising forecasts and re-optimising booking limits. The latter is done either at pre-specified times or in response to 'alarms' triggered by deviation of actual bookings from the forecast booking curve.

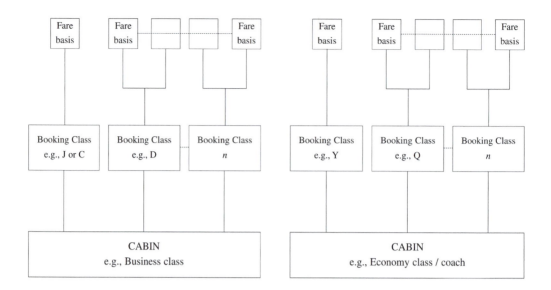

Figure 9.4   Fare bases, booking classes and aircraft cabins

Table 9.1   Typical booking data

Booking class	Empty seats	X	G	L	V	H	B	Y	J
Ticket price range	-	0	$100-199	$200-399	$400-599	$600-799	$800-999	$1,000-1,999	$2,000+
Average fare	-	0	$162.45	$324.90	$541.20	$758.10	$974.70	$1,624.50	$2,707.50
Passengers	8 empty	19	34	23	23	49	23	15	18
Load factor	4%	9%	16%	11%	11%	23%	11%	7%	8%
Revenue	-	0	$5,523	$7,473	$12,448	$37,147	$22,418	$24,368	$48,735
Average advance purchase (days)	-	-	65	46	35	32	26	14	12

As noted overleaf, the heart of the RM problem in an allocation-based system is whether to accept or reject a booking request. The object is to sell 'the right inventory unit to the right type of customer, at the right time, and for the right price' (Kimes 1997, p. 3). Put another way, the purpose of *seat inventory control* is to arrive at a revenue-maximising solution to the problem that by accepting too many low-yield reservation requests on high-demand flights an airline may sacrifice later-booking higher-yield sales, yet by rejecting too many low-yield requests it is possible that seats will be left unfilled at departure (Belobaba 1987). The fundamental rule in an allocation-based system, first formulated by Littlewoood (1972), is that a higher fare should be protected – by refusing a booking request for the lower fare – as long as the higher fare weighted by the probability of selling it in the future (i.e., expected revenue) exceeds the known revenue from selling the lower fare.

Revenue-Managing A Single Flight-Leg

Quantity-based RM can be broken down into three steps: allocation of inventory; overbooking; and management of inventory. A distinction can be drawn between allocation on a single flight-leg, on a segment, or across a hubbed network. We will look at flight-legs first, before moving on to consider revenue management of flight segments and then networks.

Initial allocation of seats on a single flight-leg   Taking the traditional approach, assume that the pricing department has designed a fare structure for a market, grouped the different fares into booking (or fare) classes applicable to each of the different aircraft cabins (i.e., compartments) being offered, and attached conditions to the purchase of anything other than unrestricted, on-demand, 'full' fares in order to prevent revenue dilution. In effect, a number of different fare products have been created, each with its own price and each defined by the rules and conditions attached to its sale. The task of the revenue management department is then to decide on the mix of products to be offered – that is, to allocate available seats on each departure to the booking classes applicable to that departure. The process of allocating seats to booking classes with a view to maximising revenue is sometimes referred to as 'fare-mix optimisation'. There are two approaches:

1. *Class-based controls* The most common of the two, this approach is based on forecasting demand at the outset and targeting an average fare for each booking class – the latter being a function of the fare bases incorporated into the booking class concerned and the number of seats sold at each of those fares. Booking limits are established to set a ceiling on the number of bookings that will be accepted in each class, and this protects remaining seats in the cabin for sale in progressively higher-yield booking classes.
2. *Revenue-based controls* A threshold or bid price is established at the outset equivalent to the lowest fare basis in each booking class, then subsequently adjusted in response to evolving demand and the time remaining to departure. A booking request is accepted only if it matches or exceeds the current threshold price in the class concerned. One advantage of using bid prices rather than booking limits is that revenue-based control can be used to discriminate between requests for different fare bases within each class, accepting or rejecting them depending on how the average revenue for the class as a whole is developing. We will come across bid-price controls used in a network context later in the chapter.

In addition to booking limits established for the allocation of inventory to booking classes, 'authorisation levels' may be set to control the number of seats released through different distribution channels or in specified geographical regions. Conversely, in some markets – particularly Asia-Pacific outbound – it is common practice for airlines to take allotments out of their seat inventory and pass them to travel agencies for retailing; where an agency is free to return unused portions of its allotment prior to departure, as frequently happens in Japan for instance, the airline needs to closely monitor agency performance (Vinod 2006).

There can be two approaches to the initial allocation of inventory:

1. *Deterministic approach* This assumes that demand can be forecast with sufficient accuracy to determine how many seats should be allocated to each booking class. The variability of air transport demand makes this approach profoundly suboptimal.
2. *Probabilistic approach* This recognises that demand is stochastic and so allocates seats to booking classes on the basis of the revenue *expected* from each marginal sale (Littlewood 1972). For example, data might show that we can be extremely confident that 20 seats on a particular departure will be sold at full fare for the cabin concerned, but that the probability of selling more seats at that fare declines marginally with each number from 21 upwards. If those declining probability figures are multiplied by the amount of the full fare, a series of declining expected marginal seat revenue (EMSR) figures will be generated. Assume that EMSR for the 24th seat sold at full fare is higher than the same seat's EMSR were it to be sold at the next lower fare, but in the case of the 25th seat the reverse is true – that is, EMSR from a discounted sale is higher than for a full-fare sale (because the probability of making a discounted sale is higher); on this assumption 24 seats would be allocated to the full-fare booking class, whilst the 25th and subsequent seats would be allocated to a lower-yield bucket.

   To summarise, what an EMSR model does is calculate a probability distribution for demand in each booking class and multiply the average fare in that booking class on the flight-leg concerned by the probability that demand will subsequently come forward, thereby arriving at an expected marginal revenue figure for each incremental seat; this figure can then be used to establish 'protection levels' or booking limits. The latter are calculated for each subordinate class by subtracting seats protected in all higher classes from the number of seats remaining available in the cabin concerned.

Having decided on an initial allocation of seats to each booking class, there are two further issues to deal with: first, the problem that not all of the seats booked will actually be occupied at flight departure; second, the problem that demand rarely arises sequentially such that the lowest-yield booking classes fill first from the bottom up. The next two subsections will look at how these problems can be addressed.

Overbooking Seats fly empty because demand forecasts were overoptimistic leading to too much capacity being flown (i.e., excess output), or because seats that had actually been booked were for some reason unoccupied at departure (i.e., spoilage). The most common reasons why bookings fail to generate boardings are:

- *Cancellations* Of particular concern are late cancellations.
- *Misconnections* A misconnection is a passenger who fails to board a flight because of the cancellation or late arrival of an incoming flight.
- *No-shows* A no-show is a booked passenger who fails to board a flight for any reason other than a missed connection, and who does not cancel the reservation.

The problem posed by no-shows and misconnections in particular is that their non-arrival is only known so close to departure that unless there are compensating numbers of unbooked go-shows or of standby passengers, seats fly empty. No-shows and late cancellations might result from a decision not to travel or from either multiple bookings (i.e., bookings held on more than one flight as a fall-back) or duplicate bookings (perhaps made in error by an agency) that the airline has failed to pick up in its CRS (most likely because it is not using revenue integrity software). More sinister sources of no-shows can be: speculative bookings by agencies claiming inventory without having a specific passenger, but wanting to have space on popular departures from the local hub to offer to any late-booking high-value clients; and possibly even abusive bookings by agencies trying to benefit from incentives offered by GDSs in return for high and rising transaction volumes – although the scope for this has been considerably reduced in recent years by airlines renegotiating contracts with GDSs to eliminate transaction-based volume incentives for agencies. We met some of these phenomena in Chapter 5 when discussing airlines' GDS costs. (There is also a small subgroup of no-shows and late cancellations called 'defections', comprising passengers with endorsable or refundable tickets who arrive at the airport in time for a flight, find it has been delayed and switch to another carrier; to predict this type of defection it is necessary to forecast the probability of departure delays.)

There are three ways to combat the problem of spoilage:

1. *Insist on payment in full at the time of booking* This is the standard LFA approach, which has been progressively adopted by network carriers in respect of their most deeply discounted fares and in some cases all but their full, unrestricted fares.
2. *Impose ticketing time limits (TTLs)* These are a somewhat less draconian way to improve the quality of bookings (i.e., reduce no-shows), the theory being that ticketed reservations are more likely to result in boarded passengers than are unticketed bookings. TTLs also offer the added advantage to new entrants onto a route that they provide some degree of control over no-shows in the absence of historical traffic data on which to base reliable overbooking models. The problem is, of course, that TTLs are difficult to enforce in unrestricted booking classes because even a ticketed passenger will be able to reschedule or obtain a refund. Another problem is that when an agency allows a TTL to expire on a flight that is still open and then rebooks, the airline might end up having to pay additional GDS fees in respect of the rollover.
3. *Overbook* Unless an airline insists on non-refundable payment at or shortly after the time of booking, the fundamental answer to the no-show and late cancellation problems is overallocation and overbooking – that is, to allocate more seats to booking classes in aggregate than are physically available on the aircraft (particularly to booking classes that do not bear heavy rebooking or cancellation penalties), and sell up to these limits. Overbooking to avoid spoilage is an essential element in RM: its purpose is to earn revenue from passengers who would otherwise have been spilled off apparently full flights, but for whom space did turn out to be available on departure. Lufthansa carries more than two-thirds of a million passengers every year who would not have flown on their preferred flights but for the extra 'capacity' created by overbooking; because some spilled passengers would have been recaptured on alternative Lufthansa services not all of them generate incremental revenue for the airline, but a substantial proportion can be assumed to do so.

    A good RMS will disaggregate no-show, go-show, and cancellation patterns and set overbooking limits appropriate to each departure. Some RMSs allow cancellations to be put back into inventory, but as departure date approaches and overbooking limits are ratcheted down towards physical capacity on the assigned aircraft, cancelled seats are progressively eliminated from inventory – in effect, eating into the overbooked inventory in order to get it down to zero by the time of departure.

Overbooking establishes an 'authorised capacity' for a flight in excess of its physical capacity; confirmed bookings at any time in advance of departure should be at or below authorised capacity but may be above physical capacity. Overbooking limits are now commonly set by optimisation models designed to minimise two sets of costs:

- *Spoilage costs* We have seen that if a booking class is closed by the sale of a refundable or re-bookable ticket to a passenger who subsequently cancels or fails to turn up and that seat could have been sold later in the booking cycle, there has been 'spoilage'. 'Spoilage cost' is an estimate of revenue forgone by flying the empty seat. This issue is not trivial: Lufthansa Group no-shows run well in excess of 5 million each year, for example, and something in the 10–15 per cent range is far from unusual for network carriers. (In the United States, trends since 2001 towards later booking of leisure fares and higher system load factors have together contributed to a marked decline in no-show rates at some carriers – to as low as 4 per cent at Continental, for example [Gorin *et al.* 2006].) Overbooking is a particularly important capacity management tool insofar as booking classes containing fully flexible and refundable fares are concerned, because this is where no-shows are likely to be the highest. The higher the proportion of an airline's fares sold on a non-cancellable, non-refundable basis the lower its no-show rate tends to be. Many LFAs – Ryanair, for example – do not overbook because all reservations are paid for at the time of booking and are non-refundable. On the other hand, because prices charged by LFAs in some markets are so low that their non-refundability may not be a particularly strong deterrent to no-shows, there can be a case even for these carriers to overbook.
  Another consideration is load factor. The higher the load factor on a flight, the greater is the likelihood that no-shows will have displaced potential customers who tried and were unable to make a reservation. Generally, the lower an airline's break-even load factor, the easier it is to adopt a conservative overbooking policy. Airlines facing low yields and high break-even load factors have an incentive to overbook more aggressively – although, as noted, less so if they place tight restrictions on cancellation and refunds. Finally, spoilage might not be limited to forgone marginal revenue on the flight-leg concerned; if that flight is in or out of a hub, the loss of a connecting O&D fare could be substantial.
- *Denied boarding costs* The most obvious cost here is the cost of a refund. Depending upon airline policy and the jurisdiction concerned, an airline bumping passengers could incur compensation costs (e.g., cash or vouchers for future flights – although the latter are often heavily conditioned), administration costs arising from rebooking, and perhaps meal and accommodation costs; particularly in high value, time-sensitive segments of demand, another significant cost is loss of customer goodwill. Overbooking policy therefore needs to be carefully monitored. Because limits are based on averages for each departure, there will be many occasions on which the number of no-shows falls below the mean. A denied-boarding problem could develop if overbooking limits are fixed too close to that mean or, over time, a change in the average goes unnoticed. Having said this, some level of denied boarding is inevitable if overbooking limits are being used to their full potential. It is therefore important that compensation packages are designed to be sufficiently attractive to ensure that as many denied boardings as possible are voluntary rather than involuntary; in practice, airlines as a whole

have not been particularly good at handling the denied boarding problem, and some have resisted even the very basic compensation requirements mandated in those few jurisdictions – notably the United States and the EU – where they have been imposed.

The above approach can be traced back to a static optimisation model formulated by Beckman (1958). What 'static' means in this case is that overbooking limits are calculated and then periodically recalculated on the basis of estimates of cancellation rates from the present going forward to departure, based on historical data for the flight concerned. Static models are in more widespread use than alternative dynamic models, which also take into account the evolution (i.e., the dynamics) of cancellations and booking requests up to the present time. Within the last few years, efforts have been made to move beyond booking and cancellation data to develop models which look at PNR characteristics; these attempt to find a link between, on the one hand, variables associated with an individual passenger (e.g., FFP membership), an itinerary (e.g., inbound leg of a return trip), and/or the booking channel (e.g., online, call centre or agency) and, on the other hand, probability of cancelling late or failing to show (Garrow and Koppelman 2004). Gorin *et al.* (2006) suggest combining passenger-specific characteristics with reservations and cancellation data.

Management of booking classes: the problem of non-sequential arrivals Having decided on the initial allocation of physical seats to booking classes in each compartment (e.g., the coach/economy or business class cabin) and the creation of 'virtual seats' by overbooking, the next task in the RM process is to manage allocations through to the day of operation. This raises the question of what the arrivals pattern will be for enquiries and bookings. The literature has modelled the problem for a single-leg flight offering multiple fare classes from two perspectives (Burger and Fuchs 2005):

1. *Static models* Booking requests are assumed to arise first for the lowest fare product, then sequentially for each higher fare class. Demand in each class is separately modelled and inventory is controlled just once at the outset of the process (Littlewood 1972; Belobaba 1987; Curry 1990; Brumelle and McGill 1993; Wollmer 1992). There have been two approaches to the establishment of booking limits and protection levels:
    *   *Optimisation* Original models, dating back to Littlewood (1972), assumed two classes and accommodated optimisation. Unfortunately, *n*-class optimisation models did not come into their own until the 1980s, and in the interim airlines having more than two classes to manage turned to heuristics as an alternative – an alternative still widely used in static single-leg models (Talluri and van Ryzin 2004).
    *   *Heuristics* The two most popular heuristics were developed by Belobaba. EMSRa (Belobaba 1987) bridges the gap between two-class and *n*-class models by applying the two-class model sequentially to each pair of classes, moving from lowest to highest. EMSRb (Belobaba 1989), now the most commonly used of the two, also adopts a two-class approach but treats as a single class *all* classes above the lower one in the pairing.
2. *Dynamic models* The arrival of booking requests is assumed not to be sequential, with the result that a subordinate fare class will not necessarily be sold out of its initial allocation before requests arise for sale of higher fare classes. The question in

this case is whether and when to close and possibly reopen classes in response to evolving demand (Lee and Hersh 1993; Subramanian *et al.* 1999). Forecasts and initial booking limits are based on historical analysis of traffic carried at different fares (i.e., the disaggregated demand distribution) on the particular departure, adjusted for any known circumstances that might impact the forecast such as a major sporting or cultural event. Thereafter, as seats are sold, a booking curve develops – a plot of reservations against time. Various points above and below the booking curve might be set to trigger the automatic opening and closing of booking classes. If actual sales take the booking curve for a class away from the forecast curve by a predetermined amount, the flight will be flagged for a revenue manager's attention. Some systems compare actual with historical data, calculate final sale probabilities under different sets of pricing assumptions, and flag individual flights if any of the probabilities fall outside a preset range. Another approach is to monitor the booking class closing rate – the rate at which low-yield booking classes are being closed to sale. (Older, less automated approaches rely not on automatic alarms or exception reports, but on revenue managers manually checking flights at specified read-points in the booking cycle to verify that bookings are evolving as predicted.)

As the departure date approaches, capacity managers generally play a more active role in releasing seats and accepting or overriding the system's reallocation recommendations. Manual overrides might be based on an intuitive reading of the current competitive environment, or they could arise from pressures exerted by other departments such as sales or scheduling which have their own agendas. If late in the booking cycle either too much space remains even for late-booking, high-yield passengers to fill or too little space remains to accommodate them, a swap to a better-sized aircraft type or variant might be the preferred option if feasible.

Managing allocated inventory within a cabin therefore requires a number of sub-problems to be addressed: how to ensure that the highest booking class is not sold out ahead of lower-yield booking classes; whether to reopen closed booking classes; how to control group bookings.

1. *How to ensure that the highest booking class is not sold out ahead of lower-yield booking classes*
    We have seen that reservation requests can be assumed to follow one of several arrival patterns: requests for fares might be assumed to arrive sequentially from low- to high-fare booking classes (the assumption in many early academic papers), or – more likely – arrivals could be interspersed (i.e., follow no particular pattern relative to booking classes). The problem of interspersed arrival is addressed by *nesting*, which has been increasingly widely practised over the last two decades. Three generic types have been applied to the single flight-leg, multiple-class inventory management problem: serial (or linear), parallel, and hybrid.
    *   *Serial nesting* This is the term used to describe a hierarchical structure of booking classes which makes all seats in lower ('subordinate') classes available to each higher (or 'prime') class. Even when a booking class is sold out to its initial allocation, it can (assuming it is not the lowest class) take available seats from a subordinate class applicable to the same aircraft cabin or 'base compartment' in response to a booking request that would otherwise be denied. The booking limit for a prime class always therefore includes inventory allocated to subordinate classes – the result being that a prime booking class can never be closed when a subordinate class remains open.

On the other hand, subordinate classes that have sold out can only access availability in a higher class once it has become clear from comparisons of actual against historical booking data that the higher class is unlikely to need all of its initial allocation – a decision that is more likely to be taken, if at all, relatively close to departure. In this way, seats in the higher class(es) are protected by booking limits imposed on subordinate classes. Some systems also impose a control limit policy that places an upper limit on the number of seats that can be sold in each booking class (or group of booking classes) at different points in time prior to departure.

- *Parallel nesting* Each subordinate booking class is nested only into the highest class for the cabin concerned (e.g., Y). Thus, the prime class can draw on the inventory of all subordinate classes, but those subordinate classes are partitioned insofar as they are not nested with each other and none can draw on the inventory of another.
- *Hybrid nesting* This combines features of parallel and serial nesting insofar as there is partitioning of some low-yield booking classes from each other, but nesting of these and intermediate classes into the full-fare booking class – which has access to all subordinate classes.

Serial nesting has clear advantages over parallel and hybrid nesting. Where demand is slow to materialise, low-yield booking classes might be expanded. If demand is stronger than expected, low-yield booking classes can be closed at levels below initial allocation and high-yield classes expanded; offers can also be opened on alternative, lightly loaded flights to redirect the more price-elastic segments whilst at the same time minimising spillage to competitors. Nonetheless, there are occasions when parallel or hybrid nesting can be useful; Weyer (1998), for example, suggests that they might be used to protect inventory for travel wholesalers or for retail promotions. All three approaches are preferable to a simple *partitioning* of booking limits at the outset, under which no booking class can draw on another irrespective of how demand develops, and most systems which use booking limit controls now apply nesting.

Figure 9.5 provides a conceptual illustration of serial, parallel, and hybrid nesting, and Table 9.2 uses hypothetical data to show what serial and hybrid nesting imply in terms of the availability of seats in progressively higher booking classes; note that in Figure 9.5 the initial allocations incorporate overbooking.

2. *Whether to reopen closed booking classes* A booking class might be closed because the seats allocated to it have been sold, or the closure might be time-determined – as when the advance purchase requirements restricting the fare bases in the class can no longer be satisfied. If sales have not developed as forecast and close to departure there is a significant number of unsold seats in the same cabin allocated to booking classes higher than one that has been closed, one response would be to reopen the lower-yield class (perhaps relaxing purchase restrictions) and use price to stimulate demand. This happens, and it accounts for the fact that advance purchase does not invariably equate to purchase at the lowest price. The problem from an RM perspective is that if done too frequently as a matter of policy, customers come to expect late-availability of cheap fares; this not only affects booking behaviour, but it could lead to the diversion to discounted fares of some late-booking and potentially high-yield passengers who would travel anyway on the departure concerned (Zhao and Zheng 2001). (Websites offering last-minute availability pose a similar problem.)

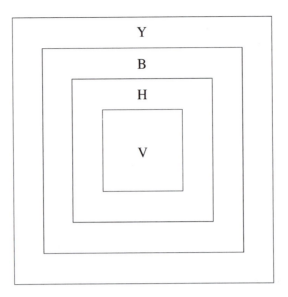

Figure 9.5a   Serial nesting of booking classes within a cabin

Note: Letters refer to booking classes, with 'V' containing the lowest fare bases and 'Y' the
highest; with the exception of 'Y', letters used can vary between markets.

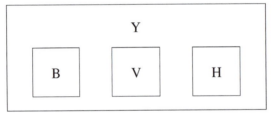

Figure 9.5b   Parallel nesting of booking classes within a cabin

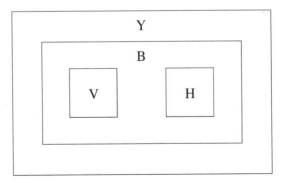

Figure 9.5c   Hybrid nesting of booking classes within a cabin

Table 9.2   **Nested booking limits for a 120-seat departure**

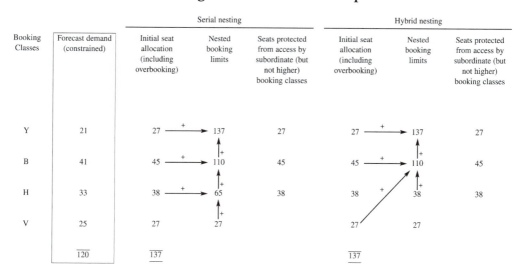

Booking Classes	Forecast demand (constrained)	Serial nesting			Hybrid nesting		
		Initial seat allocation (including overbooking)	Nested booking limits	Seats protected from access by subordinate (but not higher) booking classes	Initial seat allocation (including overbooking)	Nested booking limits	Seats protected from access by subordinate (but not higher) booking classes
Y	21	27	137	27	27	137	27
B	41	45	110	45	45	110	45
H	33	38	65	38	38	38	38
V	25	27	27		27	27	
	120	137			137		

3. *How to control group bookings* A group booking involves the sale of a significant number of seats for the same itinerary to a group of people travelling together at a rate negotiated by the group organizer with airline staff. (A 'batch booking' or 'multiple booking', on the other hand, involves several passengers travelling together on the same itinerary whose reservation requests arrive at the same time but through normal distribution channels and without any separate negotiation.) There are two significant risks when booking groups, both related to group size: first, the larger the group the greater the likelihood that it will displace some higher-fare demand; second, the larger the group the greater the risk of unsold inventory on departure if late turnback of some or all of the booking is permitted. Notwithstanding that the first is fundamentally a pricing issue and the second is fundamentally contractual, both should ideally be addressed by the sales and RM functions working together.

The proportion of a scheduled airline's traffic attributable to groups will be driven to a large extent by its geographical scope – specifically, how significant popular leisure, exhibition, incentive, and conference destinations are within its overall network. Groups usually travel on popular routes, book early in a flight's booking cycle, generate churn as a result of cancellations and additions to the party, and produce low yields. Fares negotiated by travel agencies, tour operators, cruise lines or other travel organizers with an airline's group sales desk or department will depend upon the booking status of legs on the requested itinerary at the time of booking, the size of the group, number of complimentary seats requested, expected attrition rate for the group concerned, estimated revenue displacement, and the nature of any ongoing business relationship that might exist. Sales departments whose performance and therefore planning are driven by load factors rather than quality of revenue can sometimes be in conflict with revenue managers – particularly when sales targets are established over extended periods of time, making them insensitive to the departure-specific concerns of revenue management. However, the growing trend amongst airlines to reward sales efforts on the basis of revenue rather than volume is helping improve group control. Yuen (1998) provides insight into how an airline might maximise the revenue potential of groups by redefining the internal processes used to evaluate group requests.

Conclusion   Allocation-based RMSs which control inventory on the basis of individual flight-legs remain in widespread use, contributing sometimes substantial dollar amounts of revenue enhancement. However, evaluation of booking requests on a leg-by-leg basis and consequent inability to distinguish local from flow traffic means that seats have to be available in the same class on all flight-legs for a multi-leg booking request to be accepted, which could allow a short-haul bottleneck to block remunerative long-haul bookings; this is not a problem for LFAs operating entirely point-to-point networks (which not all do, of course), but it does lead to suboptimal outcomes for network carriers. The next two sections look at developments designed to address this issue.

Revenue-Managing A Flight Segment

Travel on a segment can be synonymous with travel on a single flight-leg or – more relevant here – it can refer to travel on more than one flight-leg on a route operated under the same flight number as a direct/multi-stop/through service. For example, a London Heathrow (LHR)–Bangkok (BKK)–Sydney (SYD) through-service has three segments and two flight-legs: the LHR–BKK and LHR–SYD segments both flow over the LHR–BKK flight-leg, and the LHR–SYD and BKK–SYD segments flow over the BKK–SYD flight-leg. Broadly, we can say that aircraft operate flight-legs whilst passengers travel on segments; sometimes the two are synonymous, and sometimes they are not. Capacity in a segment-controlled system can be allocated to booking classes on each segment based on forecasted segment traffic, and the booking classes can be nested as readily as under flight-leg control.

Allocation-based RMSs have now in many cases been adapted to accommodate demand from both through- and local traffic on multi-leg flights operated under the same flight number. For example, a segment closed indicator (SCI) in a reservations control system might close a booking class for the LHR–BKK segment, but leave it open for traffic on the LHR–SYD segment. The system in effect arrives at a judgement that given the current booking curve, there is a higher probability of maximising revenue by selling each incremental seat in that booking class to LHR–SYD traffic than to LHR–BKK and BKK–SYD local traffic. What segment control cannot take into account is the value of an LHR–BKK passenger who wants to connect at BKK with a flight on the same carrier to, say, Perth.

There might, on the other hand, be circumstances where it makes sense to allocate a higher proportion of seats to high-yield local traffic than to through- or connecting traffic on a flight-leg that also serves multi-stop and connecting markets. Particularly in short- and medium-haul markets, it may be possible to extract a price premium for non-stop service in the O&D market served by that flight-leg, whereas through- and flow traffic is being offered less valuable service and so cannot sustain a premium.

Clearly, segment control is more complex than revenue-managing a single non-stop flight because decisions have to be taken regarding the probability and value of demand developing in several different markets served by the same flight (e.g., the LHR–BKK, LHR–SYD, and BKK–SYD markets). The challenge becomes more complex still when we move from considering the revenue management of a single flight-leg or a simple multi-stop flight with multiple segments to confronting the revenue management of a network of connecting flights.

Revenue-Managing A Hub-Based Network: O&D Itinerary Control

Leg- and segment-control fail to take account of network effects – the fact that sale of a seat on a single leg might close-off the opportunity to sell any of a number of O&D itineraries across the network that need that seat. The growth of hub-and-spoke networks has created a requirement for the carriers operating them to understand the network revenue value of each booking request. The RM objective has therefore shifted for these carriers from maximising EMSR on individual legs or segments, to maximising it across the network – subject, of course, to capacity constraints on each leg.

Any flight in a network designed to channel traffic over one or more hubs will be carrying passengers whose different O&D itineraries may have very different revenue implications. The O&D fare control problem is therefore a matter of how to take into account all possible passenger itineraries at all fares available between every O&D city-pair served by the network before deciding whether or not to release a seat. For example, if a low-yield booking class on an Edinburgh (EDI)–London Heathrow (LHR) flight is sold out, leg-based control would refuse a request for space in that class from a potential connecting passenger wanting to travel from EDI over LHR to Sydney (probably return) – thereby depriving the network of much more revenue than is contributed by a local EDI–LHR passenger who may just the moment before have taken the last available seat. O&D control, on the other hand, considers the 'beyond displacement cost' of selling that seat.

On any leg or segment carrying a significant amount of flow traffic connecting from origins behind or to destinations beyond, there are two issues that need to be addressed by an RMS: interline and online connecting traffic.

1. *Interline traffic* If the EDI–LHR leg channels traffic onto other carriers, particularly long-haul carriers, the need to prorate O&D fares paid by connecting passengers (i.e., to share the revenue with the other carrier(s) involved) is likely to mean that the yield earned from these passengers will be lower than the yield that would have been earned by carrying any displaced local traffic in the same booking class. (As noted in Chapter 3, this is because fares generally taper with distance.) There are two mutually compatible ways to deal with this problem:
   - The first is by negotiating favourable prorate terms – something that will be easier to achieve when the short-haul carrier concerned is predominantly a feeder of locally originating traffic rather than a receiver of overseas traffic; if specially promoted joint fares and/or code-sharing are part of the equation, the dynamics of the negotiation may be very different from the case of a more arm's-length relationship.
   - The second approach is to have an RMS able to accept or reject a booking request on the basis of its revenue implications.
2. *Online connecting traffic* This is where network O&D inventory control really comes into its own for airlines operating networks designed to channel flow traffic over integrated hubs. For example, reconsider the case where we sell the last available seat in the lowest booking class on the EDI–LHR departure to a local passenger and then have to deny space to a passenger who wants to connect at LHR for Sydney (SYD) but has been blocked from doing so by the local sale. Clearly, it can sometimes be advantageous to hold space back for online connecting traffic: one way of doing this is a technique called *virtual nesting*, which we will look at shortly. But how much space should be allocated? On an aggregate level, the answer is straightforward. We might,

for example, establish that on average over, say, 6 months or a year approximately 30 per cent of EDI–LHR passengers in each booking class on the departure concerned connect over London – so in principle we should protect up to 30 per cent of seats for flow traffic (the exact figure depending upon an assessment of the relative merit from a network revenue perspective of flow traffic in low-yield booking classes against local traffic in high-yield classes). We might also discover that over the same period on average 2 per cent of passengers on the EDI–LHR flight travel onwards to SYD.

The problem with these averages, however, is that not only can we have little confidence that on a departure-specific basis 30 per cent of passengers originating in Edinburgh will actually connect, we most certainly cannot argue that on any given departure 2 per cent will be on their way to Sydney. This latter difficulty is sometimes referred to in the context of a flow network as 'the small numbers problem' – a problem attributable to the impact of random fluctuations on small booking entities, such as EDI–SYD traffic per flight. Alliances further complicate the small-numbers problem. Whilst British Airways might, for the sake of argument, be able to arrive at a satisfactory formula for predicting EDI–SYD traffic, it will never be able to predict demand on specific flights for lightly travelled itineraries such as EDI–SYD connecting onto Qantas for Canberra; the problem is that as global alliances expand and begin to move towards joint inventory management, the revenue attributable to rare itineraries (McGill and van Ryzin 1999) is becoming quite substantial in aggregate.

But what should we do if on a particular EDI–LHR flight we have one seat remaining in a booking class that is protected for connecting traffic and a passenger bound for Cairo requests space in that class? Should the request be accepted, or should space be held in case another passenger headed for Sydney (or Tokyo, or LA, or somewhere else that generates more revenue than Cairo) appears? One answer is to plumb historical data to identify the probability that a more revenue-rich passenger will come forward, and in this way develop an opportunity cost figure which must be exceeded by the Cairo fare if that last seat is to be released. This is the heart of bid-price O&D revenue management, which we will look at shortly.

The requirement for journey control in the context of a hub-and-spoke system evidently raises complex issues. O&D RMSs need to be capable of doing three things in particular (Belobaba 1998a):

1. Giving preference to higher-revenue connecting traffic, even if that traffic generates lower yields (i.e., revenue per RPM) than local traffic.
2. Denying space to connecting passengers where the revenue they would generate is lower than the aggregate revenue earned from the local passengers on each leg who might otherwise be occupying the seats concerned, and there is a high probability that these seats will ultimately be sold to local passengers.
3. Identifying bottleneck routes on which insufficient capacity leads frequently to the denial of space for behind/beyond itineraries (as well as for local traffic).

The benefits of releasing space to local traffic to and from the hub have to be weighed against the benefits of selling the same space to passengers with connecting itineraries; furthermore, each different connecting itinerary will have its own specific costs and revenues to be considered. The impact on an airline's profitability will therefore differ depending upon whether it releases a seat to a local passenger travelling only as far as the hub, to a connecting passenger proceeding onwards down a short-haul spoke, or to a passenger connecting onto a long-haul spoke. In addition, sale to a connecting passenger of the last seat from Origin O to the hub and then the last seat from the hub to destination D might prevent future sale of *two* categories of connecting ticket: from O to the hub and on to any other final destination (the first leg now being full), and from any other origin to the hub and on to D (the second leg now being full). In the next section we will look at techniques adopted to meet these challenges.

Allocation controls within a network   On any flight into a large hub it is likely that a significant percentage of the passengers will be local and that, as we saw above, the balance will in many cases be spread so thinly across a wide range of onward connections that there are severe limits on the confidence that can be placed in the probability of demand existing for one particular behind/beyond itinerary on any given inbound flight. Compounding this problem has been the continuing reliance on booking classes themselves; even had optimal network flow solutions been developed in the past to account for the thousands of different possible itineraries in a large hub-based network, they would still have had to be mapped into a small number of controllable booking classes for space allocation purposes.

Two approaches have been used (Haerian *et al.* 2006):

- *Flight-leg optimisation*   Managing connecting flight-legs individually side-steps the knotty mathematical and technological challenge of trying to optimise an entire network – that is, accept or reject requests for space with the objective of maximising expected revenue across the network as a whole – and limits optimisation to single-leg decisions. However, network effects are clearly lost.
- *Network heuristics*   Heuristic approaches can instead be used to arrive at the best, hopefully near-optimal, network allocation decision. These are the focus of the present section.

Two types of inventory allocation control have been applied to approximate optimal solutions:

1. Virtual nesting.
2. Network bid-price control.

The following subsections briefly describe each. However, it is important to realise that some network carriers continue to store booking data by flight-leg/booking class combination, and therefore do not have data organized in such a way that forecasts by O&D itinerary/booking class combination can be generated.

Virtual nesting   This approach to O&D inventory control, which had its origins at American in the early 1980s, distinguishes between fares in different markets on the basis of the dollar revenue each generates for the network as a whole. Whilst booking classes may be managed only on a leg- or segment-basis, virtual nesting can capture the network implications of accepting or rejecting a space request. It achieves this by ordering on the basis of their revenue all the many O&D fares that passengers travelling on a particular flight-leg or segment could buy, and clustering them into a number of virtual buckets (or value classes) each comprised of itineraries which given the booking class concerned generate similar amounts of revenue. A booking limit is set for each bucket on the flight-leg or segment being managed. Every request for space triggers the indexing of the fare relevant to the O&D itinerary and booking class concerned into a bucket determined by the total revenue the journey would generate for the carrier, and a sale is made only if seats from that bucket are available on the flight(s) requested (Belobaba 1998a). The buckets are virtual in the sense that they do not correspond to any one booking class; each bucket has many different booking classes from many different possible O&D itineraries mapped into it (Smith *et al.* 1998).

It is the buckets that are used to control inventory rather than actual booking classes; they can be, and usually are, nested. The clustering of fares into buckets is accomplished by dynamic programming models designed to minimise revenue variances within buckets and maximise separation between buckets. The outcome could be, for example, that a high-yield local passenger might be in the same revenue class as a connecting passenger travelling on a deeply discounted fare.

Returning to the EDI–LHR example, it is likely that high-yield fares for long-haul connecting itineraries will be indexed into the highest value bucket because of the revenue they generate; high-yield fares for local traffic will most probably go into a lower bucket, but one that may be higher than the bucket(s) containing fares used by low-yield connecting traffic (depending, of course, on the revenue associated with the particular itinerary concerned), and low-yield local traffic will be in one of the lowest buckets. Because the buckets are nested, those supporting itineraries that generate the richest revenues have more inventory available to them in any cabin than the lower priority buckets – which therefore get closed-out more quickly.

These are, of course, generalisations, and the clustering process will depend greatly on the O&D itineraries forecast to be served on the leg concerned, the fare structures in these markets, and the algorithms used. One conclusion we can draw, however, is that although it is an improvement on leg and segment control insofar as it does allow estimation of network effects, virtual nesting will not optimise network revenue (Weatherford and Bodily 1992); this is because it is still essentially an allocation-based system.

An alternative to virtual nesting designed to overcome the mapping problems associated with that technique is *fare stratification*. This retains existing booking classes but, instead of incorporating into them only the fares available on a given flight-leg, each will contain fares in any market served by that leg which generate revenue within certain bands. For example, the full unrestricted EDI–LHR fare would no longer be a Y fare but would fall into a lower booking class – a class that would also include other itineraries/fares for travel beyond LHR which generate revenue within the same band. Only high-yield long-haul (economy class) connecting itineraries might appear as Y fares out of Edinburgh. Fares are therefore assigned to booking classes on the basis of their revenue implications for the system as a whole rather than their fare type and yield in the local market, and space is allocated accordingly (Belobaba 2002).

Both virtual nesting and fare stratification provide opportunities to enhance revenues compared to simpler allocation-based methods whilst retaining the booking class control logic built into legacy GDSs and CRSs (Talluri and van Ryzin 2004), but neither taps into the full potential of network revenue. Whilst a connecting itinerary can be given priority over a local journey provided it generates sufficient revenue, there is no absolute guarantee that the connecting itinerary will not be given priority over two or more local journeys on the same legs that together would have generated more revenue. For example, a request for space on the basis of a £400 Edinburgh–Rome fare might be given preference over both a £200 EDI–LHR fare and a £300 LHR–Rome fare simply because £400 is a higher revenue figure than either of the local revenue figures for each of the two flight-legs – even though the aggregate of the local fares exceeds £400.

What is needed is real-time evaluation of the opportunity cost, in terms of network revenue displacement, of accepting particular booking requests at a given time; ideally, each booking request should be evaluated not only in terms of the revenue it brings to the airline, but in terms of revenue net of whatever alternative revenue is lost by displacing passengers that might subsequently have come forward (or bid) for the same space.

Network bid-price (or opportunity cost) control   In order to optimise network revenue it is necessary not just to accept itineraries offering the richest revenue, but those offering the richest revenue net of upline and downline displacement costs – that is, after taking into account future revenue displaced by accepting a requested reservation. One way of achieving this is to establish a bid price for each remaining seat on a flight equivalent to the highest revenue that seat can be expected to generate from a future sale – expectation being based on feasible itineraries, the fares each will generate in available booking classes, and the probability (based on historical data and current booking trends) that demand for particular itinerary/booking class combinations will arise prior to departure. A bid price is the opportunity cost of demand that might yet come forward but would be displaced by accepting the request in hand; this future demand might be constituted by a passenger wanting to travel the same itinerary but prepared to pay a higher price, or it might represent alternative – higher revenue – O&D itineraries.

A request for space on a flight is therefore judged against two criteria (Vinod 1995):

- *Physical availability* This is determined by the type of aircraft that has been assigned to operate the flight and by the overbooking limits set for each compartment.
- *Financial availability* If the fare for an itinerary/booking class combination requested today exceeds the bid price, release of space can be authorised; if not, the seat will be held open.

Introduced in its original form by first-movers as long ago as the mid-1990s, network bid-price control – also known in this context as *continuous nesting* – is an extension of single-leg bid-price control. Multi-leg itineraries are dealt with by summing the current bid prices for each leg to determine the aggregate bid price, which then constitutes the minimum acceptable fare (MAF) for the requested O&D itinerary. Any fares in the market that exceed the current MAF and carry conditions that can be met are open for sale. For example, if the bid prices for an Omaha–Chicago O'Hare leg were $200 and for an O'Hare–London Heathrow leg $350, the current MAF for Omaha–Heathrow would be $550; valid reservation requests for fares in excess of $550 would be accepted.

Bid price controls attempt to establish a *continuous* relationship between the MAF in a cabin on a particular leg and evolving demand across the network, whereas the lumpy nature of traditional allocation-based methods at best approximates this relationship at the various points in time when decisions are taken to open and close different booking classes. A bid price is a constantly changing figure driven by what historical data and the pattern of demand as it is actually emerging lead an RMS to predict could be earned if the requested seat were held open for longer. Every sale and cancellation will lead to an increase or decrease in the bid price by an amount determined by the bid price gradient (i.e., the steepness of the booking curve that plots bookings against time) for the flight(s) concerned. Availability is not pre-stored in booking class allocations (although overbooking limits do still need to be established for each cabin); financial availability is instead recalculated each time space is requested. Thus, if there is currently a high probability that a remaining seat on a particular leg will generate more revenue by being held back for a connecting itinerary than being made available to local traffic, this will be reflected in a higher bid price than local traffic would be willing to bear.

The ultimate objective of continuous nesting and similar initiatives should be to dispense with booking classes and buckets, and to establish a bid price for each marginal seat on every flight-leg equivalent to the opportunity cost to the network as a whole of releasing that seat for sale. Challenges exist, however:

- Group and batch bookings complicate analysis insofar as it seems unlikely that the displacement cost applicable to sale of the first seat in a group or batch will be the same as for the second and subsequent seats.
- Whilst the hardware available is up to the job and software is becoming more capable all the time, relatively few airlines have the data required for building network forecasting models in the right form. The best that many can do with reasonable accuracy is estimate the local traffic that might be displaced by a multi-leg itinerary; the ability to estimate not just the potential displacement of local traffic but also the revenue from alternative connecting traffic that might be displaced across the network by accepting a particular multi-leg itinerary remains elusive for many. The bid price heuristic described above is being adopted by the still relatively few carriers that have invested in developing itinerary-, rather than just leg- and segment-, based data.
- Another issue concerns connectivity between an airline's CRS and any GDSs used to distribute its services. Airlines manage seat inventory in their CRSs, which may be either in-house or hosted in a partitioned area of an external system (perhaps another airline's CRS or a GDS). As we have seen, many legacy CRSs are capable of managing inventory only by flight-leg and segment, and so are not geared to implement continuous nesting and O&D control. Even an airline that has adapted its CRS to accommodate O&D inventory control can have problems implementing it if a significant proportion of bookings come through GDSs or other airlines' CRSs. The reason is that external channels will simply show availability by booking class on each leg and will sell against this availability notwithstanding that the airline's own CRS will be evaluating each booking request by reference to its economic value rather than simple availability; in other words, an airline might be able to exercise O&D (or itinerary) control over internal bookings received at its own counters, offices, call centres, and websites but not over booking requests made through external channels. Cases could arise where a booking request made directly to the carrier would be rejected, but the same request would be accepted if channelled through the agency system via a GDS.

    The answer is 'seamless availability'. This is an EDI standard developed under the auspices of IATA, the purpose of which is to replace periodic batch uploads of availability controls from a host CRS to a GDS with real-time access. First negotiated by several US majors in the mid-1990s, it allows each booking request into a GDS to be relayed instantly to the participating carrier's CRS, which then immediately accepts or rejects it (Belobaba 1998a). (Seamless availability can be agreed and paid for irrespective of whether a carrier uses bid price controls in its RMS, its appeal being that it allows GDSs to provide agencies and their customers with up to date price and availability information – down to the last seat. It also allows the airline to exert real-time point-of-sale control. It is mentioned here because this level of functionality can be particularly important when bid-pricing is being used.)

- The rapid growth of code-sharing has further complicated O&D revenue management because an international customer's itinerary is increasingly likely to draw on the seat inventories of two or more alliance partners. It will be recalled from Chapter 6 that code-share inventory can be handled in one of two ways:

  - *Blocked-space ('hard block')* The operating partner gives an allotment of seats to the code-share partner. This allotment is subtracted ('decremented') from the operating partner's inventory for revenue management purposes, in much the same way as if the seats had been sold to retail customers; depending on the terms of the code-share, unsold seats might be returned to the operating partner at specified times prior to departure, in which case they will be added back to its inventory. On receipt of its allotment, the code-share partner can revenue-manage those seats as though it were controlling its own flight. However, block-spacing in effect partitions the inventory and is therefore suboptimal for the flight as a whole.

  - *Free-sale and 'soft block'* Under these, more complex but more common, 'sell and report' arrangements there is no allotment and all seats are sold by both carriers from the booking classes established by the operating carrier. The operating carrier has control over the opening and closing of booking classes. This most often involves the code-share carrier mapping its booking classes onto the operating carrier's nearest equivalent codes so that changes in their respective inventories, such as sales and class closures, mirror each other. Alternatively, an operating carrier using bid-price controls might provide information on the current spot price (Talluri and van Ryzin 2003), which the code-sharing carrier could accept and mark-up for onward sale to its customer.

    There are clear advantages in partners that have antitrust immunity or its equivalent being able to manage their inventories across joint networks as though they were one integrated system – something that the transatlantic joint venture between several SkyTeam partners (immunised in 2008) was established to accomplish, for example. These carriers are free to create, price, promote, and revenue-manage what amounts to a single seat inventory even though output continues to be produced by the separate partners. Partnerships without such immunity are disadvantaged in this regard, as exemplified by British Airways and American (although a third application for antitrust immunity was being contemplated by these two at the time of writing).

- Finally, there are arguments that bid-price controls can be suboptimal under certain circumstances. These arguments, together with a variety of alternative models beyond the scope of the present book, are discussed at length and in some technical detail by Talluri and van Ryzin (2004).

This is a fast-moving field at the cutting edge of airline automation, but a note of realism is required: many of the world's airlines have yet to implement anything other than leg- or segment-based RMSs, and carriers serving only point-to-point traffic have no need for itinerary management. Legacy CRSs are expensive and difficult to adapt. On the other hand, large network airlines carrying significant volumes of connecting traffic together with the smaller airlines feeding them need to move away from local, leg-based optimisation towards something closer to network optimisation. Around 70 per cent of KLM's traffic connects, for example, and it has been reported that implementation of O&D network RM by the carrier led to a revenue benefit of approximately 5 per cent (Blom 2005). At the very least, network airlines should be looking to exert O&D revenue control over flights with high average load factors and heavy connecting traffic. In order to do this they need to store and use PNR information as a foundation for true network management. Some do, but many still do not.

PRICE-BASED APPROACH: DYNAMIC PRICING

The objective of dynamic pricing is to define and offer *a single* optimal price (the 'active fare') for *all space remaining available* at the current time – changing that price as certain dates prior to departure (e.g., 21, 14, 7, and 3 days) are reached, or in accordance with predefined booking thresholds, or in response to customers' evolving willingness to pay given the prevailing competitive conditions. It is willingness to pay that concerns us in this section.

In the case of dynamic pricing, market segmentation is based not on willingness to pay a fixed price for a fare product defined by various rules and conditions but on willingness to pay the current price for a seat on a particular flight at the time booking is being contemplated – the rules and conditions applying to all purchases being common. Using a traditional allocation-based approach to seat inventory control the sequence is first to forecast demand, then set prices (by market, not by individual flight), then allocate seats to booking classes, and finally sell-down the booking classes according to their allocation (possibly subject to some adjustment as the booking curve evolves); fare products are fenced-off from each other by rules and conditions, and so in this sense are 'differentiated'. Using a dynamic pricing approach there is just one price on sale at any one point in time for a seat on a particular flight, that price being determined by the pattern of demand relative to space remaining given the time to departure, and what the RMS is actually managing is price rather than allocation of space; there are no separate fare products fenced off from each other, because the only product sold is a one-way non-refundable fare without advance purchase restrictions, and in this sense the product can be considered to be undifferentiated.

An important distinction between traditional and dynamic pricing approaches to RM lies in how the reservation price of a customer making a booking request is estimated.

1. *Allocation-based approach* Historical data is used to forecast demand and estimate reservation prices, and from this determine seat allocations to each fare product. A common simplifying assumption is that demand for every fare product is independent of demand for any other. However, as noted earlier in the chapter, historical data might be flawed to the extent that purchase of a ticket on a flight at one price does not inevitably mean that the purchaser would not have purchased at a higher price had

the lower fare been unavailable (i.e., buy-up); in other words, demand is not in fact independent as between different fare products. In this sense, the traditional approach confuses the airline's past allocation decisions with actual demand at a particular fare (Kuhlmann 2004). (To the extent that rejected demand on one flight is recaptured by the sale of space on another, neither is demand independent as between different departures serving the same market.)

2. *Dynamic pricing approach* Historical data is used as a starting point, but the demand distribution is updated as the customer arrival rate evolves and it is this learning – rather than what remains of an initial booking class allocation – that drives which fare bucket the RMS optimiser has open at any point in time. The focus is on the prevailing price-elasticity of demand at the active price, rather than on the opportunity cost of releasing inventory at that price.

    A significant aspect of learning in this context is that it implicitly takes into account competitors' actions, which are felt via their effect on the bookings arrival rate. For example, if a competitor swamps a market with low fares this will very quickly be reflected in a decline in the other airline's customer arrival rate (until such time as the competitor is sold out). The danger in this, of course, is that where two airlines compete using dynamic pricing systems an aggressive but perhaps limited pricing move by one might provoke a competitive reaction from the other which leads to them chasing each other's fares quickly down to the lowest available level.

Dynamic pricing therefore shifts the focus of RM away from the allocation of seats to different products already having defined prices, and towards evaluation of the optimal price at a particular point in time; it effectively unites the pricing and RM functions. The idea behind dynamic pricing is millennia old. What is new is that recent developments in demand modelling and price optimisation research, together with software applications needed to apply it, have enabled dynamic pricing models to be introduced into the field of revenue management. Consumer choice modelling, which has been advancing rapidly as more online shopping data becomes available both from airline websites and Web intermediaries, is being used to develop a more accurate understanding of changes in price-elasticity and product preferences as passengers come forward and the booking curve evolves (van Ryzin 2004); the objective is to learn about consumers' willingness to pay under prevailing competitive conditions at a particular point in time rather than to forecast overall demand by fare product as traditional RMSs attempt to do. One by-product, however, is that the predictive power of historical booking data can be weakened insofar as it will now reflect demand that arose in response to perhaps multiple, fast-moving price adjustments rather than demand for a single fare product defined by a stable and identifiable price and set of conditions (Kuhlmann 2007b).

Dynamic pricing has gained traction in certain parts of the industry as LFAs offering restriction-free one-way products have won market share. That is not to say that traditional allocation-based methods cannot be used in this environment – by allocating seats to a small number of buckets, then selling the cheapest first, closing it once sold out, and repeating the process with progressively higher buckets as the departure date approaches. However, using a traditional RMS in a simplified pricing environment where one-way fares are sold subject to minimal restrictions can be problematic: there is a danger that load factors will increase but, because of a spiral down in fares, revenue will not be maximised. The fundamental reason is that traditional RMSs assume demand for each fare class is independent of demand arising at any other fare. This assumption has two consequences (Cooper *et al.* 2006):

1. The forecasting model fails to recognise that a proportion of those customers in the historical data who were able to book in a low fare class would instead have been prepared to book in a higher class had they had to (i.e., sell-up). The model therefore underestimates demand in the higher fare class (Burger and Fuchs 2005).
2. The optimisation model fails to recognise that almost all customers previously compelled to purchase high fares, because they were unable to comply with rules and restrictions attached to lower fares, will opt for a lower fare class as soon as conditions are removed (i.e., buy-down). The model responds to this new pattern of demand, and to the underestimated forecast of high-fare demand, by allocating more seats to low-fare buckets than is necessary (i.e., under-protecting high-fare buckets).

Belobaba (2006) has estimated that the revenue impact of simplifying fares but retaining a traditional RMS could amount to: -16.8 per cent if Saturday night and minimum stay restrictions are removed (an inevitable by-product of adopting one-way pricing); -29.6 per cent if all restrictions are removed but advance purchase requirements retained; and -45.0 per cent if all restrictions and advance purchase requirements are removed. Traditional models have difficulty accurately estimating customers' willingness to pay in the absence of a complex fare structure marshalled by rules and restrictions. This is why consumer choice modelling, which attempts to understand the interaction of both price and non-price (i.e., product) factors in decision-making at a given point in time under prevailing competitive conditions, is important to the newer dynamic pricing models.

Arguably, what dynamic pricing represents is acknowledgement that we are moving from a period in which airlines have managed their revenues to one in which customers are able to manage their expenditures. The enablers in this transition have been the LFAs' mission to shake-up industry pricing, and the growth of the Web; the latter has in many markets transformed airline pricing from a closed, supplier-driven system to one which is easily accessible and transparent to consumers. As consumer behaviour changes – in essence, becomes better-informed and less predictable – airline practices will also change.

Technological Issues

In principle, dynamic pricing can be continuous; in practice, for both marketing and technological reasons a limited number of discrete price buckets is usually established – again, though, it has to be stressed that unlike in the traditional allocation-based approach there will only be one open bucket at any time. Were pricing continuous, there might be a timing issue. The typical fare filing system in the United States, for example, involves transmitting data to ATPCO after which – perhaps several hours later – it is uploaded to the GDSs and ready for sale; in the meantime, fares – which may no longer be current – are sold out of cached databases. Technology allowing real-time prices to be displayed on a GDS without the need for filing is now available; however, the cost of implementing real-time availability between an airline's CRS and a GDS may not be insubstantial where one is based on a legacy mainframe and a TPF software environment – rather than on newer, more adaptable and scalable open systems architecture. (The problem inherent in caching is not limited to dynamic pricing environments. When an airline's CRS is overwhelmed by the volume of shopping enquiries coming from travel websites at peak times, those sites may have to rely on cached information which might be out of date. Another example is cross-selling between different carriers' websites: caching might not pose a problem where volumes are low, but any high-volume link-up requires real-time last-seat availability and pricing information to be exchanged.)

Dynamic Pricing In A Network Context

A network airline flying a given short-haul leg might be competing against LFAs and so need to offer undifferentiated fares, and yet also be serving medium- and long-haul flow traffic with a relatively complex structure of differentiated fare products. For example, consider the simple case of two flight-legs O–H and H–D, serving three markets O–H, O–D, and H–D. Assume that the network carrier operating these legs faces competition from an LFA offering an undifferentiated, restriction-free fare in short-haul market O–H, but competes against other network carriers using multiple fare products in a traditional pricing environment in long-haul markets O–D and H–D. To protect revenues in its two long-haul markets the network carrier might wish to close the lowest fare class available from O to H on a particular departure, but to compete effectively with an LFA offering its entire remaining capacity at a single comparable figure that class will need to be kept open. The choice is potentially quite stark:

• if the network carrier tightly controls release of it lowest fares it risks losing market share, but ...
• if it matches LFA price and availability it risks losing control of its inventory, the effect of which could be a spiral-down in revenue.

Embedded in this conundrum is actually an implied strategic choice between point-to-point and network business models. Some observers, notably amongst the management of network carriers, feel there is no dichotomy and the two models can coexist or perhaps even be merged; others, notably in the LFA community, feel the two are just as incompatible on the revenue as on the cost side of the income statement.

Using a traditional leg-based RMS to evaluate booking requests under circumstances such as those faced by the network carrier above flying O to H clearly poses difficulties insofar as it does not allow the carrier to distinguish with certainty between different types of demand in any given booking class. Notwithstanding that they will probably have adopted their systems in the first instance to solve general network optimisation problems, those (still relatively few) carriers using PNR-based RMSs to manage O&D flows will be in a better position than others to operate in the new environment because they are able to determine in real-time from the origin and destination in a booking request whether it arises in a market with differentiated or undifferentiated pricing. Difficult, and potentially strategic, choices still have to be made with regard to the allocation of inventory to different fare products in traditional markets and selection of the optimal price in the undifferentiated market – choices that a point-to-point LFA offering a single, undifferentiated fare at any given point in time does not have to make. The objective in hybrid environments such as the one described above must be to arrive at an optimal mix of passengers in each cabin, spread between those flying on the traditional fare structure and others who have bought restriction-free fares at various price points; for this there needs to be a coexistence of inventory controls (Vinod 2006), such that a bid price curve might be used to control release of inventory set aside for flow traffic, for example, and authorisation limits to control release of unrestricted fares at particular price points (ibid.).

Cathay Pacific, which in the summer of 2007 implemented an O&D RMS supplied by PROS, provides a case in point. It uses the larger capacity of its widebody fleet to offer competitive numbers of aggressively priced local seats in competition with LFAs operating narrowbodies on its intra-Asian routes, whilst still leaving plenty of seats protected for higher-yielding local and flow traffic. (In fact, this approach has its roots in the early days of revenue management. Robert Crandall, then in charge of marketing at American, recognised in the early 1980s that given the industry's low marginal costs and at that time low load factors incumbents were already flying plenty of empty seats with short-run costs as low as the costs of LFA challengers such as People Express. Revenue – or in those days 'yield' – management systems built on this insight by finding ways to segregate demand for low-priced seats. Of course, this was only a short-term solution because American's *fully allocated* costs were well above those of People Express, but by 1985 the start-up was bankrupt; hence the importance of subsequent LFA start-ups being well capitalised to ride out incumbents' initial reaction to their entry.)

Dynamic Packaging

It will be recalled from Chapter 3 that dynamic packaging is a term now commonly used to describe the sale on an airline web site of car hire, insurance, and possibly hotels and other products at the same time as sale of airline seats, but with the price points of the individual components opaque to purchasers – who are aware only of the total price of the package. As the search for ancillary revenue continues to gather momentum, it is likely that dynamic packaging will become more prevalent. The challenge will be for airlines adopting it – or, in most cases, their RMS suppliers – to learn how to revenue-manage all the components such that each service provider satisfies its margin requirements whilst at the same time still offering an appropriately priced overall package to customers. (There is also the question whether customers prefer to buy bundled packages comprised of multiple, opaquely priced components or unbundled, transparently priced products. The answer to that remains to be seen.)

III. Commercial Considerations

Many airlines now want to have control over release of space oriented not just to demand and revenue, but to the source of demand. Booking requests in this case need to be evaluated in the light of wider commercial issues (Yuen and Irrgang 1998, pp. 322–323). Examples of these issues include:

1. *Sales strategy*
    *   Biases can be established in favour of a particular route – perhaps a new route on which market share is being built. More generally, a region might be targeted for priority by a marketing department wanting to build market share in originating traffic.

- Certain distribution channels might be favoured – an agency with which a relationship is being established or which is already a preferred supplier, for example, or a direct channel which avoids commission and GDS costs.
- The lowest-yield booking class(es) in markets with heavy ethnic VFR traffic might be released only to agencies specialising in those market segments to avoid diversion from other segments of demand (Garvett and Michaels 1998).
- Some carriers use a point-of-sale control technique known as hub complex optimisation to simulate network inventory control using leg- or segment-based data (Narayanan and Yuen 1998). This involves allocating seats in each booking class into and out of a hub for sale in specific geographical areas. The idea is to try to ensure that demand from high-yield local traffic is not spilled by selling too much space to low-yield flow traffic; this is done by using historical data to impute the nature of itineraries booked in each geographical area of the network, or possibly through specific distribution channels in each area, and then allocating inventory in such a way that these average booking patterns can be used to generate the desired traffic mix.

2. *Currency issues*
   - Biases in favour of itineraries requested from points of sale offering prices and/or exchange rates favourable to the airline can be introduced. Because of competitive circumstances, exchange rate differentials, or country-of-origin pricing mechanisms in bilateral ASAs fares for round-trip journeys between two points could be lower if a journey originates at one point rather than the other, so a carrier might prefer to sell at the higher-fare end.
   - Separately, some developing countries insist that outward remittances are held for long periods in central bank queues awaiting foreign exchange, so carriers might want to limit the volume of local currency sales made in such countries.

3. *Pricing strategy* Biases in favour of itineraries encompassing markets in which a pricing initiative has been launched can be used to support competitive activity in those markets. Because O&D inventory control is market- rather than leg- or segment-oriented, it is better able to achieve this than leg- or segment-level controls.

4. *Revenue quality* Biases can be introduced in favour of high-value individual and corporate accounts – assuming the airline has a database of high-value customers and estimates of their lifetime value. Forms of bias could include protecting last-seat availability for late-booking high-value customers, or reopening a booking class to accommodate a high-value customer who might otherwise be spilled – the latter sacrificing short-term economic benefit for long-term goodwill. For this to happen, seamless connectivity between external booking channels such as GDSs on the one hand and the airline's own CRS on the other is critical: booking requests will have to be referred through to the airline's CRS for real-time approval or denial, because no carrier is likely to let external parties interface directly with its customer database.

More broadly, these considerations are symptomatic of an argument gaining force over the last decade in favour of moving revenue management away from being a technical specialism which follows on sequentially from pricing, and towards being an overarching philosophy that integrates schedule planning, sales, pricing, and inventory control. (See Venkat [2005] for a discussion of Emirates' experiences in this regard.)

IV. Revenue Management System Components

This section of the chapter will look at three topics: technology, people, and the need to integrate RM with other functions.

TECHNOLOGY

There are several critical elements in an RMS:

1. A database which contains for each departure historical records of booking build-up curves, cancellations, no-shows, go-shows, upgrades, downgrades, offloads, achieved load factors, and estimated spill – each disaggregated by booking class and, ideally, itinerary.
2. A fares database showing all published fares currently applicable to each departure, as well as unpublished net fares negotiated with individual agencies and corporate clients. Because in dynamic competitive environments fares change frequently, it is critical that the RMS has real-time access to the carrier's fares database.
3. A forecasting module (containing one or several models), an overbooking model, and an optimisation engine (containing one or several models). Their relationship is outlined in Figure 9.6. Forecasting in a quantity-based RMS is likely to rely most heavily on time-series methods, whereas a price-based RMS will rely on causal analysis – with price as a key explanatory variable.
4. A decision support system capable of providing exception reports and responding to ad hoc 'what ifs'.
5. A CRS to manage availability and record bookings. Current fare details need to be instantly accessible to the carrier's CRS. In respect of published fares filed electronically in industry-standard databases such as ATPCO and SITA, this is generally not an issue; unpublished net deals negotiated by far-flung sales offices can be more of a problem for international carriers unless the salesforce has access to a fully automated system and fares are relayed instantly back to the head office fares database (Yuen and Irrgang 1998).

    Particularly for O&D journey control, it is essential that GDSs apply the same inventory control logic as the airline's in-house CRS and that agencies accessing inventory through GDSs receive true last-seat availability on their displays. Note that an airline will not want competitors to know via a GDS precisely how many seats it is offering in each booking class. GDSs therefore show each class as either available or closed, and only when availability reaches a fairly low level (e.g., seven or nine) will numbers of remaining seats be identified; alternatively, a class may open at a low number irrespective of how many seats are really available, and continue to show this number until bookings fall below it. (Basic but readily accessible illustrations can be seen at http://www.seatcounter.com.)
6. A capability to track forward bookings up to 12 months ahead of departure, and to break down an analysis of emerging trends in the same categories listed in point 1 above to facilitate comparison.

An activity which may or may not be organized functionally as a part of revenue management but which is closely related to it is *revenue integrity*. This has gained increasing attention over the last few years and been the subject of significant software developments. The purpose of

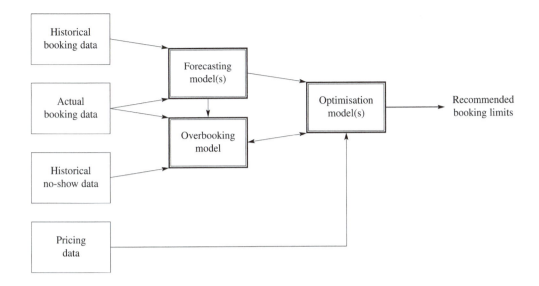

Figure 9.6   Outline architecture of an RMS

revenue integrity efforts is to ensure as far as possible that the revenue anticipated when a reservation is accepted does actually materialise. An important part of this is flight firming, which is largely a matter of verifying that bookings are ticketed and paid for, conditions are observed, duplicate bookings are minimised, and any booked connecting flights are cancelled as soon as a passenger is confirmed as a no-show at the first point of departure.

There are other possible examples of how revenue integrity software can be useful. Consider two alternatives: depending upon how markets are priced at the time, a customer with a two-segment itinerary might find it cheaper to book two single-sector, local fares rather than one through-fare; on the other hand, where a local market is not as competitive as an O&D through-market a local customer wanting just one flight-leg might find it cheaper to buy an onward connection as well but later cancel it. Taking the second example involving partial cancellation of a multi-segment itinerary, in order to maximise revenue from available seats on all the segments requested a carrier might only confirm space for a booking on the basis that each segment is 'married' to the others as a single set. Where such 'married segment control' is imposed, any subsequent alteration to the booking on one segment might cause the airline to withdraw confirmation on the other segments and require a rebooking of the entire itinerary – something which may or may not at that time be possible, depending upon how demand has developed since the original reservation was made. This is not necessarily a trivial issue: one Central American carrier recently registered a 4 per cent revenue improvement on some of its routes attributable to introducing married segment control.

Finally, a performance benchmarking system should be in place, covering at least the following indicators (tracked against same-carrier historical data and, where known, competitors' performances):

- Unsold seats, or the reciprocal of the achieved seat factor, on each route.
- Seat factor against market share.

- Dilution costs (discount percentage) in each market.
- Revenue per ASM (i.e., RASM).
- Yield (i.e., revenue per RPM).
- Denied boardings (i.e., oversales) per thousand boarded passengers, against industry average.
- Revenue share of each market (or route group, such as UK–USA) against output share.
- Closing rates of the different booking classes.
- Estimated demand spill.
- User (i.e., manual) override statistics.
- Accuracy of demand, no-show, and go-show forecasts. The problem as far as demand is concerned is that airlines do not track denied reservation requests once a booking class has been closed; in other words, they can track whether or not a booking limit has been reached but they have no records with which to calculate the demand factor, which is the ratio of demand to capacity for a given booking class or flight. However, techniques are available to model unconstrained demand; see Talluri and van Ryzin (2004), for example.

The complexity of any large RMS can be gauged by considering a single allocation-based system managing 200 daily departures, each averaging 160 seats; these 32,000 seats, augmented by overbooking, may be allocated among multiple booking classes and each departure might (particularly in medium- and long-haul international markets) be managed for up to a year ahead. In fact, none will be actively managed, beyond making initial allocations, until much closer to departure date – but the scale of the task remains considerable. If we double the number of daily departures and introduce virtual or continuous nesting, the challenge is magnified.

PEOPLE

Research by Zeni (2003) at US Airways suggested that manual overrides of output from forecasting and optimisation models were able to augment revenue from the studied flights by as much as 3 per cent. A central component of any RMS is clearly a team of revenue managers who have a sound understanding of their markets, as well as up-to-date knowledge of both their airline's marketing objectives and competitors' activities. Critically, these people need the proactive support of a senior management team whose members look upon revenue management as a philosophy – a framework within which to integrate product, network, schedule, fleet, marketing, and operational planning – rather than as just a tool.

In addition to experience, sound judgement, and technical skills, revenue managers need to be able to cooperate smoothly with other departments. Managing the release of inventory across multiple distribution channels is not a simple task, and revenue managers sometimes enter the arena long after decisions critical to flight profitability have been made elsewhere – by sales teams, for example.

The internal organization of a revenue management department might also affect revenues. A department organized by route-group, market, or region can sometimes generate suboptimal decisions for the network as a whole if units protect inventory to optimise their own revenue or profitability rather than network performance. One common approach is therefore to have analysts working at both market and network levels, with the latter able to resolve any conflicts arising at the market level.

OTHER COMPONENTS IN THE SYSTEM

It is not uncommon in large airlines for scheduling, sales (including group sales), pricing, marketing communications, and revenue management functions to operate in a less than fully coordinated way. Revenue management should in fact be looked at not as an isolated technical task, but as part of an integrated marketing effort.

1. *Pricing* Pricing and revenue management departments need to cooperate. For example, a possible response to declining load factors on a flight-leg might be to offer promotional fares in one or more of the markets served by that leg; this type of price stimulus can only be effective if adequate space is allocated to the booking class concerned.
2. *Advertising and promotion* When several flights to the same destination are showing similarly unfavourable projections, steps might be taken to promote either or both the flights and the destination. Again, this type of initiative works only if adequate space is allocated to appropriate booking classes.
3. *FFP management* Space allocated for award redemption can be varied in response to forecasted demand on a series of flights. Redemption conditions and award rates can also be varied either seasonally or as part of limited-period promotions in particular targeted markets.
4. *Sales* Group sales, corporate deals, and agency incentives can have a significant impact on revenue management. Slow reporting of unpublished net fares negotiated with travel agencies may hinder revenue managers' inventory allocation efforts. Finally, the task of revenue managers can be complicated where sales teams rewarded on the basis of volume respond to declining load factors by taking a more aggressive stance in negotiating off-tariff net fares, group deals, and corporate rates.

As already noted, RM is still widely treated as a tactical function which follows sequentially – but is separate – from the (more strategic) pricing function. In an ideal world there is a strong argument that scheduling, pricing, sales, and RM should be closely integrated.

V. Conclusion

'Yield management' is a misnomer. Booking classes with different yields are certainly being managed, but the objective is to maximise revenue – ideally, in the case of network carriers, on a network basis rather than by flight-leg or segment. What matters is whether an airline's total revenue exceeds its total cost: if costs are well-managed and are below revenues that are being maximised given current capacity constraints, declining yield need not in itself be a problem. Yield and profit are quite capable of moving in opposite directions; indeed, as noted in Chapter 3, real (i.e., inflation-adjusted) yield has been in secular decline across the industry as a whole for several decades.

If an RMS allows an airline to carry relatively low-yield traffic which would not have been carried had a simple, uniform fare been charged in each compartment and only the most inelastic market segments been targeted, this traffic will quite probably permit more frequencies to be flown on a larger network than would otherwise have been the case. Service quality will therefore be improved for all market segments, but particularly for high-yielding business travellers who value frequency. If the extra traffic is sufficiently profitable to justify use of larger aircraft than could have been supported by the smaller traffic base provided by inelastic segments alone, the lower seat-mile costs of these aircraft might lead to fare levels lower than they would otherwise have been – again benefiting consumers.

RMSs can also help impose management discipline. Traffic is tangible and clearly visible on departure whereas, in the absence of an RMS, revenues and yields might be known only days or weeks later. This can encourage over-attention to market share and a tendency towards the marginal cost pricing of ever-perishable seats. An RMS, on the other hand, is interested first in maximising revenues and only secondarily in maximising load factors – and in this sense imposes discipline on the release of space.

RMSs are important for most airlines and vital for network carriers, particularly when the competition has them. Nonetheless, they need to be treated with caution.

1.   Allocation-based RMS models are typically driven by historical data. As soon as something significant changes, such as a massive fare sale by a competitor or the entry of an aggressive challenger, historic booking curves may no longer be such an accurate guide to future demand. This problem is being addressed by research into passenger choice modelling, which uses causal models to enhance simulation capabilities, and by the development of neural nets capable of learning in response to events. In the interim, intervention by skilled and experienced analysts remains an important part of any RMS.

2.   RMSs do not necessarily eliminate the industry's generic marginal cost pricing dilemma. An RMS can only do so much to counterbalance overambitious fleet planning or poor scheduling. In particular, if too much output is scheduled, RMSs cannot fill it – this is the job of pricing and other marketing activities, pending a review of the schedule. These systems are, in fact, most valuable when used to control flights that have high load factors. When supply consistently exceeds demand on a flight, what is needed is less capacity and/or a pricing initiative.

3.   It is not unknown for overallocation of seats to low-yield booking classes to generate traffic volumes which appear to justify an increase in frequency or gauge (i.e., aircraft size) on a particular route. Insight and discipline are necessary to avoid an interlinked, and possibly unprofitable, upward spiral in output (with its attendant costs) and downward spiral in yield.

4.   Some observers argue that RMSs encourage over-segmentation of markets, perhaps even harming yields in the process. Interestingly, it was American Airlines, whose affiliates had been at the cutting edge of RMS software development, which took the lead (unsuccessfully, as it turned out) in trying to simplify the US domestic fare structure in 1992. Delta's very similar initiative in 2005 had more success, largely because by then the other majors were prepared to follow as a result of the growing threat from LFAs offering simple tariffs.

5.   As noted above, it is possible for an RMS to be undermined by incentive schemes that reward sales personnel on the basis of the volume rather than the profitability of their activities.

6.   Large airlines may house scheduling, pricing, and revenue management in different departments, and staff each area with people having different professional backgrounds and timescale orientations. Conflicts can arise when reactions to evolving patterns of demand are different. For example, high achieved load factors on a

particular departure might encourage scheduling to increase output, pricing to eliminate low fares, and revenue management to reduce allocations to low-yield booking classes; together, these reactions could lead to higher operating costs (attributable to increased output) and lower load factors (attributable to a combination of increased output and the impact of higher average fares on demand), but with an uncertain impact on revenue (dependent upon the price-elasticity of demand in the market(s) concerned). We have already seen that there is a need for scheduling, pricing, and revenue management efforts to be closely coordinated; in practice, organizational structure and incompatible information systems continue to prevent this at some carriers.

Although revenue maximisation might approximate profit maximisation in the short term, RMSs cannot create demand which is profitable in the long term if people are unwilling to pay the prices necessary to ensure profitability given the nature of the products being offered and a particular airline's cost base.

VI. Managing Freight Revenues

The objective when revenue-managing freight is the same as when revenue-managing passengers: to maximise the revenue earned from each unit of available output. However, the revenue management of freight is a less well-developed science than passenger RM. This is due in part to business strategies strongly oriented towards load factors, but also in part to some very real practical issues:

1. The much shorter booking cycles for freight than passengers – a high percentage of freight in some markets being booked within 24 hours of departure.
2. The higher variability of demand than on the passenger side, due in part to the much smaller number of customers shipping freight than buying passenger tickets.
3. The fact that provided it departs and arrives within any agreed time window, freight can take a greater number of potential paths through a multi-hub network, or be scheduled for longer connecting times at a single hub, than passengers would be prepared to tolerate.
4. The multidimensional nature of each freight shipment (i.e., volume, weight, physical dimensions, urgency, and perhaps also place in a sequential series of shipments), compared to the relative homogeneity of passenger bookings.
5. The fact that the booked volume and/or weight of a cargo shipment might not accord fully with what is tendered (hence the need for overbooking purposes to monitor show-up rates by product, shipper, and market – these being the ratios of weight and volume tendered to weight and volume booked).
6. The fact that cargo space is not as fungible as passenger seat inventories – in respect of particularly heavy shipments needing a specific onboard container or pallet location, for example.
7. The application of regulations governing carriage of certain, notably hazardous, goods.
8. The widespread use of contract rates, leaving just the spot rate to be revenue managed.
9. The fact that for one or both of two reasons precise availability of belly-hold space on a given passenger flight might not be known until very close to departure:
    *   first, where the aircraft concerned is operating at the extreme of its payload–range performance and there is a chance that under certain weather conditions freight might be offloaded to accommodate a full passenger load;

- second, where a customer (either a shipper or a forwarder) or the station's own field sales staff at the point of departure has a long-term agreement with head office for an allotment of space and (depending on the terms of that agreement) any unused space might not have to be released back to the central cargo sales function until as late as 24 or 48 hours before departure.

10. The fact that whereas on the passenger side low-yield traffic tends to book well in advance, so closing out lower booking classes and forcing later reservations into higher-yield booking classes, excess output of cargo space on many medium- and long-haul routes (primarily in the belly-holds of passenger widebodies) has contributed to the reverse situation where ad hoc late sales are often made at lower-than-contract rates (Herrmann *et al.* 1998).

11. Lack of the same precise inventory management tools that passenger CRSs provide.

A further complicating factor is that there is more scope for service customisation in respect of freight than passenger transportation, in part because there are fewer customers and their specific requirements for value-added services can often be clearly understood in advance of shipment – requirements for special handling of particular types of goods or special facilitation procedures, for example. In cases where carriers, or carriers and forwarders together, have integrated themselves into the logistics chain of a particular customer, individual commercial relationships may be sufficiently important to supersede the more transactional biases of an RMS.

Nonetheless, progress is being made in developing more sophisticated freight RM tools. For example, considerable work has been done on the use of routing algorithms: requests for space trigger a search of capacities on alternative paths a shipment could take through the particular carrier's network, and controls on the pricing and release of space are established in this context (Rao 2000). The foundations of progress are the fundamentally similar principles that underlie all traditional forms of RM: demand segmentation; forecasting by market segment; capacity allocation; overbooking; and a commitment to maximising revenues rather than load factors on high-demand flights and to optimising revenues across the network rather than by leg, segment, or geographic region.

Ideally, the revenue management of freight and passengers should be integrated by combination carriers to the point that in those relatively few cases where the value of the lowest yielding freight forecast to materialise on a payload-constrained departure exceeds the value of the lowest-yielding passengers it is space for the latter that is closed out. Average freight yields on most routes are, however, consistently lower than passenger yields (per RTM) – so in most cases it will be freight rather than passengers that loses out when payload is an issue. That said, introduction of branded, time-definite freight products by a growing number of airlines in recent years requires that carriers serious about their positioning in these market segments have to be careful when prioritising freight for shipment. A few airlines now even give their cargo divisions or subsidiaries sufficient autonomy to buy space on other carriers if this is what it takes to provide reliable service and meet high-yield customers' expectations.

Finally, in the case of some types of aircraft operating certain routes, standby cargo can on occasion be used as a revenue management tool to utilise payload capacity left unused by passengers. Particularly on widebodies, even an achieved 80 or 90 per cent seat factor may leave several thousand pounds of payload potential available for the late loading of standby cargo after passenger close-out.

VII. Conclusion to Part 3 of The Book: The Importance of Spill

Figure 9.7 outlines many of the relationships between different activities that have been discussed in the book. In particular, it isolates the role of the three capacity management tools we have been looking at in Part 3 – network management, fleet management, and revenue management – in the process that runs from design of one or more service concept(s) through to the delivery of differently priced service packages to customers. Of course, this is an idealised view of reality. In practice, it is not uncommon in large airlines for product planning, scheduling, sales (including group and cargo sales), pricing, and RM functions to operate with insufficient coordination. Efforts to improve the effectiveness of linkages between internal processes can bring significant potential benefits to the revenue side, as well as the cost side, of an airline's income statement.

The concept that unites pricing, network, fleet, and revenue management and lies at the heart of capacity management is 'spill'. Spill is demand that is unsatisfied because an airline has insufficient space in a given booking class, cabin, or airplane. It is the difference between *unconstrained demand* (i.e., the number of passengers that would book if there were no limits on the capacities of cabins and booking classes) and *constrained demand* (i.e., the number of passengers actually able to book). Clark (2007) explains how to calculate spill both in general and in particular market segments, and how to use the calculations to assist in determining appropriate aircraft size, cabin configuration, and cabin load factors.

Accurate estimates of spill and spill costs are important to fleet and network management generally, but are particularly critical to fleet management processes in order to ensure that flights are operated by aircraft with optimal capacities. With regard to revenue management, Belobaba and Farkas (1999) provide a comprehensive explanation of the linkages between RMSs and spill estimates – linkages that hinge on the impact of

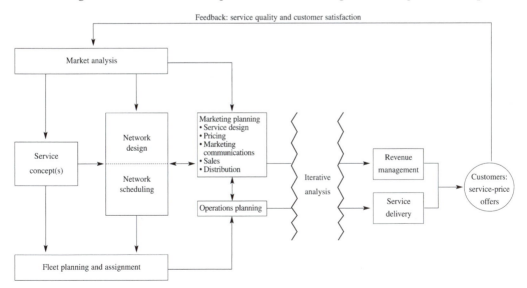

Figure 9.7   **The role of network, fleet, and revenue management relative to marketing and operations planning**

overbooking and of booking limits on spill, and on the potential use of RMS booking data to improve spill forecasting. Booking limits affect both the aggregate number of passengers spilled and their fare mix, thereby driving spill costs.

From an economic perspective, spill is inevitable; it is in almost all cases not viable to sustain the costs of meeting unconstrained demand (i.e., all demand coming forward) when it peaks, and then tolerating low load factors or punishingly low yields at other times. What adds piquancy to this analysis is that in the absence of effective revenue management, the demand most likely to be spilled at certain times (e.g., weekday peaks) comes from late-booking, high-yield travellers.

PART 4

Operating Performance

If the Wright Brothers were alive today, Wilbur would have to fire Orville to reduce costs.

Herb Kelleher

High market share is in principle no bad thing, but an important question is how it has been acquired. Specifically, has it been bought or earned? Airlines *buy* market share by pricing at levels which, given their costs, cannot generate and sustain acceptable profits. Conversely, they *earn* market share by making service–price offers (i.e., putting forward value propositions) that are both appealing to customers and rational in the context of their cost bases. Since it started operations in 1971, for example, Southwest has grown steadily to the point where it now carries more US domestic passengers than any other airline, but it has not bought market share; it has focused instead on keeping costs low enough to enable low fares to be profitably sustained over time, and in doing this has both stimulated and captured demand.

Industry downturns can present a particularly intense challenge to airline managements needing to balance the four elements in the operating performance model around which Part 2 of this book is structured: traffic, yield, output, and unit cost. Whether a cyclical downturn is more strongly reflected in figures for traffic or yield will depend in part upon the pricing decisions airlines choose to take in response to weakening demand. History suggests that in a 'regular' cyclical downturn it is likely that yields will soften as pricing becomes more aggressive in an attempt to maintain traffic, load factors, and market share; when there is a major exogenous shock as in 1990/1991 and 2001, both traffic and yield will suffer and output cuts will be essential.

Whenever significant output cuts are in fact made, they will eventually come up against a gradual recovery in demand. This situation confronts airlines with broadly two options for a return to profitability:

1. Hold output at the new level for as long as possible and then increase it only gradually, let rising demand bump up against constrained output (i.e., let load factors rise), and consolidate yields by reducing the availability of deep discounts.
2. Respond to returning demand by reinstating output as quickly as possible – with the likely result that traffic will bounce back more rapidly, but yields will take longer to recover.

From the perspective of individual carriers, particularly carriers giving a high priority to market share, the second option can be tempting. One attraction is that providing reinstated output can be sold at prices above marginal cost, the incremental revenue it earns will at least make a contribution to the fixed costs that continue to accrue irrespective of whether or not aircraft are flying. However, from an industry-wide perspective, the first option generally has more merit; it was in fact the option pursued by most US network carriers as they recovered from the post 9/11 downturn. Chapter 10 brings together the principal issues and metrics underlying this type of decision.

10

Strategy, Economics, and Operating Performance

When an industry with a reputation for difficult economics meets a manager with a reputation for excellence, it is usually the industry that keeps its reputation intact.

Warren Buffet

CHAPTER OVERVIEW

The purpose of this chapter is not to list operational performance metrics, but to bring together at a macro-level the economic fundamentals discussed in previous chapters. The opening section will discuss operating performance in general; the main body of the chapter will look at relationships between unit revenue (revenue per ASM or RASM), unit cost (cost per ASM or CASM), yield (revenue per RPM), and load factor (traffic as a percentage of output).

I. Operating Performance

Part 2 of the book highlighted four key variables: traffic, yield, output, and unit cost. Underlying each is an array of drivers, the most important of which have been discussed in preceding chapters. Figure 10.1 illustrates a sample of the pressures on airline cost and revenue streams that determine operating performance.

At this level of analysis, airlines are not materially different from other businesses: to improve operating performance it is necessary to boost revenue by selling more output and/or earning more from each sale, and to reduce costs by lowering input expenditures, raising productivity, and better matching supply to demand – all the while retaining focus on customers' expectations relative to the value being offered to them. However, there is one significant difference, at least as far as network carriers – as opposed to purely point-to-point operators – are concerned: *demand* arises in O&D markets whilst *supply* of output is generated on individual flight-legs which may simultaneously provide seats or cargo space for multiple behind/beyond markets. Not only does this complicate the allocation of costs and revenues to specific products, it makes the determination of equilibrium prices somewhat moot.

Managers will, of course, want to drill down much further than this into their cost and revenue streams. They will want the capability to make decisions based on profitability or contribution analyses by product, customer type, flight number, hub, country and/or region, distribution channel, and operating platform (i.e., mainline, affiliate, or code-

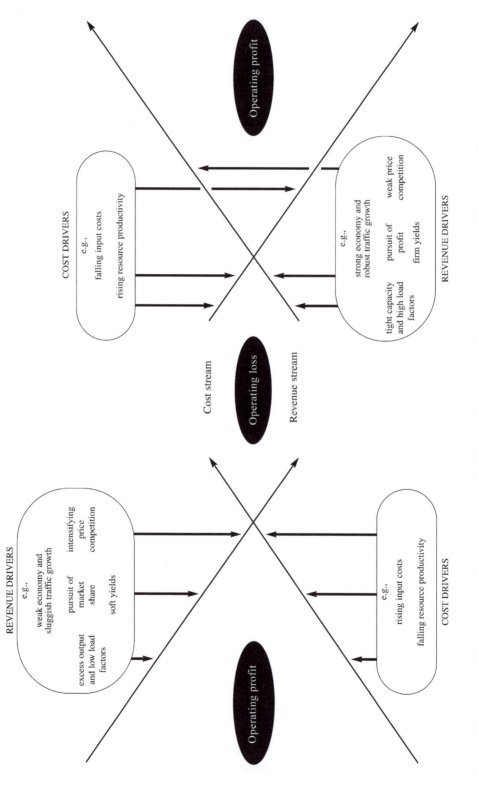

Figure 10.1 An illustration of some demand-side and supply-side pressures on airline operating performance

share) – as well as by flight-leg, route, and O&D market. These lower-level metrics will inevitably be affected by the choice, and consistency in use, of internal revenue prorate and cost allocation methods.

Discussion in the present chapter will be kept to the macro-level. First, the basic operating model around which Part 2 of the book has been structured:

Traffic × yield	=	traffic revenue		
		+ ancillary revenue	=	operating revenue
Output × unit cost			=	(operating cost)
			=	operating profit
			÷	operating revenue
			=	operating margin

Second, some additional relationships derived from the same basic metrics:

Operating revenue ÷ output	=	unit revenue (RASM)
Operating cost ÷ output	=	(unit cost)
	=	operating profit per unit of output (ASM)
Operating revenue ÷ operating cost	=	revex ratio
(Traffic ÷ output) × 100	=	load factor
(CASM ÷ yield) × 100	=	break-even load factor (BELF)
Yield × load factor	=	unit revenue (RASM)

Note the point made earlier in the book that how an airline chooses to account for ancillary revenues and for TFCs can affect these calculations. For example, there is an argument that ancillary revenue should be netted out of operating revenue before calculating RASM; also, some airlines net fuel surcharges off fuel expenditures rather than treating them as revenue. Figure 10.2 illustrates some of these relationships, and Box 10.1 exemplifies them with hypothetical figures.

The balance of the present chapter will take a closer look at these metrics and their relationships. One important point to bear in mind: whilst costs and revenues are of course critical areas for managers to focus on, the ultimate objective of managing them is not to minimise cost or maximise revenue but to earn sustainably high operating profits and margins. The problem facing US network carriers has not been that the unit costs in their domestic systems are higher than those of Southwest, jetBlue or AirTran; their problem has been that those higher costs do not contribute to the production of anything people are willing to pay a revenue premium in order to buy. This point is not semantic: it goes back to the critical concept of customer value explained in Chapter 1. The issue has been succinctly expressed from the perspective of both the consumer and the producer. From the consumer's side: 'Yes, first class on American is "better" than coach on Southwest but is it sufficiently better, as measured by real people paying real, higher prices, to justify the higher unit costs incurred by American in providing it?' (Unisys R2A 2003, p. 1). From the producer's side, in the words of a senior Continental executive: 'I don't focus on RASM or

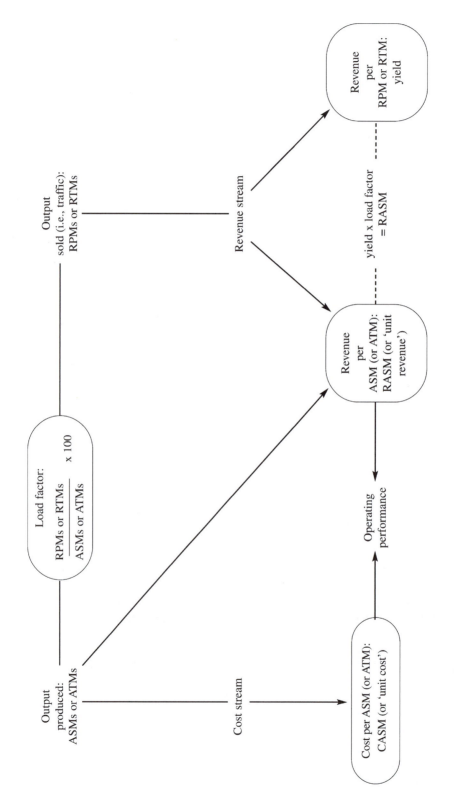

Figure 10.2   The relationship between CASM, RASM, yield and load factor

---

Box 10.1: Some Macro-Level Operating Metrics

Assume: a 150-seat aircraft flies a 1000-mile leg with 100 passengers onboard (but no cargo); operating revenue is $17,000 and operating cost is $15,000. Therefore:

Traffic is 100 passengers × 1000 miles = 100,000 RPMs.
Yield is $17,000 operating revenue ÷ 100,000 RPMs = 17 cents.
(Operating revenue has been given, but can nonetheless be seen to be: 100,000 RPMs × 17 cents = $17,000.)

Output is 150 seats × 1000 miles = 150,000 ASMs.
Unit cost is $15,000 operating cost ÷ 150,000 ASMs = 10 cents.
(Operating cost has been given, but can nonetheless be seen to be: 150,000 ASMs × 10 cents = $15,000.)

Operating profit is $17,000 − $15,000 = $2000; operating margin is ($2000 ÷ $17,000) × 100 = 11.8 per cent (which corresponds to a revex ratio of $17,000 ÷ $15,000 = 1.13).

Load factor is (100 passengers ÷ 150 seats) × 100 = 66.6 per cent.
(Technically this is a 'seat factor'; an alternative way to calculate load factor, and the method used when looking at a network as a whole rather than a single flight, is (100,000 RPMs ÷ 150,000 ASMs) × 100 = 66.6 per cent.)

Break-even load factor is (CASM 10 cents ÷ yield 17 cents) × 100 = 58.8 per cent.

Unit revenue (RASM) is $17,000 operating revenue ÷ 150,000 ASMs = 11.3 cents.
(Alternatively, RASM can be calculated as 17 cents yield × 66.6 per cent load factor = 11.3 cents.)
Unit revenue 11.3 cents − unit cost 10 cents = 1.3 cents operating profit per unit of output.

(Alternatively, this can be calculated as $2,000 ÷ 150,000 = 1.3 cents.)

CASM ... If I focused on CASM we'd have a lot less of our BusinessFirst product ... What we've said is we're happy to spend a dollar to make more than a dollar and we ought to focus on the margin' (*Air Transport World*, June 2007, p. 31).

II. Unit Cost, Unit Revenue, Yield, and Load Factor

UNIT COST, UNIT REVENUE, AND MARGIN

Irrespective of how an airline's cost and revenue streams are built up (by flight-leg, route, market, cabin, region, and so on), the ultimate measure of operating performance is whether or not RASM (i.e., unit revenue, the revenue per unit of output produced) exceeds CASM (i.e., unit cost, the cost of producing each unit of output).

1. *CASM* Improving CASM requires absolute input costs to be lowered and/or productivity to be raised.
2. *RASM* Improving RASM requires the generation of more revenue from the same level of output, or the same revenue from a reduced level of output. At any given level of

output, it is possible to improve revenue and therefore RASM either by improving yield and holding load factor (i.e., sales) steady or by improving load factor (i.e., increasing sales) while holding yields steady. The following points are important in this context:

- It is generally difficult to increase load factor and yield simultaneously; for this to be achieved, it must usually be against the background of either a strong market or significant cuts in output.
- Raising load factor within the current output range should not be expensive, but it will entail incremental traffic costs (arising from the delivery of ground and inflight service to additional passengers), incremental distribution costs (in respect of sales through agency channels), and perhaps higher marketing communication costs (to stimulate the incremental sales).
- Higher yields are also likely to have little impact on the cost side unless they arise from a product upgrade that is expensive in capital and/or operating cost terms. Again, firmer yields might lead to higher distribution costs.

Conversely, if a positive margin between RASM and CASM is to be maintained in the face of either declining yield or declining load factor, the other metric must move upwards:

- *Declining yield* Achieved load factor must rise. High price-elasticity in the market(s) concerned might help. (The revenue effect of a one basis point increase in load factor at a given yield is: yield × 0.01 × ASMs.)
- *Declining load factor* Yield must rise. This is likely to be difficult to achieve if poor load factors are indicative of carrier-specific or industry-wide demand softness and excess output. (The revenue impact of a tenth of a cent rise in yield at a given traffic level is: 0.10 × RPMs.)

If yields are falling faster than costs, it will be load factors that have to take up the slack in order to keep RASM ahead of CASM. (Note that RASM can be calculated as yield × load factor, as well as revenue/ASM.) One final point: because airline revenues are normally stated in nominal terms – that is, they are not inflation-adjusted – it is usual also to cite yields in nominal terms as well. However, when yields are being discussed at a general level it is not always clear whether the subject is real (i.e., inflation-adjusted) or nominal (i.e., current dollar) yields. Real yields have been in secular decline for decades; on the other hand, nominal yields are capable of reasonably positive growth, either in particular markets where demand is outstripping supply or across the industry as a whole when there is a marked cyclical upturn.

Unit Cost, Unit Revenue, And Output

Growing output Growing output can put downward pressure on unit cost, provided increased variable costs arising from the higher production level are outweighed by the beneficial impact of having more ASMs over which to spread fixed costs. The important question, of course, is whether the additional output also places so much downward pressure on yields that RASM declines faster than CASM and erodes operating profit. Assisted by the industry's long history as a growth business and fuelled by the apparently compelling attraction of market share to its managers, many airlines have tried in the past to grow their way out of cost problems. Uniquely, this did not happen in the US upturn that began in 2004.

Generally, we can say the following:

- Raising output within a carrier's current capacity range is often sensible because it allows broadly unchanged fixed costs to be spread over more units of output (i.e., ASMs or ATMs); the key question is whether and at what price the incremental output can be sold – specifically, whether incremental RASM exceeds incremental variable CASM (which will rise) net of incremental fixed CASM (which should fall).
- If, on the other hand, incremental output is generated not just within the existing capacity range but by adding further capacity with its own fixed costs, the challenge is greater. Because of the indivisibilities encountered in the industry – the fact that demand increases by one seat or passenger at a time per market whereas capacity increases by one aircraft (or gate or route, etc.) at a time – new capacity often brings with it more incremental output than demand is able to absorb in the short run. This can lead to softer yields as price is used to maintain load factors in the face of higher output. Not only is CASM adversely affected by higher fixed costs, albeit still being spread over higher output, but RASM might also be negatively affected by weaker yields.

Shrinking output   There are broadly two reasons why a carrier might shrink output:

1. In response to an industry downturn or carrier-specific difficulties. This is exemplified by the substantial capacity reductions initiated by US network carriers from the third quarter of 2001 and again in 2008.
2. As part of a strategic reorientation intended to underpin or boost yield. The dangers in this strategy are that high yields might be difficult to maintain in the face of a weak economy and/or competitors' upgraded products, and that costs associated with a relatively narrower system (notably smaller aircraft and perhaps reduced economies of scope) and an expensive product might put upward pressure on CASMs. Clearly, a high-yield strategy needs to be supported by a clear focus on costs just as much as does a low-fare strategy, albeit to different ends.

Although shrinking output should lead to an almost instant reduction in variable DOCs, an equally important issue is how quickly the structure of the operating system can be adjusted to bring about matching reductions in fixed DOCs and IOCs. If adjustment is slow and overhead remains at levels high enough to support previous output figures but above current needs, shrinking output can put upward pressure on unit costs; if only because it is unusual for a substantial carrier to be able to shed overhead as quickly as it can reduce frequencies or withdraw from routes, it is possible that the beneficial impact on unit costs brought about by reductions in variable DOCs may be counterbalanced in the short run by there now being fewer ASMs or ATMs over which to spread fixed costs.

Inter-Airline Comparisons: Revex Ratio, Cost Productivity, And Operating Margin

Taking up the last point, it is evident that an airline's RASM and CASM need to be analysed within some strategic context. Comparing different airlines' unit revenues and unit costs can be informative up to a point, particularly when the comparisons encompass direct competitors and are stage-length adjusted; for example, it can be analytically useful to monitor a network airline's revenue premium (i.e., RASM advantage) over a competing LFA and compare it with the cost gap between the two – an analysis which would show that US network carriers are less successful than their European counterparts in maintaining revenue premia over competing LFAs. (A similar approach sometimes used to analyse the performance of competing LFAs is to compare their respective average cost per passenger and average fare.)

However, given that unit revenue and unit cost figures cannot be adjusted to take into account different product strategies or brand positioning, where these exist, they tell at best only half the story of relative operating performances. The following can help fill in the gaps:

1. *Revex (or operating) ratio*   This is defined as: operating revenue/operating cost. Presented in this way, it is simply describing how much revenue has been earned by each dollar of expenditure. However, it is commonly turned into a percentage. One hundred per cent indicates a break-even result at the operating level, whilst a figure in excess of that is indicative of an operating profit. Revex ratios can in principle be calculated at several different levels. For example: an airline as a whole; an individual flight-leg, route or market; a cabin or a fare type (e.g., PEX or APEX) in a particular market. The finer-grained an analysis becomes, the more subjective the outcome will arguably be because of the alternative approaches available for internally prorating revenues and allocating costs to the different objects of analysis.

2. *Operating margin*   This is calculated as: (operating profit/operating revenue) × 100. It is arguably the most important macro-level performance metric. An alternative, currently favoured by analysts and very much in vogue, is EBITDAR margin: earnings before interest, tax, depreciation, amortisation, and rentals expressed as a percentage of operating revenue. Proponents favour it because by eliminating the effect of decisions pertaining to financial structure it gives a truer picture of operating performance; 'traditionalists' tend to criticise it as 'earnings with the nasty bits removed'. The debate is similar to that surrounding the increasingly common use of non-fuel CASM as an alternative to CASM, on the basis that fuel is not a controllable cost and so excluding it from CASM gives a truer impression of management's success in managing what *is* controllable; 'traditionalists' would point to the availability of hedging as a flaw in this argument.

Comparing RASM and CASM figures for very different types of airline, operating in different markets, and pursuing different competitive strategies which require operations of different complexity and scope tells us relatively little. Revex and operating margin form an arguably better basis for comparison of carriers which are not direct competitors across their networks. Such ratios and the figures on which they are based should nonetheless be treated as no more than broad descriptions of much more complex realities; only by digging down into airlines' cost and revenue streams can a rich understanding be gained of what is driving different operating performances.

Conclusion

It is common for managements to set target CASM figures. Whilst this is sound, CASM in itself means relatively little unless related to assumed RASM. What needs to be done is to target an operating margin, assume RASM based on market conditions and the carrier's brand positioning and product offering(s), and derive a CASM target. Operating margin requirements should be driven both by stakeholders' expectations and by the reinvestment needs of what is a capital-intensive industry. British Airways, for example, has very publicly committed itself to a target operating margin of 10 per cent averaged across economic cycles.

In fact, with the exception of brief periods the airline industry as a whole has historically been unable to sustain acceptable profits and margins. Too often, output has been so high that sufficient demand could only be stimulated by lowering prices to levels inadequate to generate satisfactory operating, let alone net, profits given prevailing cost structures. Restraint shown during the upturn from 2004 onwards, particularly by US network carriers in their domestic markets, represented a significant new development; further restraint was in evidence from 2008 onwards in response to high oil prices, but in many cases this was less about boosting profit margins than limiting losses and cash outflows.

YIELD

Yield – revenue per unit of output sold (i.e., per RPM or RTM) – is a highly significant metric, but it is by definition just the mathematical outcome of two even more fundamental metrics: output sold and revenue earned. When comparing revenue with cost, RASM is a more useful unit of analysis than yield because RASM and CASM have the same denominator (i.e., ASMs); since the denominator in the yield calculation is RPMs (or RTMs), yield cannot be directly compared with unit cost unless an adjustment is made for load factor. (An alternative is to compare yield with cost per RPM – something that is simple enough to calculate, but which adds little to the more usual CASM versus RASM comparison.)

Yield is nonetheless an important tool to help gain an understanding of the interplay between price and traffic figures when accounting for revenue performance in different parts of an airline's system. Figure 10.3 illustrates a simple revenue build-up approach.

For more than five decades, real (i.e., inflation-adjusted) yield across the industry as a whole has been in decline, and the price stimulus to which this has given rise accounts for a significant proportion of the traffic growth achieved during the period. However, as noted in the first section of the chapter, this is not to say that nominal (i.e., current dollar) yields reported in airline financial statements are invariably in decline, or even that real yields cannot rise periodically under certain market circumstances. Very broadly, the following generalisations apply:

1. Yields will soften when:
   - traffic growth is flat and/or insufficient to absorb output growth, and low prices are used to sustain load factors;
   - one or more carriers decides to lower prices either to stimulate the market generally or to increase market share, and competitors match on a significant scale.
2. Yields will remain firm or harden when:
   - load factors are already high and output is growing no faster than traffic;
   - traffic growth is outstripping growth in output;
   - no significant competitor feels it necessary to use price either to stimulate the market further or to build market share.

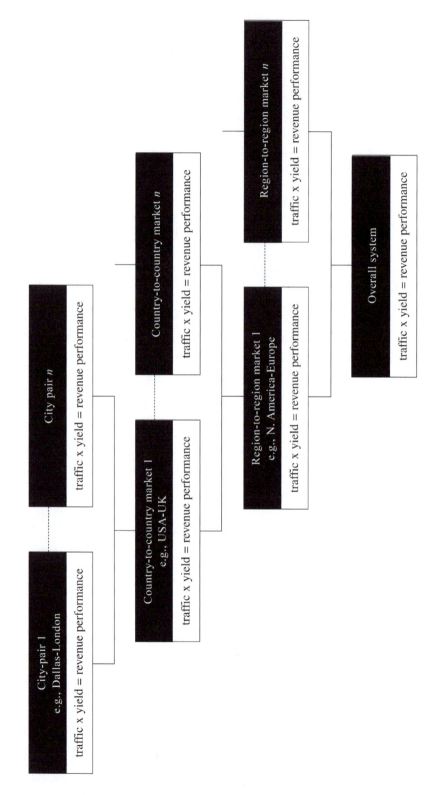

Figure 10.3   An approach to the analysis of airline revenue performance

Note that changes in yield (or, indeed, average fares) can result not just from price adjustments, but also from amending allocations to different booking classes in an RMS. Shifting inventory from high-yield to low-yield booking classes or buckets can result in lower yield, whilst reallocation in the opposite direction will harden yield (providing that the increased allocations are sold). The fact that traffic, load factor, and revenue (therefore yield) will each be affected by these types of adjustment illustrates once again how intimately connected the variables are – all within the context of available output.

Yield And Unit Costs

The higher an airline's unit cost, the more reliant it is on firm yields. Many US network carriers found their high costs 'beached above the water-line' in 2002 when revenues and yields came under downward pressure as a result of weak demand for full-fare tickets from business travellers. This, in essence, is what led several observers at the time to conclude that these airlines' short-haul business model – a model featuring high production costs underpinned by high full fares paid by a relatively small proportion of passengers travelling frequently on business – was in need of radical overhaul (particularly in markets where LFAs were, or were likely to become, part of the competitive equation). To provide a more focused example, among several strategic missteps made by former United feeder Atlantic Coast when trying to re-establish itself as Independence Air one was to fly high unit cost CRJ200s in low-yield markets.

LOAD FACTOR

Load factor measures the percentage of an airline's output that has been sold – in effect, a measure of the extent to which supply and demand are balanced at prevailing price points. Several different metrics are used:

1. *Passenger load factor* There are two calculations in common use:
    *   *Seat factor* This is the percentage of the seats available on a flight or series of flights that has been sold (with 'sold' also referring to FFP redemptions as well as revenue enplanements). It is not a distance-weighted measurement.
    *   *Distance-weighted passenger load factor* This is what is commonly meant when the expressions 'load factor' or 'passenger load factor' are used, and it is calculated as RPMs/ASMs × 100.
        The two approaches can lead to dramatically different figures. Consider a two-leg flight operated by a 200-seat aircraft: the first leg is 500 miles and is flown with 80 per cent of seats occupied (i.e., 160), whilst the second leg is 3000 miles and is flown with 40 per cent of seats occupied (i.e., 80).
    *   Distance-weighted passenger load factor is (80,000 + 240,000 RPMs)/(100,000 + 600,000 ASMs) × 100 = 45.7 per cent.
    *   Seat factor for the flight is (80 + 40)/2 = 60 per cent. (An alternative path to the same figure is (160 + 80)/(200 + 200).) In practice, this figure can be useful at the level of individual departures – with regard to aircraft assignment decisions, for example – but, as Box 10.2 suggests, there are pitfalls when it comes to averaging figures across a broader system. In the latter case, distance-weighted measures are preferable.

(It is also worth noting that average stage-length and the average distance flown by passengers are different. Average stage-length is (500 + 3000 unduplicated route-miles)/2 departures = 1750 miles. The average distance flown by passengers is (80,000 + 240,000 RPMs)/(160 + 80 passengers) = 1333 miles. The moral is that averages can be analytically useful as long as sight is not lost of the fact that they do not describe anything real. On a system-wide level, the same moral can be applied to CASM, RASM, yield, and load factor as well as average stage-length and passenger journey.)

2. *Cargo load factor* Load factors on all-cargo flights can also be measured as either: (payload capacity sold/payload capacity available) × 100; or on a distance-weighted basis as: (RTMs/ATMs) × 100.

3. *Overall (or weight) load factor* This calculation accounts for both passengers and cargo by assuming a standard weight for passengers and their baggage (often around 100–105 kg.), and combining it with cargo tonnage. As in point 2 above, this can be done on either a non-distance-weighted or a distance-weighted basis. When looking at individual flights or series of flights the former approach can be useful, whereas network analyses and comparisons tend to adopt the distance-weighted metric.

Box 10.2: The Pitfalls of Averaging

If one flight between two points is operated by a 400-seat aircraft at a 60 per cent seat factor and another is flown by a 100-seater at 80 per cent, the average seat factor is not 70 per cent; it is (240 + 80)/(400 + 100) × 100 = 64 per cent. In fact, whenever looking at anything other than a single departure (or a series of departures on the same route using aircraft with the same seating capacity), it is normally safer to calculate load factor by expressing aggregate RPMs as a percentage of aggregate ASMs.

Similar traps lie in the calculation of yield and unit cost. For example, if first class yield (i.e., revenue per RPM) on a service is $1000/1000 RPMs or $1 per RPM and economy class yield is $50,000/200,000 RPMs or 25 cents per RPM, the route yield is not the arithmetic mean of 100 cents and 25 cents. It is $51,000/201,000 or 25.4 cents per RPM. The same type of calculation needs to be applied when averaging unit costs across cabins.

Clearly, if we start with an airline's aggregate RPM figure and divide it by aggregate ASMs to calculate load factor, if we start with total revenue and divide it by aggregate RPMs to calculate yield, or if we start with total operating cost and divide it by aggregate ASMs to calculate unit cost there should not be a problem. It is usually only when calculating averages from the bottom up, by building from figures for individual routes and cabin classes, that problems sometimes arise.

The inclusion of cargo in a load factor calculation adds a number of complications:

1. Cargo payload has two facets: weight and volume. Whereas most transportation modes are more concerned with weight carried as a percentage of payload capacity available, we saw in Chapter 8 that aircraft frequently 'cube-out' before they 'weight-out' (i.e., the volume of space available for carriage of cargo is filled before the weight of cargo loaded reaches the maximum that could be uplifted). The result is that an aircraft departing absolutely full in volume terms might well have a weight load factor considerably below 100 per cent. The extent to which this matters will depend

upon the yield per pound being earned. High-volume cargo that 'wastes' payload capacity (as well as high-density cargo that 'wastes' volume capacity) should, ideally, be priced to offer attractive yields in compensation. (This was covered in Chapter 3.)

2. As far as combination carriers (uplifting both passengers and cargo) are concerned, the same flight may have different load factors depending upon which calculation is used. For example:

    *   assume that an aircraft with a payload capacity of 20 tons on a particular flight-leg actually carries passengers and cargo weighing 10 tons: its overall load factor is $(10/20) \times 100 = 50$ per cent;
    *   if on the same flight the aircraft were configured with 130 seats of which 85 were sold, the rest of the payload being cargo, the seat factor would be $(85/130) \times 100 = 65.4$ per cent.

    Although the example is hypothetical, it does illustrate an important point: overall (or weight) load factors are often lower than passenger load factors. The disparity arises because management of cargo capacity is constrained by the need to trade off payload weight against payload volume, and because the heavy directional imbalances in freight flows tend to put downward pressure on cargo load factors when they are averaged across a route network. (In the case of the US domestic system the disparity also owes much to the fact that combination carriers have conceded most of the freight market to integrated carriers and, increasingly, time-definite trucking services.)

3. On some (particularly long-haul) flight-legs, combination carriers can have difficulty maximising cargo load factor because they do not know how much cargo capacity is available until after passenger close-out (i.e., until after the passenger load has been finalised – something that might not happen until a few minutes before departure). This argues for having standby cargo ready to be loaded at the last moment when final passenger payload calculations reveal how much, if any, additional cargo can be carried.

Achieved Load Factors (ALFs)

Average load factors for the industry conceal marked variations between different types of airline, with regional carriers at the lower end of the spectrum and charter airlines generally achieving higher load factors than scheduled carriers. The average for any individual airline masks variations between different markets and cabins, with economy/coach achieving higher load factors because customers tend to book further in advance and expect lower levels of seat accessibility than is the case in premium cabins; it also conceals pronounced daily, weekly and – in particular – seasonal variations. An average annual passenger load factor of, say, 75 per cent (marginally below the 2007 global industry average) will conceal full flights and spilled demand across much of the schedule, especially during peak periods, but load factors perhaps as low as 50–60 per cent on off-peak or low-season departures. Furthermore, a year-round system load factor of 75 per cent would encompass much more dispersion around the mean (i.e., a flatter distribution curve and therefore greater spill) than would be the case were the same figure to apply either to a single route or a single month. However, advances in demand modelling and revenue management capabilities over the last decade mean that spill is now at levels that are acceptable even when ALF figures are around 80 per cent, whereas in a more rigid pricing and capacity allocation regime an ALF of 70 per cent would generate significant, perhaps unacceptable, spill.

Achieved load factors are driven to a considerable extent by the following:

1. *Output decisions relative to demand growth* 2006 was the first year on record that US network carriers reduced aggregate domestic mainline output in the face of rising demand. Not surprisingly, their load factors subsequently rose to historical peaks. The network carriers all achieved better than 80 per cent in 2007, and most regionals were in the 70–80 per cent range; with the notable exception of Southwest (72.6 per cent), the leading LFAs also exceeded 80 per cent. It remains to be seen whether the industry as a whole has finally learned to bring output growth into closer alignment with demand growth on a sustainable basis. Some observers interpret the improved performance as a cyclical phenomenon, but others believe the lessons of 2000–2005 were too painful to easily forget. Delta's March 2008 announcement that it would cut domestic capacity by ten per cent and concentrate growth into international markets in response to high fuel prices and a softening US economy supported the optimists' case, as did United's near-simultaneous grounding of up to 20 of its older aircraft for similar reasons; on the other hand, around the same time Europe was moving into what had the potential to be a period of marked short-haul overcapacity. One fact is certain: extraordinarily strong aircraft orders placed between 2005 and 2007 do not leave much room for error in the industry's bullish demand forecasts.

2. *Pricing* Fare reductions generally stimulate demand and, depending upon what decisions are taken with regard to output, generate higher load factors.

3. *Traffic mix* The 'rule' has historically been that the higher the proportion of business travellers carried by an airline, the lower its average seat factor is likely to be because:

    • demand for business travel has a random element that makes forecasting on a departure-by-departure basis relatively challenging and means that if adequate seat accessibility is to be maintained there is going to be inevitable downward pressure on load factors;

    • conversely, the more a carrier relies on advance-booking leisure and VFR traffic, the higher its load factor should be as a result of the greater predictability of booking profiles;

    • high frequencies demanded by business travellers tend to result in lower average load factors than would be achieved were the same output generated by larger aircraft operated at lower frequencies.

    This 'rule' weakens when demand growth outpaces growth in output, and load factors are forced higher. If load factors are high across all competitors – as in the US domestic market in 2006/07, for example – there is little or no seat accessibility for late bookers.

    One final point with regard to the relationship between demand characteristics and load factors is that because leisure and VFR demand is less volatile on a departure-by-departure basis, distributions around the mean tend to be tighter – and average load factor in this segment is likely to be more representative of the generality of achieved load factors – than would be the case in respect of the business segment. The fact that demand amongst business travellers is volatile and that ALFs by flight show more extreme distributions around the mean imply that demand spill will be encountered at a lower ALF in business and first class cabins (Clark 2001).

4. *Payment policies* A carrier taking non-refundable payments at the time of reservation, as most LFAs do throughout the aircraft and network carriers now do in respect of

a high proportion of their discount fares, is likely to have relatively fewer no-shows and a relatively higher seat factor than one selling a greater proportion of tickets on a fully flexible basis.

5. *Commercial success*   The success of product design, promotions, marketing communications, distribution, and service delivery will clearly influence current load factors – as will the relative success of competitors' efforts.

6. *Revenue management* The effectiveness of an RMS in minimising spoilage will influence load factors. Rising load factors were a significant driver of US airline recovery from the recessions of the early 1990s and 2000s; RMS capabilities – specifically, the refinement of demand forecasting tools – made increasingly significant contributions (alongside greater capacity discipline).

Achieved load factors are in part a measure of the success or otherwise of an airline's capacity management efforts. As we have already seen, these efforts are hindered by the fact that whilst demand fluctuates in units of single seat-departures in different O&D markets and is volatile, supply can only be produced in units equivalent to the capacity of whichever aircraft type is available to operate the flight-legs and routes designed to serve targeted O&D markets and is broadly fixed in the short run. Furthermore, the requirements to maintain both a high flight completion rate and the integrity of network connections and aircraft and crew assignments might preclude a scheduled passenger carrier from cancelling a significant number of its lightly loaded flights.

The implications of high load factors   Depending upon prevailing market circumstances, it is often the case that load factor and yield trade off against each other: unless demand is particularly strong and output growth is under firm control, it is likely that rising yield will be associated with downward pressure on load factors. Conversely, falling yield tends to be associated with higher load factors. Airline managers will generally want to arrive at a capacity plan with target load factors that strike a balance between the costs (i.e., forgone revenues) of turning passengers away and the costs (i.e., operating costs) of meeting all the peak demand coming forward and oversupplying the market at other times. High load factors might sometimes be a 'double-edged sword', however.

- On the positive side, because approximately two-thirds of an airline's costs can be directly related to the operation of aircraft and are independent of the number of passengers carried (Wells 1999), higher load factors generate lower average costs per passenger or per passenger-mile than would be the case were the same output of ASMs being produced but a lower load factor being achieved. If we assume a flight-leg DOC total of $20,000 for a 160-seater, the cost per passenger (without adjusting for changes in traffic costs) would be $167 at a 75 per cent load factor, rising to $179 at 70 per cent.

- On the negative side, we have already seen that high load factors can imply unacceptable levels of spill and, accordingly, forgone revenue. (However, recall that spill is usually less than 100 per cent of unaccommodated demand because some passengers will be booked onto earlier or later flights on the same carrier, and so recaptured rather than lost to a competitor.) At the operational level, high load factors can lead to slower turnarounds – perhaps impacting on aircraft, gate, and staff utilisation and even schedule reliability; this is a problem Southwest identified and addressed in the late 1990s, for example. They also complicate passenger reaccommodation when recovering from an operational disruption – a problem faced by most US network carriers during the summer of 2007. More generally, it is much easier from an operational perspective to manage an airline when load factors are at 64 per cent than when they are at 84 per cent – as United's were in August 2007, for example. One reason why the US national air transportation system is currently under severe strain is that there is simply not enough slack left to cope with significant disruptions, and one manifestation of the lack of slack is exceptionally high load factors. Yet only by operating at these levels can airlines hope to make money whilst offering the low fares that consumers now expect.

Conclusion   Load factors measure the percentage of output produced that has been sold. From an operating performance perspective this is important, but not as important as whether the revenue earned from sold output (i.e., from RPMs and RTMs) is sufficient to cover the costs of producing total output – both sold and unsold (i.e., the cost of producing ASMs and ATMs). We therefore need to dig deeper by comparing achieved load factor with break-even load factor.

Break-Even Load Factor

Achieved (or actual) load factor (ALF) is important, but in itself tells us nothing about operating performance until we relate it to break-even load factor (BELF). It is quite possible for an airline to achieve a higher load factor than a competitor but return a weaker operating performance (i.e., a lower operating profit or an operating loss), because the two have different BELFs.

Break-even load factor is the load factor at which costs and revenues are equal. It can be calculated at the level of:

- net costs (including non-operating items such as debt interest) and total revenue (i.e., operating and non-operating);
- total operating cost (TOC) and operating revenue;
- DOCs and operating revenue.

The focus here is on break-even at the level of TOC and operating revenue. The calculation of operating break-even is therefore as follows:

$$BELF = (TOC/ASMs)/(operating\ revenue/RPMs) \times 100$$

Expressed more simply, the calculation is (unit cost/yield) × 100.

At break-even, CASM and RASM are equal. However, it is worth keeping in mind that a carrier with high financial leverage – that is, high interest-bearing debt relative to shareholders' equity or net worth – could achieve a load factor in excess of operating break-even and so make an operating profit, yet still return a net loss because the positive operating result is insufficient to cover debt interest and other non-operating expenses net of any non-operating revenue. This has historically been a common occurrence amongst airlines during and immediately after periods of weak economic growth when profits have been poor and balance sheets have become overleveraged by heavy borrowing.

Break-even load factor can be calculated for a network as a whole or for individual flight-legs. In the case of individual flight-legs, however, a performance below fully allocated break-even (i.e., break-even calculated on the basis that all fixed costs and overhead are fully allocated to the flight) might not be critical if variable costs are being covered, a contribution is being made to fixed costs, and/or traffic profitable to the network as a whole is being carried. (This was explained in Chapter 5.) At the system level, on the other hand, BELF is a critical benchmark that needs to be beaten.

The following additional points are important:

1. An airline reaches break-even when it is selling enough output at a given yield to cover the fixed and variable costs of producing not only the output sold but also the portion of output that remains unsold (i.e., empty seats and cargo space on departed aircraft). We can therefore generalise that falling costs and/or rising yield will lower BELF, whilst rising costs and/or falling yield will raise it; we might also anticipate that introducing significant additional output could initially place upward pressure on BELF insofar as incremental fixed costs (e.g., aircraft ownership costs) have a more or less immediate impact, whilst achieving higher load factors or firmer yields to compensate may not initially be easy given the boost to output (unless, of course, increases in output are timed to lag demand). The problem with using BELF as a management tool, therefore, is that it represents a moving target: neither prices, costs, their relationship nor their behaviour in response to output changes are constant over time. Nonetheless, BELF can be a critical input into product and route decisions.

2. If we move below the system level to calculate BELF in respect of an individual cabin or flight-leg, the analysis is inevitably hostage to choices regarding cost allocation and the internal revenue prorate.

3. We saw in Chapter 5 that, at least in the short run, scheduled airlines suffer from high operating leverage – that is, high fixed costs as a proportion of total costs. What the word 'leverage' in this expression implies in practice is that once break-even is breached on either the upside or the downside, the impact of changes in revenue on operating profit are relatively greater than would be the case in a less leveraged industry. For airlines this means that what appear to be quite small differences between ALF and BELF can have a significant impact on operating results; whenever an airline is operating close to BELF, the sale of just one or two extra or fewer seats per departure can make a profound difference to system-wide operating performance.

4. An airline's BELF will be heavily influenced by its traffic mix. Break-even load factor for carriers on the North Atlantic can range from over 90 per cent in coach/economy to 40 per cent or even less in the premium cabins. At times some airlines have trouble more than breaking even on low-yield traffic but nonetheless use it to boost density and permit the operation of larger aircraft with lower seat-mile costs than high-yield traffic alone could sustain, relying on the high-yield traffic for most or all of their operating profit. This is fine as long as high-yield traffic remains robust.

    However, the interplay between traffic mix and BELF is not as straightforward as high-yield/low-BELF and low-yield/high-BELF. Ryanair appears to have its costs so firmly under control that at the time of writing its BELF is in the high 50 per cent range despite low yields and low average fares; by comparison, the equivalent figure for most US network carriers has for several years been close to 80 per cent – in some cases the wrong side of 80 per cent.

5.   Freight revenue also needs to be taken into account when calculating BELF. One approach that is commonly used is to deduct freight revenue from operating costs, including costs attributable to the carriage of freight, in order to arrive at an adjusted BELF.

Conclusion   Because airlines each have different unit costs and yields, every carrier inevitably has a different BELF. Two incontrovertible facts are that a relatively high ALF does not guarantee operating profits, and neither does a relatively low ALF guarantee operating losses (as many European regionals regularly prove). To take just one possible example of why this might be so, it is fairly obvious that if a fleet or subfleet is insufficiently utilised in terms of its aggregate time in the air – in other words, if it is not producing all the output it is capable of producing – even the sale of a high percentage of this unsatisfactory level of output (i.e., achievement of a high load factor) will not necessarily generate an operating profit.

As we have seen at various points in this book, airlines generally have high short-run fixed costs which require that:

- as much output as possible is produced over which fixed costs can be averaged (i.e., capacity utilisation should be high);
- as much of this output as possible is sold (i.e., ALF should be high);
- the output sold is sold at prices that exceed the cost of producing both sold and unsold output (i.e., BELF should be managed as low as possible and ALF should be as far as possible above it). Even a good load factor achieved on well-utilised aircraft will be inadequate if aggressive pricing and/or high costs leave BELF at a higher level.

Clearly, there is a close relationship between yield, unit cost, BELF, and ALF.

1.   *Yield*   Strategic and market positioning – specifically, the nature of the customer value being offered – provide the framework. Within this framework, how much influence an airline has over its yield depends in large measure upon the prevailing price-elasticity(ies) of demand for the particular product(s) it is offering, and on the level of competition in its markets.
   - If yield rises whilst unit cost remains unchanged, BELF will fall (i.e., improve).
   - If yield falls whilst unit cost remains unchanged, BELF will rise (i.e., deteriorate).
   - The higher the yield on a route or network, the lower will be its BELF at any given unit cost level.
   - When yield softens, unit cost must also be reduced if BELF is not to rise.
2.   *Unit cost*   As explained in Chapter 5, unit cost is a function of absolute input costs and productivity – both of which will be affected by a carrier's network and fleet structure, and by the nature of the product(s) it offers.
   - If unit cost rises whilst yield remains unchanged, BELF will rise (i.e., deteriorate).
   - If unit cost falls whilst yield remains unchanged, BELF will fall (i.e., improve).
   - The lower the unit cost of operating a route or network, the lower will be the carrier's BELF at any given level of yield.
   - If unit cost rises, yield must be improved if BELF is not to rise.
3.   *Achieved and break-even load factors*
   - A moderate ALF might be acceptable if BELF is sufficiently low – as when, for example, a high-yield (and therefore perhaps high-accessibility) product is being offered.

- A high ALF will not necessarily be enough to ensure acceptable operating performance if BELF is high – as when, for example, unit cost is high or yield is low.
- If ALF rises whilst yield and unit cost (and therefore BELF) remain constant, operating performance will improve (and vice versa).

If ALF is below BELF, what needs to be done is mathematically-speaking fairly clear: raise ALF while keeping CASM and yield constant; reduce CASM while keeping ALF and yield constant; raise yield while keeping ALF and CASM constant; or – ideally – raise ALF, reduce CASM, and raise yield. The latter route to profitability in particular is far easier said than done.

III. Concluding Comment

Part 1 of the book provided a strategic context within which to consider industry economics. Part 2 was structured around the relationship between operating revenue (traffic × yield) and operating cost (output × unit cost). Part 3 looked at several topics central to capacity management, the fundamental objective of which is to bring the relationship between revenue and cost into profitable juxtaposition.

Operating revenues can change because of changes in traffic and/or changes in the yield earned from carrying traffic. Operating costs can change because of changes in output and/or changes in the unit cost of producing output. When the two sides of this relationship balance, achieved and break-even load factors (at the operating level) will be identical. When one variable changes without a compensating change in another, achieved and break-even load factors will go their separate ways – the direction of which will quickly feed through to operating performance because of the industry's high short-run operating leverage.

Volatility in the constituent parts of each of these elements, the most significant of which have been discussed at various points throughout the book, accounts for the roller-coaster ride in airline operating performance. As this book is finalised for press in spring 2008, surging oil prices and softening demand are forcing airline finances off the cyclical peak attained in 2007. Yet that peak itself translated into an operating profit of just $16 billion and a margin of 3.2 per cent. Net profit in 2007 – the first since 2000 – was only $5.6 billion, and IATA's forecast for 2008 went from $5 billion in December 2007, to $4.5 billion in March 2008, to a loss of $2.3 billion at the time of the Association's Annual General Meeting in June (the latter based on an assumed average oil price of $107 per barrel). The word 'only' has a context: this is an already highly leveraged $500 billion industry which, according to Boeing (2007), will be ordering aircraft worth $2.8 trillion (at current list prices) between 2007 and 2026. Operating lessors can expect to be busy.

References

AeroStrategy Comment (2006), January.

Airbus (2008), *Flying by Nature: Global Market Forecast 2007–2026* (Toulouse).

Air Transport Action Group (2005), *The Economic & Social Benefits of Air Transport* (Geneva).

Air Transport Association (2001), *Annual Report* (Washington D.C.).

—— (2006), *Economic Review* (Washington D.C.).

—— (2007), <http://www.airlines.org/economics/finance/Annual+US+Results.htm> as at 1 February.

Alderson, W. (1957), *Marketing Behaviour and Executive Action* (Homewood: Irwin).

Amadeus (2007), *Future Traveller Tribes*, report produced jointly with Henley Centre Headlight Vision (<http://www.amadeus.com/amadeus/travellertribes.html>).

Areeda, P. and Turner, D. (1975), 'Predatory Prices and Related Practices Under Section 2 of the Sherman Act', *Harvard Law Review* 88: 4, 697–783.

Arinbjarnarson, K. (2007), 'Revenue Integrity', *AirCoreNews*, Q3, 5.

Bailey, E.E. and Panzar, J.C. (1981), 'The Contestability of Airline Markets During the Transition to Deregulation', *Law and Contemporary Problems* 44: Winter, 125–145.

Bailey, E.E. and Williams, J.R. (1988), 'Sources of Economic Rent in the Deregulated Airline Industry', *The Journal of Law and Economics* 31: April, 173–202.

Bailey, E.E., Graham, D.R., and Kaplan, D.P. (1985), *Deregulating the Airlines* (Cambridge: MIT Press).

Bailey, J. 'Federal Agency Investigating Airline Arrival Time Promises', *New York Times* <http://www.nytimes.com>, accessed 21 April 2007.

Bain, J.S. (1949), 'A Note on Pricing in Monopoly and Oligopoly', *American Economic Review* 39: March, 448–464.

—— (1956), *Barriers to New Competition* (Cambridge: Harvard University Press).

—— (1968), *Industrial Organization*, 2nd edition (New York: Wiley).

Baldanza, B.B. (1999), 'Measuring Airline Profitability', in Butler, G.F. and Keller, M.R. (eds.).

Baldanza, B.B. and Lipkus, L.S. (2000), 'Fundamentals of Airport Operations Staffing and Quality Assurance Measurement', in Butler, G.F. and Keller, M.R. (eds.).

BALPA (2007), *Aviation and the Environment: The Pilots' Perspective* (London).

Bamberger, G.E. and Carlton, D.W. (2002), 'Airline Networks and Fares,' in Jenkins, D. (ed.).

Barkin, T.I., Hertzell, O.S., and Young, S.J. (1995), 'Facing Low-cost Competitors: Lessons for US Airlines', *The McKinsey Quarterly*, 4, 86–99.

Barney, J.B. (1986a), 'Organizational Culture: Can it be a Source of Sustained Competitive Advantage?', *Academy of Management Review* 11: 3, 656–665.

—— (1986b), 'Strategic Factor Markets: Expectations, Luck, and Business Strategy', *Management Science* 32: 3, 1231–1241.

—— (1991), 'Firm Resources and Sustained Competitive Advantage', *Journal of Management* 17: 1, 99–120.

—— (1997), *Gaining and Sustaining Competitive Advantage* (Reading: Addison-Wesley).

Bartlik, M. (2007), *The Impact of EU Law on the Regulation of International Air Transportation* (Aldershot: Ashgate).

Basso, L.J. and Jara-Diaz, S.R. (2005), 'Calculation of Economies of Spatial Scope from Transport Cost Functions with Aggregate Output: An Application to the Airline Industry', *Journal of Transport Economics and Policy* 39: 1, 25–52.

Battersby, B. and Oczkowski, E. (2001), 'An Econometric Analysis of the Demand for Domestic Air Travel in Australia', *International Journal of Transport Economics* 28: 2, 193–204.

Baumol, W.J. (1982), 'Contestable Markets: An Uprising in the Theory of Industry Structure', *American Economic Review* 72: 1–15.

—— (2002), *The Free-Market Innovation Machine: Analyzing the Growth Miracle of Capitalism* (Princeton: Princeton University Press).

Baumol, W.J. and Willig, R.D. (1986), *Contestability: Developments Since the Book*, Research Paper 86-01, New York University.

Baumol, W.J., Panzar, J.C., and Willig, R.D. (1982), *Contestable Markets and the Theory of Industrial Structure* (New York: Harcourt, Brace, Jovanovich).

Bazargan, M. (2004), *Airline Operations and Scheduling* (Aldershot: Ashgate).

Beckman, J.M. (1958), 'Decision and Team Problems in Airline Reservations', *Econometrica* 26, 134–145.

Belobaba, P.P. (1987), 'Airline Yield Management – An Overview of Seat Inventory Control', *Transportation Science*, 21: 1, 63–73.

—— (1989), 'Application of a Probabilistic Decision Model to Airline Seat Inventory Control', *Operations Research* 37: 1, 183–197.

—— (1998a), 'The Evolution of Airline Yield Management: Fare Class to Origin-Destination Seat Inventory Control', in Butler, G.F. and Keller, M.R. (eds.).

—— (1998b), 'Airline Differential Pricing for Effective Yield Management', in Butler, G.F. and Keller, M.R. (eds.).

—— (2002), 'Airline Network Revenue Management: Recent Developments and State of the Practice', in Jenkins, D. (ed.).

—— (2006), 'Willingness to Pay and Competitive Revenue Management', paper delivered to the 12th PROS Conference, Houston, March.

Belobaba, P.P. and Farkas, A. (1999), 'Yield Management Impacts on Airline Spill Estimation', *Transportation Science* 33: 2, 217–232.

Ben-Yosef, E. (2005), *The Evolution of the US Airline Industry* (Dordrecht: Springer).

Berdy, P. (1998), 'Developing Effective Route Networks', in Butler, G.F. and Keller, M.R. (eds.).

—— (2002), 'Developing Effective Route Networks', in Jenkins, D. (ed.).

Berge, M.E. and Hopperstad, C.A. (1993), 'Demand-driven Despatch: A Method for Dynamic Aircraft Capacity Assignment, Models, and Algorithms', *Operations Research* 41: 1, 153–168.

Besanko, D., Dranove, D., and Shanley, M. (2000), *Economics of Strategy*, 2nd edition (New York: Wiley).

Beyer, B. (1999), 'Competitive Practices Under Pressure', *The Avmark Aviation Economist*, September, 1–2.

—— (2000), 'Premium Hub Fares: Reality or Myth?', *The Avmark Aviation Economist*, May, 14–16.

Bhadra, D. and Kee, J. (2008), 'The Structure and Dynamics of the Core US Air Travel Markets: A Basic Empirical Analysis of Domestic Passenger Demand', *Journal of Air Transport Management* 14, 27–39.

Bilotkach, V. (2007), 'Asymmetric Regulation and Airport Dominance in International Aviation: Evidence from the London–New York Market', *Southern Economic Journal* 74: 2, 505–523.

Binggeli, U. and Pompeo, L. (2005), 'The Battle for European Low-fare Flyers', *The McKinsey Quarterly* August, 34–42.

Bisignani, G. (2007), quoted in 'Powering into the Future', *Airlines International*, April/May, 29.

Blom, W. (2005), 'Revenue Management in Airline Transportation – New Challenges and Opportunities', presentation to the Marcus Evans Revenue Management Conference, Barcelona, March.

Boeing (1979), *Load Factor Analysis: The Relationship Between Flight Load Factor and Passenger Turnaway*, Commercial Airplane Group (Seattle).

—— (1993), *Decision Window Path Preference Methodology*, AMADWM–1, (Seattle).

—— (1997), *Current Market Outlook*, Commercial Airplane Group (Seattle).

—— (2001), 'Revenue and Yield Management', presentation by Richard Lonsdale to the *Euromoney European School of Aircraft Economics*, Vinkeveen, Netherlands, September.

—— (2004), *Fuel Conservation*, Commercial Airplane Group (Seattle).

—— (2006a), *Commercial Market Outlook*, Commercial Airplane Group (Seattle).

—— (2006b), *World Air Cargo Forecast*, Commercial Airplane Group (Seattle).

—— (2007), *Commercial Market Outlook*, Commercial Airplane Group (Seattle).

Bogner, W.C. and Thomas, H. (1996), 'From Skills to Competences: The "Playout" of Resource Bundles Across Firms', in Heene, A. and Sanchez, R. (eds.).

Borenstein, S. (1985), 'Price Discrimination in Free-Entry Markets', *RAND Journal of Economics* 16: 3, 380–397.

—— (1989), 'Hubs and High Fares: Dominance and Market Power in the U.S. Airline Industry', *RAND Journal of Economics* 20: 3, 344–365.

—— (1992), 'The Evolution of US Airline Competition', *Journal of Economic Perspectives* 6: Spring, 82–88.

—— (2005), *U.S. Domestic Airline Pricing 1995–2004*, Working Paper CPC05–48, Competition Policy Center, University of California at Berkeley.

Botimer, T.C. (1993), 'Airline Pricing and Fare Product Differentiation', Ph.D. dissertation, Massachusetts Institute of Technology.

Bowles, R. (1994), 'Air Travel: A Growth or Mature Industry?', *Canadian Aviation Forecast Conference Proceedings*, 69–73, Transport Canada.

Bowman, C. and Ambrosini, V. (1998), *Value Creation Versus Value Capture: Towards A Coherent Definition of Value in Strategy – An Exploratory Study*, Working Paper SWP 14/98, Cranfield School of Management.

Bowman, C. and Faulkner, D. (1997), *Competitive and Corporate Strategy* (London: Irwin).

Broggio, G., Falcomatà, S., Paoletti, B., Felici, G., and Gentile, C. (2000), 'An Optimization Framework for Ground Staff Roster Management Using Integer Programming', in Butler, G.F. and Keller, M.R. (eds.).

Brueckner, J.K. and Spiller, P.T. (1994), 'Economics of Traffic Density in the Deregulated Airline Industry', *Journal of Law and Economics* 37: 2, 379–391.

Brueckner, J.K. and Whalen, W.T. (1998), *The Price Effects of International Airline Alliances*, Unpublished Paper, University of Illinois at Urbana-Champaign.

Brueckner, J.K and Zhang, Y. (2001), 'Scheduling Decisions on an Airline Network', *Journal of Transport Economics and Policy* 35: 2, 195–222.

Brueckner, J.K., Dyer, N.J., and Spiller, P.T. (1992), 'Fare Determination in Airline Hub-and-Spoke Networks', *RAND Journal Of Economics* 23: 3, 309–333.

Brumelle, S.L. and McGill, J.J. (1993), 'Airline Seat Allocation with Multiple Nested Fare Classes', *Operations Research* 41: 1, 127–137.

Burger, B. and Fuchs, M. (2005), 'Dynamic Pricing – A Future Airline Business Model', *Journal of Revenue and Pricing Management* 4: 1, 39–53.

Burghouwt, G. (2007), *Airline Network Development in Europe and Its Implications for Airport Planning* (Aldershot: Ashgate).

Business Travel World (2006), 'Lord of the Wings', December, 3.

Butchers, E.R., Day, P.R., Goldie, A.P., Miller, S., Meyer, J.A., Ryan, D.M., Scott, A.C., and Wallace, C.A. (2001), 'Optimized Crew Scheduling at Air New Zealand', *Interfaces* 31: 1, 30–56.

Butler, G.F. and Keller, M.R. (eds.) (1998), *Handbook of Airline Marketing* (New York: McGraw-Hill).

Butler, G.F. and Keller, M.R. (eds.) (1999), *Handbook of Airline Finance* (New York: McGraw-Hill).

Butler, G.F. and Keller, M.R. (eds.) (2000), *Handbook of Airline Operations* (New York: McGraw-Hill).

Butler, G.F. and Keller, M.R. (eds.) (2001), *Handbook of Airline Strategy* (New York: McGraw-Hill).

Button, K.J. (ed) (1991), *Airline Deregulation: International Experiences* (London: David Fulton).

—— (1993), *Transport Economics*, 2nd edition (Cheltenham: Edward Elgar).

—— (1996), 'Liberalizing European Aviation: Is There an Empty Core Problem?', *Journal of Transport Economics and Policy* 30, 275–291.

Button, K.J. and Nijkamp, P. (2003), *Recent Advances in Air Transport Economics* (Lund: University of Lund).

Button, K.J. and Stough, R. (2000), *Air Transport Networks* (Cheltenham: Edward Elgar).

CAA (1994), *Airline Competition on European Long-Haul Routes*, CAP 639 (London).

—— (2003), *Air Passenger Growth and Airport Capacity: Advice to the Department for Transport on the Future Nature and Distribution of Demand for Air Travel* (London).

—— (2005), *Demand for Outbound Leisure Air Travel and its Key Drivers* (London).

—— (2006a), *No-frills Carriers: Revolution or Evolution*, CAP 770 (London).

—— (2006b), *UK–India Air Services – A Case Study in Liberalisation*, ERG 2006/37 (London).

—— (2006c), *Ownership and Control Liberalisation: A Discussion Paper*, CAP 769 (London).

—— (2008), *Recent Trends in Growth of UK Air Passenger Demand* (London).

Call, G.D. and Keeler, T.E. (1985), 'Airline Deregulation, Fares, and Market Behaviour: Some Empirical Evidence', in Daugherty, A.H. (ed.).

Carlton, D.W., Landes, W.M., and Posner, R.A. (1980), 'Benefits and Costs of Airline Mergers: A Case Study', *Bell Journal of Economics and Management Science* 11: spring, 65–83.

Carpenter, G.S., Glazer, R., and Nakamoto, K. (1994), 'Meaningful Brands From Meaningless Differentiation: The Dependence on Irrelevant Attributes', *Journal of Marketing Research* 31: 3, 339–350.

Carter, D.A., Rogers, D.A., and Simkins, B.J. (2006), 'Does Hedging Affect Firm Value? Evidence from the U.S. Airline Industry', *Financial Management* 35: 1, 53–87.

Caves, D.W. (1962), *Air Transport and its Regulators* (Cambridge: Harvard University Press).

Caves, D.W., Christensen, L.R., and Tretheway, M.W. (1984), 'Economies of Density Versus Economies of Scale: Why Trunk and Local Service Airline Costs Differ', *Rand Journal of Economics* 15: 4, 471–489.

Chamberlin, E.H. (1933), *The Theory of Monopolistic Competition* (Cambridge: Harvard University Press).

Chandler, A.D. (1962), *Strategy and Structure* (Cambridge: MIT Press).

Christou, I.T., Zakarian, A., Liu, J.M., and Carter, H. (1999), 'A Two-Phase Genetic Algorithm for Large-Scale Bidline-Generation Problems at Delta Air Lines', *Interfaces* 19: 5, 51-65.

Clampett, S. (1998), 'Airflite: Developing a Premium Product', *Flight Scheduling Journal*, 43–41, Sabre (Dallas).

Clark, P. (2000), 'Dynamic Fleet Management', in Butler, G.F. and Keller, M.R. (eds.).

—— (2001), *Buying the Big Jets: Fleet Planning for Airlines* (Aldershot: Ashgate).

___ (2007), *Buying the Big Jets: Fleet Planning for Airlines*, 2nd edition (Aldershot: Ashgate).

Coase, R.H. (1937), 'The Nature of the Firm', *Economica* 4, 386–405.

Comanor, W.S. and Frech, H.E. III (1993), 'Predatory Pricing and the Meaning of Intent', *Antitrust Bulletin* 38: 2, 293–308.

Cook, A. (2007a), 'The Management and Costs of Delay', in Cook (ed.).

Cook, A. (ed) (2007b), *European Air Traffic Management: Principles, Practice and Research* (Aldershot: Ashgate).

Cooper, W.L., Homem-de-Mello, T., and Kleywegt, A.J. (2006), 'Models of the Spiral-Down Effect in Revenue Management', *Operations Research*, 54: 5, 968–987.

Crandall, R.L. (1995), 'The Unique US Airline Industry', in Jenkins, D. (ed.).

Creel, M. and Farrell, M. (2001), 'Economies of Scale in the U.S. Airline Industry After Deregulation: A Fourier Series Approximation', *Transportation Research*, Part E, 321–336.

Curry, R.E. (1990), 'Optimal Airline Seat Allocation in Fare Classes Nested by Origins and Destinations', *Transportation Science* 24, 193–204.

Davies, R.E.G. (2002), 'Air Transport Directions in the 21st Century (The Lessons of History)', in Jenkins, D. (ed.).

De Boer, S.V., Freling, R., and Piersma, N. (1999), 'Mathematical Programming for Network Revenue Management Revisited', Working Paper, Erasmus Institute, Erasmus University.

Dennis, N. (1994), 'Scheduling Strategies for Airline Hub Operations', *Journal of Air Transport Management* 1, 131–144.

—— (2000), 'Scheduling Issues and Network Strategies for International Airline Alliances', *Journal of Air Transport Management* 6, 75-85.

Denton, N. and Dennis, N. (2000), 'Airline Franchising in Europe: Benefits and Disbenefits to Airlines and Consumers', *Journal of Air Transport Management* 6, 179-190.

Desrosiers, J., Lasry, A., McInnis, D., Solomon, M.M., and Soumis, F. (2000), 'Air Transat Uses ALTITUDE to Manage Its Aircraft Routing, Crew Pairing, and Work Assignment', *Interfaces* 30: 2, 41-53.

Dillon, J.E. and Kontogiorgis, S. (1999), 'US Airways Optimizes the Scheduling of Reserve Flight Crews', *Interfaces* 29: 5, 123-131.

Doganis, R.S. (2001), *The Airline Business in the 21st Century* (London: Routledge).

—— (2006), *The Airline Business in the 21st Century*, 2nd edition (London: Routledge).

DOT (1990), *Airports, Air Traffic Control and Related Concerns*, Secretary's Task Force on Competition in the U.S. Domestic Airline Industry, Office of the Secretary for Transportation (Washington D.C.).

—— (2001), *Dominated Hub Fares*, Domestic Aviation Competition Series, Office of the Assistant Secretary for Aviation and International Affairs (Washington D.C.).

—— (2006a), *Second Quarter 2006 Air Travel Price Index (ATPI)*, Press Release BTS50–06, Wednesday October 25th.

—— (2006b), *Aviation Industry Performance*, Office of the Inspector General.

DOTARS (2006), *Australia to Continue Liberalisation of International Air Services*, media release, February 22nd <http://www.ministers.dotars.gov.au/wtr/releases/ 2006/February/ 018WT.htm>.

DotEcon (2006), *Alternative Allocation Mechanisms for Slots Created by New Airport Capacity* (London).

Douglas, G.W. and Miller, J.C. (1974a), *Economic Regulation of Domestic Air Transport: Theory and Policy* (Washington: The Brookings Institution).

—— (1974b), 'Quality Competition, Industrial Equilibrium, and Efficiency in the Price-Constrained Airline Market', *American Economic Review* 64, 657–669.

Dresner, M. (2002), 'Metrics in the Airline Industry', in Jenkins, D. (ed.).

Dunleavy, H. and Westermann, D. (2005), 'Future of Airline Revenue Management', *Journal of Revenue and Pricing Management* 3: 4, 380–383.

Dussauge, R. and Garrette, B. (1995), 'Determinants of Success in International Strategic Alliances: Evidence from the Global Aerospace Industry', *Journal of International Business Studies* 26, 505–530.

ECAC (2004), *Airport Capacity: Challenges to Growth*, Joint ECAC and Eurocontrol Study (published online 14 December) <http://www.eurocontrol.int.eatm/gallery/ content/public/library/CTG04_report.pdf>.

Eden, C. and Ackermann, F. (1998), *Making Strategy: The Journey of Strategic Management* (London: Sage).

Edwards, G. (2002), 'The Perennial Problem of Predatory Pricing', *Australian Business Law Review* 30, 10–201.

ELFAA (2004), *Liberalisation of European Air Transport: The Benefits of Low Fares Airlines to Consumers, Airports, Regions and the Environment* (Brussels).

Embraer (2008), *Market Outlook 2007–2026* (São José dos Campos).

Ernst & Young and York Aviation (2007), *Analyzing the EC Proposal to Include Aviation Activities in the Emissions Trading Scheme*, June 1st.

Eurocontrol (2007), *PRR 2006* <http://www.eurocontrol.int/prc/gallery/content/public/ Docs/PRR_2006.pdf>.

European Cockpit Association (2006), *Upheaval in European Skies – Low Cost Carriers in Europe: Economic Data, Market and Pilot Demand Forecast* (2nd edition) (Brussels).

Evans, W.N. and Kessides, I.N. (1993), 'Structure, Conduct, and Performance in the Deregulated Airline Industry', *Southern Economic Journal* 59, 450–467.

FAA (2006), *Aerospace Forecasts Fiscal Years 2006–2017* (Washington D.C.).

—— (2007a), *Aerospace Forecasts Fiscal Years 2007–2018* (Washington D.C.).

—— (2007b), *Capacity Needs in the National Airspace System* (Washington D.C.).

___ (2008), *Aerospace Forecasts Fiscal Years 2008–2025* (Washington D.C.).

Fabrycky, W.J., Thuesen, G.J., and Verma, D. (1998), *Economic Decision Analysis*, 3rd edition (Upper Saddle River: Prentice-Hall).

Fershtam, C. and Muller, E. (1986), 'Capital Investment and Price Agreement in Semi-Collusive Oligopolies', *RAND Journal of Economics* 17: 2, 214–226.

Finney, P.B. (2006), 'Loading an Airliner is Rocket Science', *The New York Times*, November 14th, 14.

Fitzroy, F.R., Acs, Z.J., and Gerlowski, D.A. (1998), *Management and Economics of Organization* (Hemel Hempstead: Prentice-Hall).

Flint, P. (2001), 'Hard Times', *Air Transport World*, November, 23–27.

Ford, E. (2005), *Traffic and Fare Changes Resulting From New Nonstop Service – Recent Experience* (Reston: Eclat Consulting).

Forsyth, P. (2001), 'Promoting Trade in Airline Services', *Journal of Air Transport Management* 7, 43–50.

Forsyth, P., Gillen, D.W., Mayer, O.E., and Niemeier, H-M (eds.) (2005), *Competition versus Predation in Aviation Markets: A Survey of Experience in North America, Europe and Australia* (Aldershot: Ashgate).

Frainey, W.M. (1999), 'Network Profitability Analysis', in Butler, G.F. and Keller, M.R. (eds.).

Friend, C.H. (1992), *Aircraft Maintenance Management* (Harlow: Longman).

Fruhan, W. (1972), *The Fight for Competitive Advantage: A Study of the United States Domestic Trunk Carrier* (Cambridge: Harvard University Press).

Gale, I.L. and Holmes, T.J. (1993), 'Advance-Purchase Discounts and Monopoly Allocation of Capacity', *American Economic Review* 83: March, 135–146.

Gannon, C.A. (2005), 'An Economic Framework for Assessing Predation in Air Services: Markets, Barriers to Entry, Market Power and Tests', in Forsyth et al. (eds.).

GAO (1990), *Airline Competition: Higher Fares and Reduced Competition at Concentrated Airports*, GAO/RCED 90–102 (Washington D.C.).

—— (1991), *Airline Competition: Effects of Airline Market Concentration and Barriers to Entry on Airfares*, GAO/RCED 91–101 (Washington D.C.).

—— (1999), *Airline Deregulation: Changes in Airfares, Service Quality and Barriers to Entry*, GAO/RCED 99–92 (Washington D.C.).

—— (2001), *Aviation Competition: Challenges in Enhancing Competition in Dominated Markets*, GAO/01–518T (Washington D.C.).

—— (2003), *Airline Labor Relations: Information on Trends and Impact of Labor Actions*, GAO–03–562 (Washington D.C.).

—— (2005), *Commercial Aviation: Preliminary Observations on Legacy Airlines' Financial Condition, Bankruptcy, and Pension Issues*, GAO–05–835T (Washington D.C.).

—— (2006), *Airline Deregulation: Reregulating the Airline Industry Would Likely Reverse Current Benefits and Not Save Airline Pensions*, GAO–06–630 (Washington D.C.).

—— (2007a), *Crude Oil: Uncertainty About Future Oil Supply Makes It Important to Develop a Strategy for Addressing a Peak and Decline in Oil Production*, GAO–07–283 (Washington D.C.).

—— (2007b), *Next Generation Air Transportation System*, GAO–07–784T (Washington D.C.).

—— (2007c), *Federal Aviation Administration: Viability of Current Funding Structure for Aviation Activities and Observations on Funding Provisions of Reauthorization Proposals*, GAO–07–1104T (Washington D.C.).

—— (2007d), *Aviation and the Environment: Impact of Aviation Noise on Communities Presents Challenges for Airport Operations and Future Growth of the National Airspace System*, GAO–08–216T (Washington D.C.).

Garrow, L.A. and Koppelman, F.S. (2004), 'Predicting Air Travellers' No-show and Standby Behaviour Using Passenger and Directional Itinerary Information', *Journal of Air Transport Management* 10, 401–411.

Garvett, D.S. and Avery, A. (1998), 'Frequent Traveler Programs', in Butler, G.F. and Keller, M.R. (eds.).

Garvett, D.S. and Michaels, L. (1998), 'Price Parrying: A Direction for Quick, Decisive, and Profit-Maximizing Pricing', in Butler, G.F. and Keller, M.R. (eds.).

Garvin, M.R. Jr. (2000), 'Service Delivery System: A Regional Airline Perspective', in Butler, G.F. and Keller, M.R. (eds.).

Geil, K. (2006), 'The Single EU Aviation Market and Its External Dimension', presentation to the ICAO Global Symposium on Air Transport Liberalisation, Dubai, September.

Gertner, R. (1993), *The Role of Firm Asymmetries for Tacit Collusion in Markets With Immediate Competitive Responses*, Working Paper, University of Chicago.

Ghemawat, P. (1991), *Commitment: The Dynamic of Strategy* (New York: The Free Press).

Gialloreto, L. (1988), *Strategic Airline Management: The Global War Begins* (London: Pitman).

Gillen, D., Morrison, W., and Stewart, C. (2004), *Air Transport Demand Elasticities: Concepts, Issues and Measurement: Final Report*, Department of Transport, Ottawa.

Gillen, D., Oum, T., and Tretheway, M. (1985), *Airline Cost and Performance: Implications for Public and Industry Policies*, Centre for Transportation Studies, University of British Columbia.

—— (1990), 'Airline Cost Structures and Policy Implications', *Journal of Transport Economics and Policy* 24: 1, 9–34.

Gimeno, J. (1999), 'Reciprocal Threats in Multi-market Rivalry: Staking Out Spheres of Influence in the US Airline Industry', *Strategic Management Journal* 20, 101–129.

Golaszewski, R.S. and Ballard, B.D. (2001), 'Aviation Demand and Capacity: Do Current Institutions Promote an Efficient Balance?', in Butler, G.F. and Keller, M.R. (eds.).

Good, W. (2000), 'Flight Crew Scheduling Update: The Strategic Management of Airline Intellectual Capital and Core Competencies', in Butler, G.F. and Keller, M.R. (eds.).

Gorin, T., Brunger, W.G., and White, M.M. (2006), 'No-show Forecasting: A Blended Cost-based, PNR-adjusted Approach', *Journal of Revenue and Pricing Management* 5: 3, 188–202.

Graham, A. (2000), 'Demand for Leisure Air Travel and Limits to Growth', *Journal of Air Transport Management* 6, 109–118.

Graham, D.R. and Kaplan, D.P. (1982), 'Airline Deregulation is Working', *Regulation* 6, 26–32.

Graham, D.R., Kaplan, D.P., and Sibley, D.S. (1983), 'Efficiency and Competition in the Airline Industry', *The Bell Journal of Economics* 14, 118–138.

Grant, R.M. (1998), *Contemporary Strategy Analysis* (Malden: Blackwell).

Grubb, H. and Mason, A. (2001), 'Long Lead-time Forecasting of UK Air Passengers by Holt-Winters Methods with Damped Trend', *International Journal of Forecasting* 17, 71–82.

Gutschi, M. (2007), 'Air Canada Fliers Buy the Extras', *Wall Street Journal* (Eastern Edition), 29th March.

Haerian, L., Homem-de-Mello, T., and Mount-Campbell, C.A. (2006), 'Modeling Revenue Yield of Reservation Systems That Use Nested Capacity Protection Strategies', *International Journal of Production Economics* 104, 340–353.

Hambrick, D.C. and Frederickson, J.W. (2005), 'Are You Sure You Have a Strategy?', *Academy of Management Executive* 19: 4, 51–62.

Hanlon, P. (2007), *Global Airlines: Competition in a Transnational Industry*, 3rd edition (Oxford: Butterworth-Heinemann).

Hatton, R. (1999), 'Complexities of Air Cargo vis-à-vis Air Finance: The Economics of Wide-Body Freighter Aircraft', in Butler, G.F. and Keller, M.R. (eds.).

Havel, B.F. (1997), *In Search of Open Skies* (The Hague: Kluwer).

Heimlich, J. (2007) *2007 Outlook: Reaching for the Skies* (Washington: ATA) (published online 20th January 2007) <http://www.airlines.org/economics/review_and_outlook. htm>

Hergert, M. and Morris, D. (1989), 'Accounting Data for Value Chain Analysis', *Strategic Management Journal* 10, 175–188.

Herrmann, N., Müller, M., and Crux, A. (1998), 'Pricing and Revenue Management Can Reshape Your Competitive Position in Today's Air Cargo Business', in Butler, G.F. and Keller, M.R. (eds.).

Heskett, J.L, Jones, T.O., Loveman, G.W., Sasser, W.E. Jr., and Schlesinger, L.A. (1994), 'Putting The Service-Profit Chain to Work', *Harvard Business Review*, March–April, 164–174.

Heskett, J.L., Sasser, W.E. Jr., and Schlesinger, L.A. (1997), *The Service-Profit Chain* (New York: The Free Press).

Holloway, S. (1992), *Aircraft Acquisition Finance* (London: Pitman).

—— (1998a), *Changing Planes: A Strategic Management Perspective on an Industry in Transition (Vol. 1: Situation Analysis)* (Aldershot: Ashgate).

—— (1998b), *Changing Planes: A Strategic Management Perspective on an Industry in Transition (Vol. 2: Strategic Choice, Implementation, and Outcome)* (Aldershot: Ashgate).

—— (2002), *Airlines: Managing to Make Money* (Aldershot: Ashgate).

Homan, A.C. (2000), 'The Effect of Changes in Flight Time and On-Time Performance on Commercial Air Transport Demand', in Butler, G.F. and Keller, M.R. (eds.).

Hopperstad, C. (1994), 'The Application of Path Preference and Stochastic Demand Modelling to Market Based Forecasting', *AGIFORS Reservations and Yield Management Study Group Proceedings*, Hong Kong, June.

Hotelling, H. (1929), 'Stability in Competition', *Economic Journal* 39: 153, 41–57.

Hunt, S.D. (2000), *A General Theory of Competition: Resources, Competencies, Productivity, Economic Growth* (Thousand Oaks: Sage).

Hurdel, G.J., Johnson, R.L., Joskow, A.S., Werden, G.J., and Williams, M.A. (1989), 'Concentration, Potential Entry, and Performance in the Airline Industry', *Journal of Industrial Economics* 38, 119–139.

IATA (2001), *Flight Path to Environmental Excellence* (Geneva).

—— (2004a), *Environmental Review 2004* (Geneva).

—— (2004b), *ATM Implementation Roadmap – Short and Medium Term* (Geneva).

—— (2006a), *Value Chain Profitability*, Economics Briefing 04 (Geneva).

—— (2006b), <http://www.iata.org/pressroom/economics_facts/fact_sheets/adp.htm>, 7th November 2006.

—— (2007a), *Corporate Air Travel Survey 2007* (Geneva).

—— (2007b), *Premium Traffic Monitor* (Geneva).

—— (2007c), *CUSS Fact Sheet* (Geneva).

—— (2007d), *Building a Greener Future* (Geneva).

Iatrou, K. and Oretti, M. (2007), *Airline Choices for the Future* (Aldershot: Ashgate).

ICAO (2000), 'Report of the Conference on the Economics of Airports and Air Navigation Services – Air Transport Infrastructure for the 21st Century', Montreal, June.

—— (2004), *ICAO's Policies on Charges for Airports and Air Navigation Services*, 7th edition, Doc 9082 (Montreal).

—— (2006), *Airport Economics Manual*, 2nd edition, Doc 9562 (Montreal).

—— (2007a), *ICAO Journal*, Number 2.

—— (2007b), *Environmental Report 2007* (Montreal).

Ingold, A. and Huyton, J.R. (1997), 'Yield Management and the Airline Industry', in Yeoman, I. and Ingold, A. (eds.).

InterVISTAS Consulting (2005), *The Economic Impacts of the Open Skies Initiative – Past and Future* (Washington D.C.).

InterVISTAS-ga² (2006), *The Economic Impact of Air Service Liberalization* (Washington D.C.).

IPCC (1999), *Special Report on Aviation and the Global Atmosphere* (Geneva).

—— (2007), *Climate Change 2007* (Geneva).

Irrgang, M.E. (1995a), 'Airline Irregular Operations', in Jenkins, D. (ed.).

—— (1995b), 'Fuel Conservation', in Jenkins, D. (ed.).

—— (2000), 'Airline Operational Efficiency', in Butler, G.F. and Keller, M.R. (eds.).

Ivy, R.J. (1993), 'Variations in Hub Service in the US Domestic Air Transportation Network', *Journal of Transport Geography* 1: 4, 211–218.

Jacobs, T.L., Ratliff, R.M., and Smith, B.C. (2001), 'The Importance of Integrating Airline Scheduling, Pricing, and Yield Management Activities', in Butler, G.F. and Keller, M.R. (eds.).

James, G. (1993), 'US Commercial Aviation: A Growth or Mature Industry', *18th FAA Aviation Forecast Conference Proceedings*, FAA–APO 93–2, 182–202.

Jarrah, A.I., Goodstein, J., and Narasimhan, R. (2000), 'An Efficient Airline Re-Fleeting Model for the Incremental Modification of Planned Fleet Assignments', *Transportation Science* 34: 4, November, 349–363.

Jenkins, D. (ed.) (1995), *Handbook of Airline Economics* (New York: McGraw-Hill).

—— (ed.) (2002), *Handbook of Airline Economics*, 2nd edition (New York: McGraw-Hill).

Jenks, C.B. (2001), 'Global Alliances: Three Strategically Key Evolutionary Uncertainties', in Butler, G.F. and Keller, M.R. (eds.).

JITI (2006), *Chicago Regime Research Committee Report* (Tokyo).

Jordan, W.A. (1970), *Airline Regulation in America: Effects and Imperfections* (Baltimore: Johns Hopkins University Press).

Jorge-Calderón, J.D. (1997), 'A Demand Model for Scheduled Airline Services on International European Routes', *Journal of Air Transport Management* 3: 1, 23–35.

Joskow, P.L. and Klevorick, A.K. (1979), 'A Framework for Analyzing Predatory Pricing Policy', *Yale Law Journal* 89: 2, 213–270.

JPDO (Environmental Integrated Product Team), Partnership for AiRTransportation Noise and Emissions Reduction (2006), *Workshop on the Impacts of Aviation on Climate Change*, Cambridge MA, June.

Kahn, A.E. (1971), *The Economics of Regulation* (New York: Wiley).

—— (2004), *Lessons from Deregulation* (Washington D.C.: AEI-Brookings Joint Center for Regulatory Studies).

Kahneman, D. and Tversky, A. (1979), 'Prospect Theory: An Analysis of Decisions Under Risk', *Econometrica* 47, 263–292.

Kanellis, G.R. (1999), 'A Method for Evaluating and Selecting Avionics Equipment for Commercial Aircraft: The Head-up Guidance System (HGS®) Example', in Butler, G.F. and Keller, M.R. (eds.).

Keeler, J. and Formby, F. (1994), 'Cost, Economics and Consolidation in the U.S. Airline Industry', *International Journal of Transport Economics* 21, 21–45.

Keeler, T.E. (1972), 'Airline Regulation and Market Performance', *Bell Journal of Economics and Management* 3, 399–414.

Kelly, T. (2001), 'A Strategic Challenge: Delivering Airspace Capacity', in Butler, G.F. and Keller, M.R. (eds.).

Kimes, S.E. (1997), 'Yield Management: An Overview', in Yeoman, I. and Ingold, A. (eds.).

Kline, R. (1999), 'Managing Aircraft Costs Through Passenger Value Management', in Butler, G.F. and Keller, M.R. (eds.).

Kontogiorgis, S. and Acharya, S. (1999), 'US Airways Automates Its Weekend Fleet Assignment', *Interfaces* 29: 3, 52–62.

Kuhlmann, R. (2004), 'Why is Revenue Management Not Working?', *Journal of Revenue and Pricing Management* 2: 4, 378–387.

—— (2007a), *Unisys R2A Scorecard: Airline Industry Cost Measurement* 5: 4 <http://www. unisys.com/transportation>.

—— (2007b), *Unisys R2A Scorecard: Airline Industry Cost Measurement* 6: 2 <http://www. unisys.com/transportation>.

—— (2007c), *Unisys R2A Scorecard: Airline Industry Cost Measurement* 6: 3 <http://www. unisys.com/transportation>.

Kumbhakar, S.C. (1990), 'A Reexamination of Returns to Scale, Density and Technical Progress in U.S. Airlines', *Southern Economic Journal* 57: 2, 428–442.

Kyrou, D. (2000), *Lobbying the European Commission: The Case of Air Transport* (Aldershot: Ashgate).

Lajili, K., Madunci, M., and Mahoney, J.T. (2007), 'Testing Organizational Economics Theories of Vertical Integration', Working Paper 07-0104, University of Illinois at Urbana-Champaign, College of Business <http://www.business.uiuc.edu/Working_ Papers>

Lam, M. (1995), 'An Introduction to Airline Maintenance', in Jenkins, D. (ed.).

Laney, E. (2002), 'The Evolution of Corporate Travel Management: Reacting to the Stresses and Strains of Airline Economics', in Jenkins, D. (ed.).

Lawton, T.C. (2002), *Cleared for Take-Off: Structure and Strategy in the Low Fare Airline Business* (Aldershot: Ashgate).

Lee, D. and Luengo-Prado, M.J. (2005), 'The Impact of Passenger Mix on Reported "Hub Premiums" in the U.S. Airline Industry', *Southern Economic Journal* 72: 2, 372–387.

Lee, T.C. and Hersh, M. (1993), 'A Model for Dynamic Airline Seat Inventory Control with Multiple Seat Bookings', *Transportation Science* 27, 252–265.

Lelieur, I. (2003), *The Law and Policy of Substantial Ownership and Effective Control of Airlines: Prospects for Change* (Aldershot: Ashgate).

Levine, M.E. (1965), 'Is Regulation Necessary? California Air Transportation and National Regulatory Policy', *Yale Law Journal* 74, 1416–1485.

—— (1987), 'Airline Competition in Deregulated Markets: Theory, Firm Strategy, and Public Policy', *Yale Law Journal*, 96, 393–484.

—— (2003), 'Looking Back and Ahead: The Future of the U.S. Domestic Airline Industry', paper prepared for the MIT Global Airline Industry Program 2002–03.

Littlewood, K. (1972), 'Forecasting and Control of Passenger Bookings', paper presented to AGIFORS Symposium 12, Nathanya, May.

Lott, S. (2004), 'The U.S. Domestic Market's Need for Network Service', *Aviation Daily*, July 14th.

—— (2006), 'Navigating the Operational Landscape of U.S. Hubs', *Aviation Week & Space Technology*, December 4th.

Lovelock, C. and Wirtz, J. (2004), *Services Marketing: People, Technology, Strategy*, 5th edition, (Englewood Cliffs: Prentice-Hall).

Lu, A.C-J. (2003), *International Airline Alliances: EC Competition Law/US Antitrust Law and International Air Transport* (The Hague: Kluwer Law International).

Lufthansa (2006), *Balance: Company Social Responsibility, Environment, Corporate Citizenship* (Frankfurt).

Lyle, C. (2006), 'Trade Wins', *Airline Business*, November.

Marin, P.L. (1995), 'Competition in European Aviation: Pricing, Policy and Market Structure', *Journal of Industrial Economics* 43, 141–159.

Mason, E.S. (1939), 'Price and Production Policies of Large Scale Enterprises', *American Economic Review* 29, 61–74.

Mason, K.J. (2000), 'The Propensity of Business Travellers to Use Low-Cost Airlines', *Journal of Transport Geography* 8: 2, 107–119.

—— (2001), 'Marketing Low-Cost Airline Services to Business Travellers', *Journal of Air Transport Management* 7, 103–109.

Mason, K.J., Whelan, C., and Williams, G. (2000), *Europe's Low Cost Airlines: An Analysis of the Economics and Operating Characteristics of Europe's Charter and Low Cost Scheduled Carriers*, Cranfield University, Air Transport Group Research Report 7.

Max, M. (2007), 'Leveraging Process Documentation for Time-Driven Activity Based Costing', *Journal of Performance Management* 20: 3, 16–28.

mbs (2006), *Air Traffic Control Commercialization Policy: Has it Been Effective?* (Ottawa).

McDonald, M. (2002), 'Endangered Species?', *Air Transport World*, June.

McGill, J.I. and Van Ryzin, G.J. (1999), 'Revenue Management: Research Overview and Prospects', *Transportation Science* 33: 2, 233–256.

McShane, S. and Windle, R.J. (1989), 'The Implications of Hub-and-Spoke Routeings for Airline Costs and Competitiveness', *Logistics and Transportation Review* 25: 3, 209–230.

Medard, C.P. and Sawhney, N. (2007), 'Airline Crew Scheduling from Planning to Operations', *European Journal of Operational Research* 183: 3, 1013–1027.

Meehan, D. (2006), 'Evolution of Air Service and Changing Airline Business Models', presentation to the Sixth National Aviation System Planning Symposium, Daytona Beach, May.

Melville, J.A. (1998), 'An empirical Model of the Demand for International Air Travel,' *International Journal of Transport Economics* 25: 3, 313–322.

Meyer, J.R. and Oster, C.V. (1984), *Deregulation and The New Airline Entrepreneurs*, (Cambridge: MIT Press).

Mintzberg, H. (1994), *The Rise and Fall of Strategic Planning* (New York: The Free Press).

Moore, T.G. (1986), 'US Airline Deregulation: Its Effects on Passengers, Capital, and Labour', *Journal of Law and Economics* 29, 1–28.

Moorthy, K.S. (1984), 'Market Segmentation, Self-Selection, and Product-Line Design', *Marketing Science* 3: 4, 288–307.

Morrell, P. (2002a), 'Capital Productivity and the Role of Capital Intensity in Airline Labour Productivity', in Jenkins, D. (ed.).

—— (2002b), *Airline Finance*, 2nd edition (Aldershot: Ashgate).

—— (2005), 'Airlines Within Airlines: An Analysis of US Network Airline Responses to Low Cost Carriers', *Journal of Air Transport Management* 11, 303–312.

Morrison, S.A. and Winston, C. (1986), *The Economic Effects of Airline Deregulation* (Washington: The Brookings Institution).

—— (1987), 'Empirical Implications and Tests of the Contestability Hypothesis', *Journal of Law and Economics* 30, 53–66.

—— (1989), 'Enhancing the Performance of the Deregulated Air Transportation System', *Brookings Papers on Economic Activity*, 61–112.

—— (1995), *The Evolution of the Airline Industry* (Washington: The Brookings Institution).

—— (2000), *The Remaining Role of Government Policy in the Deregulated Airline Industry* (Washington: The Brookings Institute).

Narayanan, P.R. and Yuen, B.B. (1998), 'Point of Sale: An Alternative Form of O&D Control', in Butler, G.F. and Keller, M.R. (eds.).

Nelson, R.R., and Winter, S.G. (1982), *An Evolutionary Theory of Economic Change* (Cambridge: Belknap Press).

Newhouse, J. (1988), *The Sporty Game* (London: Random House).

Ng, C. and Seabright, P. (2001), 'Competition, Privatisation and Productive Efficiency: Evidence from the Airline Industry', *Economic Journal* 111: 591–619.

Ng, I.C.L. (2004), 'The Pricing of Services', *Proceedings of the 5th International Research Seminar in Services Management*, La Londe, June.

Ng, I.C.L. (2006), 'Differentiation, Self-selection and Revenue Management', *Journal of Revenue & Pricing Management* 5:1, 2–9.

Nichols, W.K. and Sala, S. (2000), 'Minimizing Connecting Times: A Must for Airline Competitiveness', in Butler, G.F. and Keller, M.R. (eds.).

Nickerson, J.A., Hamilton, B.H., and Wada, T. (2001), 'Market Position, Resource Profile, and Governance: Linking Porter and Williamson in the Context of International Courier and Small Package Services in Japan', *Strategic Management Journal* 22, 251–273.

Nickum, J.D. (2002), 'Airline Considerations in Avionics Equipage Decisions', in Jenkins, D. (ed.).

Nonaka, I. (1994), 'A Dynamic Theory of Organizational Knowledge Creation', *Organization Science* 5, 14–37.

OECD (1997), *The Future of International Air Transport Policy: Responding to Global Change* (Paris).

Oster, C.V. and Strong, J.S. (2001), 'Competition and Antitrust Policy', in Butler, G.F. and Keller, M.R., (eds.).

Osterwalder, A. (2004), *The Business Model Ontology: A Proposition in a Design Science Approach*, Doctoral Dissertation, Université de Lausanne Ecole Des Hautes Etudes Commerciales.

Ostrowski, P.L. and O'Brien, T.V. (1991), *Predicting Customer Loyalty for Airline Passengers*, Department of Marketing, Northern Illinois University.

Oum, T.H. and Park, J.H. (1997), 'Airline Alliances: Current Status, Policy Issues, and Future Directions' *Journal of Air Transport Management* 3, 133–144.

Oum, T.H., Park, J.H., and Zhang, A. (2000), *Globalization and Strategic Alliances* (Oxford: Pergamon).

Oum, T.H. and Yu, C. (1998), *Winning Airlines: Productivity and Cost Competitiveness of the World's Major Airlines* (Boston: Kluwer Academic Press).

—— (2000), *Shaping Air Transport in Asia Pacific* (Aldershot: Ashgate).

Pak, K., Dekker, R., and Kindervater, G. (2003), 'Airline Revenue Management with Shifting Capacity', ERIM Report Series ERS–2003–091–LIS, Erasmus Research Institute of Management, Erasmus University.

Palmeri, C. (2007), 'No "Luv" for Southwest's Changes', [website] http://www. businessweek.com, 16th November.

Panzar, J.C. and Willig, R.D. (1981), 'Economies of Scope', *American Economic Association, Papers and Proceedings* May, 268–272.

Payne, A. and Frow, P. (1999), 'Developing a Segmented Service Strategy: Improving Measurement in Relationship Marketing', *Journal of Marketing Management* 15, 797–818.

Pearce, B. (2006), *Future Challenges to Adding Value in Aviation Markets*, IATA Economics (Geneva).

Pels, E. (2001), 'A Note on Airline Alliances', *Journal of Air Transport Management* 7, 3–7.

Penrose, E.T. (1959), *Theory of the Growth of the Firm* (London: Basil Blackwell).

Perry, L.J. (1995), 'The Response of Major Airlines to Low-Cost Airlines', in Jenkins, D. (ed.).

Pickett, D.C. (2002), 'The Aircraft Engine Selection Process', in Jenkins, D. (ed.).

Pickrell, D. (1991), 'The Regulation and Deregulation of US Airlines', in Button, K.J. (ed.).

Piercy, N. (1997), *Market-Led Strategic Change*, 2nd edition (Oxford: Butterworth-Heinemann).

Pigou, A.C. (1920), *The Economics of Welfare* (London: Macmillan).

Pilarski, A.M. (2007), *Why Can't We Make Money in Aviation?* (Aldershot: Ashgate).

Pilling, M. (2001), 'Flights of Fancy', *Airline Business*, January.

—— (2007), 'After the Gold Rush', *Airline Business*, May.

Pindyck, R.S. and Rubinfeld, D.L. (2001), *Microeconomics*, 5th edition (Upper Saddle River: Prentice-Hall).

Pinkham, R. (2001), 'Bringing Delta Home', *Airline Business*, March.

Porter, M.E. (1976), *Interbrand Choice, Strategy and Bilateral Market Power* (Cambridge: Harvard University Press).

—— (1980), *Competitive Strategy* (New York: The Free Press).

—— (1985), *Competitive Advantage* (New York: The Free Press).

—— (1991), 'Towards a Dynamic Theory of Strategy', *Strategic Management Journal* 12: Winter Special Edition, 95–117.

—— (1996), 'What is Strategy?', *Harvard Business Review*, November–December, 61–78.

Prahalad, C.K. and Hamel, G. (1990), 'The Core Competence of the Corporation', *Harvard Business Review*, May-June, 79–91.

Proussaloglou, K. and Koppelman, F. (1995), 'Air Carrier Demand: An Analysis of Market Share Determinants', *Transportation* 22: 4, 371–388.

Rao, B.V. (2000), 'An Origin-Destination Model for Cargo Revenue-Mix Optimization', presentation to the *AGIFORS Cargo Study Group*, Louisville, May.

Rao, V.R. and Steckel, J.H. (1998), *Analysis for Strategic Marketing* (New York: Addison-Wesley).

Reichheld, F.F. (1996), *The Loyalty Effect* (Cambridge: Harvard Business School Press).

Reitzes, J. and Robyn, D. (2007), *An Analysis of the Economic Effects of an EU–US Open Aviation Area* <ec.europa.eu/transport/air_portal/international/pillars/global_partners/ doc/us/final_report_bah.pdf>

Rispoli, M. (1996), 'Competitive Analysis and Competence-Based Strategies in the Hotel Industry', in Sanchez, R., Heene, A., and Thomas, H. (eds.).

Robertson, R. (2002, 2008), University of New South Wales, private correspondence.

Robinson, J. (1934), 'What is Perfect Competition?', *Quarterly Journal of Economics* 49, 104–120.

Rolls-Royce (2006), *Market Outlook 2006–2025* (Derby).

Romero-Hernandez, M. and Salgado, H. (2005), 'Economies of Density, Network Size and Spatial Scope in the European Airline Industry', Working Paper UCB–ITS–WP–2005–1, Institute of Transportation Studies, University of California (Berkeley).

Rothbard, M. (1962), *Man, Economy, and State* (Princeton: Van Nostrand).

Ruehle, J., Goetsch, B., and Koch, B. (2006), 'Consequences of Feeder Delays for the Success of A380 Operations', *Journal of Air Transportation* 11: 1, 43–63.

Rumelt, R.P. (1984), 'Towards a Strategic Theory of the Firm', in Lamb, R. (ed.).

Rutherford, D. (1992), *Routledge Dictionary of Economics* (London: Routledge).

Schefczyk, M. (1993), 'Operational Performance of Airlines: An Extension of Traditional Measurement Paradigms', *Strategic Management Journal* 14, 301–317.

Schipper, Y. (2001), *Environmental Costs and Liberalization in European Air Transport: A Welfare Economic Analysis* (Cheltenham: Edward Elgar).

Schmalensee, R. (1985), 'Do Markets Differ Much?', *American Economic Review* 75: 3, 341–350.

Schnell, M.C.A. (2001), 'Managerial Perception of Barriers to Route Exit: Evidence from Europe's Civil Aviation Markets', *Journal of Air Transport Management* 7, 95–102.

—— (2005), 'Investigating Airline Managers' Perception of Route Entry Barriers: A Questionnaire-Based Approach', in Forsyth et al. (eds.).

Scott, W.R. (1995), *Institutions and Organizations* (Thousand Oaks: Sage).

Sentance, A. (2001), 'Living With Slower Growth', *Airline Business*, July.

Shaw, S. (1999), *Airline Marketing and Management*, 4th edition (Aldershot: Ashgate).

Shields, M. (1998), 'The Changing Cargo Business', in Butler, G.F. and Keller, M.R. (eds.).

Shoemaker, S. (2005), 'Pricing and the Consumer', *Journal of Revenue and Pricing Management* 4: 3, 228–237.

Sinclair, M.T. and Stabler, M. (1997), *The Economics of Tourism* (London: Routledge).

Slack, N., Chambers, S., Harland, C., Harrison, A., and Johnston, R. (1998), *Operations Management*, 2nd edition (London: Pitman).

Smith, B.C., Barlow, J., and Vinod, B. (1998), 'Airline Planning and Marketing Decision Support: A Review of Current Practices and Future Trends', in Butler, G.F. and Keller, M.R. (eds.).

Smith, B.C., Gunther, D.P., Rao, B.V., and Ratliff, R.M. (2001), 'E-Commerce and Operations Research in Airline Planning, Marketing, and Distribution', *Interfaces* 31: 2, 37–55.

Smith, B.C., Leimkuhler, J.F., and Darrow, R.M. (1992), 'Yield Management at American Airlines', *Interfaces* 22: 1, 8–31.

Smith, C. (2004), 'Strategies for Responding to Low Cost Carriers', presentation for SH&E to the Information Management 2004 conference, Athens, May.

Smith, K.G., Grimm, C.M., Gannon, M.J., and Chen, M. (1991), 'Organizational Information Processing, Competitive Responses and Performance in the US Domestic Airline Industry', *Academy of Management Journal* 34, 60–85.

Solon, D. (2001), 'Cut-price Carriers Shrug Off Worldwide Slowdown Jitters', *The Avmark Aviation Economist*, June.

Spitz, W.H. (1998), 'International Code Sharing', in Butler, G.F. and Keller, M.R. (eds.).

Starkie, D. (1998), 'Allocating Slots: A Role for the Market?', *Journal of Air Transport Management* 4, 111–116.

Stavins, J. (1996), *Price Discrimination in the Airline Market: The Effect of Market Concentration* (Boston: Federal Reserve Bank of Boston).

Steer Davies Gleave (2006), *Transparency of Airline Tickets*, Report prepared for the European Commission Directorate General, Energy and Transport, TREN/F1/22–56–2005.

Stern, N. (2006), *Stern Review on the Economics of Climate Change* (London: Her Majesty's Treasury).

Stonier, J.E. (1998), 'Marketing from a Manufacturer's Perspective: Issues in Quantifying the Economic Benefits of New Aircraft, and Making the Correct Financing Decision', in Butler, G.F. and Keller, M.R. (eds.).

Stonier, J. E. (2001), 'Airline Fleet Planning, Financing, and Hedging Decisions Under Conditions of Uncertainty', in Butler, G.F. and Keller, M.R. (eds.).

Subramanian, J., Stidham, S. jr., and Lautenbacher, C.J. (1999), 'Airline Yield Management with Overbooking, Cancellation, and No-shows', *Transportation Science* 33, 147–167.

Sudarshan, H.V. (2003), *Seamless Sky* (Aldershot: Ashgate).

Swarbrooke, J. and Horner, S. (1999), *Consumer Behaviour in Tourism* (Oxford: Butterworth-Heinemann).

Talluri, K.T. and van Ryzin, G.J. (2004), *The Theory and Practice of Revenue Management* (Boston: Kluwer Academic Press).

Taneja, N.K. (2002), *Driving Airline Business Strategies Through Emerging Technology* (Aldershot: Ashgate).

Telser, L.G. (1978), *Economic Theory and the Core* (Chicago: University of Chicago Press).

The Campbell-Hill Aviation Group, Inc. (2006), *Commercial Aviation and the American Economy*, report prepared for the ATA (Washington D.C.).

Transportation Research Board (1999), *Entry and Competition in the U.S. Airline Industry*, Special Report 255 (Washington: National Academy Press).

Treitel, D.H. (2006), *LCCs and Industry Evolution* (Washington: SH & E).

Tretheway, M.W. (1998), 'Airport Marketing: An Oxymoron', in Butler, G.F. and Keller, M.R. (eds.).

Trevett, J. (1999), 'New vs. Old', *Aircraft Economics* 44, July–August, 39–41.

Trott, P. (1998), *Innovation Management & New Product Development* (London: Pitman).

Turney, P.B.B. (1991), 'How Activity-Based Costing Helps Reduce Cost', *Journal of Cost Management*, Winter, 29–35.

UBS Investment Research (2006), *Global Airline Strategy*, October 25th.

Unisys R2A (2003), *Scorecard*, April.

—— (2006a), *Scorecard* 5: 2.

—— (2006b), *Scorecard* 5: 3.

United Nations (2004), *Population Prospects* (New York).

Van Ryzin, G.J. (2004), 'Choice-based Revenue Management: Recent Advances and Implementation Prospects', presentation to the 43rd AGIFORS Symposium, Paris, September.

Varoufakis, Y. (1998), *Foundations of Economics* (London: Routledge).

Vasigh, B. and Fleming, K. (2005), 'A Total Factor Productivity Based Structure for Tactical Cluster Assessment: Empirical Investigation in the Airline Industry', *Journal of Air Transportation* 10: 1, 3–19.

Vass, J. (1996), *Air Transport: International Comparisons of Labour Productivity* (London: National Institute of Economic and Social Research).

Venkat, R. (2005), 'Sales-centric Revenue Management', *Journal of Revenue and Pricing Management* 4: 3, 227–235

Vinod, B. (1995), 'Origin-and-Destination Yield Management', in Jenkins, D. (ed.).

—— (2005), 'Alliance Revenue Management', *Journal of Revenue and Pricing Management* 4: 1, 66–82.

—— (2006), 'Advances in Inventory Control', *Journal of Revenue and Pricing Management´* 4: 4, 367–371.

Vomhof, K. (2007), private correspondence.

Walker, S., (2002), private correspondence.

Watterson, A., Hornick, S., and Lalsare, R. (2006), 'The New Economics of Loyalty Programmes', *Mercer Management Journal* 22: November, 28–33.

Weatherford, L.R. and Bodily, S.E. (1992), 'A Taxonomy and Research Overview of Perishable Asset Revenue Management: Yield Management, Overbooking, and Pricing', *Operations Research* 40: 5, 831–844.

Wells, A.T. (1999), *Air Transportation: A Management Perspective*, 4th edition (Belmont: Wadsworth).

Weyer, T. (1998), 'Keeping Yield Management Under Control', *Aviation Strategy*, May, 16–19.

Whelan, C. (2000), 'Air Navigation Charges: Worldwide Benchmarking of Fees', *The Avmark Aviation Economist*, March, 10–17.

Wild, R. (1989), *Production and Operations Management*, 4th edition (London: Cassell).

Williams, G. (2002), *Airline Competition: Deregulation's Mixed Legacy* (Aldershot: Ashgate).

Williams, V. (2007), 'European ATM and the Environment', in Cook (ed.).

Williamson, E.L. (1992), 'Airline Network Seat Inventory Control: Methodologies and Revenue Impacts', Doctoral Dissertation, Flight Transportation Laboratory, Massachusetts Institute of Technology.

Williamson, O.E. (1968), 'Economics as an Antitrust Defense', *American Economic Review* 58: 1, 18–36.

—— (1975), *Markets and Hierarchies: Analysis and Antitrust Implications* (New York: The Free Press).

Windle, R.J. (1991), 'The World's Airlines: A Cost and Productivity Comparison', *Journal of Transport Economics and Policy* January, 31–49.

Windle, R.J. and Dresner, M.E. (1992), 'Partial Productivity Measures and Total Factor Productivity in the Air Transport Industry: Limitations and Uses', *Transportation Research – A*, 26A: 6, 435–445.

—— (1995), 'A Note on Productivity Comparisons Between Air Carriers', *The Logistics and Transportation Review* 31: 2, 125–134.

—— (1999), 'Competitive Responses to Low Cost Carrier Entry', *Transportation Research – E* 35E: 1, 59–75.

Wollmer, R.D. (1992), 'An Airline Seat Management Model for a Single Leg Route When Lower Fare Classes Book First', *Operations Research* 40, 26–37.

Wu, C-L. and Caves, R.E. (2000), 'Aircraft Operational Costs and Turnaround Efficiency at Airports', *Journal of Air Transport Management* 6, 201–208.

York Aviation (2007), *Social Benefits of Low Fares in Europe*, report prepared for the European Low Fares Airline Association, the Forum of European Regional Airports, and the Assembly of European Regions.

Yu, G., Pachan, J., Thengvall, B., Chandler, D., and Wilson, A. (2004), 'Optimizing Pilot Planning and Training for Continental Airlines', *Interfaces* 34: 4, 253–264.

Yuen, B.B. (1998), 'Group Revenue Management', in Butler, G.F. and Keller, M.R. (eds.).

Yuen, B.B. and Irrgang, M.E. (1998), 'The New Generation of Revenue Management: A Network Perspective', in Butler, G.F. and Keller, M.R. (eds.).

Zakreski, E. (1998), 'Beyond Frequent Flyers: Knowing Customers as a Foundation for Airline Growth', in Butler, G.F. and Keller, M.R. (eds.).

Zeni, R. (2003), 'The Value of Analyst Interaction with Revenue Management Systems', *Journal of Revenue and Pricing Management* 2: 1, 37–46.

Zhao, W. and Zheng, Y-S. (2001), 'A Dynamic Model for Airline Seat Allocation With Passenger Diversion and No-Shows', *Transportation Science* 35, 180–98.

Zou, S. and Cavusgil, S.T. (1996), 'Global Strategy: A Review and an Integrated Conceptual Framework', *European Journal of Marketing* 30: 1, 52–69.

Index